CONTENTS

ACKNOWLEDGEMENTS

I WANT to thank the general editor, Michael Cordner, for inviting me to do this edition, for his forbearance when it did not emerge as quickly as we had hoped, and for his guidance through successive drafts. When I have worked directly on early printed versions of these plays, it has mainly been in the Bodleian Library at Oxford, and I want to thank the staff there for their assistance. I also want to thank those who made it practically or financially possible for me to be there to do this, usually on the back of other employments; these include Paulina Kewes, Blair Worden, and my own Department of English at Lancaster. The department also made it possible for me to attend the Shakespeare Association of America meeting in Washington DC in April 1997 and, late in the day, I was able to consult the early Middleton editions and manuscripts at the Folger Shakespeare Library there.

My work on *A Game at Chess*, however, goes back a good deal longer than that on this particular edition, and involved brief fellowships at both the Folger (1987) and the Huntington Library in San Marino, California (1992), where I was able to consult all their manuscripts of the play, as well as the early printed texts. I am grateful to both libraries and their staffs for their support, and to the British Academy which on both these occasions paid for my travel.

My thanks are also due to the British Library for permission to base my edition of *A Game at Chess* on the Lansdowne manuscript of the play, *British Library Ms. Lansdowne 690*.

Thanks finally to Kate Dutton and to Alison Findlay for their help in checking the text, and to Julie Brown for hers in printing out the typescript.

OXFORD WORLD'S CLASSICS

=

THOMAS MIDDLETON

A Chaste Maid in Cheapside
Women Beware Women
The Changeling
A Game at Chess

=

Edited with an Introduction and Notes by
RICHARD DUTTON

OXFORD
UNIVERSITY PRESS

OXFORD

UNIVERSITY PRESS

Great Clarendon Street, Oxford OX2 6DP

Oxford University Press is a department of the University of Oxford.
It furthers the University's objective of excellence in research, scholarship,
and education by publishing worldwide in

Oxford New York

Auckland Bangkok Buenos Aires Cape Town Chennai
Dar es Salaam Delhi Hong Kong Istanbul Karachi Kolkata
Kuala Lumpur Madrid Melbourne Mexico City Mumbai Nairobi
São Paulo Shanghai Taipei Tokyo Toronto

Oxford is a registered trade mark of Oxford University Press
in the UK and in certain other countries

Published in the United States
by Oxford University Press Inc., New York

British Library Cataloguing in Publication Data

Data available

Library of Congress Cataloging in Publication Data

Data available

ISBN 978-0-19-953892-8

4

Typeset in Ehrhardt
by RefineCatch Limited, Bungay, Suffolk
Printed in Great Britain by
Clays Ltd, St Ives plc

OXFORD ENGLISH DRAMA

General Editor: MICHAEL CORDNER

Associate General Editors: PETER HOLLAND · MARTIN WIGGINS

WOMEN BEWARE WOMEN
AND OTHER PLAYS

THOMAS MIDDLETON was born in 1580 and died in 1627. His career as a London dramatist therefore spans the most productive, innovative, and exciting period of theatrical activity in the history of English drama. Middleton wrote nearly fifty plays during these years, either alone or in collaboration with other Jacobean dramatists. The present collection reflects the extraordinary diversity and originality of his playwriting by grouping his two greatest tragedies, *Women Beware Women* and *The Changeling*, with his most innovative city comedy, *A Chaste Maid in Cheapside*, and his daring political satire, *A Game at Chess*. By the time of his death, Middleton was reasonably well-to-do, having been appointed the City Chronologer for London in 1620, a post which obliged him to keep records of important civic events and organize public entertainments and pageants.

RICHARD DUTTON is Professor of English at Lancaster University, where he has taught since 1974. He has published widely in the field of early modern literature, especially on matters of censorship and authorship. Publications include *Mastering the Revels: The Regulation and Censorship of English Renaissance Drama* (1991) and *Ben Jonson: Authority: Criticism* (1996). He is also general editor of the Macmillan Literary Lives series. Work in progress includes *Buggeswords: Licensing and Authorship in Early Modern England* and the Revels Plays edition of Jonson's *Epicene*.

MICHAEL CORDNER is Ken Dixon Professor of Drama at the University of York. He has edited George Farquhar's *The Beaux' Stratagem*, the *Complete Plays* of Sir George Etherege, and, for Oxford English Drama, *Four Restoration Marriage Plays* and Sheridan's *The School for Scandal and Other Plays*.

PETER HOLLAND is McMeel Family Professor in Shakespeare Studies at the University of Notre Dame.

MARTIN WIGGINS is a Fellow of the Shakespeare Institute and Senior Lecturer in English at the University of Birmingham.

OXFORD WORLD'S CLASSICS

*For over 100 years Oxford World's Classics have brought
readers closer to the world's great literature. Now with over 700
titles—from the 4,000-year-old myths of Mesopotamia to the
twentieth century's greatest novels—the series makes available
lesser-known as well as celebrated writing.*

*The pocket-sized hardbacks of the early years contained
introductions by Virginia Woolf, T. S. Eliot, Graham Greene,
and other literary figures which enriched the experience of reading.
Today the series is recognized for its fine scholarship and
reliability in texts that span world literature, drama and poetry,
religion, philosophy and politics. Each edition includes perceptive
commentary and essential background information to meet the
changing needs of readers.*

INTRODUCTION

THE four plays in this volume are those on which Middleton's modern reputation principally depends. From the mid to late phases of a career that spanned thirty years they are masterpieces, variously, of comedy, tragedy and political satire. There are those (including the present editor) who would add *The Revenger's Tragedy* (*c.*1607) to this list as the earliest example of Middleton's true potential, though its early ascription to Cyril Tourneur rather than to Middleton makes that problematic. It is nevertheless a measure of these four plays that the essence of the claim for Middleton's authorship of *The Revenger's Tragedy* is that they represent the fulfilment of the potential evident in that darkly brilliant piece of blood-letting.

All five plays have characteristic qualities which not only make for drama of the highest order, but have also spoken with particular force to the last century: a sustained ironic or sardonic mode, a fascination with self-destructive violence, a penetrating insight into sexual psychology, an unblinking observation of the effects of money, lust and power on human behaviour. These and more recently discovered attractions—a drama of urban identity, of commercial ideology, and of partisan politics in an era which shaped the modern world—have all seemed particularly relevant to the generations between and after the two World Wars.

The Changeling (which Middleton co-wrote with William Rowley) led the way, quickly emerging from centuries of neglect to be seen by many as the finest of Jacobean tragedies after Shakespeare, a penetrating examination of sexual passion and self-delusion. *Women Beware Women* has also—and increasingly—been admired for similar qualities, though it has never enjoyed the same stage success. Latterly *A Chaste Maid in Cheapside* has emerged from a rather anonymous grouping of city comedies to be seen as fit to rival Jonson's finest comedies, a wry celebration of sex and money in the London which was beginning to shape the modern commercial world. *A Game at Chess* was the single most popular play of its own era, running for an unprecedented nine consecutive performances at the Globe in 1624 and causing something of a scandal: as such it has emerged as a crucial test case in historicist readings of early modern drama, the primary scholarly focus in the field for the last twenty years.

Yet the modern appeal of these plays has often been partial or selective, in the sense that the response has been to aspects of the texts rather than to their totalities. When the BBC filmed *The Changeling* with Bob Hoskins (broadcast 11 December 1993), they omitted the mad-house plot altogether. Playwrights such as Peter Barnes and Edward Bond have been moved to adapt Middleton's plays (including *A Chaste Maid in Cheapside*)—but in each case the very fact of *adaptation* suggests that not all the elements of his plays have been felt to speak to us with equal ease. When Howard Barker adapted *Women Beware Women* for the Royal Court Theatre in 1986, he preserved most of the first three and a half acts, but totally rewrote the final third of the play. He abandoned the masque and made, for example, Sordido a major character who rapes Bianca on the eve of her wedding. In a programme note he observed: 'Middleton says lust leads to the grave. I say desire alters perception. . . . Middleton knew the body was the source of politics. He did not know it was also the source of hope.'[1] Goodbye Calvin; hello Foucault and Althusser. Such decisions are symptomatic of a wider perception that *parts* of Middleton are uniquely, almost eerily, modern, while other aspects of his work remain firmly and obscurely located in a remote Jacobean world and its theatrical conventions. In that sense he has been a figure out of focus. His plays give voice to an early modern world whose priorities and values are often not our own. Yet at times *some* of the issues they raise, and the manner in which Middleton raises them, chime urgently with modern sensibilities.

I can perhaps best illustrate this (apparent) disorientating duality from a production of one of the plays. In 1978—well before Barker—Robert Osborne directed *Women Beware Women* at Lancaster University. This was set in a modern Italy, and took as its cue the closing moments of the Mike Nichols touchstone 1960s movie, *The Graduate*. In the movie Dustin Hoffman improbably snatches Katharine Ross from the altar of a conventional marriage, and the lovers head for the future in a passing bus. But in the closing shot (it is said the director kept the camera running, without telling the actors what he wanted them to do) the exhilaration slowly drains from their faces, they register confusion, doubt, and perhaps resignation as the reality of the moment takes over from the romance. This seemed to apply perfectly

[1] Programme note to William Gaskill's Royal Court Theatre production, London, February 1986; quoted in *Thomas Middleton: Five Plays*, ed. Bryan Loughrey and Neil Taylor (Harmondsworth, 1988), p. xxiv.

to the elopement of Leantio and Bianca, a fairy-tale romantic impulse which Middleton's play subjects to the sobering realities of money, sexuality, and power. Robert Osborne's production translated this into modern terms with nudity and Mafia-style hit-men. Hippolito's great death-speech, 'Lust and forgetfulness has been amongst us', was spoken to the strains of David Bowie's 'Don't Believe in Yourself'.

In all these respects *Women Beware Women* was effortlessly a play of the 1970s, of cynical style over substance, of commercialism masquerading as idealism. (It would not have been difficult to make similar 'translations' of *A Chaste Maid in Cheapside* or even *The Changeling*, as the Marcus Thompson movie has recently done.) The sticking-point, however—as Howard Barker apparently found—was the masque at the end, in which virtually all the characters die. It was not simply that this employed Jacobean theatrical conventions which were no longer current. It was as if the play had radically changed gear, or moved into another dimension, and the modes of social, psychological, and sexual realism which govern the first four acts had simply been abandoned in favour of a symbolic moralism, most apparent in the role of Cardinal—the one character whose clothes had not changed in 350 years and who is virtually the only survivor. To put it another way, a world in which characters credibly make choices for themselves, and interact within plausibly consistent social, financial, and personal rules, is suddenly superseded by one in which all human will is ruthlessly denied in a Calvinist hell of inexorable divine retribution.

Middleton was here imitating the effect (if not the staging) of the actual court masque, where a change of scene or of perspective—both *literally* possible in the complex stages Inigo Jones created at court—could reveal a new and higher truth, implicitly relegating everything that has gone before to the realm of inadequate human perception. It seems unlikely that Middleton would have shared the neo-Platonic idealism of the Stuart court masques, extravagant celebrations of the court and its values. But their apparent aesthetic capacity for transporting spectators out of their senses, taking them beyond mundane perceptions of themselves and their world, squares with a strain of Calvinist fatalism that does seem to run through Middleton's work: it overshadows the pride, lust, and self-deceit which motivates his characters most of the time at a local level, measuring their immediate pains and pleasures against an unrelenting spiritual yardstick. The vivid realism of so much of the drama, and the quasi-Freudian acuteness of the characterization, thus become forms of untruth, obstacles to a perception of what really matters. Such views of life (and death) are still comprehensible today, but may be less immediately sympathetic to modern sensibilities than other features of his work.

Yet distinctions between accessible and non-accessible elements in Middleton's writing have sometimes been drawn too easily. To return to *Women Beware Women*: with a little patience we can perhaps appreciate that the denouement is not simply an exercise in unsympathetic theology and arcane theatrical practice. There is much about it that is surprisingly modern in its self-referential awareness of its own artifice. As the masque unfolds, the on-stage audience of the Duke, Bianca, and their guests struggle to square what they are seeing with the 'plot' the Duke has been shown beforehand: 'This swerves a little from the argument, though: | Look you, my lords', 'Why, sure this plot's drawn false, here's no such thing' (5.2.124, 131). To be sure, this is still entirely consistent with a Calvinist reading: they remain blind sinners, unable to read the plots of their own damnation any better than that of the masque. At the same time, it is disconcertingly funny, a strangely postmodern distraction from the high seriousness in which they are unwitting players, exposing the fictionality of the medium even as the medium itself purports to be dealing with absolutes. In such self-consciousness Middleton seems to question, even to undermine, the theological certainties he depicts. They dissolve into tricks of the theatrical trade, in ways that audiences brought up on Tom Stoppard's *Rosencrantz and Guildenstern Are Dead* or Peter Weiss's *Marat/Sade* should have no difficulty understanding.

And this is of a piece with what Middleton does with the one character who, providentially, is not carried off by the masque or the surrounding mayhem. What are we to make of the Cardinal? A prince of the Roman Catholic Church is an unlikely emissary for John Calvin, but this may be a function of the play's Italian setting, and it has to be said that he is unlike most other Jacobean stage cardinals. Those of Webster's *The White Devil* and *The Duchess of Malfi*, for instance, are unambiguously worldly men, for whom the Church is a convenient alternative route to power. The motives of Middleton's Cardinal are much less transparent. The sermon with which he berates the Duke, his brother, on his first appearance, would certainly not disgrace a Calvinist pulpit:

> What a grief 'tis to a religious feeling
> To think a man should have a friend so goodly,
> So wise, so noble, nay, a duke, a brother,
> And all this certainly damned. (4.1.187–90)

Yet the effects of this piety are anything but holy: the Duke resolves that he must sanctify his relationship with Bianca by marriage, which will only be possible if her husband, Leantio, is first killed. Just as Beatrice-Joanna in *The Changeling* has real difficulty understanding that murder might be a more serious business than fornication, the Duke has a very self-serving view of moral priorities. And the Cardinal's own motives, which emerge when the Duke appears to show remorse, are not entirely beyond reproach: 'The powers of darkness groan, makes all Hell sorry. | First I praise Heaven, then in my work I glory' (261–2). Repentance is always the work of God's grace, but the Cardinal takes some satisfaction—smug? deserved? boastful?—in that his own 'work' was the secondary means by which God chose to operate.

When the Duke's real plan emerges, the Cardinal rages against a scheme in which 'lust usurps the bed that should be pure', but Bianca coolly challenges him with lack of charity, sardonically turning scripture against him: 'Heaven and angels | Take great delight in a converted sinner' (4.3.55–6). In private, however, she ascribes ulterior motives to what she dismisses as hypocrisy: 'Beware a brother's envy; he's next heir too' (5.2.20). The Cardinal may oppose the marriage because any child it produced would thwart his aspirations to the dukedom, should his brother die. He may well—but Middleton gives no final indication of whether this is so or not. The play offers these clues that he may not be the man of absolute piety that his rhetoric suggests, but leaves it to the actor and the audience to decide what they amount to. If he is indeed a man of worldly ambition, then we have to account for his quasi-miraculous survival throughout the final scene, when he does indeed inherit the dukedom whether he craved it or not. Why should one sinner survive when so many others perish? Are there calibrations in sin, which God carefully measures? If the ending does indeed represent the working out of an inexorable Calvinist providence, that providence is actually more inscrutable than the masque's exercise in poetic justice might suggest. The final measure of that is perhaps Bianca's death. After the tragi-comic mayhem of the masque we are allowed a moment of genuine pity for a character who is even more an outsider than she was when the play began—'What make I here? These are all strangers to me . . .' (5.2.208)—and who dies not by ironic accident but deliberately by her own hand. It is a most powerful conclusion to the play's central theme, in which 'kin' and 'kindness' take issue with 'strangeness': ideas of family and what is natural challenge what is alien and forbidden, but these categories dissolve disconcertingly (as in matters of incest) under close scrutiny.

I have pursued this discussion of a particular production, and the issues it raised, at some length because it is in many ways typical of the dramatic experience with which Middleton repeatedly confronts his audience, refusing finally to settle into the comfortable categories which it seems to propose for itself. It is one reason he is often described as an ironist. It may be true that, at some level, he measures his characters—in the comedy, *A Chaste Maid in Cheapside*, and the religious-historical allegory, *A Game at Chess*, as much as in the tragedies—against a pitilessly remorseless Calvinist universe. And yet simply to call him 'a Calvinist' is to miss the complexity of what he requires of his audience, as well as implicitly to ignore some of the more engagingly modern inflections in his writing.[2]

This is also true of the label 'puritan', which some have preferred to 'Calvinist' because, while it broadly subsumes Calvinist theology, it also implies a wider response to the economic, social and political world of Jacobean England. So, for example, 'puritanism' has often been associated with the proto-capitalist enterprise of early modern London that lies behind citizen comedies like *A Chaste Maid in Cheapside* or the mercantile world which Leantio represents in *Women Beware Women*. If more traditional strains of Christianity stressed anti-acquisitive attitudes and a spirit of communal hospitality, 'puritanism' promotes a competitive work ethic, an ideology of self-help. At the same time 'puritanism' is obsessed with the human disposition towards sin and weakness, especially in the forms of lust and pride, and not least as they manifest themselves in women, which are the recurrent themes of the plays in this volume. Yet the further we draw out this list of half-truths and popular notions, the more apparent are the inherent contradictions within them.

In *A Chaste Maid in Cheapside* Middleton depicts a number of 'puritans' who attend the christening of Mistress Allwit's baby, which they commend as a properly 'reformed' ceremony:

> well kursened, i'the right way,
> Without idolatry or superstition,
> After the pure manner of Amsterdam. (3.2.3–5)

But they prove to be as drunken, gluttonous, and lecherous as the other 'gossips' there, and more hypocritical than any of them. It is

---

[2] See John Stachniewski, 'Calvinist Psychology in Middleton's Tragedies' in R. V. Holdsworth (ed.), *Three Jacobean Revenge Tragedies: A Casebook* (Houndmills and London, 1990), 226–47.

difficult to believe that Middleton would have identified with such people. Moreover, if we take one characteristic of 'puritanism' to be a disapproval of lewd or lascivious language, we have to acknowledge the fact that—even by extremely broad Jacobean standards—Middleton sometimes achieves levels of sexual suggestiveness and innuendo that few of his contemporaries could match. Deflores's anticipation of his sexual possession of Beatrice-Joanna in *The Changeling* is as erotically charged as anything in the language, while Beatrice-Joanna's own prim protestations of virtue (this is a common trait of Middleton characters) keep betraying in their vocabulary a deeply Freudian alternative agenda. Throughout *A Chaste Maid in Cheapside* there is a remorseless equation of sexual desire with making money and social climbing, such that it is often impossible to tell where double entendre begins and ends. In the same way, in *A Game at Chess*, the religious and political ambitions of the Black House very largely manifest themselves as forms of lust; there is even a scene (3.2) which revolves almost entirely around sodomy and homosexual subjection, which the copyist Ralph Crane omitted from the Lansdowne manuscript copy, very possibly on grounds of taste. And the Black Knight comes up with a scheme for subjecting the White Queen's Pawn to a torment of unremitting pornography (2.2.256–60) which is as disturbingly perverse as it is grotesquely comic. If there is something 'puritan' in this obsession with the human capacity for depravity, there is nothing 'puritan' about Middleton's uninhibited exploration of sexual behaviour or his capacity for depicting so much of human aspiration as transposed sexual aggression.

The nub of the problem, of course, is that 'puritan' is such a broad term. In Middleton's own day it represented a very wide spectrum of religious belief, both within the Church of England and outside, including those who merely wanted to adapt Church practices further away from the Roman Catholic model, those who were unhappy with the episcopal hierarchy, those who insisted on the primacy of the Bible as the word of God, or on the inspirational working of the Holy Spirit within, as well as a variety of schismatic sects who wished to see a fundamental change in the relationship between Church and State. It was not confined to a single social group, and 'puritans' were to be found in the Privy Council, in Parliament and the clergy at all levels, as well as among the 'middling sort' who feature so strongly in Middleton's plays, a minority of whom may disgrace themselves at christening ceremonies. Since his time, moreover, 'puritan' has been overlaid with other connotations, not least because of the role played by puritans in the English Civil War and afterwards, and because of the evolution of distinctive strains of puritanism in the Americas. So, when we try to bring Middleton into focus by identifying him as a 'puritan', we are treading in a minefield.

These distinctions are particularly important in relation to recent Middleton criticism, because Margot Heinemann made one of the most impressive and influential attempts to impose an intelligible shape on his career in *Puritanism and Theatre: Thomas Middleton and Opposition Drama under the Early Stuarts* (1980). As her title suggests, she identified Middleton's puritanism with a strain of political resistance to the absolutism of James I and to a range of associated court policies and practices. These included the widespread abuse of monopolies, the undue influence of royal favourites like the Earl of Somerset and the Duke of Buckingham, supposed leniency towards Roman Catholics, and most particularly a refusal to become embroiled in the religious wars in continental Europe. The latter was widely seen as implicit support for Spain (there were long-standing expectations that the heir to the throne, Prince Charles, would marry the Spanish Infanta) and a betrayal of James's own daughter, Elizabeth, and her husband, the so-called Winter Queen and King of Bohemia, key Protestant players in the unfolding Thirty Years War. Much of Middleton's later drama can be read in the light of such associations but, as Heinemann herself argues, they are particularly relevant to *A Game at Chess*, which is so obviously an attack on Roman Catholic and Spanish ambitions.

This thesis has, nevertheless, been attacked on a number of counts. The whole concept of 'opposition drama' has been called into question for applying twentieth-century concepts of ideologically polarized party politics to an early modern world of faction and patronage which simply did not operate in that way. Revisionist historians, in particular, have argued that her view of the early Stuart era was uncritically based on dated Whiggish prejudices, reinforced by a tendency to read the conflicts of the Civil War back into earlier generations. In respect of *A Game at Chess*, her suggestion that Middleton's puritanism was ideologically consonant with the grouping around the Earl of Pembroke, who had for many years resisted Buckingham's influence and advocated anti-Spanish policies, and who as Lord Chamberlain would have been well placed to facilitate the staging of so 'dangerous' a play, has been challenged on several counts. It has particularly been pointed out that by the time the play was staged all the key political players—the King, Prince Charles, Buckingham, and Pembroke (the latter pair having come to a reconciliation)—were agreed on an anti-Spanish policy, so that the play was neither so controversial nor so 'oppositional' as she suggested.[3]

On the contrary, as T. H. Howard-Hill puts it: 'It is possible then to view the play's performances during a summer season otherwise barren of public festivals as a carnivalistic celebration of a national deliverance, as the triumph of the common people over a foreign policy they had neither wanted nor supported.'[4] Nevertheless, Heinemann has defended her thesis vigorously, and Gary Taylor, the general editor of the forthcoming complete *Oxford Middleton*, has agreed to the extent of proposing a Middleton who was a genuinely 'subversive' dramatist, by explicit contrast with Shakespeare.[5] And critics as various as Albert Tricomi, Tony Bromham and Zara Bruzzi, and Cristina Malcomson (all listed in the bibliography) have in different ways followed Heinemann's lead. In provoking such different responses, Middleton as a 'puritan' remains out of focus, lacking final definition. But he has become the centre of debate.

Heinemann's book was a major early contribution to the general rehistoricization of early modern drama, which has dominated criticism of the genre for the last twenty years in waves of Marxist, feminist, new historicist, cultural materialist, and revisionist readings. And in that wider debate Middleton occupies a more central place than earlier New Critical, moralist, and formalist schools of criticism accorded him, however impressed they were, in particular, by *The Changeling*. He was always implicitly inferior to the major canonical figures, Shakespeare and Jonson, but also even to Webster and Marlowe by those critical lights. That has now changed, and Middleton is appreciated as a key voice of London as it grew to phenomenal size and commercial prosperity in the first quarter of the seventeenth century, a voice of the tensions between an earlier festive culture and an evolving competitive work ethic, of new economic and social structures rubbing shoulders with those of the old landed gentry,

---

[3] See J. Limon, *Dangerous Matter: English Drama and Politics in 1623/4* (Cambridge, 1986) and T. H. Howard-Hill, 'Political Interpretations of Middleton's *A Game at Chess*', *Yearbook of English Studies*, 21 (1991), 274–85.

[4] T. H. Howard-Hill, *Middleton's 'Vulgar Pasquin': Essays on 'A Game at Chess'* (Newark, DE, 1995), 226.

[5] See Margot Heinemann, 'Drama and Opinion in the 1620s: Middleton and Massinger' in J. R. Mulryne and M. Shewring (eds.), *Theatre and Government under the Early Stuarts* (Cambridge, 1993), and G. Taylor, 'Shakespeare and Middleton', *English Literary Renaissance*, 24 (1994), 283–314.

of the old oral and scribal culture coexisting alongside the world of print, of deeply spiritual anxieties running through a time intensely attuned to material and sensual realities. That is, we have begun to see him as one of the more important authors to have delineated the early modern world as it laid down the conditions from which our own world would emerge.

A Chaste Maid in Cheapside

The title-page of the earliest printed copy (1630) declares *A Chaste Maid in Cheapside* to be 'A pleasant conceited comedy . . . as it hath often been acted at the Swan on the Bankside, by the Lady Elizabeth her servants'. Princess Elizabeth was King James's only daughter, and she first became patron of an acting company in 1611; they performed at the unpopular Swan—a theatre with an unfortunate history, and this is the only extant play known to have been played there—until 1613. So this limits the dating of the play. R. B. Parker, in his Revels edition of the play, argues plausibly that it was first staged by a combined troupe of Lady Elizabeth's Men and the Queen's Revels Children, the grouping that performed Jonson's *Bartholomew Fair* in 1614. If so, that settles the date of *A Chaste Maid in Cheapside* as 1613.

Though he was writing for a new company, Middleton reverted to a form with which he was familiarly associated, that of city or citizen comedy, openly depicting contemporary London life. The 'negotiation' of new, commercial money (as represented by the goldsmith, Yellowhammer) by the indigent landed gentry (Sir Walter Whorehound), and conversely the aspirations of that new money towards its own gentrification; the problems of even respectable gentry (the Touchwood Seniors) living beyond their means, and of their younger sons (Touchwood Junior) having to fend for themselves in a system of strict primogeniture; the wider difficulties stemming from debt sustained by the expectation of inheritance (Sir Walter and the Kixes): these were all familiar social and economic themes which Middleton had addressed before in earlier plays, such as *A Mad World, My Masters*, *Michaelmas Term*, and *A Trick to Catch the Old One* (all *c*.1605/6).

These themes all reflected actual social problems of the day, exacerbated by rampant inflation in the early years of the seventeenth century, which particularly depressed the real value of land, on which the gentry's fortunes traditionally rested.[6] But these plays are not, as was once thought, merely slices of naïve or journalistic realism. 'City comedies' were written for a range of acting companies, theatres, and prospective audiences, and this clearly coloured their approaches to the subjects and situations they depicted. The earlier Middleton plays I have mentioned were all written for Paul's Boys, a company which specialized in topical local satire and was more likely to sympathize with (say) resourceful sons of the gentry than with either their elders or tradespeople of 'the middling sort'. And this makes them very different from a play like Dekker's *The Shoemaker's Holiday* (1599) which romanticizes and celebrates London and its merchant classes. *A Chaste Maid in Cheapside* skilfully blends the intrigue comedy of Middleton's earlier 'city comedies' with some elements of 'popular comedy' such as Dekker's, making it in many ways a more complex and multi-vocal work than any of its immediate models.[7]

Another measure of the sophistication of city comedies is the clear debt of so many of them to the Roman Comedy of Plautus and Terence, with its ingenious plotting and stock characters of grumpy older men, spendthrift heirs, young lovers, witty servant/slaves, and women of loose morals.[8] But there is nothing narrowly pedantic about this imitation of the classics. It seems clear that Middleton, Jonson, and other writers in this mode appreciated that Roman Comedy constituted one of the few pre-existing models for depicting *urban* affairs, a world of unstable money, of social and sexual aspiration, of competitive and individualist psychology—very different from the romantic and festive comedy we associate, for example, with the Shakespeare of the 1590s, which reflects variously courtly and agrarian societies. Of course, there were major differences between Jacobean London and Republican Rome, but there were enough similarities for the dramatists of the former to create their city in the image left them by the dramatists of the latter, in a reciprocity that denies any casual 'realism'.

Middleton's education actually progressed further than that of either Shakespeare or Jonson; he attended Queen's College, Oxford, in

[6] See Lawrence Stone, *The Crisis of the Aristocracy 1558–1641* (Oxford, 1965).

[7] The 'mixed' modelling of the play is discussed in detail by Brian Gibbons in his pioneering study of these plays, *Jacobean City Comedy* (2nd edn; London: Methuen 1980), 127–30. For a different approach to such plays, see Alexander Leggatt, *Citizen Comedy in the Age of Shakespeare* (1973).

[8] The most thorough and rewarding study of this in relation to Middleton is George E. Rowe, *Thomas Middleton and the New Comedy Tradition* (Lincoln: University of Nebraska Press, 1979).

1598, though there is no record of his ever graduating.[9] His wry humour at the attempts of Tim Yellowhammer and his parents to master Latin mirrors the condescension of an audience secure in its socially privileged learning, rather than the envy of those excluded from such knowledge.[10] And those educated enough to recognize for themselves the derivation of his plot-lines would have appreciated how far, in some ways, he went beyond them. Plautus' plays usually have a strong single plot, while Terence's are noted for their double-plotting. *A Chaste Maid in Cheapside* has no less than four plots, all intricately interweaved around the crucial figure of Sir Walter Whorehound: (i) the Yellowhammers are trying to marry their daughter, Moll, to Sir Walter, but are thwarted by her attachment to Touchwood Junior; (ii) they also plan to marry Tim to a supposed 'Welsh gentlewoman', in reality Sir Walter's former whore; (iii) Sir Walter has been maintaining the family of the complacent cuckold, Allwit, whose children he has actually fathered for him; (iv) Sir Walter has been sustaining himself financially on expectations of inheritance from his kin, the infertile Kixes, but these evaporate when Touchwood Senior—an impoverished but over-fertile gentleman—provides a remedy for the Kixes' childlessness.[11]

So the play out-Terences Terence in its ingenuity, and the impression it may give of artless realism—fostered by a very careful adaptation of the action to a specific and familiar locale—is itself a product of art. We see this also in other measures Middleton takes to prevent a play with so many constituent elements from collapsing into shapelessness. I have already pointed to the crucial role of Sir Walter Whorehound, a centripetal figure among so many centrifugal forces. We should also note how pointedly the play is constructed around a key phase of the Church year—the transition from Lent to Easter—and around its key ceremonial rites of passage, a christening, a funeral and a wedding, birth, death, and new generation.

These are in fact the structural elements of the play which generate such mordant ironies. Lent is a period of abstinence, of repression of the desires of the flesh—the antithesis of the carnival that precedes it—in a spiritual preparation for the death and resurrection of Easter.

---

[9] Neither Shakespeare nor Jonson attended university, though in 1619 Jonson was made an honorary MA by Oxford.

[10] For those who appreciate the ancient rivalry between Oxford and Cambridge, it will be apparent that it is probably not an accident that Tim is a Cambridge man.

[11] See R. Levin, *The Multiple Plot in English Renaissance Drama* (Madison: University of Wisconsin Press, 1971).

Yet the characters still pursue the flesh, both literally and metaphorically, and the observance of Lent is reduced to a corrupt policing of the laws that forbade most eating of meat in that period. The punch-line when the 'promoters' are left literally holding the baby, thinking that it is a joint of illicit lamb, recalls the famous *Second Shepherds' Pageant* in the Wakefield pageants from the Towneley Cycle of mystery plays, where a lamb substitutes for a child. The overtones of Christ's body, sacrificed for man and left symbolically to be eaten in commemoration of him, are very strong—and the indifference of the characters to these religious echoes very telling.

The christening of Allwit's (or rather, Sir Walter's) son degenerates into a drunken farrago of lust, greed, and social pretension—the holy water of baptism draining away to leave spilled wine and urine ('Nothing but wet, sir, | Some wine spilt here, belike ... Is't no worse, thinkst thou?' 3.2.184–5) as the gossips stagger off for more entertainment by the aptly named Pissing Conduit near the Royal Exchange. The mixed associations of water—with purification and spiritual rebirth, but also with death—surface again later in the Thames itself, where Moll 'drowns' in order to provide the Easter resurrection, which is the catalyst for the play's festive conclusion. The play's recurrent emphasis on these religious ceremonies and rites of passage is what gives context and conviction to what is in fact the major climax and necessary precursor of that festive conclusion—Sir Walter's brush with death and spiritual reawakening: 'If ever eyes were open, these are they; | Gamesters, farewell, I have nothing left to play' (5.1.149–50). Of course Middleton milks the comedy here for all that it is worth, as all Sir Walter's sins with the Allwits come back to haunt him, in one misguided attempt after another to make him feel better. But at the same time there is an important sense in which Sir Walter really has seen the light, and is appalled by what it shows him—the whole texture of Jacobean London life to which he has been so integral is rotten through and through, spiritually dead. When he says he has 'nothing left to play' he sees life revealed both as a gambling game and as a theatrical charade.

But this is not quite Middleton's last word in this play: if it were, it would be so much easier to label the play as a whole as 'puritan', endorsing the view of what today we might call a born-again Christian. Firstly, the Allwits are totally unmoved by Sir Walter's conversion and seem bent on a career of high-class prostitution. Secondly, life in general goes on, Sir Walter's departure meaning that Moll's 'resurrection' allows her something suspiciously like a romantic happy ending with Touchwood Junior. Then Lady Kix's 'miraculous' pregnancy gives a dubious lease of financial life to the Touchwood Seniors, and even Tim is persuaded, against all his training in logic, that life with his 'Welsh Gentlewoman' is for the best. It is as if no serious lessons have been learnt, unless the audience have been more attentive than the characters themselves. The ending above all lends support to the view that Middleton is not a satirist, in the sense of having a clear agenda which he wishes to promote in place of the world as he currently sees it, but an ironist who demonstrates that human beings are born to behave exactly as they do and are simultaneously a disappointment to their own potential when they do so.

Women Beware Women

The date of *Women Beware Women* has never been established with any certainty, nor has the company for which it was written. It is usually dated around either 1613/14 or 1619/23, on the basis primarily of two types of evidence: supposed affinities with other works by Middleton (early-daters point to the Lord Mayor's Show, *The Triumphs of Truth*, 1613, late-daters to *The Changeling*, 1622); and supposed allusions to contemporary events at court, usually involving either the Earl of Somerset and Lady Frances Howard (early) or the Duke of Buckingham (late). But all such arguments are inevitably circular and inconclusive. The sources are not a lot more helpful. Middleton's main source for the story of Bianca and the Duke was Celio Malespini's *Ducento Novelle* (Venice, 1609), but that did not include the tragic ending, for which it seems he turned to Fynes Moryson's *Itinerary*, which introduces the Cardinal and Bianca's ill-fated plot to kill him. It was entered in the Stationers' Register in 1617, but never printed until 1903. So it would only help us with the dating if we knew how and when Middleton had access to it. Similarly, *The True History of the Tragicke Loves of Hipolito and Isabella Neapolitans*, from which Middleton took the Isabella–Hippolito plot, was printed in French in 1597 and English in 1628, but there is no knowing which version he drew on, or when.

There is a final consideration, which has not been given as much attention as the others. The play requires an unusually large cast, many of whom have to be on stage simultaneously in the final scene, which eliminates opportunities for doubling; that scene calls for at least 23 parts (modestly counting Lords, Ladies, and cupids as only two apiece, and with no provision at all for attendants). Furthermore, there are four prominent female roles, as well as nymphs, cupids, and pages, who were all (except perhaps the Mother, and maybe Livia) presumably played by boy actors. This would have tested the resources of most companies of the day—and may well explain why there is no early history of performance of the play, beyond Nathaniel Richards's late prefatory testimony that 'I . . . have seen't.' Is it possible that the play was performed by the same grouping of the Lady Elizabeth's Men and the Queen's Revels Boys which R. B. Parker hypothesized for *A Chaste Maid in Cheapside*? If so, the earlier dating of 1613/14 is indicated. That runs against the general recent consensus, which favours the later dating. But that in turn is largely governed by a critical fashion for seeing the play, along with *The Changeling*, as an example of anti-court or opposition drama, which supposedly flourished in the early 1620s. The fact is that we do not know when *Women Beware Women* was written and performed, and should beware of over-easy assumptions that we do.

The title of the play announces that it is an intervention in the long and often rancorous debate between those (implicitly men) who denounced women as the daughters of Eve, weak, vain, and untrustworthy, necessarily subject to their fathers and husbands, and those (both men and women) who defended them from such attacks, seeing them as equal partners in God's creation. The debate stretched back well into the Middle Ages, as we can see in several of Chaucer's *Canterbury Tales*. But during Middleton's lifetime it became particularly acute, for a variety of reasons. Firstly, a number of humanists in the early sixteenth century had argued the case for the education of women as well as men (if not necessarily to the same extent). Sir Thomas More famously educated his own daughter; Juan Luys Vives wrote *The Education of a Christian Woman* and was tutor, among others, to the later Queens, Mary I and Katherine Parr. The fact that England was then ruled successively by educated women, Mary and Elizabeth, for over fifty years also left its mark—albeit mainly in the circles of the aristocracy.

By the end of the century other voices—mainly puritan in complexion—were arguing for a greater equality between the sexes, for seeing marriage as a genuine partnership, and even for the possibility of divorce. All of these developments were met, however, by an equally ferocious misogynist backlash, epitomized by Joseph Swetnam's *The Arraignment of Lewd, Idle, Froward, and Unconstant Women* (1615) and fuelled to some extent by King James, who denounced female cross-dressing and women's extravagance in clothes, and who besides had a noted preference for male company. Middleton and Dekker collaborated on *The Roaring Girl* (*c*.1608–11), a romanticized account of the real-life cross-dressing Moll Frith, which clearly engages in this debate, rather less ambiguously than does *Women Beware Women*.

The issue with this play can thus readily be summed up: just how ironic, or otherwise, is the title? It would be easy to conclude that it is not ironic at all: Livia is a multiple bawd and murderer; Bianca slips easily from adultery to attempted murder; even Isabella settles with discomforting ease into adultery once she is convinced that it does not involve incest. Yet, as with the ambiguities about the Cardinal which I outlined earlier, this is a totally inadequate response to these characters and the complexity of the situations in which they find themselves, all of which are the products of a harshly repressive patriarchy. Isabella's lot, to be paraded like a prize mare for the lascivious scrutiny of the cretinous and phallically obsessed Ward, is a graphic reminder of the condition to which they all either are, or have been, or could be subject. Her protests about the social realities that place women in such situations are unanswerable: 'O the heart-breakings | Of miserable maids, where love's enforced . . . ' (1.2.164–5). The fact that her own situation is all an adjunct to the financial negotiations between Guardiano and Fabritio graphically underlines the subjection and sexual commodification of all the women.

By comparison with this, Hippolito's deeply-felt and scrupulous regard for Isabella cannot but seem attractive; and her preference for him, arguably, excusable. Similarly, in the case of Bianca, her elopement with Leantio seems at first to be the antithesis of such demeaning horse-trading. She has escaped the potential trap of her parents' inflexible will, exercised her own preference (against all class imperatives) in choosing Leantio, and honourably married. But once he has her back home, Leantio's idealized vision of his wife dwindles into patriarchal normality; she becomes a prize possession (a 'purchase', 'treasure', 'jewel'), to be hidden from the eyes of other men, and their passionate love-life has to be weighed in the balance against his need to earn a living. Her change of affection from Leantio to the Duke is not, then, simply unprincipled. Leantio has in effect betrayed her, even before the Duke—not to mince words—rapes her. And just as Isabella surrenders to the Ward because it means she can have Hippolito, Bianca settles for being the Duke's mistress, because if she has to be a man's possession (as life has taught her) she might as well be a possession to whom others must defer. It gives her wealth, prestige, even power of a kind—and we can understand why she would not want to let the Cardinal take that from her.[12]

Livia is the most complex case of all.[13] Old by the standards of the day ('nine and thirty') for someone in the sexual market-place, she has already buried two husbands, learning in the process bitter lessons about the patriarchy and how to make the most of it. And indeed when we first see her she seems to have settled for what might seem the most enviable role for a woman of her era, that of the rich widow. This gave her considerable independence and power in her own right—though at the price of sexual abstinence. Within that role she is free to voice markedly liberated views on the situation of women in general, telling Fabritio (when he insists Isabella shall marry whomever he chooses):

> You may compel out of the power of father
> Things merely harsh to a maid's flesh and blood;
> But when you come to love, there the soil alters:
> Y'are in another country. (1.2.131–4)

She also points out to him that there is a double standard in monogamy, because it ties women to a life of obedient subservience which is not part of a man's experience (39–45).

But there is always a sense in which Livia's free-thinking is contained by, and subject to, the patriarchy with which she has reached an accommodation of sorts. This perhaps explains why she agrees to play the bawd in the Duke's assault on Bianca. The much-admired scene in which Livia's game of chess with (Leantio's) Mother parallels and comments upon the seduction taking place on the upper stage has many implications: the Duke 'mates' Bianca as Livia 'mates' the Mother.[14] But it is less commonly perceived how much Livia herself is a pawn in the process. Though she deploys her considerable wit and

---

[12] Una Ellis Fermor praised Middleton's 'supreme gift, his discernment of the minds of women' in *The Jacobean Tragedy*, originally published in 1935. For a sympathetic reading of Bianca's role, see V. A. Foster, 'The Deed's Creature: The Tragedy of Bianca in *Women Beware Women*', *Journal of European and Germanic Philology*, 78 (1979), 508–21.

[13] For an analysis of Livia's role, see K. Muir, 'The Role of Livia in *Women Beware Women*', in A. Coleman and A. Hammond (eds.), *Essays in Honour of Harold F. Brooks* (London: Methuen), 76–89.

[14] On the staging of this scene, and of the play in general, see M. S. Lancaster, 'Middleton's Use of the Upper Stage in *Women Beware Women*', *Tulane Studies in English*, 22 (1977), 65–85; G. B. Shand, 'The Stagecraft of *Women Beware Women*', *Research Opportunities in Renaissance Drama*, 28 (1985), 29–36; L. Thomson, '"Enter Above": The Staging of *Women Beware Women*', *SEL* 26 (1986), 331–43.

sophistication, she never questions the Duke's right to do what he does, and effectively accepts it (and her role in furthering it) as the way of the world. When Bianca calls her a 'damned bawd', she shrugs it off: ''Tis but a qualm of honour, 'twill away; | A little bitter for the time, but lasts not' (2.2.472–3). Her cynicism here, and her resignation to the fact that it is only a matter of time before Bianca sees things the same way, is a measure of just how deeply implicated she is within the patriarchal structures which have created a relatively comfortable space for her.

This is perhaps best seen in her handling of the Isabella–Hippolito relationship where, although she is concerned about her niece's fate with the Ward, she seems more driven by her own feelings for Hippolito. It does not take a Freudian to see, in her supposed removal of the incest impediment between uncle and niece, a displaced removal of the same impediment between herself and her brother, Hippolito. Or that, in facilitating that sexual relationship, she reawakens her own suppressed sexuality and, denied Hippolito, displaces those feelings on to Leantio. That is, her initial motivation is the male sexual agenda: it is only because, here, the man concerned is a brother for whom her own feelings are extreme that she begins to act like a truly liberated woman. And in doing that she breaks the implicit contract—the sexual abstinence—that gave her relative freedom in the first place. In a retribution which echoes that of the Duchess in Webster's *The Duchess of Malfi*, the brother she loves is appalled by her liaison with a social inferior, and puts patriarchal family honour above her self-fulfilment. So Livia is paid back by the patriarchy whose tool in some respects she had been, and resolves in turn on a revenge which will be instrumental in destroying an entire sexual economy based on force, lies, rape, and deceit.

The strength of the play, in short, lies in refusing to be simplistic in its view of women, any more than in its view of men. As Flaubert put it, to know everything is to excuse everything, and Middleton seems close to flirting with such moral relativism in the sympathetic psychological realism of this play (as he is again in *The Changeling*). There is a remorseless logic in this society (dictated largely, it must be said, by the Duke at its head) in which innocence and idealism become indistinguishable from selfishness and power. Yet all of this is played out on a chess-board of fixed rules and known penalties, the enforcement of which is as ruthless as it is inscrutable. Middleton leaves it to his audience to determine the relationship between all these elements.

The Changeling

We can date and place *The Changeling* with a precision impossible for the first two plays in this collection. It was licensed on 7 May 1622 by the Master of the Revels to the Lady Elizabeth's Men, for performance at the small indoor theatre known as the Phoenix in Drury Lane. It was also performed at the court at Whitehall on 4 January 1624, in the presence of Prince Charles. The precise dating allows us to speak with some confidence about the play in relation to the reputation of the court in the early 1620s, and in the context of British relations with Spain; we may even suppose that the court performance is a measure of the change in Anglo-Spanish relations between these two dates, which is a key issue in relation to *A Game at Chess* (see below). These have been a theme in a good deal of recent writing on the play.[15]

The intimacy of the original theatre (which the authors would have known they were writing for) must help to account for the unusual intensity of psychological 'close-up' in the play, the narrow, charged focus on small groups of characters (notably the pairing of Beatrice-Joanna and Deflores)—qualities which the 1974 BBC version, with Stanley Baker as Deflores and Helen Mirren as Beatrice-Joanna, translated perfectly to television, but which have been lost (one of several deficiencies) in the recent (1997/8) widescreen version directed by Marcus Thompson, with Ian Dury and Amanda Ray-King in the lead roles.[16] We do know that the play was extremely successful in its own day, so much so that it seems to have popularized the name Antonio or 'Tony' (from the madhouse plot) as synonymous with a fool. Queen

---

[15] Apart from M. Heinemann, *Puritanism and Theatre: Thomas Middleton and Opposition Drama under the Early Stuarts* (Cambridge: Cambridge University Press, 1980), see A. H. Tricomi, *Anticourt Drama in England 1603–1642* (Charlottesville: University Press of Virginia, 1989); A. A. Bromham and Z. Bruzzi, *'The Changeling' and the Year of Crisis* (London: Pinter, 1990); C. Malcolmson, '"As Tame as the Ladies": Politics and Gender in *The Changeling*', *ELR* 20 (1990), 320–39.

[16] The 1993 BBC version, despite a powerful performance by Bob Hoskins, was not considered particularly successful. This may say something about the importance to the play as a whole of the madhouse plot, which was unaccountably omitted. But I think it also said something about the use of videotape, which contributed to a raw authenticity that did not substitute adequately for theatrical intimacy. Marcus Thompson's movie seems to have been an attempt to emulate the success of Baz Luhrmann's *Romeo and Juliet* in its uninhibited translation of Renaissance passion to a modern setting, or as Philip French put it in *The Observer* (8 March 1998): 'This being School of Derek Jarman, the central characters wear Jacobean costumes but drive around in stretch limos with police outriders.' But critics have unanimously pronounced it a failure.

Henrietta's Men took it over after 1625, and the Duke of York's Men revived it early in the Restoration. Thereafter it fell out of fashion until this century, when Eliot's early enthusiasm for it was symptomatic of a wider interest, and since around 1930 it has been staged as regularly as any non-Shakespearean play of its period.[17] Significant recent productions include those by Terry Hands for the Royal Shakespeare Company (RSC) at the Aldwych (both 1978), by Richard Eyre for the National Theatre in 1988, and by Michael Attenborough for the RSC at the Swan (1992) and the Pit (1993), with Malcolm Storry as Deflores and Cheryl Campbell as Beatrice-Joanna—these latter both using the small-scale intimacy of the venues to good effect.

The early publishing history of *The Changeling* raises some interesting questions, which still in a way have a bearing on our response to the play. When it was entered for copyright purposes in the Stationers' Register on 19 October 1652, it was described as a comedy by William Rowley. The printed text that appeared the next year said nothing about genre, but ascribed it jointly to 'Thomas Middleton and William Rowley, Gents'. Middleton and Rowley had actually collaborated on at least four plays before this, and it should be said that the majority of Middleton's work for the theatre was written in collaboration—not only with Rowley, but with Dekker, Webster, Munday, possibly Fletcher, even possibly (if modern theories about *Timon of Athens* are to be credited) with Shakespeare. But post-Romantic sensibility has largely balked at the multiple authorship of so much of early modern drama which (like writing for the Hollywood studios in the 1930s and 1940s) smacks of the production line rather than inspiration.[18] Many plays written in this way are unfairly neglected. *The Changeling* is the great exception to that rule—but it is an exception that has only been achieved by some wilful misrepresentation of the evidence.[19]

That is, the play is almost universally ascribed to Middleton 'with William Rowley' (i.e. Rowley is given the lesser role). Yet scholarship is fairly unanimous, on stylistic grounds, about which parts are by which author: Rowley wrote 1.1, 1.2, 3.3, 4.2.1–16, 4.3, and 5.3, while Middleton wrote the rest. So Rowley actually wrote more than half of the text, including the crucial opening and closing scenes. But

---

[17] Lisa Cronin, *Professional Productions in the British Isles since 1880 of Plays by Tudor and Early Stuart Dramatists (Excluding Shakespeare)* (University of Warwick, 1987), lists 42 productions between 1950 and 1984.

[18] T. S. Eliot observed that Middleton 'collaborated shamelessly'.

[19] Marcus Thompson's movie perpetuates this, being called *Middleton's Changeling*.

Middleton is almost always credited as the presiding genius of the play, on the grounds that he authored most of the Beatrice-Joanna/Alsemero/Deflores plot, the tragedy which has been the focus of most modern attention. Whereas Rowley's authorship of the Isabella/Alibius/Lollio/Antonio/Franciscus 'comedy' is relegated to a distinct second-place, that of a serviceable 'sub-plot' which is most to be commended for being so thematically well-integrated with the 'main action'. Doubtless this is partly because that side of the play (as William Empson long ago observed) 'forces one to take the unembarrassed Elizabethan view of lunatics'.[20] But it is also because of a modern critical predilection for tragedy over comedy, and because Rowley is usually categorized as a journeyman playwright, in a lesser league than Middleton.

This is a catalogue of self-reinforcing prejudices which needs to be seen as such, circling around the still-vexed status of theatrical texts as 'literature'. Rowley (c.1585–1626) was a long-standing man of the theatre, who served successively with Queen Anne's, Prince Charles's, and latterly the King's Men, sometimes in positions of responsibility. He regularly wrote plays, either alone or in collaboration, between 1607 and 1624, including (of his unaided work) *A Shoemaker a Gentleman* and *All's Lost by Lust*. He seems to have been particularly well known for playing fat fool roles, like Lollio in *The Changeling*. (The Fat Bishop in *A Game at Chess* is an elaboration of such roles.) Yet little of this is traditionally credited, at least with any force, in respect of his part in *The Changeling*. Although Middleton has never been an assured canonical literary figure like Shakespeare and Jonson, it is his presence which validates the play as literature, overshadowing the theatrical journeyman.

Rowley deserves at least an equal billing with Middleton. All the evidence suggests that it was his 'comedy' which impressed early audiences and, besides, what I shall call the castle plot and the madhouse plot (implying no hierarchy) are so closely integrated that it would be impertinent to suggest that one author was more important than the

---

[20] W. Empson, *Some Versions of Pastoral* (London: Chatto and Windus, 1935; cited here from Harmondsworth: Penguin, 1966), 46. Empson himself does not distinguish between 'main' and 'sub' plots. Nor does Richard Levin in his major study, *The Multiple Plot in English Renaissance Drama*. I am discussing a general tendency which can be found in many earlier popular editions of the play. Gamini Salgado, for example, in *Three Jacobean Tragedies* (Harmondsworth, 1965), describes Rowley as 'a hardworking hack with a nose for what the public wanted' who contributed 'the farcical sub-plot' (p. 34).

other. The integration operates at any number of levels. Antonio and Franciscus, the pretend fool and madman respectively who pursue Isabella in the madhouse, are absentees from Vermandero's castle, and so become suspects in Alonzo's murder; Alibius and Lollio prepare their patients to perform a grotesque dance of antics as a climax to the wedding celebrations of Alsemero and Beatrice-Joanna, but Deflores and Beatrice-Joanna are revealed as the truly insane ones, performing their own dance of death instead. In a seminal essay Christopher Ricks showed how the play revolves around the sexual *double entendre* of a key group of words—blood, will, act, deed, service—consistently trans- muting the languages of family honour and of courtly love into those of lust and personal satisfaction.[21] This applies equally to the castle and the madhouse plots. But it is significant how central Deflores is to this linguistic transmutation, as if his own social slippage (a gentleman reduced by financial necessity to working for Vermandero) mirrors the degrading of high ideals: the courtly 'service' of a monarch or a lady becomes the demeaning servitude of paid employment and animal sexual gratification; the 'blood' that binds the family in the honour code flows into lust and murder.

The title itself is a measure of the integration of the work. The *OED* lists the following senses of 'changeling': (1) 'One given to change; a fickle or inconstant person'; (2) 'A Person or thing (surrepti- tiously) put in exchange for another'; (3) 'A child secretly substituted for another in infancy; *esp.* a child (usually stupid or ugly) supposed to have been left by fairies for one stolen'; (4) 'A half-witted person, idiot, imbecile'; (5) 'The rhetorical figure *Hypallage*' [defined else- where as 'A figure of speech in which there is an interchange of two elements of a proposition, the natural relations of these being reversed'], citing George Puttenham's *Art of English Poesie* (1589): 'Hipallage or the Changeling . . . as, he that should say, for tell me troth and lie not, lie me troth and tell not'. All of these apply to the play, in both its plots, in a variety of ways. The 'changeling' of the title is probably Antonio, who substitutes himself in the role of a fool; in this he is matched by Franciscus, who substitutes himself as a madman—the operative legal distinction being that a 'fool' was men- tally abnormal from birth, while a 'madman' was someone who was born sane but went mad. Alibius's madhouse is divided into separate wards for these two categories, and is presided over by a theatrical

[21] C. Ricks, 'The Moral and Political Structure of *The Changeling*', *Essays in Criticism*, 10 (1960), 290–306.

'fool' (a role which always exploits the fact of 'substitution' involved in acting), Lollio, who is himself sex-obsessed and underlines the sexual nature of all the insanity in the play.

Beatrice-Joanna is another 'changeling', fickle in her sexual preferences, choosing Alonzo and then almost immediately preferring Alsemero, but finally obsessed with Deflores, to whom she once had a pathological aversion. That change in her relationship, however, goes well beyond fickleness: the coming together of her striking beauty and what (to her at least) seems his repulsive appearance is precisely the kind of inversion of the properties in their relationship which we might call *hypallage*. So Beatrice-Joanna proves to be, at least metaphorically, a child left by the fairies, in some way not her father's daughter. That notion is picked up in some of the play's fascinating psychological half-lights, such as Vermandero's revelation to Alsemero that Beatrice-Joanna once had a 'fellow' but she died (3.4.4–6). The text is ambiguous about whether Vermandero means his wife or another daughter (even twin), but in either case there are dark suggestions of doubleness or substitution. This may or may not be linked to Beatrice-Joanna's double name: for those watching the play (i.e. without the text to guide them) she is 'Joanna' and it comes as some surprise when, late in 3.3, the double name is first voiced. Its real force emerges in the closing moments when her bewildered father calls 'Joanna! Beatrice! Joanna' (5.3.148). This points, of course, to her double identity, the corrupt self beneath the beautiful appearance, but also suggests that she has somehow taken on the identity of 'her fellow'. At the same time, Vermandero's ill-concealed enthusiasm at the prospect of acquiring a 'son' in Alonzo speaks volumes about his relationship with his daughter. In all these senses Beatrice-Joanna is a child left by the fairies, though her own metaphor expresses it differently: 'I am that of your blood was taken from you | For your better health' (5.3.150–1).

The essential attribute of 'the changeling' is not that of changing, but that of revealing its true nature, in spite of efforts—conscious or otherwise—to conceal them. Antonio is indeed a fool, and Franciscus in some important senses truly mad (morally blind, self-deluded by his own cleverness), to pay court to a chastely married woman, just as Alibius's jealousy borders on insanity in keeping Isabella locked up in this way. Beatrice-Joanna's fickleness, her assumption that it is only a small matter to transfer her affections from Alonzo to Alsemero, is belied by the devastating truth that she is indeed 'the deed's creature' (3.4.136), inescapably driven by a lust that takes murder casually in its stride. This is a truth she resists recognizing as long as she can, in those electrifying scenes with Deflores, until she is completely consumed by, at one with, his remorseless sexual agenda, dedicated only to its fulfilment and equally indifferent to murder. Hence the aptness of the climax to their relationship when, their crimes revealed and no future to look forward to, they indulge in one last frenzied act of adultery in the closet before Deflores stabs her, and then himself. Alonzo's severed finger, with its ring still attached, is a brutally revealing symbol of the forces that drive this play; phallic power, vaginal lustful tenacity, and death.

A Game at Chess

A Game at Chess was licensed for performance by the Master of the Revels on 12 June 1624, and performed by the King's Men at the Globe from 5 to 14 August 1624 (excepting only Sunday 8 August, when all theatres were closed). Performances were halted after 14 August by the Privy Council, following complaints to the King by the Spanish Ambassador. Middleton's last surviving play is unique among the plays of its era on at least three counts, which all derive from its phenomenal contemporary popularity: in having been performed nine days running (when plays were normally spaced out in a changing repertory, to maintain the interest of regular playgoers); in having survived in no less than eight different forms, six of them manuscript and two distinct printed versions; and in having left a wealth of contemporary record and comment, including one detailed eye-witness account of a performance, unrivalled by any other dramatic text of the time.

Each of these features is as problematic as it is special. The popular appeal of the play was undoubtedly connected with its relatively frank discussion of recent political events, including the melodramatic business of the visit in 1623 by Prince Charles and the Duke of Buckingham to Madrid, in order to negotiate the marriage of the Prince to the Spanish Infanta. These negotiations failed. The Prince and Duke returned and reversed British foreign policy, declaring for war with Spain—all developments which were met with popular rejoicing in London. The play thus represented on stage figures who, though notionally chess-pieces, were unmistakably members of the Spanish and British royal families, and various important politicians, including the former Spanish Ambassador, Gondomar (the Black Knight), and Buckingham himself. In the case of Gondomar (though perhaps not most other characters) the actors went to extraordinary lengths to make the impersonation unmistakable, acquiring a cast suit of his clothes, the litter in which he was carried around town, and the chair of ease he needed because of a painful anal fistula. How did Middleton and the actors think they could get away with staging such a work? How did they get it licensed? Did they deliberately delay performance until the King and the court were well removed from London (they were in the Midlands, some two days' ride away, when the scandal broke)? Did they have support behind the scenes, from someone like the Duke of Buckingham himself, or the Lord Chamberlain, the Earl of Pembroke, a long-standing friend of the actors and supporter of anti-Spanish policies? We have no sure answers to any of these questions.

The plethora of texts is fascinating, and a luxury we have for no other play of the period. Middleton himself and the professional copyist, Ralph Crane, set up a production line for manuscript copies to meet demand, at a time when no printed text would have been licensed. But this creates as many problems as it solves, not least in determining the 'best' text for modern readers. Briefly, the six manuscripts are: (1) *Archdall-Folger Ms. v.a. 231* (hereafter Ar.). Although dated 13 August 1624 (i.e. one of the days of performance), this is an early version of the play prepared by Crane, is more than 300 lines shorter than the fullest versions, lacks the character of the Fat Bishop and some of the ending, and is significantly different from later versions in the character of the White King's Pawn. (2) *Trinity College, Cambridge Ms. o.2.66* (Tr.). The only copy entirely in Middleton's own hand, but apparently written before the play was fully ready for the stage. It omits 4.5 and ten lines of 5.1, and is quite careless in some respects. (3) *Bridgewater-Huntington Ms. EL 34 B17* (Bri.). It is partly in Middleton's own hand, partly in the hands of two unidentified amateur scribes. It is quite late in the evolution of the play, and Middleton's own versions of 5.2, 5.3, and the Epilogue perhaps reflect his last thoughts on these scenes. But overall the text compounds some earlier errors, and there is a major gap in 2.2, which Middleton himself unsatisfactorily tried to bridge. (4) *Rosenbach-Folger Ms. v.a.342* (Ros.). Despite a title-page in Middleton's own hand this is the work of inexperienced scribes, and it shows. It unsatisfactorily mixes early and late stages of the play's composition. (5) *British Library Ms. Lansdowne 690* (Lan.). This is a finely crafted Crane copy of quite a late version of the play, adopted as the copy-text for this edition (see 'Note on the Texts'). (6) *Bodleian Library Ms. Malone 25*. Another fine Crane copy (with a holograph dedication by Middleton to make it a

New Year's gift), but radically trimmed; it has about 785 lines fewer than *Tr.* and includes unique bridging passages to cover gaps. Neither of the two early printed quartos (*c.*1625, and unlicensed) is of much textual interest; one (*Short Title Catalogue* 17882; hereafter Q1) seems to derive mainly from the *Bri.* and *Ros.* line of manuscripts, though with evidence of Crane in the later scenes, and is very clumsily printed (*STC* 17883 is simply a reprint; Q2); the other (*STC* 17884; Q3) seems to derive from the line of manuscripts in Crane's hand. The quartos are of most interest for their title-pages, the latter apparently based on the former; they show quite accurate pictures of three of the major figures behind the play, Archbishop De Dominis (the Fat Bishop), Count Gondomar (the Black Knight), and Prince Charles (the White Knight), but it is doubtful if they represent the play as it was staged.

The sheer weight of contemporary comment on the play, much of it as surprised as modern commentators have been by its daring, inevitably fuels speculation about the staging of the play, and whether it was somehow specially sanctioned. (The Appendix reprints the two fullest contemporary descriptions of the play, a report by the Spanish Ambassador and an eye-witness account by John Holles.) My own view, in brief, is that this is an *unnecessary* assumption. The play was duly licensed by the Master of the Revels, Sir Henry Herbert, and while it is true that he owed his post to his patron and kinsman, the Earl of Pembroke, the play's anti-Spanish sentiments were by 1624 fully—and publicly—shared by Prince Charles, the Duke of Buckingham, and (however reluctantly) King James himself. In such circumstances, Herbert need not have had strong qualms about licensing a play which veiled its subject-matter under the discreet fiction of the chess-game. I suspect that the unusual lengths the actors went to impersonate Gondomar may have created more of a stir than Herbert anticipated, and the Spanish Ambassador—already highly excited by the wave of anti-Spanish sentiment, and not even sure he should still be in England—felt he had no alternative but to make an issue of it all. By the same token, the King had little option but to respond to the grievances of the Ambassador of a country with whom he was still, however notionally, negotiating. And he may have been genuinely aggrieved that those Privy Councillors still in London had let the scandal of the play get out of hand.

This, however, is a revisionist view of the matter, which basically sees the play as a relatively normal (albeit superbly crafted) play of the period, which just happened to fall foul of abnormal circumstances.

Others—notably Margot Heinemann and Albert Tricomi—would argue that the play and its production are symptomatic of deeper divisions in the society of the day, of forces opposed (whatever immediate factional accommodations may have been operative) to Stuart absolutism and its creation, Buckingham. When the White Duke is in the Black House he does pretend to admit to a number of vices to which Buckingham was in actuality prone—but it is not easy to know how much weight such details should be accorded. Indeed, because the play is unique in so many ways it is difficult to determine what terms of judgement to apply to any of its features. Was the play itself unusual, or the manner or timing of its performance, or the way it was published in manuscript, or the political context within which it was written and received, or a mixture of these? We actually know so much about it (by contrast with virtually every other play of the period) that we finally have nothing with which we can properly compare it. And all judgements are ultimately a reading of the ideology of early modern theatre history as a whole, rather than of this single play.

A most unfortunate consequence of the scandal surrounding it is that the play itself has been completely overshadowed by its notoriety. This is a pity because it is one of the finest of Middleton's plays, a tragicomic study in temptation, sin, and retribution in many guises. The Black Knight in particular is a splendid example of the bravura villain, in the tradition of Shakespeare's Richard III, or Marlowe's Jew of Malta, or Jonson's Volpone, a Machiavel-master in the art of seduction, so in love with his own skill that it is impossible not to fall partly under the spell of his infectious enthusiasm. Yet the type is so familiar that we feel it can only be a matter of time before he overreaches himself, as he does when (having 'seduced' the White King's Pawn and the Fat Bishop) he tries to take on the White Knight, in a move that precipitates 'checkmate by discovery' for the whole Black House.

'Seduction' is a central concept in the play, fusing together the play's sexual, religious, and political intrigues. When the Black Bishop's Pawn pursues the White Queen's Pawn, he is after her body every bit as much as her soul, and the implications of his success in either sphere would be serious for the political balance between the Black and White Houses. Lust is in fact the besetting vice of the Black House, but it is indivisible from their attempts (however cynical) to achieve spiritual hegemony, and from their long-term ambitions for 'universal monarchy'. It is precisely because these different forms of motivation are so interchangeable that the complex plotting of the play all holds together (there can be as many as five 'seductions' in progress at any one time). It is also a key to the play's allegorical mode, and to the way it tantalizingly involves the audience in its decoding: in a sense we are always as much objects of seduction as any member of the White House.

The play is presented as a game of chess, a polysemous metaphor of any conflict between white and black, right and wrong, good and evil, but one organized by contrasting states, with their monarchs, aristocrats, bishops, knights, and lower orders. And this is not just any game of chess: it is one seen (in the Induction) in a dream-vision by Error, and expounded to Ignatius Loyola, founder of the Jesuits. This immediately places us in the Counter-Reformation politics of the Jesuits, and indirectly (because Loyola himself had been Spanish) of Spanish ambitions against Protestant Europe. If the play is, in a sense, inevitably anti-Catholic, it is specifically aimed at what are presented as these twin vanguards of militant Catholicism, rather than at the Church in general: the Black Bishop in the play is the Father General of the Jesuits (and both his Pawn and the Black Queen's Pawn, two of the chief mischief-makers, belong to his order), while the Black Knight is unmistakably Count Gondomar, formerly Spanish Ambassador in London, whose charm and guile were popularly credited with increasing Spanish influence at King James's court. It is broadly hinted that the other Black Bishop is the Pope himself, but he never appears, leaving the Jesuits and the Spanish as the real villains of the piece.

But if Gondomar is unmistakable (and the actors made sure of this with his costume and properties), most of the other characters are only inferentially identifiable with counterparts in actuality. There is an exception to this in the conceited and gluttonous Fat Bishop, a late addition to the plot (which, incidentally, tipped the balance of the play more decisively towards comedy), whose circumstances—a Catholic convert to the Church of England, who later reverted to Rome—could only fit Marc Antonio De Dominis, Archbishop of Spalato, and contemporaries readily identified him. But when we look beyond these two, the issue becomes much less clear-cut. The kings are obviously, at some level, the Kings of Spain and of England, just as the dukes are their respective favourites, Olivares and Buckingham, and the White Knight has to be Prince Charles. But all of these roles are kept as brief as their functions within the plot allow, and largely devoid of individual characteristics; they may well, in fact, not have been *impersonated* at all, though the Spanish Ambassador did report home that 'the king of the blacks has easily been taken for our lord the King, because of his youth, dress, and other details' (see Appendix, p. 311).

And some details do not 'fit': the White Queen cannot 'be' Queen Anne, in the aftermath of the Charles/Buckingham visit to Madrid, since she had died in 1619. The Black King's lust for her, moreover, makes no *biographical* sense. It is probably more appropriate, therefore, to follow those who have seen her as embodying the Church of England, a Protestant Church under siege from various Roman Catholic forces, to whom the King was 'married' as its Supreme Head: in which context the White Queen's Pawn could represent some of the virtues espoused by the Church, such as truth and purity. But this may be over-literal. In the first place, the play's time-scale is studiously unspecific. Both Gondomar and De Dominis had left England two years before the play, in 1622, and while the former might still plausibly be seen as a threat, the Archbishop had lost favour with the Catholic Church to which he had returned and died in prison at around the time the play was staged, awaiting trial for heresy. Inasmuch as the play depicts their activities in England, this is out of sync with the trip of Charles and Buckingham to Spain in 1623. Middleton is also inexact, either deliberately or through ignorance, about details like the date of the canonization of Ignatius Loyola, which reinforces a sense of the play's fluid, dream-like time-scale. And this reopens the possibility that the White Queen might in a sense 'shadow' Queen Anne, who was known to have been a Roman Catholic convert, and who might aptly represent the vulnerability of the English Church right at the centre of the court. If that were so, the plight of her Pawn might the more credibly be taken to represent that of Anne's own daughter, Elizabeth, Queen of Bohemia, whose perilous situation in the Thirty Years War was the object of much Protestant sympathy and anti-Spanish feeling in England.

It is in the nature of allegory that it prompts such speculations, without finally confirming or denying their validity. It titillates, or seduces, but denies us the satisfaction of closure. This is probably what allowed the Master of the Revels to license the play with a clear conscience. And it does have to be said that none of the very extensive contemporary documentation relating to the play so much as hints an 'identity' for the White Queen or her Pawn. John Chamberlain discreetly mentions that 'the worst is in playing him [Gondomar], they played somebody else', which is probably an allusion to King James himself or Prince Charles, while the later correspondence between Secretary Conway and the Privy Council in London makes it clear that 'the representing of any modern Christian kings' on stage was an issue. But none of this takes us below the surface of the allegory. And this remains true, perhaps the more oddly, even in the case of the White King's Pawn, a traitor to the White cause, whose role Middleton adapted between the early Archdall text and the later versions.

In Archdall, the character seems largely to have been based on someone with pro-Catholic, indeed pro-Jesuit, leanings. The Black Knight describes him as a 'Poor Jesuit-ridden soul' (1.1.324) and promises to reward him with the 'red hat' of a cardinal (2.2.219). This would seem to apply most aptly to Sir Toby Matthew, son of the Archbishop of York, who had become a Jesuit, advocated restoration of the Catholic bishops in England, and was sent to Madrid in 1623 to help with Prince Charles's marriage negotiations. All of this remains in the later versions of the play, yet none of the correspondence identifies the Pawn with Matthew. Indeed, John Chamberlain seems to imply that he was expected to figure in the play but did not, inasmuch as the depiction of Gondomar 'lacked nothing but . . . Sir G. Peter, or Sir T. Matthew to bear him company'. This is presumably because by then the original conception had been elaborated with suggestions of someone much more senior in court or government circles (see particularly the additions at 1.1.315–19 and 3.1.261–6), whom modern commentators usually identify as Lionel Cranfield, Earl of Middlesex. As Lord Treasurer he had opposed war with Spain on the grounds of cost, and paid for crossing Buckingham with impeachment. Yet, again, no contemporary commentator makes this identification. The only person to make any definite identification of the role is John Holles, who says 'this by the character is supposed Bristol: yet it is hard players should judge him in jest, before the State in earnest'. John Digby, Earl of Bristol, had been central to negotiations for a Spanish marriage since 1614, but had been recalled from Madrid in disgrace at the end of 1623, another person to fall foul of Buckingham and indeed Prince Charles. He hardly fits the characterizations of being either 'Jesuit-ridden' or in a position 'To cross . . . with my counsel, purse and power' English resistance to Gondomar and his ambitions. Yet that is the identification made by Holles, a true eye-witness of the play in performance, a friend of Bristol, and an experienced political commentator.

So the play's allegory (and indeed its contextual mysteries of licensing and eventual suppression) seduce us into ever more sophisticated readings, just as the members of the Black House attempt to seduce those of the White House into sexual and theological indiscretions. It is an endless process. The Fat Bishop and the White King's Pawn succumb to the seduction, but the White Queen's Pawn is saved, and the 'checkmate by discovery' of the whole Black House is a moment of pure triumph. Yet it is implicit in Middleton's 'game' metaphor that the playing is never really over, that the pieces can always be put back on the board; Spanish and Jesuit plots have only been thwarted, not eradicated. Hence the warnings in the Epilogue about 'their depraving work' and (more an exhortation than a promise) the determination that 'what they'd commit to bane, | Her White friends' loves will build up fair again'.

NOTE ON THE TEXTS

THERE are relatively few textual difficulties associated with the first three plays in this selection. In each case there is only one early text of any authority, and these were all printed with care by the standards of the day. Over the past ten years I have been able to consult these originals in the Folger, Huntington and Bodleian Libraries; those in the Bodleian have been the most accessible during the preparation of this edition. The one issue that foxed compositors then, as it does editors today, is that it is often difficult to tell when Middleton is writing verse and when he is writing prose. As Michael Taylor, the editor of a companion volume of Middleton plays in this series, admirably puts it:

The problem is no doubt due in part to Middleton's habits as a writer of manuscripts. He uses small capitals or minuscules at the heads of lines, crowds lines into a small space, and occasionally completes verse lines at the left of the margin. But I suspect that the compositors' confusion was mainly caused by a general tendency in Middleton to write a prose that often sounds like indifferent verse and a verse that would have been better off for having been prose.[1]

On the whole I have tended to assume that verse was intended, except where there are relatively clear indications that it wasn't (as, for examples, when documents are read aloud, or in sequences where clown figures like Lollio in *The Changeling* and Sordido in *Women Beware Women* have dominant roles). But there are no hard-and-fast rules.

I have silently modernized spelling and punctuation in line with series policy, only commenting on matters in the notes when they affect interpretation. Forms of the past participle ending in 'ed' are given in full, though they are normally elided in the originals (so e.g. the 'play'd' in the first line of *Chaste Maid* becomes 'played'); where it is required to be stressed, it is rendered as 'èd'. Speech prefixes are given in full. The place of the action is rarely indicated in the original texts, and I have not supplied spurious 'locations' for what would have been performed on a mainly bare stage. Editorial stage directions (or

[1] M. Taylor (ed.), *A Mad World, My Masters and Other Plays by Thomas Middleton* (Oxford World's Classics; Oxford: Oxford University Press, 1995), p. xx.

amendments to original stage directions) are indicated by square brackets, and should be treated as speculative suggestions only.

A Chaste Maid in Cheapside was entered in the Stationers' Register on 8 April 1630 for Francis Constable, and printed for him in quarto (Q) shortly thereafter. This is the copy-text for this edition. The Scholar Press (Menston, 1969) produced a facsimile of a British Library copy. I have also consulted various modern editions, notably those by R. B. Parker for the Revels Plays (London, 1969) and by Bryan Loughrey and Neil Taylor in *Thomas Middleton: Five Plays* for Penguin Classics (Harmondsworth, 1988).

Women Beware Women was entered in the Stationers' Register on 9 September 1653 for Humphrey Moseley, and printed for him in a 1657 octavo (O), called *Two New Plays, viz. More Dissemblers besides Women . . . Women Beware Women*. That is the copy-text for this edition. I have also consulted the Revels Plays edition by J. R. Mulryne (London, 1975), the first (Roma Gill: London, 1968) and second (William C. Carroll: London, 1994) New Mermaid editions, and the Penguin Classics edition by Bryan Loughrey and Neil Taylor.

The Changeling was entered in the Stationers' Register on 19 October 1652 for Humphrey Moseley, and printed for him in quarto (Q) in 1653. That is the copy-text for this edition. The Scholar Press (Menston, 1973) produced a facsimile of a British Library copy. I have also consulted the Revels Plays edition by N. W. Bawcutt (London, 1958), the Penguin Classics edition by Bryan Loughrey and Neil Taylor, and the New Mermaids second edition by Joost Daalder (London, 1990).

I have described in the introduction the phenomenally complex textual state of *A Game at Chess*. Although R. C. Bald's landmark 1929 edition of the play remains useful, not least for its reproduction of many putative sources, all modern editors must start from the exhaustive and exacting labours of T. H. Howard-Hill. These have produced (to mention only the most striking items) a Revels Plays edition (Manchester, 1992), a Malone Society Reprints old-spelling edition (Oxford, 1990), and a collection of essays on both textual and contextual matters, *Middleton's 'Vulgar Pasquin': Essays on 'A Game at Chess'* (Newark: University of Delaware Press, 1995). Between these he has subjected the text and its production to the most minute enquiry, exploding many myths and over-easy assumptions. In textual matters he has followed the normal assumption that the author's own versions of the play are of paramount authority. So the Malone Society Reprint is a version of the Trinity holograph, with an appendix of those parts of the Bridgewater-Huntington manuscript also in

Middleton's own hand; and those are the principal copy-texts for his Revels edition.

Subsequent editors who follow the same assumptions must, to all intents and purposes, reproduce most of Howard-Hill's conclusions. This seems inherently wasteful, and there are in this instance grounds for not following those assumptions. Firstly, the Trinity holograph represents a relatively early version of the play; secondly, Middleton's penmanship was far from perfect either in the act of composition or, as here, when he was his own copyist: see Michael Taylor's comments, quoted above, on Middleton's authorial habits. What emerged in the Trinity text, as Howard-Hill concedes, was 'a careless transcript of Middleton's foul papers [i.e. his first complete draft] somewhat revised' (Revels edn, p. 4). While it undoubtedly reflects Middleton's own thoughts, at that stage of the play's evolution, it does so imperfectly and in ways that need substantial decoding and supplementing with evidence from other versions.

I have therefore opted instead to use as my copy text the Lansdowne manuscript, which Howard-Hill describes as 'the most elegant and readable of all the *Game* texts' (*Middleton's 'Vulgar Pasquin'*, 171). This nevertheless requires some justification, since it is clear that Ralph Crane—the sole hand in this manuscript—was by this stage acting as an editor of the text, as much as a copyist, and was not heavily constrained by considerations of what precisely Middleton wrote. So, for example, Crane punctuated far more heavily than Middleton did, and represented elisions in more elaborate forms (e.g. 'they'had' for Middleton's 'theyde'). Many of these sophistications largely disappear in the process of modernization anyway. But I have retained (largely, though not dogmatically) Crane's use of brackets. Middleton often wrote long, loosely structured periods, with explanatory insertions and sub-clauses that make it difficult to determine where ideas begin and end, or to see the shape of the whole passage. Modern editors tend to steer us through these with commas and semicolons, but Crane's brackets often seem to me to do the job much more clearly. There are also times when I suspect they indicate a change of tone or register— something Crane could even have picked up from performances— which the modern recourse to commas would not capture. At the risk, therefore, of contravening anodyne modern conventions I have preserved many of these brackets to allow readers to make up their own minds.

There are a number of other usages where Crane's instincts often overrode his copying brief, such as a preference for 'It's' over ' 'Tis', 'mine/thine' over 'my/thy', 'hath/doth' over 'has/does'—not in all cases or systematically, but enough to be noticeable. I have retained these for the sake of consistency. Crane also omitted 3.2 altogether, possibly because of its heavy sexual innuendo, but equally possibly because it was—in his judgement—more an opportunity for extensive stage business than an integral part of the text; and there are a few other minor omissions which look more deliberate than accidental. Some of these, at least, seem to represent a doctoring of the text to make it more suitable for its intended recipient, who would have been known to Crane though his identity is lost to us. If so, it reflects a form of self-censorship as intriguing as the non-censorship of the play for the stage. (The omitted passages are supplied from other witnesses, as indicated in the notes, and marked in the text by square brackets.)

One further objection to the Lansdowne manuscript as copy-text is that, while none of the early copies gives us anything like a detailed account of the play as it was staged, this version is the one that is most indifferent to the play's theatrical provenance. It is, as Howard-Hill says, 'an elaborately calligraphic manuscript . . . intended to give pleasure to a reader' (Revels edn, pp. 8–9): to a reader, not to someone trying to recreate the experience of an audience. Given, however, that no version of the play offers an authoritative account of the staging, there is some virtue in starting with a text that tells us relatively little, and then drawing on all the other witnesses (textual and otherwise) to supply what we can.

My principal justification for choosing this as my copy-text is precisely that it *is* a carefully *edited* version of what Middleton wrote, prepared by someone who worked in close (but not slavish) proximity to Middleton, and with an accuracy and attention to the needs of a reader which Middleton himself lacked. If we use the copies in which Middleton's own hand is prominent as the basis for a modern text we will inevitably find ourselves engaged in a heavy process of editing and reconstruction simply to establish what Middleton himself intended— in matters of staging as much as anything else. By starting from Crane's Lansdowne manuscript, we start with a version of things in which Middleton's associate has done much of that for us, with more authority than any modern editor can claim. It would have been possible, of course, to produce a totally hybrid text, based on eclectic selection from all the originals. I have preferred, rather, to produce an edition of the most readable and consistent of the early texts, with thorough annotation to indicate where it differs from other texts and where it does not tell us what we may infer was meant to happen on stage.

SELECT BIBLIOGRAPHY

ELR	*English Literary Renaissance*	*MLR*	*Modern Language Review*
E&S	*Essays and Studies*	*N&Q*	*Notes and Queries*
HLQ	*Huntington Library Quarterly*	*SEL*	*Studies in English Literature*
MLQ	*Modern Language Quarterly*	*RES*	*Review of English Studies*

I HAVE suggested in the Introduction that Margot Heinemann's *Puritanism and Theatre* (1980) marks a watershed in Middleton studies. Earlier criticism was mainly concerned with formalist matters such as the generic categorization of his plays—tragedies, tragicomedies, city comedies, New Comedy—or with largely New Critical explorations of his imagery, or the nature of his 'realism', or the rhetorical strategies of his satiric/ironic vision. This is all helpfully categorized in the reviews of work on Middleton by Sara Jayne Steen (*Thomas Middleton: A Reference Guide*, 1984), J. B. Brooks ('Recent Studies in Middleton, 1971–1981', *ELR* 14 (1984), 114–28), and G. De Souza ('Thomas Middleton: Criticism Since T. S. Eliot', *Research Opportunities in Renaissance Drama*, 28 (1985), 73–85). Steen's study *Ambrosia in an Earthen Vessel* (1993) is the most comprehensive account of the vagaries of Middleton's reputation over the centuries. Heinemann's book signals a shift towards a closer interest in the historical, theatrical and ideological contexts within which he wrote, and their implication for the political orientation, social psychology, and sexual agenda of what he wrote. Much of this is apparent in such recent work on Middleton as Swapan Chakravorty's *Society and Politics in the Plays of Thomas Middleton*, who treats his subject as 'a great chronicler of early modern culture's loss of innocence'.

This does not mean that earlier criticism is no longer useful, only that we should approach it in the knowledge that it is not directly attuned to the concerns which have largely preoccupied the most recent generation. Yet the earlier work often set the agenda for what has followed, and can still usefully inform our appreciation of the plays. So, for example, we can trace through the pioneering works of L. C. Knights (*Drama and Society in the Age of Jonson*, 1937), Muriel Bradbrook (*The Growth and Structure of Elizabethan Comedy*, 1955) and Brian Gibbons (*Jacobean City Comedy*, 1968, rev. edn, 1980) a range of questions about city or citizen comedy, and Middleton's distinctive contribution to the form, which still usefully inform our reading of *A Chaste Maid in Cheapside*. Anthony Covatta's *Thomas Middleton's City Comedies* (1973) and Alexander Leggatt's *Citizen Comedy in the Age of Shakespeare* (1973) problematized their work, the former largely by challenging the entrenched view of Middleton as a realist and satirist (preferring instead to see him as an ironist), the latter by examining in more detail the various types and theatrical provenances of city comedy. None of these debates disappeared in the 1980s and 1990s, but they were recast in more openly theoretical and historicist terms, as in Gail K. Paster's *The Idea of the City* (1985), which looks at the way Middleton inverts and parodies traditional ideas of community, or T. B. Leinwand's argument in *The City Staged: Jacobean Comedy, 1603–1613* (1986) that the plays present a provocatively sceptical view of the city and its values, or Douglas Bruster's materialist and Bakhtinian reading (*Drama and the Market in the Age of Shakespeare*, 1992) which sees the plays as celebrating the commodification of city life even as they satirize it. Joanne Altieri adds a modern perspective to another long debate about Jacobean drama in 'Against Moralizing Jacobean Comedy: Middleton's *Chaste Maid*', *Criticism*, 30 (1988), 171–87.

Similar—though more extensive—critical genealogies can be drawn for the two tragedies, which feature in virtually every survey of Jacobean tragedy. I mention here only some of the more influential treatments, starting with those that consider both. George Hibbard is concerned with the generic indeterminacies of both *Women Beware Women* and *The Changeling,* in relation to the supposed 'decadence' of Jacobean tragedy, emphasizing the 'mongrel' qualities of the former ('The Tragedies of Thomas Middleton and the Decadence of the Drama', *Nottingham Renaissance and Modern Studies*, 1 (1957), 35–64). Richard Levin is searchingly thorough on the question of multiple-plotting plotting (*The Multiple Plot in English Renaissance Drama*, 1971). Nicholas Brooke has some perceptive things to say, in *Horrid Laughter in Jacobean Tragedy* (1979), in particular about the social nuancing of the plays and about the relationship between their emotional intensity and dramatic techniques. Heinemann and Tricomi (*Anticourt Drama in England 1603–1642*, 1989) both consider the plays in terms of the theatrical politics of the 1620s, the former as examples of puritan 'oppositional' drama, the latter as instances of what he calls anti-court drama. The collection, *Three Jacobean Tragedies: A Casebook*, ed. R. V. Holdsworth (1990), contains a number of useful essays on both plays, including one by the late John Stachniewski on

Calvinism and Middleton's tragedies, and one by the editor himself on their staging.

Individual essays on *Women Beware Women* include two seminal pieces, one by Christopher Ricks on its word-play ('Word Play in *Women Beware Women*', *RES* NS 12 (1961), 238–50), one by Brian Parker on its experiments with comic form ('Middleton's Experiments with Comedy and Judgement', in J. R. Brown and B. Harris (eds), *Stratford-Upon-Avon Studies 1: Jacobean Theatre*, 1960). Inga-Stina Ewbank reformulates questions about morality and 'realism' in 'Realism and Morality in *Women Beware Women*', *E&S* 22 (1969), 57–70; Neil Taylor and Brian Loughrey focus on the chess motif in 'Middleton's Chess Strategies in *Women Beware Women*', *SEL* 24 (1984), 341–54; J. Potter relates the structure of the play to 'public festivals' in '"In Time of Sports": Masques and Masquing in Middleton's *Women Beware Women*', *Papers on Language and Literature* 18 (1982), 268–83; and Anthony B. Dawson trenchantly dissects an 'economy of rape' running through it in '*Women Beware Women* and the Economy of Rape', *SEL* 27 (1987), 303–20. There have been a number of suggestive studies of the play's original staging, including those by M. S. Lancaster ('Middleton's Use of the Upper Stage in *Women Beware Women*', *Tulane Studies in English* 22 (1977), 65–85), G. B. Shand ('The Stagecraft of *Women Beware Women*', *Research Opportunities in Renaissance Drama*, 28 (1985), 29–36) and L. Thomson ('"Enter Above": The Staging of *Women Beware Women*', *SEL* 26 (1986), 331–43). On *The Changeling*, the debate about the double plot goes back to William Empson's *Some Versions of Pastoral* (1935) and runs through Bradbrook's *Themes and Conventions of Elizabethan Tragedy* (1935), S. Schoenbaum's *Middleton's Tragedies: A Critical Study* (1955), the works by Hibbard and Levin already cited, and implicitly through most other studies of the play, one way or another, including another seminal essay by Ricks ('The Moral and Poetical Structure of *The Changeling*', *Essays in Criticism* 10 (1960), 290–306). There is a parallel debate about the relative culpability of Beatrice-Joanna and Deflores, with earlier commentators (on the whole) gallantly finding excuses for her as a spoiled child and castigating him as an embodiment of evil; later readings, exemplified by P. B. R. Doob's 'A Reading of *The Changeling*', *ELR* 3 (1973), 183–206; D. B. J. Randall's 'Some Observations on the Theme of Chastity in *The Changeling*', *ELR* 14 (1984), 347–66; and Martin Wiggins's *Journeymen in Murder: The Assassin in English Renaissance Drama* (1991), have found more sympathy for a man marginalized in a rigid social hierarchy. More recently these themes have been opened out to see the play as an allegorical warning about gender politics, and marriage and alliance with Spain: see Cristina Malcolmson, '"As Tame as the Ladies": Politics and Gender in *The Changeling*', *ELR* 20 (1990), 320–39; and A. A. Bromham and Z. Bruzzi, *'The Changeling' and the Years of Crisis* (1990). On the dumb show and its conventions, see Dieter Mehl, *The Elizabethan Dumb Show* (1965).

As mentioned earlier, *A Game at Chess* has always stood to one side of Middleton's general reputation, and most of the early criticism is concerned with often rather fanciful attempts to decode the allegory, and the play's complex textual status. Heinemann's elevation of it as a key puritan-inspired 'oppositional' play has made it much more central, but has incurred considerable resistance. Jerzy Limon, in *Dangerous Matter: English Drama and Politics in 1623/4* (1986), denies its 'oppositional' status, seeing it as in line with the general views of the most powerful figures at court at the time. In 'Thomas Middleton and the Court, 1624: *A Game of Chess* in Context', *HLQ* 47 (1984), 273–88, Thomas Cogswell more comprehensively challenges the readings of history and politics implicit in many readings of the play. Paul Yachnin has also questioned the modern politicization of the play ('*A Game at Chess*: Thomas Middleton's "Praise of Folly"', *MLQ* 48 (1987), 105–23) and more generally of Jacobean theatre ('The Powerless Theater', *ELR* 21 (1991), 49–74), as—from various perspectives —has Trevor Howard-Hill, in 'Political Interpretations of Middleton's *A Game at Chess*', *Yearbook of English Studies*, 21 (1991), 274–85, and *Middleton's 'Vulgar Pasquin': Essays on 'A Game at Chess'* (1995). Most of Middleton's sources were reproduced in R. C. Bald's edition of the play, *A Game at Chesse by Thomas Middleton* (1929) but others have been discovered since by G. R. Price ('The Latin Oration in *A Game at Chess*', *HLQ* 23 (1960), 389–93) and Paul Yachnin ('A New Source for Middleton's *A Game at Chess*', *N&Q* 225 (1990), 157–8). There are two assessments of John Holles's letter describing a performance of the play: A. R. Braunmuller's '"To the Globe I Rowed": John Holles Sees *A Game at Chess*', *ELR* 20 (1990), 340–56, and Trevor Howard-Hill's 'The Unique Eye-Witness Report of Middleton's *A Game at Chess*', *RES* NS 42 (1991), 168–78.

Feminists have generally found Middleton fairly unsympathetic, largely in being so representative of prevailing Jacobean male attitudes. An exception to this was C. L. Cherry, in *The Most Unvaluedst Purchase: Women in the Plays of Thomas Middleton* (1972), who argued for a positive construction to be put on his contribution to the early modern debate on the role of women. This was briskly refuted by Ingrid Hotz-Davies in '*A Chaste Maid in Cheapside* and *Women Beware Women*: Feminism, Anti-Feminism and the Limitations of Satire', *Cahiers Élisabéthains*, 39 (1991), 29–38. Mary Beth Rose, in *The Expense of Spirit: Love and Sexuality in English Renaissance Drama* (1988), Gail K. Paster, in *The Body Embarrassed: Drama and the Disciplines of Shame in Early Modern England* (1993), and some of the essays in Susan Zimmerman's *Erotic Politics: Desire on the Renaissance Stage* (1992) all invoke Middleton in relation to the construction or commodification of the female body, and the politics of desire. Malcolmson, cited above, shows how some of these approaches can open out into the wider politics of the drama.

A CHRONOLOGY OF
THOMAS MIDDLETON

1580 Birth of Thomas Middleton; christened at St Lawrence Jewry 18 April.

1586 Death of father, William; mother, Anne, marries Thomas Harvey, November.

1597 *The Wisdom of Solomon Paraphrased* (poem) published.

1598 Matriculates at Queen's College, Oxford, 9 April.

1599 *Micro-Cynicon: Six Snarling Satires* (poem) published.

1600 *Ghost of Lucrece* (poem) published.

1601 Described in legal document as 'here daily in London accompanying the players'.

c.1602 Marries Magdalen (Mary) Marbeck. Writes *The Chester Tragedy, or Randall Earl of Chester* (lost play); *Caesar's Fall, or Two Lost Shapes* (lost play, with Dekker, Drayton, Munday, and Webster). [*Blurt, Master Constable* and *The Family of Love*, formerly ascribed to Middleton, are now generally thought to be by Dekker.]

1604 Son, Edward, born. Speech of Zeal in Thomas Dekker's part of *The Magnificent Entertainment* for King James's formal entry into London; writes *The Phoenix* (play, pub. 1607); *The Ant and the Nightingale, or Father Hubburd's Tales* published (pamphlet); *The Black Book* published (pamphlet); *The Honest Whore, Part 1* published (play, with Dekker); *The Meeting of the Gallants at an Ordinary, or The Walks in Paul's* published (pamphlet, with Dekker).

c.1605 Writes *A Trick to Catch the Old One* (pub. 1608), *Your Five Gallants* (pub. 1608), *Timon of Athens* (with William Shakespeare, pub. 1623).

c.1606 Writes *A Mad World, My Masters* (pub. 1608), *Michaelmas Term* (pub. 1607), *The Puritan, or the Widow of Watling Street* (pub. 1607), *The Viper and Her Brood* (lost play), *The Revenger's Tragedy* (pub. 1607).

c.1607 Writes *A Yorkshire Tragedy* (pub. 1608).

1609 *Sir Robert Sherley's Entertainment in Cracovia* (pamphlet).

1611 Writes *The Second Maiden's Tragedy* (first pub. 1824), *The Roaring Girl, or Moll Cutpurse* (with Dekker, pub. 1611), *No Wit, No Help Like a Woman's* (pub. 1657, possibly as revised by James Shirley).

1613 Writes and publishes *The New River Entertainment* (performed 29 Sept.) and *The Triumphs of Truth* (performed 29 Oct.; pageants).

c.1613 Writes *A Chaste Maid in Cheapside* (pub. 1630).

1614   *The Masque of Cupid* (lost).

*c.*1614–15   Writes *Wit at Several Weapons* (with William Rowley, pub. 1647), *The Witch* (not pub. till 1778). *Women Beware Women* (pub. 1657; or *c.*1621: see Introduction).

1616   Writes and publishes *Civitatis Amor, The City's Love* (pageant), performed 4 Nov.

*c.*1616   Writes *The Nice Valour, or the Passionate Madman* (perhaps with John Fletcher, pub. 1647), *The Widow* (pub. 1652).

1617   Writes and publishes *The Triumphs of Honour and Industry* (pageant), performed 29 Oct.; *A Fair Quarrel* (with Rowley), published.

*c.*1618   Writes *The Mayor of Queenborough, or Hengist King of Kent* (pub. 1661), *The Old Law, or A New Way to Please You* (with Rowley, pub. 1656).

1619   Writes and publishes *The Inner Temple Masque, or Masque of Heroes*, performed at the Inner Temple, 6 Jan.–2 Feb.; also *The Triumphs of Love and Antiquity, A Noble Solemnity* (pageant), performed 29 Oct. [Verses 'On the Death of Richard Burbage', ascribed to Middleton, probably a 19thC forgery.]

*c.*1619   Writes *More Dissemblers Besides Women* (pub. with *Women Beware Women*, 1657).

1620   Appointed Chronologer to the City of London. Writes and publishes *A Courtly Masque: The Device Called the World Tossed at Tennis* (with Rowley; performed at the Cockpit Theatre).

1621   Writes and publishes *The Sun in Aries, A Noble Solemnity* (pageant); performed 29 Oct.

*c.*1621   Writes *Anything for a Quiet Life* (with Webster, pub. 1662).

1622   Writes *The Changeling* (with Rowley; pub. 1653); writes and publishes *The Triumphs of Honour and Virtue* (pageant), performed 29 October.

1623   Writes and publishes *The Triumphs of Integrity* (pageant), performed 29 October.

*c.*1623   Writes *The Puritan Maid, Modest Wife, and Wanton Widow* (lost play).

1624   Writes *A Game at Chess*; performed 6–16 Aug.; pub. 1625; sought by Privy Council to explain his part in the play; his son, Edward, answered in his absence.

1626   Writes and publishes *The Triumphs of Health and Prosperity* (pageant), performed 30 Oct.; payment delayed on grounds of 'ill performance'. Pageant for the entry of Charles I and Henrietta Maria (not performed).

*c.*1626   Writes *The Conqueror's Custom, or The Fair Penitent* (lost play).

1627   Middleton buried, 4 July, in Newington Butts, Southwark.

A CHASTE MAID IN CHEAPSIDE

THE CHARACTERS OF THE PLAY°

Master Yellowhammer, a goldsmith°
Maudline, his wife°
Tim, their son [a Cambridge student]°
Moll, their daughter°
[Susan, maid to Moll]
Tutor, to Tim
Sir Walter Whorehound, a suitor to Moll
Sir Oliver Kix, and his Wife [Lady Kix], kin to Sir Walter°
Master Allwit, and his Wife [Mistress Allwit], whom Sir Walter
    keeps°
Welsh Gentlewoman, Sir Walter's whore°
Wat and Nick, his bastards [i.e. Sir Walter's sons by Mistress Allwit]
Davy Dahumma, his man [personal servant, also distant relative to Sir
    Walter]°
Touchwood Senior, and his Wife [Mistress Touchwood], a decayed
    gentleman°
Touchwood Junior [brother of Touchwood Senior], another suitor to
    Moll
Two Promoters°
Servants [Nine in all: two to Allwit, one to a Comfit-maker, four to the
    Kixes, two to Sir Walter]
[Three or Four] Watermen°

[Parson
Jugg, maid to Lady Kix
Country Wench, formerly whore to Touchwood Senior, with a child
Porter
Gentleman
Dry Nurse to Mistress Allwit's latest baby
Wet Nurse to Mistress Allwit's latest baby
Midwife
Two Men with meat baskets
Two Puritan Women
Five Gossips]°

A Chaste Maid in Cheapside°

1.1

Enter Maudline and Moll, a shop being discovered°

MAUDLINE Have you played over all your old lessons
  O' the virginals?

MOLL   Yes.°

MAUDLINE Yes? You are a dull maid o'late, methinks;
  You had need have somewhat to quicken°
  Your green sickness—do you weep?—a husband.   5
  Had not such a piece of flesh been ordained,
  What had us wives been good for?—to make salads,°
  Or else cried up and down for samphire.°
  To see the difference of these seasons!
  When I was of your youth, I was lightsome   10
  And quick two years before I was married.°
  You fit for a knight's bed—
  Drowsy-browed, dull eyed, drossy spirited!°
  I hold my life you have forgot your dancing—°
  When was the dancer with you?

MOLL   The last week.

MAUDLINE   Last week!   15
  When I was of your bord he missed me not a night;°
  I was kept at it; I took delight to learn,
  And he to teach me; pretty brown gentleman,
  He took pleasure in my company;
  But you are dull, nothing comes nimbly from you—   20
  You dance like a plumber's daughter and deserve°
  Two thousand pound in lead to your marriage,
  And not in goldsmith's ware.

Enter Yellowhammer

YELLOWHAMMER   Now, what's the din
  Betwixt mother and daughter, ha?

MAUDLINE   Faith, small—
  Telling your daughter Mary of her errors.   25

YELLOWHAMMER Errors? Nay, the city cannot hold you, wife,°
  But you must needs fetch words from Westminster.—°

I ha'done, i'faith—°
Has no attorney's clerk been here o'late
And changed his half-crown piece his mother sent him,°   30
Or rather cozened you with a gilded twopence,°
To bring the word in fashion for her faults   *flaw of Eve*
Or cracks in duty and obedience?
Term 'em e'en so, sweet wife.
As there is no woman made without a flaw,   35
Your purest lawns have frays and cambrics bracks.°

MAUDLINE But 'tis a husband solders up all cracks.°

MOLL What, is he come, sir?

YELLOWHAMMER   Sir Walter's come:
He was met at Holborn bridge, and in his company°
A proper fair young gentlewoman, which I guess   40
By her red hair and other rank descriptions
To be his landed niece brought out of Wales,
Which Tim our son (the Cambridge boy) must marry.
'Tis a match of Sir Walter's own making,
To bind us to him and our heirs for ever.   45

MAUDLINE We are honoured then, if this baggage would be humble
And kiss him with devotion when he enters.°
I cannot get her for my life
To instruct her hand thus, before and after,
Which a knight will look for—before and after.°   50
I have told her still, 'tis the waving of a woman°
Does often move a man and prevails strongly.
But, sweet, ha' you sent to Cambridge? Has Tim word on't?°

YELLOWHAMMER Had word just the day after, when you sent him
The silver spoon to eat his broth in the hall   55
Amongst the gentlemen commoners.

MAUDLINE   O, 'twas timely.

        Enter Porter

YELLOWHAMMER   How now?°

PORTER A letter from a gentleman in Cambridge.

YELLOWHAMMER O, one of Hobson's porters: thou art welcome—°
I told thee, Maud, we should hear from Tim.
    [*Reads*] *Amantissimis carissimisque ambobus parentibus patri et matri.*°   60

MAUDLINE What's the matter?

YELLOWHAMMER   Nay, by my troth, I know not,
Ask not me: he's grown too verbal; this learning is
A great witch.

4

MAUDLINE   Pray, let me see it; I was wont
To understand him—
Amantissimus charissimus:° he has sent the carrier's man, he says;
ambobus parentibus: for a pair of boots; *patri et matri*: pay the porter   65
or it makes no matter.
PORTER° Yes, by my faith, mistress! There's no true construction° in
that; I have took a great deal of pains and come from the Bell°
sweating. Let me come to't, for I was a scholar forty years ago. 'Tis   70
thus, I warrant you—*Matri*: it makes no matter; *ambobus parenti-*
bus: for a pair of boots; *patri*: pay the porter; *amantissimis carissimis*:
he's the carrier's man, and his name is Sims—And there he says
true, forsooth; my name is Sims indeed. I have not forgot all my
learning! A money matter; I thought I should hit on't.°   75
YELLOWHAMMER Go, thou art an old fox! [*Gives money*] There's a
tester for thee.
PORTER If I see your worship at Goose Fair, I have
A dish of birds for you.
YELLOWHAMMER   Why, dost dwell at Bow?°
PORTER All my lifetime, sir; I could ever say
Boo to a goose. Farewell to your worship.°   80
        Exit [*Porter*]
YELLOWHAMMER A merry porter!
MAUDLINE   How can he choose but be so,
Coming with Cambridge letters from our son Tim?
YELLOWHAMMER What's here? [*Reads*] *Maxime diligo*? Faith,°
I must to my learned counsel with this gear,
'Twill ne'er be discerned else.
MAUDLINE   Go to my cousin, then,   85
At Inns of Court
YELLOWHAMMER Fie, they are all for French;°
They speak no Latin.
MAUDLINE   The parson then will do it.
        Enter a Gentleman with a chain
YELLOWHAMMER Nay, he disclaims it, calls Latin papistry;°
He will not deal with it.—What is't you lack, gentleman?
GENTLEMAN Pray, weigh this chain.
        [*Yellowhammer weighs the chain.*] *Enter Sir Walter*
        Whorehound, Welsh Gentlewoman and Davy Dahumma. [*They*
        talk apart from the Yellowhammers]
SIR WALTER   Now, wench, thou art welcome   90
To the heart of the city of London.

5

WELSH GENTLEWOMAN *Dugat a whee*°
SIR WALTER You can thank me in English, if you list.°
WELSH GENTLEWOMAN I can, sir, simply. [*She kisses him*]
SIR WALTER   'Twill serve to pass, wench;°
   'Twas strange that I should lie with thee so often°   95
   To leave thee without English; that were unnatural.
   I bring thee up to turn thee into gold, wench,
   And make thy fortune shine like your bright trade;
   A goldsmith's shop sets out a city maid.
   Davy Dahumma, not a word!
DAVY DAHUMMA   Mum, mum, sir.°   100
SIR WALTER Here you must pass for a pure virgin.
DAVY DAHUMMA [*aside*] Pure Welsh virgin—
   She lost her maidenhead in Brecknockshire.°
SIR WALTER I hear you mumble, Davy.
DAVY DAHUMMA   I have teeth, sir;°
   I need not mumble yet this forty years.   105
SIR WALTER [*aside*] The knave bites plaguily.
YELLOWHAMMER [*to Gentleman with chain*] What's your price, sir?
GENTLEMAN A hundred pound, sir.
YELLOWHAMMER   A hundred marks the utmost,
   'Tis not for me else.—What, Sir Walter Whorehound?
     [*Exit Gentleman*]
MOLL O death!
     Exit [*Moll*]
MAUDLINE   Why, daughter! Faith, the baggage!
   [*To Sir Walter*] A bashful girl, sir; these young things are
     shamefaced;   110
   Besides, you have a presence, sweet Sir Walter,
   Able to daunt a maid brought up i'the city:°
     Enter Moll°
   A brave court-spirit makes our virgins quiver
   And kiss with trembling thighs. Yet see, she comes, sir.°
SIR WALTER [*to Moll*] Why, how now, pretty mistress. Now I have   115
   Caught you. What, can you injure so your time
   To stray thus from your faithful servant?
YELLOWHAMMER   Pish!°
   Stop your words, good knight—'twill make her blush else—
   Which sound too high for the daughters of the freedom.°
   'Honour' and 'faithful servant'! They are compliments   120
   For the worthies of Whitehall or Greenwich.°

E'en plain, sufficient, subsidy words serves us, sir.°
And is this gentlewoman your worthy niece?
SIR WALTER You may be bold with her on these terms; 'tis she, sir,°
   Heir to some nineteen mountains.
YELLOWHAMMER   Bless us all!°   125
   You overwhelm me, sir, with love and riches.
SIR WALTER And all as high as Paul's.
DAVY DAHUMMA [aside]   Here's work,i'faith.°
SIR WALTER How sayest thou, Davy?
DAVY DAHUMMA   Higher, sir, by far;
   You cannot see the top of'em.
YELLOWHAMMER   What, man!
   Maudline, salute this gentlewoman, our daughter,   130
   If things hit right.°
      Enter Touchwood Junior
TOUCHWOOD JUNIOR [aside] My knight, with a brace of footmen,
   Is come, and brought up his ewe-mutton to find
   A ram at London; I must hasten it,°
   Or else pick a famine; her blood's mine,°
   And that's the surest. Well, knight, that choice spoil°   135
   Is only kept for me. [*He catches Moll's attention from behind*]
MOLL   Sir?
TOUCHWOOD JUNIOR   Turn not to me°
   Till thou may'st lawfully; it but whets°
   My stomach, which is too sharp-set already.°
   Read that note carefully.
      [*He secretly gives her a letter*]
   Keep me from suspicion still, nor know my zeal   140
   But in thy heart. Read, and send but thy liking°
   In three words; I'll be at hand to take it.°
YELLOWHAMMER [*to Sir Walter*] O, Tim, sir, Tim:°
   A poor plain boy, an university man;
   Proceeds next Lent to a bachelor of art;° *Easter*   145
   He will be called Sir Yellowhammer then°
   Over all Cambridge, and that's half a knight.
MAUDLINE   Please you, draw near
   And taste the welcome of the city, sir.
YELLOWHAMMER Come, good Sir Walter, and your virtuous niece
   here.
SIR WALTER 'Tis manners to take kindness.
YELLOWHAMMER   Lead 'em in, wife.   150

7

SIR WALTER Your company, sir?

YELLOWHAMMER   I'll give it you instantly.
    [*Exeunt Maudline, Sir Walter, Davy and Welsh Gentlewoman*]

TOUCHWOOD JUNIOR [*aside*] How strangely busy is the devil and
    riches!
    Poor soul, kept in too hard, her mother's eye
    Is cruel toward her, being to him.°
    'Twere a good mirth now to set him a-work   155
    To make her wedding-ring; I must about it;
    Rather than the gain should fall to a stranger
    'Twas honesty in me to enrich my father.°

YELLOWHAMMER [*aside*] The girl is wondrous peevish. I fear
    nothing
    But that she's taken with some other love,   160
    Then all's quite dashed: that must be narrowly looked to.
    We cannot be too wary in our children.
    [*To Touchwood Junior*] What is't you lack?

TOUCHWOOD JUNIOR O, nothing now; all that I wish is present—°
    I would have a wedding ring made for a gentlewoman   165
    With all speed that may be.

YELLOWHAMMER   Of what weight, sir?

TOUCHWOOD JUNIOR Of some half ounce; stand fair and comely°
    With the spark of a diamond, sir; 'twere pity°
    To lose the least grace.

YELLOWHAMMER   Pray, let's see it.
    [*Takes jewel from Touchwood Junior*]
    Indeed, sir, 'tis a pure one.

TOUCHWOOD JUNIOR   So is the mistress.   170

YELLOWHAMMER Have you the wideness of her finger, sir?°

TOUCHWOOD JUNIOR Yes, sure, I think I have her measure about me.
    Good faith, 'tis down; I cannot show't you,°
    I must pull too many things out to be certain.
    Let me see: long and slender, and neatly jointed;   175
    Just such another gentlewoman that's your daughter, sir.

YELLOWHAMMER And therefore, sir, no gentlewoman.

TOUCHWOOD JUNIOR   I protest°
    I never saw two maids handed more alike;
    I'll ne'er seek farther, if you'll give me leave, sir.

YELLOWHAMMER If you dare venture by her finger, sir.   180

TOUCHWOOD JUNIOR Ay, and I'll bide all loss, sir.

YELLOWHAMMER   Say you so, sir?°

Let's see hither, girl.
TOUCHWOOD JUNIOR Shall I make bold
With your finger, gentlewoman? [*He examines Moll's finger*]
MOLL   Your pleasure, sir.
TOUCHWOOD JUNIOR That fits her to a hair, sir.
YELLOWHAMMER   What's your posy, now, sir?°
TOUCHWOOD JUNIOR Mass, that's true: posy? I'faith, e'en thus, sir: 185
                        'Love that's wise
                        Blinds parents' eyes.'
YELLOWHAMMER How, how? If I may speak without offence, sir,°
I hold my life—
TOUCHWOOD JUNIOR What, sir?
YELLOWHAMMER   Go to. You'll pardon me?°
TOUCHWOOD JUNIOR Pardon you? Ay, sir.
YELLOWHAMMER   Will you, i'faith?
TOUCHWOOD JUNIOR   Yes, faith, I will.   190
YELLOWHAMMER You'll steal away some man's daughter: am I near
    you?°
Do you turn aside? You gentlemen are mad wags!°
I wonder things can be so warily carried,
And parents blinded so; but they're served right
That have two eyes and wear so dull a sight.°   195
TOUCHWOOD JUNIOR [*aside*] Thy doom take hold of thee.
YELLOWHAMMER   Tomorrow noon
Shall show your ring well done.
TOUCHWOOD JUNIOR   Being so, 'tis soon.
Thanks—[*to Moll*] and your leave, sweet gentlewoman.
MOLL Sir, you are welcome.
            Exit [*Touchwood Junior*]
[*Aside*] O, were I made of wishes, I went with thee.°   200
YELLOWHAMMER Come now, we'll see how the rules go within.°
MOLL [*aside*] That robs my joy; there I lose all I win.°
            Exeunt°

1.2

        Enter Davy and Allwit severally°
DAVY DAHUMMA [*aside*] Honesty wash my eyes! I have spied a
    wittol.°

9

ALLWIT What, Davy Dahumma? Welcome from North Wales,
    i'faith;
  And is Sir Walter come?
DAVY DAHUMMA   New come to town, sir.
ALLWIT In to the maids, sweet Davy, and give order
  His chamber be made ready instantly.   5
  My wife's as great as she can wallow, Davy, and longs°
  For nothing but pickled cucumbers and his coming;°
  And now she shall ha't, boy.
DAVY DAHUMMA   She's sure of them, sir.
ALLWIT Thy very sight will hold my wife in pleasure
  Till the knight come himself. Go in, in, in, Davy.   10
     Exit [Davy]
  The founder's come to town: I am like a man
  Finding a table furnished to his hand,°
  As mine is still to me, prays for the founder—
  'Bless the right worshipful the good founder's life.'
  I thank him, h'as maintained my house this ten years,°   15
  Not only keeps my wife, but a keeps me
  And all my family: I am at his table.
  He gets me all my children and pays the nurse
  Monthly or weekly; puts me to nothing,°
  Rent nor church duties, not so much as the scavenger:°   20
  The happiest state that ever man was born to!
  I walk out in a morning, come to breakfast,
  Find excellent cheer; a good fire in winter;
  Look in my coal-house about midsummer eve—
  That's full, five or six chaldron new laid up;   25
  Look in my backyard, I shall find a steeple
  Made up with Kentish faggots, which o'erlooks°
  The water-house and the windmills: I say nothing,°
  But smile and pin the door. When she lies in,°
  As now she's even upon the point of grunting,   30
  A lady lies in not like her; there's her embossings,
  Embroid'rings, spanglings and I know not what,
  As if she lay with all the gaudy-shops
  In Gresham's Burse about her; then her restoratives,°
  Able to set up a young pothecary   35
  And richly stock the foreman of a drug shop;°
  Her sugar by whole loaves, her wines by runlets.
  I see these things, but like a happy man

I pay for none at all; yet fools think's mine;°
I have the name, and in his gold I shine;   40
And where some merchants would in soul kiss hell
To buy a paradise for their wives, and dye
Their conscience in the bloods of prodigal heirs
To deck their night-piece, yet all this being done,
Eaten with jealousy to the inmost bone—   45
As what affliction nature more constrains
Than feed the wife plump for another's veins?—
These torments stand I freed of. I am as clear
From jealousy of a wife as from the charge:
O, two miraculous blessings! 'Tis the knight   50
Hath took that labour all out of my hands:
I may sit still and play; he's jealous for me,
Watches her steps, sets spies; I live at ease,
He has both the cost and torment: when the strings
Of his heart frets, I feed, laugh or sing:°   55
[*Sings*] *La dildo, dildo la dildo, la dildo dildo de dildo.*
        Enter Two Servants
FIRST SERVANT What, has he got a singing in his head now?°
SECOND SERVANT Now's out of work, he falls to making dildoes.
ALLWIT Now, sirs, Sir Walter's come.
FIRST SERVANT   Is our master come?
ALLWIT Your master? What am I?
FIRST SERVANT   Do not you know, sir?   60
ALLWIT Pray, am not I your master?
FIRST SERVANT   O, you are but
  Our mistress's husband.
ALLWIT   *Ergo*, knave, your master.°
       Enter Sir Walter and Davy
FIRST SERVANT *Negatur argumentum*—Here comes Sir Walter.°
  [*Aside to Second Servant*] Now a stands bare as well as we; make the
    most of him,
  He's but one pip above a serving man,°   65
  And so much his horns make him.
SIR WALTER   How dost, Jack?°
ALLWIT Proud of your worship's health, sir.
SIR WALTER   How does your wife?
ALLWIT E'en after your own making, sir; she's a tumbler, o'faith;
  The nose and belly meets.
SIR WALTER   They'll part in time again.°

ALLWIT At the good hour they will, an please your worship.°   70
SIR WALTER [*to Servant*] Here, sirrah, pull off my boots. [*To Allwit*]
    Put on, put on, Jack.°
ALLWIT I thank your kind worship, sir.
SIR WALTER   Slippers! [*To Servant bringing slippers*] Heart,
    You are sleepy.
ALLWIT [*aside*]   The game begins already.
SIR WALTER Pish! Put on, Jack.
ALLWIT [*aside*]   Now must I do it, or he'll be
    As angry now as if I had put it on   75
    At first bidding. 'Tis but observing—[*He puts on hat*]
    'Tis but observing a man's humour once,
    And he may ha'him by the nose all his life.
SIR WALTER [*to Servant*] What entertainment has lain open here?
    No strangers in my absence?
FIRST SERVANT   Sure, sir, not any.   80
ALLWIT [*aside*] His jealousy begins. Am not I happy now?
    That can laugh inward whilst his marrow melts?
SIR WALTER How do you satisfy me?
FIRST SERVANT   Good sir, be patient.
SIR WALTER For two months' absence I'll be satisfied.
FIRST SERVANT No living creature entered—
SIR WALTER   Entered? Come, swear.   85
FIRST SERVANT You will not hear me out, sir.
SIR WALTER   Yes, I'll hear't out, sir.
FIRST SERVANT [*indicates Allwit*] Sir, he can tell, himself.
SIR WALTER   Heart, he can tell!
    Do you think I'll trust him?—as a usurer
    With forfeited lordships. Him? O monstrous injury!°
    Believe him? Can the devil speak ill of darkness?   90
    [*To Allwit*] What can you say, sir?
ALLWIT   Of my soul and conscience, sir,
    She's a wife as honest of her body to me
    As any lord's proud lady can be.
SIR WALTER Yet, by your leave, I heard you were once off'ring
    To go to bed to her.
ALLWIT   No, I protest, sir!   95
SIR WALTER Heart, if you do, you shall take all. I'll marry!
ALLWIT O, I beseech you, sir.
SIR WALTER [*aside*]   That wakes the slave,
    And keeps his flesh in awe.

ALLWIT [*aside*]   I'll stop that gap
  Where'er I find it open. I have poisoned
  His hopes in marriage already—   100
  Some old rich widows and some landed virgins,
     Enter Two Children [Wat and Nick]
  And I'll fall to work still before I'll lose him,
  He's yet too sweet to part from.
WAT [*to Allwit*]   God-den, father.
ALLWIT Ha, villain, peace.
NICK   God-den, father.
ALLWIT   Peace, bastard!
  [*Aside*] Should he hear 'em! [*Aloud*] These are two foolish children,   105
  They do not know the gentleman that sits there.
SIR WALTER O, Wat! How dost, Nick? Go to school, ply your books,
  boys, ha?
ALLWIT [*aside to boys*] Where's your legs, whoresons? [*Aside*] They
  should kneel indeed,°
  If they could say their prayers.
SIR WALTER [*aside*]   Let me see, stay;
  How shall I dispose of these two brats now   110
  When I am married? For they must not mingle
  Amongst my children that I get in wedlock;
  'Twill make foul work, that, and raise many storms.
  I'll bind Wat prentice to a goldsmith—
  My father Yellowhammer, as fit as can be!   115
  Nick with some vintner; good, goldsmith and vintner,
  There will be wine in bowls, i'faith.
     Enter Allwit's Wife
MISTRESS ALLWIT [*embracing Sir Walter*] Sweet knight,
  Welcome! I have all my longings now in town;
  Now, welcome the good hour.°
SIR WALTER How cheers my mistress?
MISTRESS ALLWIT   Made lightsome e'en by him   120
  That made me heavy.
SIR WALTER   Methinks she shows gallantly,°
  Like a moon at full, sir.
ALLWIT   True, and if she bear
  A male child, there's the man in the moon, sir.
SIR WALTER 'Tis but the boy in the moon yet, goodman calf.°
ALLWIT There was a man, the boy had never been there else.   125
SIR WALTER It shall be yours, sir.

13

ALLWIT   No, by my troth, I'll swear
   It's none of mine. Let him that got it
   Keep it! [*Aside*] Thus do I rid myself of fear,
   Lie soft, sleep hard, drink wine and eat good cheer.
        [*Exeunt*]

2.1

Enter Touchwood Senior and his Wife

MISTRESS TOUCHWOOD 'Twill be so tedious, sir, to live from you,
    But that necessity must be obeyed.
TOUCHWOOD SENIOR I would it might not, wife. The tediousness
    Will be the most part mine, that understand
    The blessings I have in thee; so to part,°   5
    That drives the torment to a knowing heart.
    But as thou say'st, we must give way to need,
    And live awhile asunder; our desires
    Are both too fruitful for our barren fortunes.
    How adverse runs the destiny of some creatures: 10
    Some only can get riches and no children,
    We can only get children and no riches!
    Then 'tis the prudent'st part to check our wills°
    And, till our state rise, make our bloods lie still.
    Life, every year a child, and some years two;   15
    Besides drinkings abroad, that's never reckoned;°
    This gear will not hold out.
MISTRESS TOUCHWOOD   Sir, for a time°
    I'll take the courtesy of my uncle's house,
    If you will be pleased to like on't, till prosperity°
    Look with a friendly eye upon our states.   20
TOUCHWOOD SENIOR Honest wife, I thank thee; I ne'er knew°
    The perfect treasure thou brought'st with thee more
    Than at this instant minute. A man's happy
    When he's at poorest that has matched his soul
    As rightly as his body. Had I married   25
    A sensual fool now, as 'tis hard to 'scape it°
    'Mongst gentlewomen of our time, she would ha' hanged
    About my neck, and never left her hold
    Till she had kissed me into wanton businesses,
    Which at the waking of my better judgement   30
    I should have cursed most bitterly,
    And laid a thicker vengeance on my act°
    Than misery of the birth—which were enough
    If it were born to greatness, whereas mine
    Is sure of beggary, though it were got in wine.   35

Fulness of joy showeth the goodness in thee;
Thou art a matchless wife: farewell, my joy.
MISTRESS TOUCHWOOD I shall not want your sight?
TOUCHWOOD SENIOR   I'll see thee often,
    Talk in mirth and play at kisses with thee,
    Anything, wench, but what may beget beggars;   40
    There I give o'er the set, throw down the cards,°
    And dare not take them up.
MISTRESS TOUCHWOOD   Your will be mine, sir.
        Exit [*Mistress Touchwood*]
TOUCHWOOD SENIOR This does not only make her honesty
        perfect,
    But her discretion, and approves her judgement.°
    Had her desires been wanton, they'd been blameless   45
    In being lawful ever, but of all creatures°
    I hold that wife a most unmatched treasure
    That can unto her fortunes fix her pleasure
    And not unto her blood: this is like wedlock;°
    The feast of marriage is not lust but love   50
    And care of the estate; when I please blood,
    Merely I sing and suck out others'; then°
    'Tis many a wise man's fault, but of all men
    I am the most unfortunate in that game
    That ever pleased both genders: I ne'er played yet°   55
    Under a bastard; the poor wenches curse me°
    To the pit where'er I come; they were ne'er served so,°
    But used to have more words than one to a bargain.°
    I have such a fatal finger in such business
    I must forth with't, chiefly for country wenches,°   60
    For every harvest I shall hinder hay-making:
        Enter a Wench with a child
    I had no less than seven lay in last progress°
    Within three weeks of one another's time.
WENCH O, snap-hance, have I found you?
TOUCHWOOD SENIOR   How snap-hance?
WENCH [*showing him the child*] Do you see your workmanship? Nay,
        turn not from it,   65
    Nor offer to escape; for if you do
    I'll cry it through the streets and follow you.
    Your name may well be called Touchwood—
    A pox on you!—you do but touch and take;°

Thou hast undone me; I was a maid before,   70
   I can bring a certificate for it
   From both the churchwardens.
TOUCHWOOD SENIOR   I'll have the parson's°
   Hand too, or I'll not yield to't.
WENCH   Thou shalt have more,
   Thou villain. Nothing grieves me but Ellen,°
   My poor cousin in Derbyshire; thou hast cracked°   75
   Her marriage quite; she'll have a bout with thee.°
TOUCHWOOD SENIOR Faith, when she will, I'll have a bout with her!
WENCH A law bout, sir, I mean.
TOUCHWOOD SENIOR   True, lawyers use
   Such bouts as other men do. And if that
   Be all thy grief, I'll tender her a husband.   80
   I keep of purpose two or three gulls in pickle
   To eat such mutton with, and she shall choose one.°
   Do but in courtesy, faith, wench, excuse me
   Of this half yard of flesh, in which, I think,°
   It wants a nail or two.
WENCH   No, thou shalt find, villain,°   85
   It hath right shape and all the nails it should have.
TOUCHWOOD SENIOR Faith, I am poor. Do a charitable deed, wench;
   I am a younger brother and have nothing.°
WENCH Nothing! Thou hast too much, thou lying villain,
   Unless thou wert more thankful.
TOUCHWOOD SENIOR   I have no dwelling;°   90
   I brake up house but this morning. Pray thee, pity me;°
   I am a goodfellow, faith, have been too kind
   To people of your gender; if I ha't
   Without my belly, none of your sex shall want it.°
   [*Aside*] That word has been of force to move a woman.°   95
   [*To her*] There's tricks enough to rid thy hand on't, wench:°
   Some rich man's porch, tomorrow before day,
   Or else anon i'the evening; twenty devices.°
   [*Giving her money*] Here's all I have, i'faith, take purse and all;
   [*Aside*] And would I were rid of all the ware i'the shop so!°   100
WENCH Where I find manly dealings, I am pitiful:°
   This shall not trouble you.
TOUCHWOOD SENIOR   And I protest, wench,°
   The next I'll keep myself.
WENCH   Soft, let it be got first!

[*Aside*] This is the fifth; if e'er I venture more,°
Where I now go for a maid, may I ride for a whore.°   105
        Exit [*Wench*]
TOUCHWOOD SENIOR What shift she'll make now with this piece of
    flesh°
In this strict time of Lent, I cannot imagine;°
Flesh dare not peep abroad now. I have known
This city now above this seven years,
But, I protest, in better state of government   110
I never knew it yet, nor ever heard of.°
There has been more religious wholesome laws
In the half circle of a year erected°
For common good than memory ever knew of,
        Enter Sir Oliver Kix and his Lady
Setting apart corruption of promoters,°   115
And other poisonous officers that infect
And with a venomous breath taint every goodness.
LADY KIX O, that e'er I was begot, or bred, or born!
SIR OLIVER Be content, sweet wife.
TOUCHWOOD SENIOR [*aside*]   What's here to do, now?°
I hold my life she's in deep passion°   120
For the imprisonment of veal and mutton
Now kept in garrets; weeps for some calf's head now.
Methinks her husband's head might serve with bacon.°
        Enter Touchwood Junior
LADY KIX Hist!
SIR OLIVER   Patience, sweet wife. [*The Kixes walk aside*]
TOUCHWOOD JUNIOR   Brother, I have sought you strangely.°
TOUCHWOOD SENIOR Why, what's the business?
TOUCHWOOD JUNIOR With all the speed thou canst   125
    Procure a licence for me.
TOUCHWOOD SENIOR   How, a licence?°
TOUCHWOOD JUNIOR Cud's foot, she's lost else! I shall miss her ever.
TOUCHWOOD SENIOR Nay, sure, thou shalt not miss so fair a mark
    For thirteen shillings fourpence.
TOUCHWOOD JUNIOR   Thanks by hundreds!°
        [*Exit Touchwood Junior. Touchwood Senior remains and
        overhears the Kixes*]°
SIR OLIVER Nay, pray thee, cease; I'll be at more cost yet,°   130
    Thou know'st we are rich enough.
LADY KIX   All but in blessings,°

18

And there the beggar goes beyond us. O, O, O!
To be seven years a wife and not a child,
O, not a child!

SIR OLIVER Sweet wife, have patience.

LADY KIX   Can any woman have a greater cut?°   135

SIR OLIVER I know 'tis great, but what of that, wife?
I cannot do withal; there's things making,°
By thine own doctor's advice, at pothecary's;
I spare for nothing, wife, no, if the price°
Were forty marks a spoonful,   140
I'd give a thousand pound to purchase fruitfulness:
'Tis but 'bating so many good works°
In the erecting of bridewells and spital-houses,°
And so fetch it up again; for, having none,°
I mean to make good deeds my children.   145

LADY KIX Give me but those good deeds, and I'll find children.
        [*Exit*° Touchwood Senior]

SIR OLIVER Hang thee, thou hast had too many!

LADY KIX   Thou liest, brevity.°

SIR OLIVER O, horrible! Dar'st thou call me 'brevity'?
Dar'st thou be so short with me?

LADY KIX   Thou deservest worse.
Think but upon the goodly lands and livings   150
That's kept back through want on't.

SIR OLIVER   Talk not on't, pray thee;°
Thou'lt make me play the woman and weep too.°

LADY KIX 'Tis our dry barrenness puffs up Sir Walter;
None gets by your not-getting but that knight;°
He's made by th'means, and fats his fortunes shortly   155
In a great dowry with a goldsmith's daughter.

SIR OLIVER They may be all deceived; be but you patient, wife.

LADY KIX I have suff'red a long time.

SIR OLIVER   Suffer thy heart out,
A pox suffer thee!

LADY KIX   Nay, thee, thou desertless slave!

SIR OLIVER Come, come, I ha' done; you'll to the gossiping   160
Of Master Allwit's child?

LADY KIX   Yes, to my much joy!°
Everyone gets before me; there's my sister
Was married but at Barthol'mew-eve last,°
And she can have two children at a birth:

O, one of them, one of them, would ha' served my turn.   165
SIR OLIVER Sorrow consume thee, thou art still crossing me,
    And know'st my nature—
       Enter a Maid
MAID   O, mistress—
    [*Aside*] Weeping or railing, that's our house harmony!°
LADY KIX What say'st, Jug?
MAID   The sweetest news!
LADY KIX   What is't, wench?°
MAID Throw down your doctor's drugs, they're all   170
    But heretics; I bring certain remedy°
    That has been taught and proved and never failed.
SIR OLIVER O, that, that, that, or nothing!
MAID   There's a gentleman,
    I haply have his name too, that has got°
    Nine children by one water that he useth: 175
    It never misses; they come so fast upon him°
    He was fain to give it over.
LADY KIX   His name, sweet Jug?
MAID One Master Touchwood, a fine gentleman,
    But run behindhand much with getting children.°
SIR OLIVER Is't possible?
MAID   Why, sir, he'll undertake,   180
    Using that water, within fifteen year,
    For all your wealth, to make you a poor man,
    You shall so swarm with children.
SIR OLIVER   I'll venture that, i'faith.
LADY KIX That shall you, husband.
MAID   But I must tell you first,
    He's very dear.
SIR OLIVER   No matter: what serves wealth for?°   185
LADY KIX True, sweet husband.
SIR OLIVER   There's land to come. Put case his water°
    Stands me in some five hundred pound a pint,°
    'Twill fetch a thousand, and a kersten soul.
LADY KIX And that's worth all, sweet husband.
SIR OLIVER   I'll about it.
       Exeunt

2.2

Enter Allwit

ALLWIT I'll go bid gossips presently myself.°
    That's all the work I'll do; nor need I stir,
    But that it is my pleasure to walk forth
    And air myself a little: I am tied
    To nothing in this business; what I do   5
    Is merely recreation, not constraint.
    Here's running to and fro—nurse upon nurse,°
    Three charwomen, besides maids and neighbour's children!
    Fie, what a trouble have I rid my hands on;
    It makes me sweat to think on't.
    Enter Sir Walter Whorehound

SIR WALTER   How now, Jack?   10

ALLWIT I am going to bid gossips for your worship's child, sir;
    A goodly girl, i'faith—give you joy on her!
    She looks as if she had two thousand pound
    To her portion, and run away with a tailor;°
    A fine, plump, black-eyed slut: under correction, sir.°   15
    I take delight to see her. Nurse!
    Enter Dry Nurse

DRY NURSE   Do you call, sir?

ALLWIT I call not you, I call the wet nurse hither.
    Exit [Dry Nurse]
    Give me the wet nurse—!
    Enter Wet Nurse [with Child]

                  Ay, 'tis thou; come hither, come hither!
    Let's see her once again; I cannot choose
    But buss her thrice an hour.

WET NURSE   You may be proud on't, sir;   20
    'Tis the best piece of work that e'er you did.

ALLWIT Think'st thou so, nurse? What sayest to Wat and Nick?

WET NURSE They're pretty children both, but here's a wench
    Will be a knocker.

ALLWIT *[to Child]* Pup!—Say'st thou me so?—Pup, little
    countess—°
    Faith, sir, I thank your worship for this girl   25
    Ten thousand times and upward.

SIR WALTER   I am glad

I have her for you, sir.
ALLWIT   Here, take her in, nurse;
    Wipe her, and give her spoon-meat.
WET NURSE   Wipe your mouth, sir.°
        Exit [Wet Nurse, with Child]
ALLWIT And now about these gossips.
SIR WALTER   Get but two;
    I'll stand for one myself.
ALLWIT   To your own child, sir?°   30
SIR WALTER The better policy: it prevents suspicion;
    'Tis good to play with rumour at all weapons.°
ALLWIT Troth, I commend your care, sir; 'tis a thing
    That I should ne'er have thought on.
SIR WALTER *[aside]*   The more slave!
    When man turns base, out goes his soul's pure flame: 35
    The fat of ease o'erthrows the eyes of shame.°
ALLWIT I am studying who to get for godmother
    Suitable to your worship. Now I ha' thought on't.°
SIR WALTER I'll ease you of that care, and please myself in't—
    [Aside] My love, the goldsmith's daughter; if I send,   40
    Her father will command her.—Davy Dahumma!
        Enter Davy [Dahumma]
ALLWIT I'll fit your worship then with a male partner.
SIR WALTER What is he?
ALLWIT   A kind, proper gentleman,
    Brother to Master Touchwood.
SIR WALTER   I know Touchwood:
    Has he a brother living?
ALLWIT   A neat bachelor.°   45
SIR WALTER Now we know him, we'll make shift with him:
    Despatch, the time draws near.—Come hither, Davy.
        Exit [Sir Walter Whorehound, with Davy Dahumma]
ALLWIT In troth, I pity him, he ne'er stands still;
    Poor knight, what pains he takes: sends this way one,
    That way another; has not an hour's leisure: 50
    I would not have thy toil for all thy pleasure.
        Enter Two Promoters
    [Aside] Ha, how now? What are these that stand so close
    At the street-corner, pricking up their ears
    And snuffing up their noses, like rich men's dogs
    When the first course goes in? By the mass, promoters!°   55

'Tis so, I hold my life; and planted there
To arrest the dead corpse of poor calves and sheep,°
Like ravenous creditors, that will not suffer
The bodies of their poor departed debtors
To go to th'grave, but e'en in death to vex   60
And stay the corpse with bills of Middlesex.°
This Lent will fat the whoresons up with sweetbreads,
And lard their whores with lamb-stones; what their golls°
Can clutch goes presently to their Molls and Dolls:
The bawds will be so fat with what they earn,   65
Their chins will hang like udders by Easter-eve°
And, being stroked, will give the milk of witches.°
How did the mongrels hear my wife lies in?°
Well, I may baffle'em; gallantly. [*To them*] By your favour,
    gentlemen,°
I am a stranger both unto the city   70
And to her carnal strictness.
FIRST PROMOTER   Good. Your will, sir?°
ALLWIT Pray, tell me where one dwells that kills this Lent?°
FIRST PROMOTER How, kills? [*To his fellow*] Come hither, Dick; a
    bird, a bird!°
SECOND PROMOTER [*to Allwit*] What is't that you would have?
ALLWIT   Faith, any flesh;
But I long especially for veal and green-sauce.°   75
FIRST PROMOTER [*aside*] Green-goose, you shall be sauced.
ALLWIT   I have half a scornful stomach,°
No fish will be admitted.
FIRST PROMOTER   Not this Lent, sir?
ALLWIT Lent? What cares colon here for Lent?°
FIRST PROMOTER You say well, sir:
Good reason that the colon of the gentleman   80
As you were lately pleased to term your worship's, sir,
Should be fulfilled with answerable food,°
To sharpen the blood, delight health, and tickle nature.
Were you directed hither to this street, sir?°
ALLWIT That I was, ay, marry.
SECOND PROMOTER   And the butcher, belike,   85
Should kill and sell close in some upper room?°
ALLWIT Some apple-loft, as I take it, or a coal-house;
I know not which, i'faith.
SECOND PROMOTER   Either will serve:

[*Aside*] This butcher shall kiss Newgate, 'less he turn up
The bottom of the pocket of his apron.—° 90
You go to see him?
ALLWIT   Where you shall not find him:
I'll buy, walk by your noses with my flesh,
Sheep-biting mongrels, hand-basket freebooters!°
My wife lies in—a foutra for promoters.°
            Exit [*Allwit*]
FIRST PROMOTER That shall not serve your turn. What a rogue's
      this!   95
How cunningly he came over us.
            Enter a Man with meat in a basket
SECOND PROMOTER   Hush't, stand close.
MAN I have 'scaped well thus far; they say the knaves
Are wondrous hot and busy.
FIRST PROMOTER   By your leave, sir,°
We must see what you have under your cloak there.
MAN Have! I have nothing.
FIRST PROMOTER   No? Do you tell us that?   100
What makes this lump stick out then? We must see, sir.
MAN What will you see, sir? A pair of sheets and two
Of my wife's foul smocks going to the washers?
SECOND PROMOTER O, we love that sight well! You cannot please us
      better.
            [*He removes meat*]
What, do you gull us? Call you these shirts and smocks?   105
MAN Now, a pox choke you!
You have cozened me and five of my wife's kindred
Of a good dinner; we must make it up now
With herrings and milk-pottage.
            [*Exit Man*]
FIRST PROMOTER   'Tis all veal.
SECOND PROMOTER All veal? Pox, the worse luck! I promised
      faithfully   110
To send this morning a fat quarter of lamb
To a kind gentlewoman in Turnbull Street°
That longs; and how I'm crossed!°
FIRST PROMOTER Let's share this, and see what hap comes next then.
            Enter another [*Man*] *with a basket*
SECOND PROMOTER Agreed. Stand close again: another booty.°   115
What's he?

FIRST PROMOTER [*addressing the newcomer*] Sir, by your favour.
SECOND MAN   Meaning me, sir?
FIRST PROMOTER Good Master Oliver? Cry thee mercy, i'faith.°
    What hast thou there?
SECOND MAN   A rack of mutton, sir,
    And half a lamb; you know my mistress's diet.
FIRST PROMOTER Go, go, we see thee not; away, keep close—   120
    [*To Second Promoter*] Heart, let him pass. Thou'lt never have the
      wit°
    To know our benefactors.
        [*Exit Second Man*]
SECOND PROMOTER   I have forgot him.
FIRST PROMOTER 'Tis Master Beggarland's man, the wealthy
    merchant°
    That is in fee with us.
SECOND PROMOTER   Now I have a feeling of him.
FIRST PROMOTER You know he purchased the whole Lent together,°   125
    Gave us ten groats a-piece on Ash Wednesday.°
SECOND PROMOTER True, true.
      Enter a Wench with a basket and a child in it under a loin of
      mutton
FIRST PROMOTER   A wench!
SECOND PROMOTER   Why then, stand close indeed.
WENCH [*aside*] Women had need of wit, if they'll shift here,°
    And she that hath wit may shift anywhere.
FIRST PROMOTER Look, look! Poor fool, she has left the rump
    uncovered too,°   130
    More to betray her. This is like a murd'rer
    That will outface the deed with a bloody band.°
SECOND PROMOTER What time of the year is't, sister?°
WENCH   O, sweet gentlemen,
    I am a poor servant, let me go.
FIRST PROMOTER   You shall, wench,
    But this must stay with us.
WENCH   O, you undo me, sir,°   135
    'Tis for a wealthy gentlewoman that takes physic, sir;
    The doctor does allow my mistress mutton.
    O, as you tender the dear life of a gentlewoman!°
    I'll bring my master to you; he shall show you
    A true authority from the higher powers,°   140
    And I'll run every foot.

SECOND PROMOTER   Well, leave your basket then,
  And run and spare not.
WENCH   Will you swear then to me°
  To keep it till I come?
FIRST PROMOTER   Now by this light I will.
WENCH What say you, gentleman?
SECOND PROMOTER   What a strange wench 'tis!
  Would we might perish else.
WENCH   Nay, then I run, sir.°   145
  [*Wench leaves basket and*] *Exit* [*running*]
FIRST PROMOTER And ne'er return, I hope.
SECOND PROMOTER   A politic baggage!
  She makes us swear to keep it: I prithee
  Look what market she hath made.
FIRST PROMOTER   *Imprimis*, sir,°
  A good fat loin of mutton. What comes next
  Under this cloth? Now for a quarter of lamb.   150
SECOND PROMOTER Now for a shoulder of mutton.
FIRST PROMOTER   Done!°
SECOND PROMOTER Why, done, sir!
FIRST PROMOTER   By the mass, I feel I have lost;
  'Tis of more weight, i'faith.
SECOND PROMOTER   Some loin of veal?
FIRST PROMOTER No, faith, here's a lamb's head, I feel that plainly;
  Why, I'll yet win my wager. [*He discovers a child*]°
SECOND PROMOTER   Ha?
FIRST PROMOTER   'Swounds, what's here?   155
SECOND PROMOTER A child!
FIRST PROMOTER   A pox of all dissembling cunning whores!
SECOND PROMOTER Here's an unlucky breakfast!
FIRST PROMOTER   What shall's do?
SECOND PROMOTER The quean made us swear to keep it too.
FIRST PROMOTER We might leave it else.
SECOND PROMOTER   Villainous strange!°
  Life, had she none to gull but poor promoters   160
  That watch hard for a living?
FIRST PROMOTER   Half our gettings°
  Must run in sugar-sops and nurses' wages now,
  Besides many a pound of soap and tallow;°
  We have need to get loins of mutton still,
  To have suet to change for candles.°   165

SECOND PROMOTER Nothing mads me but this was a lamb's head
    with you;
  You felt it! She has made calves' heads of us.°
FIRST PROMOTER Prithee, no more on't. There's time to get it up;
  It is not come to Mid-Lent Sunday yet.°
SECOND PROMOTER I am so angry, I'll watch no more today.   170
FIRST PROMOTER Faith, nor I neither.
SECOND PROMOTER   Why then, I'll make a motion.°
FIRST PROMOTER Well, what is't?
SECOND PROMOTER   Let's e'en go to the Checker
  At Queenhive, and roast the loin of mutton°
  Till young flood; then send the child to Brainford.°
        [*Exeunt*]

2.3

*Enter Allwit in one of Sir Walter [Whorehound]'s suits and
Davy [Dahumma] trussing him°*
ALLWIT 'Tis a busy day at our house, Davy.
DAVY DAHUMMA Always the kurs'ning -day, sir.
ALLWIT   Truss, truss me, Davy.°
DAVY DAHUMMA [*aside*] No matter an you were hanged, sir.
ALLWIT   How does°
  This suit fit me, Davy?
DAVY DAHUMMA   Excellent neatly;
  My master's things were ever fit for you, sir,   5
  E'en to a hair, you know.
ALLWIT   Thou hast hit it right, Davy,°
  We ever jumped in one this ten years, Davy;°
  So, well said.
        Enter a Servant with a box
              What art thou?
SERVANT   Your comfit-maker's man, sir.°
ALLWIT O, sweet youth, in to the nurse, quick, quick,
  'Tis time, i'faith; your mistress will be here?   10
SERVANT She was setting forth, sir.
        Enter two Puritans
ALLWIT   Here comes our gossips now;°
  O, I shall have such kissing work today—°

Sweet Mistress Underman, welcome, i'faith.°
FIRST PURITAN Give you joy of your fine girl, sir:
    Grant that her education may be pure   15
    And become one of the faithful
ALLWIT   Thanks to your°
    Sisterly wishes, Mistress Underman.
SECOND PURITAN Are any of the brethren's wives yet come?°
ALLWIT There are some wives within, and some at home.
FIRST PURITAN Verily, thanks, sir.
    Exeunt [Puritans]
ALLWIT   Verily, you are an ass, forsooth: 20
    I must fit all these times, or there's no music.°
    Enter two Gossips
    Here comes a friendly and familiar pair:
    Now I like these wenches well.
FIRST GOSSIP   How dost, sirrah?°
ALLWIT Faith, well, I thank you, neighbour, and how dost thou?
SECOND GOSSIP Want nothing but such getting, sir, as thine.°   25
ALLWIT My gettings, wench? They are poor.
FIRST GOSSIP   Fie that thou'lt say so!
    Th'hast as fine children as a man can get.
DAVY DAHUMMA [*aside*] Ay, as a man can get, and that's my master.
ALLWIT They are pretty foolish things, put to making
    In minutes; I ne'er stand long about 'em.°   30
    Will you walk in, wenches?
    [*Exeunt Gossips.*] *Enter Touchwood Junior and Moll*
TOUCHWOOD JUNIOR The happiest meeting that our souls could
    wish for!
    Here's the ring ready; I am beholding
    Unto your father's haste, h'as kept his hour.°
MOLL He never kept it better.
    Enter Sir Walter Whorehound
TOUCHWOOD JUNIOR   Back, be silent.°   35
SIR WALTER Mistress and partner, I will put you both
    Into one cup. [*He drinks their health*]
DAVY DAHUMMA [*aside*]   Into one cup! Most proper:°
    A fitting compliment for a goldsmith's daughter.
ALLWIT Yes, sir, that's he must be your worship's partner
    In this day's business, Master Touchwood's brother.   40
SIR WALTER I embrace your acquaintance, sir.
TOUCHWOOD JUNIOR   It vows your service, sir.

SIR WALTER It's near high time. Come, Master Allwit.
ALLWIT   Ready, sir.
SIR WALTER Wilt please you walk?
TOUCHWOOD JUNIOR   Sir, I obey your time.°
    [*Exeunt*]

2.4

Enter Midwife with the Child, [Maudline, the two Puritans,]
and the [five] Gossips to the kurs'ning. [Exit Midwife with the
Child.]°

FIRST GOSSIP [*making way*] Good Mistress Yellowhammer.
MAUDLINE   In faith, I will not.°
FIRST GOSSIP Indeed, it shall be yours.
MAUDLINE   I have sworn, i'faith.
FIRST GOSSIP I stand still then.
MAUDLINE   So will you let the child
  Go without company, and make me forsworn.
FIRST GOSSIP You are such another creature.
    [*Exeunt First Gossip and Maudline*]
SECOND GOSSIP   Before me?°   5
  I pray, come down a little.
THIRD GOSSIP   Not a whit;
  I hope I know my place.
SECOND GOSSIP   Your place? Great wonder, sure!
  Are you any better than a comfit-maker's wife?
THIRD GOSSIP And that's as good at all times as a pothecary's.
SECOND GOSSIP Ye lie! Yet I forbear you too.
    [*Exeunt Second and Third Gossips*]
FIRST PURITAN   Come, sweet sister;°   10
  We go in unity, and show the fruits of peace,
  Like children of the spirit.
SECOND PURITAN   I love lowliness.°
    [*Exeunt Puritans*]
FOURTH GOSSIP True, so say I: though they strive more,
  There comes as proud behind as goes before.°
FIFTH GOSSIP Every inch, i'faith.   15
    Exeunt

3.1

Enter Touchwood Junior and a Parson

TOUCHWOOD JUNIOR O sir, if ever you felt the force of love,
  Pity it in me.
PARSON   Yes, though I ne'er was married, sir,
  I have felt the force of love from good men's daughters,
  And some that will be maids yet three years hence.°
  Have you got a licence?
TOUCHWOOD JUNIOR   Here, 'tis ready, sir.°   5
PARSON That's well.
TOUCHWOOD JUNIOR The ring and all things perfect.
  She'll steal hither.
PARSON   She shall be welcome, sir;
  I'll not be long a-clapping you together.
    Enter Moll and Touchwood Senior
TOUCHWOOD JUNIOR O, here she's come, sir.
PARSON   What's he?
TOUCHWOOD JUNIOR   My honest brother.
TOUCHWOOD SENIOR Quick, make haste, sirs!
MOLL   You must despatch with all° 10
  Speed you can, for I shall be missed straight;
  I made hard shift for this small time I have.°
PARSON Then I'll not linger.
  Place that ring upon her finger:
  This the finger plays the part,   15
  Whose master-vein shoots from the heart.°
    [*Touchwood Junior puts the ring on Moll's finger*]
  Now join hands—
    Enter Yellowhammer and Sir Walter [*Whorehound*]
YELLOWHAMMER   Which I will sever,
  And so ne'er again meet never!
MOLL O, we are betrayed.
TOUCHWOOD JUNIOR   Hard fate!
SIR WALTER   I am struck with wonder!
YELLOWHAMMER Was this the politic fetch, thou mystical
  baggage,°   20
  Thou disobedient strumpet? [*To Sir Walter*] And were you°
  So wise to send for her to such an end?

SIR WALTER Now I disclaim the end; you'll make me mad.

YELLOWHAMMER [*to Touchwood Junior*] And what are you, sir?

TOUCHWOOD JUNIOR   An you cannot see
    With those two glasses, put on a pair more.°   25

YELLOWHAMMER I dreamed of anger still!—Here, take your ring,
    sir.°
        [*He takes the ring off Moll's finger*]
    Ha, this? Life, 'tis the same! Abominable!
    Did not I sell this ring?

TOUCHWOOD JUNIOR   I think you did;
    You received money for't.

YELLOWHAMMER   Heart, hark you, knight;
    Here's no inconscionable villainy!°   30
    Set me a-work to make this wedding-ring,
    And come with an intent to steal my daughter:
    Did ever runaway match it?

SIR WALTER [*to Touchwood Senior*] 'This your brother, sir?

TOUCHWOOD SENIOR He can tell that as well as I.

YELLOWHAMMER The very posy mocks me to my face: 35
            'Love that's wise,
            Blinds parents' eyes!'
    I thank your wisdom, sir, for blinding us;
    We have good hope to recover our sight shortly;
    In the meantime I will lock up this baggage   40
    As carefully as my gold: she shall see
    As little sun, if a close room or so°
    Can keep her from the light on't.

MOLL   O, sweet father,
    For love's sake, pity me!

YELLOWHAMMER   Away!

MOLL [*to Touchwood Junior*]   Farewell, sir,
    All content bless thee, and take this for comfort: 45
    Though violence keep me, thou canst lose me never,
    I am ever thine although we part for ever.

YELLOWHAMMER Ay, we shall part you, minx.
        Exit [*Yellowhammer with Moll*]

SIR WALTER [*to Touchwood Junior*]   Your acquaintance, sir,
    Came very lately, yet it came too soon;
    I must hereafter know you for no friend,   50
    But one that I must shun like pestilence
    Or the disease of lust.

TOUCHWOOD JUNIOR   Like enough, sir:°
  You ha' ta'en me at the worst time for words
  That e'er you picked out: faith, do not wrong me, sir.°
     Exit [Touchwood Junior with Parson]
TOUCHWOOD SENIOR   Look after him, and spare not: there he
    walks   55
  That never yet received baffling: you're blest°
  More than e'er I knew; go, take your rest.
     Exit [Touchwood Senior]
SIR WALTER   I pardon you, you are both losers.°
     Exit

3.2

    A bed thrust out upon the stage, Allwit's Wife in it. Enter all the
    Gossips [the Puritans, Maudline, Lady Kix, and Dry Nurse with
    the Child]°
FIRST GOSSIP   How is't, woman? We have brought you home
  A kersen soul.
MISTRESS ALLWIT   Ay, I thank your pains.°
FIRST PURITAN   And verily, well kursened, i' the right way,
  Without idolatry or superstition,
  After the pure manner of Amsterdam.°   5
MISTRESS ALLWIT   Sit down, good neighbours. Nurse!
NURSE   At hand, forsooth.
MISTRESS ALLWIT   Look they have all low stools.
NURSE   They have, forsooth.°
SECOND GOSSIP   Bring the child hither, nurse. How say you now,
    gossip,
  Is't not a chopping girl? So like the father.
THIRD GOSSIP   As if it had been spit out of his mouth!°   10
  Eyed, nosed and browed as like a girl can be,
  Only indeed it has the mother's mouth.
SECOND GOSSIP   The mother's mouth up and down, up and down!°
THIRD GOSSIP   'Tis a large child; she's but a little woman.
FIRST PURITAN   No, believe me,   15
  A very spiny creature, but all heart;
  Well mettled, like the faithful, to endure°
  Her tribulation here and raise up seed.

SECOND GOSSIP She had a sore labour on't, I warrant you;
    You can tell, neighbour.
THIRD GOSSIP   O, she had great speed;°   20
    We were afraid once, but she made us all
    Have joyful hearts again; 'tis a good soul, i'faith;
    The midwife found her a most cheerful daughter.
FIRST PURITAN 'Tis the spirit; the sisters are all like her.°
    Enter Sir Walter with two spoons and plate, and Allwit.°
SECOND GOSSIP O, here comes the chief gossip, neighbours.   25
    [*Exit Nurse with Child*]
SIR WALTER The fatness of your wishes to you all, ladies.°
THIRD GOSSIP O dear, sweet gentleman, what fine words he has:
    'The fatness of our wishes'!
SECOND GOSSIP   Calls us all 'ladies'!°
FOURTH GOSSIP I promise you, a fine gentleman and a courteous.
SECOND GOSSIP Methinks her husband shows like a clown to him.°   30
THIRD GOSSIP I would not care what clown my husband were too,
    So I had such fine children.
SECOND GOSSIP   She's all fine children, gossip.°
THIRD GOSSIP Ay, and see how fast they come.
FIRST PURITAN   Children are blessings,
    If they be got with zeal by the brethren,
    As I have five at home.
SIR WALTER [*to Mistress Allwit*] The worst is past,   35
    I hope now, gossip.
MISTRESS ALLWIT   So I hope, too, good sir.
ALLWIT [*aside*] Why, then, so hope I too for company;
    I have nothing to do else.
SIR WALTER [*giving presents*] A poor remembrance, lady,°
    To the love of the babe; I pray, accept of it.
MISTRESS ALLWIT O, you are at too much charge, sir.
SECOND GOSSIP   Look, look!   40
    What has he given her? What is't, gossip?
THIRD GOSSIP Now, by my faith, a fair high standing-cup
    And two great 'postle spoons, one of them gilt.°
FIRST PURITAN Sure that was Judas then with the red beard.°
SECOND PURITAN I would not feed my daughter with that spoon   45
    For all the world, for fear of colouring her hair;
    Red hair the brethren like not, it consumes them much:°
    'Tis not the sisters' colour.
        Enter Nurse with comfits and wine

ALLWIT   Well said, nurse;°
About, about with them amongst the gossips!—
[*Aside*] Now out comes all the tasselled handkerchers,°   50
They are spread abroad between their knees already;
Now in goes the long fingers that are washed
Some thrice a day in urine; my wife uses it.°
Now we shall have such pocketing: see how
They lurch at the lower end!
FIRST PURITAN   Come hither, nurse.   55
ALLWIT [*aside*] Again? She has taken twice already.
FIRST PURITAN [*taking comfits*] I had forgot a sister's child that's sick.
ALLWIT [*aside*] A pox! It seems your purity loves sweet things well
That puts in thrice together. Had this been
All my cost now, I had been beggared;   60
These women have no consciences at sweetmeats,
Where'er they come; see an they have not culled out
All the long plums too, they have left nothing here°
But short wriggle-tail comfits, not worth mouthing:
No mar'l I heard a citizen complain once   65
That his wife's belly only broke his back;°
Mine had been all in fitters seven years since,
But for this worthy knight,
That with a prop upholds my wife and me,
And all my estate buried in Bucklersbury.°   70
MISTRESS ALLWIT [*toasting them*] Here, Mistress Yellowhammer
    and neighbours,
To you all that have taken pains with me,
All the good wives at once.
FIRST PURITAN   I'll answer for them.
They wish all health and strength, and that you may
Courageously go forward, to perform   75
The like and many such, like a true sister,°
With motherly bearing. [*Drinks*]
ALLWIT [*aside*]   Now the cups troll about
To wet the gossips' whistles. It pours down, i'faith;
They never think of payment.
FIRST PURITAN   Fill again, nurse. [*Drinks*]
ALLWIT [*aside*] Now, bless thee, two at once! I'll stay no longer;   80
It would kill me and if I paid for't—
[*To Sir Walter*] Will it please you to walk down and leave the
    women?

34

SIR WALTER With all my heart, Jack.

ALLWIT   Troth, I cannot blame you.

SIR WALTER Sit you all merry, ladies.

ALL GOSSIPS   Thank your worship, sir.

FIRST PURITAN Thank your worship, sir.   85

ALLWIT [aside] A pox twice tipple ye, you are last and lowest!
    Exeunt [Sir Walter Whorehound and Allwit]

FIRST PURITAN Bring hither that same cup, nurse, I would fain
    Drive away this—hup!—antichristian grief. [Drinks]

THIRD GOSSIP See, gossip, an she lies not in like a countess;°
    Would I had such a husband for my daughter!   90

FOURTH GOSSIP Is not she toward marriage?

THIRD GOSSIP   O no, sweet gossip!°

FOURTH GOSSIP Why, she's nineteen.

THIRD GOSSIP   Ay, that she was last Lammas,°
    But she has a fault, gossip, a secret fault.
    [Nurse refills glasses, then exits]

FOURTH GOSSIP A fault? What is't?

THIRD GOSSIP   I'll tell you when I have drunk. [Drinks]

FOURTH GOSSIP [aside] Wine can do that, I see, that friendship
    cannot.   95

THIRD GOSSIP And now I'll tell you, gossip: she's too free.

FOURTH GOSSIP Too free?

THIRD GOSSIP   O ay, she cannot lie dry in her bed.°

FOURTH GOSSIP What, and nineteen?

THIRD GOSSIP   'Tis as I tell you, gossip.
    [Enter Nurse and talks to Maudline]

MAUDLINE Speak with me, nurse? Who is't?

NURSE   A gentleman
    From Cambridge; I think it be your son, forsooth.   100

MAUDLINE 'Tis my son Tim, i'faith; prithee, call him up
    Among the women, 'twill embolden him well,
    [Exit Nurse]
    For he wants nothing but audacity.
    'Would the Welsh gentlewoman at home
    Were here now.

LADY KIX   Is you son come, forsooth?   105

MAUDLINE Yes, from the university, forsooth.

LADY KIX 'Tis great joy on ye.

MAUDLINE   There's a great marriage
    Toward for him.

LADY KIX   A marriage?
MAUDLINE   Yes, sure,°
  A huge heir in Wales at least to nineteen mountains,
  Besides her goods and cattle.
      Enter [Nurse with] Tim
TIM   O, I am betrayed!°   110
     Exit [Tim]
MAUDLINE What, gone again? Run after him, good nurse.
     [Exit Nurse]
  He's so bashful, that's the spoil of youth:
  In the university they're kept still to men,
  And ne'er trained up to women's company.°
LADY KIX 'Tis a great spoil of youth, indeed.   115
     Enter Nurse and Tim
NURSE Your mother will have it so.
MAUDLINE   Why son, why Tim!
  What, must I rise and fetch you? For shame, son!
TIM Mother, you do entreat like a freshwoman;°
  'Tis against the laws of the university
  For any that has answered under bachelor   120
  To thrust 'mongst married wives.
MAUDLINE   Come, we'll excuse you here.°
TIM Call up my tutor, mother, and I care not.°
MAUDLINE What, is your tutor come? Have you brought him up?
TIM I ha'not brought him up, he stands at the door:
  Negatur. There's logic to begin with you, mother.°   125
MAUDLINE Run, call the gentleman, nurse; he's my son's tutor.
     [Exit Nurse]
  [To Tim] Here, eat some plums.
TIM   Come I from Cambridge,
  And offer me six plums!
MAUDLINE   Why, how now, Tim!
  Will not your old tricks yet be left?
TIM   Served like a child,
  When I have answered under bachelor!   130
MAUDLINE You'll never lin till I make your tutor whip you;
  You know how I served you once at the free-school°
  In Paul's church-yard.
TIM   O monstrous absurdity!
  Ne'er was the like in Cambridge since my time;
  Life, whip a bachelor! You'd be laughed at soundly;   135

Let not my tutor hear you! 'Twould be a jest
Through the whole university. No more words, mother.
    Enter Tutor
MAUDLINE Is this your tutor, Tim?
TUTOR   Yes, surely, lady;
  I am the man that brought him in league
  With logic and read the Dunces to him.°   140
TIM That did he, mother, but now I have 'em all
  In my own pate, and can as well read 'em°
  To others.
TUTOR   That can he, mistress, for they flow
  Naturally from him.
MAUDLINE   I'm the more beholding°
  To your pains, sir.
TUTOR   *Non ideo sane.*°   145
MAUDLINE True, he was an idiot indeed, when he
  Went out of London, but now he's well mended.
  Did you receive the two goose-pies I sent you?
TUTOR And eat them heartily, thanks to your worship.
MAUDLINE [*to Gossips*] 'Tis my son Tim; I pray you, bid him
    welcome, gentlewomen.   150
TIM 'Tim'? Hark you: 'Timotheus', mother, 'Timotheus'.°
MAUDLINE How, shall I deny your name? 'Timotheus', quoth he.
  Faith, there's a name! 'Tis my son Tim, forsooth.
LADY KIX (*kiss[es Tim]*) You're welcome, Master Tim.
TIM [*aside to Tutor*]   O this is horrible,
  She wets as she kisses! Your handkercher, sweet tutor,   155
  To wipe them off as fast as they come on.
SECOND GOSSIP (*kiss[es Tim]*) Welcome from Cambridge.
TIM [*aside to Tutor*]   This is intolerable!
  This woman had a villainous sweet breath,°
  Did she not stink of comfits. Help me, sweet tutor,°
  Or I shall rub my lips off.
TUTOR   I'll go kiss   160
  The lower end the whilst.
TIM   Perhaps that's the sweeter°,
  And we shall despatch the sooner.
FIRST PURITAN   Let me come next.°
  Welcome from the wellspring of discipline
  That waters all the brethren.
    Reels and falls

TIM   Hoist, I beseech thee!°

THIRD GOSSIP O bless the woman!—Mistress Underman!   165

FIRST PURITAN 'Tis but the common affliction of the faithful;
  We must embrace our falls.

TIM [*aside to Tutor*]   I am glad I 'scaped it;°
  It was some rotten kiss, sure, it dropped down
  Before it came at me.
          Enter Allwit and Davy

ALLWIT [*aside*]   Here's a noise!°
  Not parted yet? Heyday, a looking glass!°   170
  They have drunk so hard in plate that some of them°
  Have need of other vessels. [*Aloud*] Yonder's
  The bravest show!

ALL GOSSIPS   Where, where, sir?

ALLWIT   Come along presently°
  By the Pissing-Conduit, with two brave drums°
  And a standard-bearer.

ALL GOSSIPS   O, brave!

TIM   Come, tutor!   175
          Exit [Tim with Tutor]

ALL GOSSIPS [*to Mistress Allwit*] Farewell, sweet gossip.
          Exeunt [Gossips]

MISTRESS ALLWIT   I thank you all for your pains.

FIRST PURITAN Feed and grow strong.
          [*Exeunt Mistress Allwit, Maudline, Moll, Lady Kix, and
          Puritans*]°

ALLWIT   You had more need to sleep than eat;
  Go, take a nap with some of the brethren, go,°
  And rise up a well-edified, boldified sister!
  O, here's a day of toil well passed o'er,   180
  Able to make a citizen hare-mad!°
  How hot they have made the rooms with their thick bums;°
  Dost not feel it, Davy?

DAVY DAHUMMA   Monstrous strong, sir.

ALLWIT What's here under the stools?

DAVY DAHUMMA   Nothing but wet, sir,°
  Some wine spilt here belike.

ALLWIT   Is't no worse, think'st thou?°   185
  Fair needlework stools cost nothing with them, Davy.°

DAVY DAHUMMA [*aside*] Nor you neither, i'faith.

ALLWIT   Look how they have laid them,

E'en as they lie themselves, with their heels up!
How they have shuffled up the rushes too, Davy,°
With their short figging little shittle-cork-heels!°   190
These women can let nothing stand as they find it.
But what's the secret thou'st about to tell me,
My honest Davy?
DAVY DAHUMMA   If you should disclose it, sir—
ALLWIT Life, rip my belly up to the throat then, Davy.
DAVY DAHUMMA My master's upon marriage.°   195
ALLWIT Marriage, Davy? Send me to hanging, rather!
DAVY DAHUMMA [aside] I have stung him!
ALLWIT   When, where? What is she, Davy?
DAVY DAHUMMA E'en the same was gossip, and gave the spoon.
ALLWIT I have no time to stay, nor scarce can speak,
   I'll stop those wheels, or all the work will break.°   200
      Exit [Allwit]
DAVY DAHUMMA I knew 'twould prick. Thus do I fashion still°
   All mine own ends by him and his rank toil:°
   'Tis my desire to keep him still from marriage;
   Being his poor nearest kinsman, I may fare
   The better at his death; there my hopes build,   205
   Since my Lady Kix is dry and hath no child.
      Exit

3.3

      Enter [Touchwood Senior and Touchwood Junior]
TOUCHWOOD JUNIOR Y'are in the happiest way to enrich yourself
   And pleasure me, brother, as man's feet can tread in;°
   For though she be locked up, her vow is fixed
   Only to me; then time shall never grieve me,
   For by that vow e'en absent I enjoy her,°   5
   Assuredly confirmed that none else shall,
   Which will make tedious years seem gameful to me.°
   In the mean space, lose you no time, sweet brother;
   You have the means to strike at this knight's fortunes
   And lay him level with his bankrout merit;°   10
   Get but his wife with child, perch at tree-top
   And shake the golden fruit into her lap;°

About it, before she weep herself to a dry ground
And whine out all her goodness.
TOUCHWOOD SENIOR   Prithee, cease;°
I find too much aptness in my blood   15
For such a business without provocation;°
You might' well spared this banquet of eringoes,°
Artichokes, potatoes, and your buttered crab:°
They were fitter kept for your own wedding dinner.
TOUCHWOOD JUNIOR Nay, an you'll follow my suit and save my
      purse too,   20
Fortune dotes on me: he's in happy case°
Finds such an honest friend i'the common-place.°
TOUCHWOOD SENIOR Life, what makes thee so merry? Thou hast no
      cause
That I could hear of lately since thy crosses,°
Unless there be news come with new additions.   25
TOUCHWOOD JUNIOR Why, there thou hast it right: I look for her
This evening, brother.
TOUCHWOOD SENIOR   How's that? Look for her?
TOUCHWOOD JUNIOR I will deliver you of the wonder straight,
      brother:°
By the firm secrecy and kind assistance
Of a good wench i'the house, who, made of pity,   30
Weighing the case her own, she's led through gutters,°
Strange hidden ways, which none but love could find,
Or ha' the heart to venture; I expect her
Where you would little think.
TOUCHWOOD SENIOR   I care not where,
So she be safe, and yours.
TOUCHWOOD JUNIOR   Hope tells me so: 35
But from your love and time my peace must grow.
      Exit [Touchwood Junior]
TOUCHWOOD SENIOR You know the worst, then, brother. Now to my
      Kix,
The barren he and she; they're i'the next room;
But to say which of their two humours hold them°
Now at this instant, I cannot say truly.   40
SIR OLIVER [*to Lady Kix, both within*] Thou liest, barrenness!°
TOUCHWOOD SENIOR O, is't that time of day? Give you joy of your
      tongue,
There's nothing else good in you: this their life

The whole day, from eyes open to eyes shut,
Kissing or scolding, and then must be made friends;   45
Then rail the second part of the first fit out,°
And then be pleased again, no man knows which way:
Fall out like giants and fall in like children;°
Their fruit can witness as much.°
    Enter Sir Oliver Kix and his Lady
SIR OLIVER   'Tis thy fault.   50
LADY KIX Mine, drouth and coldness?
SIR OLIVER   Thine; 'tis thou art barren.
LADY KIX I barren? O life, that I durst but speak now
  In mine own justice, in mine own right! I barren?°
  'Twas otherways with me when I was at court;
  I was never called so till I was married.   55
SIR OLIVER I'll be divorced.
LADY KIX   Be hanged! I need not wish it.°
  That will come too soon to thee: I may say°
  'Marriage and hanging goes by destiny,'
  For all the goodness I can find in't yet.°
SIR OLIVER I'll give up house, and keep some fruitful whore,   60
  Like an old bachelor, in a tradesman's chamber;
  She and her children shall have all.
LADY KIX   Where be they?
TOUCHWOOD SENIOR   Pray, cease;°
  When there are friendlier courses took for you
  To get and multiply within your house
  At your own proper costs; in spite of censure,   65
  Methinks an honest peace might be established.°
SIR OLIVER What, with her? Never.
TOUCHWOOD SENIOR   Sweet sir—
SIR OLIVER   You work all in vain.
LADY KIX Then he doth all like thee.
TOUCHWOOD SENIOR   Let me entreat, sir—°
SIR OLIVER Singleness confound her! I took her with one smock.°
LADY KIX But, indeed, you came not so single when°   70
  You came from shipboard.
SIR OLIVER Heart, she bit sore there! [*To Touchwood Senior*] Prithee,
  make's friends.
TOUCHWOOD SENIOR [*aside*] Is't come to that? The peal begins to
  cease.°
SIR OLIVER [*to Lady Kix*] I'll sell all at an outcry!

LADY KIX   Do thy worst, slave!°
   [*To Touchwood Senior*] Good sweet sir, bring us into love again.   75
TOUCHWOOD SENIOR [*aside*] Some would think this impossible to
     compass—
   [*To them*] Pray, let this storm fly over.
SIR OLIVER   Good sir, pardon me;
   I'm master of this house, which I'll sell presently;
   I'll clap up bills this evening.
TOUCHWOOD SENIOR   Lady, friends, come!°
LADY KIX If e'er ye loved woman, talk not on't, sir.°   80
   What, friends with him! Good faith, do you think I'm mad?
   With one that's scarce the hinder quarter of a man!°
SIR OLIVER Thou art nothing of a woman.
LADY KIX (*weeps*)   Would I were
   Less than nothing!
SIR OLIVER   Nay, prithee, what dost mean?
LADY KIX I cannot please you.
SIR OLIVER   I'faith, thou art a good soul;   85
   He lies that says it; [*kisses her*] buss, buss, pretty rogue.°
LADY KIX You care not for me.
TOUCHWOOD SENIOR [*aside*] Can any man tell now
   Which way they came in? By this light, I'll be hanged then!°
SIR OLIVER Is the drink come?
TOUCHWOOD SENIOR *aside*   Here's a little vial of°
   Almond-milk, that stood me in some threepence.°   90
SIR OLIVER I hope to see thee, wench, within these few years,
   Circled with children, pranking up a girl,
   And putting jewels in their little ears;
   Fine sport, i'faith!
LADY KIX   Ay, had you been ought, husband,
   It had been done ere this time.
SIR OLIVER   Had I been ought!°   95
   Hang thee! Hadst thou been ought! But a cross thing
   I ever found thee.
LADY KIX   Thou art a grub to say so.°
SIR OLIVER A pox on thee!
TOUCHWOOD SENIOR [*aside*] By this light, they are out again
   At the same door, and no man can tell which way!   100
   [*To Sir Oliver*] Come, here's your drink, sir.
SIR OLIVER   I will not take it now, sir,
   An I were sure to get three boys ere midnight.

LADY KIX Why, there thou show'st now of what breed thou
    comest,°
    To hinder generation. O thou villain,
    That knows how crookedly the world goes with us   105
    For want of heirs, yet put by all good fortune.°
SIR OLIVER Hang, strumpet! I will take it now in spite!°
TOUCHWOOD SENIOR [giving vial to Sir Oliver] Then you must ride
    upon't five hours.
SIR OLIVER   I mean so.°
    Within there!
        Enter a Servant
SERVANT   Sir?
SIR OLIVER   Saddle the white mare:
        [*Exit Servant*]
    I'll take a whore along and ride to Ware.°   110
LADY KIX Ride to the devil!
SIR OLIVER   I'll plague you every way.
    Look ye, do you see? (*Drinks*) 'Tis gone.
LADY KIX   A pox go with it!
SIR OLIVER Ay, curse and spare not now.
TOUCHWOOD SENIOR   Stir up and down, sir,
    You must not stand.
SIR OLIVER   Nay, I'm not given to standing.°
TOUCHWOOD SENIOR So much the better, sir, for the —°   115
SIR OLIVER I never could stand long in one place yet;
    I learned it of my father, ever figient.
    How if I crossed this, sir?
        [*He*] *capers*
TOUCHWOOD SENIOR   O passing good, sir,°
    And would show well a-horseback: when you come to your inn,°
    If you leaped over a joint-stool or two,°   120
    'Twere not amiss—(*aside*) although you break your neck, sir.°
SIR OLIVER What say you to a table thus high, sir?
        [*He capers*]
TOUCHWOOD SENIOR Nothing better, sir;—[*aside*] if it be
    furnished
    With good victuals. [*To him*] You remember how
    The bargain runs about this business?   125
SIR OLIVER Or else I had a bad head: you must receive, sir,°
    Four hundred pounds of me at four several payments:
    One hundred pound now in hand.

TOUCHWOOD SENIOR   Right, that I have, sir.
SIR OLIVER Another hundred when my wife is quick;
   The third when she's brought a-bed; and the last hundred°   130
   When the child cries, for if it should be still-born,
   It doth no good, sir.
TOUCHWOOD SENIOR All this is even still:
   A little faster, sir.
SIR OLIVER   Not a whit, sir;°
   I'm in an excellent pace for any physic.
        Enter a Servant
SERVANT Your white mare's ready.
SIR OLIVER   I shall up presently—   135
        [*Exit Servant*]
   [*To Lady Kix*] One kiss, and farewell.
LADY KIX   Thou shalt have two, love.
SIR OLIVER Expect me about three.
        Exit [*Sir Oliver Kix*]
LADY KIX   With all my heart, sweet.
TOUCHWOOD SENIOR [*aside*] By this light, they have forgot their
      anger since,°
   And are as far in again as e'er they were.
   Which way the devil came they? Heart, I saw 'em not.   140
   Their ways are beyond finding out. [*To Lady Kix*] Come, sweet
      lady.
LADY KIX How must I take mine, sir?
TOUCHWOOD SENIOR   Clean contrary;°
   Yours must be taken lying.
LADY KIX   A-bed, sir?
TOUCHWOOD SENIOR A-bed, or where you will for your own ease,
   Your coach will serve.
LADY KIX   The physic must needs please.°   145
        Exeunt

4.1

Enter Tim and Tutor

TIM *Negatur argumentum*, tutor.

TUTOR *Probo tibi*, pupil, *stultus non est animal rationale.*

TIM *Falleris sane.*

TUTOR *Quaeso ut taceas: probo tibi—*

TIM *Quomodo probas, domine?*   5

TUTOR *Stultus non habet rationem, ergo non est animal rationale.*

TIM *Sic argumentaris, domine: stultus non habet rationem, ergo non est*
     animal rationale. Negatur argumentum again, tutor.

TUTOR *Argumentum iterum probo tibi, domine: qui non participat de*
       ratione, nullo modo potest vocari rationalis; but *stultus non participat*   10
       de ratione, ergo stultus nullo modo potest dici rationalis.

TIM *Participat.*

TUTOR *Sic disputas: qui participat, quomodo participat?*

TIM *Ut homo, probabo tibi in syllogismo.*

TUTOR *Hunc proba.*   15

TIM *Sic probo, domine: stultus est homo sicut tu et ego sumus; homo est*
     animal rationale, sicut stultus est animal rationale.°

      Enter Maudline

MAUDLINE Here's nothing but disputing all the day long with'em!

TUTOR *Sic disputas: stultus est homo sicut tu et ego sumus; homo est*
       animal rationale, sicut stultus est animal rationale.°   20

MAUDLINE Your reasons are both good, whate'er they be;
          Pray, give them o'er; faith, you'll tire yourselves;
          What's the matter between you?

TIM   Nothing but reasoning
          About a fool, mother.

MAUDLINE   About a fool, son?
          Alas, what need you trouble your heads about that?   25
          None of us all but knows what a fool is.

TIM Why, what's a fool, mother? I come to you now.°

MAUDLINE Why, one that's married before he has wit.°

TIM 'Tis pretty, i'faith, and well guessed of a woman
     Never brought up at the university;   30
     But bring forth what fool you will, mother, I'll prove him
     To be as reasonable a creature as myself
     Or my tutor here.

MAUDLINE   Fie, 'tis impossible.

TUTOR Nay, he shall do't, forsooth.

TIM   'Tis the easiest thing
  To prove a fool by logic; by logic   35
  I'll prove anything.

MAUDLINE   What, thou wilt not!

TIM I'll prove a whore to be an honest woman.

MAUDLINE Nay, by my faith, she must prove that herself,
  Or logic will never do't.

TIM   'Twill do't, I tell you.

MAUDLINE Some in the street would give a thousand pounds   40
  That you could prove their wives so.

TIM   Faith, I can,°
  And all their daughters too, though they had three bastards!°
  When comes your tailor hither?

MAUDLINE   Why, what of him?°

TIM By logic I'll prove him to be a man,
  Let him come when he will.

MAUDLINE [to Tutor]   How hard at first°   45
  Was learning to him! Truly, sir, I thought
  He would never ha'took the Latin tongue.
  How many accidences do you think he wore out°
  Ere he came to his grammar?

TUTOR   Some three or four?

MAUDLINE Believe me, sir, some four and thirty.

TIM   Pish,   50
  I made haberdines° of'em in church porches.°

MAUDLINE He was eight years in his grammar, and stuck horribly
  At a foolish place there called as in praesenti.°

TIM [pointing to his head] Pox, I have it here now.

MAUDLINE   He so shamed me once
  Before an honest gentleman that knew me   55
  When I was a maid.

TIM   These women must have all out!°

MAUDLINE 'Quid est grammatica?' says the gentleman to him—°
  I shall remember by a sweet, sweet token—°
  But nothing could he answer.

TUTOR   How now, pupil, ha?
    Quid est grammatica?

TIM   Grammatica? Ha, ha, ha!   60

MAUDLINE Nay, do not laugh, son, but let me hear you say it now:
  There was one word went so prettily off
  The gentleman's tongue, I shall remember it
  The longest day of my life.
TUTOR   Come, *quid est grammatica?*
TIM Are you not ashamed, tutor? *Grammatica*:   65
  Why, *recte scribendi atque loquendi ars,*°
  Sir-reverence of my mother.
MAUDLINE   That was it, i'faith!°
  Why now, son, I see you are a deep scholar.
  And, Master Tutor, a word I pray: let us
  Withdraw a little into my husband's chamber;   70
  I'll send in the North Wales gentlewoman to him,°
  She looks for wooing. I'll put together both
  And lock the door.
TUTOR   I give great approbation
  To your conclusion.°
          Exeunt [Maudline and Tutor]
TIM   I mar'l what this gentlewoman°
  Should be that I should have in marriage: 75
  She's a stranger to me: I wonder what
  My parents mean, i'faith, to match me with a stranger so,
  A maid that's neither kiff nor kin to me.°
  Life, do they think I have no more care of my body
  Than to lie with one that I ne'er knew, a mere stranger,   80
  One that ne'er went to school with me neither,
  Nor ever play-fellows together?
  They're mightily o'erseen in't, methinks.
  They say she has mountains to her marriage;°
  She's full of cattle, some two thousand runts:°   85
  Now what the meaning of these runts should be
  My tutor cannot tell me; I have looked
  In Rider's Dictionary for the letter R.°
  And there I can hear no tidings of these runts neither;
  Unless they should be Romford hogs, I know them not.°   90
          Enter Welsh Gentlewoman
  And here she comes. If I know what to say to her now
  In the way of marriage, I'm no graduate!°
  Methinks, i'faith, 'tis boldly done of her
  To come into my chamber, being but a stranger;
  She shall not say I'm so proud yet but I'll speak   95

To her: marry, as I will order it,°
She shall take no hold of my words, I'll warrant her.°
　　　[*Welsh Gentlewoman curtsies.*]
She looks and makes a cur'sey! [*To her*] *Salve tu quoque, puella
pulcherrima; quid vis nescio nec sane curo—.* Tully's own phrase to a
heart!°

WELSH GENTLEWOMAN [*aside*]　I know not what he means: a suitor,　100
　　quoth a?°
I hold my life he understands no English.

TIM　*Ferter, mehercule, tu virgo, Wallia ut opibus abundis maximis.*°

WELSH GENTLEWOMAN [*aside*]　What's this *fertur* and *abundundis*?
He mocks me sure, and calls me a bundle of farts.　105

TIM [*aside*]　I have no Latin word now for runts;
　I'll make some shift or other:°
　[*To her*] *Iterum dico, opibus abundat maximis montibus et fontibus et,
　ut ita dicam, rontibus; attamen vero homunculus ego sum natura simule
　arte baccalaureus, lecto profecto non parata*°　110

WELSH GENTLEWOMAN [*aside*]　This is most strange: maybe he can
　　speak Welsh—
　[*To him*] *Avedera whee comrage, der due cog foginis.*°

TIM [*aside*]　*Cog foggin?* I scorn to cog with her; I'll tell her so too,
　In a word near her own language. [*To her*] *Ego non cogo.*°

WELSH GENTLEWOMAN　*Rhegosin a whiggin harle ron corid ambre.*°　115

TIM [*aside*]　By my faith, she's a good scholar, I see that already:
　She has the tongues plain; I hold my life she has travelled.°
　What will folks say? 'There goes the learned couple!'
　Faith, if the truth were known, she hath proceeded!°
　　　Enter Maudline

MAUDLINE　How now, how speeds your business?

TIM [*aside*]　　　　　　　　　　　I'm glad my mother's come　120
　To part us.

MAUDLINE [*to Welsh Gentlewoman*]　How do you agree, forsooth?°

WELSH GENTLEWOMAN　As well as e'er we did before we met.

MAUDLINE　　　　　　　　　　　　　　　How's that?

WELSH GENTLEWOMAN　You put me to a man I understand not;
　Your son's no Englishman, methinks.

MAUDLINE　　　　　　　　　　No Englishman!
　Bless my boy, and born i'the heart of London?　125

WELSH GENTLEWOMAN　I ha' been long enough in the chamber with
　　him,
　And I find neither Welsh nor English in him.

MAUDLINE Why, Tim, how have you used the gentlewoman?

TIM As well as a man might do, mother, in modest Latin.

MAUDLINE Latin, fool?

TIM   And she recoiled in Hebrew.°   130

MAUDLINE In Hebrew, fool? 'Tis Welsh!

TIM   All comes to one, mother.

MAUDLINE She can speak English too.

TIM   Who told me so much?
    Heart, an she can speak English, I'll clap to her;°
    I thought you'd marry me to a stranger.°

MAUDLINE [to Welsh Gentlewoman] You must forgive him; he's so
    inured to Latin,   135
    He and his tutor, that he hath quite forgot
    To use the Protestant tongue.

WELSH GENTLEWOMAN   'Tis quickly°
    Pardoned, forsooth.

MAUDLINE   Tim, make amends and kiss her.—
    [To Welsh Gentlewoman] He makes towards you, forsooth.

TIM [kissing Welsh Gentlewoman]   O delicious!°
    One may discover her country by her kissing;°   140
    'Tis a true saying: 'There's nothing tastes so sweet
    As your Welsh mutton'—°
    [To Welsh Gentlewoman] It was reported you could sing.°

MAUDLINE O, rarely, Tim, the sweetest British songs.°

TIM And 'tis my mind, I swear, before I marry,
    I would see all my wife's good parts at once,°   145
    To view how rich I were.

MAUDLINE   Thou shalt hear sweet music, Tim—
    [To Welsh Gentlewoman] Pray, forsooth.°
      Music and Welsh [Gentlewoman sings]°

              Cupid is Venus' only joy°
              But he is a wanton boy,   150
              A very, very, wanton boy;
              He shoots at ladies' naked breasts,
              He is the cause of most men's crests—°
              I mean upon the forehead,
              Invisible but horrid;   155
              'Twas he first taught upon the way
              To keep a lady's lips in play.°

              Why should not Venus chide her son

> For the pranks that he hath done,
> The wanton pranks that he hath done?   160
> He shoots his fiery darts so thick,
> They hurt poor ladies to the quick,°
> Ah me, the cruel wounding!
> His darts are so confounding,
> That life and sense would soon decay   165
> But that he keeps their lips in play.
>
> Can there be any part of bliss,
> In a quickly fleeting kiss,
> A quickly fleeting kiss?
> To one's pleasure leisures are but waste,°   170
> The slowest kiss makes too much haste,
> We lose it ere we find it.°
> The pleasing sport they only know
> That close above and close below.°

TIM I would not change my wife for a kingdom;   175
   I can do somewhat too in my own lodging.°
     Enter Yellowhammer and Allwit
YELLOWHAMMER Why, well said, Tim! The bells go merrily;
   I love such peals o'life. Wife, lead them in a while;°
   Here's a strange gentleman desires private conference.°
     [*Exeunt Maudline, Welsh Gentlewoman, and Tim*]
   [*To Allwit*] You're welcome, sir, the more for your name's sake,   180
   Good Master Yellowhammer; I love my name well:
   And which o'the Yellowhammers take you descent from,
   If I may be so bold with you? which, I pray?
ALLWIT The Yellowhammers in Oxfordshire near Abingdon.°
YELLOWHAMMER And those are the best Yellowhammers, and truest
    bred;   185
   I came from thence myself, though now a citizen:°
   I'll be bold with you; you are most welcome.
ALLWIT I hope the zeal I bring with me shall deserve it.°
YELLOWHAMMER I hope no less; what is your will, sir?
ALLWIT I understand, by rumours, you have a daughter,   190
   Which my bold love shall henceforth title 'cousin'.
YELLOWHAMMER I thank you for her, sir.
ALLWIT   I heard of her virtues
   And other confirmed graces.
YELLOWHAMMER   A plaguy girl, sir!°

ALLWIT Fame sets her out with richer ornaments
  Than you are pleased to boast of; 'tis done modestly:°   195
  I hear she's towards marriage.
YELLOWHAMMER   You hear truth, sir.
ALLWIT And with a knight in town, Sir Walter Whorehound.
YELLOWHAMMER The very same, sir.
ALLWIT   I am the sorrier for't.
YELLOWHAMMER The sorrier? Why, cousin?
ALLWIT   'Tis not too far past,
    is't?
  It may yet be recalled?
YELLOWHAMMER   Recalled? Why, good sir?   200
ALLWIT Resolve me in that point, ye shall hear from me.°
YELLOWHAMMER There's no contract passed.
ALLWIT   I am very joyful, sir.
YELLOWHAMMER But he's the man must bed her.
ALLWIT   By no means, coz;
  She's quite undone then, and you'll curse the time
  That e'er you made the match; he's an arrant whoremaster,   205
  Consumes his time and state—°
  Whom in my knowledge he hath kept this seven years;
  Nay, coz, another man's wife, too.
YELLOWHAMMER   O, abominable!
ALLWIT Maintains the whole house, apparels the husband,
  Pays servants' wages, not so much but—°   210
YELLOWHAMMER Worse and worse! And doth the husband know
    this?
ALLWIT Knows? Ay, and glad he may too, 'tis his living;
  As other trades thrive, butchers by selling flesh,
  Poulters by vending conies, or the like, coz.°
YELLOWHAMMER What an incomparable wittol's this!   215
ALLWIT Tush, what cares he for that? Believe me, coz,
  No more than do I.
YELLOWHAMMER   What a base slave is that!
ALLWIT All's one to him: he feeds and takes his ease,
  Was ne'er the man that ever broke his sleep
  To get a child yet, by his own confession,   220
  And yet his wife has seven.
YELLOWHAMMER   What, by Sir Walter?
ALLWIT Sir Walter's like to keep'em and maintain'em
  In excellent fashion: he dares do no less, sir.

YELLOWHAMMER Life, has he children, too?

ALLWIT   Children! boys thus high,
   In their Cato and Corderius.

YELLOWHAMMER   What? You jest, sir!°   225

ALLWIT Why, one can make a verse and is now at Eton College.°

YELLOWHAMMER O, this is news has cut into my heart, coz.

ALLWIT It had eaten nearer, if it had not been prevented:°
   One Allwit's wife.

YELLOWHAMMER   Allwit? Foot, I have heard of him;
   He had a girl kursened lately?

ALLWIT   Ay, that work°   230
   Did cost the knight above a hundred mark.

YELLOWHAMMER I'll mark him for a knave and villain for't;
   A thousand thanks and blessings! I have done with him.

ALLWIT [aside] Ha, ha, ha! This knight will stick by my ribs still;
   I shall not lose him yet; no wife will come;   235
   Where'er he woos, I find him still at home. Ha, ha!
          Exit [Allwit]

YELLOWHAMMER Well, grant all this, say now his deeds are black,
   Pray, what serves marriage but to call him back?°
   I've kept a whore myself, and had a bastard
   By Mistress Anne, in anno—°   240
   I care not who knows it; he's now a jolly fellow,
   H'as been twice warden; so may his fruit be,°
   They were but base begot, and so was he.
   The knight is rich, he shall be my son-in-law;
   No matter, so the whore he keeps be wholesome,°   245
   My daughter takes no hurt then; so let them wed:
   I'll have him sweat well ere they go to bed.°
          Enter Maudline

MAUDLINE O, husband, husband!

YELLOWHAMMER   How now, Maudline?

MAUDLINE   We are all undone!
   She's gone, she's gone!

YELLOWHAMMER   Again? Death! Which way?

MAUDLINE Over the houses. Lay the waterside;   250
   She's gone for ever, else.

YELLOWHAMMER   O vent'rous baggage!
          Exeunt

4.2

Enter Tim and Tutor

TIM Thieves, thieves! My sister's stol'n! Some thief hath got her:
   O, how miraculously did my father's plate 'scape!
   'Twas all left out, tutor.

TUTOR   Is't possible?

TIM Besides three chains of pearl and a box of coral!
   My sister's gone. Let's look at Trig-stairs for her;°   5
   My mother's gone to lay the common stairs
   At Puddle-wharf; and at the dock below°
   Stands my poor silly father. Run, sweet tutor, run!°
      Exeunt

4.3

Enter both the Touchwoods

TOUCHWOOD SENIOR I had been taken, brother, by eight
      sergeants,°
   But for the honest watermen; I am bound to them;°
   They are the most requitefull'st people living,°
   For as they get their means by gentlemen,
   They are still the forwardest to help gentlemen:°   5
   You heard how one 'scaped out of the Blackfriars,°
   But a while since, from two or three varlets came°
   Into the house with all their rapiers drawn,
   As if they'd dance the sword-dance on the stage,
   With candles in their hands, like chandlers' ghosts,   10
   Whilst the poor gentleman so pursued and bandied°
   Was by an honest pair of oars safely landed.

TOUCHWOOD JUNIOR I love them with my heart for't.

      Enter three or four Watermen

FIRST WATERMAN   Your first man, sir.°

SECOND WATERMAN Shall I carry you gentlemen with a pair of oars?

TOUCHWOOD SENIOR These be the honest fellows. Take one pair   15
   And leave the rest for her.

TOUCHWOOD JUNIOR   Barn Elms.

TOUCHWOOD SENIOR   No more, brother.°

FIRST WATERMAN Your first man.
SECOND WATERMAN   Shall I carry your worship?
TOUCHWOOD JUNIOR   Go.
     [Exit Touchwood Senior with First Waterman]
  And you honest watermen that stay,
  Here's a French crown for you.
     [He gives a coin]°
  There comes a maid with all speed to take water,   20
  Row her lustily to Barn Elms after me.°
SECOND WATERMAN To Barn Elms, good sir. Make ready the boat,
  Sam;
  We'll wait below.
     Exeunt [Watermen.] Enter Moll
TOUCHWOOD JUNIOR What made you stay so long?
MOLL I found the way more dangerous than I looked for.
TOUCHWOOD JUNIOR Away, quick! There's a boat waits for you; and
  I'll   25
  Take water at Paul's wharf and overtake you.°
MOLL Good sir, do; we cannot be too safe.°
     [Exeunt]

4.4

     Enter Sir Walter Whorehound, Yellowhammer, Tim and Tutor
SIR WALTER Life, call you this close keeping?
YELLOWHAMMER   She was kept°
  Under a double lock.
SIR WALTER   A double devil!
TIM That's a buff sergeant, tutor; he'll ne'er wear out.°
YELLOWHAMMER How would you have women locked?
TIM   With padlocks, father;
  The Venetian uses it; my tutor reads it.°   5
SIR WALTER Heart, if she were so locked up, how got she out?
YELLOWHAMMER There was a little hole looked into the gutter;°
  But who would have dreamt of that?
SIR WALTER   A wiser man would!
TIM He says true, father; a wise man for love
  Will seek every hole; my tutor knows it.°   10
TUTOR *Verum poeta dicta.*
TIM   *Dicit Virgilius*, father.°

YELLOWHAMMER Prithee, talk of thy jills somewhere else, she's
played
The jill with me. Where's your wise mother now?°
TIM Run mad, I think; I thought she would have drowned herself;
She would not stay for oars but took a smelt-boat:°   15
Sure, I think she be gone a-fishing for her!
YELLOWHAMMER She'll catch a goodly dish of gudgeons now,
Will serve us all to supper.°

Enter Maudline drawing Moll by the hair, and Watermen.

MAUDLINE I'll tug thee home by the hair.
FIRST WATERMAN   Good mistress, spare her.
MAUDLINE Tend your own business.
SECOND WATERMAN   You are a cruel mother.   20

Exeunt [Watermen]

MOLL O, my heart dies!
MAUDLINE   I'll make thee an example
For all the neighbours' daughters.
MOLL   Farewell, life!
MAUDLINE You that have tricks can counterfeit.
YELLOWHAMMER   Hold, hold, Maudline!
MAUDLINE I have brought your jewel by the hair.
YELLOWHAMMER   She's here, knight.
SIR WALTER Forbear, or I'll grow worse.
TIM   Look on her, tutor;°   25
She hath brought her from the water like a mermaid;°
She's but half my sister now, as far as the flesh goes,
The rest may be sold to fishwives.
MAUDLINE Dissembling, cunning baggage.
YELLOWHAMMER   Impudent strumpet!
SIR WALTER Either give over, both, or I'll give over!—°   30
[*To Moll*] Why have you used me thus, unkind mistress?
Wherein have I deservèd?
YELLOWHAMMER   You talk too fondly, sir:°
We'll take another course and prevent all;°
We might have done't long since; we'll lose no time now,
Nor trust to't any longer. Tomorrow morn,°   35
As early as sunrise, we'll have you joined.
MOLL O, bring me death tonight, love-pitying fates;
Let me not see tomorrow up upon the world.
YELLOWHAMMER Are you content, sir? Till then she shall be
watched!

MAUDLINE Baggage, you shall!
      Exit [Maudline with Moll]
TIM   Why, father, my tutor and I   40
  Will both watch in armour.
      [Exit Yellowhammer]
TUTOR   How shall we do for weapons?
TIM Take you no care for that; if need be I can send
  For conquering metal, tutor, ne'er lost day yet;°
  'Tis but at Westminster: I am acquainted°
  With him that keeps the monuments; I can borrow   45
  Harry the Fifth's sword. 'Twill serve us both
  To watch with.
      Exeunt [Tim and Tutor]
SIR WALTER   I never was so near my wish
  As this chance makes me: ere tomorrow noon
  I shall receive two thousand pound in gold
  And a sweet maidenhead worth forty.°   50
      Enter Touchwood Junior with [First] Waterman
TOUCHWOOD JUNIOR O, thy news splits me!
FIRST WATERMAN   Half drowned! She cruelly°
  Tugged her by the hair, forced her disgracefully,
  Not like a mother.
TOUCHWOOD JUNIOR Enough! Leave me, like my joys.°
      Exit [First] Waterman
  [To Sir Walter] Sir, saw you not a wretched maid pass this way?
  Heart, villain, is it thou?
SIR WALTER   Yes, slave, 'tis I!   55
      Both draw and fight
TOUCHWOOD JUNIOR I must break through thee, then: there is no
    stop
  That checks my tongue and all my hopeful fortunes,
  That breast excepted, and I must have way.°
SIR WALTER *[wounding Touchwood Junior]* Sir, I believe 'twill hold
    your life in play.°
TOUCHWOOD JUNIOR *[fighting back]* Sir, you'll gain the heart in my
    breast at first?°   60
SIR WALTER There is no dealing, then? Think on the dowry
  For two thousand pounds.
TOUCHWOOD JUNIOR   O, now 'tis quit, sir.°
      [Touchwood Junior wounds Sir Walter]
SIR WALTER And being of even hand, I'll play no longer.°

TOUCHWOOD JUNIOR No longer, slave?
SIR WALTER   I have certain things to think on
    Before I dare go further.
        [*Exit Sir Walter*]
TOUCHWOOD JUNIOR   But one bout!°   65
    I'll follow thee to death, but ha"t out.°
        Exit

5.1

Enter Allwit, his Wife, and Davy Dahumma

MISTRESS ALLWIT A misery of a house!

ALLWIT   What shall become of us?

DAVY DAHUMMA I think his wound be mortal.

ALLWIT   Think'st thou so,
　　Davy?
　　Then am I mortal too, but a dead man, Davy;°
　　This is no world for me whene'er he goes;
　　I must e'en truss up all and after him, Davy;   5
　　A sheet with two knots, and away!

　　　　　Enter Sir Walter Whorehound, led in hurt [by two Servants]

DAVY DAHUMMA   O, see, sir,°
　　How faint he goes! Two of my fellows lead him.

MISTRESS ALLWIT [*fainting*]   O me!

ALLWIT Heyday, my wife's laid down too! Here's like to be
　　A good house kept, when we are all together down:
　　Take pains with her, good Davy, cheer her up there.   10
　　Let me come to his worship, let me come.

　　　　　[*Exeunt Servants*]

SIR WALTER Touch me not, villain! My wound aches at thee,
　　Thou poison to my heart!

ALLWIT   He raves already,
　　His senses are quite gone, he knows me not—
　　[*To him*] Look up, an't like your worship; heave those eyes,   15
　　Call me to mind; is your remembrance left?°
　　Look in my face: who am I, an't like your worship?

SIR WALTER If anything be worse than slave or villain,
　　Thou art the man!

ALLWIT   Alas, his poor worship's weakness!
　　He will begin to know me by little and little.   20

SIR WALTER No devil can be like thee!

ALLWIT   Ah, poor gentleman,
　　Methinks the pain that thou endurest—

SIR WALTER Thou know'st me to be wicked, for thy baseness
　　Kept the eyes open still on all my sins;
　　None knew the dear account my soul stood charged with   25
　　So well as thou, yet, like hell's flattering angel,

Would'st never tell me on't, let'st me go on,
And join with death in sleep; that if I had not
Waked now by chance, even by a stranger's pity,
I had everlastingly slept out all hope   30
Of grace and mercy.
ALLWIT   Now he is worse and worse.
  Wife, to him, wife: thou wast wont to do good on him.
MISTRESS ALLWIT How is't with you, sir?
SIR WALTER   Not as with you,
  Thou loathsome strumpet! Some good pitying man
  Remove my sins out of my sight a little;   35
  I tremble to behold her, she keeps back
  All comfort while she stays. Is this a time,°
  Unconscionable woman, to see thee?
  Art thou so cruel to the peace of man
  Not to give liberty now? The devil himself   40
  Shows a far fairer reverence and respect
  To goodness than thyself; he dares not do this,
  But parts in time of penitence, hides his face;°
  When man withdraws from him, he leaves the place.
  Hast thou less manners and more impudence   45
  Than thy instructor? Prithee show thy modesty,°
  If the least grain be left, and get thee from me:
  Thou shouldst be rather locked many rooms hence
  From the poor miserable sight of me,
  If either love or grace had part in thee.   50
MISTRESS ALLWIT He is lost for ever!
ALLWIT   Run, sweet Davy, quickly,°
  And fetch the children hither; sight of them
  Will make him cheerful straight.
      [*Exit Davy Dahumma*]
SIR WALTER [*to Mistress Allwit*]   O death! Is this
  A place for you to weep? What tears are those?
  Get you away with them, I shall fare the worse,   55
  As long as they are a-weeping; they work against me;
  There's nothing but thy appetite in that sorrow,
  Thou weep'st for lust; I feel it in the slackness
  Of comforts coming towards me: I was well°
  Till thou began'st to undo me. This shows like°   60
  The fruitless sorrow of a careless mother
  That brings her son with dalliance to the gallows°

And then stands by and weeps to see him suffer.
>*Enter Davy Dahumma with* [*Nick, Wat and the baby*]

DAVY DAHUMMA There are the children, sir; an't like your worship,°
    Your last fine girl: in troth she smiles;°   65
    Look, look, in faith, sir.
SIR WALTER   O, my vengeance!°
    Let me for ever hide my cursèd face
    From sight of those that darkens all my hopes,°
    And stands between me and the sight of heaven!
    Who sees me now, he too and those so near me,°   70
    May rightly say I am o'ergrown with sin.
    O, how my offences wrestle with my repentance!
    It hath scarce breath;°
    Still my adulterous guilt hovers aloft,
    And with her black wings beats down all my prayers   75
    Ere they be half way up. What's he knows now°
    How long I have to live? O, what comes then?
    My taste grows bitter; the round world all gall now;
    Her pleasing pleasures now hath poisoned me,
    Which I exchanged my soul for:°   80
    Make way a hundred sighs at once for me!°
ALLWIT Speak to him, Nick.
NICK   I dare not, I am afraid.
ALLWIT Tell him he hurts his wounds, Wat, with making moan.°
SIR WALTER Wretched, death of seven.
ALLWIT   Come, let's be talking°
    Somewhat to keep him alive. Ah, sirrah Wat,   85
    And did my lord bestow that jewel on thee
    For an epistle thou mad'st in Latin?
    Thou art a good forward boy, there's great joy on thee.
SIR WALTER O sorrow!
ALLWIT [*aside*]   Heart, will nothing comfort him?
    If he be so far gone, 'tis time to moan.   90
    [*To him*] Here's pen and ink and paper, and all things ready;
    Will't please your worship for to make your will?
SIR WALTER My will? Yes, yes, what else? Who writes apace, now?°
ALLWIT That can your man, Davy, an't like your worship,
    A fair, fast, legible hand.
SIR WALTER   Set it down, then: [*Davy Dahumma writes*] 95
    Imprimis, I bequeath to yonder wittol
    Three times his weight in curses.

ALLWIT   How!
SIR WALTER   All plagues
   Of body and of mind.
ALLWIT   Write them not down, Davy.
DAVY DAHUMMA It is his will; I must.
SIR WALTER   Together also°
   With such a sickness ten days ere his death.°   100
ALLWIT There's a sweet legacy! I am almost choked with it.
SIR WALTER Next I bequeath to that foul whore his wife
   All barrenness of joy, a drouth of virtue,
   And dearth of all repentance: for her end,°
   The common misery of an English strumpet,   105
   In French and Dutch; beholding ere she dies°
   Confusion of her brats before her eyes,°
   And never shed a tear for it.
       Enter a Servant
FIRST SERVANT   Where's the knight?
   O sir, the gentleman you wounded is
   Newly departed!
SIR WALTER   Dead? Lift, lift! Who helps me?   110
ALLWIT Let the law lift you now, that must have all;
   I have done lifting on you, and my wife too.°
FIRST SERVANT You were best lock yourself close.
ALLWIT   Not in my house, sir,
   I'll harbour no such persons as men-slayers;
   Lock yourself where you will.
SIR WALTER   What's this?
MISTRESS ALLWIT   Why, husband!   115
ALLWIT I know what I do, wife.
MISTRESS ALLWIT [*aside to Allwit*] You cannot tell yet;°
   For having killed the man in his defence,
   Neither his life nor estate will be touched, husband.
ALLWIT Away, wife! Hear a fool! His lands will hang him.°   120
SIR WALTER Am I denied a chamber? [*To Mistress Allwit*] What say
   you, forsooth?
MISTRESS ALLWIT Alas, sir, I am one that would have all well°
   But must obey my husband—[*To Allwit*] Prithee, love,
   Let the poor gentleman stay, being so sore wounded:
   There's a close chamber at one end of the garret°   125
   We never use; let him have that I prithee.
ALLWIT We never use? You forget sickness then,

And physic-times; is't not a place of easement?
> *Enter a [second] Servant*

SIR WALTER O death! do I hear this with part
Of former life in me? What's the news now?   130

SECOND SERVANT Troth, worse and worse; you're like to lose your
    land,
If the law save your life, sir, or the surgeon.

ALLWIT [*aside*] Hark you there, wife?

SIR WALTER   Why, how, sir?

SECOND SERVANT Sir Oliver Kix's wife is new quickened;
That child undoes you, sir.

SIR WALTER   All ill at once!°   135

ALLWIT I wonder what he makes here with his consorts?
Cannot our house be private to ourselves
But we must have such guests? I pray, depart, sirs,
And take your murderer along with you;
Good he were apprehended ere he go,   140
H'as killed some honest gentleman: send for officers!°

SIR WALTER I'll soon save you that labour.

ALLWIT   I must tell you, sir,°
You have been somewhat bolder in my house
Than I could well like of; I suffered you
Till it stuck here at my heart; I tell you truly   145
I thought you had been familiar with my wife once.

MISTRESS ALLWIT With me? I'll see him hanged first: I defy him,
And all such gentlemen in the like extremity.°

SIR WALTER If ever eyes were open, these are they:
Gamesters, farewell, I have nothing left to play.°   150
> *Exit [Sir Walter Whorehound with Servants]*

ALLWIT [*to Davy*] And therefore get you gone, sir.

DAVY DAHUMMA   Of all wittols
Be thou the head! [*To Mistress Allwit*] Thou, the grand whore of
    spittles!
> *Exit [Davy Dahumma]*

ALLWIT So, since he's like now to be rid of all,°
I am right glad I am so well rid of him.

MISTRESS ALLWIT I knew he durst not stay when you named
    officers.   155

ALLWIT That stopped his spirits straight. What shall we do now,
    wife?

MISTRESS ALLWIT As we were wont to do.

ALLWIT   We are richly furnished, wife,
  With household stuff.
MISTRESS ALLWIT   Let's let out lodgings then,
  And take a house in the Strand.
ALLWIT   In troth, a match, wench:°
  We are simply stocked with cloth-of-tissue cushions   160
  To furnish out bay-windows; push, what not that's quaint°
  And costly, from the top to the bottom;
  Life, for furniture, we may lodge a countess!
  There's a close-stool of tawny velvet too,°
  Now I think on't, wife.
MISTRESS ALLWIT   There's that should be, sir;   165
  Your nose must be in everything!
ALLWIT   I have done, wench;
  And let this stand in every gallant's chamber:°
  'There's no gamester like a politic sinner,
  For whoe'er games, the box is sure a winner.'°
    Exeunt

5.2

    Enter Yellowhammer and his Wife
MAUDLINE O husband, husband, she will die, she will die!°
  There is no sign but death.
YELLOWHAMMER   'Twill be our shame, then.
MAUDLINE O, how she's changed in compass of an hour!°
YELLOWHAMMER Ah, my poor girl! Good faith, thou wert too
    cruel
  To drag her by the hair.
MAUDLINE   You would have done as much, sir,   5
  To curb her of her humour.
YELLOWHAMMER   'Tis curbed sweetly!°
  She catched her bane o'th'water!
    Enter Tim
MAUDLINE   How now, Tim?°
TIM Faith, busy, mother, about an epitaph
  Upon my sister's death.
MAUDLINE   Death? She is not dead, I hope?
TIM No, but she means to be, and that's as good,   10

And when a thing's done, 'tis done; you taught me°
That, mother.
YELLOWHAMMER What is your tutor doing?
TIM Making one too, in principal pure Latin,
    Culled out of Ovid *de Tristibus*.°
YELLOWHAMMER How does your sister look? Is she not changed?   15
TIM Changed? Gold into white money was never so changed°
    As is my sister's colour into paleness.
            Enter Moll [carried in sick by Servants]
YELLOWHAMMER O, here she's brought; see how she looks like death!
TIM Looks she like death, and ne'er a word made yet?°
    I must go beat my brains against a bed-post   20
    And get before my tutor.
            [Exit Tim]
YELLOWHAMMER *[to Moll]* Speak, how dost thou?°
MOLL I hope I shall be well, for I am as sick
    At heart as I can be.
YELLOWHAMMER   'Las, my poor girl!
    The doctor's making a most sovereign drink for thee,
    The worst ingredients dissolved pearl and amber;°   25
    We spare no cost, girl.
MOLL   Your love comes too late,
    Yet timely thanks reward it. What is comfort,°
    When the poor patient's heart is past relief?
    It is no doctor's art can cure my grief.
YELLOWHAMMER All is cast away then;°   30
    Prithee look upon me cheerfully.
MAUDLINE Sing but a strain or two, thou wilt not think°
    How 'twill revive thy spirits: strive with thy fit,°
    Prithee, sweet Moll.
MOLL   You shall have my goodwill, mother.°
MAUDLINE Why, well said, wench.   35
[MOLL *(sings)*]

> *Weep eyes, break heart,*
> *My love and I must part.*
> *Cruel fates true love do soonest sever:*
> *O, I shall see thee never, never, never!*
> *O, happy is the maid whose life takes end*   40
> *Ere it knows parents' frown or loss of friend.*
> *Weep eyes, break heart,*
> *My love and I must part.*

Enter Touchwood Senior with a letter

MAUDLINE O, I could die with music!—Well sung, girl.

MOLL If you call it so, it was.

YELLOWHAMMER   She plays the swan°   45
    And sings herself to death.

TOUCHWOOD SENIOR   By your leave, sir.°

YELLOWHAMMER What are you, sir? Or what's your business, pray?

TOUCHWOOD SENIOR I may be now admitted, though the brother
    Of him your hate pursued: it spreads no further;
    Your malice sets in death, does it not, sir?   50

YELLOWHAMMER In death?

TOUCHWOOD SENIOR   He's dead: 'twas a dear love to him,°
    It cost him but his life, that was all, sir;
    He paid enough, poor gentleman, for his love.

YELLOWHAMMER [*aside*] There's all our ill removed, if she were well
    now—
    [*To Touchwood Senior*] Impute not, sir, his end to any hate   55
    That sprung from us; he had a fair wound brought that.

TOUCHWOOD SENIOR That helped him forward, I must needs
    confess;
    But the restraint of love, and your unkindness,
    Those were the wounds that from his heart drew blood;
    But being past help, let words forget it too: 60
    Scarcely three minutes ere his eyelids closed
    And took eternal leave of this world's light,
    He wrote this letter, which by oath he bound me
    To give to her own hand: that's all my business.

YELLOWHAMMER You may perform it then: there she sits.   65

TOUCHWOOD SENIOR O, with a following look!

YELLOWHAMMER   Ay, trust me, sir,°
    I think she'll follow him quickly.

TOUCHWOOD SENIOR   Here's some gold
    He willed me to distribute faithfully
    Amongst your servants. [*He gives gold to the Servants*]

YELLOWHAMMER   'Las, what doth he mean, sir?°

TOUCHWOOD SENIOR [*to Moll*] How cheer you, mistress?

MOLL   I must learn of you, sir.°   70

TOUCHWOOD SENIOR [*giving letter to Moll*] Here's a letter from a
    friend of yours,
    And where that fails in satisfaction,°
    I have a sad tongue ready to supply.

MOLL How does he, ere I look on't?
TOUCHWOOD SENIOR   Seldom better;
    H'as a contented health now.°   75
MOLL [*reading*] I am most glad on't.
MAUDLINE [*to Yellowhammer*]   Dead, sir?
YELLOWHAMMER   He is. Now, wife, let's but get the girl
    Upon her legs again, and to church roundly with her.
MOLL O, sick to death he tells me: how does he after this?
TOUCHWOOD SENIOR Faith, feels no pain at all: he's dead, sweet
    mistress.
MOLL [*collapsing*] Peace close mine eyes!
YELLOWHAMMER   The girl, look to the girl, wife!   80
MAUDLINE Moll, daughter, sweet girl, speak! Look but once up,°
    Thou shalt have all the wishes of thy heart
    That wealth can purchase!
YELLOWHAMMER   O, she's gone for ever!
    That letter broke her heart.
TOUCHWOOD SENIOR   As good now, then,
    As let her lie in torment and then break it.   85
        Enter Susan
MAUDLINE O Susan, she thou loved'st so dear is gone!
SUSAN O sweet maid!
TOUCHWOOD SENIOR [*aside*] This is she that helped her still.—
    [*Giving Susan money and a note*] I've a reward here for thee.
YELLOWHAMMER   Take her in,°
    Remove her from our sight, our shame and sorrow.
TOUCHWOOD SENIOR Stay, let me help thee; 'tis the last cold
        kindness   90
    I can perform for my sweet brother's sake.
        [*Exeunt Touchwood Senior, Susan and Servants, carrying Moll*]
YELLOWHAMMER All the whole street will hate us, and the world
    Point me out cruel: it is our best course, wife,
    After we have given order for the funeral,
    To absent ourselves till she be laid in ground.   95
MAUDLINE Where shall we spend that time?
YELLOWHAMMER   I'll tell thee where, wench:
    Go to some private church and marry Tim°
    To the rich Brecknock gentlewoman.
MAUDLINE   Mass, a match!
    We'll not lose all at once, somewhat we'll catch.°
        Exeunt

5.3

Enter Sir Oliver [Kix] and [four] Servants

SIR OLIVER Ho, my wife's quickened; I am a man for ever!
  I think I have bestirred my stumps, i'faith.°
  Run, get your fellows all together instantly,
  Then to the parish church and ring the bells.°

FIRST SERVANT It shall be done, sir.
    [Exit First Servant]

SIR OLIVER   Upon my love   5
  I charge you, villain, that you make a bonfire
  Before the door at night.

SECOND SERVANT   A bonfire, sir?

SIR OLIVER A thwacking one, I charge you.

SECOND SERVANT *[aside]*   This is monstrous!°
    [Exit Second Servant]

SIR OLIVER Run, tell a hundred pound out for the gentleman
  That gave my wife the drink, the first thing you do.   10

THIRD SERVANT A hundred pounds, sir?

SIR OLIVER   A bargain! As our joys grows,
  We must remember still from whence it flows,
  Or else we prove ungrateful multipliers.
    [Exit Third Servant]
  The child is coming and the land comes after;°
  The news of this will make a poor Sir Walter.   15
  I have struck it home, i'faith!

FOURTH SERVANT   That you have, marry, sir;°
  But will not your worship go to the funeral
  Of both these lovers?

SIR OLIVER   Both? Go both together?

FOURTH SERVANT Ay, sir, the gentleman's brother will have it so;
  'Twill be the pitifullest sight. There's such running,   20
  Such rumours, and such throngs, a pair of lovers
  Had never more spectators, more men's pities,
  Or women's wet eyes.

SIR OLIVER   My wife helps the number then?°

FOURTH SERVANT There's such drawing out of handkerchers;
  And those that have no handkerchers, lift up aprons.   25

SIR OLIVER Her parents may have joyful hearts at this!
  I would not have my cruelty so talked on

To any child of mine, for a monopoly.°
FOURTH SERVANT I believe you, sir.
   'Tis cast so too, that both their coffins meet,°   30
   Which will be lamentable.
SIR OLIVER   Come, we'll see't.
     Exeunt.

5.4

*Recorders° dolefully playing, enter at one door the coffin of
the Gentleman [Touchwood Junior], solemnly decked,° his
sword upon it, attended by many in black [including Sir Oliver
Kix, and a Parson], his brother [Touchwood Senior] being the
chief mourner; at the other door the coffin of the virgin [Moll],
with a garland of flowers, with epitaphs° pinned on't, attended
by maids and women [including Lady Kix, Mistress Allwit, and
Susan]. Then set them down one right over-against the other;
while all the company seem to weep and mourn, there is a sad
song in the music-room*

TOUCHWOOD SENIOR Never could death boast of a richer prize
   From the first parent; let the world bring forth°
   A pair of truer hearts. To speak but truth°
   Of this departed gentleman, in a brother
   Might, by hard censure, be called flattery,°   5
   Which makes me rather silent in his right
   Than so to be delivered to the thoughts°
   Of any envious hearer, starved in virtue,
   And therefore pining to hear others thrive;
   But for this maid, whom envy cannot hurt   10
   With all her poisons, having left to ages
   The true, chaste monument of her living name,
   Which no time can deface, I say of her°
   The full truth freely, without fear of censure:
   What nature could there shine, that might redeem   15
   Perfection home to woman, but in her
   Was fully glorious? Beauty set in goodness°
   Speaks what she was: that jewel so infixed,°
   There was no want of anything of life
   To make these virtuous precedents man and wife.°   20

ALLWIT Great pity of their deaths!

ALL   Ne'er more pity!

LADY KIX It makes a hundred weeping eyes, sweet gossip.

TOUCHWOOD SENIOR I cannot think there's anyone amongst you
    In this full fair assembly, maid, man or wife,
    Whose heart would not have sprung with joy and gladness   25
    To have seen their marriage day.

ALL   It would have made
    A thousand joyful hearts.

TOUCHWOOD SENIOR [*to Touchwood Junior and Moll*] Up then apace,
    And take your fortunes, make these joyful hearts;
    Here's none but friends.
        [*Touchwood Junior and Moll rise out of their coffins*]

ALL   Alive, sir? O, sweet, dear couple!°

TOUCHWOOD SENIOR Nay, do not hinder'em now, stand from about
    'em;   30
    If she be caught again, and have this time,°
    I'll ne'er plot further for 'em, nor this honest chambermaid
    That helped all at a push.

TOUCHWOOD JUNIOR [*to Parson*] Good sir, apace!°

PARSON Hands join now, but hearts forever,°
    Which no parents' mood shall sever: 35
    [*To Touchwood Junior*] You shall forsake all widows, wives, and
        maids—
    [*To Moll*] You, lords, knights, gentlemen, and men of trades—
    And if in haste any article misses,
    Go interline it with a brace of kisses.°

TOUCHWOOD SENIOR Here's a thing trolled nimbly! Give you joy,
    brother;°   40
    Were't not better thou shouldst have her than
    The maid should die?

MISTRESS ALLWIT   To you, sweet mistress bride.

ALL Joy, joy to you both.

TOUCHWOOD SENIOR   Here be your wedding sheets°
    You brought along with you; you may both go to bed
    When you please to.

TOUCHWOOD JUNIOR My joy wants utterance.   45

TOUCHWOOD SENIOR Utter all at night then, brother.

MOLL   I am°
    Silent with delight.

TOUCHWOOD SENIOR Sister, delight will silence

Any woman, but you'll find your tongue again
Among maid servants now you keep house, sister.°
ALL Never was hour so filled with joy and wonder.   50
TOUCHWOOD SENIOR To tell you the full story of this chambermaid,
    And of her kindness in this business to us,
    'Twould ask an hour's discourse; in brief, 'twas she
    That wrought it to this purpose cunningly.°
ALL We shall all love her for't.
      Enter Yellowhammer and his Wife [*Maudline*]
ALLWIT   See who comes here now!   55
TOUCHWOOD SENIOR A storm, a storm, but we are sheltered
    for it.
YELLOWHAMMER I will prevent you all and mock you thus,°
    You and your expectations: I stand happy
    Both in your lives and your hearts' combination!
TOUCHWOOD SENIOR Here's a strange day again!
YELLOWHAMMER   The knight's proved villain: 60
    All's come out now, his niece an arrant baggage;°
    My poor boy Tim is cast away this morning,
    Even before breakfast, married a whore
    Next to his heart.
ALL   A whore?
YELLOWHAMMER   His 'niece', forsooth!°
ALLWIT [*aside to his Wife*] I think we rid our hands in good time of
    him.   65
MISTRESS ALLWIT I knew he was past the best when I gave him
    over.
    [*To Yellowhammer*] What is become of him, pray, sir?
YELLOWHAMMER   Who, the knight?
    He lies i'th'knight's ward—[*To Lady Kix*] Now your belly, lady,°
    Begins to blossom, there's no peace for him,
    His creditors are so greedy.
SIR OLIVER [*to Touchwood Senior*] Master Touchwood,   70
    Hear'st thou this news? I am so endeared to thee
    For my wife's fruitfulness that I charge you both,
    Your wife and thee, to live no more asunder
    For the world's frowns: I have purse, and bed, and board for you:°
    Be not afraid to go to your business roundly;   75
    Get children, and I'll keep them.
TOUCHWOOD SENIOR   Say you so, sir?
SIR OLIVER Prove me with three at a birth, an thou dar'st now.°

TOUCHWOOD SENIOR Take heed how you dare a man, while you live,
    sir,
    That has good skill at his weapon.
        Enter Tim, Welsh Gentlewoman [and Tutor]
SIR OLIVER   Foot, I dare you, sir!°
YELLOWHAMMER Look, gentlemen, if ever you saw the picture°   80
    Of the unfortunate marriage, yonder 'tis.
WELSH GENTLEWOMAN Nay, good sweet Tim—
TIM   Come from the university
    To marry a whore in London, with my tutor too!
    O tempora! O mors!
TUTOR   Prithee, Tim,°
    Be patient!
TIM   I bought a jade at Cambridge;°   85
    I'll let her out to execution, tutor,°
    For eighteen pence a day, or Brainford horse-races,
    She'll serve to carry seven miles out of town well.°
    Where be these mountains? I was promised mountains,
    But there's such a mist, I can see none of 'em.   90
    What are become of those two thousand runts?
    Let's have a bout with them in the meantime;
    A vengeance runt thee!
MAUDLINE   Good, sweet Tim, have patience.
TIM *Flectere si neguro superos, Acheronta mourbo*, mother.°
MAUDLINE I think you have married her in logic, Tim.   95
    You told me once by logic you would prove
    A whore an honest woman; prove her so, Tim,
    And take her for thy labour.
TIM   Troth, I thank you:
    I grant you I may prove another man's wife so,
    But not mine own.
MAUDLINE   There's no remedy now, Tim;   100
    You must prove her so as well as you may.
TIM Why then, my tutor and I will about her
    As well as we can.
    Uxor non est meretrix, ergo falacis.°
WELSH GENTLEWOMAN Sir, if your logic cannot prove me honest,   105
    There's a thing called marriage, and that makes me honest.°
MAUDLINE O, there's a trick beyond your logic, Tim.
TIM I perceive then a woman may be honest
    According to the English print, when she is

A whore in the Latin; so much for marriage and logic!°   110
I'll love her for her wit, I'll pick out my runts there;
And for my mountains, I'll mount upon—°
YELLOWHAMMER So Fortune seldom deals two marriages
With one hand, and both lucky; the best is,
One feast will serve them both! Marry, for room,   115
I'll have the dinner kept in Goldsmiths' Hall,°
To which, kind gallants, I invite you all.
    [*Exeunt*]

WOMEN BEWARE WOMEN

[PUBLISHER'S PREFACE]

When these° amongst others of Mr Thomas Middleton's excellent   1
poems came to my hands, I was not a little confident but that his name
would prove as great an inducement for thee to read, as to me to print
them, since those issues of his brain that have already seen the sun
have by their worth gained themselves a free entertainment amongst   5
all that are ingenious;° and I am most certain that these will no way
lessen his reputation, nor hinder his admission to any noble and recreative spirits.° All that I require at thy hands is to continue the author
in his deserved esteem, and to accept of my endeavours which have
ever been to please thee.

Farewell.

[COMMENDATORY VERSES]

Upon the Tragedy of My Familiar Acquaintance,
Tho[mas] Middleton.

Women Beware Women: 'tis a true text
Never to be forgot. Drabs of state, vexed,°
Have plots, poisons, mischiefs, that seldom miss,
To murder virtue with a venom kiss.
Witness this worthy tragedy, expressed   5
By him that well deserved among the best
Of poets in his time: he knew the rage,
Madness of women crossed; and for the stage
Fitted their humours—hell-bred malice, strife
Acted in state, presented to the life.°   10
I that have seen't can say, having just cause,
Never came tragedy off with more applause.

Nath[aniel] Richards°

74

[THE CHARACTERS OF THE PLAY]°

Duke of Florence.
Lord Cardinal, brother to the Duke.
Two Cardinals more.
A Lord.
Fabritio, father to Isabella.
Hippolito, brother to Fabritio.
Guardiano, uncle to the foolish Ward.
Ward, a rich young heir.
Leantio, a factor, husband to Bianca.°
Sordido, the Ward's man.

Livia, sister to Fabritio [and Hippolito].
Isabella, niece to Livia.
Bianca, Leantio's wife.°
Widow, his mother [i.e. Mother to Leantio].
States of Florence; Citizens; Apprentices; Boys; Messenger;
Servants.°
[Lords; Ladies; Nymphs; Hebe; Hymen; Ganymede; Attendants.]

The Scene: Florence

1.1

Enter Leantio with Bianca, and Mother

MOTHER Thy sight was never yet more precious to me;
 Welcome with all the affection of a mother,
 That comfort can express from natural love.°
 Since thy birth-joy, a mother's chiefest gladness,
 After sh'as undergone her curse of sorrows,°   5
 Thou wast not more dear to me than this hour
 Presents thee to my heart. Welcome again.
LEANTIO [*aside*] 'Las poor affectionate soul, how her joys speak to
  me!°
 I have observed it often, and I know it is
 The fortune commonly of knavish children   10
 To have the loving'st mothers.
MOTHER   What's this gentlewoman?
LEANTIO Oh you have named the most unvalued'st purchase°
 That youth of man had ever knowledge of.
 As often as I look upon that treasure
 And know it to be mine—there lies the blessing—   15
 It joys me that I ever was ordained
 To have a being, and to live 'mongst men;
 Which is a fearful living, and a poor one,
 Let a man truly think on't.
 To have the toil and griefs of fourscore years   20
 Put up in a white sheet, tied with two knots—°
 Methinks it should strike earthquakes in adulterers,
 When e'en the very sheets they commit sin in
 May prove, for ought they know, all their last garments:
 Oh what a mark were there for women then!°   25
 But beauty able to content a conqueror,
 Whom earth could scarce content, keeps me in compass;°
 I find no wish in me bent sinfully
 To this man's sister, or to that man's wife:
 In love's name let 'em keep their honesties,   30
 And cleave to their own husbands, 'tis their duties.
 Now when I go to church I can pray handsomely,°
 Not come like gallants only to see faces,°
 As if lust went to market still on Sundays.

I must confess I am guilty of one sin, Mother,   35
More than I brought into the world with me;°
But that I glory in: 'tis theft, but noble
As ever greatness yet shot up withal.°
MOTHER How's that?
LEANTIO   Never to be repented, Mother,
Though sin be death; I had died, if I had not sinned.°   40
And here's my masterpiece: do you now behold her!
Look on her well, she's mine. Look on her better.
Now say if't be not the best piece of theft
That ever was committed; and I have my pardon for't:
'Tis sealed from heaven by marriage.
MOTHER   Married to her!   45
LEANTIO You must keep counsel, Mother, I am undone else;°
If it be known, I have lost her; do but think now
What that loss is—life's but a trifle to't.
From Venice, her consent and I have brought her
From parents great in wealth, more now in rage.   50
But let storms spend their furies; now we have got
A shelter o'er our quiet innocent loves,
We are contented. Little money sh'as brought me;
View but her face, you may see all her dowry,
Save that which lies locked up in hidden virtues,   55
Like jewels kept in cabinets.
MOTHER   Y'are too blame,°
If your obedience will give way to a check,°
To wrong such a perfection.
LEANTIO   How?
MOTHER   Such a creature,
To draw her from her fortune—which no doubt,
At the full time, might have proved rich and noble—°   60
You know not what you have done. My life can give you
But little helps, and my death lesser hopes;°
And hitherto your own means has but made shift
To keep you single, and that hardly too.°
What ableness have you to do her right then   65
In maintenance fitting her birth and virtues?
Which ev'ry woman of necessity looks for,
And most to go above it; not confined
By their conditions, virtues, bloods, or births,°
But flowing to affections, wills, and humours.°   70

LEANTIO Speak low, sweet Mother; you are able to spoil as many°
          As come within the hearing; if it be not
          Your fortune to mar all, I have much marvel.°
          I pray do not you teach her to rebel
          When she's in a good way to obedience;   75
          To rise with other women in commotion°
          Against their husbands, for six gowns a year,
          And so maintain their cause, when they're once up,°
          In all things else that require cost enough.
          They are all of 'em a kind of spirits—soon raised   80
          But not so soon laid, Mother. As for example,°
          A woman's belly is got up in a trice—
          A simple charge ere it be laid down again:°
          So ever in all their quarrels, and their courses.°
          And I'm a proud man, I hear nothing of 'em,   85
          They're very still, I thank my happiness,
          And sound asleep; pray let not your tongue wake 'em.
          If you can but rest quiet, she's contented
          With all conditions that my fortunes bring her to:
          To keep close as a wife that loves her husband;   90
          To go after the rate of my ability,°
          Not the licentious swindge of her own will,
          Like some of her old school-fellows. She intends°
          To take out other works in a new sampler,°
          And frame the fashion of an honest love,°   95
          Which knows no wants but, mocking poverty,
          Brings forth more children—to make rich men wonder
          At divine Providence, that feeds mouths of infants,
          And sends them none to feed, but stuffs their rooms
          With fruitful bags, their beds with barren wombs.°   100
          Good Mother, make not you things worse than they are,
          Out of your too much openness—pray take heed on't—
          Nor imitate the envy of old people,
          That strive to mar good sport, because they are perfect.°
          I would have you more pitiful to youth,   105
          Especially to your own flesh and blood.
          I'll prove an excellent husband, here's my hand;
          Lay in provision, follow my business roundly,°
          And make you a grandmother in forty weeks.
          Go, pray salute her, bid her welcome cheerfully.°   110
MOTHER Gentlewoman, thus much is a debt of courtesy [*kisses her*]

Which fashionable strangers pay each other
At a kind meeting; then there's more than one
Due to the knowledge I have of your nearness:°
I am bold to come again, [*kisses her*] and now salute you   115
By th'name of daughter, which may challenge more°
Than ordinary respect. [*Kisses her again*].

LEANTIO   Why this is well now,
And I think few mothers of threescore will mend it.°

MOTHER What I can bid you welcome to is mean,
But make it all your own; we are full of wants,   120
And cannot welcome worth.

LEANTIO   Now this is scurvy°
And spake as if a woman lacked her teeth.°
These old folks talk of nothing but defects,
Because they grow so full of 'em themselves.

BIANCA Kind Mother, there is nothing can be wanting°   125
To her that does enjoy all her desires.
Heaven send a quiet peace with this man's love
And I am rich as virtue can be poor:
Which were enough after the rate of mind
To erect temples for content placed here.°   130
I have forsook friends, fortunes, and my country,
And hourly I rejoice in't: here's my friends,
And few is the good number. [*To Leantio*] Thy successes,°
Howe'er they look, I will still name my fortunes;
Hopeful or spiteful, they shall all be welcome.   135
Who invites many guests has of all sorts,°
As he that traffics much drinks of all fortunes;
Yet they must all be welcome, and used well.
I'll call this place the place of my new birth now,
And rightly too: for here my love was born,   140
And that's the birth-day of a woman's joys.
You have not bid me welcome since I came.

LEANTIO That I did questionless.

BIANCA   No, sure, how was't?
I have quite forgot it.

LEANTIO   Thus. [*Kisses her*]

BIANCA   Oh sir, 'tis true,
Now I remember well. I have done thee wrong,   145
Pray take't again, sir.
        [*They kiss again*]

LEANTIO   How many of these wrongs
  Could I put up in an hour. And turn up the glass°
  For twice as many more!
MOTHER Will't please you walk in, daughter?
BIANCA   Thanks, sweet Mother;
  The voice of her that bare me is not more pleasing.°   150
    Exeunt [Mother and Bianca]
LEANTIO Though my own care and my rich master's trust
  Lay their commands both on my factorship,°
  This day and night I'll know no other business
  But her and her dear welcome. 'Tis a bitterness
  To think upon tomorrow: that I must leave her   155
  Still to the sweet hopes of the week's end.°
  That pleasure should be so restrained and curbed,
  After the course of a rich workmaster°
  That never pays till Saturday night. Marry,
  It comes together in a round sum then,   160
  And does more good, you'll say. Oh fair-eyed Florence,
  Didst thou but know what a most matchless jewel
  Thou now art mistress of, a pride would take thee,°
  Able to shoot destruction through the bloods
  Of all thy youthful sons! But 'tis great policy   165
  To keep choice treasures in obscurest places:°
  Should we show thieves our wealth, 'twould make 'em bolder.
  Temptation is a devil will not stick°
  To fasten upon a saint—take heed of that.
  The jewel is cased up from all men's eyes;   170
  Who could imagine now a gem were kept
  Of that great value under this plain roof?
  But how in times of absence? What assurance
  Of this restraint then? Yes, yes, there's one with her:
  Old mothers know the world, and such as these,   175
  When sons lock chests, are good to look to keys.
    Exit

1.2

Enter Guardiano, Fabritio, and Livia [with Servant]

GUARDIANO What, has your daughter seen him yet? Know you that?

FABRITIO No matter, she shall love him.

GUARDIANO   Nay, let's have fair play:
    He has been now my ward some fifteen year,°
    And 'tis my purpose, as time calls upon me,°
    By custom seconded and such moral virtues,°   5
    To tender him a wife. Now, sir, this wife
    I'd fain elect out of a daughter of yours:
    You see my meaning's fair. If now this daughter°
    So tendered (let me come to your own phrase, sir)
    Should offer to refuse him, I were hanselled.°   10
    [*Aside*] Thus am I fain to calculate all my words
    For the meridian of a foolish old man,
    To take his understanding. [*To him*] What do you answer, sir?°

FABRITIO I say still she shall love him.

GUARDIANO   Yet again?
    And shall she have no reason for this love?   15

FABRITIO Why, do you think that women love with reason?

GUARDIANO [*aside*] I perceive fools are not at all hours foolish,°
    No more than wise men wise.

FABRITIO   I had a wife,
    She ran mad for me; she had no reason for't
    For aught I could perceive. [*To Livia*] What think you,   20
    Lady sister?

GUARDIANO [*aside*]   'Twas a fit match that,
    Being both out of their wits. [*To him*] A loving wife, it seemed
    She strove to come as near you as she could.

FABRITIO And if her daughter prove not mad for love too,
    She takes not after her; nor after me,   25
    If she prefer reason before my pleasure.°
    [*To Livia*] You're an experienced widow, lady sister,
    I pray let your opinion come amongst us.

LIVIA I must offend you then, if truth will do't,
    And take my niece's part, and call't injustice   30
    To force her love to one she never saw.
    Maids should both see and like: all little enough;
    If they love truly after that, 'tis well.

Counting the time she takes one man till death,°
That's a hard task, I tell you. But one may   35
Enquire at three years' end amongst young wives
And mark how the game goes.

FABRITIO   Why, is not man
Tied to the same observance, lady sister,°
And in one woman?

LIVIA   'Tis enough for him;
Besides, he tastes of many sundry dishes°   40
That we poor wretches never lay our lips to:
As obedience forsooth, subjection, duty, and such kickshaws,
All of our making, but served in to them.
And if we lick a finger then sometimes
We are not to blame; your best cooks use it.   45

FABRITIO Th'art a sweet lady, sister, and a witty—

LIVIA A witty! Oh the bud of commendation
Fit for a girl of sixteen; I am blown, man,°
I should be wise by this time; and for instance
I have buried my two husbands in good fashion,   50
And never mean more to marry.

GUARDIANO   No? Why so, lady?

LIVIA Because the third shall never bury me.
I think I am more than witty; how think you, sir?

FABRITIO I have paid often fees to a counsellor°
Has had a weaker brain.

LIVIA   Then I must tell you,   55
Your money was soon parted.

GUARDIANO [to Fabritio]   Light her now, brother!°

LIVIA Where is my niece? Let her be sent for straight.
    [Exit Servant]
If you have any hope 'twill prove a wedding,
'Tis fit i'faith she should have one sight of him,
And stop upon't, and not be joined in haste,°   60
As if they went to stock a new-found land.°

FABRITIO Look out her uncle, and y'are sure of her.°
Those two are never asunder; they've been heard
In argument at midnight; moonshine nights
Are noondays with them: they walk out their sleeps,°   65
Or rather at those hours appear like those
That walk in'em, for so they did to me.°
Look you, I told you truth; they're like a chain:

Draw but one link, all follows.
   Enter [Servant with] Hippolito, and Isabella the niece.

GUARDIANO   Oh affinity,
 What piece of excellent workmanship art thou!   70
 'Tis work clean wrought, for there's no lust, but love in't,
 And that abundantly; when in stranger things°
 There is no love at all, but what lust brings.

FABRITIO [*to Isabella*] On with your mask, for 'tis your part to see now
 And not be seen. Go to, make use of your time;   75
 See what you mean to like; nay, and I charge you,°
 Like what you see. Do you hear me? There's no dallying,
 The gentleman's almost twenty, and 'tis time
 He were getting lawful heirs, and you a-breeding on 'em.

ISABELLA Good father!

FABRITIO   Tell me not of tongues and rumours.° 80
 You'll say the gentleman is somewhat simple—
 The better for a husband, were you wise,
 For those that marry fools live ladies' lives.
 On with the mask, I'll hear no more; he's rich,
 The fool's hid under bushels. [*Isabella puts on mask*]°

LIVIA   Not so hid neither, 85
 But here's a foul great piece of him, methinks;°
 What will he be, when he comes altogether?
   Enter the Ward with a trap-stick, and Sordido his man.°

WARD   Beat him?
 I beat him out o'th'field with his own cat-stick,
 Yet gave him the first hand.

SORDIDO   Oh strange!

WARD   I did it,°
 Then he set jacks on me.

SORDIDO   What, my ladies' tailor?° 90

WARD Ay, and I beat him too.

SORDIDO   Nay, that's no wonder,
 He's used to beating.

WARD   Nay, I tickled him°
 When I came once to my tippings.°

SORDIDO Now you talk on'em, there was a poulterer's wife made a
 great complaint of you last night to your guardianer, that you 95
 struck a bump in her child's head, as big as an egg.°

WARD An egg may prove a chicken, then in time the poulterer's wife
 will get by't. When I am in game, I am furious;° came my mother's

eyes in my way, I would not lose a fair end.° No, were she alive, but
with one tooth in her head, I should venture the striking out of   100
that. I think of nobody when I am in play, I am so earnest. Coads
me, my guardianer! Prithee lay up my cat and cat-stick safe.

SORDIDO Where, sir, i'the chimney-corner?

WARD   Chimney-corner?°

SORDIDO Yes, sir, your cats are always safe i'th'chimney-corner,
unless they burn their coats.°   105

WARD Marry, that I am afraid on!

SORDIDO Why, then I will bestow your cat i'th'gutter, and there she's
safe I am sure.

WARD If I but live to keep a house, I'll make thee a great° man, if meat
and drink can do't. I can stoop gallantly, and pitch out when I list;   110
I'm dog at a hole.° I mar'l my guardianer does not seek a wife for
me; I protest I'll have a bout° with the maids else, or contract°
myself at midnight to the larder-woman, in presence of a fool, or a
sack-posset.°

GUARDIANO Ward!   115

WARD I feel myself after any exercise horribly prone: let me but ride,
I'm lusty; a cock-horse° straight, i'faith.

GUARDIANO Why, Ward, I say!

WARD I'll forswear eating eggs in moon-shine nights. There's ne'er a
one I eat but turns into a cock° in four and twenty hours; if my hot   120
blood be not took down in time, sure 'twill crow shortly.

GUARDIANO Do you hear, sir? Follow me, I must new school you.

WARD School me? I scorn that, now; I am past schooling. I am not so
base to learn to write and read; I was born to better fortunes in my
cradle.   125

    Exeunt [Guardiano, Ward, Sordido]

FABRITIO [*to Isabella*] How do you like him, girl? This is your
    husband.
Like him or like him not, wench, you shall have him,
And you shall love him.

LIVIA Oh soft there, brother! Though you be a Justice,
Your warrant cannot be served out of your liberty; °   130
You may compel out of the power of father
Things merely harsh to a maid's flesh and blood;
But when you come to love, there the soil alters:°
Y'are in another country, where your laws
Are no more set by than the cacklings of geese   135
In Rome's great Capitol.

FABRITIO   Marry him she shall, then;°
    Let her agree upon love afterwards.
       Exit [*Fabritio*]
LIVIA You speak now, brother, like an honest mortal
    That walks upon th'earth with a staff; you were°
    Up i'th'clouds before. You'd command love—   140
    And so do most old folks that go without it.°
    [*To Hippolito*] My best and dearest brother, I could dwell here;°
    There is not such another seat on earth
    Where all good parts better express themselves.°
HIPPOLITO You'll make me blush anon.   145
LIVIA 'Tis but like saying grace before a feast then,
    And that's most comely; thou art all a feast,
    And she that has thee, a most happy guest.
    Prithee cheer up thy niece with special counsel.°
       [*Exit Livia*]
HIPPOLITO [*aside*] I would 'twere fit to speak to her what I would, but   150
    'Twas not a thing ordained, Heaven has forbid it;
    And 'tis most meet that I should rather perish
    Than the decree divine receive least blemish.
    Feed inward, you my sorrows; make no noise,
    Consume me silent, let me be stark dead   155
    Ere the world know I'm sick. You see my honesty;
    If you befriend me—so.
ISABELLA [*aside*]   Marry a fool!°
    Can there be greater misery to a woman
    That means to keep her days true to her husband,
    And know no other man? So virtue wills it.   160
    Why, how can I obey and honour him
    But I must needs commit idolatry?°
    A fool is but the image of a man,
    And that but ill made neither. Oh the heart-breakings°
    Of miserable maids, where love's enforced!   165
    The best condition is but bad enough:
    When women have their choices, commonly
    They do but buy their thraldoms, and bring great portions°
    To men to keep 'em in subjection—
    As if a fearful prisoner should bribe   170
    The keeper to be good to him, yet lies in still,°
    And glad of a good usage, a good look sometimes.°
    By'r Lady, no misery surmounts a woman's:

Men buy their slaves, but women buy their masters.
Yet honesty and love makes all this happy,   175
And, next to angels', the most blest estate.
That Providence that has made ev'ry poison
Good for some use, and sets four warring elements°
At peace in man, can make a harmony
In things that are most strange to human reason.   180
Oh but this marriage! [*To Hippolito*] What, are you sad too, uncle?
'Faith, then there's a whole household down together!
Where shall I go to seek my comfort now
When my best friend's distressed? What is't afflicts you, sir?

HIPPOLITO 'Faith, nothing but one grief that will not leave me,   185
And now 'tis welcome. Ev'ry man has something
To bring him to his end, and this will serve,
Joined with your father's cruelty to you—
That helps it forward.

ISABELLA   Oh be cheered, sweet uncle!
How long has't been upon you? I ne'er spied it;   190
What a dull sight have I. How long, I pray, sir?

HIPPOLITO Since I first saw you, niece, and left Bologna.

ISABELLA And could you deal so unkindly with my heart
To keep it up so long hid from my pity?
Alas, how shall I trust your love hereafter?   195
Have we passed through so many arguments°
And missed of that still, the most needful one?
Walked out whole nights together in discourses,
And the main point forgot? We are to blame both;
This is an obstinate, wilful forgetfulness,°   200
And faulty on both parts. Let's lose no time now:
Begin, good uncle, you that feel't, what is't?

HIPPOLITO You of all creatures, niece, must never hear on't;
'Tis not a thing ordained for you to know.

ISABELLA Not I, sir? All my joys that word cuts off.   205
You made profession once you loved me best;
'Twas but profession!

HIPPOLITO   Yes, I do't too truly,°
And fear I shall be chid for't. Know the worst then:
I love thee dearlier than an uncle can.

ISABELLA Why, so you ever said, and I believed it.   210

HIPPOLITO [*aside*] So simple is the goodness of her thoughts,
They understand not yet th'unhallowed language

Of a near sinner. I must yet be forced
(Though blushes be my venture) to come nearer.°
[*To her*] As a man loves his wife, so love I thee.   215
ISABELLA What's that? Methought I heard ill news come toward me,
Which commonly we understand too soon,
Than over-quick at hearing. I'll prevent it,
Though my joys fare the harder, welcome it:°
It shall ne'er come so near mine ear again.   220
Farewell all friendly solaces and discourses,
I'll learn to live without ye, for your dangers
Are greater than your comforts. What's become
Of truth in love, if such we cannot trust—°
When blood that should be love is mixed with lust?   225
        Exit [*Isabella*]
HIPPOLITO The worst can be but death, and let it come;
He that lives joyless, ev'ry day's his doom.
        Exit

1.3

Enter Leantio alone
LEANTIO Methinks I am e'en as dull now at departure
As men observe great gallants the next day
After a revels; you shall see'em look
Much of my fashion, if you mark'em well.
'Tis e'en a second hell to part from pleasure   5
When man has got a smack on't. As many holidays
Coming together makes your poor heads idle°
A great while after, and are said to stick
Fast in their fingers' ends, e'en so does game°
In a new-married couple: for the time   10
It spoils all thrift, and indeed lies abed
To invent all the new ways for great expenses.°
        [*Enter*] *Bianca and Mother above*
See an she be not got on purpose now
Into the window to look after me.
I have no power to go now, an I should be hanged.   15
Farewell all business, I desire no more
Than I see yonder; let the goods at quay

Look to themselves; why should I toil my youth out?
It is but begging two or three year sooner,°
And stay with her continually—is't a match?°   20
O fie, what a religion have I leaped into!
Get out again for shame; the man loves best
When his care's most: that shows his zeal to love.
Fondness is but the idiot to affection,°
That plays at hot–cockles with rich merchants' wives—°   25
Good to make sport withal when the chest's full,
And the long warehouse cracks. 'Tis time of day°
For us to be more wise, 'tis early with us;
And if they lose the morning of their affairs
They commonly lose the best part of the day.   30
Those that are wealthy, and have got enough,
'Tis after sunset with'em; they may rest,
Grow fat with ease, banquet and toy and play,
When such as I enter the heat o'th'day;
And I'll do't cheerfully.

BIANCA   I perceive, sir,   35
Y'are not gone yet; I have good hope you'll stay now.

LEANTIO Farewell, I must not.

BIANCA   Come, come, pray return;
Tomorrow, adding but a little care more
Will dispatch all as well; believe me 'twill, sir.

LEANTIO I could well wish myself where you would have me.   40
But love that's wanton must be ruled awhile
By that that's careful, or all goes to ruin:
As fitting is a government in love
As in a kingdom; where 'tis all mere lust
'Tis like an insurrection in the people,   45
That, raised in self-will, wars against all reason.
But love that is respective for increase°
Is like a good king that keeps all in peace.°
Once more farewell.

BIANCA   But this one night, I prithee.

LEANTIO Alas I'm in for twenty if I stay,   50
And then for forty more: I have such luck to flesh,
I never bought a horse but he bore double.°
If I stay any longer I shall turn
An everlasting spendthrift. As you love
To be maintained well, do not call me again,   55

For then I shall not care which end goes forward—°
Again farewell to thee.

BIANCA   Since it must, farewell too.

      Exit [Leantio]

MOTHER 'Faith, daughter, y'are too blame, you take the course
To make him an ill husband, troth you do.
And that disease is catching, I can tell you,°   60
Ay, and soon taken by a young man's blood,
And that with little urging. Nay, fie, see now,
What cause have you to weep? Would I had no more
That have lived three score years—there were a cause
And 'twere well thought on. Trust me, y'are too blame,   65
His absence cannot last five days at utmost.
Why should those tears be fetched forth? Cannot love
Be e'en as well expressed in a good look,
But it must see her face still in a fountain?°
It shows like a country maid dressing her head   70
By a dish of water. Come, 'tis an old custom°
To weep for love.

      Enter two or three Boys, and a Citizen or two, with an Apprentice

BOYS Now they come, now they come!

2 BOY   The Duke!

3 BOY   The State!°

CITIZEN How near, boy?

1 BOY   I'th'next street, sir, hard at hand.

CITIZEN You sirrah, get a standing for your mistress,°   75
The best in all the city.

APPRENTICE   I have't for her, sir,
'Twas a thing I provided for her overnight,
'Tis ready at her pleasure.

CITIZEN   Fetch her to't then,
Away, sir.

      [Exit Apprentice]

BIANCA   What's the meaning of this hurry,
Can you tell me, Mother?

MOTHER   What a memory   80
Have I! I see by that years come upon me.
Why, 'tis a yearly custom and solemnity,°
Religiously observed by th'Duke and State
To St Mark's Temple, the fifteenth of April.°
See if my dull brains had not quite forgot it.   85

'Twas happily questioned of thee, I had gone down else,°
Sat like a drone below, and never thought on't.
I would not to be ten years younger again
That you had lost the sight; now you shall see°
Our Duke, a goodly gentleman, of his years.   90
BIANCA Is he old then?
MOTHER   About some fifty-five.
BIANCA That's no great age in man, he's then at best
    For wisdom, and for judgement.
MOTHER   The Lord Cardinal
    His noble brother, there's a comely gentleman,
    And greater in devotion than in blood.°   95
BIANCA He's worthy to be marked.
MOTHER   You shall behold
    All our chief States of Florence; you came fortunately
    Against this solemn day.
BIANCA   I hope so always.°
        Music
MOTHER I hear'em near us now; do you stand easily?
BIANCA Exceeding well, good Mother.
MOTHER   Take this stool.   100
BIANCA I need it not, I thank you.
MOTHER   Use your will, then.
        Enter in great solemnity six Knights bareheaded, then two
        Cardinals, and then the Lord Cardinal, then the Duke; after him
        the States of Florence by two and two, with variety of music and
        song. Exeunt [those in the procession]
MOTHER How like you, daughter?
BIANCA   'Tis a noble State.
    Methinks my soul could dwell upon the reverence°
    Of such a solemn and most worthy custom.
    Did not the Duke look up? Methought he saw us.   105
MOTHER That's ev'ry one's conceit that sees a duke;
    If he looks steadfastly, he looks straight at them;
    When he perhaps, good careful gentleman,
    Never minds any; but the look he casts°
    Is at his own intentions, and his object   110
    Only the public good.
BIANCA   Most likely so.
MOTHER Come, come, we'll end this argument below.
        Exeunt

2.1

Enter Hippolito, and Lady Livia the Widow

LIVIA A strange affection, brother, when I think on't;
  I wonder how thou camest by't.

HIPPOLITO   E'en as easily
  As man comes by destruction, which oft-times
  He wears in his own bosom.

LIVIA   Is the world
  So populous in women, and creation   5
  So prodigal in beauty and so various,
  Yet does love turn thy point to thine own blood?°
  'Tis somewhat too unkindly. Must thy eye
  Dwell evilly on the fairness of thy kindred,
  And seek not where it should? It is confined   10
  Now in a narrower prison than was made for't—
  It is allowed a stranger; and where bounty°
  Is made the great man's honour, 'tis ill husbandry
  To spare, and servants shall have small thanks for't.°
  So he heaven's bounty seems to scorn and mock   15
  That spares free means, and spends of his own stock.°

HIPPOLITO Never was man's misery so soon sowed up,°
  Counting how truly.

LIVIA   Nay, I love you so
  That I shall venture much to keep a change from you°
  So fearful as this grief will bring upon you.   20
  'Faith, it even kills me, when I see you faint
  Under a reprehension, and I'll leave it°
  Though I know nothing can be better for you.
  Prithee, sweet brother, let not passion waste°
  The goodness of thy time, and of thy fortune.   25
  Thou keep'st the treasure of that life I love°
  As dearly as mine own; and if you think
  My former words too bitter, which were ministered°
  By truth and zeal, 'tis but a hazarding
  Of grace and virtue, and I can bring forth°   30
  As pleasant fruits as sensuality wishes
  In all her teeming longings. This I can do.

HIPPOLITO Oh nothing that can make my wishes perfect!°

LIVIA I would that love of yours were pawned to't, brother,
And as soon lost that way as I could win.°   35
Sir, I could give as shrewd a lift to chastity°
As any she that wears a tongue in Florence:
Sh'ad need be a good horsewoman, and sit fast,
Whom my strong argument could not fling at last.°
Prithee take courage, man; though I should counsel   40
Another to despair, yet I am pitiful
To thy afflictions and will venture hard—
I will not name for what, 'tis not handsome.
Find you the proof, and praise me.°
HIPPOLITO   Then I fear me,
I shall not praise you in haste.
LIVIA   This is the comfort.   45
You are not the first, brother, has attempted
Things more forbidden than this seems to be.
I'll minister all cordials now to you°
Because I'll cheer you up, sir.
HIPPOLITO   I am past hope.
LIVIA Love, thou shalt see me do a strange cure then,   50
As e'er was wrought on a disease so mortal,
And near akin to shame. When shall you see her?
HIPPOLITO Never in comfort more.
LIVIA   Y'are so impatient too.
HIPPOLITO Will you believe? 'Death, sh'as forsworn my company,
And sealed it with a blush.
LIVIA   So I perceive°   55
All lies upon my hands then; well, the more glory
When the work's finished.
          Enter Servant
                            How now, sir, the news?
SERVANT Madam, your niece the virtuous Isabella
Is 'lighted now to see you.
LIVIA [*to Hippolito*]   That's great fortune;°
Sir, your stars bless. [*To Servant*] You simple, lead her in.°   60
          Exit Servant
HIPPOLITO What's this to me?
LIVIA   Your absence, gentle brother;
I must bestir my wits for you.
HIPPOLITO   Ay, to great purpose.
          Exit Hippolito

LIVIA   Beshrew you, would I loved you not so well!
    I'll go to bed, and leave this deed undone.
    I am the fondest where I once affect,°   65
    The carefull'st of their healths, and of their ease, forsooth,
    That I look still but slenderly to mine own.
    I take a course to pity him so much now
    That I have none left for modesty and myself.
    This 'tis to grow so liberal—y'have few sisters   70
    That love their brothers' ease 'bove their own honesties;°
    But if you question my affections,°
    That will be found my fault.
        Enter Isabella the niece
                                    Niece, your love's welcome.
    Alas, what draws that paleness to thy cheeks?
    This enforced marriage towards?
ISABELLA   It helps, good aunt,   75
    Amongst some other griefs; but those I'll keep
    Locked up in modest silence, for they're sorrows
    Would shame the tongue more than they grieve the thought.
LIVIA   Indeed the Ward is simple.
ISABELLA   Simple! that were well:
    Why one might make good shift with such a husband.°   80
    But he's a fool entailed, he halts downright in't.°
LIVIA   And knowing this, I hope 'tis at your choice
    To take or refuse, niece?
ISABELLA   You see it is not.
    I loathe him more than beauty can hate death
    Or age, her spiteful neighbour.
LIVIA   Let't appear, then.°   85
ISABELLA   How can I, being born with that obedience
    That must submit unto a father's will?
    If he command, I must of force consent.
LIVIA   Alas, poor soul, be not offended, prithee,
    If I set by the name of niece awhile   90
    And bring in pity in a stranger fashion—°
    It lies here in this breast, would cross this match.°
ISABELLA   How, cross it, aunt?
LIVIA   Ay, and give thee more liberty
    Than thou hast reason yet to apprehend.
ISABELLA   Sweet aunt, in goodness keep not hid from me   95
    What may befriend my life.

LIVIA   Yes, yes, I must;
  When I return to reputation,
  And think upon the solemn vow I made
  To your dead mother, my most loving sister—
  As long as I have her memory 'twixt mine eyelids,°   100
  Look for no pity now.
ISABELLA   Kind, sweet, dear aunt—
LIVIA No, 'twas a secret I have took special care of,
  Delivered by your mother on her death-bed;
  That's nine years now, and I'll not part from't yet,
  Though ne'er was fitter time, nor greater cause for't.   105
ISABELLA As you desire the praises of a virgin—
LIVIA Good sorrow! I would do thee any kindness,
  Not wronging secrecy or reputation.°
ISABELLA Neither of which, as I have hope of fruitfulness,°
  Shall receive wrong from me.
LIVIA   Nay, 'twould be your own wrong,   110
  As much as any's, should it come to that once.°
ISABELLA I need no better means to work persuasion, then.
LIVIA Let it suffice, you may refuse this fool,
  Or you may take him, as you see occasion
  For your advantage; the best wits will do't.   115
  Y'have liberty enough in your own will,
  You cannot be enforced: there grows the flower
  If you could pick it out, makes whole life sweet to you.
  That which you call your father's command's nothing;
  Then your obedience must needs be as little.   120
  If you can make shift here to taste your happiness,
  Or pick out aught that likes you, much good do you;
  You see your cheer, I'll make you no set dinner.°
ISABELLA And trust me, I may starve for all the good
  I can find yet in this. Sweet aunt, deal plainlier.°   125
LIVIA Say I should trust you now upon an oath,
  And give you in a secret that would start you,°
  How am I sure of you, in faith and silence?°
ISABELLA Equal assurance may I find in mercy,°
  As you for that in me.
LIVIA   It shall suffice.   130
  Then know, how ever custom has made good,°
  For reputation's sake, the names of niece
  And aunt 'twixt you and I, w'are nothing less.

ISABELLA How's that?

LIVIA   I told you I should start your blood.
  You are no more allied to any of us,   135
  Save what the courtesy of opinion casts°
  Upon your mother's memory and your name,
  Than the merest stranger is, or one begot
  At Naples when the husband lies at Rome:
  There's so much odds betwixt us. Since your knowledge°   140
  Wished more instruction, and I have your oath
  In pledge for silence, it makes me talk the freelier:
  Did never the report of that famed Spaniard,
  Marquis of Coria, since your time was ripe
  For understanding, fill your ear with wonder?°   145

ISABELLA Yes, what of him? I have heard his deeds of honour
  Often related when we lived in Naples.

LIVIA You heard the praises of your father then.

ISABELLA My father!

LIVIA   That was he. But all the business
  So carefully and so discreetly carried   150
  That fame received no spot by't, not a blemish.
  Your mother was so wary to her end
  None knew of it but her conscience and her friend,°
  Till penitent confession made it mine,
  And now my pity, yours. It had been long else—°   155
  And I hope care and love alike in you,
  Made good by oath, will see it take no wrong now.
  How weak his commands now, whom you call father?°
  How vain all his enforcements, your obedience?
  And what a largeness in your will and liberty,°   160
  To take, or to reject, or to do both?
  For fools will serve to father wise men's children.°
  All this y'have time to think on. Oh my wench,°
  Nothing o'erthrows our sex but indiscretion;
  We might do well else of a brittle people   165
  As any under the great canopy.°
  I pray forget not but to call me aunt still;
  Take heed of that, it may be marked in time else.
  But keep your thoughts to yourself, from all the world,
  Kindred, or dearest friend, nay, I entreat you   170
  From him that all this while you have called uncle;
  And though you love him dearly, as I know

His deserts claim as much e'en from a stranger,
Yet let not him know this, I prithee do not—
As ever thou hast hope of second pity,°   175
If thou shouldst stand in need on't, do not do't.
ISABELLA Believe my oath, I will not.
LIVIA   Why, well said.
    [*Aside*] Who shows more craft t'undo a maidenhead,
    I'll resign my part to her.
            Enter Hippolito
    [*To him*]   She's thine own, go.
            Exit [Livia]
HIPPOLITO [*aside*] Alas, fair flattery cannot cure my
    sorrows!   180
ISABELLA [*aside*] Have I passed so much time in ignorance,
    And never had the means to know myself°
    Till this blest hour? Thanks to her virtuous pity
    That brought it now to light. Would I had known it
    But one day sooner, he had then received   185
    In favours what—poor gentleman—he took°
    In bitter words: a slight and harsh reward
    For one of his deserts.
HIPPOLITO [*aside*]   There seems to me now
    More anger and distraction in her looks.
    I'm gone, I'll not endure a second storm;   190
    The memory of the first is not past yet.
ISABELLA [*aside*] Are you returned, you comforts of my life?
    In this man's presence I will keep you fast now,
    And sooner part eternally from the world
    Than my good joys in you. [*To him*] Prithee, forgive me, 195
    I did but chide in jest; the best loves use it
    Sometimes, it sets an edge upon affection.°
    When we invite our best friends to a feast
    'Tis not all sweetmeats that we set before them:
    There's somewhat sharp and salt, both to whet appetite, 200
    And make'em taste their wine well. So methinks
    After a friendly, sharp and savoury chiding
    A kiss tastes wondrous well, and full o'th'grape. [*Kisses him*].
    How think'st thou, does't not?
HIPPOLITO   'Tis so excellent,
    I know not how to praise it, what to say to't.   205
ISABELLA This marriage shall go forward.

HIPPOLITO   With the Ward?
   Are you in earnest?
ISABELLA   'Twould be ill for us else.
HIPPOLITO [*aside*] For us? How means she that?
ISABELLA [*aside*]   Troth, I begin
   To be so well methinks within this hour—
   For all this match able to kill one's heart—   210
   Nothing can pull me down. Should my father
   Provide a worse fool yet (which I should think
   Were a hard thing to compass) I'd have him either:°
   The worse the better, none can come amiss now,
   If he want wit enough. So discretion love me,°   215
   Desert and judgement, I have content sufficient.°
   [*To him*] She that comes once to be a housekeeper
   Must not look every day to fare well, sir,°
   Like a young waiting-gentlewoman in service:
   For she feeds commonly as her lady does,   220
   No good bit passes her, but she gets a taste on't.
   But when she comes to keep house for herself,
   She's glad of some choice cates then once a week,
   Or twice at most, and glad if she can get'em:
   So must affection learn to fare with thankfulness.   225
   Pray make your love no stranger, sir, that's all.
   [*Aside*] Though you be one yourself, and know not on't,°
   And I have sworn you must not.
        Exit [Isabella]
HIPPOLITO   This is beyond me!
   Never came joys so unexpectedly
   To meet desires in man. How came she thus?   230
   What has she done to her, can any tell?°
   'Tis beyond sorcery this, drugs, or love-powders.
   Some art that has no name, sure, strange to me°
   Of all the wonders I e'er met withal
   Throughout my ten years' travels; but I'm thankful for't.   235
   This marriage now must of necessity forward,
   It is the only veil wit can devise
   To keep our acts from sin-piercing eyes.
        Exit

2.2

Enter Guardiano and Livia

LIVIA How, sir, a gentlewoman so young, so fair
    As you set forth, spied from the widow's window?°
GUARDIANO She!
LIVIA   Our Sunday-dinner woman?
GUARDIANO And Thursday-supper woman, the same
    still.°
    I know not how she came by her, but I'll swear   5
    She's the prime gallant for a face in Florence;
    And no doubt other parts follow their leader.°
    The Duke himself first spied her at the window;
    Then in a rapture, as if admiration
    Were poor when it were single, beckoned me,°   10
    And pointed to the wonder warily
    As one that feared she would draw in her splendour°
    Too soon, if too much gazed at. I ne'er knew him
    So infinitely taken with a woman,
    Nor can I blame his appetite, or tax   15
    His raptures of slight folly: she's a creature°
    Able to draw a State from serious business,
    And make it their best piece to do her service.°
    What course shall we devise? H'as spoke twice now.
LIVIA Twice?
GUARDIANO 'Tis beyond your apprehension   20
    How strangely that one look has catched his heart;
    'Twould prove but too much worth in wealth and favour
    To those should work his peace.
LIVIA   And if I do't not,
    Or at least come as near it (if your art
    Will take a little pains and second me)°   25
    As any wench in Florence of my standing,
    I'll quite give o'er, and shut up shop in cunning.
GUARDIANO 'Tis for the Duke, and if I fail your purpose
    All means to come by riches or advancement°
    Miss me, and skip me over.
LIVIA   Let the old woman then   30
    Be sent for with all speed, then I'll begin.
GUARDIANO A good conclusion follow, and a sweet one,

After this stale beginning with old ware.
Within there!
    Enter Servant
SERVANT   Sir, do you call?
GUARDIANO   Come near, list hither. [*They talk aside*]
LIVIA I long myself to see this absolute creature,°   35
    That wins the heart of love and praise so much.
GUARDIANO Go, sir, make haste.
LIVIA   Say I entreat her company;
    Do you hear, sir?
SERVANT   Yes, madam.
    Exit [*Servant*]
LIVIA   That brings her quickly.
GUARDIANO I would 'twere done; the Duke waits the good hour°
    And I wait the good fortune that may spring from't.   40
    I have had a lucky hand these fifteen year
    At such court passage with three dice in a dish.°
    Enter Fabritio
    Signior Fabritio!
FABRITIO Oh sir, I bring an alteration in my mouth now.°
GUARDIANO An alteration! [*Aside*] No wise speech, I hope;   45
    He means not to talk wisely, does he, trow?
    [*To him*] Good! What's the change, I pray, sir?
FABRITIO   A new change.
GUARDIANO [*aside*] Another yet! Faith there's enough already.°
FABRITIO My daughter loves him now.
GUARDIANO   What, does she, sir?
FABRITIO Affects him beyond thought, who but the Ward forsooth!   50
    No talk but of the Ward—she would have him
    To choose 'bove all the men she ever saw.
    My will goes not so fast as her consent now;
    Her duty gets before my command still.°
GUARDIANO Why then, sir, if you'll have me speak my thoughts,   55
    I smell 'twill be a match.
FABRITIO   Ay, and a sweet young couple,°
    If I have any judgement.
GUARDIANO [*aside*]   'Faith, that's little.
    [*To him*] Let her be sent tomorrow before noon,
    And handsomely tricked up; for 'bout that time
    I mean to bring her in, and tender her to him.   60
FABRITIO I warrant you for handsome. I will see°

Her things laid ready, every one in order,
And have some part of her tricked up tonight.
GUARDIANO Why, well said.
FABRITIO   'Twas a use her mother had,
  When she was invited to an early wedding: 65
  She'd dress her head o'er night, sponge up herself,
  And give her neck three lathers—
GUARDIANO [*aside*]   Ne'er a halter?°
FABRITIO On with her chain of pearl, her ruby bracelets,
  Lay ready all her tricks, and jiggam-bobs—°
GUARDIANO So must your daughter.
FABRITIO   I'll about it straight, sir.   70
     Exit Fabritio
LIVIA How he sweats in the foolish zeal of fatherhood
  After six ounces an hour, and seems°
  To toil as much as if his cares were wise ones!
GUARDIANO Y'have let his folly blood in the right vein, lady.°
LIVIA And here comes his sweet son-in-law that shall be.   75
  They're both allied in wit before the marriage;
  What will they be hereafter, when they are nearer?
  Yet they can go no further than the fool:
  There's the world's end in both of 'em.°
     Enter Ward and Sordido, one with a shittlecock, the other a
     battledore°
GUARDIANO   Now, young heir!
WARD What's the next business after shittlecock now?   80
GUARDIANO Tomorrow you shall see the gentlewoman—
  Must be your wife.
WARD   There's e'en another thing too
  Must be kept up with a pair of battledores.°
  My wife! What can she do?
GUARDIANO Nay, that's a question you should ask yourself, Ward,   85
  When y'are alone together. [*Guardiano and Livia talk separately*]
WARD   That's as I list.°
  A wife's to be asked anywhere, I hope; I'll ask her in a congregation,
  if I have a mind to't, and so save a licence. My guardianer has no
  more wit than a herb-woman, that sells away all her sweet herbs and
  nose-gays, and keeps a stinking breath for her own pottage.°   90
SORDIDO Let me be at the choosing of your beloved, if you desire a
  woman of good parts.
WARD Thou shalt, sweet Sordido.

SORDIDO I have a plaguy guess: let me alone to see what she is; if I
  but look upon her—'way, I know all the faults to a hair that you   95
  may refuse her for.°

WARD Dost thou? I prithee let me hear'em, Sordido.

SORDIDO Well, mark'em then; I have'em all in rhyme.°
  The wife your guardiner ought to tender
  Should be pretty, straight and slender;   100
  Her hair not short, her foot not long,
  Her hand not huge, nor too too loud her tongue;
  No pearl in eye, nor ruby in her nose,°
  No burn or cut, but what the catalogue shows.°
  She must have teeth, and that no black ones,   105
  And kiss most sweet when she does smack once;
  Her skin must be both white and plumped,
  Her body straight, not hopper-rumped,°
  Or wriggle sideways like a crab;
  She must be neither slut nor drab,   110
  Nor go too splay-foot with her shoes,°
  To make her smock lick up the dews.
  And two things more, which I forgot to tell ye:
  She neither must have bump in back, nor belly—°
  These are the faults that will not make her pass.   115

WARD And if I spy not these, I am a rank ass.

SORDIDO Nay more: by right, sir, you should see her naked,
  For that's the ancient order.

WARD   See her naked?
  That were good sport, i'faith. I'll have the books turned over,
  And if I find her naked on record,°   120
  She shall not have a rag on. But stay, stay,
  How if she should desire to see me so too?
  I were in a sweet case then, such a foul skin.°

SORDIDO But y'have a clean shirt, and that makes amends, sir.

WARD I will not see her naked for that trick, though.°   125
  Exit [Ward]

SORDIDO Then take her with all her faults, with her clothes
    on!
  And they may hide a number with a bum-roll;°
  'Faith, choosing of a wench in a huge farthingale
  Is like the buying of ware under a great
  Penthouse: what with the deceit of one,°   130
  And the false light of th'other, mark my speeches,

He may have a diseased wench in's bed,
And rotten stuff in's breeches.
    Exit [Sordido]
GUARDIANO It may take handsomely.
LIVIA   I see small hindrance:°
    Enter [Servant with] Mother
[*To Servant*] How now, so soon returned?
GUARDIANO   She's come.
    [*Exit Servant*]
LIVIA   That's well.   135
[*To Mother*] Widow, come, come, I have a great quarrel
    to you;
'Faith, I must chide you, that you must be sent for!
You make yourself so strange, never come at us,°
And yet so near a neighbour, and so unkind.
Troth, y'are to blame, you cannot be more welcome   140
To any house in Florence, that I'll tell you.
MOTHER My thanks must needs acknowledge so much, madam.
LIVIA How can you be so strange, then? I sit here,
Sometimes whole days together without company,
When business draws this gentleman from home;   145
And should be happy in society°
Which I so well affect as that of yours.
I know y'are alone too; why should not we,
Like two kind neighbours, then supply the wants
Of one another, having tongue-discourse,°   150
Experience in the world, and such kind helps
To laugh down time, and meet age merrily?°
MOTHER Age! Madam, you speak mirth! 'Tis at my door,
But a long journey from your ladyship yet.
LIVIA My faith, I'm nine and thirty, ev'ry stroke, wench;°   155
And 'tis a general observation
'Mongst knights' wives, or widows, we account ourselves°
Then old when young men's eyes leave looking at's.
'Tis a true rule amongst us, and ne'er failed yet
In any but in one that I remember—   160
Indeed, she had a friend at nine and forty;°
Marry, she paid well for him, and in th'end
He kept a quean or two with her own money,
That robbed her of her plate, and cut her throat.
MOTHER She had her punishment in this world, madam,   165

And a fair warning to all other women
That they live chaste at fifty.
LIVIA   Ay, or never, wench.
Come, now I have thy company I'll not part with't
Till after supper.
MOTHER   Yes, I must crave pardon, madam.
LIVIA I swear you shall stay supper. We have no strangers, woman,   170
None but my sojourners and I, this gentleman°
And the young heir his ward; you know our company.
MOTHER Some other time I will make bold with you, madam.
GUARDIANO Nay, pray stay, widow.
LIVIA   'Faith, she shall not go;
Do you think I'll be forsworn?   *Table and chess*°
MOTHER   'Tis a great while°   175
Till supper-time; I'll take my leave then, now, madam,
And come again i'th'evening, since your ladyship
Will have it so.
LIVIA   I'the'evening! By my troth, wench,
I'll keep you while I have you; you have great business, sure,
To sit alone at home; I wonder strangely   180
What pleasure you take in't! Were't to me now,
I should be ever at one neighbour's house
Or other all day long. Having no charge,°
Or none to chide you, if you go, or stay,
Who may live merrier, ay, or more at heart's ease?   185
Come, we'll to chess, or draughts; there are an hundred tricks
To drive out time till supper, never fear't, wench.
MOTHER I'll but make one step home, and return straight, madam.
LIVIA Come, I'll not trust you; you use more excuses
To your kind friends than ever I knew any.   190
What business can you have, if you be sure
Y'have locked the doors? And that being all you have°
I know y'are careful on't. One afternoon
So much to spend here! Say I should entreat you now
To lie a night or two, or a week with me,   195
Or leave your own house for a month together—
It were a kindness that long neighbourhood
And friendship might well hope to prevail in.
Would you deny such a request? I'faith,
Speak truth, and freely.
MOTHER   I were then uncivil, madam.   200

LIVIA Go to then, set your men; we'll have whole nights°
    Of mirth together, ere we be much older, wench.
MOTHER [*aside*] As good now tell her then, for she will know't;°
    I have always found her a most friendly lady.
LIVIA Why, widow, where's your mind?
MOTHER   'Troth e'en at home, madam. 205
    To tell you truth, I left a gentlewoman°
    E'en sitting all alone, which is uncomfortable,
    Especially to young bloods.
LIVIA   Another excuse!
MOTHER No, as I hope for health, madam, that's a truth;
    Please you to send and see.
LIVIA   What gentlewoman? Pish! 210
MOTHER Wife to my son, indeed; but not known, madam,
    To any but yourself.
LIVIA   Now I beshrew you,
    Could you be so unkind to her and me
    To come and not bring her? 'Faith, 'tis not friendly.
MOTHER I feared to be too bold.
LIVIA   Too bold? Oh what's become 215
    Of the true hearty love was wont to be
    'Mongst neighbours in old time?
MOTHER   And she's a stranger, madam.°
LIVIA The more should be her welcome. When is courtesy
    In better practice, than when 'tis employed
    In entertaining strangers? I could chide, i'faith— 220
    Leave her behind, poor gentlewoman, alone too!
    Make some amends, and send for her betimes, go.
MOTHER Please you command one of your servants, madam.
LIVIA Within there!
    Enter Servant
SERVANT   Madam?
LIVIA   Attend the gentlewoman.
MOTHER [*aside*] It must be carried wondrous privately° 225
    From my son's knowledge; he'll break out in storms else.
    [*To Servant*] Hark you, sir.
      [*Mother and Servant talk apart. Exit Servant*]
LIVIA [*to Guardiano*]   Now comes in the heat of your part.°
GUARDIANO [*to Livia*] True, I know it, lady, and if I be out
    May the Duke banish me from all employments,
    Wanton or serious.

LIVIA   So, have you sent, widow?   230
MOTHER Yes, madam, he's almost at home by this.°
LIVIA And 'faith let me entreat you that henceforward
    All such unkind faults may be swept from friendship,
    Which does but dim the lustre. And think thus much:
    It is a wrong to me, that have ability   235
    To bid friends welcome, when you keep'em from me;
    You cannot set greater dishonour near me
    For bounty is the credit and the glory°
    Of those that have enough. I see y'are sorry,
    And the good 'mends is made by't.°
MOTHER   Here she's, madam.   240
    Enter Bianca and Servant
BIANCA [*aside*] I wonder how she comes to send for me now?
    [*Exit Servant*]
LIVIA Gentlewoman, y'are most welcome, trust me y'are,
    As courtesy can make one, or respect
    Due to the presence of you.
BIANCA   I give you thanks, lady.°
LIVIA I heard you were alone, and't had appeared   245
    An ill condition in me, though I knew you not,°
    Nor ever saw you (yet humanity
    Thinks ev'ry case her own) to have kept your company°
    Here from you, and left you all solitary.
    I rather ventured upon boldness then   250
    As the least fault, and wished your presence here—
    A thing most happily motioned of that gentleman,°
    Whom I request you, for his care and pity
    To honour and reward with your acquaintance:
    A gentleman that ladies' rights stands for,   255
    That's his profession.
BIANCA   'Tis a noble one,°
    And honours my acquaintance.
GUARDIANO   All my intentions°
    Are servants to such mistresses.
BIANCA   'Tis your modesty
    It seems, that makes your deserts speak so low, sir.
LIVIA Come, widow. Look you, lady, here's our business.   260
    [*Points to the chess-board*]
    Are we not well employed, think you? An old quarrel°
    Between us, that will never be at an end.

BIANCA No, and methinks there's men enough to part you,
    lady.
LIVIA Ho! but they set us on, let us come off°
    As well as we can, poor souls, men care no farther.   265
    I pray sit down, forsooth, if you have the patience
    To look upon two weak and tedious gamesters.
GUARDIANO 'Faith, madam, set these by till evening,
    You'll have enough on't then; the gentlewoman,
    Being a stranger, would take more delight   270
    To see your rooms and pictures.
LIVIA   Marry, good sir,
    And well remembered; I beseech you show 'em her—
    That will beguile time well. Pray heartily do, sir,
    I'll do as much for you; here, take these keys,
    Show her the monument too; and that's a thing°   275
    Everyone sees not—you can witness that, widow.
MOTHER And that's worth sight indeed, madam.
BIANCA   Kind lady,
    I fear I came to be a trouble to you.
LIVIA Oh nothing less forsooth.
BIANCA   And to this courteous
    gentleman
    That wears a kindness in his breast so noble   280
    And bounteous to the welcome of a stranger.
GUARDIANO If you but give acceptance to my service,
    You do the greatest grace and honour to me°
    That courtesy can merit.
BIANCA   I were to blame else,
    And out of fashion much. I pray you lead, sir.   285
LIVIA After a game or two, w'are for you, gentlefolks.
GUARDIANO We wish no better seconds in society°
    Than your discourses, madam, and your partner's there.
MOTHER I thank your praise. I listened to you, sir,
    Though when you spoke there came a paltry rook°   290
    Full in my way, and chokes up all my game.
        Exit Guardiano and Bianca
LIVIA Alas, poor widow, I shall be too hard for thee.
MOTHER Y'are cunning at the game, I'll be sworn, madam.°
LIVIA It will be found so, ere I give you over.
    She that can place her man well—
MOTHER   As you do, madam.   295

LIVIA As I shall, wench—can never lose her game.
  Nay, nay, the black king's mine.
MOTHER   Cry you mercy, madam.°
LIVIA And this my queen.
MOTHER   I see't now.
LIVIA   Here's a duke°
  Will strike a sure stroke for the game anon—
  Your pawn cannot come back to relieve itself.°   300
MOTHER I know that, madam.
LIVIA   You play well the whilst.
  How she belies her skill! I hold two ducats°
  I give you check and mate to your white king,
  Simplicity itself, your saintish king there.°
MOTHER Well ere now, lady,   305
  I have seen the fall of subtlety. Jest on.
LIVIA Ay, but simplicity receives two for one.°
MOTHER What remedy but patience!
          Enter above Guardiano and Bianca
BIANCA   Trust me, sir,
  Mine eye ne'er met with fairer ornaments.
GUARDIANO Nay, livelier, I am persuaded, neither Florence   310
  Nor Venice can produce.
BIANCA   Sir, my opinion°
  Takes your part highly.
GUARDIANO   There's a better piece°
  Yet than all these.
          [Enter] Duke above [unseen by Bianca]
BIANCA   Not possible, sir!
GUARDIANO   Believe it;
  You'll say so when you see't. Turn but your eye now
  Y'are upon't presently.
          Exit [Guardiano]
BIANCA *[sees the Duke]* Oh sir!
DUKE   He's gone, beauty!   315
  Pish, look not after him. He's but a vapour
  That when the sun appears is seen no more.
BIANCA Oh treachery to honour!
DUKE   Prithee tremble not.
  I feel thy breast shake like a turtle panting°
  Under a loving hand that makes much on't.   320
  Why art so fearful? As I'm friend to brightness,°

107

There's nothing but respect and honour near thee.
You know me, you have seen me; here's a heart
Can witness I have seen thee.
BIANCA   The more's my danger.
DUKE The more's my happiness. Pish, strive not, sweet;   325
This strength were excellent employed in love now,
But here 'tis spent amiss. Strive not to seek
Thy liberty, and keep me still in prison.°
I'faith you shall not out, till I'm released now;
We'll be both freed together, or stay still by't;   330
So is captivity pleasant.
BIANCA   Oh my lord!
DUKE I am not here in vain; have but the leisure°
To think on that, and thou'lt be soon resolved.
The lifting of thy voice is but like one
That does exalt his enemy, who proving high   335
Lays all the plots to confound him that raised him.°
Take warning, I beseech thee; thou seem'st to me
A creature so composed of gentleness,
And delicate meekness—such as bless the faces
Of figures that are drawn for goddesses,   340
And makes art proud to look upon her work—
I should be sorry the least force should lay
An unkind touch upon thee.
BIANCA   Oh my extremity!
My lord, what seek you?
DUKE   Love.
BIANCA   'Tis gone already,
I have a husband.
DUKE   That's a single comfort;°   345
Take a friend to him.
BIANCA   That's a double mischief,°
Or else there's no religion.
DUKE   Do not tremble
At fears of thine own making.
BIANCA   Nor, great lord,
Make me not bold with death and deeds of ruin°
Because they fear not you; me they must fright.   350
Then am I best in health. Should thunder speak°
And none regard it, it had lost the name
And were as good be still. I'm not like those

That take their soundest sleeps in greatest tempests;
Then wake I most, the weather fearfullest,   355
And call for strength to virtue.
DUKE   Sure I think°
   Thou know'st the way to please me. I affect°
   A passionate pleading 'bove an easy yielding,
   But never pitied any—they deserved none—
   That will not pity me. I can command,   360
   Think upon that. Yet if thou truly knewest
   The infinite pleasure my affection takes
   In gentle, fair entreatings, when love's businesses
   Are carried courteously 'twixt heart and heart,
   You'd make more haste to please me.
BIANCA   Why should you seek, sir,   365
   To take away that you can never give?
DUKE   But I give better in exchange: wealth, honour.
   She that is fortunate in a duke's favour
   Lights on a tree that bears all women's wishes;
   If your own mother saw you pluck fruit there,°   370
   She would commend your wit, and praise the time
   Of your nativity. Take hold of glory.
   Do not I know y'have cast away your life
   Upon necessities, means merely doubtful°
   To keep you in indifferent health and fashion—   375
   A thing I heard too lately, and soon pitied?
   And can you be so much your beauty's enemy
   To kiss away a month or two in wedlock,
   And weep whole years in wants for ever after?
   Come, play the wise wench and provide for ever;°   380
   Let storms come when they list, they find thee sheltered.
   Should any doubt arise, let nothing trouble thee;
   Put trust in our love for the managing
   Of all to thy heart's peace. We'll walk together,
   And show a thankful joy for both our fortunes.   385
      Exeunt [Duke, Bianca] above
LIVIA   Did not I say my duke would fetch you over, widow?°
MOTHER   I think you spoke in earnest when you said it,
   madam.
LIVIA   And my black king makes all the haste he can, too.
MOTHER   Well, madam, we may meet with him in time yet.°
LIVIA   I have given thee blind mate twice.°

MOTHER   You may see, madam,°   390
  My eyes begin to fail.
LIVIA   I'll swear they do, wench.
      Enter Guardiano
GUARDIANO [*aside*] I can but smile as often as I think on't:
  How prettily the poor fool was beguiled,
  How unexpectedly; it's a witty age.°
  Never were finer snares for women's honesties   395
  Than are devised in these days; no spider's web
  Made of a daintier thread than are now practised
  To catch love's flesh-fly by the silver wing.°
  Yet to prepare her stomach by degrees
  To Cupid's feast, because I saw 'twas queasy,°   400
  I showed her naked pictures by the way:
  A bit to stay the appetite. Well, advancement,°
  I venture hard to find thee; if thou comest
  With a greater title set upon thy crest,
  I'll take that first cross patiently, and wait   405
  Until some other comes greater than that:
  I'll endure all.°
LIVIA The game's e'en at the best now; you may see, widow,
  How all things draw to an end.
MOTHER   E'en so do I, madam.
LIVIA I pray take some of your neighbours along with you.°   410
MOTHER They must be those are almost twice your years then,
  If they be chose fit matches for my time, madam.°
LIVIA Has not my duke bestirred himself?
MOTHER   Yes 'faith, madam,
  H'as done me all the mischief in this game.
LIVIA H'as showed himself in's kind.
MOTHER   In's kind, call you it?°   415
  I may swear that.
LIVIA   Yes 'faith, and keep your oath.
GUARDIANO [*aside*] Hark, list, there's somebody coming down; 'tis
    she.
      Enter Bianca
BIANCA [*aside*] Now bless me from a blasting; I saw that now°
  Fearful for any woman's eye to look on.
  Infectious mists and mildews hang at's eyes,°   420
  The weather of a doomsday dwells upon him.
  Yet since mine honour's leprous, why should I

Preserve that fair that caused the leprosy?°
Come, poison all at once. [*To Guardiano*] Thou in whose
   baseness
The bane of virtue broods, I'm bound in soul°   425
Eternally to curse thy smooth-browed treachery,°
That wore the fair veil of a friendly welcome,
And I a stranger; think upon't, 'tis worth it.
Murders piled up upon a guilty spirit
At his last breath will not lie heavier   430
Than this betraying act upon thy conscience.
Beware of off'ring the first-fruits to sin:°
His weight is deadly, who commits with strumpets
After they have been abased, and made for use;°
If they offend to th'death, as wise men know,   435
How much more they, then, that first make'em so?°
I give thee that to feed on. I'm made bold now;
I thank thy treachery; sin and I'm acquainted,
No couple greater. And I'm like that great one
Who, making politic use of a base villain,   440
He likes the treason well, but hates the traitor.°
So I hate thee, slave.
GUARDIANO [*aside*]   Well, so the Duke loves me,°
I fare not much amiss then: two great feasts°
Do seldom come together in one day,
We must not look for'em.
BIANCA   What, at it still, Mother?   445
MOTHER You see we sit by't. Are you so soon returned?
LIVIA [*aside*] So lively and so cheerful, a good sign that.
MOTHER You have not seen all since, sure?
BIANCA   That have I, Mother.°
The monument and all. I'm so beholding
To this kind, honest, courteous gentleman,   450
You'd little think it, Mother, showed me all,
Had me from place to place, so fashionably—
The kindness of some people, how't exceeds!
'Faith, I have seen that I little thought to see,
I'th'morning when I rose.
MOTHER   Nay, so I told you°   455
Before you saw't, it would prove worth your sight.
I give you great thanks for my daughter, sir,
And all your kindness towards her.

GUARDIANO   Oh good widow!
    Much good may't do her—[*aside*] forty weeks hence, i'faith.°
       Enter Servant
LIVIA Now, sir?
SERVANT   May't please you, madam, to walk in?   460
    Supper's upon the table.
LIVIA   Yes, we come;
    Will't please you, gentlewoman?
BIANCA   Thanks, virtuous lady.
    [*Aside to Livia*] Y'are a damned bawd! [*Aloud*] I'll follow you
      forsooth;
    Pray take my mother in. [*Aside to Livia*] An old ass go with you.°
    [*Aloud*] This gentleman and I vow not to part.   465
LIVIA Then get you both before.
BIANCA [*aside*]   There lies his art.°
      Exeunt [*Bianca, Guardiano and Servant*]
LIVIA Widow, I'll follow you.
      [*Exit Mother*]
                 Is't so: damned bawd?
    Are you so bitter? 'Tis but want of use—
    Her tender modesty is sea-sick a little,°
    Being not accustomed to the breaking billow   470
    Of woman's wavering faith, blown with temptations.
    'Tis but a qualm of honour, 'twill away,
    A little bitter for the time, but lasts not.
    Sin tastes at the first draught like wormwood water,°
    But drunk again, 'tis nectar ever after.   475
      Exit

3.1

Enter Mother

MOTHER   I would my son would either keep at home,
     Or I were in my grave!
     She was but one day abroad, but ever since°
     She's grown so cutted, there's no speaking to her.
     Whether the sight of great cheer at my lady's°   5
     And such mean fare at home work discontent in her,
     I know not, but I'm sure she's strangely altered.
     I'll ne'er keep daughter-in-law i'th'house with me
     Again, if I had an hundred. When read I of any
     That agreed long together, but she and her mother°   10
     Fell out in the first quarter—nay, sometime°
     A grudging of a scolding the first week, by'r Lady?
     So takes the new disease methinks in my house.°
     I'm weary of my part, there's nothing likes her,°
     I know not how to please her here a-late;   15
     And here she comes.

Enter Bianca

BIANCA   This is the strangest house
     For all defects as ever gentlewoman
     Made shift withal to pass away her love in.°
     Why is there not a cushion-cloth of drawn work,
     Or some fair cut-work pinned up in my bedchamber,°   20
     A silver-gilt casting-bottle hung up by't?
     Nay, since I am content to be so kind to you
     To spare you for a silver basin and ewer,
     Which one of my fashion looks for of duty—°
     She's never offered under, where she sleeps—   25

MOTHER [*aside*]   She talks of things here my whole state's not
     worth.°

BIANCA   Never a green silk quilt is there i'th'house, Mother,
     To cast upon my bed?

MOTHER   No, by my troth is there,
     Nor orange tawny neither.

BIANCA   Here's a house°
     For a young gentlewoman to be got with child in?   30

MOTHER   Yes, simple though you make it, there has been three

Got in a year in't, since you move me to't; °
And all as sweet-faced children, and as lovely,
As you'll be mother of. I will not spare you.
What, cannot children be begot, think you,   35
Without gilt casting-bottles? Yes, and as sweet ones:
The miller's daughter brings forth as white boys,°
As she that bathes herself with milk and bean-flour.°
'Tis an old saying: 'one may keep good cheer
In a mean house'; so may true love affect   40
After the rate of princes, in a cottage.°

BIANCA   Troth, you speak wondrous well for your old house here;
'Twill shortly fall down at your feet to thank you,
Or stoop when you go to bed, like a good child°
To ask you blessing. Must I live in want,   45
Because my fortune matched me with your son?
Wives do not give away themselves to husbands,
To the end to be quite cast away; they look°
To be the better used, and tendered rather,
Highlier respected, and maintained the richer—   50
They're well rewarded else for the free gift
Of their whole life to a husband. I ask less now
Than what I had at home when I was a maid,°
And at my father's house; kept short of that
Which a wife knows she must have, nay, and will,   55
Will, Mother, if she be not a fool born;
And report went of me, that I could wrangle
For what I wanted when I was two hours old,
And by that copy, this land still I hold.°
You hear me, Mother.
          Exit [Bianca]
MOTHER   Ay, too plain methinks;   60
And were I somewhat deafer when you spake,
'Twere ne'er a whit the worse for my quietness.°
'Tis the most sudden'st, strangest alteration,
And the most subtlest that e'er wit at threescore°
Was puzzled to find out. I know no cause for't; but   65
She's no more like the gentlewoman at first
Than I am like her that never lay with man yet;
(And she's a very young thing where'er she be).
When she first lighted here, I told her then
How mean she should find all things; she was pleased forsooth,   70

None better. I laid open all defects to her,
She was contented still. But the devil's in her,
Nothing contents her now. Tonight my son
Promised to be at home; would he were come once,°
For I'm weary of my charge, and life too.   75
She'd be served all in silver by her good will,°
By night and day; she hates the name of pewterer°
More than sick men the noise, or diseased bones°
That quake at fall o'th'hammer, seeming to have
A fellow-feeling with't at every blow.   80
What course shall I think on? She frets me so.
    [*Exit the Mother.*] *Enter Leantio*°
LEANTIO How near am I now to a happiness
That earth exceeds not! Not another like it;
The treasures of the deep are not so precious
As are the concealed comforts of a man,   85
Locked in a woman's love. I scent the air
Of blessings when I come but near the house.
What a delicious breath marriage sends forth!
The violet-bed's not sweeter. Honest wedlock
Is like a banqueting-house built in a garden,°   90
On which the spring's chaste flowers take delight
To cast their modest odours; when base lust
With all her powders, paintings, and best pride,°
Is but a fair house built by a ditch side.
When I behold a glorious dangerous strumpet,   95
Sparkling in beauty and destruction too,
Both at a twinkling, I do liken straight
Her beautified body to a goodly temple
That's built on vaults where carcasses lie rotting;°
And so by little and little I shrink back again,°   100
And quench desire with a cool meditation;
And I'm as well methinks. Now for a welcome°
Able to draw men's envies upon man:
A kiss now that will hang upon my lip
As sweet as morning dew upon a rose,   105
And full as long. After a five days' fast
She'll be so greedy now, and cling about me,
I take care how I shall be rid of her;°
And here't begins.
    [*Enter Bianca and the Mother*]

BIANCA   Oh sir, y'are welcome home.
MOTHER Oh is he come? I am glad on't.
LEANTIO   Is that all?   110
  [*Aside*] Why this as dreadful now as sudden death°
  To some rich man, that flatters all his sins
  With promise of repentance when he's old,
  And dies in the midway before he comes to't.
  [*To her*] Sure y'are not well, Bianca! How dost, prithee?   115
BIANCA I have been better than I am at this time.
LEANTIO Alas, I thought so.
BIANCA   Nay, I have been worse too,
  Than now you see me, sir.
LEANTIO   I'm glad thou mend'st yet,°
  I feel my heart mend too. How came it to thee?
  Has anything disliked thee in my absence?   120
BIANCA No, certain, I have had the best content°
  That Florence can afford.
LEANTIO   Thou makest the best on't;
  Speak, Mother, what's the cause? You must needs know.
MOTHER Troth I know none, son, let her speak herself.
  [*Aside*] Unless it be the same gave Lucifer   125
  A tumbling cast: that's pride.
BIANCA Methinks this house stands nothing to my mind;°
  I'd have some pleasant lodging i'th'high street, sir,
  Or if 'twere near the court, sir, that were much better:
  'Tis a sweet recreation for a gentlewoman   130
  To stand in a bay window, and see gallants.°
LEANTIO Now I have another temper, a mere stranger°
  To that of yours, it seems; I should delight
  To see none but yourself.
BIANCA   I praise not that:
  Too fond is as unseemly as too churlish.°   135
  I would not have a husband of that proneness
  To kiss me before company, for a world.
  Beside 'tis tedious to see one thing still, sir,
  Be it the best that ever heart affected;
  Nay, were't yourself, whose love had power you know   140
  To bring me from my friends, I would not stand thus,
  And gaze upon you always. Troth, I could not, sir;
  As good be blind, and have no use of sight
  As look on one thing still. What's the eye's treasure,

But change of objects? You are learnèd, sir,   145
And know I speak not ill; 'tis full as virtuous°
For woman's eye to look on several men
As for her heart, sir, to be fixed on one.
LEANTIO Now thou comest home to me; a kiss for that word.
BIANCA No matter for a kiss, sir; let it pass,   150
'Tis a toy, we'll not so much as mind it;°
Let's talk of other business and forget it.
What news now of the pirates, any stirring?°
Prithee, discourse a little.
MOTHER [aside]   I am glad he's here yet
To see her tricks himself; I had lied monstrously,°   155
If I had told'em first.
LEANTIO   Speak, what's the humour, sweet,
You make your lip so strange? This was not wont.°
BIANCA Is there no kindness betwixt man and wife,
Unless they make a pigeon-house of friendship,°
And be still billing? 'Tis the idlest fondness   160
That ever was invented, and 'tis pity
It's grown a fashion for poor gentlewomen;
There's many a disease kissed in a year by't,
And a French curtsy made to't. Alas, sir,°
Think of the world, how we shall live; grow serious—   165
We have been married a whole fortnight now.
LEANTIO How, a whole fortnight! Why, is that so long?
BIANCA 'Tis time to leave off dalliance; 'tis a doctrine
Of your own teaching, if you be remembered,
And I was bound to obey it.
MOTHER [aside]   Here's one fits him;   170
This was well catched, i'faith, son, like a fellow°
That rids another country of the plague,
And brings it home with him to his own house.   *Knock within*
Who knocks?
LEANTIO   Who's there now? Withdraw you, Bianca,
Thou art a gem no stranger's eye must see,   175
Howe'er thou pleased now to look dull on me.°
        Exit [Bianca.] Enter Messenger
Y'are welcome, sir; to whom your business, pray?
MESSENGER To one I see not here now.
LEANTIO   Who should that be, sir?
MESSENGER A young gentlewoman I was sent to.

LEANTIO A young gentlewoman?

MESSENGER   Ay, sir, about sixteen;   180
    Why look you wildly, sir?

LEANTIO   At your strange error.
    Y'have mistook the house, sir. There's none such here,
    I assure you.

MESSENGER   I assure you too,
    The man that sent me cannot be mistook.

LEANTIO Why, who is't sent you, sir?

MESSENGER   The Duke.

LEANTIO   The Duke?   185

MESSENGER Yes, he entreats her company at a banquet
    At Lady Livia's house.

LEANTIO   Troth, shall I tell you, sir,
    It is the most erroneous business
    That e'er your honest pains was abused with.
    I pray forgive me, if I smile a little   190
    (I cannot choose, i'faith, sir) at an error
    So comical as this—I mean no harm though.
    His Grace has been most wondrous ill informed;
    Pray so return it, sir. What should her name be?°

MESSENGER That I shall tell you straight too: Bianca Capella.   195

LEANTIO How, sir, Bianca? What do you call th'other?°

MESSENGER Capella. Sir, it seems you know no such then?

LEANTIO Who should this be? I never heard o'th'name.

MESSENGER Then 'tis a sure mistake.

LEANTIO   What if you enquired
    In the next street, sir? I saw gallants there   200
    In the new houses that are built of late.
    Ten to one, there you find her.

MESSENGER   Nay, no matter,
    I will return the mistake, and seek no further.

LEANTIO Use your own will and pleasure, sir, y'are welcome.
    Exit Messenger
    What shall I think of first? Come forth, Bianca—   205
    Enter Bianca
    Thou art betrayed, I fear me.

BIANCA   Betrayed! How, sir?

LEANTIO The Duke knows thee.

BIANCA   Knows me? How know you that, sir?°

LEANTIO H'as got thy name.

BIANCA [*aside*]   Ay, and my good name too,
  That's the worse o'th'twain.
LEANTIO   How comes this work about?°
BIANCA How should the Duke know me? Can you guess,
    Mother?   210
MOTHER Not I with all my wits, sure we kept house close.°
LEANTIO Kept close! Not all the locks in Italy
  Can keep you women so; you have been gadding,°
  And ventured out at twilight to th'court-green yonder,°
  And met the gallant bowlers coming home—   215
  Without your masks too, both of you, I'll be hanged else!°
  Thou hast been seen, Bianca, by some stranger,
  Never excuse it.
BIANCA   I'll not seek the way, sir.
  Do you think y'have married me to mew me up
  Not to be seen; what would you make of me?   220
LEANTIO A good wife, nothing else.
BIANCA   Why, so are some
  That are seen ev'ry day, else the devil take'em.
LEANTIO No more then, I believe all virtuous in thee
  Without an argument; 'twas but thy hard chance°
  To be seen somewhere, there lies all the mischief.   225
  But I have devised a riddance.
MOTHER   Now I can tell you, son,°
  The time and place.
LEANTIO   When, where?
MOTHER   What wits have I?
  When you last took your leave, if you remember,
  You left us both at window.
LEANTIO   Right, I know that.
MOTHER And not the third part of an hour after   230
  The Duke passed by in a great solemnity,
  To St Mark's temple, and to my apprehension°
  He looked up twice to th'window.
LEANTIO   Oh there quickened°
  The mischief of this hour!
BIANCA [*aside*]   If you call't mischief—
  It is a thing I fear I am conceived with.   235
LEANTIO Looked he up twice, and could you take no warning?
MOTHER Why, once may do as much harm, son, as a
    thousand:

Do not you know one spark has fired an house
As well as a whole furnace?
LEANTIO   My heart flames for't!
Yet let's be wise, and keep all smothered closely;   240
I have bethought a means; is the door fast?
MOTHER I locked it myself after him.
LEANTIO   You know, Mother,
At the end of the dark parlour there's a place
So artificially contrived for a conveyance,°
No search could ever find it. When my father   245
Kept in for manslaughter, it was his sanctuary.°
There will I lock my life's best treasure up,
Bianca.
BIANCA   Would you keep me closer yet?
Have you the conscience? Y'are best e'en choke me up, sir!°
You make me fearful of your health and wits,   250
You cleave to such wild courses. What's the matter?
LEANTIO Why, are you so insensible of your danger
To ask that now? The Duke himself has sent for you
To Lady Livia's, to a banquet forsooth.°
BIANCA Now I beshrew you heartily, has he so?   255
And you the man would never yet vouchsafe
To tell me on't till now. You show your loyalty
And honesty at once; and so farewell, sir.
LEANTIO Bianca, whither now?
BIANCA   Why, to the Duke, sir:
You say he sent for me.
LEANTIO   But thou dost not mean   260
To go, I hope?
BIANCA   No? I shall prove unmannerly,
Rude and uncivil, mad—and imitate you.
Come, mother, come, follow his humour no longer;
We shall all be executed for treason shortly.
MOTHER Not I, i'faith. I'll first obey the Duke,   265
And taste of a good banquet; I'm of thy mind,
I'll step but up and fetch two handkerchiefs°
To pocket up some sweetmeats, and o'ertake thee.
          Exit [Mother]
BIANCA [aside] Why here's an old wench would trot into a bawd now,
For some dry sucket, or a colt in marchpane.°   270
          Exit [Bianca]

LEANTIO Oh thou the ripe time of man's misery, wedlock,
       When all his thoughts, like over-laden trees,
       Crack with the fruits they bear, in cares, in jealousies.
       Oh that's a fruit that ripens hastily,
       After 'tis knit to marriage; it begins   275
       As soon as the sun shines upon the bride
       A little to show colour. Blessed Powers,°
       Whence comes this alteration? The distractions,
       The fears and doubts it brings are numberless,
       And yet the cause I know not. What a peace   280
       Has he that never marries! If he knew
       The benefit he enjoyed, or had the fortune
       To come and speak with me, he should know then
       The infinite wealth he had, and discern rightly
       The greatness of his treasure by my loss.   285
       Nay, what a quietness has he 'bove mine,
       That wears his youth out in a strumpet's arms,
       And never spends more care upon a woman°
       Than at the time of lust; but walks away,
       And if he find her dead at his return,   290
       His pity is soon done—he breaks a sigh
       In many parts, and gives her but a piece on't!
       But all the fears, shames, jealousies, costs and troubles,
       And still renewed cares of a marriage bed
       Live in the issue, when the wife is dead.   295
           Enter Messenger
MESSENGER A good perfection to your thoughts.°
LEANTIO   The news, sir?
MESSENGER Though you were pleased of late to pin an error on me,
       You must not shift another in your stead too:°
       The Duke has sent me for you.
LEANTIO   How, for me, sir?
       [*Aside*] I see then 'tis my theft; w'are both betrayed.°   300
       Well, I'm not the first has stol'n away a maid,
       My countrymen have used it. [*To him*] I'll along with you, sir.
           Exeunt

3.2

A banquet prepared. Enter Guardiano and Ward

GUARDIANO Take you especial note of such a gentlewoman,°
    She's here on purpose; I have invited her,
    Her father and her uncle, to this banquet.
    Mark her behaviour well, it does concern you;
    And what her good parts are, as far as time   5
    And place can modestly require a knowledge of,
    Shall be laid open to your understanding.
    You know I'm both your guardian and your uncle,
    My care of you is double, ward and nephew,
    And I'll express it here.
WARD   'Faith, I should know her°   10
    Now by her mark among a thousand women:
    A little, pretty, deft and tidy thing, you say?°
GUARDIANO Right.
WARD   With a lusty sprouting sprig in her hair.°
GUARDIANO Thou goest the right way still; take one mark more:
    Thou shalt ne'er find her hand out of her uncle's,   15
    Or else his out of hers, if she be near him.
    The love of kindred never yet stuck closer
    Than theirs to one another; he that weds her
    Marries her uncle's heart too.
WARD   Say you so, sir,
    Then I'll be asked i'th'church to both of them.   *Cornets [sound]*°   20
GUARDIANO Fall back, here comes the Duke.
WARD *[aside]*   He brings a gentlewoman,
    I should fall forward rather.
       Enter Duke, Bianca, Fabritio, Hippolito, Livia, Mother,
       Isabella and Attendants
DUKE   Come, Bianca,°
    Of purpose sent into the world to show
    Perfection once in woman; I'll believe
    Henceforward they have ev'ry one a soul too,°   25
    'Gainst all the uncourteous opinions
    That man's uncivil rudeness ever held of 'em.
    Glory of Florence, light into mine arms!°
       Enter Leantio
BIANCA Yon comes a grudging man will chide you, sir;°

The storm is now in's heart, and would get nearer,   30
And fall here if it durst—it pours down yonder.°
DUKE   If that be he, the weather shall soon clear.
List, and I'll tell thee how. [*Whispers in her ear*]
LEANTIO [*aside*]   A-kissing too?
I see 'tis plain lust now, adultery boldened.
What will it prove anon, when 'tis stuffed full   35
Of wine and sweetmeats, being so impudent fasting?°
DUKE [*to Leantio*] We have heard of your good parts, sir, which we
    honour°
With our embrace and love. [*To Attendant*] Is not the captainship
Of Rouans citadel, since the late deceased,
Supplied by any yet?°
GENTLEMAN   By none, my lord.°   40
DUKE [*to Leantio*] Take it, the place is yours then, and as
    faithfulness
And desert grows, our favour shall grow with't. [*Leantio kneels*]
Rise now the Captain of our fort at Rouans.
LEANTIO   The service of whole life give your Grace thanks.
DUKE   Come sit, Bianca.
LEANTIO [*aside*]   This is some good yet,   45
And more than e'er I looked for; a fine bit
To stay a cuckold's stomach. All preferment°
That springs from sin and lust, it shoots up quickly,
As gardener's crops do in the rotten'st grounds;
So is all means raised from base prostitution,°   50
E'en like a sallet growing upon a dunghill.
I'm like a thing that never was yet heard of,
Half merry and half mad: much like a fellow
That eats his meat with a good appetite,
And wears a plague-sore that would fright a country;°   55
Or rather like the barren, hardened ass,°
That feeds on thistles till he bleeds again—
And such is the condition of my misery.°
LIVIA   Is that your son, widow?
MOTHER   Yes, did your ladyship
Never know that till now?
LIVIA   No, trust me, did I.   60
[*Aside*] Nor ever truly felt the power of love
And pity to a man, till now I knew him.
I have enough to buy me my desires,

And yet to spare; that's one good comfort. [*To Leantio*] Hark you,
  Pray let me speak with you, sir, before you go.   65
LEANTIO With me, lady? You shall, I am at your service.
  [*Aside*] What will she say now, trow, more goodness yet?°
WARD I shall see her now, I'm sure: the ape's so little,°
  I shall scarce feel her; I have seen almost
  As tall as she sold in the fair for ten pence.°   70
  See how she simpers it, as if marmalade°
  Would not melt in her mouth. She might have the kindness,
    i'faith,
  To send me a gilded bull from her own trencher,°
  A ram, a goat, or somewhat to be nibbling.
  These women when they come to sweet things once,   75
  They forget all their friends, they grow so greedy;
  Nay, oftentimes their husbands.
DUKE   Here's a health now, gallants,
  To the best beauty at this day in Florence.
BIANCA Whoe'er she be, she shall not go unpledged, sir.°
DUKE Nay, you're excused for this.
BIANCA   Who, I, my lord?   80
DUKE Yes, by the law of Bacchus—plead your benefit;°
  You are not bound to pledge your own health, lady.
BIANCA That's a good way, my lord, to keep me dry.°
DUKE Nay, then I will not offend Venus so much,°
  Let Bacchus seek his 'mends in another court.°   85
  Here's to thyself, Bianca. [*He drinks*]
BIANCA   Nothing comes
  More welcome to that name than your Grace.
LEANTIO [*aside*]   So, so;
  Here stands the poor thief, now, that stole the treasure,°
  And he's not thought on. Ours is near kin now
  To a twin-misery born into the world: 90
  First the hard-conscienced worldling, he hoards wealth up;
  Then comes the next, and he feasts all upon't—
  One's damned for getting, th'other for spending on't.
  Oh equal justice, thou hast met my sin
  With a full weight; I'm rightly now oppressed;°   95
  All her friends' heavy hearts lie in my breast.°
DUKE Methinks there is no spirit amongst us, gallants,
  But what divinely sparkles from the eyes
  Of bright Bianca; we sat all in darkness,°

But for that splendour. Who was't told us lately   100
  Of a match-making rite, a marriage tender?°
GUARDIANO 'Twas I, my lord.
DUKE   'Twas you indeed; where is she?
GUARDIANO This is the gentlewoman.
FABRITIO   My lord, my daughter.
DUKE Why, here's some stirring yet.
FABRITIO   She's a dear child to me.°
DUKE That must needs be; you say she is your daughter.   105
FABRITIO Nay, my good lord, dear to my purse I mean—
  Beside my person; I ne'er reckoned that.
  She has the full qualities of a gentlewoman:
  I have brought her up to music, dancing, what not
  That may commend her sex, and stir her husband.   110
DUKE And which is he now?
GUARDIANO   This young heir, my lord.
DUKE What is he brought up to?
HIPPOLITO [aside]   To cat-and-trap.°
GUARDIANO My lord, he's a great ward, wealthy, but simple;
  His parts consist in acres.
DUKE   Oh, wise-acres.°
GUARDIANO Y'have spoken him in a word, sir.
BIANCA   'Las, poor gentlewoman,   115
  She's ill bestead, unless sh'as dealt the wiselier
  And laid in more provision for her youth:°
  Fools will not keep in summer.
LEANTIO [aside]   No, nor such wives°
  From whores in winter.
DUKE [to Fabritio]   Yea, the voice too, sir?°
FABRITIO Ay, and a sweet breast too, my lord, I hope,°   120
  Or I have cast away my money wisely.°
  She took her pricksong earlier, my lord,°
  Than any of her kindred ever did:
  A rare child, though I say't—but I'd not have
  The baggage hear so much, 'twould make her swell straight;°   125
  And maids of all things must not be puffed up.°
DUKE Let's turn us to a better banquet then,
  For music bids the soul of man to a feast,°
  And that's indeed a noble entertainment,
  Worthy Bianca's self. [To Bianca] You shall perceive, beauty,   130
  Our Florentine damsels are not brought up idly.

BIANCA They are wiser of themselves, it seems, my lord,°
    And can take gifts when goodness offers 'em.   *Music*
LEANTIO [*aside*] True, and damnation has taught you that wisdom;
    You can take gifts too. Oh that music mocks me!   135
LIVIA [*aside*] I am as dumb to any language now
    But love's, as one that never learned to speak.°
    I'm not yet so old but he may think of me;
    My own fault, I have been idle a long time;
    But I'll begin the week, and paint tomorrow,°   140
    So follow my true labour day by day—
    I never thrived so well as when I used it.

        Song [sung by Isabella]°

What harder chance can fall to woman   WARD Here's a tune
Who was born to cleave to some man,   indeed! Pish, I had
Than to bestow her time, youth, beauty, rather hear one ballad   145
Life's observance, honour, duty,°   sung i'th'nose now, of
On a thing for no use good,   the lamentable
But to make physic work, or blood°   drowning of fat sheep
Force fresh in an old lady's cheek?°   and oxen, than all these
She that would be   simpering tunes played   150
Mother of fools,   upon cats' guts, and
Let her compound with me.   sung by little kitlings.°

FABRITIO How like you her breast now, my lord?
BIANCA [*aside to Duke*]   Her breast?°
    He talks as if his daughter had given suck
    Before she were married, as her betters have;   155
    The next he praises sure will be her nipples.
DUKE [*aside to Bianca*] Methinks now, such a voice to such a
        husband
    Is like a jewel of unvalued worth,°
    Hung at a fool's ear.
FABRITIO   May it please your Grace
    To give her leave to show another quality?   160
DUKE Marry as many good ones as you will, sir,
    The more the better welcome.
LEANTIO [*aside*]   But the less
    The better practised. The soul's black indeed°
    That cannot commend virtue: but who keeps it?°
    The extortioner will say to a sick beggar,   165

Heaven comfort thee, though he give none himself:
This good is common.
FABRITIO   Will it please you now, sir,°
To entreat your ward to take her by the hand,
And lead her in a dance before the Duke?
GUARDIANO That will I, sir, 'tis needful; hark you, nephew.   170
FABRITIO Nay, you shall see, young heir, what y'have for your
    money,
Without fraud or imposture.
WARD   Dance with her?
Not I, sweet guardiner, do not urge my heart to't,
'Tis clean against my blood; dance with a stranger!°
Let whoso will do't, I'll not begin first with her.°   175
HIPPOLITO [aside] No, fear't not, fool, sh'as took a better order.°
GUARDIANO Why, who shall take her then?
WARD   Some other gentleman.
Look, there's her uncle, a fine-timbered reveller;°
Perhaps he knows the manner of her dancing too—
I'll have him do't before me: I have sworn, guardiner,   180
Then may I learn the better.
GUARDIANO   Thou'lt be an ass still.
WARD Ay, all that, uncle, shall not fool me out:°
Pish, I stick closer to myself than so.°
GUARDIANO [to Hippolito] I must entreat you, sir, to take your niece
And dance with her; my ward's a little wilful,   185
He would have you show him the way.
HIPPOLITO   Me, sir?
He shall command it at all hours, pray tell him so.
GUARDIANO I thank you for him, he has not wit himself, sir.
HIPPOLITO [to Isabella] Come, my life's peace. I have a strange office
    on't here:°
'Tis some man's luck to keep the joys he likes   190
Concealed for his own bosom, but my fortune
To set'em out now, for another's liking—°
Like the mad misery of necessitous man°
That parts from his good horse with many praises,
And goes on foot himself; need must be obeyed   195
In ev'ry action, it mars man and maid.
        Music. A dance [by Hippolito and Isabella], making honours°
        to the Duke and curtsy to themselves, both before and after
DUKE Signior Fabritio, y'are a happy father,

Your cares and pains are fortunate; you see°
Your cost bears noble fruits. Hippolito, thanks.

FABRITIO Here's some amends for all my charges yet: 200
She wins both prick and praise, where'er she comes.°

DUKE How likest, Bianca?

BIANCA   All things well, my lord;
But this poor gentlewoman's fortune, that's the worst.

DUKE There is no doubt, Bianca, she'll find leisure
To make that good enough; he's rich and simple.   205

BIANCA She has the better hope o'th'upper hand indeed,
Which women strive for most.

GUARDIANO [to Ward]   Do't when I bid you, sir.

WARD I'll venture but a hornpipe with her, guardiner,°
Or some such married man's dance.

GUARDIANO   Well, venture something, sir.°

WARD I have rhyme for what I do.

GUARDIANO [aside]   But little reason, I think.   210

WARD Plain men dance the measures, the cinquepace the gay:
Cuckolds dance the hornpipe, and farmers dance the hay:
Your soldiers dance the round, and maidens that grow big:
You drunkards, the canaries; you whore and bawd the jig.°
Here's your eight kinds of dancers; he that finds the ninth—   215
Let him pay the minstrels.

DUKE Oh here he appears once in his own person;
I thought he would have married her by attorney,°
And lain with her so too.

BIANCA   Nay, my kind lord,
There's very seldom any found so foolish   220
To give away his part there.

LEANTIO [aside]   Bitter scoff!
Yet I must do't—with what a cruel pride
The glory of her sin strikes by my afflictions.°

        Music. Ward and Isabella dance; he ridiculously imitates
        Hippolito

DUKE This thing will make shift, sirs, to make a husband,°
For aught I see in him; how think'st, Bianca?   225

BIANCA 'Faith, an ill-favoured shift, my lord, methinks;
If he would take some voyage when he's married
Dangerous, or long enough, and scarce be seen
Once in nine year together, a wife then
Might make indifferent shift to be content with him.   230

DUKE A kiss! [*Kisses her*] That wit deserves to be made much on.°
   Come, our caroch.
GUARDIANO   Stands ready for your Grace.
DUKE My thanks to all your loves. Come, fair Bianca,°
   We have took special care of you, and provided
   Your lodging near us now.
BIANCA   Your love is great, my lord.   235
DUKE Once more, our thanks to all.
ALL   All blest honours guard you.
         Cornets flourish. Exeunt all but Leantio and Livia
LEANTIO [*aside*] Oh hast thou left me then, Bianca, utterly!
   Bianca, now I miss thee! Oh return,
   And save the faith of woman. I ne'er felt°
   The loss of thee till now; 'tis an affliction   240
   Of greater weight than youth was made to bear,
   As if a punishment of after-life°
   Were fallen upon man here; so new it is
   To flesh and blood, so strange, so insupportable
   A torment, e'en mistook, as if a body   245
   Whose death were drowning must needs therefore suffer it°
   In scalding oil.
LIVIA   Sweet sir!
LEANTIO [*aside*]   As long as mine eye saw thee,
   I half enjoyed thee.
LIVIA   Sir?
LEANTIO [*aside*]   Canst thou forget
   The dear pains my love took? How it has watched°
   Whole nights together, in all weathers for thee,   250
   Yet stood in heart more merry than the tempests
   That sung about mine ears (like dangerous flatterers
   That can set all their mischief to sweet tunes)
   And then received thee from thy father's window
   Into these arms at midnight; when we embraced   255
   As if we had been statues only made for't,
   To show art's life, so silent were our comforts,°
   And kissed as if our lips had grown together.
LIVIA [*aside*] This makes me madder to enjoy him now.°
LEANTIO [*aside*] Canst thou forget all this? And better joys 260
   That we met after this, which then new kisses
   Took pride to praise?
LIVIA [*aside*]   I shall grow madder yet. [*To him*] Sir.°

LEANTIO [*aside*] This cannot be but of some close bawd's working.°
    [*To her*] Cry mercy, lady. What would you say to me?
    My sorrow makes me so unmannerly,   265
    So comfort bless me, I had quite forgot you.
LIVIA Nothing but, e'en in pity to that passion,
    Would give your grief good counsel.°
LEANTIO   Marry, and welcome, lady,
    It never could come better.
LIVIA   Then first, sir,
    To make away all your good thoughts at once of her,   270
    Know most assuredly she is a strumpet.
LEANTIO Ha? 'Most assuredly'! Speak not a thing
    So vile so certainly, leave it more doubtful.°
LIVIA Then I must leave all truth, and spare my knowledge;
    A sin which I too lately found and wept for.   275
LEANTIO Found you it?
LIVIA   Ay, with wet eyes.
LEANTIO   Oh perjurious friendship!°
LIVIA You missed your fortunes when you met with her, sir:
    Young gentlemen that only love for beauty,
    They love not wisely; such a marriage rather
    Proves the destruction of affection—   280
    It brings on want, and want's the key of whoredom.
    I think y'had small means with her.°
LEANTIO   Oh not any, lady.
LIVIA Alas, poor gentleman, what meant'st thou, sir,
    Quite to undo thyself with thine own kind heart?
    Thou art too good and pitiful to woman.   285
    Marry, sir, thank thy stars for this blest fortune
    That rids the summer of thy youth so well
    From many beggars that had lain a-sunning°
    In thy beams only else, till thou hadst wasted°
    The whole days of thy life in heat and labour.°   290
    What would you say now to a creature found
    As pitiful to you, and as it were°
    E'en sent on purpose from the whole sex general,°
    To requite all that kindness you have shown to't.
LEANTIO What's that, madam?
LIVIA   Nay, a gentlewoman, and one able   295
    To reward good things; ay, and bears a conscience to't.°
    Couldst thou love such a one that (blow all fortunes)°

WOMEN BEWARE WOMEN   3.2

Would never see thee want?
Nay more, maintain thee to thine enemy's envy?
And shalt not spend a care for't, stir a thought,°   300
Nor break a sleep; unless love's music waked thee,
No storm of fortune should. Look upon me,
And know that woman.
LEANTIO   Oh my life's wealth, Bianca!
LIVIA [*aside*] Still with her name? Will nothing wear it out?
     [*To him*] That deep sigh went but for a strumpet, sir.   305
LEANTIO It can go for no other that loves me.
LIVIA [*aside*] He's vexed in mind; I came too soon to him;
     Where's my discretion now, my skill, my judgement?
     I'm cunning in all arts but my own love.
     'Tis as unseasonable to tempt him now   310
     So soon, as for a widow to be courted
     Following the husband's corpse, or to make bargain
     By the grave side, and take a young man there:
     Her strange departure stands like a hearse yet°
     Before his eyes; which time will take down shortly.   315
          Exit [*Livia*]
LEANTIO Is she my wife till death, yet no more mine?
     That's a hard measure; then what's marriage good for?°
     Methinks, by right, I should not now be living,
     And then 'twere all well. What a happiness
     Had I been made of, had I never seen her;   320
     For nothing makes man's loss grievous to him
     But knowledge of the worth of what he loses;
     For what he never had he never misses.
     She's gone for ever, utterly; there is
     As much redemption of a soul from hell   325
     As a fair woman's body from his palace.
     Why should my love last longer than her truth?°
     What is there good in woman to be loved,
     When only that which makes her so has left her?
     I cannot love her now, but I must like   330
     Her sin, and my own shame too, and be guilty
     Of law's breach with her, and mine own abusing—°
     All which were monstrous. Then my safest course,
     For health of mind and body, is to turn
     My heart, and hate her, most extremely hate her;   335
     I have no other way. Those virtuous powers

131

Which were chaste witnesses of both our troths
Can witness she breaks first. And I'm rewarded
With captainship o'th'fort! A place of credit
I must confess, but poor; my factorship   340
Shall not exchange means with't. He that died last in't,°
He was no drunkard, yet he died a beggar
For all his thrift; besides the place not fits me—
It suits my resolution, not my breeding.°
    Enter Livia
LIVIA [*aside*] I have tried all ways I can, and have not power   345
    To keep from sight of him. [*To him*] How are you now, sir?
LEANTIO I feel a better ease, madam.
LIVIA   Thanks to blessedness.
    You will do well, I warrant you, fear it not, sir;
    Join but your own good will to't. He's not wise
    That loves his pain or sickness, or grows fond   350
    Of a disease, whose property is to vex him
    And spitefully drink his blood up. Out upon't, sir,°
    Youth knows no greater loss. I pray let's walk, sir;
    You never saw the beauty of my house yet,°
    Nor how abundantly fortune has blessed me   355
    In worldly treasure; trust me, I have enough, sir,
    To make my friend a rich man in my life,
    A great man at my death—yourself will say so.
    If you want anything, and spare to speak,
    Troth, I'll condemn you for a wilful man, sir.   360
LEANTIO Why, sure this can be but the flattery of some dream.
LIVIA Now by this kiss, my love, my soul and riches,
    'Tis all true substance. [*Kisses him*]°
    Come, you shall see my wealth; take what you list;
    The gallanter you go, the more you please me.   365
    I will allow you, too, your page and footman,°
    Your race-horses, or any various pleasure
    Exercised youth delights in; but to me
    Only, sir, wear your heart of constant stuff—°
    Do but you love enough, I'll give enough.   370
LEANTIO Troth then, I'll love enough, and take enough.
LIVIA Then we are both pleased enough.
    Exeunt

3.3

Enter Guardiano and Isabella at one door, and the Ward and
Sordido at another

GUARDIANO Now, nephew, here's the gentlewoman again.

WARD Mass, here's she come again; mark her now, Sordido.

GUARDIANO   This is the maid my love and care has chose
    Out for your wife, and so I tender her to you;
    Yourself has been eye-witness of some qualities   5
    That speak a courtly breeding, and are costly.°
    I bring you both to talk together now,
    'Tis time you grew familiar in your tongues;
    Tomorrow you join hands, and one ring ties you,
    And one bed holds you—if you like the choice.   10
    Her father and her friends are i'th'next room,
    And stay to see the contract ere they part.
    Therefore dispatch, good Ward, be sweet and short;°
    Like her, or like her not, there's but two ways—
    And one your body, th'other your purse pays.°   15

WARD I warrant you, guardiner, I'll not stand all day thrumming,
    But quickly shoot my bolt at your next coming.°

GUARDIANO   Well said: good fortune to your birding then.
    [*Exit Guardiano*]

WARD I never missed mark yet.

SORDIDO Troth, I think, master, if the truth were known,   20
    You never shot at any but the kitchen-wench,
    And that was a she-woodcock, a mere innocent,°
    That was oft lost and cried, at eight and twenty.

WARD   No more of that meat, Sordido, here's eggs o'the'spit now,°
    We must turn gingerly. Draw out the catalogue   25
    Of all the faults of women.

SORDIDO How, all the faults! Have you so little reason to think so
    much paper will lie in my breeches? Why, ten carts will not carry it,
    if you set down but the bawds. All the faults? Pray let's be content
    with a few of 'em; and if they were less, you would find 'em enough,   30
    I warrant you. Look you, sir. [*They examine her closely*]

ISABELLA [*aside*] But that I have th'advantage of the fool,
    And as much as woman's heart can wish and joy at,
    What an infernal torment 'twere to be
    Thus bought and sold, and turned and pried into; when, alas,   35

The worst bit is too good for him! And the comfort is
H'as but a cater's place on't, and provides°
All for another's table; yet how curious
The ass is, like some nice professor on't,°
That buys up all the daintiest food i'th'markets,   40
And seldom licks his lips after a taste on't!

SORDIDO Now to her, now y'have scanned all her parts over.

WARD But at what end shall I begin now, Sordido?°

SORDIDO Oh ever at a woman's lip, while you live, sir; do you ask that
    question?   45

WARD Methinks, Sordido, sh'as but a crabbed face to begin with.°

SORDIDO A crabbed face? That will save money.

WARD How, save money, Sordido?

SORDIDO Ay, sir: for having a crabbed face of her own, she'll eat the
    less verjuice with her mutton; 'twill save verjuice at year's end, sir.   50

WARD Nay, an your jests begin to be saucy once, I'll make you eat your
    meat without mustard.°

SORDIDO And that in some kind is a punishment.

WARD Gentlewoman, they say 'tis your pleasure to be my wife, and
    you shall know shortly whether it be mine or no, to be your
    husband; and thereupon thus I first enter upon° you. [Kisses her]   55
    Oh most delicious scent! [Aside] Methinks it tasted as if a man had
    stepped into a comfit-maker's shop° to let a cart go by, all the while
    I kissed her. [To her] It is reported, gentlewoman, you'll run mad
    for me, if you have me not.   60

ISABELLA I should be in great danger of my wits, sir;°
    [Aside] For being so forward, should this ass kick backward now.°

WARD Alas, poor soul! And is that hair your own?°

ISABELLA Mine own? Yes sure, sir, I owe nothing for't.

WARD 'Tis a good hearing;° I shall have the less to pay when I have   65
    married you. [To Sordido] Look, does her eyes stand well?

SORDIDO They cannot stand better than in her head, I think; where
    would you have them? And for her nose, 'tis of a very good last.°

WARD I have known as good as that has not lasted a year, though.

SORDIDO That's in the using of a thing; will not any strong bridge fall   70
    down in time, if we do nothing but beat at the bottom? A nose of
    buff would not last always, sir, especially if it came into th'camp
    once.°

WARD But, Sordido, how shall we do to make her laugh, that I may see
    what teeth she has? For I'll not bate her a tooth,° nor take a black   75
    one into th'bargain.

SORDIDO Why, do but you fall in talk with her, you cannot choose but
    one time or other make her laugh, sir.

WARD It shall go hard but I will. [*To her*] Pray what qualities have you
    beside singing and dancing? Can you play at shittlecock forsooth?   80

ISABELLA Ay, and at stool-ball too, sir; I have great luck at it.

WARD Why, can you catch a ball well?

ISABELLA I have catched two in my lap° at one game.

WARD What, have you, woman? I must have you learn to play at trap
    too, then y'are full and whole.   85

ISABELLA Anything that you please to bring me up to° I shall take
    pains to practise.

WARD [*aside to Sordido*] 'Twill not do, Sordido, we shall never get her
    mouth opened wide enough.

SORDIDO No, sir? That's strange! Then here's a trick for your learning.   90
    He yawns. [*Isabella yawns too, but covers her mouth*]
    Look now, look now; quick, quick there!

WARD Pox of that scurvy mannerly trick with handkerchief;° it hin-
    dered me a little, but I am satisfied. When a fair woman gapes, and
    stops her mouth so, it shows like a cloth-stopple in a cream pot; I
    have fair hope of her teeth now, Sordido.   95

SORDIDO Why then, y'have all well, sir; for aught I see, she's right
    and straight enough, now as she stands. They'll commonly lie
    crookèd, that's no matter: wise gamesters° never find fault with
    that, let'em lie still so.

WARD I'd fain mark how she goes, and then I have all. For of all   100
    creatures I cannot abide a splay-footed° woman, she's an unlucky
    thing to meet in a morning; her heels keep together so, as if she
    were beginning an Irish dance still, and the wriggling of her bum
    playing the tune to't. But I have bethought a cleanly shift to find it:
    dab down° as you see me, and peep of one side, when her back's   105
    toward you; I'll show you the way.

SORDIDO And you shall find me apt enough to peeping,
    I have been one of them has seen mad sights
    Under your scaffolds.

WARD [*to Isabella*]   Will it please you walk, forsooth,°
    A turn or two by yourself? You are so pleasing to me,   110
    I take delight to view you on both sides.

ISABELLA I shall be glad to fetch a walk to your love, sir;
    'Twill get affection a good stomach, sir.
    [*Aside*] Which I had need have, to fall to such coarse victuals.°
    [*She walks around. Ward and Sordido peer up her skirt*]

WARD Now go thy ways for a clean-treading wench,°   115
    As ever man in modesty peeped under.
SORDIDO I see the sweetest sight to please my master:
    Never went Frenchman righter upon ropes
    Than she on Florentine rushes.
WARD [*to Isabella*]   'Tis enough, forsooth.°
ISABELLA And how do you like me now, sir?
WARD   'Faith, so well,   120
    I never mean to part with thee, sweetheart,
    Under some sixteen children, and all boys.
ISABELLA You'll be at simple pains, if you prove kind,°
    And breed 'em all in your teeth.
WARD   Nay by my faith,°
    What serves your belly for? 'Twould make my cheeks   125
    Look like blown bagpipes.
        Enter Guardiano
GUARDIANO   How now, ward and nephew.
    Gentlewoman and niece! Speak, is it so or not?
WARD 'Tis so, we are both agreed, sir.
GUARDIANO   In to your kindred, then;
    There's friends, and wine, and music waits to welcome you.
WARD Then I'll be drunk for joy.
SORDIDO   And I for company,   130
    I cannot break my nose in a better action.°
        Exeunt

4.1

Enter Bianca attended by two Ladies

BIANCA How goes your watches, ladies? What's o'clock now?°

1 LADY By mine, full nine.

2 LADY   By mine, a quarter past.

1 LADY I set mine by St Mark's.

2 LADY   St Anthony's, they say,°
Goes truer.

1 LADY   That's but your opinion, madam,
Because you love a gentleman o'th'name.   5

2 LADY He's a true gentleman, then.

1 LADY   So may he be
That comes to me tonight, for aught you know.

BIANCA I'll end this strife straight. I set mine by the sun,°
I love to set by th'best; one shall not then
Be troubled to set often.

2 LADY   You do wisely in't.   10

BIANCA If I should set my watch as some girls do
By ev'ry clock i'th'town, 'twould ne'er go true;
And too much turning of the dial's point,
Or tamp'ring with the spring, might in small time
Spoil the whole work too. Here it wants of nine now.°   15

1 LADY It does indeed, forsooth; mine's nearest truth yet.

2 LADY Yet I have found her lying with an advocate, which
    showed°
Like two false clocks together in one parish.

BIANCA So now I thank you, ladies, I desire
A while to be alone.

1 LADY   And I am nobody,   20
Methinks, unless I have one or other with me.°
'Faith, my desire and hers will ne'er be sisters.
            Exeunt Ladies

BIANCA How strangely woman's fortune comes about!
This was the farthest way to come to me,°
All would have judged, that knew me born in Venice   25
And there with many jealous eyes brought up,
That never thought they had me sure enough
But when they were upon me. Yet my hap°

To meet it here, so far off from my birth-place,
My friends, or kindred; 'tis not good, in sadness,°   30
To keep a maid so strict in her young days;
Restraint breeds wand'ring thoughts, as many fasting days
A great desire to see flesh stirring again.°
I'll ne'er use any girl of mine so strictly:
Howe'er they're kept, their fortunes find 'em out;   35
I see't in me: if they be got in court,
I'll never forbid 'em the country, nor the court,
Though they be born i'th'country; they will come to't
And fetch their falls a thousand mile about,°
Where one would little think on't.   40
          Enter Leantio
LEANTIO [*aside*] I long to see how my despiser looks,
     Now she's come here to court. These are her lodgings;
     She's simply now advanced. I took her out
     Of no such window, I remember, first:°
     That was a great deal lower, and less carved.   45
BIANCA [*aside*] How now? What silk-worm's this, i'th'name of
          pride?°
     What, is it he?
LEANTIO   A bow i'th'ham to your greatness;
     You must have now three legs, I take it, must you not?°
BIANCA Then I must take another, I shall want else
     The service I should have; you have but two there.   50
LEANTIO Y'are richly placed.
BIANCA   Methinks y'are wondrous brave,
          sir.°
LEANTIO A sumptuous lodging.
BIANCA   Y'have an excellent suit.
LEANTIO A chair of velvet.
BIANCA   Is your cloak lined through, sir?
LEANTIO Y'are very stately here.
BIANCA   Faith, something proud, sir.°
LEANTIO Stay, stay, let's see your cloth-of-silver slippers. 55
BIANCA Who's your shoemaker? H'as made you a neat boot.
LEANTIO Will you have a pair? The Duke will lend you spurs.°
BIANCA Yes, when I ride.
LEANTIO   'Tis a brave life you lead.
BIANCA I could ne'er see you in such good clothes
     In my time.

LEANTIO   In your time?

BIANCA   Sure, I think, sir,   60
  We both thrive best asunder.

LEANTIO   Y'are a whore!

BIANCA Fear nothing, sir.

LEANTIO   An impudent, spiteful strumpet!°

BIANCA Oh sir, you give me thanks for your captainship;
  I thought you had forgot all your good manners.

LEANTIO And to spite thee as much, look there, there read!   65
      [*Gives her a letter*]
  Vex, gnaw; thou shalt find there I am not love-starved.
  The world was never yet so cold, or pitiless,
  But there was ever still more charity found out
  Than at one proud fool's door; and 'twere hard, 'faith,
  If I could not pass that. Read to thy shame there;°   70
  A cheerful and a beauteous benefactor too,
  As e'er erected the good works of love.°

BIANCA [*aside*] Lady Livia!
  Is't possible? Her worship was my pandress.
  She dote, and send and give, and all to him!   75
  Why here's a bawd plagued home. [*To him*] Y'are simply happy,
      sir,°
  Yet I'll not envy you.

LEANTIO   No, court-saint, not thou!
  You keep some friend of a new fashion;°
  There's no harm in your devil, he's a suckling;°
  But he will breed teeth shortly, will he not?   80

BIANCA Take heed you play not then too long with him.

LEANTIO Yes, and the great one too. I shall find time°
  To play a hot religious bout with some of you,
  And perhaps drive you and your course of sins
  To their eternal kennels. I speak softly now,°   85
  'Tis manners in a noble woman's lodgings,
  And I well know all my degrees of duty.°
  But come I to your everlasting parting once,
  Thunder shall seem soft music to that tempest.

BIANCA 'Twas said last week there would be change of weather,   90
  When the moon hung so, and belike you heard it.°

LEANTIO Why, here's sin made, and ne'er a conscience put to't;
  A monster with all forehead, and no eyes.°
  Why do I talk to thee of sense or virtue,

That art as dark as death? And as much madness°   95
To set light before thee, as to lead blind folks
To see the monuments, which they may smell as soon
As they behold—marry, ofttimes their heads,
For want of light, may feel the hardness of 'em.°
So shall thy blind pride my revenge and anger,   100
That canst not see it now; and it may fall
At such an hour when thou least seest of all;
So to an ignorance darker than thy womb
I leave thy perjured soul: a plague will come!
          Exit [Leantio]
BIANCA Get you gone first, and then I fear no greater;   105
     Nor thee will I fear long; I'll have this sauciness
     Soon banished from these lodgings, and the rooms
     Perfumed well after the corrupt air it leaves:
     His breath has made me almost sick, in troth.
     A poor base start-up! Life! because h'as got   110
     Fair clothes by foul means, comes to rail, and show 'em.°
          Enter the Duke
DUKE Who's that?
BIANCA   Cry you mercy, sir.
DUKE   Prithee, who's that?
BIANCA The former thing, my lord, to whom you gave
     The captainship; he eats his meat with grudging still.
DUKE Still!
BIANCA   He comes vaunting here of his new love,   115
     And the new clothes she gave him. Lady Livia,
     Who but she now his mistress?
DUKE   Lady Livia?
     Be sure of what you say.
BIANCA   He showed me her name, sir,
     In perfumed paper, her vows, her letter,
     With an intent to spite me; so his heart said,   120
     And his threats made it good; they were as spiteful
     As ever malice uttered, and as dangerous,
     Should his hand follow the copy.
DUKE   But that must not;°
     Do not vex your mind, prithee to bed, go.
     And all shall be well and quiet.
BIANCA   I love peace, sir.   125
DUKE And so do all that love; take you no care for 't,°

It shall be still provided to your hand.
  Exit [*Bianca*]
Who's near us there?
  Enter Messenger
MESSENGER   My lord.
DUKE   Seek out Hippolito,
 Brother to Lady Livia, with all speed.
MESSENGER He was the last man I saw, my lord.
DUKE   Make haste.   130
  Exit [*Messenger*]
 He is a blood soon stirred, and as he's quick
 To apprehend a wrong, he's bold and sudden°
 In bringing forth a ruin. I know likewise
 The reputation of his sister's honour's
 As dear to him as life-blood to his heart.   135
 Beside, I'll flatter him with a goodness to her,°
 Which I now thought on, but ne'er meant to practise°
 (Because I know her base) and that wind drives him.
 The ulcerous reputation feels the poise°
 Of lightest wrongs, as sores are vexed with flies: 140
  Enter Hippolito
 He comes; Hippolito, welcome.
HIPPOLITO   My loved lord.
DUKE How does that lusty widow, thy kind sister?
 Is she not sped yet of a second husband?°
 A bed-fellow she has, I ask not that,
 I know she's sped of him.
HIPPOLITO   Of him, my lord?   145
DUKE Yes, of a bed-fellow; is the news so strange to you?
HIPPOLITO I hope 'tis so to all.
DUKE   I wish it were, sir,
 But 'tis confessed too fast; her ignorant pleasures,°
 Only by lust instructed, have received
 Into their services an impudent boaster:°   150
 One that does raise his glory from her shame,
 And tells the midday sun what's done in darkness—
 Yet blinded with her appetite, wastes her wealth,
 Buys her disgraces at a dearer rate
 Than bounteous house-keepers purchase their honour.°   155
 Nothing sads me so much, as that in love
 To thee, and to thy blood, I had picked out°

A worthy match for her, the great Vincentio,
High in our favour, and in all men's thoughts.

HIPPOLITO Oh thou destruction of all happy fortunes,   160
Unsated blood! Know you the name, my lord,°
Of her abuser?

DUKE   One Leantio.

HIPPOLITO He's a factor!

DUKE   He ne'er made so brave a voyage
By his own talk.

HIPPOLITO   The poor old widow's son;
I humbly take my leave.

DUKE [aside]   I see 'tis done.   165
[To him] Give her good counsel, make her see her error,
I know she'll hearken to you.

HIPPOLITO   Yes, my lord,
I make no doubt, as I shall take the course
Which she shall never know till it be acted;
And when she wakes to honour, then she'll thank me for't.   170
I'll imitate the pities of old surgeons°
To this lost limb, who ere they show their art
Cast one asleep, then cut the diseased part.
So out of love to her I pity most,
She shall not feel him going till he's lost;   175
Then she'll commend the cure.
            Exit [Hippolito]

DUKE   The great cure's past;°
I count this done already. His wrath's sure,
And speaks an injury deep; farewell, Leantio,°
This place will never hear thee murmur more.
            Enter Lord Cardinal attended
Our noble brother, welcome.

CARDINAL   Set those lights down;   180
Depart till you be called.
            [Exeunt Attendants]

DUKE [aside]   There's serious business
Fixed in his look; nay, it inclines a little
To the dark colour of a discontentment.
[To him] Brother, what is't commands your eye so powerfully?
Speak, you seem lost.

CARDINAL   The thing I look on seems so,°   185
To my eyes lost for ever.

DUKE   You look on me.
CARDINAL What a grief 'tis to a religious feeling
    To think a man should have a friend so goodly,
    So wise, so noble, nay, a duke, a brother,
    And all this certainly damned!
DUKE   How?
CARDINAL   'Tis no wonder,   190
    If your great sin can do't. Dare you look up
    For thinking of a vengeance? Dare you sleep°
    For fear of never waking but to death,
    And dedicate unto a strumpet's love
    The strength of your affections, zeal and health?   195
    Here you stand now; can you assure your pleasures
    You shall once more enjoy her, but once more?
    Alas, you cannot; what a misery 'tis then
    To be more certain of eternal death
    Than of a next embrace! Nay, shall I show you   200
    How more unfortunate you stand in sin
    Than the low private man? All his offences,°
    Like enclosed grounds, keep but about himself,°
    And seldom stretch beyond his own soul's bounds;
    And when a man grows miserable, 'tis some comfort   205
    When he's no further charged than with himself; °
    'Tis a sweet ease to wretchedness. But, great man,
    Ev'ry sin thou commit'st shows like a flame
    Upon a mountain; 'tis seen far about,
    And with a big wind made of popular breath°   210
    The sparkles fly through cities—here one takes,
    Another catches there, and in short time
    Waste all to cinders. But remember still,
    What burnt the valleys first came from the hill.
    Ev'ry offence draws his particular pain,   215
    But 'tis example proves the great man's bane:°
    The sins of mean men lie like scattered parcels
    Of an unperfect bill; but when such fall,°
    Then comes example, and that sums up all.°
    And this your reason grants. If men of good lives,   220
    Who by their virtuous actions stir up others
    To noble and religious imitation,
    Receive the greater glory after death
    (As sin must needs confess) what may they feel

In height of torments, and in weight of vengeance,   225
  Not only they themselves not doing well,
  But sets a light up to show men to hell?°
DUKE If you have done, I have; no more, sweet brother.
CARDINAL I know time spent in goodness is too tedious;
  This had not been a moment's space in lust now.   230
  How dare you venture on eternal pain
  That cannot bear a minute's reprehension?°
  Methinks you should endure to hear that talked of
  Which you so strive to suffer. Oh my brother!
  What were you, if you were taken now?°   235
  My heart weeps blood to think on't; 'tis a work
  Of infinite mercy you can never merit
  That yet you are not death-struck, no, not yet—
  I dare not stay you long, for fear you should not°
  Have time enough allowed you to repent in.   240
  There's but this wall between you and destruction,°
  When y'are at strongest, and but poor thin clay.
  Think upon't, brother; can you come so near it°
  For a fair strumpet's love? And fall into
  A torment that knows neither end nor bottom   245
  For beauty, but the deepness of a skin,
  And that not of their own neither? Is she a thing°
  Whom sickness dare not visit, or age look on,
  Or death resist? Does the worm shun her grave?
  If not (as your soul knows it) why should lust   250
  Bring man to lasting pain, for rotten dust?
DUKE Brother of spotless honour, let me weep
  The first of my repentance in thy bosom,
  And show the blest fruits of a thankful spirit;
  And if I e'er keep woman more unlawfully,   255
  May I want penitence at my greatest need—
  And wise men know there is no barren place
  Threatens more famine, than a dearth in grace.°
CARDINAL Why, here's a conversion at this time, brother,
  Sung for a hymn in Heaven; and at this instant°   260
  The powers of darkness groan, makes all Hell sorry.
  First I praise Heaven, then in my work I glory.°
  Who's there attends without?
       Enter Servants
SERVANTS   My lord!

CARDINAL Take up those lights; there was a thicker darkness,
⠀⠀When they came first. The peace of a fair soul ⠀⠀⠀⠀⠀⠀⠀265
⠀⠀Keep with my noble brother.
⠀⠀⠀⠀⠀*Exit Cardinal [and Servants]*
DUKE⠀⠀⠀⠀⠀⠀⠀⠀⠀⠀⠀⠀⠀⠀Joys be with you, sir.
⠀⠀She lies alone tonight for't, and must still,
⠀⠀Though it be hard to conquer; but I have vowed°
⠀⠀Never to know her as a strumpet more,
⠀⠀And I must save my oath. If fury fail not,° ⠀⠀⠀⠀⠀⠀⠀270
⠀⠀Her husband dies tonight, or at the most
⠀⠀Lives not to see the morning spent tomorrow;°
⠀⠀Then will I make her lawfully mine own,
⠀⠀Without this sin and horror. Now I'm chidden,
⠀⠀For what I shall enjoy then unforbidden, ⠀⠀⠀⠀⠀⠀⠀275
⠀⠀And I'll not freeze in stoves. 'Tis but a while,°
⠀⠀Live like a hopeful bridegroom, chaste from flesh;
⠀⠀And pleasure then will seem new, fair and fresh.
⠀⠀⠀⠀⠀*Exit*

4.2

⠀⠀⠀⠀*Enter Hippolito*
HIPPOLITO The morning so far wasted, yet his baseness so
⠀⠀⠀impudent?
⠀⠀See if the very sun do not blush at him!
⠀⠀Dare he do thus much, and know me alive?
⠀⠀Put case one must be vicious, as I know myself
⠀⠀Monstrously guilty, there's a blind time made for't;° ⠀⠀⠀⠀5
⠀⠀He might use only that, 'twere conscionable—°
⠀⠀Art, silence, closeness, subtlety, and darkness°
⠀⠀Are fit for such a business; but there's no pity
⠀⠀To be bestowed on an apparent sinner,°
⠀⠀An impudent daylight lecher! The great zeal ⠀⠀⠀⠀⠀⠀10
⠀⠀I bear to her advancement in this match
⠀⠀With Lord Vincentio, as the Duke has wrought it
⠀⠀To the perpetual honour of our house,
⠀⠀Puts fire into my blood, to purge the air
⠀⠀Of this corruption, fear it spread too far,° ⠀⠀⠀⠀⠀⠀⠀15
⠀⠀And poison the whole hopes of this fair fortune.

I love her good so dearly, that no brother
Shall venture farther for a sister's glory,
Than I for her preferment.
    Enter Leantio and a Page

LEANTIO   Once again
I'll see that glist'ring whore, shines like a serpent°   20
Now the court's sun's upon her. Page!

PAGE   Anon, sir.

LEANTIO I'll go in state too. [*To Page*] See the coach be ready.°
I'll hurry away presently.
    [*Exit Page*]

HIPPOLITO   Yes, you shall hurry,
And the devil after you; take that at setting forth. [*Strikes him*]
Now, an you'll draw, we are upon equal terms, sir:°   25
Thou took'st advantage of my name in honour
Upon my sister—I ne'er saw the stroke
Come, till I found my reputation bleeding;
And therefore count it I no sin to valour°
To serve thy lust so. Now we are of even hand,   30
Take your best course against me. You must die.°

LEANTIO How close sticks envy to man's happiness!
When I was poor, and little cared for life,
I had no such means offered me to die;
No man's wrath minded me. [*Draws his sword*] Slave, I turn this to
    thee,   35
To call thee to account for a wound lately
Of a base stamp upon me.°

HIPPOLITO   'Twas most fit
For a base mettle. Come and fetch one now°
More noble then, for I will use thee fairer
Than thou hast done thine own soul, or our honour.°   40
    [*They fight, and Leantio is wounded*]
And there, I think, 'tis for thee.

[VOICES] (*within*)   Help, help, oh part'em.

LEANTIO False wife! I feel now th'hast prayed heartily for me.
Rise, strumpet, by my fall; thy lust may reign now;
My heart-string and the marriage-knot that tied thee°
Breaks both together. [*Dies*]

HIPPOLITO   There I heard the sound on't,   45
And never liked string better.
    Enter Guardiano, Livia, Isabella, Ward and Sordido

LIVIA   'Tis my brother;°
  Are you hurt, sir?
HIPPOLITO   Not anything.
LIVIA   Blessed fortune;
  Shift for thyself. What is he thou hast killed?°
HIPPOLITO Our honour's enemy.
GUARDIANO   Know you this man, lady?
LIVIA Leantio? My love's joy? [*To Hippolito*] Wounds stick upon thee   50
  As deadly as thy sins; art thou not hurt?
  The devil take that fortune. And he dead!
  Drop plagues into thy bowels without voice,°
  Secret and fearful. [*To others*] Run for officers,
  Let him be apprehended with all speed,   55
  For fear he 'scape away; lay hands on him,
  We cannot be too sure; 'tis wilful murder!°
  You do Heaven's vengeance and the law just service—
  You know him not as I do: he's a villain,
  As monstrous as a prodigy and as dreadful.°   60
HIPPOLITO Will you but entertain a noble patience,
  Till you but hear the reason, worthy sister?
LIVIA The reason! That's a jest Hell falls a-laughing at:
  Is there a reason found for the destruction
  Of our more lawful loves? And there was none°   65
  To kill the black lust 'twixt thy niece and thee,
  That has kept close so long?°
GUARDIANO   How's that, good madam?
LIVIA Too true, sir, there she stands, let her deny't;
  The deed cries shortly in the midwife's arms,
  Unless the parents' sins strike it still-born—   70
  And if you be not deaf and ignorant,°
  You'll hear strange notes ere long. [*To Isabella*] Look upon me,
    wench!°
  'Twas I betrayed thy honour subtly to him
  Under a false tale; it lights upon me now;
  His arm has paid me home upon thy breast,°   75
  My sweet, beloved Leantio!
GUARDIANO [*aside*]   Was my judgement
  And care in choice so dev'lishly abused,
  So beyond shamefully? All the world will grin at me.
WARD Oh Sordido, Sordido, I'm damned, I'm damned!
SORDIDO Damned, why sir?   80

147

WARD One of the wicked; dost not see't? A cuckold, a plain reprobate
    cuckold.°

SORDIDO Nay, an you be damned for that, be of good cheer, sir, y'have
    gallant company of all professions; I'll have a wife next Sunday°
    too, because I'll along with you myself.   85

WARD That will be some comfort yet.

LIVIA [to Guardiano] You, sir, that bear your load of injuries,
    As I of sorrows, lend me your grieved strength
    To this sad burden, who in life wore actions,°
    Flames were not nimbler. We will talk of things°   90
    May have the luck to break our hearts together.

GUARDIANO I'll list to nothing but revenge and anger°
    Whose counsels I will follow.

            Exeunt Livia and Guardiano [with Leantio's body]

SORDIDO   A wife, quotha!
    Here's a sweet plum-tree of your guardiner's graffing!°

WARD Nay, there's a worse name belongs to this fruit yet, and you   95
    could hit on't; a more open one. For he that marries a whore looks
    like a fellow bound all his lifetime to a medlar-tree;° and that's good
    stuff, 'tis no sooner ripe, but it looks rotten—and so do some
    queans at nineteen. A pox on't, I thought there was some knavery
    abroach,° for something stirred in her belly, the first night I lay   100
    with her.

SORDIDO What, what, sir?

WARD This is she brought up so courtly! Can sing, and dance—and
    tumble° too, methinks. I'll never marry wife again that has so many
    qualities.   105

SORDIDO Indeed they are seldom good, master; for likely when they
    are taught so many, they will have one trick more of their own
    finding out. Well, give me a wench but with one good quality, to lie
    with none but her husband, and that's bringing-up enough for any
    woman breathing.   110

WARD This was the fault, when she was tendered to me; you never
    looked to this.

SORDIDO Alas, how would you have me see through a great farthin-
    gale, sir? I cannot peep through a millstone,° or in the going, to see
    what's done i'th'bottom.°   ~ 115

WARD Her father praised her breast, sh'had the voice forsooth; I mar-
    velled she sung so small indeed, being no maid.° Now I perceive
    there's a young chorister in her belly—this breeds a singing in my
    head,° I'm sure.

SORDIDO 'Tis but the tune of your wives' cinquepace,° danced in a   120
    feather-bed. 'Faith, go lie down, master—[*aside*] but take heed
    your horns do not make holes in the pillowbeers. I would not batter
    brows with him for a hogshead of angels,° he would prick my skull
    as full of holes as a scrivener's sand-box.°
       Exeunt Ward and Sordido
ISABELLA [*aside*] Was ever maid so cruelly beguiled   125
    To the confusion of life, soul, and honour,°
    All of one woman's murd'ring? I'd fain bring
    Her name no nearer to my blood than woman,
    And 'tis too much of that. Oh shame and horror!
    In that small distance from yon man to me°   130
    Lies sin enough to make a whole world perish.
    [*To Hippolito*] 'Tis time we parted, sir, and left the sight
    Of one another; nothing can be worse
    To hurt repentance; for our very eyes°
    Are far more poisonous to religion   135
    Than basilisks to them. If any goodness
    Rest in you, hope of comforts, fear of judgements,
    My request is I ne'er may see you more;
    And so I turn me from you everlastingly,
    So is my hope to miss you. [*Aside*] But for her°   140
    That durst so dally with a sin so dangerous,
    And lay a snare so spitefully for my youth,
    If the least means but favour my revenge,°
    That I may practice the like cruel cunning
    Upon her life as she has on mine honour,   145
    I'll act it without pity.
HIPPOLITO   Here's a care
    Of reputation, and a sister's fortune
    Sweetly rewarded by her. Would a silence,
    As great as that which keeps among the graves,
    Had everlastingly chained up her tongue;   150
    My love to her has made mine miserable.
       Enter Guardiano and Livia [*who talk aside*]
GUARDIANO If you can but dissemble your heart's griefs now,
    Be but a woman so far.
LIVIA   Peace! I'll strive, sir.°
GUARDIANO As I can wear my injuries in a smile,°
    Here's an occasion offered that gives anger   155
    Both liberty and safety to perform

Things worth the fire it holds, without the fear
Of danger or of law; for mischiefs acted
Under the privilege of a marriage-triumph°
At the Duke's hasty nuptials, will be thought   160
Things merely accidental—all's by chance,°
Not got of their own natures.

LIVIA   I conceive you, sir,°
Even to a longing for performance on't;
And here behold some fruits.

[*Kneels before Hippolito and Isabella*]
                                    Forgive me both;
What I am now, returned to sense and judgement,   165
Is not the same rage and distraction
Presented lately to you; that rude form
Is gone for ever. I am now myself,
That speaks all peace and friendship; and these tears
Are the true springs of hearty, penitent sorrow   170
For those foul wrongs, which my forgetful fury
Slandered your virtues with. This gentleman
Is well resolved now.

GUARDIANO   I was never otherways;°
I knew, alas, 'twas but your anger spake it,
And I ne'er thought on't more.

HIPPOLITO   Pray rise, good sister.   175

ISABELLA [*aside*] Here's e'en as sweet amends made for a wrong now,
As one that gives a wound, and pays the surgeon;
All the smart's nothing, the great loss of blood,
Or time of hindrance. Well, I had a mother,°
I can dissemble too. [*To Livia*] What wrongs have slipped   180
Through anger's ignorance, aunt, my heart forgives.

GUARDIANO Why, this is tuneful now!

HIPPOLITO   And what I did, sister,°
Was all for honour's cause, which time to come
Will approve to you.

LIVIA   Being awaked to goodness,°
I understand so much, sir, and praise now   185
The fortune of your arm, and of your safety;
For by his death y'have rid me of a sin
As costly as e'er woman doted on.
T'has pleased the Duke so well too, that (behold, sir)
H'as sent you here your pardon [*gives him a letter*] which I kissed   190

With most affectionate comfort. When 'twas brought°
Then was my fit just past; it came so well, methought,
To glad my heart.
HIPPOLITO   I see his Grace thinks on me.
LIVIA There's no talk now but of the preparation
For the great marriage.
HIPPOLITO   Does he marry her, then?   195
LIVIA With all speed, suddenly, as fast as cost
Can be laid on with many thousand hands.
This gentleman and I had once a purpose
To have honoured the first marriage of the Duke
With an invention of his own; 'twas ready,°   200
The pains well past, most of the charge bestowed on't,°
Then came the death of your good mother, niece,
And turned the glory of it all to black.
'Tis a device would fit these times so well too,°
Art's treasury not better; if you'll join,   205
It shall be done, the cost shall all be mine.
HIPPOLITO Y'have my voice first, 'twill well approve my
    thankfulness°
For the Duke's love and favour.
LIVIA   What say you, niece?
ISABELLA I am content to make one.
GUARDIANO   The plot's full then;°
Your pages, madam, will make shift for Cupids.   210
LIVIA That will they, sir.
GUARDIANO   You'll play your old part still.
LIVIA What is't? Good troth, I have e'en forgot it,
GUARDIANO Why, Juno Pronuba, the marriage-goddess.°
LIVIA 'Tis right indeed.
GUARDIANO [to Isabella] And you shall play the nymph
That offers sacrifice to appease her wrath.   215
ISABELLA Sacrifice, good sir?
LIVIA   Must I be appeased, then?
GUARDIANO That's as you list yourself, as you see cause.
LIVIA Methinks 'twould show the more state in her deity
To be incensed.
ISABELLA   'Twould, but my sacrifice°
Shall take a course to appease you, or I'll fail in't—   220
[Aside] And teach a sinful bawd to play a goddess.
GUARDIANO For our parts, we'll not be ambitious, sir;

Please you walk in, and see the project drawn,
Then take your choice.
HIPPOLITO   I weigh not, so I have one.°
    Exeunt [Isabella, Guardiano and Hippolito]
LIVIA How much ado have I to restrain fury   225
From breaking into curses! Oh how painful 'tis
To keep great sorrow smothered! Sure I think
'Tis harder to dissemble grief than love.
Leantio, here the weight of thy loss lies,°
Which nothing but destruction can suffice.   230
    Exit

4.3

Hoboys. Enter in great state the Duke and Bianca, richly attired,
with Lords, Cardinals, Ladies, and other Attendants; they pass
solemnly over.° Enter Lord Cardinal in a rage, seeming to break
off the ceremony

CARDINAL Cease, cease! Religious honours done to sin
Disparage virtue's reverence, and will pull
Heaven's thunder upon Florence—holy ceremonies
Were made for sacred uses, not for sinful.
Are these the fruits of your repentance, brother?   5
Better it had been you had never sorrowed
Than to abuse the benefit, and return
To worse than where sin left you.
Vowed you then never to keep strumpet more,
And are you now so swift in your desires   10
To knit your honours and your life fast to her?
Is not sin sure enough to wretched man,°
But he must bind himself in chains to't? Worse!
Must marriage, that immaculate robe of honour,
That renders virtue glorious, fair, and fruitful   15
To her great master, be now made the garment°
Of leprosy and foulness? Is this penitence,
To sanctify hot lust? What is it otherways
Than worship done to devils? Is this the best
Amends that sin can make after her riots?   20
As if a drunkard, to appease Heaven's wrath,

Should offer up his surfeit for a sacrifice?°
If that be comely, then lust's offerings are
On wedlock's sacred altar.

DUKE   Here y'are bitter
Without cause, brother. What I vowed, I keep   25
As safe as your conscience, and this needs not—°
I taste more wrath in't, than I do religion,
And envy more than goodness. The path now
I tread is honest, leads to lawful love,
Which virtue in her strictness would not check.   30
I vowed no more to keep a sensual woman:
'Tis done; I mean to make a lawful wife of her.

CARDINAL He that taught you that craft,°
Call him not master long: he will undo you.
Grow not too cunning for your soul, good brother;   35
Is it enough to use adulterous thefts,
And then take sanctuary in marriage?
I grant, so long as an offender keeps
Close in a privileged temple, his life's safe;°
But if he ever venture to come out,   40
And so be taken, then he surely dies for't.
So now y'are safe; but when you leave this body,
Man's only privileged temple upon earth,
In which the guilty soul takes sanctuary,
Then you'll perceive what wrongs chaste vows endure,   45
When lust usurps the bed that should be pure.

BIANCA Sir, I have read you over this while°
In silence, and I find great knowledge in you,
And severe learning; yet 'mongst all your virtues°
I see not charity written, which some call   50
The first-born of religion, and I wonder°
I cannot see't in yours. Believe it, sir,
There is no virtue can be sooner missed
Or later welcomed; it begins the rest,
And sets 'em all in order. Heaven and angels   55
Take great delight in a converted sinner;
Why should you then, a servant and professor,°
Differ so much from them? If ev'ry woman
That commits evil should be therefore kept
Back in desires of goodness, how should virtue   60
Be known and honoured? From a man that's blind

153

To take a burning taper, 'tis no wrong;
He never misses it. But to take light
From one that sees, that's injury and spite.
Pray, whether is religion better served,°   65
When lives that are licentious are made honest,
Than when they still run through a sinful blood?
'Tis nothing virtue's temples to deface,
But build the ruins, there's a work of grace.°
DUKE I kiss thee for that spirit; thou hast praised thy wit   70
A modest way. On, on there!
      Hoboys. [Exeunt Duke, Bianca and Attendants]
CARDINAL   Lust is bold,
And will have vengeance speak, ere't be controlled.°
      Exit

5.1

Enter Guardiano and Ward

GUARDIANO Speak, hast thou any sense of thy abuse? Dost thou know what wrong's done thee?

WARD I were an ass else—I cannot wash my face, but I am feeling° on't.

GUARDIANO Here take this galtrop, then; convey it secretly into the place I showed you; look you, sir, this is the trap-door° to't. 5

WARD I know't of old, uncle, since the last triumph;° here rose up a devil with one eye, I remember, with a company of fireworks° at's tail.

GUARDIANO Prithee leave squibbing° now, mark me, and fail not; but when thou hear'st me give a stamp, down with't—the villain's caught then. 10

WARD If I miss you, hang me; I love to catch a villain, and your stamp shall go current I warrant you. But how shall I rise up and let him down too, all at one hole?° That will be a horrible puzzle. You know 15 I have a part in't, I play Slander.

GUARDIANO True, but never make you ready for't.

WARD No? My clothes are bought and all, and a foul fiend's head with a long contumelious tongue i'th'chaps on't,° a very fit shape for Slander i'th'out-parishes.° 20

GUARDIANO It shall not come so far, thou understand'st it not.°

WARD Oh, oh!

GUARDIANO He shall lie deep enough ere that time, and stick first upon those.

[Indicates the points of the galtrop]

WARD Now I conceive you, guardiner. 25

GUARDIANO Away, list to the privy stamp, that's all thy part.

WARD Stamp° my horns in a mortar if I miss you, and give the powder in white wine to sick cuckolds; a very present remedy for the headache.°

Exit [Ward]

GUARDIANO If this should any way miscarry now, 30
(As, if the fool be nimble enough, 'tis certain)°
The pages that present the swift-winged Cupids°
Are taught to hit him with their shafts of love
(Fitting his part) which I have cunningly poisoned.°

He cannot 'scape my fury; and those ills   35
Will be laid all on fortune, not our wills.
That's all the sport on't; for who will imagine,
That at the celebration of this night
Any mischance that haps can flow from spite?
    Exit

5.2

Flourish. Enter above° Duke, Bianca, Lord Cardinal,
Fabritio, and other Cardinals, Lords and Ladies in state
DUKE Now our fair duchess, your delight shall witness
How y'are beloved and honoured; all the glories
Bestowed upon the gladness of this night
Are done for your bright sake.
BIANCA   I am the more
In debt, my lord, to loves and courtesies   5
That offer up themselves so bounteously
To do me honoured grace, without my merit.°
DUKE A goodness set in greatness; how it sparkles
Afar off, like pure diamonds set in gold!
How perfect my desires were, might I witness   10
But a fair noble peace 'twixt your two spirits!°
The reconcilement would be more sweet to me
Than longer life to him that fears to die.
[*To Lord Cardinal*] Good sir?
CARDINAL   I profess peace, and am content.
DUKE I'll see the seal upon't, and then 'tis firm.°   15
CARDINAL You shall have all you wish. [*Kisses Bianca*]
DUKE   I have all indeed now.
BIANCA [*aside*] But I have made surer work; this shall not blind
    me.°
He that begins so early to reprove,
Quickly rid him or look for little love.
Beware a brother's envy; he's next heir too.   20
Cardinal, you die this night, the plot's laid surely—
In time of sports death may steal in securely,
Then 'tis least thought on.
For he that's most religious, holy friend,°

Does not at all hours think upon his end;   25
He has his times of frailty, and his thoughts
Their transportations too, through flesh and blood°
(For all his zeal, his learning, and his light)
As well as we, poor soul, that sin by night.
    [*Fabritio hands the Duke a paper*]°
DUKE What's this, Fabritio?
FABRITIO   Marry, my lord, the model°   30
Of what's presented.
DUKE   Oh we thank their loves;
    Sweet Duchess, take your seat, list to the argument.°
    [*Reads*] 'There is a nymph that haunts the woods and springs,
    In love with two at once, and they with her.
    Equal it runs; but to decide these things,   35
    The cause to mighty Juno they refer,
    She being the marriage-goddess. The two lovers
    They offer sighs, the nymph a sacrifice,
    All to please Juno, who by signs discovers
    How the event shall be; so that strife dies.°   40
    Then springs a second; for the man refused
    Grows discontent, and out of love abused,°
    He raises Slander up, like a black fiend,
    To disgrace th'other, which pays him i'th'end.'°
BIANCA In troth, my lord, a pretty pleasing argument,   45
    And fits th'occasion well; Envy and Slander
    Are things soon raised against two faithful lovers;
    But comfort is, they are not long unrewarded.
        Music
DUKE This music shows they're upon entrance now.
BIANCA [*aside*] Then enter all my wishes!   50
        Enter Hymen in yellow, Ganymede in a blue robe powdered with
        stars, and Hebe in a white robe with golden stars, with covered
        cups in their hands. They dance a short dance, then bowing to the
        Duke &c., Hymen speaks
HYMEN [*giving Bianca a cup*] 'To thee, fair bride, Hymen offers up
    Of nuptial joys this the celestial cup.
    Taste it, and thou shalt ever find
    Love in thy bed, peace in thy mind.'
BIANCA We'll taste you, sure, 'twere pity to disgrace   55
    So pretty a beginning.

DUKE   'Twas spoke nobly.
GANYMEDE *'Two cups of nectar have we begged from Jove;*
    Hebe, give that to innocence, I this to love.'
       [Hebe gives a cup to the Cardinal, Ganymede one to the Duke.
       Both drink]
    'Take heed of stumbling more, look to your way;
    Remember still the Via Lactea.'°   60
HEBE *'Well, Ganymede, you have more faults, though not so known;*
    I spilled one cup, but you have filched many a one.'
HYMEN *'No more, forbear for Hymen's sake;*
    In love we met, and so let's parting take.'°
       Exeunt [Masque characters]
DUKE But soft! Here's no such persons in the argument   65
    As these three, Hymen, Hebe, Ganymede.
    The actors that this model here discovers
    Are only four, Juno, a nymph, two lovers.
BIANCA This is some antemasque belike, my lord,°
    To entertain time. Now my peace is perfect,°   70
    Let sports come on apace. Now is their time, my lord: *Music*
    Hark you, you hear from'em!
DUKE   The nymph indeed!
    Enter two dressed like Nymphs, bearing two tapers lighted; then
    Isabella dressed with flowers and garlands, bearing a censer with
    fire in it; they set the censer and tapers on Juno's altar with much
    reverence; this ditty being sung in parts°

DITTY

    Juno, nuptial goddess,
    Thou that rul'st o'er coupled bodies,
    Tiest man to woman, never to forsake her,   75
    Thou only powerful marriage-maker,
    Pity this amazed affection;°
    I love both, and both love me;
    Nor know I where to give rejection,
    My heart likes so equally,   80
    Till thou set'st right my peace of life,
    And with thy power conclude this strife.

ISABELLA *[to the Nymphs]* 'Now with my thanks depart you to the
    springs,°

I to these wells of love.'
        [*Exeunt Nymphs*]
                            'Thou sacred goddess,
And queen of nuptials, daughter to great Saturn,   85
Sister and wife to Jove, imperial Juno,
Pity this passionate conflict in my breast,
This tedious war 'twixt two affections;
Crown one with victory, and my heart's at peace.'°

        Enter Hippolito and Guardiano, like shepherds
HIPPOLITO *'Make me that happy man, thou mighty goddess.'*   90
GUARDIANO *'But I live most in hope, if truest love*
    Merit the greatest comfort.'
ISABELLA   *'I love both*
    With such an even and fair affection
    I know not which to speak for, which to wish for,
    Till thou, great arbitress 'twixt lovers' hearts,   95
    By thy auspicious grace, design the man;°
    Which pity I implore.'
BOTH [*Hippolito and Guardiano*] *'We all implore it.'*
        Livia descends like Juno [accompanied by Cupids with bows]°
ISABELLA *'And after sighs, contrition's truest odours,*
    I offer to thy powerful deity   100
    This precious incense; may it ascend peacefully—'
        [*The incense sends up a poisoned smoke*]
    [*Aside*] And if it keeps true touch, my good aunt Juno,°
    'Twill try your immortality ere't be long; °
    I fear you'll never get so nigh heaven again,
    When you're once down.
LIVIA   *'Though you and your affections*   105
    Seem all as dark to our illustrious brightness°
    As night's inheritance, hell, we pity you,
    And your requests are granted. You ask signs;
    They shall be given you, we'll be gracious to you.
    He of those twain which we determine for you   110
    Love's arrows shall wound twice; the later wound
    Betokens love in age, for so are all
    Whose love continues firmly all their life-time
    Twice wounded at their marriage; else affection
    Dies when youth ends.' [*Aside*] This savour overcomes me.°   115

[As Juno] 'Now for a sign of wealth and golden days,
Bright-eyed prosperity which all couples love,
Ay, and makes love, take that—'
    [Throws flaming gold upon Isabella, who dies]
                  'Our brother Jove°
Never denies us of his burning treasure,
T'express bounty.'

DUKE   She falls down upon't,   120
What's the conceit of that?

FABRITIO   As overjoyed, belike.°
Too much prosperity overjoys us all,
And she has her lapful it seems, my lord.°

DUKE This swerves a little from the argument, though:°
Look you, my lords!   125

GUARDIANO All's fast; now comes my part to tole him hither;°
Then with a stamp given, he's dispatched as cunningly.
    [Hippolito discovers Isabella dead]

HIPPOLITO Stark dead. O treachery, cruelly made away!
    [Hippolito stamps. Guardiano falls through the trap-door]
                  How's that?°

FABRITIO Look, there's one of the lovers dropped away too.   130

DUKE Why, sure this plot's drawn false, here's no such thing.

LIVIA Oh I am sick to th'death, let me down quickly;
This fume is deadly. Oh 'thas poisoned me!
My subtlety is sped, her art has quitted me;°
My own ambition pulls me down to ruin. *[Falls and dies]°*   135

HIPPOLITO Nay, then I kiss thy cold lips, and applaud
This thy revenge in death. *[Kisses the dead Isabella]*

FABRITIO Look, Juno's down too. *Cupids shoot [at Hippolito]*
What makes she there? Her pride should keep aloft;
She was wont to scorn the earth in other shows—°
Methinks her peacocks' feathers are much pulled.°   140

HIPPOLITO Oh death runs through my blood; in a wild flame too.
Plague of those Cupids. Some lay hold on'em;
Let'em not 'scape, they have spoiled me; the shaft's deadly.°

DUKE I have lost myself in this quite.

HIPPOLITO My great lords, we are all confounded.

DUKE   How?   145

HIPPOLITO Dead; and I worse. *[Hippolito points to Isabella's body]°*

FABRITIO   Dead? My girl dead? I hope
My sister Juno has not served me so.

HIPPOLITO Lust and forgetfulness has been amongst us,°
    And we are brought to nothing. Some blest charity
    Lend me the speeding pity of his sword   150
    To quench this fire in blood. Leantio's death°
    Has brought all this upon us—now I taste it—°
    And made us lay plots to confound each other.
    The event so proves it, and man's understanding°
    Is riper at his fall than all his life-time.   155
    She, in a madness for her lover's death,
    Revealed a fearful lust in our near bloods,°
    For which I am punished dreadfully and unlooked for;
    Proved her own ruin too: vengeance met vengeance
    Like a set match, as if the plagues of sin°   160
    Had been agreed to meet here altogether.
    But how her fawning partner fell, I reach not,°
    Unless caught by some springe of his own setting;
    For, on my pain, he never dreamed of dying,
    The plot was all his own, and he had cunning   165
    Enough to save himself—but 'tis the property
    Of guilty deeds to draw your wise men downward.°
    Therefore the wonder ceases. Oh this torment!
DUKE Our guard below there!
       Enter a Lord with a Guard°
LORD   My lord.
HIPPOLITO   Run and meet death then,
    And cut off time and pain. [*Runs on Guard's halberd and dies*]°
LORD   Behold, my lord,   170
    H'as run his breast upon a weapon's point.
DUKE Upon the first night of our nuptial honours
    Destruction plays her triumph, and great mischiefs
    Mask in expected pleasures; 'tis prodigious!°
    They're things most fearfully ominous, I like 'em not.   175
    [*To Guards*] Remove these ruined bodies from our eyes.
       [*Guards remove bodies*]
BIANCA [*aside*] Not yet, no change? When falls he to the earth?°
LORD Please but your Excellence to peruse that paper,
    Which is a brief confession from the heart
    Of him that fell first, ere his soul departed;°   180
    And there the darkness of these deeds speaks plainly.
    'Tis the full scope, the manner, and intent;
    His ward, that ignorantly let him down,

Fear put to present flight at the voice of him.°
BIANCA [*aside*] Nor yet?
DUKE [*to Lord Cardinal*] Read, read; for I am lost in sight and
    strength.   185
CARDINAL My noble brother!
BIANCA   Oh the curse of wretchedness!
    My deadly hand is fallen upon my lord.
    Destruction take me to thee; give me way;°
    The pains and plagues of a lost soul upon him
    That hinders me a moment!   190
DUKE My heart swells bigger yet; help here, break't ope,°
    My breast flies open next. [*Dies*]
BIANCA   Oh, with the poison
    That was prepared for thee, thee, Cardinal!
    'Twas meant for thee.
CARDINAL   Poor Prince!
BIANCA   Accursed error!
    Give me thy last breath, thou infected bosom,   195
    And wrap two spirits in one poisoned vapour.
       [*Kisses the dead Duke*]
    Thus, thus, reward thy murderer, and turn death
    Into a parting kiss. My soul stands ready at my lips,
    E'en vexed to stay one minute after thee.
CARDINAL The greatest sorrow and astonishment   200
    That ever struck the general peace of Florence
    Dwells in this hour.
BIANCA   So my desires are satisfied,
    I feel death's power within me.
    Thou hast prevailed in something, cursed poison,
    Though thy chief force was spent in my lord's bosom;   205
    But my deformity in spirit's more foul—
    A blemished face best fits a leprous soul.°
    What make I here? These are all strangers to me,°
    Not known but by their malice, now th'art gone;
    Nor do I seek their pities. [*Drinks from the poisoned cup*]
CARDINAL   O restrain   210
    Her ignorant wilful hand!
BIANCA   Now do; 'tis done.°
    Leantio, now I feel the breach of marriage
    At my heart-breaking. Oh the deadly snares°
    That women set for women, without pity

Either to soul or honour! Learn by me   215
To know your foes; in this belief I die:
Like our own sex, we have no enemy, no enemy!°

LORD See, my lord,
What shift sh'as made to be her own destruction.

BIANCA Pride, greatness, honours, beauty, youth, ambition,   220
You must all down together, there's no help for't.
Yet this my gladness is, that I remove,°
Tasting the same death in a cup of love.
    [Bianca dies]

CARDINAL Sin, what thou art, these ruins show too piteously.
Two kings on one throne cannot sit together,   225
But one must needs down, for his title's wrong;
So where lust reigns, that prince cannot reign long.
    Exeunt

THE CHANGELING

THE CHARACTERS OF THE PLAY°

Vermandero, father to Beatrice-Joanna.
Tomazo de Piracquo, a noble lord.
Alonzo de Piracquo, his brother, suitor to Beatrice-Joanna.
Alsemero, a nobleman, afterwards married to Beatrice-Joanna.
Jasperino, his friend.
Alibius, a jealous doctor.
Lollio, his man.
Pedro, friend to Antonio.
Antonio, the changeling.°
Franciscus, the counterfeit madman.
Deflores, servant to Vermandero.°
Madmen.
Servants.

Beatrice-Joanna, daughter to Vermandero.°
Diaphanta, her waiting woman.
Isabella, wife to Alibius.

The Scene: Alicante°

1.1

Enter Alsemero

ALSEMERO 'Twas in the temple where I first beheld her,°
And now again the same; what omen yet
Follows of that? None but imaginary;
Why should my hopes or fate be timorous?°
The place is holy, so is my intent: 5
I love her beauties to the holy purpose.
And that, methinks, admits comparison°
With man's first creation, the place blest,°
And is his right home back, if he achieve it.
The church hath first begun our interview,°   10
And that's the place must join us into one,
So there's beginning and perfection too.°

Enter Jasperino

JASPERINO Oh sir, are you here? Come, the wind's fair with you,
Y'are like to have a swift and pleasant passage.

ALSEMERO Sure y'are deceived, friend, 'tis contrary°   15
In my best judgement.

JASPERINO   What, for Malta?
If you could buy a gale amongst the witches,°
They could not serve you such a lucky pennyworth
As comes a'God's name.

ALSEMERO   Even now I observed°
The temple's vane to turn full in my face,   20
I know 'tis against me.

JASPERINO   Against you?
Then you know not where you are.

ALSEMERO   Not well, indeed.

JASPERINO Are you not well, sir?

ALSEMERO   Yes, Jasperino.
Unless there be some hidden malady
Within me that I understand not.

JASPERINO   And that   25
I begin to doubt, sir; I never knew°
Your inclinations to travels at a pause
With any cause to hinder it, till now.°
Ashore you were wont to call your servants up,

And help to trap your horses for the speed;°   30
At sea I have seen you weigh the anchor with'em,
Hoist sails for fear to lose the foremost breath,
Be in continual prayers for fair winds!
And have you changed your orisons?°
ALSEMERO   No, friend,
I keep the same church, same devotion.   35
JASPERINO Lover I'm sure y'are none, the stoic°
Was found in you long ago; your mother
Nor best friends who have set snares of beauty°
(Ay, and choice ones too) could never trap you that way.
What might be the cause?
ALSEMERO   Lord, how violent   40
Thou art. I was but meditating of
Somewhat I heard within the temple.
JASPERINO Is this violence? 'tis but idleness
Compared with your haste yesterday.
ALSEMERO I'm all this while a-going, man.   45
        Enter Servants
JASPERINO Backwards, I think, sir. Look, your servants.
FIRST SERVANT The seamen call; shall we board your trunks?
ALSEMERO No, not today.
JASPERINO 'Tis the critical day, it seems, and the sign in Aquarius.°
SECOND SERVANT [*aside*] We must not to sea today; this smoke will   50
    bring forth fire.°
ALSEMERO Keep all on shore; I do not know the end
    (Which needs I must do) of an affair in hand
    Ere I can go to sea.
FIRST SERVANT Well, your pleasure.   55
SECOND SERVANT [*aside*] Let him e'en take his leisure, too, we are
    safer on land.
        Exeunt Servants. Enter Beatrice-Joanna, Diaphanta, and
        Servants.° [Alsemero greets Beatrice-Joanna with a kiss]
JASPERINO [*aside*] How now? The laws of the Medes° are changed,
    sure: salute a woman? He kisses too: wonderful! Where learnt he
    this? And does it perfectly too; in my conscience° he ne'er   60
    rehearsed it before. Nay, go on, this will be stranger and better news
    at Valencia than if he had ransomed half Greece from the Turk.°
BEATRICE-JOANNA You are a scholar, sir?
ALSEMERO   ·   A weak one, lady.
BEATRICE-JOANNA Which of the sciences is this love you speak of?

ALSEMERO From your tongue I take it to be music.   65
BEATRICE-JOANNA You are skilful in't, can sing at first
    sight.°
ALSEMERO And I have showed you all my skill at once.
    I want more words to express me further,
    And must be forced to repetition:
    I love you dearly.
BEATRICE-JOANNA Be better advised, sir: 70
    Our eyes are sentinels unto our judgements,
    And should give certain judgement what they see;
    But they are rash sometimes, and tell us wonders
    Of common things, which when our judgements find,
    They can then check the eyes and call them blind.   75
ALSEMERO But I am further, lady; yesterday
    Was mine eyes' employment, and hither now
    They brought my judgement, where are both agreed.
    Both houses then consenting, 'tis agreed;°
    Only there wants the confirmation   80
    By the hand royal; that's your part, lady.
BEATRICE-JOANNA Oh, there's one above me, sir. [*Aside*] For five
    days past°
    To be recalled! Sure, mine eyes were mistaken,°
    This was the man was meant me; that he should come°
    So near his time, and miss it!   85
JASPERINO [*aside*] We might have come by the carriers from Valencia,
    I see, and saved all our sea-provision: we are at farthest° sure.
    Methinks I should do something too; I meant to be a venturer in
    this voyage. Yonder's another vessel, I'll board her; if she be lawful
    prize, down goes her top-sail.°   90
    [*Jasperino greets Diaphanta.*] *Enter Deflores*
DEFLORES Lady, your father—
BEATRICE-JOANNA   Is in health, I hope.
DEFLORES Your eye shall instantly instruct you, lady.
    He's coming hitherward.
BEATRICE-JOANNA   What needed then
    Your duteous preface? I had rather
    He had come unexpected; you must stall   95
    A good presence with unnecessary blabbing:°
    And how welcome for your part you are,
    I'm sure you know.
DEFLORES [*aside*]   Will't never mend this scorn

One side nor other? Must I be enjoined°
To follow still while she flies from me? Well,   100
Fates do your worst, I'll please myself with sight
Of her, at all opportunities,
If but to spite her anger; I know she had
Rather see me dead than living, and yet
She knows no cause for it, but a peevish will.   105

ALSEMERO You seem displeased, lady, on the sudden.

BEATRICE-JOANNA Your pardon, sir, 'tis my infirmity;
　Nor can I other reason render you
　Than his or hers, of some particular thing
　They must abandon as a deadly poison,   110
　Which to a thousand other tastes were wholesome;°
　Such to mine eyes is that same fellow there,
　The same that report speaks of the basilisk.

ALSEMERO This is a frequent frailty in our nature;
　There's scarce a man amongst a thousand sound°   115
　But hath his imperfection: one distastes
　The scent of roses, which to infinites
　Most pleasing is, and odoriferous;
　One oil, the enemy of poison;°
　Another wine, the cheerer of the heart   120
　And lively refresher of the countenance.°
　Indeed this fault (if so it be) is general;
　There's scarce a thing but is both loved and loathed:
　Myself, I must confess, have the same frailty.

BEATRICE-JOANNA And what may be your poison, sir? I am bold
　with you.   125

ALSEMERO What might be your desire, perhaps: a cherry.°

BEATRICE-JOANNA I am no enemy to any creature
　My memory has, but yon gentleman.

ALSEMERO He does ill to tempt your sight, if he knew it.

BEATRICE-JOANNA He cannot be ignorant of that, sir,   130
　I have not spared to tell him so; and I want
　To help myself, since he's a gentleman
　In good respect with my father, and follows him.°

ALSEMERO He's out of his place then now.
　　　　[Alsemero and Beatrice-Joanna talk apart]

JASPERINO I am a mad wag, wench.   135

DIAPHANTA So methinks; but for your comfort I can tell you we have
　a doctor° in the city that undertakes the cure of such.

JASPERINO Tush, I know what physic is best for the state of mine
    own body.
DIAPHANTA 'Tis scarce a well-governed state, I believe.   140
JASPERINO I could show thee such a thing with an ingredient that we
    two would compound together, and if it did not tame the maddest
    blood i'th'town for two hours after,° I'll ne'er profess physic again.
DIAPHANTA A little poppy, sir, were good to cause you sleep.°
JASPERINO Poppy! I'll give thee a pop i'th'lips for that first and begin   145
    there. [*Kisses her*] Poppy is one simple indeed, and cuckoo (what
    you call't)° another: I'll discover° no more now, another time I'll
    show thee all.
BEATRICE-JOANNA My father, sir.
      Enter Vermandero and Servants
VERMANDERO   Oh, Joanna, I came to meet thee;°
    Your devotion's ended?
BEATRICE-JOANNA   For this time, sir.   150
    [*Aside*] I shall change my saint, I fear me, I find°
    A giddy turning in me. [*To Vermandero*] Sir, this while
    I am beholding to this gentleman,
    Who left his own way to keep me company,
    And in discourse I find him much desirous   155
    To see your castle: he hath deserved it, sir,
    If ye please to grant it.
VERMANDERO   With all my heart, sir.
    Yet there's an article between: I must know
    Your country; we use not to give survey°
    Of our chief strengths to strangers; our citadels°   160
    Are placed conspicuous to outward view,
    On promonts' tops; but within are secrets.
ALSEMERO A Valencian, sir.
VERMANDERO   A Valencian?
    That's native, sir; of what name, I beseech you?
ALSEMERO Alsemero, sir.
VERMANDERO   Alsemero; not the son   165
    Of John de Alsemero?
ALSEMERO   The same, sir.
VERMANDERO My best love bids you welcome.
BEATRICE-JOANNA [*aside*]   He was wont
    To call me so, and then he speaks a most
    Unfeignèd truth.
VERMANDERO   Oh sir, I knew your father;°

We two were in acquaintance long ago,   170
Before our chins were worth iulan down,°
And so continued till the stamp of time
Had coined us into silver: well, he's gone;°
A good soldier went with him.

ALSEMERO You went together in that, sir.°   175

VERMANDERO No, by Saint Jacques, I came behind him.°
Yet I have done somewhat too; an unhappy day
Swallowed him at last at Gibraltar
In fight with those rebellious Hollanders,
Was it not so?

ALSEMERO   Whose death I had revenged,   180
Or followed him in fate, had not the late league°
Prevented me.

VERMANDERO   Ay, ay, 'twas time to breathe:
Oh, Joanna, I should ha'told thee news,
I saw Piracquo lately.

BEATRICE-JOANNA [aside] That's ill news.

VERMANDERO He's hot preparing for this day of triumph,   185
Thou must be a bride within this sevennight.

ALSEMERO [aside]   Ha!

BEATRICE-JOANNA Nay, good sir, be not so violent; with speed
I cannot render satisfaction
Unto the dear companion of my soul,
Virginity, whom I thus long have lived with,   190
And part with it so rude and suddenly;
Can such friends divide, never to meet again,
Without a solemn farewell?

VERMANDERO   Tush, tush, there's a toy.

ALSEMERO [aside] I must now part, and never meet again
With any joy on earth. [To Vermandero] Sir, your pardon,   195
My affairs call on me.

VERMANDERO   How, sir? By no means;
Not changed so soon, I hope? You must see my castle,
And her best entertainment, ere we part,
I shall think myself unkindly used else.
Come, come, let's on; I had good hope your stay   200
Had been a while with us in Alicant;
I might have bid you to my daughter's wedding.

ALSEMERO [aside] He means to feast me, and poisons me
    beforehand.

[*To Vermandero*] I should be dearly glad to be there, sir,
Did my occasions suit as I could wish.°   205
BEATRICE-JOANNA I shall be sorry if you be not there
    When it is done, sir—but not so suddenly.
VERMANDERO I tell you, sir, the gentleman's complete,°
    A courtier and a gallant, enriched
    With many fair and noble ornaments;°   210
    I would not change him for a son-in-law
    For any he in Spain, the proudest he,
    And we have great ones, that you know.
ALSEMERO   He's much
    Bound to you, sir.
VERMANDERO   He shall be bound to me,°
    As fast as this tie can hold him; I'll want°   215
    My will else.
BEATRICE-JOANNA [*aside*] I shall want mine if you do it.
VERMANDERO But come, by the way I'll tell you more of him.
ALSEMERO [*aside*] How shall I dare to venture in his castle,
    When he discharges murderers at the gate?°
    But I must on, for back I cannot go.   220
BEATRICE-JOANNA [*aside*] Not this serpent gone yet?
        [*Beatrice-Joanna drops a glove*]
VERMANDERO   Look, girl, thy glove's fall'n;°
    Stay, stay—Deflores, help a little.
DEFLORES   Here, lady. [*He offers Beatrice-Joanna the glove*]
BEATRICE-JOANNA Mischief on your officious forwardness!
    Who bade you stoop? They touch my hand no more:
    There, for t'other's sake I part with this.   225
        [*Takes off other glove and throws it to him*]
    Take 'em and draw thine own skin off with 'em.°
        Exeunt [*Beatrice-Joanna, Vermandero, Alsemero, Jasperino,
        Diaphanta*]°
DEFLORES Here's a favour come, with a mischief! Now I know°
    She had rather wear my pelt tanned in a pair
    Of dancing pumps, than I should thrust my fingers
    Into her sockets here; I know she hates me,°   230
    Yet cannot choose but love her:
    No matter, if but to vex her I'll haunt her still;
    Though I get nothing else, I'll have my will.
        Exit

1.2

Enter Alibius and Lollio

ALIBIUS Lollio, I must trust thee with a secret,
But thou must keep it.

LOLLIO I was ever close to a secret, sir.°

ALIBIUS The diligence that I have found in thee,
The care and industry already past,   5
Assures me of thy good continuance.
Lollio, I have a wife.

LOLLIO Fie, sir, 'tis too late to keep her secret; she's known to be
married all the town and country over.

ALIBIUS Thou goest too fast, my Lollio, that knowledge   10
I allow no man can be barred it;
But there is a knowledge which is nearer,
Deeper and sweeter, Lollio.

LOLLIO Well, sir, let us handle that between you and I.

ALIBIUS 'Tis that I go about, man; Lollio,°   15
My wife is young.

LOLLIO So much the worse to be kept secret, sir.

ALIBIUS Why, now thou meet'st the substance of the point:
I am old, Lollio.

LOLLIO No, sir, 'tis I am old Lollio.°   20

ALIBIUS Yet why may not this concord and sympathise?°
Old trees and young plants often grow together,°
Well enough agreeing.

LOLLIO Ay, sir, but the old trees raise themselves higher and broader
than the young plants.°   25

ALIBIUS Shrewd application! There's the fear, man;
I would wear my ring on my own finger;°
Whilst it is borrowed it is none of mine,
But his that useth it.

LOLLIO You must keep it on still then; if it but lie by, one or other will   30
be thrusting into it.

ALIBIUS Thou conceiv'st me, Lollio; here thy watchful eye
Must have employment; I cannot always be
At home.

LOLLIO I dare swear you cannot.

ALIBIUS   I must look out°.   35

LOLLIO I know't, you must look out, 'tis every man's case.

ALIBIUS Here I do say must thy employment be,
  To watch her treadings, and in my absence°
  Supply my place.
LOLLIO I'll do my best, sir, yet surely I cannot see who you should   40
  have cause to be jealous of.
ALIBIUS Thy reason for that, Lollio? 'Tis a comfortable question.°
LOLLIO We have but two sorts of people in the house, and both under
  the whip, that's fools and madmen; the one has not wit enough to
  be knaves, and the other not knavery enough to be fools.   45
ALIBIUS Ay, those are all my patients, Lollio.
  I do profess the cure of either sort:°
  My trade, my living 'tis, I thrive by it;
  But here's the care that mixes with my thrift:
  The daily visitants that come to see°   50
  My brainsick patients, I would not have
  To see my wife. Gallants I do observe
  Of quick enticing eyes, rich in habits,
  Of stature and proportion very comely:
  These are most shrewd temptations, Lollio.   55
LOLLIO They may be easily answered, sir; if they come to see the
  fools and madmen, you and I may serve the turn,° and let my
  mistress alone, she's of neither sort.
ALIBIUS 'Tis a good ward; indeed, come they to see°
  Our madmen or our fools, let'em see no more   60
  Than what they come for; by that consequent°
  They must not see her. I'm sure she's no fool.
LOLLIO And I'm sure she's no madman.
ALIBIUS Hold that buckler fast, Lollio; my trust°
  Is on thee, and I account it firm and strong.   65
  What hour is't, Lollio?
LOLLIO Towards belly-hour, sir.
ALIBIUS Dinner time? Thou mean'st twelve o'clock.
LOLLIO Yes, sir, for every part has his hour: we wake at six and look
  about us, that's eye-hour; at seven we should pray, that's knee-   70
  hour; at eight walk, that's leg-hour; at nine gather flowers and
  pluck a rose,° that's nose hour; at ten we drink, that's mouth hour;
  at eleven lay about us for victuals,° that's hand-hour; at twelve go to
  dinner, that's belly hour.
ALIBIUS Profoundly, Lollio! It will be long   75
  Ere all thy scholars learn this lesson, and
  I did look to have a new one entered. Stay,°

I think my expectation is come home.°
     Enter Pedro, and Antonio like an idiot°
PEDRO Save you, sir; my business speaks itself;
     This sight takes off the labour of my tongue.°   80
ALIBIUS Ay, ay, sir; 'tis plain enough, you mean him
     For my patient.
PEDRO And if your pains prove but commodious, to give but some
     little strength to his sick and weak part of nature in him, these are
     [*Pedro gives money*] but patterns° to show you of the whole pieces   85
     that will follow to you, beside the charge of diet, washing, and other
     necessaries fully defrayed.
ALIBIUS Believe it, sir, there shall be no care wanting.
LOLLIO Sir, an officer in this place may deserve something; the
     trouble will pass through my hands.°   90
PEDRO 'Tis fit something should come to your hands then, sir.
          [*Pedro gives him money*]
LOLLIO Yes, sir, 'tis I must keep him sweet, and read to him; what is
     his name?
PEDRO His name is Antonio; marry, we use but half to him, only   95
     Tony.°
LOLLIO Tony, Tony, 'tis enough, and a very good name for a fool;
     what's your name, Tony?
ANTONIO He, he, he! well, I thank you, cousin; he, he, he!
LOLLIO Good boy! Hold up your head: he can laugh, I perceive by   100
     that he is no beast.°
PEDRO Well, sir,
     If you can raise him but to any height,
     Any degree of wit, might he attain
     (As I might say) to creep but on all four   105
     Towards the chair of wit, or walk on crutches,
     'Twould add an honour to your worthy pains,
     And a great family might pray for you,
     To which he should be heir, had he discretion°
     To claim and guide his own; assure you, sir.   110
     He is a gentleman.°
LOLLIO Nay, there's nobody doubted that; at first sight I knew him
     for a gentleman, he looks no other yet.°
PEDRO Let him have good attendance and sweet lodging.°
LOLLIO As good as my mistress lies in, sir; and as you allow us time   115
     and means, we can raise him to the higher degree of discretion.
PEDRO Nay, there shall no cost want, sir.

LOLLIO He will hardly be stretched up to the wit of a magnifico.°

PEDRO Oh no, that's not to be expected, far shorter will be enough.

LOLLIO I warrant you I'll° make him fit to bear office in five weeks;   120
I'll undertake to wind him up to the wit of constable.

PEDRO If it be lower than that it might serve turn.

LOLLIO No, fie, to level him with a headborough, beadle, or watchman were but little better than he is; constable I'll able him:° if he
do come to be a justice afterwards, let him thank the keeper. Or I'll   125
go further with you; say I do bring him up to my own pitch, say I
make him as wise as myself.

PEDRO Why, there I would have it.

LOLLIO Well, go to, either I'll be as arrant° a fool as he, or he shall be
as wise as I, and then I think 'twill serve his turn.   130

PEDRO Nay, I do like thy wit passing well.

LOLLIO Yes, you may; yet if I had not been a fool, I had had more wit
than I have too; remember what state° you find me in.

PEDRO I will, and so leave you: your best cares, I beseech you.
        Exit Pedro

ALIBIUS Take you none° with you, leave 'em all with us.   135

ANTONIO Oh, my cousin's gone, cousin, cousin, oh!

LOLLIO Peace, peace, Tony, you must not cry, child—you must be
whipped° if you do; your cousin is here still, I am your cousin,
Tony.

ANTONIO He, he, then I'll not cry, if thou be'st my cousin, he, he, he!   140

LOLLIO I were best try his wit a little, that I may know what form° to
place him in.

ALIBIUS Ay, do, Lollio, do.

LOLLIO I must ask him easy questions at first. Tony, how many true°
fingers has a tailor on his right hand?   145

ANTONIO As many as on his left, cousin.

LOLLIO Good; and how many on both?

ANTONIO Two less than a deuce, cousin.°

LOLLIO Very well answered; I come to you again, cousin Tony: how
many fools goes to a wise man?°   150

ANTONIO Forty in a day sometimes, cousin.

LOLLIO Forty in a day? How prove you that?

ANTONIO All that fall out amongst themselves, and go to a lawyer to
be made friends.°

LOLLIO A parlous fool! He must sit in the fourth form at least, I   155
perceive that; I come again, Tony: how many knaves make an
honest man?

ANTONIO I know not that, cousin.

LOLLIO No, the question is too hard for you: I'll tell you, cousin, there's three knaves may make an honest man—a sergeant, a jailer, and a beadle; the sergeant catches him, the jailer holds him, and the beadle lashes him; and if he be not honest then, the hangman must cure him.   160

ANTONIO Ha, ha, ha, that's fine sport, cousin!

ALIBIUS This was too deep a question for the fool, Lollio.   165

LOLLIO Yes, this might have served yourself,° though I say't; once more, and you shall go play, Tony.

ANTONIO Ay, play at push-pin, cousin, ha, he!°

LOLLIO So thou shalt; say how many fools are here—

ANTONIO Two, cousin, thou and I.   170

LOLLIO Nay, y'are too forward there, Tony; mark my question: how many fools and knaves are here? A fool before a knave, a fool behind a knave, between every two fools a knave; how many fools, how many knaves?

ANTONIO I never learnt so far, cousin.   175

ALIBIUS Thou put'st too hard questions to him, Lollio.

LOLLIO I'll make him understand it easily; cousin, stand there.°

ANTONIO Ay, cousin.

LOLLIO Master, stand you next the fool.

ALIBIUS Well, Lollio?   180

LOLLIO Here's my place: mark now, Tony, there a fool before knave.

ANTONIO That's I, cousin.

LOLLIO Here's a fool behind a knave, that's I, and between us two fools there is a knave, that's my master; 'tis but we three, that's all.°

ANTONIO We three, we three, cousin!   185

Madmen [make noise] within

FIRST MADMEN [*within*] Put's head i'th'pillory, the bread's too little.

SECOND MADMEN [*within*] Fly, fly and he catches the swallow.°

THIRD MADMEN [*within*] Give her more onion, or the devil put the rope about her crag.°

LOLLIO You may hear what time of day it is, the chimes of Bedlam goes.   190

ALIBIUS Peace, peace, or the wire° comes!

THIRD MADMEN [*within*] Cat-whore, cat-whore, her permasant, her permasant!°

ALIBIUS Peace, I say. Their hour's come, they must be fed, Lollio.   195

LOLLIO There's no hope of recovery of that Welsh madman, was°

undone by a mouse, that spoiled him a permasant; lost his wits
for't.

ALIBIUS Go to your charge, Lollio, I'll to mine.

LOLLIO Go you to your madmen's ward, let me alone with your fools.

ALIBIUS And remember my last charge, Lollio.   200
        Exit [Alibius]

LOLLIO Of which your patients do you think I am? Come, Tony, you
    must amongst your school-fellows now; there's pretty scholars
    amongst'em, I can tell you, there's some of'em at *stultus, stulta,*
    stultum.°

ANTONIO I would see° the madmen, cousin, if they would not bite   205
    me.

LOLLIO No, they shall not bite thee, Tony.

ANTONIO They bite when they are at dinner, do they not, coz?

LOLLIO They bite at dinner indeed, Tony. Well, I hope to get credit
    by thee; I like thee the best of all the scholars that ever I brought 210
    up, and thou shalt prove a wise man, or I'll prove a fool myself.°
        Exeunt

2.1

Enter Beatrice-Joanna and Jasperino severally°
BEATRICE-JOANNA Oh sir, I'm ready now for that fair service,°
   Which makes the name of friend sit glorious on you.
   Good angels and this conduct be your guide.
      [*She hands over a document*]°
   Fitness of time and place is there set down, sir.
JASPERINO The joy I shall return rewards my service.°   5
      Exit [*Jasperino*]
BEATRICE-JOANNA How wise is Alsemero in his friend!
   It is a sign he makes his choice with judgement.
   Then I appear in nothing more approved°
   Than making choice of him;
   For 'tis a principle, he that can choose   10
   That bosom well, who of his thoughts partakes,
   Proves most discreet in every choice he makes.°
   Methinks I love now with the eyes of judgement,
   And see the way to merit, clearly see it.°
   A true deserver like a diamond sparkles;   15
   In darkness you may see him, that's in absence,
   Which is the greatest darkness falls on love;
   Yet is he best discerned then
   With intellectual eyesight. What's Piracquo
   My father spends his breath for? And his blessing°   20
   Is only mine, as I regard his name,
   Else it goes from me, and turns head against me,
   Transformed into a curse: some speedy way°
   Must be remembered; he's so forward too.°
   So urgent that way, scarce allows me breath   25
   To speak to my new comforts.°
      Enter Deflores
DEFLORES [*aside*]   Yonder's she.
   Whatever ails me? Now a-late especially
   I can as well be hanged as refrain seeing her;
   Some twenty times a day, nay, not so little,
   Do I force errands, frame ways and excuses   30
   To come into her sight, and I have small reason for't,
   And less encouragement; for she baits me still

Every time worse than other, does profess herself
The cruellest enemy to my face in town,
At no hand can abide the sight of me,°   35
As if danger or ill luck hung in my looks.
I must confess my face is bad enough,
But I know far worse has better fortune,
And not endured alone, but dotèd on:°
And yet such pick-haired faces, chins like witches',   40
Here and there five hairs, whispering in a corner,
As if they grew in fear one of another,
Wrinkles like troughs, where swine-deformity swills
The tears of perjury that lie there like wash°
Fallen from the slimy and dishonest eye—   45
Yet such a one plucks sweets without restraint,°
And has the grace of beauty to his sweet.°
Though my hard fate has thrust me out to servitude,
I tumbled into th'world a gentleman.°
She turns her blessèd eye upon me now,   50
And I'll endure all storms before I part with't.
BEATRICE-JOANNA [aside]   Again!
This ominous ill-faced fellow more disturbs me
Than all my other passions.
DEFLORES [aside]   Now't begins again;
I'll stand the storm of hail though the stones pelt me.
BEATRICE-JOANNA Thy business, what's thy business?
DEFLORES [aside]   Soft and fair,   55
I cannot part so soon now.
BEATRICE-JOANNA [aside]   The villain's fixed.
[To him] Thou standing toad-pool!°
DEFLORES [aside] The shower falls amain now.
BEATRICE-JOANNA Who sent thee? What's thy errand? Leave my
    sight.
DEFLORES My lord your father charged me to deliver
    A message to you.
BEATRICE-JOANNA What, another since?°   60
    Do't and be hanged then, let me be rid of thee.
DEFLORES True service merits mercy.
BEATRICE-JOANNA   What's thy message?
DEFLORES Let beauty settle but in patience,
    You shall hear all.
BEATRICE-JOANNA A dallying, trifling torment!

DEFLORES Signor Alonzo de Piracquo, lady,   65
    Sole brother to Tomazo de Piracquo—
BEATRICE-JOANNA Slave, when wilt make an end?
DEFLORES   Too soon I shall.°
BEATRICE-JOANNA What all this while of him?
DEFLORES   The said Alonzo,
    With the foresaid Tomazo—
BEATRICE-JOANNA   Yet again?
DEFLORES Is new alighted.
BEATRICE-JOANNA   Vengeance strike the news!   70
    Thou thing most loathed, what cause was there in this
    To bring thee to my sight?
DEFLORES   My lord your father
    Charged me to seek you out.
BEATRICE-JOANNA   Is there no other
    To send his errand by?
DEFLORES   It seems 'tis my luck
    To be i'th'way still.
BEATRICE-JOANNA Get thee from me.
DEFLORES [*aside*]   So—   75
    Why, am not I an ass to devise ways
    Thus to be railed at? I must see her still!
    I shall have a mad qualm within this hour again,°
    I know't, and like a common Garden bull°
    I do but take breath to be lugged again.   80
    What this may bode I know not; I'll despair the less,
    Because there's daily precedents of bad faces
    Beloved beyond all reason; these foul chops
    May come into favour one day 'mongst his fellows:
    Wrangling has proved the mistress of good pastime;°   85
    As children cry themselves to sleep, I ha'seen
    Women have chid themselves abed to men.
       Exit Deflores
BEATRICE-JOANNA I never see this fellow, but I think
    Of some harm towards me, danger's in my mind still;
    I scarce leave trembling of an hour after.°   90
    The next good mood I find my father in,
    I'll get him quite discarded: oh, I was
    Lost in this small disturbance, and forgot
    Affliction's fiercer torrent that now comes°
    To bear down all my comforts.

Enter Vermandero, Alonzo, Tomazo

VERMANDERO   Y'are both welcome,   95
  But an especial one belongs to you, sir,
  To whose most noble name our love presents
  The addition of a son, our son Alonzo.°
ALONZO The treasury of honour cannot bring forth
  A title I should more rejoice in, sir.   100
VERMANDERO You have improved it well; daughter, prepare,
  The day will steal upon thee suddenly.
BEATRICE-JOANNA [*aside*] Howe'er I will be sure to keep the night,°
  If it should come so near me.
     [*Beatrice-Joanna and Vermandero talk apart*]
TOMAZO   Alonzo.
ALONZO   Brother?
TOMAZO In troth I see small welcome in her eye.   105
ALONZO Fie, you are too severe a censurer
  Of love in all points, there's no bringing on you;°
  If lovers should mark everything a fault°
  Affection would be like an ill-set book,
  Whose faults might prove as big as half the volume.   110
BEATRICE-JOANNA That's all I do entreat.
VERMANDERO   It is but reasonable;
  I'll see what my son says to't: son Alonzo,
  Here's a motion made but to reprieve
  A maidenhead three days longer; the request
  Is not far out of reason, for indeed   115
  The former time is pinching.
ALONZO   Though my joys
  Be set back so much time as I could wish
  They had been forward, yet since she desires it
  The time is set as pleasing as before,
  I find no gladness wanting.   120
VERMANDERO May I ever meet it in that point still:
  Y'are nobly welcome, sirs.
     Exeunt Vermandero and Beatrice-Joanna
TOMAZO So: did you mark the dullness of her parting now?
ALONZO What dullness? Thou art so exceptious still.
TOMAZO Why, let it go then, I am but a fool   125
  To mark your harms so heedfully.
ALONZO   Where's the oversight?
TOMAZO Come, your faith's cozened in her, strongly cozened;

Unsettle your affection with all speed°
Wisdom can bring it to, your peace is ruined else.
Think what a torment 'tis to marry one   130
Whose heart is leaped into another's bosom:
If ever pleasure she receive from thee,°
It comes not in thy name or of thy gift;
She lies but with another in thine arms,
He is the half-father unto all thy children   135
In the conception; if he get 'em not,
She helps to get 'em for him; and how dangerous°
And shameful her restraint may go in time to,°
It is not to be thought on without sufferings.
ALONZO You speak as if she loved some other, then.   140
TOMAZO Do you apprehend so slowly?
ALONZO   Nay, an that
    Be your fear only, I am safe enough.
    Preserve your friendship and your counsel, brother,
    For times of more distress; I should depart
    An enemy, a dangerous, deadly one   145
    To any but thyself, that should but think°
    She knew the meaning of inconstancy,
    Much less the use and practice; yet w'are friends.°
    Pray, let no more be urged; I can endure
    Much, till I meet an injury to her,°   150
    Then I am not myself. Farewell, sweet brother,
    How much w'are bound to heaven to depart lovingly.°
        Exit [Alonzo]
TOMAZO Why, here is love's tame madness; thus a man
    Quickly steals into his vexation.
        Exit

2.2

Enter Diaphanta and Alsemero
DIAPHANTA The place is my charge, you have kept your hour,°
    And the reward of a just meeting bless you.
    I hear my lady coming; complete gentleman,°
    I dare not be too busy with my praises,
    Th'are dangerous things to deal with.°

Exit [*Diaphanta*]

ALSEMERO   This goes well;   5
    These women are the ladies' cabinets,
    Things of most precious trust are locked into'em.°
    Enter Beatrice-Joanna

BEATRICE-JOANNA I have within mine eye all my desires;
    Requests that holy prayers ascend heaven for,
    And brings'em down to furnish our defects,°   10
    Come not more sweet to our necessities
    Than thou unto my wishes.

ALSEMERO   W'are so like
    In our expressions, lady, that unless I borrow
    The same words, I shall never find their equals. [*Kisses her*]

BEATRICE-JOANNA How happy were this meeting, this
       embrace,   15
    If it were free from envy! This poor kiss,
    It has an enemy, a hateful one,
    That wishes poison to't: how well were I now°
    If there were none such name known as Piracquo,
    Nor no such tie as the command of parents!   20
    I should be but too much blessed.

ALSEMERO   One good service
    Would strike off both your fears, and I'll go near it too,°
    Since you are so distressed; remove the cause,
    The command ceases, so there's two fears blown out°
    With one and the same blast.

BEATRICE-JOANNA   Pray let me find you, sir.°   25
    What might that service be so strangely happy?

ALSEMERO The honourablest piece 'bout man, valour.°
    I'll send a challenge to Piracquo instantly.

BEATRICE-JOANNA How? Call you that extinguishing of fear,
    When 'tis the only way to keep it flaming?   30
    Are you not ventured in the action,
    That's all my joys and comforts? Pray, no more, sir.
    Say you prevailed, y'are danger's and not mine then;°
    The law would claim you from me, or obscurity
    Be made the grave to bury you alive.   35
    I'm glad these thoughts come forth; oh keep not one
    Of this condition, sir. Here was a course°
    Found to bring sorrow on her way to death:
    The tears would ne'er ha'dried, till dust had choked'em.

Blood-guiltiness becomes a fouler visage;   40
And now I think on one—[*aside*] I was too blame,°
I ha' marred so good a market with my scorn;°
'T had been done questionless; the ugliest creature
Creation framed for some use, yet to see
I could not mark so much where it should be.   45
ALSEMERO Lady—
BEATRICE-JOANNA [*aside*]   Why, men of art make much of poison,°
  Keep one to expel another; where was my art?
ALSEMERO Lady, you hear not me.
BEATRICE-JOANNA   I do especially, sir;
  The present times are not so sure of our side°
  As those hereafter may be; we must use 'em then   50
  As thrifty folks their wealth, sparingly now,
  Till the time opens.
ALSEMERO   You teach wisdom, lady.°
BEATRICE-JOANNA Within there, Diaphanta!
          Enter Diaphanta
DIAPHANTA   Do you call, madam?
BEATRICE-JOANNA Perfect your service, and conduct this
      gentleman°
  The private way you brought him.
DIAPHANTA   I shall, madam.   55
ALSEMERO My love's as firm as love e'er built upon.°
        Exeunt Diaphanta and Alsemero. Enter Deflores
DEFLORES [*aside*] I have watched this meeting, and do wonder much
  What shall become of t'other; I'm sure both°
  Cannot be served unless she transgress; happily°
  Then I'll put in for one: for if a woman°   60
  Fly from one point, from him she makes a husband,
  She spreads and mounts then like arithmetic,°
  One, ten, a hundred, a thousand, ten thousand,
  Proves in time sutler to an army royal.°
  Now do I look to be most richly railed at,   65
  Yet I must see her.
BEATRICE-JOANNA [*aside*]   Why, put case I loathed him°
  As much as youth and beauty hates a sepulchre,
  Must I needs show it? Cannot I keep that secret,
  And serve my turn upon him? See, he's here.°
  [*To him*] Deflores.
DEFLORES [*aside*]   Ha, I shall run mad with joy;   70

She called me fairly by my name Deflores,
And neither rogue nor rascal!

BEATRICE-JOANNA   What ha'you done
To your face a-late? Y'have met with some good physician;
Y'have pruned yourself, methinks; you were not wont°
To look so amorously.

DEFLORES [*aside*]   Not I;°   75
'Tis the same physnomy, to a hair and pimple,
Which she called scurvy scarce an hour ago:
How is this?

BEATRICE-JOANNA Come hither; nearer, man!

DEFLORES [*aside*] I'm up to the chin in heaven.

BEATRICE-JOANNA   Turn, let me see;
Faugh, 'tis but the heat of the liver, I perceiv't.°   80
I thought it had been worse.

DEFLORES [*aside*]   Her fingers touched me!
She smells all amber.

BEATRICE-JOANNA I'll make a water for you shall cleanse this°
Within a fortnight.

DEFLORES   With your own hands, lady?

BEATRICE-JOANNA Yes, mine own, sir; in a work of cure   85
I'll trust no other.

DEFLORES [*aside*]   'Tis half an act of pleasure°
To hear her talk thus to me.

BEATRICE-JOANNA   When w'are used
To a hard face, 'tis not so unpleasing;
It mends still in opinion, hourly mends,
I see it by experience.

DEFLORES [*aside*]   I was blest   90
To light upon this minute; I'll make use on't.

BEATRICE-JOANNA Hardness becomes the visage of a man well,
It argues service, resolution, manhood,
If cause were of employment.

DEFLORES   'Twould be soon seen,°
If e'er your ladyship had cause to use it.   95
I would but wish the honour of a service
So happy as that mounts to.

BEATRICE-JOANNA   We shall try you.°
Oh my Deflores!

DEFLORES [*aside*]   How's that?
She calls me hers already, *my* Deflores!

[*To her*] You were about to sigh out somewhat, madam.   100
BEATRICE-JOANNA No, was I? I forgot. Oh!
DEFLORES   There 'tis again,
   The very fellow on't.
BEATRICE-JOANNA   You are too quick, sir.°
DEFLORES There's no excuse for't now, I heard it twice, madam;
   That sigh would fain have utterance, take pity on't,
   And lend it a free word; 'las, how it labours°   105
   For liberty! I hear the murmur yet
   Beat at your bosom.
BEATRICE-JOANNA   Would creation—
DEFLORES Ay, well said, that's it.
BEATRICE-JOANNA   Had formed me man.
DEFLORES Nay, that's not it.
BEATRICE-JOANNA   Oh, 'tis the soul of freedom!
   I should not then be forced to marry one   110
   I hate beyond all depths; I should have power
   Then to oppose my loathings, nay, remove'em
   For ever from my sight.
DEFLORES   Oh blest occasion!°
   Without change to your sex, you have your wishes.
   Claim so much man in me.
BEATRICE-JOANNA   In thee, Deflores?°   115
   There's small cause for that.
DEFLORES   Put it not from me,
   It's a service that I kneel for to you. [*Kneels*]
BEATRICE-JOANNA You are too violent to mean faithfully;°
   There's horror in my service, blood and danger,
   Can those be things to sue for?
DEFLORES   If you knew   120
   How sweet it were to me to be employed
   In any act of yours, you would say then
   I failed, and used not reverence enough
   When I receive the charge on't.
BEATRICE-JOANNA [*aside*]   This is much, methinks;
   Belike his wants are greedy, and to such   125
   Gold tastes like angels' food. [*To him*] Rise.
DEFLORES I'll have the work first.
BEATRICE-JOANNA [*aside*]   Possible his need°
   Is strong upon him; there's to encourage thee.
      [*She gives him money*]

As thou art forward and thy service dangerous,°
Thy reward shall be precious.
DEFLORES   That I have thought on;   130
I have assured myself of that beforehand,
And know it will be precious, the thought ravishes.°
BEATRICE–JOANNA Then take him to thy fury.
DEFLORES   I thirst for him.
BEATRICE–JOANNA Alonzo de Piracquo.
DEFLORES   His end's upon him;
He shall be seen no more. [*Rises*]
BEATRICE–JOANNA   How lovely now   135
Dost thou appear to me! Never was man
Dearlier rewarded.
DEFLORES   I do think of that.
BEATRICE–JOANNA Be wondrous careful in the execution.
DEFLORES Why, are not both our lives upon the cast?°
BEATRICE–JOANNA Then I throw all my fears upon thy service.   140
DEFLORES They ne'er shall rise to hurt you.
BEATRICE–JOANNA   When the deed's done,
I'll furnish thee with all things for thy flight;
Thou may'st live bravely in another country.°
DEFLORES Ay, ay, we'll talk of that hereafter.
BEATRICE–JOANNA [*aside*]   I shall rid myself
Of two inveterate loathings at one time,   145
Piracquo and his dog-face.
          Exit [Beatrice-Joanna]
DEFLORES   Oh my blood!°
Methinks I feel her in mine arms already,
Her wanton fingers combing out this beard,
And being pleased, praising this bad face.
Hunger and pleasure, they'll commend sometimes   150
Slovenly dishes, and feed heartily on'em,°
Nay, which is stranger, refuse daintier for'em.
Some women are odd feeders. I'm too loud.
Here comes the man goes supperless to bed,
Yet shall not rise tomorrow to his dinner.   155
          Enter Alonzo
ALONZO Deflores.
DEFLORES   My kind, honourable lord?
ALONZO I am glad I ha'met with thee.
DEFLORES   Sir.

ALONZO   Thou canst show me
  The full strength of the castle?
DEFLORES   That I can, sir.
ALONZO I much desire it.
DEFLORES   And if the ways and straits
  Of some of the passages be not too tedious for you,   160
  I will assure you, worth your time and sight, my lord.
ALONZO Puh! That shall be no hindrance.
DEFLORES   I'm your servant, then:
  'Tis now near dinner-time; 'gainst your lordship's rising°
  I'll have the keys about me.
ALONZO   Thanks, kind Deflores.
DEFLORES [*aside*] He's safely thrust upon me beyond hopes.°   165
    Exeunt

3.1

*In the act-time Deflores hides a naked rapier.° Enter Alonzo
and Deflores*

DEFLORES Yes, here are all the keys; I was afraid, my lord,
    I'd wanted for the postern, this is it.°
    I've all, I've all, my lord: this for the sconce.
ALONZO 'Tis a most spacious and impregnable fort.
DEFLORES You'll tell me more, my lord: this descent   5
    Is somewhat narrow, we shall never pass
    Well with our weapons; they'll but trouble us.
        [*Deflores removes his sword-belt*]
ALONZO Thou say'st true.
DEFLORES   Pray let me help your lordship.
        [*Deflores helps Alonzo remove his sword-belt*]
ALONZO 'Tis done. Thanks, kind Deflores.
DEFLORES   Here are hooks, my lord,
    To hang such things on purpose.
        [*Deflores hangs up the sword-belts*]
ALONZO   Lead, I'll follow thee.   10
        Exeunt at one door

3.2

Enter Deflores and Alonzo at the other door
DEFLORES All this is nothing; you shall see anon
    A place you little dream on.
ALONZO   I am glad°
    I have this leisure: all your master's house°
    Imagine I ha'taken a gondola.
DEFLORES All but myself, sir—[*aside*] which makes up my safety.—   5
    [*To Alonzo*] My lord, I'll place you at a casement here
    Will show you the full strength of all the castle.
    Look, spend your eye awhile upon that object.
ALONZO Here's rich variety, Deflores.
DEFLORES   Yes, sir.
ALONZO Goodly munition.

DEFLORES   Ay, there's ordnance, sir,   10
  No bastard metal, will ring you a peal like bells°
  At great men's funerals; keep your eye straight, my lord,
  Take special notice of that sconce before you,
  There you may dwell awhile.
          [*Takes out the hidden rapier*]°
ALONZO   I am upon't.
DEFLORES And so am I. [*Stabs him*]
ALONZO   Deflores! Oh, Deflores!   15
  Whose malice hast thou put on?
DEFLORES   Do you question°
  A work of secrecy? I must silence you.
          [*Stabs him*]
ALONZO Oh, oh, oh.
DEFLORES   I must silence you.
          [*Stabs him. Alonzo dies*]
  So, here's an undertaking well accomplished.
  This vault serves to good use now. Ha! what's that   20
  Threw sparkles in my eye? Oh, 'tis a diamond
  He wears upon his finger: it was well found,
  This will approve the work. What, so fast on?°
  Not part in death? I'll take a speedy course then,
  Finger and all shall off. [*Cuts off the finger*] So, now I'll clear   25
  The passages from all suspect or fear.°
          Exit with body

3.3

          Enter Isabella and Lollio
ISABELLA Why, sirrah? Whence have you commission
  To fetter the doors against me?
  If you keep me in a cage, pray whistle to me,
  Let me be doing something.
LOLLIO You shall be doing, if it please you; I'll whistle to you if you'll   5
  pipe after.°
ISABELLA Is it your master's pleasure, or your own,
  To keep me in this pinfold?
LOLLIO 'Tis for my master's pleasure, lest being taken in another
  man's corn, you might be pounded° in another place.   10

ISABELLA 'Tis very well, and he'll prove very wise.

LOLLIO He says you have company enough in the house, if you please
to be sociable, of all sorts of people.

ISABELLA Of all sorts? Why, here's none but fools and madmen.

LOLLIO Very well: and where will you find any other, if you should go   15
abroad? There's my master and I to boot° too.

ISABELLA Of either sort one, a madman and a fool.

LOLLIO I would ev'n participate° of both then, if I were as you; I
know y'are half mad already; be half foolish too.

ISABELLA Y'are a brave saucy rascal! Come on, sir,   20
Afford me then the pleasure of your bedlam;°
You were commending once today to me
Your last-come lunatic, what a proper°
Body there was without brains to guide it,
And what a pitiful delight appeared   25
In that defect, as if your wisdom had found
A mirth in madness; pray, sir, let me partake
If there be such a pleasure.

LOLLIO If I do not show you the handsomest, discreetest madman,
one that I may call the understanding madman, then say I am a fool.   30

ISABELLA Well, a match, I will say so.

LOLLIO When you have a taste of the madman, you shall (if you
please) see Fools' College, o'th'side; I seldom lock there, 'tis but
shooting a bolt or two,° and you are amongst'em.
        Exit [Lollio]°

LOLLIO [*offstage*] Come on, sir, let me see how handsomely you'll   35
behave yourself now.
        Enter Lollio [with] Franciscus

FRANCISCUS How sweetly she looks! Oh, but there's a wrinkle in her
brow as deep as philosophy; Anacreon, drink to my mistress'
health, I'll pledge it: stay, stay, there's a spider in the cup! No, 'tis
but a grapestone; swallow it, fear nothing, poet;° so, so, lift higher.   40

ISABELLA Alack, alack, 'tis too full of pity
To be laughed at; how fell he mad? Canst thou tell?

LOLLIO For love, mistress: he was a pretty poet too, and that set him
forwards° first; the muses then forsook him, he ran mad for a
chambermaid, yet she was but a dwarf neither.°   45

FRANCISCUS Hail, bright Titania!
Why stand'st thou idle on these flowery banks?
Oberon is dancing with his dryades;°
I'll gather daisies, primrose, violets,

And bind them in a verse of poesie. [*Approaches Isabella*]   50
LOLLIO Not too near; you see your danger. [*Shows a whip*]
FRANCISCUS Oh hold thy hand, great Diomede,°
    Thou feed'st thy horses well, they shall obey thee;
    Get up, Bucephalus kneels. [*Kneels*]°
LOLLIO You see how I awe my flock; a shepherd has not his dog at   55
    more obedience.
ISABELLA His conscience is unquiet, sure that was
    The cause of this. A proper gentleman.
FRANCISCUS Come hither, Esculapius; hide the poison.°
LOLLIO Well, 'tis hid.   60
FRANCISCUS Didst thou never hear of one Tiresias,°
    A famous poet? [*Rises*]
LOLLIO Yes, that kept tame wild-geese.°
FRANCISCUS That's he; I am the man.
LOLLIO No!   65
FRANCISCUS Yes; but make no words on't; I was a man
    Seven years ago.
LOLLIO A stripling, I think you might.°
FRANCISCUS Now I'm a woman, all feminine.
LOLLIO I would I might see that.   70
FRANCISCUS Juno struck me blind.
LOLLIO I'll ne'er believe that; for a woman, they say, has an eye° more
    than a man.
FRANCISCUS I say she struck me blind.
LOLLIO And Luna made you mad; you have two trades° to beg with.   75
FRANCISCUS Luna is now big-bellied, and there's room
    For both of us to ride with Hecate;°
    I'll drag thee up into her silver sphere,
    And there we'll kick the dog, and beat the bush°
    That barks against the witches of the night: 80
    The swift lycanthropi that walks the round,°
    We'll tear their wolvish skins, and save the sheep.
       [*Franciscus seizes Lollio*]
LOLLIO Is't come to this? Nay, then my poison comes forth again;
    mad slave, indeed, abuse your keeper! [*Lollio produces a whip*]
ISABELLA I prithee hence with him, now he grows dangerous.   85
FRANCISCUS (*sings*)
        Sweet love, pity me,
        Give me leave to lie with thee.
LOLLIO No, I'll see you wiser first: to your own kennel.

FRANCISCUS No noise, she sleeps, draw all the curtains round;
    Let no soft sound molest the pretty soul   90
    But love, and love creeps in at a mouse-hole.°
LOLLIO I would you would get into your hole.
    Exit Franciscus
  Now, mistress, I will bring you another sort; you shall be fooled
  another while; Tony, come hither, Tony; look who's yonder,
  Tony.   95
    Enter Antonio
ANTONIO Cousin, is it not my aunt?°
LOLLIO Yes, 'tis one of 'em, Tony.
ANTONIO He, he, how do you, uncle?
LOLLIO Fear him not, mistress, 'tis a gentle nidget;° you may play
  with him, as safely with him as with his bauble.°   100
ISABELLA How long hast thou been a fool?
ANTONIO Ever since I came hither, cousin.
ISABELLA Cousin, I am none of thy cousins,° fool.
LOLLIO Oh mistress, fools have always so much wit as to claim their
  kindred.   105
MADMEN (*within*) Bounce, bounce, he falls, he falls.
ISABELLA Hark you, your scholars in the upper room
    Are out of order.
LOLLIO Must I come amongst you there? Keep you the fool, mistress;
  I'll go up and play left-handed Orlando° amongst the madmen.   110
    Exit [Lollio]
ISABELLA Well, sir.
ANTONIO 'Tis opportuneful now, sweet lady! Nay,
    Cast no amazing eye upon this change.°
ISABELLA Ha!
ANTONIO This shape of folly shrouds your dearest love,   115
    The truest servant to your powerful beauties,
    Whose magic had this force thus to transform me.
ISABELLA You are a fine fool indeed.
ANTONIO   Oh, 'tis not strange;
    Love has an intellect that runs through all
    The scrutinous sciences, and like   120
    A cunning poet, catches a quantity
    Of every knowledge, yet brings all home
    Into one mystery, into one secret
    That he proceeds in.
ISABELLA   Y'are a parlous fool.°

ANTONIO No danger in me: I bring nought but love,   125
   And his soft-wounding shafts to strike you with:
   Try but one arrow; if it hurt you,°
   I'll stand you twenty back in recompense. [*Tries to kiss her*]
ISABELLA A forward fool too!
ANTONIO   This was love's teaching:
   A thousand ways he fashioned out my way,   130
   And this I found the safest and nearest
   To tread the Galaxia to my star.°
ISABELLA Profound withal! Certain, you dreamed of this;
   Love never taught it waking.
ANTONIO   Take no acquaintance°
   Of these outward follies; there is within   135
   A gentleman that loves you.
ISABELLA   When I see him,
   I'll speak with him; so in the meantime keep
   Your habit, it becomes you well enough.
   As you are a gentleman, I'll not discover you;°
   That's all the favour that you must expect: 140
   When you are weary, you may leave the school,
   For all this while you have but played the fool.
     Enter Lollio
ANTONIO And must again. He, he, I thank you, cousin;°
   I'll be your valentine tomorrow morning.
LOLLIO How do you like the fool, mistress?   145
ISABELLA Passing well, sir.°
LOLLIO Is he not witty, pretty well for a fool?
ISABELLA If he hold on as he begins, he is like
   To come to something.
LOLLIO Ay, thank a good tutor: you may put him to't; he begins to   150
   answer pretty hard questions. Tony, how many is five times six?
ANTONIO Five times six is six times five.
LOLLIO What arithmetician could have answered better? How many
   is one hundred and seven?
ANTONIO One hundred and seven is seven hundred and one, cousin.   155
LOLLIO This is no wit to speak on; will you be rid of the fool now?
ISABELLA By no means, let him stay a little.
MADMEN (*within*) Catch there, catch the last couple in hell!°
LOLLIO Again? Must I come amongst you? Would my master were
   come home! I am not able to govern both these wards° together.   160
     Exit [*Lollio*]

ANTONIO Why should a minute of love's hour be lost?

ISABELLA Fie, out again? I had rather you kept
  Your other posture: you become not your tongue,
  When you speak from your clothes.°

ANTONIO   How can he freeze
  Lives near so sweet a warmth? Shall I alone   165
  Walk through the orchard of the Hesperides,°
  And cowardly not dare to pull an apple?
  This with the red cheeks I must venture for.
      Enter Lollio above. [*Antonio tries to kiss Isabella*]

ISABELLA Take heed, there's giants keep'em.°

LOLLIO [*aside*] How now, fool, are you good at that? Have your read 170
  Lipsius?° He's past *Ars Amandi*;° I believe I must put harder questions to him, I perceive that.

ISABELLA You are bold without fear too.

ANTONIO   What should I fear,
  Having all joys about me? Do you smile,°
  And love shall play the wanton on your lip,   175
  Meet and retire, retire and meet again:
  Look you but cheerfully, and in your eyes
  I shall behold mine own deformity,
  And dress myself up fairer; I know this shape
  Becomes me not, but in those bright mirrors°   180
  I shall array me handsomely.

LOLLIO Cuckoo! cuckoo!°
      Exit [*Lollio above.*] [*Enter*] *Madmen above, some as birds, others*
      as beasts°

ANTONIO What are these?

ISABELLA   Of fear enough to part us;
  Yet are they but our schools of lunatics,°
  That act their fantasies in any shapes   185
  Suiting their present thoughts; if sad, they cry;
  If mirth be their conceit, they laugh again;°
  Sometimes they imitate the beasts and birds,
  Singing or howling, braying, barking; all
  As their wild fancies prompt'em.
      [*Exeunt Madmen above.*] *Enter Lollio*

ANTONIO   These are no fears.   190

ISABELLA But here's a large one—my man.°

ANTONIO Ha, he, that's fine sport indeed, cousin.

LOLLIO I would my master were come home, 'tis too much for one

shepherd to govern two of these flocks; nor can I believe that one
churchman can instruct two benefices° at once; there will be some   195
incurable mad of the one side, and very fools on the other. Come,
Tony.

ANTONIO   Prithee, cousin, let me stay here still.

LOLLIO   No, you must to your book, now you have played sufficiently.

ISABELLA   Your fool is grown wondrous witty.   200

LOLLIO   Well, I'll say nothing; but I do not think but he will put you
down° one of these days.
        Exit Lollio and Antonio

ISABELLA   Here the restrainèd current might make a breach,
        Spite of the watchful bankers; would a woman stray,°
        She need not gad abroad to seek her sin,   205
        It would be brought home one ways or other:
        The needle's point will to the fixèd north;°
        Such drawing arctics women's beauties are.
        Enter Lollio

LOLLIO   How does thou, sweet rogue?

ISABELLA   How now?   210

LOLLIO   Come, there are degrees, one fool may be better than
another.°

ISABELLA   What's the matter?

LOLLIO   Nay, if thou giv'st thy mind to fool's-flesh, have at thee!
        [*Lollio tries to kiss her*]

ISABELLA   You bold slave, you!   215

LOLLIO   I could follow now as t'other fool did:
        'What should I fear,
        Having all joys about me? Do you smile,
        And love shall play the wanton on your lip,
        Meet and retire, retire and meet again: 220
        Look you but cheerfully, and in your eyes
        I shall behold my own deformity,
        And dress myself up fairer; I know this shape
        Becomes me not—'°
        And so as it follows; but is not this the more foolish way? Come, 225
        sweet rogue, kiss me, my little Lacedemonian.° Let me feel how thy
        pulses beat; thou hast a thing about thee would do a man pleasure,
        I'll lay my hand on't.

ISABELLA   Sirrah, no more! I see you have discovered
        This love's knight-errant, who hath made adventure°   230
        For purchase of my love; be silent, mute,°

Mute as a statue, or his injunction
For me enjoying, shall be to cut thy throat:°
I'll do it, though for no other purpose,
And be sure he'll not refuse it.   235
LOLLIO My share, that's all; I'll have my fool's part with you.
ISABELLA No more—your master.
    Enter Alibius
ALIBIUS   Sweet, how dost thou?
ISABELLA Your bounden servant, sir.
ALIBIUS   Fie, fie, sweetheart,°
No more of that.
ISABELLA   You were best lock me up.
ALIBIUS In my arms and bosom, my sweet Isabella,   240
I'll lock thee up most nearly. Lollio,
We have employment, we have task in hand;
At noble Vermandero's, our castle-captain,
There is a nuptial to be solemnised
(Beatrice-Joanna, his fair daughter, bride)°   245
For which the gentleman hath bespoke our pains:°
A mixture of our madmen and our fools,
To finish, as it were, and make the fag
Of all the revels, the third night from the first;
Only an unexpected passage over,   250
To make a frightful pleasure, that is all,°
But not the all I aim at. Could we so act it,
To teach it in a wild distracted measure,
Though out of form and figure, breaking time's head,
It were no matter; 'twould be healed again   255
In one age or other, if not in this:
This, this, Lollio, there's a good reward begun
And will beget a bounty, be it known.°
LOLLIO This is easy, sir, I'll warrant you: you have about you fools
and madmen that can dance very well; and 'tis no wonder, your best   260
dancers are not the wisest men; the reason is, with often jumping
they jolt their brains down into their feet, that their wits lie more in
their heels than in their heads.
ALIBIUS Honest Lollio, thou giv'st me a good reason,
And a comfort in it.
ISABELLA   Y'have a fine trade on't,   265
Madmen and fools are a staple commodity.°
ALIBIUS Oh wife, we must eat, wear clothes, and live;

Just at the lawyers' haven we arrive,°
By madmen and by fools we both do thrive.
    Exeunt

3.4

   Enter Vermandero, Alsemero, Jasperino, and
   Beatrice-Joanna

VERMANDERO Valencia speaks so nobly of you, sir,
  I wish I had a daughter now for you.
ALSEMERO The fellow of this creature were a partner°
  For a king's love.
VERMANDERO   I had her fellow once, sir,°
  But heaven has married her to joys eternal;   5
  'Twere sin to wish her in this vale again.°
  Come, sir, your friend and you shall see the pleasures
  Which my health chiefly joys in.
ALSEMERO I hear the beauty of this seat largely.°
VERMANDERO It falls much short of that.
    Exeunt [Vermandero, Alsemero and Jasperine]. Beatrice-Joanna
    remains
BEATRICE-JOANNA   So, here's one step   10
  Into my father's favour; time will fix him.
  I have got him now the liberty of the house:
  So wisdom by degrees works out her freedom;
  And if that eye be darkened that offends me°
  (I wait but that eclipse), this gentleman   15
  Shall soon shine glorious in my father's liking,
  Through the refulgent virtue of my love.°
    Enter Deflores
DEFLORES [*aside*] My thoughts are at a banquet for the deed;
  I feel no weight in't, 'tis but light and cheap°
  For the sweet recompense that I set down for't.   20
BEATRICE-JOANNA Deflores.
DEFLORES   Lady.
BEATRICE-JOANNA   Thy looks promise cheerfully.
DEFLORES All things are answerable, time, circumstance,
  Your wishes, and my service.
BEATRICE-JOANNA   Is it done then?

DEFLORES Piracquo is no more.

BEATRICE-JOANNA My joys start at mine eyes; our sweet'st delights   25
  Are evermore born weeping.

DEFLORES   I've a token for you.°

BEATRICE-JOANNA For me?

DEFLORES   But it was sent somewhat unwillingly,
  I could not get the ring without the finger.
        [*Deflores shows her the finger*]

BEATRICE-JOANNA Bless me! What hast thou done?

DEFLORES   Why, is that more
  Than killing the whole man? I cut his heart-strings.   30
  A greedy hand thrust in a dish at court
  In a mistake hath had as much as this.°

BEATRICE-JOANNA 'Tis the first token my father made me send him.

DEFLORES And I made him send it back again
  For his last token; I was loath to leave it,   35
  And I'm sure dead men have no use of jewels.
  He was as loath to part with't, for it stuck
  As if the flesh and it were both one substance.

BEATRICE-JOANNA At the stag's fall the keeper has his fees;°
  'Tis soon applied: all dead men's fees are yours, sir;   40
  I pray, bury the finger, but the stone
  You may make use on shortly; the true value,
  Take't of my truth, is near three hundred ducats.

DEFLORES 'Twill hardly buy a capcase for one's conscience, though,
  To keep it from the worm, as fine as 'tis.°   45
  Well, being my fees, I'll take it;
  Great men have taught me that, or else my merit
  Would scorn the way on't.

BEATRICE-JOANNA   It might justly, sir:°
  Why, thou mistak'st, Deflores, 'tis not given
  In state of recompense.

DEFLORES   No, I hope so, lady°   50
  You should soon witness my contempt to't then.

BEATRICE-JOANNA Prithee, thou look'st as if thou wert
  offended.

DEFLORES That were strange, lady; 'tis not possible
  My service should draw such a cause from you.
  Offended? Could you think so? That were much   55
  For one of my performance, and so warm°
  Yet in my service.

BEATRICE-JOANNA 'Twere misery in me to give you cause, sir.
DEFLORES I know so much; it were so, misery
 In her most sharp condition.
BEATRICE-JOANNA   'Tis resolved then;
 Look you, sir, here's three thousand golden florins: 60
 I have not meanly thought upon thy merit.
DEFLORES What, salary? Now you move me.
BEATRICE-JOANNA   How, Deflores?
DEFLORES Do you place me in the rank of verminous fellows,
 To destroy things for wages? Offer gold?
 The life blood of man! Is anything°   65
 Valued too precious for my recompense?
BEATRICE-JOANNA I understand thee not.
DEFLORES   I could ha' hired
 A journeyman in murder at this rate,°
 And mine own conscience might have slept at ease,°
 And have had the work brought home.
BEATRICE-JOANNA [*aside*]   I'm in a labyrinth.° 70
 What will content him? I would fain be rid of him.
 [*To him*] I'll double the sum, sir.
DEFLORES   You take a course
 To double my vexation, that's the good you do.
BEATRICE-JOANNA [*aside*] Bless me! I am now in worse plight than I
  was;
 I know not what will please him. [*To him*] For my fear's sake, 75
 I prithee make away with all speed possible.
 And if thou be'st so modest not to name
 The sum that will content thee, paper blushes not;
 Send thy demand in writing, it shall follow thee,
 But prithee take thy flight.
DEFLORES   You must fly too then.   80
BEATRICE-JOANNA I?
DEFLORES   I'll not stir a foot else.
BEATRICE-JOANNA   What's your meaning?
DEFLORES Why, are not you as guilty? In, I'm sure,
 As deep as I? And we should stick together.
 Come, your fears counsel you but ill, my absence°
 Would draw suspect upon you instantly;   85
 There were no rescue for you.
BEATRICE-JOANNA [*aside*] He speaks home.
DEFLORES Nor is it fit we two, engaged so jointly,

Should part and live asunder. [*Deflores tries to kiss her*]
BEATRICE-JOANNA   How now, sir?
   This shows not well.
DEFLORES   What makes your lip so strange?
   This must not be betwixt us.
BEATRICE-JOANNA [*aside*]   The man talks wildly.   90
DEFLORES   Come, kiss me with a zeal now.
BEATRICE-JOANNA [*aside*]   Heaven, I doubt him!
DEFLORES   I will not stand so long to beg'em shortly.
BEATRICE-JOANNA   Take heed, Deflores, of forgetfulness,°
   'Twill soon betray us.
DEFLORES   Take you heed first;
   Faith, y'are grown much forgetful, y'are too blame in't.°   95
BEATRICE-JOANNA [*aside*] He's bold, and I am blamed for't!
DEFLORES   I have eased you
   Of your trouble, think on't; I'm in pain
   And must be eased of you; 'tis a charity.°
   Justice invites your blood to understand me.
BEATRICE-JOANNA   I dare not.
DEFLORES   Quickly!
BEATRICE-JOANNA   Oh, I never shall!   100
   Speak it yet further off, that I may lose
   What has been spoken, and no sound remain on't.°
   I would not hear so much offence again
   For such another deed.
DEFLORES   Soft, lady, soft;
   The last is not yet paid for! Oh, this act   105
   Has put me into spirit; I was as greedy on't°
   As the parched earth of moisture, when the clouds weep.
   Did you not mark I wrought myself into't?°
   Nay, sued and kneeled for it? Why was all that pains took?
   You see I have thrown contempt upon your gold,   110
   Not that I want it not, for I do piteously:
   In order I will come unto't, and make use on't,°
   But 'twas not held so precious to begin with;
   For I place wealth after the heels of pleasure,
   And were I not resolved in my belief   115
   That thy virginity were perfect in thee,
   I should but take my recompense with grudging,
   As if I had but half my hopes I agreed for.
BEATRICE-JOANNA   Why, 'tis impossible thou canst be so wicked,

Or shelter such a cunning cruelty,   120
To make his death the murderer of my honour.
Thy language is so bold and vicious,
I cannot see which way I can forgive it
With any modesty.
DEFLORES   Push, you forget yourself!
A woman dipped in blood and talk of modesty?   125
BEATRICE-JOANNA Oh misery of sin! Would I had been bound°
Perpetually unto my living hate
In that Piracquo, than to hear these words.
Think but upon the distance that creation
Set 'twixt thy blood and mine, and keep thee there.°   130
DEFLORES Look but into your conscience, read me there,
'Tis a true book, you'll find me there your equal:
Push, fly not to your birth, but settle you
In what the act has made you, y'are no more now;°
You must forget your parentage to me;°   135
Y'are the deed's creature; by that name°
You lost your first condition, and I challenge you,°
As peace and innocency has turn'd you out,°
And made you one with me.
BEATRICE-JOANNA   With thee, foul villain?
DEFLORES Yes, my fair murderess; do you urge me?   140
Though thou writ'st 'maid', thou whore in thy affection;°
'Twas changed from thy first love, and that's a kind
Of whoredom in thy heart; and he's changed now
To bring thy second on, thy Alsemero.
Whom (by all sweets that ever darkness tasted)   145
If I enjoy thee not, thou ne'er enjoy'st;
I'll blast the hopes and joys of marriage—
I'll confess all; my life I rate at nothing.
BEATRICE-JOANNA Deflores!
DEFLORES I shall rest from all lovers' plagues then;   150
I live in pain now: that shooting eye°
Will burn my heart to cinders.
BEATRICE-JOANNA   Oh sir, hear me.
DEFLORES She that in life and love refuses me,
In death and shame my partner she shall be.
BEATRICE-JOANNA Stay, hear me once for all. [*Kneels*] I make thee
    master   155
Of all the wealth I have in gold and jewels:

Let me go poor unto my bed with honour,
And I am rich in all things.
DEFLORES Let this silence thee:
The wealth of all Valencia shall not buy
My pleasure from me;   160
Can you weep fate from its determined purpose?
So soon may you weep me.
BEATRICE-JOANNA   Vengeance begins;°
Murder I see is followed by more sins.
Was my creation in the womb so cursed
It must engender with a viper first?°   165
DEFLORES Come, rise and shroud your blushes in my bosom.
     [*Lifts her*]
Silence is one of pleasure's best receipts:
Thy peace is wrought for ever in this yielding.
'Las, how the turtle pants! Thou'lt love anon
What thou so fear'st and faint'st to venture on.   170
     Exeunt

4.1

*[Dumb-show] Enter Gentlemen, Vermandero meeting them
with action of wonderment at the flight of Piracquo. Enter
Alsemero, with Jasperino, and Gallants. Vermandero points to
him, the Gentlemen seeming to applaud the choice.° [Exeunt in
procession Vermandero,°] Alsemero, Jasperino, and Gentlemen.
Beatrice-Joanna the bride following in great state,°
accompanied with Diaphanta, Isabella and other
Gentlewomen. Deflores after all, smiling at the accident.°
Alonzo's ghost appears to Deflores in the midst of his smile,
startles him, showing him the hand whose finger he had cut
off. They pass over° in great solemnity. Enter Beatrice-
Joanna*

BEATRICE-JOANNA This fellow has undone me endlessly,°
  Never was bride so fearfully distressed;
  The more I think upon the ensuing night,
  And whom I am to cope with in embraces,°
  One that's ennobled both in blood and mind,° 5
  So clear in understanding (that's my plague now),
  Before whose judgement will my fault appear
  Like malefactors' crimes before tribunals;
  There is no hiding on't, the more I dive
  Into my own distress. How a wise man° 10
  Stands for a great calamity! There's no venturing°
  Into his bed, what course soe'er I light upon,°
  Without my shame, which may grow up to danger;°
  He cannot but in justice strangle me
  As I lie by him, as a cheater use me;° 15
  'Tis a precious craft to play with a false die°
  Before a cunning gamester. Here's his closet,
  The key left in't, and he abroad i'th' park:°
  Sure 'twas forgot; I'll be so bold as look in't. *[Opens closet]*
  Bless me! A right physician's closet 'tis, 20
  Set round with vials, every one her mark too.
  Sure he does practise physic for his own use,°
  Which may be safely called your great man's wisdom.
  What manuscript lies here? 'The Book of Experiment.
  Called *Secrets in Nature*'; so 'tis, 'tis so;° 25

'How to know whether a woman be with child or no.'
I hope I am not yet; if he should try though!
Let me see, folio forty-five. Here 'tis;°
The leaf tucked down upon't, the place suspicious.
'If you would know whether a woman be with child or not, give her   30
two spoonfuls of the white water in glass C . . . '
Where's that glass C? Oh yonder, I see't now—
' . . . and if she be with child, she sleeps full twelve hours after,
if not, not.'
None of that water comes into my belly.   35
I'll know you from a hundred; I could break you now,°
Or turn you into milk, and so beguile
The master of the mystery, but I'll look to you.°
Ha! That which is next is ten times worse.
'How to know whether a woman be a maid or not.'   40
If that should be applied, what would become of me?
Belike he has a strong faith of my purity,
That never yet made proof; but this he calls
'A merry sleight,° but true experiment, the author Antonius Mizal-
dus. Give the party you suspect the quantity of a spoonful of the   45
water in glass M, which upon her that is a maid makes three several
effects: 'twill make her incontinently gape, then fall into a sudden
sneezing, last into a violent laughing; else dull, heavy, and lumpish.'
Where had I been?°
I fear it, yet 'tis seven hours to bedtime.   50

        Enter Diaphanta
DIAPHANTA Cuds, madam, are you here?
BEATRICE-JOANNA [*aside*]   Seeing that wench now,
    A trick comes in my mind; 'tis a nice piece
    Gold cannot purchase. [*To her*] I come hither, wench,°
    To look my lord.
DIAPHANTA [*aside*] Would I had such a cause
    To look him too. [*To her*] Why, he's i'th'park, madam.°   55
BEATRICE-JOANNA There let him be.
DIAPHANTA   Ay, madam, let him compass
    Whole parks and forests, as great rangers do;
    At roosting time a little lodge can hold'em.°
    Earth-conquering Alexander, that thought the world
    Too narrow for him, in the end had but his pit-hole.°   60
BEATRICE-JOANNA I fear thou art not modest, Diaphanta.
DIAPHANTA Your thoughts are so unwilling to be known, madam;

207

'Tis ever the bride's fashion towards bed-time
To set light by her joys, as if she owed 'em not.°
BEATRICE-JOANNA Her joys? Her fears, thou would'st say.
DIAPHANTA   Fear of what?   65
BEATRICE-JOANNA Art thou a maid and talk'st so to a maid?
You leave a blushing business behind,°
Beshrew your heart for't!
DIAPHANTA   Do you mean good sooth, madam?°
BEATRICE-JOANNA Well, if I'd thought upon the fear at first
Man should have been unknown.
DIAPHANTA   Is't possible?   70
BEATRICE-JOANNA I will give a thousand ducats to that woman
Would try what my fear were, and tell me true
Tomorrow, when she gets from't: as she likes
I might perhaps be drawn to't.
DIAPHANTA   Are you in earnest?°
BEATRICE-JOANNA Do you get the woman, then challenge me°   75
And see if I'll fly from't; but I must tell you
This by the way, she must be a true maid,
Else there's no trial, my fears are not hers else.
DIAPHANTA Nay, she that I would put into your hands, madam,
Shall be a maid.
BEATRICE-JOANNA You know I should be shamed else,   80
Because she lies for me.
DIAPHANTA   'Tis a strange humour:
But are you serious still? Would you resign
Your first night's pleasure, and give money too?
BEATRICE-JOANNA As willingly as live. [Aside] Alas, the gold
Is but a by-bet to wedge in the honour.°   85
DIAPHANTA I do not know how the world goes abroad
For faith or honesty, there's both required in this.°
Madam, what say you to me, and stray no further?
I've a good mind, in troth, to earn your money.
BEATRICE-JOANNA Y'are too quick, I fear, to be a maid.   90
DIAPHANTA How? Not a maid? Nay, then you urge me, madam;°
Your honourable self is not a truer
With all your fears upon you—
BEATRICE-JOANNA [aside]   Bad enough then.
DIAPHANTA Than I with all my lightsome joys about me.
BEATRICE-JOANNA I'm glad to hear't then; you dare put your
honesty°   95

Upon an easy trial?
DIAPHANTA   Easy? Anything.
BEATRICE-JOANNA I'll come to you straight.
        [*Beatrice-Joanna goes to the closet*]
DIAPHANTA [*aside*]   She will not search me, will she,
    Like the forewoman of a female jury?°
BEATRICE-JOANNA Glass M: ay, this is it; look, Diaphanta,
    You take no worse than I do. [*Beatrice-Joanna drinks*]
DIAPHANTA   And in so doing   100
    I will not question what 'tis, but take it. [*Diaphanta drinks*]
BEATRICE-JOANNA [*aside*] Now if the experiment be true, 'twill
        praise itself°
    And give me noble ease. [*Diaphanta gapes*] Begins already.
    There's the first symptom; and what haste it makes
    To fall into the second, [*Diaphanta sneezes*] there by this time. 105
    Most admirable secret. On the contrary,
    It stirs not me a whit, which most concerns it.°
DIAPHANTA Ha, ha, ha!
BEATRICE-JOANNA [*aside*] Just in all things and in order
    As if 'twere circumscribed; one accident°
    Gives way unto another.
DIAPHANTA   Ha, ha, ha!
BEATRICE-JOANNA   How now, wench?   110
DIAPHANTA Ha, ha, ha! I am so, so light at heart—ha, ha, ha!—so
        pleasurable!
    But one swig more, sweet madam.
BEATRICE-JOANNA   Ay, tomorrow;
    We shall have time to sit by't.
DIAPHANTA   Now I'm sad again.
BEATRICE-JOANNA [*aside*] It lays itself so gently too. [*To her*] Come,
    wench,°
    Most honest Diaphanta I dare call thee now.   115
DIAPHANTA Pray tell me, madam, what trick call you this?
BEATRICE-JOANNA I'll tell thee all hereafter; we must study
    The carriage of this business.
DIAPHANTA   I shall carry't well°
    Because I love the burden.
BEATRICE-JOANNA   About midnight°
    You must not fail to steal forth gently,   120
    That I may use the place.
DIAPHANTA   Oh, fear not, madam,°

I shall be cool by that time. [*Aside*] The bride's place,
And with a thousand ducats. I'm for a justice now,
I bring a portion with me; I scorn small fools.°
    Exeunt

4.2

    Enter Vermandero and Servant
VERMANDERO I tell thee, knave, mine honour is in question°
  A thing till now free from suspicion,
  Nor ever was there cause. Who of my gentlemen
  Are absent? Tell me and truly how many and who.
SERVANT Antonio, sir, and Franciscus.   5
VERMANDERO When did they leave the castle?
SERVANT Some ten days since, sir, the one intending to Briamata,°
    th'other for Valencia.
VERMANDERO The time accuses 'em; a charge of murder°
  Is brought within my castle gate, Piracquo's murder;   10
  I dare not answer faithfully their absence:
  A strict command of apprehension°
  Shall pursue 'em suddenly, and either wipe
  The stain off clear or openly discover it.
  Provide me wingèd warrants for the purpose.   15
    Exit Servant
  See, I am set on again.°
    Enter Tomazo
TOMAZO I claim a brother of you.
VERMANDERO   Y'are too hot,
  Seek him not here.
TOMAZO   Yes, 'mongst your dearest bloods,
  If my peace find no fairer satisfaction;
  This is the place must yield account for him,°   20
  For here I left him, and the hasty tie
  Of this snatched marriage gives strong testimony
  Of his most certain ruin.
VERMANDERO   Certain falsehood!
  This is the place indeed; his breach of faith°
  Has too much marred both my abusèd love,   25
  The honourable love I reserved for him,

And mocked my daughter's joy; the prepared morning°
Blushed at his infidelity; he left
Contempt and scorn to throw upon those friends
Whose belief hurt'em: oh, 'twas most ignoble   30
To take his flight so unexpectedly,
And throw such public wrongs on those that loved him.
TOMAZO Then this is all your answer?
VERMANDERO   'Tis too fair
For one of his alliance; and I warn you°
That this place no more see you.
       Exit [Vermandero.] Enter Deflores
TOMAZO   The best is°   35
There is more ground to meet a man's revenge on.°
Honest Deflores!
DEFLORES   That's my name indeed.
Saw you the bride? Good sweet sir, which way took she?
TOMAZO I have blessed mine eyes from seeing such a false one.°
DEFLORES [*aside*] I'd fain get off. This man's not for my company,° 40
I smell his brother's blood when I come near him.
TOMAZO Come hither, kind and true one; I remember
My brother loved thee well.
DEFLORES   Oh purely, dear sir.
[*Aside*] Methinks I am now again a-killing on him,
He brings it so fresh to me.
TOMAZO   Thou canst guess, sirrah,   45
(One honest friend has an instinct of jealousy)
At some foul guilty person?°
DEFLORES 'Las, sir, I am so charitable, I think none
Worse than myself. You did not see the bride then?
TOMAZO I prithee, name her not. Is she not wicked?   50
DEFLORES No, no, a pretty, easy, round-packed sinner°
As your most ladies are (else you might think
I flattered her); but, sir, at no hand wicked
Till th'are so old their chins and noses meet,°
And they salute witches. I am called, I think, sir.   55
[*Aside*] His company ev'n o'erlays my conscience.°
       Exit [Deflores]
TOMAZO That Deflores has a wondrous honest heart;
He'll bring it out in time, I am assured on't.°
Oh, here's the glorious master of the day's joy.
'Twill not be long till he and I do reckon.°   60

Enter Alsemero

Sir.

ALSEMERO You are most welcome.

TOMAZO   You may call that word back.
    I do not think I am, nor wish to be.

ALSEMERO 'Tis strange you found the way to this house then.

TOMAZO Would I'd ne'er known the cause! I'm none of those, sir,   65
    That come to give you joy, and swill your wine;°
    'Tis a more precious liquor that must lay°
    The fiery thirst I bring.

ALSEMERO   Your words and you
    Appear to me great strangers.

TOMAZO   Time and our swords
    May make us more acquainted. This the business: 70
    I should have a brother in your place.
    How treachery and malice have disposed of him
    I am bound to enquire of him which holds his right,
    Which never could come fairly.

ALSEMERO   You must look°
    To answer for that word, sir.

TOMAZO   Fear you not,   75
    I'll have it ready drawn at our next meeting.°
    Keep your day solemn. Farewell, I disturb it not;°
    I'll bear the smart with patience for a time.

      Exit [Tomazo]

ALSEMERO 'Tis somewhat ominous this: a quarrel entered
    Upon this day. My innocence relieves me.°   80

      Enter Jasperino

    I should be wondrous sad else. Jasperino,
    I have news to tell thee, strange news.

JASPERINO   I ha'some too,
    I think as strange as yours. Would I might keep
    Mine, so my faith and friendship might be kept in't.°
    Faith, sir, dispense a little with my zeal   85
    And let it cool in this.

ALSEMERO   This puts me on,°
    And blames thee for thy slowness.

JASPERINO   All may prove nothing;°
    Only a friendly fear that leapt from me, sir.

ALSEMERO No question it may prove nothing; let's partake it,
    though.°

JASPERINO 'Twas Diaphanta's chance (for to that wench   90
    I pretend honest love, and she deserves it)°
    To leave me in a back part of the house,
    A place we chose for private conference;
    She was no sooner gone but instantly
    I heard your bride's voice in the next room to me;   95
    And lending more attention, found Deflores
    Louder than she.
ALSEMERO   Deflores? Thou art out now.°
JASPERINO You'll tell me more anon.
ALSEMERO   Still I'll prevent thee;°
    The very sight of him is poison to her.
JASPERINO That made me stagger too, but Diaphanta   100
    At her return confirmed it.
ALSEMERO   Diaphanta!
JASPERINO Then fell we both to listen, and words passed
    Like those that challenge interest in a woman.
ALSEMERO Peace, quench thy zeal; 'tis dangerous to thy bosom.°
JASPERINO Then truth is full of peril.
ALSEMERO   Such truths are;   105
    Oh, were she the sole glory of the earth,
    Had eyes that could shoot fire into kings' breasts,
    And touched, she sleeps not here. Yet I have time,°
    Though night be near, to be resolved hereof;°
    And prithee do not weigh me by my passions.   110
JASPERINO I never weighed friend so.
ALSEMERO   Done charitably. [*Alsemero gives Jasperino a key*]
    That key will lead thee to a pretty secret
    By a Chaldean taught me, and I've made°
    My study upon some; bring from my closet
    A glass inscribed there with the letter M,   115
    And question not my purpose.
JASPERINO   It shall be done, sir.
      Exit [*Jasperino*]
ALSEMERO How can this hang together? Not an hour since,°
    Her woman came pleading her lady's fears,
    Delivered her for the most timorous virgin°
    That ever shrunk at man's name, and so modest   120
    She charged her weep out her request to me,
    That she might come obscurely to my bosom.°
    Enter Beatrice-Joanna

BEATRICE-JOANNA [*aside*] All things go well. My woman's preparing
    yonder
    For her sweet voyage, which grieves me to lose;°
    Necessity compels it; I lose all else.   125

ALSEMERO [*aside*] Push, modesty's shrine is set in yonder forehead.
    I cannot be too sure though. [*To her*] My Joanna!

BEATRICE-JOANNA Sir, I was bold to weep a message to you;
    Pardon my modest fears.

ALSEMERO [*aside*]   The dove's not meeker;
    She's abused, questionless.

       Enter Jasperino [*with a glass*]

                    Oh, are you come, sir?°   130

BEATRICE-JOANNA [*aside*] The glass, upon my life! I see the letter.

JASPERINO Sir, this is M.

ALSEMERO   'Tis it.

BEATRICE-JOANNA [*aside*]   I am suspected.

ALSEMERO How fitly our bride comes to partake with us!

BEATRICE-JOANNA What is't, my lord?

ALSEMERO   No hurt.

BEATRICE-JOANNA   Sir, pardon me,
    I seldom taste of any composition.   135

ALSEMERO But this, upon my warrant, you shall venture on.

BEATRICE-JOANNA I fear 'twill make me ill.

ALSEMERO   Heaven forbid that.

BEATRICE-JOANNA [*aside*] I'm put now to my cunning; th'effects I
    know,
    If I can now but feign'em handsomely.

      [*Beatrice-Joanna drinks*]

ALSEMERO [*to Jasperino*] It has that secret virtue, it ne'er missed, sir,   140
    Upon a virgin.

JASPERINO   Treble qualitied?°

      [*Beatrice-Joanna gapes, then sneezes*]

ALSEMERO By all that's virtuous it takes there, proceeds!

JASPERINO This is the strangest trick to know a maid by.

BEATRICE-JOANNA Ha, ha, ha!
    You have given me joy of heart to drink, my lord.   145

ALSEMERO No, thou hast given me such joy of heart,
    That never can be blasted.

BEATRICE-JOANNA   What's the matter, sir?°

ALSEMERO [*to Jasperino*] See, now 'tis settled in a melancholy,
    Keeps both the time and method. [*To her*] My Joanna,°

Chaste as the breath of heaven, or morning's womb   150
That brings the day forth, thus my love encloses thee.
    [*Embraces her.*] *Exeunt*

4.3

    Enter Isabella and Lollio

ISABELLA Oh heaven! Is this the waiting moon?°
  Does love turn fool, run mad, and all at once?
  Sirrah, here's a madman akin to the fool too,°
  A lunatic lover.
LOLLIO No, no, not he I brought the letter from?   5
ISABELLA Compare his inside with his out, and tell me. [*Gives him the
  letter*]°
LOLLIO The out's mad, I'm sure of that; I had a taste° on't.
  [*Reads*] 'To the bright Andromeda, chief chambermaid to the
  Knight of the Sun, at the sign of Scorpio, in the middle region, sent
  by the bellows mender of Aeolus. Pay the post.' This is stark   10
  madness.°
ISABELLA Now mark the inside. [*Takes letter and reads*] 'Sweet lady,
  having now cast off this counterfeit cover of a madman, I appear to°
  your best judgement a true and faithful lover of your beauty.'
LOLLIO He is mad still.   15
ISABELLA 'If any fault you find, chide those perfections in you which
  have made° me imperfect; 'tis the same sun that causeth to grow,
  and enforceth to wither . . .'
LOLLIO Oh rogue!
ISABELLA ' . . . Shapes and transshapes, destroys and builds again; I   20
  come in winter to you dismantled of my proper ornaments:° by the
  sweet splendour of your cheerful smiles I spring and live a lover.'
LOLLIO Mad rascal still.
ISABELLA 'Tread him not under foot that shall appear an honour to
  your bounties. I remain—mad till I speak with you, from whom I   25
  expect my cure. Yours all, or one beside himself, Franciscus.'
LOLLIO You are like to have a fine time on't; my master and I may
  give over our professions; I do not think but you can cure fools and
  madmen° faster than we, with little pains too.
ISABELLA Very likely.   30
LOLLIO One thing I must tell you, mistress: you perceive that I am

privy to your skill; if I find you minister once and set up the trade, I
put in for my thirds;° I shall be mad or fool else.

ISABELLA The first place is thine, believe it, Lollio;
    If I do fall—°   35

LOLLIO I fall upon you.

ISABELLA So.

LOLLIO Well, I stand to° my venture.

ISABELLA But thy counsel now, how shall I deal with° 'em?

LOLLIO Why,° do you mean to deal with 'em?   40

ISABELLA Nay, the fair understanding,° how to use 'em.

LOLLIO Abuse 'em; that's the way to mad the fool, and make a fool of
    the madman, and then you use 'em kindly.°

ISABELLA 'Tis easy, I'll practise; do thou observe it;
    The key of thy wardrobe.°   45

LOLLIO There, fit yourself for 'em, and I'll fit 'em° both for you.
    [Lollio gives her the key]

ISABELLA Take thou no further notice than the outside.
    Exit [Isabella]

LOLLIO Not an inch, I'll put you to the inside.°
    Enter Alibius

ALIBIUS Lollio, art there? Will all be perfect, think'st thou?
    Tomorrow night, as if to close up the solemnity,   50
    Vermandero expects us.

LOLLIO I mistrust the madmen most; the fools will do well enough; I
    have taken pains° with them.

ALIBIUS Tush, they cannot miss; the more absurdity,
    The more commends it, so no rough behaviours°   55
    Affright the ladies; they are nice things, thou know'st.°

LOLLIO You need not fear, sir; so long as we are there with our com-
    manding pizzles,° they'll be as tame as the ladies themselves.

ALIBIUS I will see them once more rehearse before they go.

LOLLIO I was about it, sir; look you to the madmen's morris,° and let   60
    me alone with the other; there is one or two that I mistrust their
    fooling; I'll instruct them, and then they shall rehearse the whole
    measure.°

ALIBIUS Do so; I'll see the music prepared. But Lollio,
    By the way, how does my wife brook her restraint?   65
    Does she not grudge at it?

LOLLIO So, so; she takes some pleasure in the house, she would
    abroad else; you must allow her a little more length, she's kept too
    short.°

ALIBIUS She shall along to Vermandero's with us;   70
    That will serve her for a month's liberty.

LOLLIO What's that on your face, sir?

ALIBIUS Where, Lollio? I see nothing.

LOLLIO Cry you mercy, sir, 'tis your nose; it showed like the trunk of
    a young elephant.°   75

ALIBIUS Away, rascal! I'll prepare the music, Lollio.
       Exit Alibius

LOLLIO Do, sir, and I'll dance the whilst; Tony, where art thou,
    Tony?
       Enter Antonio

ANTONIO Here, cousin: where art thou?

LOLLIO Come, Tony, the footmanship I taught you.   80

ANTONIO I had rather ride, cousin.°

LOLLIO Ay, a whip take you; but I'll keep you out. Vault in;° look you,
    Tony: fa, la la, la la. [*Lollio dances*]

ANTONIO Fa, la la, la la. [*Antonio dances*]

LOLLIO There, an honour.°   85

ANTONIO Is this an honour, coz? [*Bows*]

LOLLIO Yes, an it please your worship.

ANTONIO Does honour bend in the hams, coz?°

LOLLIO Marry does it; as low as worship, squireship, nay, yeomanry°
    itself sometimes, from whence it first stiffened. There rise, a caper.   90

ANTONIO Caper after an honour, coz?

LOLLIO Very proper, for honour is but a caper, rises° as fast and high,
    has a knee or two, and falls to th'ground again. You can remember
    your figure,° Tony?
       Exit [Lollio]

ANTONIO Yes, cousin; when I see thy figure, I can remember mine.   95
    [*Antonio dances.*] *Enter Isabella* [*like a madwoman*]

ISABELLA Hey, how he° treads the air; shoo, shoo, t'other way, he
    burns his wings else; here's wax enough below, Icarus, more than
    will be cancelled these eighteen moons; he's down, he's down, what
    a terrible fall he had. [*Antonio falls.*] Stand up, thou son of Cretan
    Daedalus, and let us tread the lower labyrinth; I'll bring thee to the   100
    clue.° [*Isabella helps him up*]

ANTONIO Prithee, coz, let me alone.

ISABELLA   Art thou not drowned?°
    About thy head I saw a heap of clouds,
    Wrapped like a Turkish turban; on thy back
    A crooked chameleon-coloured rainbow hung   105

Like a tiara down unto thy hams.°
Let me suck out those billows in thy belly;
Hark how they roar and rumble in the straits!°
Bless thee from the pirates.

ANTONIO Pox upon you, let me alone.   110

ISABELLA Why shouldst thou mount so high as Mercury,
Unless thou hadst reversion of his place?°
Stay in the moon with me, Endymion,°
And we will rule these wild rebellious waves,
That would have drowned my love.   115

ANTONIO I'll kick thee if again thou touch me,
Thou wild unshapen antic; I am no fool,°
You bedlam.

ISABELLA   But you are, as sure as I am, mad.°
Have I put on this habit of a frantic,
With love as full of fury to beguile   120
The nimble eye of watchful jealousy,
And am I thus rewarded? [*Isabella reveals herself*]

ANTONIO Ha! Dearest beauty!

ISABELLA   No, I have no beauty now,
Nor never had, but what was in my garments.
You a quick-sighted lover? Come not near me.   125
Keep your caparisons, y'are aptly clad;
I came a feigner to return stark mad.°
        Exit [Isabella.] Enter Lollio

ANTONIO Stay, or I shall change condition,
And become as you are.

LOLLIO Why, Tony, whither now? Why, fool?   130

ANTONIO Whose fool, usher of idiots? You coxcomb!°
I have fooled too much.

LOLLIO You were best be mad another while then.°

ANTONIO So I am stark mad, I have cause enough;
And I could throw the full effects on thee,   135
And beat thee like a fury.

LOLLIO Do not, do not; I shall not forbear the gentleman under the
fool, if you do; alas, I saw through your fox-skin° before now: come,
I can give you comfort; my mistress loves you, and there is as arrant
a madman i'th'house as you are a fool, your rival, whom she loves   140
not; if after the masque we can rid her of him, you earn her love,
she says, and the fool shall ride her.°

ANTONIO May I believe thee?

LOLLIO Yes, or you may choose whether you will or no.

ANTONIO She's eased of him; I have a good quarrel on't.   145

LOLLIO Well, keep your old station yet, and be quiet.

ANTONIO Tell her I will deserve her love.

    [Exit Antonio]

LOLLIO And you are like to have your desire.

    Enter Franciscus

FRANCISCUS *[sings]* 'Down, down, down a-down a-down'; and then
    with a horse-trick,   150
    To kick Latona's forehead and break her bowstring.°

LOLLIO *[aside]* This is t'other counterfeit; I'll put him out of his
    humour. *[Lollio takes out letter and reads]* 'Sweet lady, having now
    cast off this counterfeit cover of a madman, I appear to your best
    judgement a true and faithful lover of your beauty.' This is pretty   155
    well for a madman.

FRANCISCUS Ha, what's that?

LOLLIO 'Chide those perfections in you, which [have] made me
    imperfect.'

FRANCISCUS I am discovered to the fool.   160

LOLLIO I hope to discover the fool in you, ere I have done with you.
    'Yours all, or one beside himself, Franciscus.' This madman will
    mend sure.

FRANCISCUS What do you read, sirrah?

LOLLIO Your destiny, sir; you'll be hanged for this trick, and another°   165
    that I know.

FRANCISCUS Art thou of counsel with thy mistress?°

LOLLIO Next her apron strings.

FRANCISCUS Give me thy hand.°

LOLLIO Stay, let me put yours in my pocket first. *[Lollio puts away the*   170
    letter.] Your hand is true, is it not? It will not pick? I partly fear it,
    because I think it does lie.

FRANCISCUS Not in a syllable.

LOLLIO So; if you love my mistress so well as you have handled the
    matter here, you are like to be cured of your madness.   175

FRANCISCUS And none but she can cure it.

LOLLIO Well, I'll give you over then, and she shall cast your water°
    next.

FRANCISCUS Take for thy pains past. *[Franciscus gives Lollio money]*

LOLLIO I shall deserve more, sir, I hope; my mistress loves you,° but   180
    must have some proof of your love to her.

FRANCISCUS There I meet my wishes.°

LOLLIO   That will not serve, you must meet° her enemy and yours.

FRANCISCUS   He's dead already.

LOLLIO   Will you tell me that, and I parted but now with him?   185

FRANCISCUS   Show me the man.

LOLLIO   Ay, that's a right course now, see him before you kill him in any case, and yet it needs not go so far neither; 'tis but a fool that haunts the house and my mistress in the shape of an idiot; bang but his fool's coat well-favouredly, and 'tis well.   190

FRANCISCUS   Soundly, soundly.

LOLLIO   Only reserve him till the masque be past,° and if you find him not now in the dance yourself, I'll show you. In, in. My master.°

FRANCISCUS   He handles him like a feather. Hey!   195

     [*Exit Franciscus dancing.*]   *Enter Alibius*

ALIBIUS   Well said; in a readiness, Lollio?°

LOLLIO   Yes, sir.

ALIBIUS   Away then, and guide them in, Lollio;

Entreat your mistress to see this sight.

     [*Exit Lollio*]

Hark, is there not one incurable fool   200

That might be begged? I have friends.°

LOLLIO [*within*]   I have him° for you, one that shall deserve it too.

ALIBIUS   Good boy, Lollio.

     [*Enter Isabella. Then Lollio with Madmen and Fools.*] *The Madmen and Fools dance*

'Tis perfect; well, fit but once these strains,°

We shall have coin and credit for our pains.   205

     Exeunt

5.1

Enter Beatrice-Joanna. A clock strikes°

BEATRICE-JOANNA One struck, and yet she lies by't. Oh my
　　fears!°
　This strumpet serves her own ends, 'tis apparent now,
　Devours the pleasure with a greedy appetite,
　And never minds my honour or my peace,
　Makes havoc of my right; but she pays dearly for't:°　　　　5
　No trusting of her life with such a secret,
　That cannot rule her blood to keep her promise.°
　Beside, I have some suspicion of her faith to me
　Because I was suspected of my lord,
　And it must come from her. Hark, by my horrors,°　　　　10
　Another clock strikes two.

Strikes two. Enter Deflores

DEFLORES　　　　　　　　Pist, where are you?°
BEATRICE-JOANNA Deflores?
DEFLORES　　　　　　　　Ay. Is she not come from him yet?
BEATRICE-JOANNA As I am a living soul, not.
DEFLORES　　　　　　　　　　　　Sure the devil
　Has sowed his itch within her; who'd trust
　A waiting-woman?
BEATRICE-JOANNA I must trust somebody.°　　　　　　　15
DEFLORES Push, they are termagants,
　Especially when they fall upon their masters
　And have their ladies' first-fruits; th'are mad whelps,°
　You cannot stave 'em off from game royal then.°
　You are so harsh and hardy, ask no counsel,°　　　　　20
　And I could have helped you to an apothecary's daughter,
　Would have fallen off before eleven, and thanked you too.°
BEATRICE-JOANNA Oh me, not yet? This whore forgets herself.
DEFLORES The rascal fares so well; look, y'are undone,
　The day-star, by this hand. See Phosphorus plain yonder.°　25
BEATRICE-JOANNA Advise me now to fall upon some ruin;
　There is no counsel safe else.
DEFLORES　　　　　　　　Peace, I ha't now;°
　We must force a rising; there's no remedy.°
BEATRICE-JOANNA How? Take heed of that.

DEFLORES   Tush, be you quiet,
  Or else give over all.
BEATRICE-JOANNA   Prithee, I ha'done then.   30
DEFLORES This is my reach: I'll set some part a-fire°
  Of Diaphanta's chamber.
BEATRICE-JOANNA   How? Fire, sir?
  That may endanger the whole house.
DEFLORES You talk of danger when your fame's on fire?
BEATRICE-JOANNA That's true; do what thou wilt now.
DEFLORES   Push, I aim   35
  At a most rich success, strikes all dead sure;°
  The chimney being afire and some light parcels
  Of the least danger in her chamber only,
  If Diaphanta should be met by chance then
  Far from her lodging, which is now suspicious,   40
  It would be thought her fears and affrights then
  Drove her to seek for succour; if not seen
  Or met at all, as that's the likeliest,
  For her own shame she'll hasten towards her lodging;
  I will be ready with a piece high-charged   45
  As 'twere to cleanse the chimney. There 'tis proper now,°
  But she shall be the mark.
BEATRICE-JOANNA   I'm forced to love thee now°
  'Cause thou provid'st so carefully for my honour.°
DEFLORES 'Slid, it concerns the safety of us both,
  Our pleasure and continuance.
BEATRICE-JOANNA   One word now, prithee;   50
  How for the servants?
DEFLORES   I'll despatch them
  Some one way, some another in the hurry,
  For buckets, hooks, ladders; fear not you,
  The deed shall find its time. And I've thought since
  Upon a safe conveyance for the body too.   55
  How this fire purifies wit! Watch you your minute.°
BEATRICE-JOANNA Fear keeps my soul upon't; I cannot stray
    from't.
    Enter Alonzo's Ghost
DEFLORES Ha! What art thou that tak'st away the light
  'Twixt that star and me? I dread thee not;°
  'Twas but a mist of conscience. All's clear again.   60
    Exit [*Deflores*]

BEATRICE-JOANNA Who's that, Deflores? Bless me! It slides by.
    [*Exit Ghost*]
  Some ill thing haunts the house; 't has left behind it
  A shivering sweat upon me: I'm afraid now.
  This night hath been so tedious. Oh, this strumpet!
  Had she a thousand lives, he should not leave her°   65
  Till he had destroyed the last. List, oh my terrors,
    Struck three o'clock
  Three struck by Saint Sebastian's!°
[VOICE] (*within*) Fire, fire, fire!
BEATRICE-JOANNA Already? How rare is that man's speed!
  How heartily he serves me! His face loathes one,°   70
  But look upon his care, who would not love him?
  The east is not more beauteous than his service.°
[VOICE] (*within*) Fire, fire, fire!
    Enter Deflores. Servants pass over, ring a bell
DEFLORES Away, despatch! Hooks, buckets, ladders; that's well
  said!
  The fire-bell rings, the chimney works; my charge,   75
  The piece is ready.
    Exit [Deflores]
BEATRICE-JOANNA Here's a man worth loving!°
    Enter Diaphanta
  Oh, y'are a jewel!
DIAPHANTA   Pardon frailty, madam;
  In troth I was so well, I even forgot myself.
BEATRICE-JOANNA Y'have made trim work.
DIAPHANTA   What?
BEATRICE-JOANNA   Hie quickly to your chamber;°
  Your reward follows you.
DIAPHANTA   I never made   80
  So sweet a bargain.
    Exit [Diaphanta.] Enter Alsemero
ALSEMERO   Oh, my dear Joanna,
  Alas art thou risen too? I was coming,
  My absolute treasure.
BEATRICE-JOANNA   When I missed you,
  I could not choose but follow.
ALSEMERO   Th'art all sweetness!
  The fire is not so dangerous.
BEATRICE-JOANNA   Think you so, sir?   85

ALSEMERO I prithee, tremble not: believe me, 'tis not.

     Enter Vermandero, Jasperino

VERMANDERO Oh bless my house and me.

ALSEMERO [*to Beatrice-Joanna*]   My lord your father.

     Enter Deflores with a piece

VERMANDERO Knave, whither goes that piece?

DEFLORES To scour the chimney.

     Exit [Deflores]

VERMANDERO   Oh, well said, well said;°

  That fellow's good on all occasions.   90

BEATRICE-JOANNA A wondrous necessary man, my lord.°

VERMANDERO He hath a ready wit; he's worth'em all, sir.

  Dog at a house of fire; I ha' seen him singed ere now.°

     The piece goes off

  Ha, there he goes.

BEATRICE-JOANNA [*aside*] 'Tis done.

ALSEMERO   Come, sweet, to bed now;

  Alas, thou wilt get cold.

BEATRICE-JOANNA   Alas, the fear keeps that out!   95

  My heart will find no quiet till I hear

  How Diaphanta, my poor woman, fares;

  It is her chamber, sir, her lodging chamber.

VERMANDERO How should the fire come there?

BEATRICE-JOANNA As good a soul as ever lady countenanced,   100

  But in her chamber negligent and heavy;

  She 'scaped a mine twice.

VERMANDERO   Twice?

BEATRICE-JOANNA   Strangely twice, sir.°

VERMANDERO Those sleepy sluts are dangerous in a house,°

  An they be ne'er so good.°

     Enter Deflores°

DEFLORES   Oh poor virginity!°

  Thou hast paid dearly for't.

VERMANDERO   Bless us, what's that?   105

DEFLORES A thing you all knew once; Diaphanta's burnt.

BEATRICE-JOANNA My woman, oh, my woman!

DEFLORES   Now the flames

  Are greedy of her; burnt, burnt, burnt to death, sir!

BEATRICE-JOANNA Oh my presaging soul!

ALSEMERO   Not a tear more;°

  I charge you by the last embrace I gave you   110

In bed before this raised us.

BEATRICE-JOANNA   Now you tie me;
Were it my sister, now she gets no more.°
  Enter Servant

VERMANDERO How now?

SERVANT All danger's past, you may now take your rests, my lords;
the fire is throughly quenched; ah, poor gentlewoman, how soon   115
was she stifled!

BEATRICE-JOANNA Deflores, what is left of her inter,
And we as mourners all will follow her:
I will entreat that honour to my servant,
Ev'n of my lord himself.

ALSEMERO   Command it, sweetness.   120

BEATRICE-JOANNA Which of you spied the fire first?

DEFLORES   'Twas I, madam.

BEATRICE-JOANNA And took such pains in't too? A double goodness!
'Twere well he were rewarded.

VERMANDERO   He shall be;
Deflores, call upon me.

ALSEMERO   And upon me, sir.°
  Exeunt [Vermandero, Alsemero, Beatrice-Joanna, Servant]

DEFLORES Rewarded? Precious, here's a trick beyond me!°   125
I see in all bouts, both of sport and wit,
Always a woman strives for the last hit.
  Exit

5.2

  Enter Tomazo

TOMAZO I cannot taste the benefits of life
With the same relish I was wont to do.°
Man I grow weary of, and hold his fellowship
A treacherous bloody friendship; and because
I am ignorant in whom my wrath should settle;°   5
I must think all men villains, and the next
I meet (whoe'er he be) the murderer
Of my most worthy brother. Ha, what's he?
  Enter Deflores, passes over the stage
Oh, the fellow that some call honest Deflores.°

But methinks honesty was hard bested   10
To come there for a lodging; as if a queen°
Should make her palace of a pest-house.
I find a contrariety in nature°
Betwixt that face and me: the least occasion
Would give me game upon him; yet he's so foul,°   15
One would scarce touch with a sword he loved
And made account of. So most deadly venomous,°
He would go near to poison any weapon
That should draw blood on him; one must resolve
Never to use that sword again in fight,   20
In way of honest manhood, that strikes him;°
Some river must devour it, 'twere not fit
That any man should find it. What, again?
        Enter Deflores
He walks a'purpose by, sure, to choke me up,°
To infect my blood.
DEFLORES   My worthy noble lord.   25
TOMAZO Dost offer to come near and breathe upon me?
        [*Tomazo strikes Deflores*]
DEFLORES A blow?
        [*Deflores draws his sword*]
TOMAZO   Yea, are you so prepared?
    I'll rather like a soldier die by th'sword
    Than like a politician by thy poison.
        [*Tomazo draws his sword*]°
DEFLORES Hold, my lord, as you are honourable.   30
TOMAZO All slaves that kill by poison are still cowards.
DEFLORES [*aside*] I cannot strike; I see his brother's wounds
    Fresh bleeding in his eye, as in a crystal.°
    [*To him*] I will not question this, I know y'are noble.
        [*Deflores sheathes his sword*]
    I take my injury with thanks given, sir,   35
    Like a wise lawyer; and as a favour
    Will wear it for the worthy hand that gave it.°
    [*Aside*] Why this from him, that yesterday appeared
    So strangely loving to me?
    Oh, but instinct is of a subtler strain.°   40
    Guilt must not walk so near his lodge again;
    He came near me now.°
        Exit [*Deflores*]

        226

TOMAZO All league with mankind I renounce for ever,°
    Till I find this murderer; not so much
    As common courtesy but I'll lock up:°   45
    For in the state of ignorance I live in
    A brother may salute his brother's murderer,
    And wish good speed to th'villain in a greeting.
     Enter Vermandero, Alibius and Isabella
VERMANDERO Noble Piracquo!
TOMAZO   Pray keep on your way, sir,
    I've nothing to say to you.
VERMANDERO   Comforts bless you, sir.   50
TOMAZO I have forsworn compliment; in troth I have, sir;
    As you are merely man I have not left
    A good wish for you, nor any here.
VERMANDERO Unless you be so far in love with grief
    You will not part from't upon any terms,
    We bring that news will make a welcome for us.   55
TOMAZO What news can that be?
VERMANDERO   Throw no scornful smile
    Upon the zeal I bring you, 'tis worth more, sir.
    Two of the chiefest men I kept about me°
    I hide not from the law, or your just vengeance.   60
TOMAZO Ha!
VERMANDERO To give your peace more ample satisfaction,°
    Thank these discoverers.
TOMAZO   If you bring that calm,
    Name but the manner I shall ask forgiveness in°
    For that contemptuous smile upon you:
    I'll perfect it with reverence that belongs°   65
    Unto a sacred altar.
     [*Tomazo kneels*]
VERMANDERO   Good sir, rise.
     [*Vermandero raises him*]
    Why, now you overdo as much a'this hand
    As you fell short a't'other. Speak, Alibius.°
ALIBIUS 'Twas my wife's fortune (as she is most lucky
    At a discovery) to find out lately   70
    Within our hospital of fools and madmen
    Two counterfeits slipped into these disguises;
    Their names Franciscus and Antonio.
VERMANDERO Both mine, sir, and I ask no favour for'em.

ALIBIUS Now that which draws suspicion to their habits—   75
    The time of their disguisings agrees justly°
    With the day of the murder.
TOMAZO   O blest revelation!
VERMANDERO Nay more, nay more, sir, I'll not spare mine own
    In way of justice. They both feigned a journey
    To Briamata and so wrought out their leaves;°   80
    My love was so abused in't.
TOMAZO   Time's too precious
    To run in waste now; you have brought a peace
    The riches of five kingdoms could not purchase.
    Be my most happy conduct; I thirst for'em:°
    Like subtle lightning will I wind about'em,   85
    And melt their marrow in'em.°
       Exeunt

5.3

     Enter Alsemero and Jasperino
JASPERINO Your confidence, I'm sure, is now of proof.°
    The prospect from the garden has showed°
    Enough for deep suspicion.
ALSEMERO   The black mask°
    That so continually was worn upon't
    Condemns the face for ugly ere't be seen—   5
    Her despite to him, and so seeming-bottomless.°
JASPERINO Touch it home then: 'tis not a shallow probe°
    Can search this ulcer soundly; I fear you'll find it
    Full of corruption. 'Tis fit I leave you;
    She meets you opportunely from that walk: 10
    She took the back door at his parting with her.°
       Exit Jasperino
ALSEMERO Did my fate wait for this unhappy stroke
    At my first sight of woman?—She's here.
       Enter Beatrice-Joanna
BEATRICE-JOANNA Alsemero!
ALSEMERO   How do you?
BEATRICE-JOANNA   How do I?
    Alas! How do you? You look not well.   15
ALSEMERO You read me well enough; I am not well.

BEATRICE-JOANNA Not well, sir? Is't in my power to better you?
ALSEMERO Yes.
BEATRICE-JOANNA Nay, then y'are cured again.
ALSEMERO Pray resolve me one question, lady.°
BEATRICE-JOANNA   If I can.
ALSEMERO None can so sure. Are you honest?   20
BEATRICE-JOANNA Ha, ha, ha! That's a broad question, my lord.°
ALSEMERO But that's not a modest answer, my lady:
   Do you laugh? My doubts are strong upon me.
BEATRICE-JOANNA 'Tis innocence that smiles and no rough
      brow°
   Can take away the dimple in her cheek.   25
   Say I should strain a tear to fill the vault,
   Which would you give the better faith to?°
ALSEMERO 'Twere but hypocrisy of a sadder colour,
   But the same stuff; neither your smiles nor tears
   Shall move or flatter me from my belief: 30
   You are a whore!
BEATRICE-JOANNA What a horrid sound it hath!
   It blasts a beauty to deformity;
   Upon what face soever that breath falls
   It strikes it ugly: oh, you have ruined
   What you can ne'er repair again.   35
ALSEMERO I'll all demolish, and seek out truth within you,
   If there be any left; let your sweet tongue
   Prevent your heart's rifling; there I'll ransack°
   And tear out my suspicion.
BEATRICE-JOANNA   You may, sir;
   'Tis an easy passage. Yet, if you please,   40
   Show me the ground whereon you lost your love:
   My spotless virtue may but tread on that°
   Before I perish.
ALSEMERO   Unanswerable!
   A ground you cannot stand on; you fall down
   Beneath all grace and goodness when you set   45
   Your ticklish heel on't; there was a visor°
   O'er that cunning face, and that became you.
   Now impudence in triumph rides upon't.°
   How comes this tender reconcilement else
   'Twixt you and your despite, your rancorous loathing,   50
   Deflores? He that your eye was sore at sight of,°

He's now become your arms' supporter, your°
Lips' saint!
BEATRICE-JOANNA Is there the cause?
ALSEMERO   Worse: your lust's devil,°
Your adultery!
BEATRICE-JOANNA Would any but yourself say that,
'Twould turn him to a villain.
ALSEMERO   'Twas witnessed   55
By the counsel of your bosom, Diaphanta.°
BEATRICE-JOANNA Is your witness dead then?
ALSEMERO   'Tis to be feared
It was the wages of her knowledge; poor soul,
She lived not long after the discovery.
BEATRICE-JOANNA Then hear a story of not much less horror   60
Than this your false suspicion is beguiled with.°
To your bed's scandal, I stand up innocence,
Which even the guilt of one black other deed
Will stand for proof of: your love has made me°
A cruel murd'ress.
ALSEMERO   Ha!
BEATRICE-JOANNA   A bloody one;   65
I have kissed poison for't, stroked a serpent:
That thing of hate (worthy in my esteem
Of no better employment, and him most worthy
To be so employed) I caused to murder°
That innocent Piracquo, having no   70
Better means than that worst to assure
Yourself to me.
ALSEMERO   Oh, the place itself e'er since°
Has crying been for vengeance, the temple
Where blood and beauty first unlawfully
Fired their devotion and quenched the right one;   75
'Twas in my fears at first, 'twill have it now;°
Oh, thou art all deformed!
BEATRICE-JOANNA   Forget not, sir,
It for your sake was done; shall greater dangers
Make the less welcome?
ALSEMERO   Oh, thou shouldst have gone
A thousand leagues about to have avoided   80
This dangerous bridge of blood; here we are lost.
BEATRICE-JOANNA Remember I am true unto your bed.°

ALSEMERO The bed itself's a charnel, the sheets shrouds
    For murdered carcasses; it must ask pause°
    What I must do in this; meantime you shall   85
    Be my prisoner only: enter my closet.°
      Exit Beatrice-Joanna [into the closet]
    I'll be your keeper yet. Oh, in what part
    Of this sad story shall I first begin? Ha!
      Enter Deflores
    This same fellow has put me in. Deflores!°

DEFLORES Noble Alsemero?

ALSEMERO   I can tell you   90
    News, sir; my wife has her commended to you.°

DEFLORES That's news indeed, my lord; I think she would
    Commend me to the gallows if she could,
    She ever loved me so well; I thank her.°

ALSEMERO What's this blood upon your band, Deflores?   95

DEFLORES Blood? No, sure, 'twas washed since.

ALSEMERO   Since when, man?

DEFLORES Since t'other day I got a knock
    In a sword and dagger school; I think 'tis out.°

ALSEMERO Yes, 'tis almost out, but 'tis perceived, though.
    I had forgot my message; this it is: 100
    What price goes murder?

DEFLORES   How, sir?

ALSEMERO   I ask you, sir;
    My wife's behindhand with you, she tells me,°
    For a brave bloody blow you gave for her sake
    Upon Piracquo.

DEFLORES   Upon? 'Twas quite through him, sure;
    Has she confessed it?

ALSEMERO   As sure as death to both of you,   105
    And much more than that.

DEFLORES   It could not be much more;
    'Twas but one thing, and that she's a whore.°

ALSEMERO It could not choose but follow; oh cunning devils!°
    How should blind men know you from fair-faced saints?

BEATRICE-JOANNA *(within)* He lies; the villain does belie me.   110

DEFLORES Let me go to her, sir.

ALSEMERO   Nay, you shall to her.
    [To her, through the door] Peace, crying crocodile, your sounds are
      heard.°

Take your prey to you, get you in to her, sir.°
Exit Deflores [into the closet]
I'll be your pander now; rehearse again
Your scene of lust, that you may be perfect   115
When you shall come to act it to the black audience°
Where howls and gnashings shall be music to you.
Clip your adult'ress freely, 'tis the pilot°
Will guide you to the Mare Mortuum,°
Where you shall sink to fathoms bottomless.   120
    Enter Vermandero, Alibius, Isabella, Tomazo, Franciscus and
    Antonio
VERMANDERO Oh, Alsemero, I have a wonder for you.°
ALSEMERO No, sir, 'tis I, I have a wonder for you.
VERMANDERO I have suspicion near as proof itself
  For Piracquo's murder.
ALSEMERO   Sir, I have proof
  Beyond suspicion for Piracquo's murder.   125
VERMANDERO Beseech you, hear me; these two have been disguised
  E'er since the deed was done.
    [Vermandero indicates Franciscus and Antonio]
ALSEMERO   I have two other
  That were more close disguised than your two could be,
  E'er since the deed was done.
VERMANDERO You'll hear me, these mine own servants—   130
ALSEMERO Hear me. Those nearer than your servants,°
  That shall acquit them and prove them guiltless.
FRANCISCUS That may be done with easy truth, sir.
TOMAZO How is my cause bandied through your delays!°
  'Tis urgent in blood and calls for haste;°   135
  Give me a brother alive or dead:
  Alive, a wife with him; if dead, for both
  A recompense, for murder and adultery.°
BEATRICE-JOANNA (*within*) Oh, oh, oh!
ALSEMERO   Hark, 'tis coming to you.°
DEFLORES (*within*) Nay, I'll along for company.
BEATRICE-JOANNA (*within*)   Oh, oh!   140
VERMANDERO What horrid sounds are these?
ALSEMERO Come forth, you twins of mischief.
    [Alsemero opens the door.] Enter Deflores bringing in Beatrice-
    Joanna [wounded]
DEFLORES Here we are. If you have any more

To say to us, speak quickly, I shall not
Give you the hearing else; I am so stout yet   145
And so, I think, that broken rib of mankind.°
VERMANDERO An host of enemies entered my citadel
   Could not amaze like this: Joanna! Beatrice! Joanna!
BEATRICE-JOANNA Oh come not near me, sir, I shall defile
      you.
   I am that of your blood was taken from you   150
   For your better health; look no more upon't,°
   But cast it to the ground regardlessly:°
   Let the common sewer take it from distinction.°
   Beneath the stars, upon yon meteor°
   Ever hung my fate, 'mongst things corruptible.   155
   I ne'er could pluck it from him: my loathing°
   Was prophet to the rest, but ne'er believed;
   Mine honour fell with him, and now my life.
   Alsemero, I am a stranger to your bed;
   Your bed was cozened on the nuptial night,   160
   For which your false bride died.
ALSEMERO   Diaphanta!
DEFLORES Yes. And the while I coupled with your mate
   At barley-brake; now we are left in hell.°
VERMANDERO We are all there; it circumscribes here.°
DEFLORES I loved this woman in spite of her heart;   165
   Her love I earned out of Piracquo's murder.
TOMAZO Ha! My brother's murderer.
DEFLORES   Yes, and her honour's prize°
   Was my reward. I thank life for nothing
   But that pleasure: it was so sweet to me
   That I have drunk up all, left none behind   170
   For any man to pledge me.
VERMANDERO   Horrid villain!°
   Keep life in him for further tortures.
DEFLORES   No!
   I can prevent you; here's my penknife still.
   It is but one thread more [*he stabs himself*] and now 'tis cut.
   Make haste, Joanna, by that token to thee.°   175
   Canst not forget, so lately put in mind,
   I would not go to leave thee far behind.   *Dies*
BEATRICE-JOANNA Forgive me, Alsemero, all forgive;
   'Tis time to die, when 'tis a shame to live.   *Dies*

VERMANDERO Oh, my name is entered now in that record°   180
    Where till this fatal hour 'twas never read.
ALSEMERO Let it be blotted out, let your heart lose it,°
    And it can never look you in the face,
    Nor tell a tale behind the back of life
    To your dishonour. Justice hath so right   185
    The guilty hit, that innocence is quit
    By proclamation and may joy again.°
    [*To Tomazo*] Sir, you are sensible of what truth hath done;
    'Tis the best comfort that your grief can find.
TOMAZO [*to Vermandero*] Sir, I am satisfied, my injuries   190
    Lie dead before me; I can exact no more,°
    Unless my soul were loose and could o'ertake
    Those black fugitives that are fled from thence,°
    To take a second vengeance. But there are wraths
    Deeper than mine, 'tis to be feared, about 'em.   195
ALSEMERO What an opacous body had that moon°
    That last changed on us. Here's beauty changed
    To ugly whoredom; here, servant obedience
    To a master sin, imperious murder;
    I, a supposed husband, changed embraces   200
    With wantonness, but that was paid before;°
    [*To Tomazo*] Your change is come too, from an ignorant wrath
    To knowing friendship. Are there any more on's?°
ANTONIO Yes, sir; I was changed too, from a little ass as I was to a
    great fool as I am; and had like to ha'been changed to the gallows,°   205
    but that you know my innocence° always excuses me.
FRANCISCUS I was changed from a little wit to be stark mad,
    Almost for the same purpose.
ISABELLA [*to Alibius*]   Your change is still behind,
    But deserve best your transformation:°
    You are a jealous coxcomb, keep schools of folly,   210
    And teach your scholars how to break your own head.°
ALIBIUS I see all apparent, wife, and will change now
    Into a better husband, and never keep
    Scholars that shall be wiser than myself.
ALSEMERO [*to Vermandero*] Sir, you have yet a son's duty living,   215
    Please you accept it; let that your sorrow°
    As it goes from your eye, go from your heart;
    Man and his sorrow at the grave must part.

Epilogue

ALSEMERO All we can do to comfort one another,
 To stay a brother's sorrow for a brother,
 To dry a child from the kind father's eyes,
 Is to no purpose; it rather multiplies.
 Your only smiles have power to cause re-live   5
 The dead again, or in their rooms to give°
 Brother a new brother, father a child;
 If these appear, all griefs are reconciled.
  Exeunt

A GAME AT CHESS

THE CHARACTERS OF THE PLAY°

White King
White King's Pawn
White Knight
White Knight's Pawn
White Duke
White Bishop
White Bishop's Pawn
White Pawn

Black King
Black Knight
Black Knight's Pawn
Black Duke
Black Bishop
Black Bishop's Pawn
Black Jesting Pawn
Black Pawn

Fat Bishop
Fat Bishop's Pawn

White Queen
White Queen's Pawn

Black Queen
Black Queen's Pawn

Ignatius Loyola
Error

Prologue°

What of the game called chess-play can be made
To make a stage-play, shall this day be played.
First you shall see the men in order set,
States and their pawns, when both the sides are met,°
The Houses well distinguished; in the game°   5
Some men entrapped and taken, to their shame,
Rewarded by their play: and in the close°
You shall see checkmate given to virtue's foes.°
But the fairest jewel that our hopes can deck°
Is so to play our game, to avoid your check.°   10

The Induction°

Ignatius Loyola [appearing] and Error [at his feet]°
IGNATIUS Hah! Where? What angle of the world is this,°
    That I can neither see the politic face
    Nor with my refined nostrils taste the footsteps
    Of any of my disciples, sons and heirs
    As well of my designs as institution?°   5
    I thought they'd spread over the world by this time,
    Covered the earth's face and made dark the land
    Like the Egyptian grasshoppers.°
    Here's too much light appears, shot from the eyes
    Of truth and goodness (never yet deflowered.)°   10
    Sure they were never here. Then is their monarchy
    Unperfect yet: a just reward I see°
    For their ingratitude so long to me,
    (Their father and their founder.)
    It's not five years since I was sainted by'em;   15
    Where slept mine honour all the time before?
    Could they be so forgetful to canonise
    Their prosperous institutor? When they had sainted me°
    They found no room in all their calendar°
    To place my name, that should have removed princes,   20
    Pulled the most eminent prelates by the roots up
    For my dear coming, to make way for me.
    Let every petty-martyr and saint-homily,°
    Roch, Main, and Petronill (itch- and ague-curers),°
    Your Abbess Aldegund, and Cunegund,°   25
    The widow Marcell, parson Polycarp,°
    Cecily and Ursula, all take place of me;°
    And but for the bisextile or leap-year°
    (And that's but one in three), I fall by chance
    Into the nine and twentieth day of February.   30
    There were no room else for me. See their love
    (Their conscience too) to thrust me, a lame soldier,°
    Into leap-year. My wrath's up, and methinks
    I could with the first syllable of my name°
    Blow up their colleges. Up, Error, wake,°   35

Father of Supererogation, rise,°
It is Ignatius calls thee, Loyola!

ERROR What have you done? O I could sleep in ignorance
Immortally, the slumber is so pleasing.
I saw the bravest setting for a game now°   40
That ever mine eye fixed on.

IGNATIUS   What game, prithee?

ERROR The noblest game of all, a game at chess°
Betwixt our side and the White House, the men set
In their just order, ready to go to it.

IGNATIUS Were any of my sons placed for the game?   45

ERROR Yes, and a daughter too, a secular daughter°
That plays the Black Queen's Pawn, he the Black Bishop's.

IGNATIUS If ever power could show a mastery in thee
Let it appear in this.

ERROR   It's but a dream,°
A vision you must think.

IGNATIUS   I care not what   50
So I behold the children of my cunning
And see what rank they keep.

          [*Music.*] *Enter the White House and Black* [*as in order of the
          game*]°

ERROR   You have your wish;
Behold, there's the full number of the game,
Kings and their pawns, queens, bishops, knights and dukes.

IGNATIUS Dukes? They are called rooks by some.

ERROR   Corruptively!   55
Le Roc the word, *Custode de la Roche*,
The keeper of the forts, in whom both kings
Repose much confidence, and for their trust-sake,
Courage and worth, do well deserve those titles.°

IGNATIUS The answer's high. I see my son and daughter.   60

ERROR Those are two pawns, the Black Queen's and the Bishop's.°

IGNATIUS Pawns argue but poor spirits, and slight preferments,°
Not worthy of the name of my disciples.
If I had stood so nigh, I would have cut
That Bishop's throat but I would have had his place,°   65
And told the Queen a love-tale in her ear
Would make her best pulse dance. There's no elixir
Of brain or spirit amongst'em.

ERROR Why, would you have them play against themselves?

241

That's quite against the rule of the game, Ignatius.   70
IGNATIUS Pish, I would rule myself, not observe rule.
ERROR Why then you'd play a game all by yourself.
IGNATIUS I would do anything to rule alone;
    It's rare to have the world reigned in by one.°
ERROR See'em anon, and mark'em in their play;   75
    Observe (as in a dance) they glide away.°
IGNATIUS O, with what longings will this breast be tossed°
    Until I see this great game won and lost.
        Exeunt°

1.1°

Enter the White Queen's Pawn and the Black Queen's Pawn°

BLACK QUEEN'S PAWN I never see that face but my pity rises;°
  When I behold so clear a masterpiece
  Of heaven's art, wrought out of dust and ashes,°
  And, at next thought, to give her lost eternally,
  In being not ours but the daughter of heresy°   5
  My soul bleeds at mine eyes.°
WHITE QUEEN'S PAWN   Where should truth speak°
  If not in such a sorrow? These are tears plainly.°
  Beshrew me if she weep not heartily.
  What is my peace to her, to take such pains in't?°
  If I wander to loss and with broad eyes   10
  Yet miss the path she can run blindfold in
  (Through often exercise) why should my oversight
  (Though in the best game that e'er Christian lost)
  Raise the least spring of pity in her eye?°
  It's doubtless a great charity, and no virtue   15
  Could win me sooner.
BLACK QUEEN'S PAWN Blessed things prevail with't!°
  If ever goodness made a gracious promise°
  It is in yonder look. What little pains
  Would build a fort for virtue to all memory
  In that sweet creature, were the ground-work firmer.°   20
WHITE QUEEN'S PAWN It hath been all my glory to be firm
  In what I have professed.
BLACK QUEEN'S PAWN   That is the enemy°
  That steals your strength away, and fights against you,
  Disarms your soul even in the heat of battle.
  Your firmness that way makes you more infirm   25
  For the right Christian conflict. There I spied°
  A zealous primitive sparkle but now flew
  From your devoted eye, able to blow up all heresies
  That ever sat in council with your spirit.°
    Enter the Black Bishop's Pawn, [a Jesuit]°
  And here comes he whose sanctimonious breath   30
  Will make that spark a flame. List to him, virgin,°

At whose first entrance princes will fall prostrate;
Women are weaker vessels.
WHITE QUEEN'S PAWN   By my penitence°
A comely presentation, and the habit,
To admiration reverend.
BLACK QUEEN'S PAWN   But the heart, lady, so meek,°   35
That as you see good Charity pictured still
With young ones in her arms, so will he cherish°
All his young tractable sweet obedient daughters
E'en in his bosom, in his own dear bosom.
I am myself a secular Jesuitess,   40
(As many ladies are of wealth and greatness;)°
A second sort are Jesuits *in voto*,
Giving their vow in to the Father General
(That's the Black Bishop of our House, whose Pawn
This gentleman now stands for) to receive   45
The college habit at his holy pleasure.°
WHITE QUEEN'S PAWN But how are those *in voto* employed, lady,
Till they receive the habit?
BLACK QUEEN'S PAWN   They're not idle;
He finds'em all true labourers in the work
Of the universal monarchy, which he   50
And his disciples principally aim at.
Those are maintained in many courts and palaces,
And are induced by noble personages
Into great princes' services, and prove°
Some councillors of state, some secretaries,   55
All serving in notes of intelligence°
(As parish clerks their mortuary bills)°
To the Father General; so are designs
Oft times prevented, and important secrets°
Of states discovered, yet no author found   60
But those suspected oft that are most sound.
This mystery is too deep yet for your entrance°
And I offend to set your zeal so back.°
Checked by obedience, with desire to hasten
Your progress to perfection, I commit you   65
To the great worker's hands, to whose grave worth
I fit my reverence, as to you my wishes.°
BLACK BISHOP'S PAWN [*aside to Black Queen's Pawn*] Do you find
her supple?°

244

BLACK QUEEN'S PAWN There's a little passage.°
    Exit [Black Queen's Pawn]
BLACK BISHOP'S PAWN Let me contemplate,
  With holy wonder season my access,° 70
  And by degrees approach the sanctuary
  Of unmatched beauty set in grace and goodness.°
  Amongst the daughters of men I have not found
  A more catholical aspect; that eye°
  Does promise single life and meek obedience;° 75
  Upon those lips (the sweet fresh buds of youth)
  The holy dew of prayer lies like a pearl
  Dropped from the opening eyelids of the morn
  Upon the bashful rose. How beauteously°
  A gentle fast, not rigorously imposed, 80
  Would look upon that cheek, and how delightfully
  The courteous physic of a tender penance
  (Whose utmost cruelty should not exceed
  The first fear of a bride) to beat down frailty,°
  Would work to sound health your long festered judgement, 85
  And make your merit (which through erring ignorance
  Appears but spotted righteousness to me)°
  Far clearer than the innocence of infants.
WHITE QUEEN'S PAWN To that good work I bow, and will become
  Obedience's humblest daughter, since I find° 90
  Th'assistance of a sacred strength to aid me;
  The labour is as easy to serve virtue
  The right way (since 'tis she I ever served
  In my desire, though I transgressed in judgement.)°
BLACK BISHOP'S PAWN That's easily absolved amongst the rest. 95
  You shall not find the virtue you serve now°
  A sharp and cruel mistress; her ear's open
  To all your supplications, you may boldly
  And safely let in the most secret sin
  Into her knowledge, which (like vanished man) 100
  Never returns into the world again;°
  Fate locks not up more trulier.
WHITE QUEEN'S PAWN   To the guilty°
  That may appear some benefit.
BLACK BISHOP'S PAWN   Who is so innocent°
  That never stands in need on't, in some kind?
  If every thought were blabbed that's so confessed, 105

The very air we breathe would be unblest.
[*Aside*] Now to the work indeed, which is to catch
Her inclination; that's the special use
We make of all our practice, in all kingdoms,
For by disclosing their most secret frailties,   110
Things, which once ours they must not hide from us,
(That's the first article in the creed we teach'em)
Finding to what point their blood most inclines,
Know best to apt them to our designs.°
[*To White Queen's Pawn*] Daughter, the sooner you disperse your
        errors,°   115
The sooner you make haste to your recovery.
You must part with'em: to be nice or modest
Toward this good action is to imitate
The bashfulness of one conceals an ulcer,°
For the uncomely parts the tumor vexes,°   120
Till't be past cure. Resolve you thus far, lady,
The privat'st thought that runs to hide itself
In the most secret corner of your heart now
Must be of my acquaintance, so familiarly
Never she-friend of your night-counsel nearer.°   125
WHITE QUEEN'S PAWN I stand not much in fear of any action
Guilty of that black time, most noble holiness.°
I must confess—as in a sacred temple
Thronged with an auditory, some come rather
To feed on human object than to taste   130
Of angels' food;
So in the congregation of quick thoughts
Which are more infinite than such assemblies
(I cannot with truth's safety speak for all)
Some have been wanderers, some fond, some sinful   135
(But those found ever but poor entertainment;
They'd small encouragement to come again)—
The single life which strongly I profess now,°
Heaven pardon me, I was about to part from.
BLACK BISHOP'S PAWN Then you have passed through love?
WHITE QUEEN'S PAWN   But left no stain   140
In all my passage, sir, no print of wrong
For the most chaste maid that may trace my footsteps.°
BLACK BISHOP'S PAWN How came you off so clear?
WHITE QUEEN'S PAWN   I was discharged

By an inhuman accident, which modesty
Forbids me to put any language to.°   145
BLACK BISHOP'S PAWN How you forget yourself! All actions
  Clad in their proper language, though most sordid,
  My ear is bound by duty to let in
  And shut up everlastingly. Shall I help you?°
  He was not found to answer his creation.°   150
  A vestal virgin in a slip of prayer
  Could not deliver man's loss modestlier:°
  'Twas the White Bishop's Pawn.
WHITE QUEEN'S PAWN   The same, blessed sir.
BLACK BISHOP'S PAWN A heretic well pickled.
WHITE QUEEN'S PAWN   By base treachery°
  And violence prepared by his competitor   155
  (The Black Knight's Pawn) whom I shall ever hate for it.
BLACK BISHOP'S PAWN 'Twas (of revenges) the unmanliest way
  That ever rival took, a villainy
  That for your sake I'll ne'er absolve him of.
WHITE QUEEN'S PAWN I wish it not so heavy.
BLACK BISHOP'S PAWN   He must feel it;°   160
  I never yet gave absolution
  To any crime of that unmanning nature.
  It seems then you refused him for defect;°
  Therein you stand not pure from the desire
  That other women have in ends of marriage.°   165
  Pardon my boldness, if I sift your goodness
  To the last grain.
WHITE QUEEN'S PAWN I reverence your pains, sir,
  And must acknowledge custom to enjoy
  What other women challenge and possess°   170
  More ruled me than desire: for my desires
  Dwell all in ignorance, and I'll never wish
  To know that fond way may redeem them thence.°
BLACK BISHOP'S PAWN [aside] I never was so taken, beset doubly
  Now with her judgement; what a strength it puts forth.°   175
  [To her] I bring work nearer to you: when you have seen°
  A masterpiece of man, composed by heaven
  For a great prince's favour, kingdom's love,
  So exact, envy could not find a place°
  To stick a blot, on person or on fame;   180
  Have you not found ambition swell your wish then,

247

And desire steer your blood?

WHITE QUEEN'S PAWN   By virtue, never.
   I have only in the dignity of the creature
   Admired the Maker's glory.

BLACK BISHOP'S PAWN [*aside*] She's impregnable;
   A second siege must not fall off so tamely.   185
   She's one of those must be informed to know
   A daughter's duty, which some take untaught.°
   Her modesty brings her behind-hand much;
   My old means I must fly to, yes, 'tis it.°
        [*He gives the White Queen's Pawn a book*]
   Please you peruse this small tract of obedience,°   190
   'Twill help you forward well.

WHITE QUEEN'S PAWN   Sir, that's a virtue
   I have ever thought on with especial reverence.

BLACK BISHOP'S PAWN You will conceive by that my power, your
   duty.

WHITE QUEEN'S PAWN The knowledge will be precious of both, sir.
        Enter the White Bishop's Pawn

WHITE BISHOP'S PAWN [*aside*] What makes yond troubler of all
   Christian waters   195
   So near the blessed spring? But that I know°
   Her goodness is the rock from whence it issues,
   Unmovable as fate, 'twould more afflict me
   Than all my suff'rings for her; which, so long
   As she holds constant to the House she comes of,   200
   The whiteness of the cause, the side, the quality,
   Are sacrifices to her worth, and virtue,
   And (though confined) in my religious joys°
   I would marry her and possess her.
        Enter the Black Knight's Pawn

BLACK BISHOP'S PAWN   Behold, lady,
   The two inhuman enemies, the Black Knight's Pawn,°   205
   And the White Bishop's (the gelder and the gelded.)

WHITE QUEEN'S PAWN There's my grief, my hate.

BLACK KNIGHT'S PAWN [*aside*]   What, in the Jesuit's fingers?°
   I'll give my part now for a parrot's feather°
   She never returns virtuous; 'tis impossible.
   I'll undertake more wagers will be laid   210
   Upon a usurer's return from hell
   Than upon hers from him now; I'have been guilty°

Of such base malice that my very conscience
Shakes at the memory of, and when I look
To gather fruit find nothing but the savin tree,°   215
Too frequent in nuns' orchards, and there planted
By all conjecture to destroy fruit rather.
I will be resolved now. [*To White Queen's Pawn*] Most noble
    virgin—°
WHITE BISHOP'S PAWN Ignoble villain! Dare that unhallowed tongue
Lay hold upon a sound so gracious?°   220
What's nobleness to thee? Or virgin chastity?
They're out of thy acquaintance. Talk of violence°
That shames creation; deeds would make night blush,
That's company for thee. Hast thou the impudence
To court me with a leprosy upon thee°   225
Able t'infect the walls of a great building?
BLACK BISHOP'S PAWN Son of offence, forbear, go set your evil
Before your eyes. A penitential vesture°
Would better become you, some shirt of hair.°
BLACK KNIGHT'S PAWN And you, a three pound smock 'stead of an
    alb,   230
An epicene chasuble. [*Aside*] This holy felon°
Robs safe and close. I feel a sting that's worse too.°
[*To White Bishop's Pawn*] White Pawn! hast so much charity to
    accept
A reconcilement? Make thy own conditions,
For I begin to be extremely burdened.°   235
WHITE BISHOP'S PAWN [*aside*] No truth or peace of that Black House
    protested
Is to be trusted; but for hope of quittance
And warned by diffidence I may entrap him soonest.°
[*To Black Knight's Pawn*] I admit conference.
BLACK KNIGHT'S PAWN   It is nobleness°
That makes confusion cleave to all my merits.°   240
        [*Exeunt White Bishop's Pawn and Black Knight's Pawn.*] *Enter*
        Black Knight.° [*Black Bishop's Pawn takes White Queen's*
        Pawn to one side.]
BLACK BISHOP'S PAWN [*to her*] That treatise will instruct you fully.
BLACK KNIGHT [*aside*]   So, so,
The business of the universal monarchy
Goes forward well now, the great college pot
That should be always boiling, with the fuel

Of all intelligencies possible°   245
Through the Christian kingdoms. Is this fellow°
Our prime incendiary, and one of those°
That promised the White Kingdom seven year since°
To our Black House? Put a new daughter to him,
The great work stands; he minds nor monarchy, nor hierarchy°   250
(Diviner principality). I've bragged less,°
But I've done more than all the conclave of 'em,°
Take their Assistant Fathers in all parts,°
Yea, and their Father General in to boot.
And what I have done, I have done facetiously,°   255
With pleasant subtlety and bewitching courtship,
Abused all my believers with delight;°
They took a comfort to be cozened by me.°
To many a soul I have let in mortal poison
Whose cheeks have cracked with laughter to receive it;   260
I could so roll my pills in sugared syllables
And strew such kindly mirth o'er all my mischiefs,
They took their bane in way of recreation
As pleasure steals corruption into youth.
He spies me now, I must uphold his reverence,°   265
Especially in public, though I know
[Priapus, guardian of the cherry gardens,]
Bacchus and Venus' chit, is not more vicious.°
BLACK BISHOP'S PAWN Blessings' accumulation keep with you, sir.
BLACK KNIGHT Honour's dissimulation be your due, sir.°   270
    [*Bows to Black Bishop's Pawn*]
WHITE QUEEN'S PAWN [*aside*] How deep in duty his observance
    plunges;
His charge must needs be reverend.
BLACK BISHOP'S PAWN [*to her*]   I am confessor°
To this Black Knight too; you see devotion's fruitful,
Sh'ath many sons and daughters.
BLACK KNIGHT [*aside*]   I do this the more
T'amaze our adversaries to behold   275
The reverence we give these guitonens,
And to beget a sound opinion
Of holiness in them and zeal in us,
As also to invite the like obedience
In other pusills, by our meek example.°   280
    [*Exit White Queen's Pawn*]

So, is your trifle vanished?
BLACK BISHOP'S PAWN Trifle call you her? It's a good pawn, sir;
Sure she's the second pawn in the White House,
And to the opening of the game I hold her.°
BLACK KNIGHT [*aside*] Ay, you hold well for that, I know your play of
    old.   285
If there were more Queen's Pawns you'd ply your game
A great deal harder. [*To him*] Now, sir, we're in private:°
But what for the main work, the great existence,
The hope monarchal?
BLACK BISHOP'S PAWN   It goes on in this.°
BLACK KNIGHT In this? I cannot see't.
BLACK BISHOP'S PAWN   You may deny so   290
A dial's motion, 'cause you cannot see
The hand move, or a wind that rends the cedar.°
BLACK KNIGHT Where stops the current of intelligence?°
Your Father General, Bishop of the Black House,
Complains for want of work.
BLACK BISHOP'S PAWN   Here's from all parts   295
Sufficient to employ him; I received
A packet from the Assistant Fathers lately;
    [*Gives letters to the Black Knight*]
Look, there's Anglica, this Gallica.
BLACK KNIGHT Ay, marry, sir, there's some quick flesh in this.
BLACK BISHOP'S PAWN [*giving another letter*]   Germanica!°
BLACK KNIGHT I think they've sealed this with butter.
BLACK BISHOP'S PAWN [*giving another letter*]   This Italica!°   300
BLACK KNIGHT They've put their pens the Hebrew way methinks.°
BLACK BISHOP'S PAWN [*giving another letter*] Hispanica here!
BLACK KNIGHT   Hispanica, blind work this;°
The Jesuit has writ this with juice of lemons, sure.
It must be held close to the fire of purgatory°
Ere't can be read.
BLACK BISHOP'S PAWN You will not lose your jest, Knight,   305
Though it wound your own name.
    Enter the White King's Pawn
BLACK KNIGHT   *Curanda pecunia!*°
BLACK BISHOP'S PAWN Take heed, sir, we're entrapped. The White
    King's Pawn!
BLACK KNIGHT He's made our own, man, half *in voto* yours;°
His heart's in the Black House, leave him to me.

[*Exit Black Bishop's Pawn.*]

[*To White King's Pawn*] Most of all friends endeared, preciously
    special.°   310

WHITE KING'S PAWN You see my outside, but you know my heart,
    Knight,

Great difference in the colour. There's some intelligence
    [*Gives the Black Knight letters*]

And as more ripens so your knowledge still

Shall prove the richer; there shall nothing happen,

Believe it, to extenuate your cause   315

Or to oppress her friends, but I will strive

To cross it with my counsel, purse and power,

Keep all supplies back, both in means and men,

That may raise strength against you. We must part;°

I dare not longer of this theme discuss.   320

The ear of the state is quick and jealous.
    Exit [*White King's Pawn.*]°

BLACK KNIGHT Excellent estimation, thou art valued

Above the fleet of gold, that came short home.°

Poor Jesuit-ridden soul, how art thou fooled°

Out of thy faith, from thy allegiance drawn;   325

Which way soe'er thou tak'st thou'rt a lost pawn.°
    [*Exit*]

2.1

Enter the White Queen's Pawn [reading,] and to her the Black Bishop's Pawn°

WHITE QUEEN'S PAWN And here again: it is the daughter's duty°
To obey her confessor's command in all things
Without exception or expostulation.
It's the most general rule that e'er I read of,°
Yet when I think how boundless virtue is,   5
Goodness and grace, it's gently reconciled°
And then it appears well to have the power
Of the dispenser as uncircumscribed.°

BLACK BISHOP'S PAWN [*aside*] She's hard upon't: 'twas the most modest key
That I could use to open my intents;°   10
What little or no pains goes to some people.°
Hah! what have we here? a sealed note, whence this?°
[*Reads*] 'To the Black Bishop's Pawn there.' How? to me? Strange, who subscribes it? The Black King! What would he? 'Pawn, suf-
ficiently holy, but unmeasurably politic:° we had late intelligence   15
from our most industrious servant (famous in all parts of Europe) our Knight of the Black House, that you have at this instant in chase the White Queen's Pawn, and very likely by the carriage of your game to entrap and take her. These° are therefore to require you by the burning affection I bear to the rape of devotion,° that 20
speedily upon the surprisal of her, by all watchful advantage you make some attempt upon the White Queen's person,° whose fall or prostitution our lust most violently rages for.'
Sir, after my desire has took a julep
For its own inflammation, that yet scorches me,   25
I shall have cooler time to think of yours.
She's passed the general rule, the large extent°
Of our prescription for obedience,
And yet with what alacrity of soul
Her eye moves on the letters.

WHITE QUEEN'S PAWN   Holy sir,   30
Too long I have missed you; O, your absence starves me.
Hasten for time's redemption, worthy sir,°

Lay your commands as thick and fast upon me
As you can speak'em; how I thirst to hear'em!
Set me to work upon this spacious virtue   35
Which the poor span of life's too narrow for,
Boundless obedience,
The humblest yet the mightiest of all duties;
Well here set down a universal goodness.°
BLACK BISHOP'S PAWN [*aside*] By holiness of garment, her safe
    innocence°   40
Has frighted the full meaning from itself;
She's farther off from understanding now
The language of my intent than at first meeting.
WHITE QUEEN'S PAWN For virtue's sake, good sir, command me
    something;
Make trial of my duty in some small service   45
And as you find the faith of my obedience there,
Then trust it with a greater.
BLACK BISHOP'S PAWN   You speak sweetly,
I do commend you first then—
WHITE QUEEN'S PAWN   With what joy
I do prepare my duty.
BLACK BISHOP'S PAWN To meet me
And seal a kiss of love upon my lip.   50
WHITE QUEEN'S PAWN Ha!
BLACK BISHOP'S PAWN   At first disobedient, in so little too?
How shall I trust you with a greater then,
Which was your own request?
WHITE QUEEN'S PAWN   Pray send not back
My innocence to wound me, be more courteous;
I must confess much like an ignorant plaintiff   55
Who presuming on the fair path of his meaning°
Goes rashly on, till on a sudden brought
Into the wilderness of law by words
Dropped unadvisedly, hurts his own cause°
And gives his adversary advantage by it.   60
Apply it you can best, sir, if my obedience
And your command can find no better way;
Fond men command, and wantons best obey.°
BLACK BISHOP'S PAWN If I can at that distance send you a
    blessing,
Is it not nearer to you in mine arms?   65

It flies from these lips dealt abroad in parcels,°
And I (to honour thee above all daughters)
Invite thee home to the House, where thou mayst surfeit
On that which others miserably pine for,
A favour which the daughters of great potentates   70
Would look of envy's colour but to hear.°

WHITE QUEEN'S PAWN Good men may err sometimes; you are
 mistaken sure.
If this be virtue's path, 'tis a most strange one.
I never came this way before.

BLACK BISHOP'S PAWN   That's your ignorance,
And therefore shall that idiot still conduct you°   75
That knows no way but one, nor ever seeks it?
If there be twenty ways to some poor village,
'Tis strange that virtue should be put to one;°
Your fear is wondrous faulty, cast it from you;°
'Twill gather else in time a disobedience   80
Too stubborn for my pardon.

WHITE QUEEN'S PAWN   Have I locked myself
At unawares into sin's servitude
With more desire of goodness? Is this the top°
Of all strict order? And the holiest
Of all societies, the three-vowed people   85
For poverty, obedience, chastity,
The last the most forgot? When a virgin's ruined°
I see the great work of obedience
Is better than half finished.

BLACK BISHOP'S PAWN   What a stranger
Are you to duty grown, what distance keep you!   90
Must I bid you come forward to a happiness
Yourself should sue for? 'Twas never so with me;°
I dare not let this stubbornness be known—
'Twould bring such fierce hate on you; yet presume not
To make that courteous care a privilege°   95
For wilful disobedience; it turns then
Into the blackness of a curse upon you.
Come, come, be nearer.

WHITE QUEEN'S PAWN Nearer?

BLACK BISHOP'S PAWN   Was that scorn?
I would not have it prove so, for the hopes
Of the grand monarchy; if it were like it°   100

Let it not stir abroad again;
A stronger ill will cope with't.

WHITE QUEEN'S PAWN   Bless me, threatens me°
And quite dismays the good strength that should help me.°
I never was so doubtful of my safety.

BLACK BISHOP'S PAWN 'Twas but my jealousy; forgive me,
    sweetness;°   105
Yond is the house of meekness and no venom lives°
Under the roof. Be nearer, why so fearful?
Nearer the altar the more safe and sacred.

WHITE QUEEN'S PAWN But nearer to the offerer oft more wicked.

BLACK BISHOP'S PAWN A plain and most insufferable contempt!   110
My glory I have lost upon this woman:
In freely offering that she should have kneeled
A year in vain for, my respect is darkened;°
Give me my reverence again thou hast robbed me of
In thy repulse; thou shalt not carry it hence.°   115

WHITE QUEEN'S PAWN Sir—

BLACK BISHOP'S PAWN Thou'rt too great a winner to depart so°
And I too deep a loser to give way to it.

WHITE QUEEN'S PAWN O heaven!

BLACK BISHOP'S PAWN   Lay me down reputation°
Before thou stir'st; thy nice virginity
Is recompense too little for my love:°   120
'Tis well if I accept of that for both.°
Thy loss is but thine own, there's art to help thee
And fools to pass thee to; in my discovery°
The whole Society suffers, and in that°
The hope of absolute monarchy eclipsed.   125
Assurance thou canst make none for thy secrecy
But thy honour's loss; that act must awe thee.°

WHITE QUEEN'S PAWN O my distressed condition!

BLACK BISHOP'S PAWN   Dost weep?°
If thou hadst any pity this necessity°
Would wring it from thee. I must else destroy thee: 130
We must not trust the policy of Europe
Upon a woman's tongue.

WHITE QUEEN'S PAWN   Then take my life,°
And leave mine honour for my guide to heaven.

BLACK BISHOP'S PAWN Take heed I take not both, which I have
    vowed;°

If longer thou resist me—
WHITE QUEEN'S PAWN   Help, O help!   135
BLACK BISHOP'S PAWN Art thou so cruel for an honour's bubble
    T'undo a whole fraternity, and disperse
    The secrets of most princes locked in us?°
WHITE QUEEN'S PAWN For heaven and virtue's sake—
BLACK BISHOP'S PAWN   Must force confound—°
    Noise within
    Ha! What's that? Silence, if fair worth be in thee.   140
WHITE QUEEN'S PAWN I'll venture my escape upon all dangers now.°
BLACK BISHOP'S PAWN Who comes to take me? Let me see that
    pawn's face
    Or his proud tympanous master, swelled with state wind,
    Which being once pricked in the convocation house
    The corrupt air puffs out and he falls shrivelled.°   145
WHITE QUEEN'S PAWN I will discover thee, arch-hypocrite,
    To all the kindreds of the earth.
    [*Exit° White Queen's Pawn*]
BLACK BISHOP'S PAWN   Confusion!
    In that voice rings the alarm of my undoing.
    How! Which way 'scaped she from me.
    Enter the Black Queen's Pawn
BLACK QUEEN'S PAWN   Are you mad?
    Can lust infatuate a man so hopeful?   150
    No patience in your blood? The dog-star reigns sure;°
    Time and fair temper would have wrought her pleasant.°
    I spied a pawn o'the White House walk near us
    And made that noise o'purpose to give warning—
    [*Aside*] For mine own turn, which end is all I work for.°   155
BLACK BISHOP'S PAWN Methinks I stand over a powder-vault
    And the match now akindling. What's to be done?°
BLACK QUEEN'S PAWN Ask the Black Bishop's counsel; you're his
    pawn,
    It's his own case, he will defend you mainly;°
    Enter the Black Bishop and the Black Knight
    And happily here he comes, with the Black Knight too.   160
BLACK BISHOP O, you've made noble work for the White House
    yonder,
    This act will fill the adversary's mouth
    And blow the Lutherans' cheeks, till they crack again.°
BLACK KNIGHT This will advance the great monarchal business

In all parts well, and help the agents forward.°   165
What I in seven years laboured to accomplish
One minute sets back by some codpiece college still.°
BLACK BISHOP'S PAWN I dwell not, sir, alone in this default;
  The Black House yields me partners.
BLACK BISHOP   All more cautelous.°
BLACK KNIGHT *Qui cauté, casté,* that's my motto ever.   170
  I have travelled with that word over most kingdoms°
  And lain safe with most nations: of a leaking bottom,°
  I have been as often tossed on Venus' seas
  As trimmer fresher barks, when sounder vessels
  Have lain at anchor, that is, kept the door.°   175
BLACK BISHOP She has no witness then?
BLACK BISHOP'S PAWN   None, none.
BLACK KNIGHT   Gross, witness?°
  When went a man of his Society
  To mischief with a witness?
BLACK BISHOP   I have done't then.°
  Away, upon the wings of speed: take post-horse,
  Cast thirty leagues of earth behind thee suddenly;°   180
  Leave letters (antedated) with our House
  Ten days at least from this.
BLACK KNIGHT   Bishop, I taste thee;°
  Good strong episcopal counsel, take a bottle on't;°
  'Twill serve thee all the journey.
BLACK BISHOP'S PAWN   But, good sir,
  How for my getting forth, unspied?
BLACK KNIGHT   There's check again.°   185
BALCK QUEEN'S PAWN No, I'll help that!
BLACK KNIGHT   Well said, my bouncing Jesuitess.
BLACK QUEEN'S PAWN There lies a secret vault.
BLACK KNIGHT   Away, make haste then.
BLACK BISHOP'S PAWN Run for my cabinet of intelligences°
  For fear they search the House.
      [*Exit Black Queen's Pawn*]
                            Good Bishop, burn 'em rather,
  I cannot stand to pick 'em now.
BLACK BISHOP   Be gone,°   190
  The danger's all in you.
      [*Exit Black Bishop's Pawn. Enter Black Queen's Pawn, with a
      case*]

BLACK KNIGHT   Let me see, Queen's Pawn.°
How formally he's packed up his intelligences;
'Hath laid'em all in truckle-beds, methinks,
And (like court-harbingers) he hath writ their names°
In chalk upon their chambers. Anglica!   195
O, this is the English House; what news there, trow?
Anglica, most of these are bawdy epistles;°
Time they were burnt indeed, whole bundles of'em.
Here's from his daughter Blanche, and daughter Bridget,
From their safe sanctuary in the Whitefriars;°   200
These from two tender Sisters of Compassion°
In the bowels of Bloomsbury;
These from the nunnery in Drury Lane.°
A fire, a fire, good Jesuitess, a fire—
What have you there?
BLACK BISHOP   A note, sir, of state policy,   205
And an exceeding safe one.
BLACK KNIGHT   Pray, let's see it—°
[Reads] 'To sell away all the powder in a kingdom
To prevent blowing up.' That's safe, I'll able it.°
Here's a facetious observation now,
And suits my humour better: he writes here   210
Some wives in England will commit adultery,
And then send to Rome for a bull for their husbands.
BLACK BISHOP Have they those shifts?
BLACK KNIGHT   O there's no female breathing°
Sweeter and subtler; here, wench, take these papers,
Scorch'em me soundly, burn'em to French russet   215
And put'em in again.
BLACK BISHOP   Why, what's your mystery?°
BLACK KNIGHT O sir, 'twill mock the adversary strangely
If e'er the House be searched. 'Twas done in Venice
Upon the Jesuitical expulse there,°
When the inquisitors came all spectacled°   220
To pick out syllables out of the dung of treason
As children pick out cherry-stones, yet found none°
But what they made themselves with ends of letters.
Do as I bid you, Pawn.
          Exit [Black Knight and Black Bishop]
BLACK QUEEN'S PAWN Fear not: in all,
I love roguery too well to let it fall.   225

Enter the Black Knight's Pawn
How now? What news with you?
BLACK KNIGHT'S PAWN   The sting of conscience
Afflicts me so, for that inhuman violence°
On the White Bishop's Pawn, it takes away
My joy, my rest.
BLACK QUEEN'S PAWN This 'tis to make a eunuch;
You made a sport on't then.
BLACK KNIGHT'S PAWN   Cease aggravation;°   230
I come to be absolved for't. Where's my confessor?
Why dost thou point to the ground?
BLACK QUEEN'S PAWN   'Cause he went that way.°
BLACK KNIGHT'S PAWN What's that?
BLACK QUEEN'S PAWN   Come, help me with this
      cabinet°
And after I have singed these papers thoroughly
I'll tell thee a strange story.
BLACK KNIGHT'S PAWN   If 't be sad   235
It's welcome.
BLACK QUEEN'S PAWN 'Tis not troubled with much mirth, sir.
      Exeunt

2.2

Enter Fat Bishop and his Pawn°
FAT BISHOP Pawn!
FAT BISHOP'S PAWN I attend at your great holiness' service.
FAT BISHOP For great I grant you, but for greatly holy,
There the soil alters. Fat cathedral bodies°
Have very often but lean little souls   5
Much like the lady in the lobster's head,°
A great deal of shell and garbage of all colours,
But the pure part that should take wings and mount°
Is at last gasp, as if a man should gape
And from his huge bulk let forth a butterfly,   10
Like those big-bellied mountains which the poet
Delivers, that are brought abed with mouse-flesh.°
Are my books printed, Pawn? My last invectives
'Gainst the Black House?

FAT BISHOP'S PAWN   Ready for publication,°
    For I saw perfect books this morning, sir.°   15
FAT BISHOP Fetch me a few which I will instantly
    Distribute 'mongst the White House.
FAT BISHOP'S PAWN   With all speed, sir.
     Exit [Fat Bishop's Pawn]
FAT BISHOP It's a most lordly life to rail at ease,°
    Sit, eat, and feed upon the fat of one kingdom,
    And rail upon another with the juice on't.   20
    [I have writ this book out of the strength and marrow°
    Of six and thirty dishes at a meal,
    But most on't out of cullis of cock-sparrows;°
    'Twill stick and glue the faster to the adversary.
    'Twill slit the throat of their most calvish cause,   25
    And yet I eat but little butcher's meat°
    In the conception.]°
    Of all things I commend the White House best
    For plenty and variety of victuals.
    When I was one of the Black House professed   30
    My flesh fell half a cubit; time to turn°
    When mine own ribs revolted. But (to say true)
    I have no preferment yet that's suitable
    To the greatness of my person and my parts;°
    I grant I live at ease, for I am made   35
    The master of the beds (the long acre of beds.)°
    But there's no marigolds that shuts and opens,
    Flower-gentles, Venus-baths, apples of love,°
    Pinks, hyacinths, honeysuckles, daffadowndillies.
    There was a time I had more such drabs than beds,   40
    Now I have more beds than drabs;
    Yet there's no eminent trader deals in wholesale
    But she and I have clapped a bargain up,°
    Let in at watergate, for which I have racked°
    My tenants' purse-strings, they have twanged again.°   45
     Enter Black Knight and Black Bishop.
    Yonder's Black Knight (the fistula of Europe)°
    Whose disease once I undertook to cure
    With a High Holborn halter. When he last°
    Vouchsafed to peep into my privileged lodgings
    He saw good store of plate there and rich hangings;   50
    He knew I brought none to the White House with me.°

I have not lost the use of my profession
Since I turned White House Bishop.
   Enter [his] Pawn with Books.
BLACK KNIGHT   Look, more books yet.
 Yond greasy-turn-coat, gormandising prelate
 Has wrought our House more mischief by his scripts,   55
 His fat and fulsome volumes,
 Than the whole body of the adverse party.
BLACK BISHOP O, 'twere a masterpiece of serpent subtlety°
 To fetch him on this side again.
BLACK KNIGHT   And then damn him
 Into the bag for ever, or expose him°   60
 Against the adverse part (which now he feeds upon)°
 And that would double-damn him. My revenge
 Hath prompted me already; I'll confound him
 On both sides for the physic he prescribed°
 And the base surgeon he provided for me.°   65
 I'll tell you what a most uncatholic jest
 He put upon me once, when my pain tortured me;
 He told me he had found a present cure for me
 Which I grew proud on, and observed him seriously.°
 What think you 'twas? Being execution-day   70
 He showed the hangman to me out at window,
 The common hangman.
BLACK BISHOP   Insufferable.
BLACK KNIGHT I'll make him the balloon-ball of the churches°
 And both the sides shall toss him; he looks like one,
 A thing swelled up with mingled drink and urine,   75
 And will bound well from one side to another!
 Come, you shall write, our second Bishop absent°
 (Which has yet no employment in the game,
 Perhaps nor ever shall; it may be won
 Without his motion, it rests most in ours)°   80
 He shall be flattered with *sede vacante*;°
 Make him believe he comes into his place
 And that will fetch him with a vengeance to us,
 For I know powder is not more ambitious
 When the match meets it, than his mind for mounting;° 85
 As covetous, and lecherous—
BLACK BISHOP   No more now, sir,°
 Both the sides fill.

Enter the White House [including White King, Queen, Bishop,
Duke, Knight, and King's and Bishop's Pawns] and the Black
House [including Black King, Queen, Duke, and at least one
Pawn] (severally)

WHITE KING   This hath been looked for long.°

FAT BISHOP The stronger sting it shoots into the blood
  Of the Black adversary. I am ashamed now
  I was theirs ever; what a lump was I   90
  When I was led in ignorance and blindness;
  I must confess, I have all my lifetime played
  The fool till now.

BLACK KNIGHT [*aside*] And now he plays two parts, the fool and
    knave.°

FAT BISHOP There is my recantation in the last leaf,°   95
  Writ like a Ciceronian in pure Latin.°

WHITE BISHOP Pure honesty, the plainer Latin serves then.

BLACK KNIGHT Out on these pestilent pamphlets, those are they°
  That wound our cause to the heart.
          Enter the White Queen's Pawn.

BLACK BISHOP   Here comes more anger.

BLACK KNIGHT But we come well provided for this storm.°   100

WHITE QUEEN Is this my Pawn? She that should guard our
    person?
  Or some pale figure of dejection
  Her shape usurping? Sorrow and affrightment°
  Hath prevailed strangely with her.

WHITE QUEEN'S PAWN   King of integrity!
  Queen of the same, and all the House professors   105
  Of noble candour, uncorrupted justice°
  And truth of heart: through my alone discovery—°
  My life and honour wondrously preserved—
  I bring into your knowledge with my sufferings,
  Fearful affrightments and heart-killing terrors,   110
  The great incendiary of Christendom,°
  The absolut'st abuser of true sanctity,
  Fair peace and holy order, can be found°
  In any part of the universal globe;
  Who making meek devotion keep the door—°   115
  His lips being full of holy zeal at first—
  Would have committed a foul rape upon me.°

WHITE KING A rape? That's foul indeed, the very sound

To our ear fouler than the offence itself
To some kings of the earth.

WHITE QUEEN'S PAWN   Sir, to proceed: 120
Gladly I offered life to preserve honour
Which would not be accepted without both,°
The chief of his ill aim being at my honour,
Till heaven was pleased (by some unlooked-for accident)
To give me courage to redeem myself.   125

WHITE KING When we find desperate sins in ill men's
    companies
We place a charitable sorrow there,
But custom and their leprous inclination
Quits us of wonder, for our expectation
Is answered in their lives. But to find sin,°   130
Ay, and a masterpiece of darkness, sheltered
Under a robe of sanctity, is able
To draw all wonder to that monster only
And leave created monsters unadmired.°
The pride of him that took first fall for pride   135
Is to be angel-shaped, and imitate
The form from whence he fell; but this offender°
(Far baser than sin's master) fixed by vow
To holy order, which is angels' method,°
Takes pride to use that shape to be a devil.   140
It grieves me that my knowledge must be tainted
With his infested name;°
O rather with thy finger point him out.

WHITE QUEEN'S PAWN The place which he should fill is void, my
    lord;
His guilt hath seized him: the Black Bishop's Pawn.   145

BLACK BISHOP Hah! Mine? My pawn? The glory of his order,
The prime and president zealot of the earth?°
Impudent Pawn! For thy sake at this minute
Modesty suffers, all that's virtuous blushes,
And truth's self (like the sun vexed with a mist)   150
Looks red with anger.

WHITE BISHOP   Be not you drunk with rage too.

BLACK KNIGHT Sober sincerity! Nor you a cup
Spiced with hypocrisy.

WHITE KNIGHT [to the Black Bishop] You name there, Bishop,°
But your own Christmas-bowl, your morning's draught

Next your episcopal heart all the twelve days,   155
Which smack you cannot leave all the year following.°
BLACK KNIGHT [*aside*] [A shrewd retort!
He's made our Bishop smell of burning too;°
Would I stood further off; were't no impeachment
To my honour or the game, would they'd play faster.—]°   160
White Knight! there is acknowledged from our House
A reverence to you, and a respect
To that loved Duke stands next to you; with the favour°
Of the White King, and the aforenamed respected,
I combat with this cause. [*To White Queen's Pawn*] If with all
    speed—°   165
Waste not one syllable, unfortunate Pawn,°
Of what I speak—thou dost not plead distraction,
A plea which will but faintly take thee off neither
From this leviathan-scandal that lies rolling°
Upon the crystal waters of devotion;   170
Or (what may quit thee more, though enough nothing)
Fall down and foam, and by that pang discover
The vexing spirit of falsehood strong within thee;
Make thyself ready for perdition.
There's no remove in all the game to 'scape it;°   175
This pawn, or this, the Bishop or myself,
Will take thee in the end, play how thou canst.°
WHITE QUEEN'S PAWN Spite of sin's glorious ostentation,°
And all loud threats (those thunder-cracks of pride)
Ush'ring a storm of malice, house of impudence,   180
Craft and equivocation, my true cause°
Shall keep the path it treads in.
BLACK KNIGHT   I play thus then:
Now in the hearing of this high assembly
Bring forth the time of this attempt's conception.°
WHITE QUEEN'S PAWN Conception! O how tenderly you handle it.   185
WHITE BISHOP It seems, Black Knight, you are afraid to touch it.
BLACK KNIGHT Well, its eruption. Will she have it so then?°
Or you, White Bishop, for her? The uncleaner,
Vile and more impious that you urge the strain to,°
The greater will her shame's heap show i'th'end   190
And the wronged meek-man's glory. The time, Pawn?°
WHITE QUEEN'S PAWN Yesterday's hapless evening.
BLACK KNIGHT   O, the treasure°

Of my revenge I cannot spend all on thee;
Ruin enough to spare for all thy kindred too.°
For honour's sake call in more slanderers: 195
I have such plentiful confusion,°
I know not how to waste it. I'll be nobler yet
And put her to her own House. [*To the White King*] King of
    meekness,°
Take the cause to thee, for our hands too heavy;°
Our proofs will fall upon her like a tower   200
And grind her bones to powder.
WHITE QUEEN'S PAWN   What new engine
Hath the devil raised in him now?
BLACK KNIGHT   Is it he,
And that the time? Stand firm now to your scandal;°
Pray do not shift your slander.
WHITE QUEEN'S PAWN   Shift your treacheries;°
They've worn one suit too long.
BLACK KNIGHT   That holy man,   205
So wrongfully accused by this lost pawn,
Has not been seen these ten days in these parts.
WHITE KING How?°
BLACK KNIGHT Nay, at this instant, thirty leagues from hence.
WHITE QUEEN'S PAWN Fathomless falsehood! Will't 'scape
    unblasted?   210
WHITE KING Can you make this appear?
BLACK KNIGHT   Light is not clearer;°
By his own letters, most impartial monarch!
WHITE KING'S PAWN How wrongfully may sacred virtue suffer, sir.°
BLACK KNIGHT [*aside*] Bishop, we have a treasure of that false heart.
WHITE KING Step forth and reach those proofs.
        [*Exit a Black Pawn. He returns with papers*]
WHITE QUEEN'S PAWN   Amazement covers me!° 215
Can I be so forsaken of a cause°
So strong in truth and equity? Will virtue
Send me no aid in this hard time of friendship?
BLACK KNIGHT [*aside to White King's Pawn*] There's an infallible
    staff and a red hat°
Reserved for you.
WHITE KING'S PAWN O sir endeared!
BLACK KNIGHT   A staff°   220
That will not easily break, you may trust to it.

[*Aside*] And such a one had your corruption need of;
There's a state-fig for you now.
WHITE KING   Behold all,°
How they cohere in one. I always held°
A charity so good to holiness   225
Professed that I ever believed rather°
The accuser false than the professor vicious.
BLACK KNIGHT A charity like all your virtues else,
Gracious and glorious.
WHITE KING   Where settles the offence,
Let the fault's punishment be derived from thence:°   230
We leave her to your censure.
BLACK KNIGHT   Most just Majesty!
     [*Exeunt White King, Queen, Bishop, King's Pawn, Fat Bishop,
     and Fat Bishop's Pawn*]
WHITE QUEEN'S PAWN Calamity of virtue! My Queen leave me too?°
Am I cast off as th'olive casts her flower?°
Poor friendless innocence, art thou left a prey°
To the devourer?
WHITE KNIGHT   No, thou art not lost;   235
Let 'em put on their bloodiest resolutions,
If the fair policy I aim at prospers.
Thy counsel, noble Duke?
WHITE DUKE   For that work cheerfully.°
WHITE KNIGHT A man for speed now?
WHITE BISHOP'S PAWN   Let it be mine honour, sir:°
Make me that flight that owes her my life's service.°   240
     Exeunt [*White Knight, Duke, and Bishop's Pawn*]
BLACK KNIGHT Was not this brought about well for our honours?
BLACK BISHOP Pish, that Galician brain can work out wonders.°
BLACK KNIGHT Let's use her as upon the like discovery°
A maid was used at Venice; everyone
Be ready with a penance. Begin, majesty.°   245
Vessel of foolish scandal! Take thy freight:°
Had there been in that cabinet of niceness°
Half the virginities of the earth locked up
And all swept at one cast by the dexterity°
Of a Jesuitical gamester, it had not valued   250
The least part of that general worth thou hast tainted.°
BLACK KING First I enjoin thee to a three days' fast for 't.
BLACK QUEEN You are too penurious, sir; I'll make it four.

BLACK BISHOP I, to a twelve hours' kneeling at one time.
BLACK KNIGHT And in a room filled all with Aretine's pictures,°   255
　　More than the twice twelve labours of luxury;°
　　Thou shalt not see so much as the chaste pommel
　　Of Lucrece' dagger peeping; nay, I'll punish thee°
　　For a discoverer, I'll torment thy modesty.
BLACK DUKE After that four days' fast, to the Inquisition house,°   260
　　Strengthened with bread and water, for worse penance.
BLACK KNIGHT Well said, Duke of our House, nobly aggravated!°
WHITE QUEEN'S PAWN Virtue (to show her influence more strong)
　　Fits me with patience mightier than my wrong.°
　　　　Exeunt

3.1

Enter the Fat Bishop

FAT BISHOP I know my pen draws blood of the Black House;
There's never a book I write but their cause bleeds.
It hath lost many an ounce of reputation°
Since I came of this side: I strike deep in
And leave the orifex gushing where I come;   5
But where is my advancement all this while?°
I'd have some round preferment, corpulent dignity,
That bears some breadth and compass in the gift on't;
I am persuaded that this flesh would fill
The biggest chair ecclesiastical°   10
If it were put to trial.
To be made master of an hospital
Is but a kind of diseased bed-rid honour,
Or dean of the poor alms-knights that wear badges.
There's but two lazy beggarly preferments°   15
In the White Kingdom, and I have got'em both;
My merit doth begin to be crop-sick°
For want of other titles.

Enter Black Knight

BLACK KNIGHT [*aside*]   O here walks
His fulsome holiness; now for the master-trick
T'undo him everlastingly that's put home°   20
And make him hang in hell most seriously
That jested with a halter upon me.

FAT BISHOP [*aside*] The Black Knight! I must look to my play
then.

BLACK KNIGHT I bring fair greetings to your reverend virtues
From Cardinal Paulus, your most princely kinsman.
     [*Gives him a letter*]°   25

FAT BISHOP Our princely kinsman, say'st thou? We accept'em.
Pray keep your side and distance; I am chary°
Of my episcopal person.
[*Aside*] I know the Knight's walk in this game too well;°
He may skip over me, and where am I then?   30

BLACK KNIGHT [*aside*] There where thou shalt be shortly if art fail
not.

FAT BISHOP *Reads*: 'Right reverend and holy'°—meaning me—'our
   true kinsman in blood but alienated in affection, your unkind disobedience to the Mother Cause proves at this time the only cause
   of° your ill fortune. My present remove, by general election, to the   35
   papal dignity had° now auspiciously settled you in my *sede
   vacente*'—how? had it so?—'which at my next remove by death
   might have proved your step to supremacy.'°
   Hah! All my body's blood mounts to my face°
   To look upon this letter.
BLACK KNIGHT   The pill works with him!   40
FAT BISHOP (*reads*) 'Think on't seriously. It is not yet too late through
   the submissive° acknowledgement of your disobedience to be lov-
   ingly received into the brotherly bosom of the conclave.'
   [*Aside*] This was the chair of ease I ever aimed at.°
   I'll make a bonfire of my books immediately;   45
   All that are left against that side I'll sacrifice,
   Pack up my plate and goods and steal away
   By night at watergate. It is but penning°
   Another recantation, and inventing°
   Two or three bitter books against the White House   50
   And then I'm in, on th'other side again
   As firm as e'er I was, as fat and flourishing.—
   Black Knight! expect a wonder ere't be long;
   Thou shalt see me one of the Black House shortly.
BLACK KNIGHT Your holiness is merry with the messenger,   55
   Too happy to be true; you speak what should be,°
   If natural compunction touched you truly.°
   O you've drawn blood, life-blood, the blood of honour,
   From your most dear, your primitive mother's heart.°
   Your sharp invectives have been points of spears   60
   In her sweet tender sides; the unkind wounds°
   Which a son gives (a son of reverence specially)
   They rankle ten times more than the adversaries'.
   I tell you, sir, your reverend revolt
   Did give the fearful'st blow to adoration°   65
   Our cause e'er felt; it shook the very statues,
   The urns and ashes of the sainted sleepers.°
FAT BISHOP Forbear, or I shall melt i'the place I stand°
   [And let forth a fat bishop in sad syrup;]°
   Suffices, I am yours when they least dream on't.   70
   Ambition's fodder (power and riches) draws me;

270

When I smell honour, that's the lock of hay
That leads me through the world's field every way.°
    Exit [Fat Bishop]
BLACK KNIGHT Here's a sweet paunch to propagate belief on,
    Like the foundation of a chapel laid   75
    Upon a quagmire. I may number him now
    Amongst my inferior policies and not shame'em;°
    But let me a little solace my designs
    With the remembrance of some brave ones past,
    To cherish the futurity of project   80
    Whose motion must be restless, till that great work°
    (Called the possession of the world) be ours.
    Was it not I procured a gallant fleet
    From the White Kingdom to secure our coasts
    'Gainst the infidel pirates, under pretext   85
    Of more necessitous expedition?°
    Who made the jails fly open (without miracle)
    And let the locusts out, those dangerous flies
    Whose property is to burn corn with touching?
    The heretic granaries feel it to this minute,   90
    And now they've got amongst the country-crops
    They stick so fast to the converted ears
    The loudest tempest that authority rouses
    Will hardly shake'em off; they have their dens
    In ladies' couches, there's safe groves and fens.   95
    Nay, were they followed and found out by th'scent,
    Palm-oil will make a pursuivant relent.°
    Whose policy was't to put a silenced muzzle
    On all the barking tongue-men of the time,
    Made pictures that were dumb enough before   100
    Poor sufferers in that politic restraint?°
    My light spleen skips and shakes my ribs to think on't.°
    Whilst our drifts walked uncensured but in thought,
    A whisper or a whistle would be questioned
    In the most fortunate angle of the world.°   105
    The court hath held the city by the horns
    While I have milked her; I have got good sops too°
    From country ladies for their liberties,°
    From some, for their most vainly hoped preferments,
    High offices in the air. I should not live°   110
    But for this *mel aerium*, this mirth-manna.°

My pawn! How now? The news?
                    Enter the Black Knight's Pawn
BLACK KNIGHT'S PAWN   Expect none very pleasing
   That comes, sir, of my bringing; I'm for sad things.
BLACK KNIGHT Thy conscience is so tender-hoofed o'late;
   Every nail pricks it.
BLACK KNIGHT'S PAWN   This may prick yours too   115
   If there be any quick flesh in a yard on't.°
BLACK KNIGHT Mine?
   Mischief must find a deep nail and a driver°
   Beyond the strength of any Machiavel
   The politic kingdoms fatten, to reach mine.   120
   Prithee compunction, needle-pricked a little:
   Unbind this sore wound.
BLACK KNIGHT'S PAWN   Sir, your plot's discovered.°
BLACK KNIGHT Which of the twenty thousand and nine hundred,
   Three score and five, canst tell?
BLACK KNIGHT'S PAWN   Bless us, so many?°
   How do poor countrymen have but one plot   125
   To keep a cow on, yet in law for that?°
   You cannot know'em all sure by their names, sir.°
BLACK KNIGHT Yes, were the number trebled. Thou hast seen°
   A globe stands on the table in my closet?
BLACK KNIGHT'S PAWN A thing, sir, full of countries and hard
      words?   130
BLACK KNIGHT True, with lines drawn some tropical, some oblique.°
BLACK KNIGHT'S PAWN I scarce can read; I was brought up in
      blindness.°
BLACK KNIGHT Just such a thing (if e'er my skull be opened)
   Will my brains look like.
BLACK KNIGHT'S PAWN   Like a globe of countries.
BLACK KNIGHT Yes, and some master-politician   135
   That hath sharp state-eyes will go near to pick out
   The plots, and every climate where they fastened;°
   It will puzzle'em too.
BLACK KNIGHT'S PAWN   I'm of your mind for that, sir.°
BLACK KNIGHT They'll find'em to fall thick upon some countries;
   They'd need of spectacles. But I turn to you now: 140
   What plot is that discovered?
BLACK KNIGHT'S PAWN   Your last brat, sir,°
   Begot betwixt the Black Bishop and yourself,

Your antedated letters 'bout the Jesuit.°
BLACK KNIGHT Discovered? How?
BLACK KNIGHT'S PAWN   The White Knight's policy
Has outstripped yours, it seems,   145
Joined with th'assistant counsel of his Duke.
The White Bishop's Pawn undertook the journey
Who (as they say) discharged it like a flight;
I made him for the business fit and light.°
BLACK KNIGHT It's but a bawdy pawn out of the way a little,   150
Enough of them in all parts.
     Enter the White and Black Houses (*severally*) [*including*
     minimally the Black Bishop, King, Queen and Duke, and the
     White King, Queen, Duke, Knight, Bishop, King's Pawn and one
     other Pawn, and the Fat Bishop]°
BLACK BISHOP   You have heard all then?
BLACK KNIGHT The wonder's past with me, but some shall down
    for't.°
WHITE KING Set free that virtuous pawn from all her wrongs;°
Let her be brought with honour to the face
Of her malicious adversary.
    [*Exit a White Pawn*]
BLACK KNIGHT   Good!°   155
WHITE KING [*to the White Knight*] Noble chaste Knight, a title of that
    candour
The greatest prince on earth without impeachment
May have the dignity of his worth comprised in,°
This fair delivering act of virtue will register
In that white book of the defence of virgins   160
Where the clear fames of all preserving knights
Are to eternal memory consecrated;°
And we embrace (as partner of that honour)
This worthy Duke (the counsel of the act)
Whom we shall ever place in our respect.   165
WHITE DUKE Most blessed of kings, throned in all royal graces!
Every good deed sends back its own reward
Into the bosom of the enterpriser;°
But you to express yourself as well to be
King of munificence as integrity   170
Adds glory to the gift.
WHITE KING   Thy desert claims it,°
Zeal and fidelity.—Appear, thou beauty

Of truth and innocence, best ornament
Of patience, thou that mak'st thy suff'rings glorious.°
        [*Enter White Pawn with White Queen's Pawn*]
BLACK KNIGHT [*aside*] I'll take no knowledge on't. [*To all*] What
        makes she here?°   175
How dares yond pawn unpenanced, with a cheek
Fresh as her falsehood yet, where castigation
Hath left no pale print of her visiting anguish,°
Appear in this assembly? [*Aside*] Let me alone;
Sin must be bold, that's all the grace 'tis born to.°   180
WHITE KNIGHT What's this?
WHITE KING   I'm wonder-struck!
WHITE QUEEN'S PAWN   Assist me, goodness;°
I shall to prison again.
BLACK KNIGHT [*aside*]   At least I've 'mazed'em;°
Scattered their admiration of her innocence
As the fired ships put in severed the fleet
In eighty-eight. I'll on with't; impudence°   185
Is mischief's patrimony.—[*To all*] Is this justice?
Is injured reverence no sharplier righted?°
I ever held that majesty impartial
That (like most equal heaven) looks on the manners,°
Not on the shapes they shroud in.
WHITE KING   This Black Knight   190
Will never take an answer; 'tis a victory°
To make him understand he doth amiss
When he knows in his own clear understanding
That he doth nothing else. Show him the testimony
(Confirmed by good men) how that foul attempter   195
Got, but this morning, to the place from whence
He dated his forged lines for ten days past.
BLACK KNIGHT Why may not that corruption sleep in this
By some connivance, as you have waked in ours
By too rash confidence?
WHITE DUKE   I'll undertake°   200
This Knight shall teach the devil how to lie.°
WHITE KNIGHT If sin were half as wise as impudent
She'd ne'er seek farther for an advocate.
        [*Enter Black Queen's Pawn*]°
BLACK QUEEN'S PAWN [*aside*] Now to act treachery with an angel's
        tongue;

Since all's come out, I'll bring him strangely in again.° 205
[*To all*] Where is this injured chastity, this goodness
Whose worth no transitory piece can value,°
This rock of constant and invincible virtue
That made sin's tempest weary of his fury?
BLACK QUEEN What, is my pawn distracted?
BLACK KNIGHT   I think rather° 210
There is some notable masterprize of roguery
This drum strikes up for.
BLACK QUEEN'S PAWN   Let me fall with reverence
Before this blessed altar.
BLACK QUEEN   This is madness.°
BLACK KNIGHT Well, mark the end; I stand for roguery still,
I will not change my side.
BLACK QUEEN'S PAWN   I shall be taxed, I know;° 215
I care not what the Black House thinks of me.
BLACK QUEEN What say you now?
BLACK KNIGHT   I shall not be unlaid yet.
BLACK QUEEN'S PAWN How any censure flies, I honour sanctity;°
That is my object, I intend no other,
I saw this glorious and most valiant virtue 220
Fight the most noblest combat with the devil.
BLACK KNIGHT If both the Bishops had been there for seconds
'T had been a complete duel.
WHITE KING   Then thou heard'st°
The violence intended.
BLACK QUEEN'S PAWN   'Tis a truth
I joy to justify. I was an agent,° 225
On virtue's part, and raised that confused noise
That startled him, and gave her liberty.°
BLACK QUEEN'S PAWN O 'tis a righteous story she has told, sir;
My life and fame stand mutually engaged,°
Both to the truth and goodness of this pawn. 230
WHITE KING Does it appear to you yet, clear as the sun?
BLACK KNIGHT 'Las, I believed it long before 'twas done.°
BLACK KING Degenerate.
BLACK QUEEN   Base.
BLACK BISHOP   Perfidious.
BLACK DUKE   Traitorous pawn!
BLACK QUEEN'S PAWN What, are you all beside yourselves?
BLACK KNIGHT   But I.°

275

Remember that, Pawn!

BLACK QUEEN'S PAWN   May a fearful barrenness   235
    Blast both my hopes and pleasures, if I brought not
    Her ruin in my pity, a new trap°
    For her more sure confusion.

BLACK KNIGHT   Have I won now?
    Did not I say 'twas craft and machination?°
    I smelt conspiracy all the way it went   240
    Although the mess were covered, I'm so used to it.°

BLACK KING   That Queen would I fain finger.

BLACK KNIGHT   You are too hot, sir;°
    If she were took, the game would be ours quickly.
    My aim's at that White Knight; entrap him first
    The Duke will follow too.

BLACK BISHOP   I would that Bishop   245
    Were in my diocese; I would soon change his whiteness.°

BLACK KNIGHT   Sir, I could whip you up a pawn immediately;°
    I know where my game stands.

BLACK KING   Do it suddenly:
    Advantage least must not be lost in this play.

        [*Black Knight seizes White King's Pawn*]

BLACK KNIGHT   Pawn, thou art ours! He's taken by default.°   250

WHITE KNIGHT   By wilful negligence. Guard the sacred persons;°
    Look well to the White Bishop, for that pawn
    Gave guard to the Queen and him in the third place.°

BLACK KNIGHT   See what sure piece you lock your confidence in.°
    I made this pawn here by corruption ours,   255
    As soon as honour by creation yours;°
    This whiteness upon him is but the leprosy°
    Of pure dissimulation. View him now:
    His heart and his intents are of our colour.

        [*His upper garment taken off*] he appears black underneath

WHITE KNIGHT   Most dangerous hypocrite!

WHITE DUKE   One made against us!°   260

WHITE QUEEN   His truth of their complexion!

WHITE KING   Has my goodness,°
    Clemency, love, and favour gracious raised thee
    From a condition next to popular labour,
    Took thee from all the dubitable hazards
    Of fortune, her most unsecure adventures,   265
    And grafted thee into a branch of honour,°

And dost thou fall from the top-bough by the rottenness
Of thy alone corruption, like a fruit°
That's over-ripened by the beams of favour?
Let thine own weight reward thee, I have forgot thee;°   270
Integrity of life is so dear to me
Where I find falsehood or a crying trespass,°
Be it in any whom our grace shines most on,°
I would tear him from my heart.

WHITE BISHOP   Spoke like heaven's substitute.°

WHITE KING You have him, we can spare him, and his shame   275
    Will make the rest look better to their game.°

BLACK KING The more cunning we must use then.

BLACK KNIGHT   We shall match you,°
    Play how you can, perhaps and mate you too.

FAT BISHOP Is there so much amazement spent on him°
    That's but half black? (There might be hope of that man.)°   280
    But how will this House wonder if I stand forth
    And show a whole one, instantly discover
    One that's all black? Where there's no hope at all?

WHITE KING I'll say thy heart then justifies thy books;
    I long for that discovery.

FAT BISHOP   Look no farther then: 285
    Bear witness all the House I am the man
    And turn myself into the Black House freely;
    I am of this side now.

WHITE KNIGHT   Monster ne'er matched him!

BLACK KING This is your noble work, Knight.

BLACK KNIGHT   Now I'll halter him.

FAT BISHOP Next news you hear, expect my books against you   290
    Printed at Douay, Brussels, or Spalato.°

WHITE KING See his goods seized on.

FAT BISHOP   'Las, they were all conveyed°
    Last night by water to a tailor's house,
    A friend of the Black cause.

WHITE KING   A prepared hypocrite.°

WHITE DUKE Premeditated turncoat.
      Exeunt [*White King, Queen, Bishop, Knight, and Duke*]

FAT BISHOP   Yes, rail on;   295
    I'll reach you in my writings when I am gone.

BLACK KNIGHT [*aside to Black House*] Flatter him a while with
    honour, till we put him°

Upon some dangerous service and then burn him.°

BLACK KING [*to Fat Bishop*] This came unlooked for.

BLACK DUKE   How we joy to see you.

FAT BISHOP Now I'll discover all the White House to you.   300

BLACK DUKE Indeed, that will both reconcile and raise you.

    [*Exeunt Black King, Queen, Duke, Bishop and Fat Bishop*]

WHITE KING'S PAWN I rest upon you, Knight, for my advancement
    now.°

BLACK KNIGHT O, for the staff, the strong staff that will hold,
    And the red hat fit for the guilty mazard.°
    Into the empty bag know thy first way;°   305
    Pawns that are lost are ever out of play.

WHITE KING'S PAWN How's this?

BLACK KNIGHT No replications, you know me;
    No doubt ere long you'll have more company;
    The bag is big enough, 'twill hold us all.   310

    Exeunt [*Black Knight, Black Knight's Pawn, and White King's
    Pawn*]

WHITE QUEEN'S PAWN I sue to thee, prithee be one of us,
    Let my love win thee. Thou hast done truth this day
    And yesterday my honour, noble service;
    The best pawn of our House could not transcend it.°

BLACK QUEEN'S PAWN My pity flamed with zeal, especially   315
    When I foresaw your marriage; then it mounted.°

WHITE QUEEN'S PAWN How, marriage?

BLACK QUEEN'S PAWN   That contaminating act
    Would have spoiled all your fortunes—a rape, bless us!°

WHITE QUEEN'S PAWN Thou talk'st of marriage.

BLACK QUEEN'S PAWN   Yes, yes, you do marry;
    I saw the man.

WHITE QUEEN'S PAWN The man?   320

BLACK QUEEN'S PAWN An absolute handsome gentleman, a complete
    one;°
    You'll say so when you see him, heir to three red hats
    Besides his general hopes in the Black House.°

WHITE QUEEN'S PAWN Why, sure thou'rt much mistaken in this man;
    I have promised single life to all my affections.   325

BLACK QUEEN'S PAWN Promise you what you will, or I, or all on's,°
    There's a fate rules and over-rules us all, methinks.

WHITE QUEEN'S PAWN Why, how came you to see, or know this
    mystery?

BLACK QUEEN'S PAWN A magical glass I bought of an Egyptian,
 Whose stone retains that speculative virtue,°   330
 Presented the man to me. Your name brings him
 As often as I use it, and methinks
 I never have enough, persons and postures°
 Are all so pleasing.
WHITE QUEEN'S PAWN This is wondrous strange.
 The faculties of soul are still the same;°   335
 I can feel no one motion tend that way.
BLACK QUEEN'S PAWN We do not always feel our faith we live by,
 Nor ever see our growth, yet both work upward.°
WHITE QUEEN'S PAWN 'Twas well applied, but may I see him too?°
BLACK QUEEN'S PAWN Surely you may without all doubt or fear, 340
 Observing the right use as I was taught it,
 Nor looking back or questioning the spectre.°
WHITE QUEEN'S PAWN That's no hard observation, trust it with me.°
 Is't possible? I long to see this man.
BLACK QUEEN'S PAWN Why then observe; I'll ease you instantly.° 345
  [*Exeunt*]°

[3.2°

 Enter a Black Jesting Pawn°
BLACK JESTING PAWN I would so fain take one of these white pawns
  now;°
 I'd make him do all under-drudgery,°
 Feed him with asses' milk crumbed with goat's cheese,°
 And all the whitemeats could be devised for him.
 I'd make him my white jennet when I pranced°   5
 After the Black Knight's litter.
  Enter a White Pawn
WHITE PAWN   And you would look then°
 Just like a devil striding o'er a nightmare
 Made of a miller's daughter.
BLACK JESTING PAWN   A pox on you,°
 Were you so near? I'm taken like a blackbird
 In the great snow, this White pawn grinning over me.°   10
WHITE PAWN And now because I will not foul my clothes°
 Ever hereafter, for white quickly soils, you know—

BLACK JESTING PAWN I prithee get thee gone then; I shall smut
    thee.
WHITE PAWN Nay, I'll put that to venture now I have snapped thee;
    Thou shalt do all the dirty drudgery   15
    That slavery was e'er put to.
BLACK JESTING PAWN   I shall cozen you:
    You may chance come and find your work undone then,
    For I'm too proud to labour; I'll starve first,
    I tell you that beforehand.
WHITE PAWN   I will fit you then°
    With a black whip that shall not be behind-hand.   20
BLACK JESTING PAWN Pugh, I have been used to whipping, I have
    whipped°
    Myself three mile out of town in a morning; and
    I can fast a fortnight and make all your meat°
    Stink and lie o'your hands!°
WHITE PAWN To prevent that, your food shall be blackberries,   25
    And upon gaudy-days a pickled spider
    Cut out like an anchovy; I'm not to learn
    A monkey's ordinary. Come, sir, will you frisk?°
      Enter a Second Black Pawn.°
SECOND BLACK PAWN Soft, soft; you have no such bargain of it,°
    If you look well about you.
WHITE PAWN   By this hand,   30
    I am snapped too, a Black Pawn in the breech of me.°
    We three look like a birdspit, a white chick°
    Between two russet woodcocks.
BLACK JESTING PAWN   I'm so glad of this.°
WHITE PAWN But you shall have small cause, for I'll firk you.°
SECOND BLACK PAWN Then I'll firk you again.
WHITE PAWN   And I'll firk him again.   35
BLACK JESTING PAWN Mass, here will be old firking; I shall have°
    The worst on't for I can firk nobody.°
    We draw together now for all the world
    Like three flies with one straw through their buttocks.
      [*Exeunt.*]

3.3

[*Enter Black Queen's Pawn and White Queen's Pawn*]°

BLACK QUEEN'S PAWN This is the room he did appear to me in;
And (look you) this the magical glass that showed him.°

WHITE QUEEN'S PAWN I find no motion yet; what should I think
on't?°
A sudden fear invades me, a faint trembling
Under this omen, as is oft felt like the panting of a turtle°   5
Under a stroking hand.

BLACK QUEEN'S PAWN   That bodes good luck still,
Sign you shall change state speedily, for that trembling
Is always the first symptom of a bride.
For any vainer fears that may accompany°
His apparition, by my truth to friendship   10
I quit you of the least. Never was object°
More gracefully presented; the very air
Conspires to do him honour, and creates
Sweet vocal sounds, as if a bridegroom entered,
Which argues the blessed harmony of your loves.°   15

WHITE QUEEN'S PAWN And will the using of my name produce him?

BLACK QUEEN'S PAWN Nay, of yours only, else the wonder halted.°
To clear you of that doubt, I'll put the difference
In practice the first thing I do, and make
His invocation in the name of others.

WHITE QUEEN'S PAWN   'Twill satisfy me much, that.

BLACK QUEEN'S PAWN   It shall be done.   20
Thou, whose gentle form and face
Filled lately this Egyptic glass,
By the imperious powerful name
And the universal fame
Of the mighty Black House Queen,   25
I conjure thee to be seen.
What, see you nothing yet?

WHITE QUEEN'S PAWN   Not any part;
Pray, try another.

BLACK QUEEN'S PAWN You shall have your will.°
I double my command and power
And at the instant of this hour   30
Invoke thee in the White Queen's name,

With stay for time, and shape the same.°
What see you yet?
WHITE QUEEN'S PAWN There's nothing shows at all.
BLACK QUEEN'S PAWN My truth reflects the clearer; then now fix°
    And bless your fair eye with your own for ever.°   35
        Thou well-composed, by fate's hand drawn°
        To enjoy the White Queen's Pawn,
        Of whom thou shalt (by virtue met)
        Many graceful issues get,°
        By the beauty of her fame,   40
        By the whiteness of her name,
        By her fair and fruitful love,
        By her truth that mates the dove,
        By the meekness of her mind,
        By the softness of her kind,   45
        By the lustre of her grace,
        By all these thou art summoned to this place.
Hark, how the air, enchanted with your praises°
And his approach, these words to sweet notes raises.
      Music. The Black Bishop's Pawn° enters (as in an apparition)
      richly habited; [presents himself before the glass; then exits]°
WHITE QUEEN'S PAWN O let him stay a while, a little longer!   50
BLACK QUEEN'S PAWN That's a good hearing.°
WHITE QUEEN'S PAWN If he be mine, why should he part so
  soon?
BLACK QUEEN'S PAWN Why, this is but the shadow of yours.°
WHITE QUEEN'S PAWN O I did ill to give consent to see it.
    What certainty is in our blood or state?°   55
    What we still write is blotted out by fate.°
    Our wills are like a cause that is law-tossed;
    What one court orders is by another crossed.
BLACK QUEEN'S PAWN I find no fit place for this passion here;
    It's merely an intruder. He is a gentleman°   60
    Most wishfully composed; honour grows on him°
    And wealth piled up for him; h'ath youth enough, too,
    And yet in the sobriety of his countenance,
    Grave as a tetrarch (which is gracious
    In th'eye of modest pleasure.) Where's the emptiness?°   65
    What can you more request?
WHITE QUEEN'S PAWN   I do not know
  What answer yet to make. It doth require

A meeting 'twixt my fear and my desire.
    Exit [White Queen's Pawn]
BLACK QUEEN'S PAWN She's caught, and (which is strange) by her
    most wronger.°
        Exit

4.1

Enter the Black Bishop's Pawn and the Black Knight's Pawn°
BLACK KNIGHT'S PAWN [*aside*] 'Tis he, my confessor! He might have
    passed me
  Seven years together, had I not by chance°
  Advanced mine eye upon that lettered hatband,°
  The Jesuitical symbol to be known by,
  Worn by the brave collegians by consent.°   5
  It's a strange habit for a holy father,
  (A president of poverty especially.)°
  But we (the sons and daughters of obedience)
  Dare not once think awry, but must confess ourselves°
  As humbly to the father of that feather,   10
  Long spur and poniard, as to the alb and altar,°
  And happy we're so highly graced to attain it.
  [*To him*] Holy and reverend!
BLACK BISHOP'S PAWN   How hast found me out?
BLACK KNIGHT'S PAWN O sir, put on the sparklingest trim of glory,°
  Perfection will shine foremost, and I knew you   15
  By the catholical mark you wear about you,°
  The mark above your forehead.
BLACK BISHOP'S PAWN   Are you grown
  So ambitious in your observance? Well, your business?°
  I have my game to follow.
BLACK KNIGHT'S PAWN   I have a worm°
  Follows me so that I can follow no game;   20
  The most faint-hearted pawn, if he could see
  His play, might snap me up at pleasure. I desire, sir,°
  To be absolved; my conscience being at ease,
  I could then with more courage ply my game.
BLACK BISHOP'S PAWN 'Twas a base fact.
BLACK KNIGHT'S PAWN   'Twas to a schismatic pawn, sir.° 25
BLACK BISHOP'S PAWN What's that to the nobility of revenge?°
  Suffices, I have neither will nor power
  To give you absolution for that violence.
  Make your petition to the Penance-chamber.°
  If the tax-register relieve you in't°   30
  By the Fat Bishop's clemency, you have wrought out°

A singular piece of favour with your money;
That's all your refuge now.

BLACK KNIGHT'S PAWN   The sting shoots deeper.°

　　　　Exit [the Black Knight's Pawn]. Enter the White and the Black
　　　　Queens' Pawns

BLACK BISHOP'S PAWN Yonder's my game, which, like a politic
　　chess-master,
I must not seem to see.

WHITE QUEEN'S PAWN O my heart, 'tis he!°

BLACK QUEEN'S PAWN   That 'tis!   35

WHITE QUEEN'S PAWN The very self-same that the magical mirror
Presented lately to me.

BLACK QUEEN'S PAWN   And how like
A most regardless stranger he walks by,°
Merely ignorant of his fate; you are not minded
(The principal'st part of him.) What strange mysteries°   40
Inscrutable love works by!

WHITE QUEEN'S PAWN   The time you see°
Is not yet come!

BLACK QUEEN'S PAWN   But 'tis in our power now
[To bring time nearer—knowledge is a mastery—]°
And make it observe us, and not we it.°

WHITE QUEEN'S PAWN I would force nothing from its proper virtue.°   45
Let time have his full course; I had rather die
The modest death of undiscovered love
Than have heaven's least and lowest servant suffer
Or in his motion receive check for me.°
How is my soul's growth altered that single life,   50
(The fittest garment that peace ever made for't)
Is grown too strait, too stubborn on the sudden.°

BLACK QUEEN'S PAWN He comes this way again.

WHITE QUEEN'S PAWN   O there's a traitor°
Leaped from my heart into my cheek already   55
That will betray all to his powerful eye
If it but glance upon me.

BLACK QUEEN'S PAWN   By my verity,
　Look, he's passed by again, drowned in neglect
Without the prosperous hint of so much happiness
To look upon his fortune. How close fate°
Seals up the eye of human understanding   60
Till (like the sunflower) time and love uncloses it.

'Twere pity he should dwell in ignorance longer.°
WHITE QUEEN'S PAWN What will you do?
BLACK QUEEN'S PAWN   Yes, die a bashful death, do,°
　　And let the remedy pass by unused still.
　　You're changed enough already if you'd look int'it.°   65
　　[To Black Bishop's Pawn] Absolute sir (with your most noble
　　　　pardon
　　For this my rude intrusion) I am bold
　　To bring the knowledge of a secret nearer
　　By many days, sir, than it would arrive
　　In its own proper revelation with you.°   70
　　Pray turn and fix: do you know yond noble goodness?°
BLACK BISHOP'S PAWN 'Tis the first minute mine eye blessed me
　　with her,
　　And clearly shows how much my knowledge wanted,
　　Not knowing her till now.
BLACK QUEEN'S PAWN   She's to be liked then?°
　　Pray view advisedly: there is strong reason   75
　　That I'm so bold to urge it, you must guess;°
　　The work concerns you nearer than you think for.
BLACK BISHOP'S PAWN Her glory, and the wonder of this secret
　　Puts a reciprocal amazement on me.°
BLACK QUEEN'S PAWN And 'tis not without worth; you two must be 80
　　Better acquainted.
BLACK BISHOP'S PAWN Is there cause? Affinity?°
　　Or any courteous help creation joys in
　　To bring that forward?
BLACK QUEEN'S PAWN Yes, yes, I can show you°
　　The nearest way to that perfection
　　(Of a most virtuous one) that joy e'er found.°   85
　　Pray mark her once again, then follow me
　　And I will show you her must be your wife, sir.°
BLACK BISHOP'S PAWN The mystery extends, or else creation
　　Hath set that admirable piece before us
　　To choose our chaste delights by.
BLACK QUEEN'S PAWN   Please you follow, sir.°   90
BLACK BISHOP'S PAWN What art have you to put me on an object
　　And cannot get me off? 'Tis pain to part from it.°
　　　　　　Exit [Black Bishop's Pawn, with Black Queen's Pawn].
WHITE QUEEN'S PAWN If there prove no check in that magical glass
　　now,°

But my proportion come as fair and full°
Into his eye as his into mine lately,   95
Then I am confirmed, he is mine own for ever.
    Enter [Black Bishop's Pawn and Black Queen's Pawn]
BLACK BISHOP'S PAWN The very self-same that the mirror blessed
   me with,
   From head to foot, the beauty and the habit.
   Kept you this place still? Did you not remove, lady?
WHITE QUEEN'S PAWN Not a foot farther, sir.
BLACK BISHOP'S PAWN   Is't possible?   100
   I would have sworn I'd seen the substance yonder,°
   'Twas to that lustre, to that life presented.
WHITE QUEEN'S PAWN Even so was yours to me, sir.
BLACK BISHOP'S PAWN   Saw you mine?
WHITE QUEEN'S PAWN Perfectly clear; no sooner my name used
   But yours appeared.
BLACK BISHOP'S PAWN Just so did yours at mine now.   105
BLACK QUEEN'S PAWN Why stand you idle? Will you let time
   cozen you,°
   Protracting time, of those delicious beauties°
   That fate hath marked to you, you modest pair
   Of blushing gamesters—and you, sir, the bashfullest;
   I cannot flatter a foul fault in any—   110
   Can you be more than man and wife assigned,°
   And by a power the most irrevocable?
   Others that may be adventurers in delight
   May meet with crosses, shame, or separation,
   [Their fortunes hid, and the events locked from'em;]°   115
   You know the mind of fate; you must be coupled.
BLACK BISHOP'S PAWN She speaks but truth in this. I see no reason
   then,
   That we should miss the relish of this night
   But that we are both shamefaced.
WHITE QUEEN'S PAWN   How? This night, sir?
   Did not I know you must be mine, and therein   120
   Your privilege runs strong, for that loose motion
   You never should be. Is it not my fortune°
   To match with a pure mind? Then am I miserable.
   The doves and all chaste loving winged creatures
   Have their pairs fit, their desires justly mated;   125
   Is woman more unfortunate? A virgin,

The May of woman! Fate that hath ordained, sir,°
We should be man and wife hath not given warrant
For any act of knowledge till we are so.°
BLACK BISHOP'S PAWN Tender-eyed modesty, how it gives at this!   130
  [*Aside to Black Queen's Pawn*] I'm as far off for all this strange
    imposture°
As at first interview. Where lies our game now?
You know I cannot marry by mine order.
BLACK QUEEN'S PAWN I know you cannot, sir, yet you may venture
  Upon a contract.
BLACK BISHOP'S PAWN   Ha!
BLACK QUEEN'S PAWN   Surely you may, sir,°   135
  Without all question, so far, without danger
Or any stain to your vow, and that may take her.
Nay, do't with speed; she'll think you mean the better, too.
BLACK BISHOP'S PAWN [*to White Queen's Pawn*] Be not so lavish of
  that blessed spring;
You've wasted that upon a cold occasion now°   140
Would wash a sinful soul white. By our love-joys,
That motion shall ne'er light upon my tongue more
Till we are contracted, then I hope you're mine.
WHITE QUEEN'S PAWN In all just duty ever.
BLACK QUEEN'S PAWN   Then do you question it?
  Pish, then you're man and wife (all but church ceremony.)   145
  [*To Black Bishop's Pawn*] Pray, let's see that done first; she shall do
    reason then.°
  [*Aside*] Now I'll enjoy the sport and cozen 'em both;
My blood's game is the wages I have worked for.°
    Exeunt

4.2

Enter the Black Knight and his Pawn
BLACK KNIGHT Pawn, I have spoken to the Fat Bishop for thee;°
I'll get thee absolution from his own mouth.
Reach me to my chair of ease, my chair of cozenage;°
Seven thousand pound in woman, reach me that.°
I love o'life to sit upon a bank   5
Of heretic gold. O soft and gentle, sirrah!

There's a foul flaw in the bottom of my drum, Pawn.°
I ne'er shall make sound soldier, but sound treacher
With any he in Europe. How now, qualm?°
Thou hast the pukingest soul that e'er I met with;   10
It cannot bear one suckling villainy.
Mine can digest a monster without crudity,
A sin as weighty as an elephant,
And never wamble for it.
BLACK KNIGHT'S PAWN   Ay, you have been used t'it, sir;
That's a great help; the swallow of my conscience°   15
Has but a narrow passage you must think, yet
It lies in the penitent pipe and will not down.°
If I had got seven thousand pound by offices
And gulled down that, the bore would have been bigger.°
BLACK KNIGHT Nay, if thou prov'st facetious I shall hug thee.   20
Can a soft, rare, poor-poached iniquity
So ride upon thy conscience? I'm ashamed of thee.
Hadst thou betrayed the White House to the Black,
Beggared a kingdom by dissimulation,
Unjointed the fair frame of peace and traffic,   25
Poisoned allegiance, set faith back, and wrought
Women's soft souls even up to masculine malice°
To pursue truth to death if the cause roused 'em,
That stares and parrots are first taught to curse thee—°
BLACK KNIGHT'S PAWN Ay, marry sir, here's swapping sins indeed.   30
BLACK KNIGHT All these and ten times trebled has this brain
Been parent to; they are my offsprings all.
BLACK KNIGHT'S PAWN A goodly brood!
BLACK KNIGHT   Yet I can jest as tightly,°
Laugh and tell stirring stories to court madams
(Daughters of my seducement) with alacrity°   35
As high and hearty as youth's time of innocence
That never knew a sin to shape a sorrow by.°
I never feel a tempest, [nor] a leaf-wind stirring°
To shake a fault; my conscience is becalmed rather.
BLACK KNIGHT'S PAWN I am sure there is a whirlwind huffs in mine,
    sir.   40
BLACK KNIGHT Sirrah, I have sold the groom o'the stool six times,°
And received money of six several ladies
Ambitious to take place of baronets' wives;°
To three old mummy-matrons I have promised

The mothership o'the maids; I have taught our friends, too,° 45
To convey White House gold to our Black Kingdom
In cold baked pasties, and so cozen searchers.
For venting hallowed oil, beads, medals, pardons,
Pictures, Veronica's heads in private presses,°
That's done by one in th'habit of a pedlar; 50
Letters conveyed in rolls, tobacco-balls.
When a restraint comes, by my politic counsel°
Some of our Jesuits turn gentlemen-ushers,
Some falconers, some park-keepers, and some huntsmen;
One took the shape of an old lady's cook once 55
And despatched two chores on a Sunday morning,°
The altar and the dresser! Pray what use°
Put I my summer recreation to?
But more to inform my knowledge in the state
And strength of the White Kingdom! No fortification,° 60
Haven, creek, landing-place 'bout the White coast
But I got draught and platform, learned the depth°
Of all their channels, knowledge of all sands,
Shelves, rocks, and rivers for invasion properest;
A catalogue of all the navy royal, 65
The burden of each ship, the brassy murderers,°
The number of the men, to what cape bound;
Again, for the discovery of the islands,
Never a shire but the state better known
To me than to her breast inhabitants,° 70
What power of men and horse, gentry's revenues,
Who well affected to our side, who ill,
Who neither well nor ill, all the neutrality.
Thirty-eight thousand souls have been seduced, Pawn,
Since the jails vomited with the pill I gave'em.° 75

BLACK KNIGHT'S PAWN Sure you put oil of toad into that physic,
    sir.°
BLACK KNIGHT I'm now about a masterpiece of play
    To entrap the White Knight and with false allurements
    Entice him to the Black House—more will follow:°
    Whilst our Fat Bishop sets upon the Queen; 80
    Then will our game lie sweetly.
        Enter Fat Bishop [with a book]
BLACK KNIGHT'S PAWN   He's come now, sir.°
FAT BISHOP Here's *Taxa Poenitentiara*, Knight,°

The book of general pardons of all prices;
I have been searching for his sin this half-hour°
And cannot light upon't.

BLACK KNIGHT   That's strange, let me see't.   85

BLACK KNIGHT'S PAWN Pawn wretched that I am: hath my rage done
        that
There is no precedent of pardon for?

BLACK KNIGHT [*reads*] 'For wilful murder, thirteen pounds, four shil-
    lings and six pence'° (that's reasonable cheap) 'For killing, killing,
    killing &c'—°   90
Why here's nothing but killing, Bishop, on this side.

FAT BISHOP Turn the sheet over, you shall find adultery
And other trivial sins.

BLACK KNIGHT   Adultery?
O, I'm in't now.—'For adultery a couple°
Of shillings, and for fornication five pence'—   95
These are two good pennyworths! I cannot see
How a man can mend himself.—'For lying°
With mother, sister, and daughter'—ay, marry, sir—
'Thirteen pound, three shillings, three pence'—°
The sin's gradation right; paid all in threes.°   100

FAT BISHOP You have read the story of that monster, sir,°
That got his daughter, sister, and his wife
Of his own mother—

BLACK KNIGHT   'Simony, nine pound.'

FAT BISHOP They may thank me for that, 'twas nineteen
Before I came; I have mitigated many of the sums.   105

BLACK KNIGHT 'Sodomy, sixpence.' (You should put that sum
    Ever in the backside of your book, Bishop.)

FAT BISHOP There's few on's very forward, sir.

BLACK KNIGHT   What's here, sir?°
'Two old precedents of encouragement . . .'°

FAT BISHOP Ay, those are ancient notes.   110

BLACK KNIGHT 'Given as a gratuity for the killing of a heretical
    prince° with a poisoned knife, ducats five thousand.'

FAT BISHOP True,° that was paid.

BLACK KNIGHT 'Promised also to Doctor Lopez for poisoning the
    maiden Queen of the White Kingdom, ducats twenty thousand;   115
    which said sum was afterwards given as a meritorious alms to the
    nunnery at Lisbon,° having at this present ten thousand pound
    more at use in the townhouse at° Antwerp.'

BLACK KNIGHT'S PAWN What's all this to° my conscience, worthy
    holiness?   120
    I sue for pardon, I have brought money with me.

FAT BISHOP You must depart; you see there is no precedent
    Of any price or pardon for your fact.°

BLACK KNIGHT'S PAWN Most miserable! Are fouler sins remitted?
    Killing, nay, wilful murder?

FAT BISHOP   True, there's instance.   125
    Were you to kill him I would pardon you;
    There's precedent for that, and price set down,
    But none for gelding.

BLACK KNIGHT'S PAWN I have picked out understanding now for ever
    Out of that cabalistic bloody riddle:°   130
    I'll make away all my estate and kill him
    And by that act obtain full absolution.°
        Exit [Black Knight's Pawn]. Enter Black King

BLACK KING Why, Bishop! Knight! Where's your removes? Your
    traps?°
    Stand you now idle in the heat of game?

BLACK KNIGHT My life for yours, Black Sovereign, the game's ours;   135
    I have wrought underhand for the White Knight
    And his brave Duke, and find'em coming both.

FAT BISHOP Then for their sanctimonious Queen's surprisal°
    In that state-puzzle and distracted hurry°
    Trust my arch-subtlety with.

BLACK KING   O eagle pride!°   140
    Never was game more hopeful of our side.
        [*Exeunt Black King and Fat Bishop*]

BLACK KNIGHT If Bishop Bull-beef be not snapped at next bout
    (As the men stand) I'll never trust art more.°
        Exit

4.3

*A Dumb show. [Recorders].° Enter the Black Queen's Pawn
(with a taper in her hand) and conducts the White Queen's Pawn
in her night attire into one chamber; and then conveys the Black
Bishop's Pawn (in his night habit) into another chamber; so puts
out the light, and follows him°*

4.4

Enter the White Knight and White Duke

WHITE KNIGHT True noble Duke, fair virtue's most endeared one,°
    Let us prevent their rank insinuation°
    With truth of cause and courage: meet their plots
    With confident goodness that shall strike'em grovelling.

WHITE DUKE Sir, all the gins, traps and alluring snares   5
    The devil hath been at work since 'eighty-eight on°
    Are laid for the great hope of this game only.

WHITE KNIGHT Why, the more noble will truth's triumph be;
    When they have wound about our constant courages
    The glitteringest serpent that e'er falsehood fashioned   10
    And glorying most in his resplendent poisons,
    Just heaven can find a bolt to bruise his head.°

Enter Black Knight

WHITE DUKE Look, would you see destruction lie asunning?°
    In yonder smile sits blood and treachery basking;
    In that perfidious model of face-falsehood   15
    Hell is drawn grinning.

WHITE KNIGHT   What pain it is
    For truth to feign a little.

BLACK KNIGHT   O fair Knight!
    The rising glory of that House of candour,
    Have I so many protestations lost,°
    Lost, lost, quite lost? Am I not worth your confidence?   20
    I that have vowed the faculties of soul,
    Life, spirit and brain to your sweet game of youth,
    Your noble fruitful game. Can you mistrust
    Any foul play in me that have been ever
    The most submiss observer of your virtues   25
    And no way tainted with ambition
    Save only to be thought your first admirer?°
    How often have I changed for your delight
    The royal presentation of my place
    Into a mimic-jester, and become   30
    (For your sake and th'expulsion of sad thoughts)°
    Of a grave state-sire a light son of pastime,
    Made three score years a tomboy, a mere wanton?°

I'll tell you what I told a Savoy dame once,°
Now wed, high, plump, and lusting for an issue: 35
Within the year I promised her a child
If she could stride over St Rumold's breeches,
(A relic kept at Mechlin.) The next morning°
One of my followers' old hose was conveyed
Into her chamber where she tried the feat,   40
By that, and a court friend, after grew great.°
WHITE KNIGHT Why, who could be without thee?
BLACK KNIGHT   I will change
    To any shape to please you, and my aim
    Has been to win your love in all this game.
WHITE KNIGHT Thou hast it nobly, and we long to see   45
    The Black House pleasure, state and dignity.
BLACK KNIGHT Of honour you'll so surfeit and delight°
    You'll ne'er desire again to see the White.
        Exeunt

4.5°

    Enter the White Queen
WHITE QUEEN My love, my hope, my dearest! O he's gone,
    Ensnared, entrapped, surprised amongst the Black ones.°
    I never felt extremity like this;
    Thick darkness dwells upon this hour, integrity
    (Like one of heaven's bright luminaries now   5
    By error's dullest element interposed)°
    Suffers a black eclipse. I never was
    More sick of love than now I am of horror.
        Enter Fat Bishop
    I shall be taken, the game's lost, I'm set upon!
    O 'tis the turncoat Bishop, having watched   10
    The advantage of his play, comes now to seize on me.°
    O I am hard beset, distressed most miserably.°
FAT BISHOP 'Tis vain to stir; remove which way you can
    I take you now. This is the time we have hoped for;
    Queen, you must down.
WHITE QUEEN   No rescue, no deliverer?°   15
FAT BISHOP The Black King's blood burns for thy prostitution

And nothing but the spring of thy chaste virtue
Can cool his inflammation; instantly
He dies upon a pleurisy of luxury°
If he deflower thee not.
     Enter White Bishop
WHITE QUEEN   O strait of misery!°   20
WHITE BISHOP And is your holiness his divine procurer?
FAT BISHOP The devil's in't, I'm taken by a ring–dove!°
   Where stood this Bishop that I saw him not?
WHITE BISHOP You were so ambitious you looked over me.
   You aimed at no less person than the Queen,   25
     Enter White King
   The glory of the game; if she were won
   The way were open to the master check
   Which, look you, he and his lives to give you;°
   Honour and virtue guide him in his station.
WHITE QUEEN O my safe sanctuary.
WHITE KING   Let heaven's blessings   30
   Be mine no longer than I am thy sure one,°
   The dove's house is not safer in the rock°
   Than thou in my firm bosom.
WHITE QUEEN   I am blessed in't.
WHITE KING [*looking at Fat Bishop*] Is it that lump of rank
   ingratitude°
   Swelled with the poison of hypocrisy?   35
   Could he be so malicious, hath partaken°
   Of the sweet fertile blessings of our kingdom?
   [*To White Bishop*] Bishop, thou hast done our White House
   gracious service
   And worthy the fair reverence of thy place.
   [*To Fat Bishop*] For thee, Black Holiness, that work'st out thy
   death°   40
   As the blind mole (the proper'st son of earth)°
   Who in the casting his ambitious hills up
   Is often taken, and destroyed i'th'midst
   Of his advanced work, 'twere well with thee
   If like that verminous labourer, which thou imitat'st   45
   In hills of pride and malice, when death puts thee up°
   The silent grave might prove thy bag for ever,
   No deeper pit than that. For thy vain hope°
   Of the White Knight and his most firm assistant,

Two princely pieces which I know thy thoughts   50
Give lost for ever now, my strong assurance°
Of their fixed virtues, could you let in seas
Of populous untruths against that fort,
'Twould burst the proudest billows.
WHITE QUEEN   My fear's past then.°
WHITE KING Fear? You were never guilty of an injury   55
    To goodness but in that.
WHITE QUEEN   It stayed not with me, sir.
WHITE KING It was too much if it usurped a thought;
    Place a good guard there.
WHITE QUEEN   Confidence is set, sir.°
WHITE KING Take that prize hence; go (reverend of men)
    Put covetousness into the bag again.°   60
FAT BISHOP The bag had need be sound, or it goes to wrack;
    Sin and my weight will make a strong one crack.°
        Exeunt

5.1

[*Music.*]° *Enter the Black Knight* (*in his litter*)° [*as passing in haste over the stage*] *and the Black Bishop's Pawn* (*above*)

BLACK KNIGHT Hold, hold!°
Is the Black Bishop's Pawn, the Jesuit,
Planted above for his concise oration?

BLACK BISHOP'S PAWN *Ecce triumphante me fixum Caesaris arce.*°

BLACK KNIGHT Art there, my holy boy? Sirrah, Bishop Tumbrel°   5
Is snapped, i'th'bag by this time.

BLACK BISHOP'S PAWN *Haeretici pereant sic.*°

BLACK KNIGHT All Latin? Sure the oration hath infected him.
Away, make haste, they're coming.

[*Hautboys.*]° *Enter Black House* [*including the Black King, Queen, Duke and some Pawns*] *meeting the White Knight and Duke.* [*The Black Bishop's Pawn entertains them with this Latin oration*]°

BLACK BISHOP'S PAWN *Si quid mortalibus unquam oculis hilarem et*   10
gratum aperuit diem, si quid peramantibus amicorum animis gaudium
attulit peperitve laetitiam, Eques Candidissime, praelucentissime,
felicem profecto tuum a Domo Candoris ad Domum Nigritudinis acces-
sum promisisse, peperisse, atulisse fatemur. Omnes adventus tui confla-
grantissimi, omni qua possumus laetitia, gaudio, congratulatione,   15
acclamatione, animis observantissimis, affectibus devotissimis, obsequiis
venerabundis, te sospitem congratulamur.°

BLACK KING Sir, in this short congratulatory speech
You may conceive how the whole House affects you.

BLACK KNIGHT The colleges and sanctimonious seed-plots.°   20

WHITE KNIGHT 'Tis clear, and so acknowledged, royal sir.

BLACK KING What honours, pleasures, rarities, delights
Your noble thought can think—

BLACK QUEEN   Your fair eye fix on,
That's comprehended in the spacious circuit
Of our Black Kingdom, they are your servants all.   25

WHITE KNIGHT How amply you endear us.

WHITE DUKE   They are favours°
That equally enrich the royal giver
As the receiver, in the free donation.

BLACK KNIGHT Hark (to enlarge your welcome) from all parts
Is heard sweet sounding airs, abstruse things open   30

Of voluntary freeness, and yond altar°
(The seat of adoration) seems t'adore°
The virtues you bring with you.
WHITE KNIGHT [*aside to the White Duke*]   There's a taste
Of the old vessel still.
WHITE DUKE   The erroneous relish.°
   Music. An altar discovered with tapers on it and divers images
   about it°

       Song   35

   Wonder work some strange delight°
   (This place was never yet without)
   To welcome the fair White House Knight,
   And to bring our hopes about.
   May from the altar flames aspire,   40
   Those tapers set themselves on fire.°
   May senseless things our joys approve°
   And those brazen statues move
      The images move in a dance
   Quickened by some power above,
   Or what more strange, to show our love. 45

BLACK KNIGHT A happy omen waits upon this hour;
 All move portentously, the right-hand way.°
BLACK KING Come, let's set free all the most choice delights
 That ever adorned days or quickened nights.
   Exeunt

5.2

   Enter the White Queen's Pawn and the Black Bishop's Pawn [in
   his reverend habit, meeting her]
WHITE QUEEN'S PAWN I see 'twas but a trial of my duty now;
 H'as a more modest mind, and in that virtue
 Most worthily has fate provided for me.—°
 Ha! 'Tis the bad man in the reverend habit.
 Dares he be seen again? Traitor to holiness!° 5
 O marble-fronted impudence! And knows°

How ill 'hath used me; I'm ashamed he blushes not.°

BLACK BISHOP'S PAWN Are you yet stored with any woman's pity?
Are you the mistress of so much devotion,
Kindness and charity, as to bestow   10
An alms of love on your poor sufferer yet,
For your sake only?°

WHITE QUEEN'S PAWN Sir, for the reverend respect you ought°
To give to sanctity, though none to me,
In being her servant vowed and wear her livery,°   15
If I might counsel you, you never should speak
The language of unchasteness in that habit;
You would not think how ill it does with you.°
The world's a stage on which all parts are played:
You'd think it most absurd to see a devil°   20
Presented there not in a devil's shape,
Or (wanting one) to send him out in yours;°
You'd rail at that for an absurdity
No college e'er committed. For decorum's sake then,
For pity's cause, for sacred virtue's honour,   25
If you'll persist still in your devil's part,
Present him as you should do, and let one
That carries up the goodness of the play
Come in that habit, and I'll speak with him;°
Then will the parts be fitted and the spectators°   30
Know which is which. They must have cunning judgements
To find it else, for such a one as you°
Is able to deceive a mighty auditory;°
Nay, those you have seduced (if there be any
In the assembly) when they see what manner   35
You play your game with me, they cannot love you.°
Is there so little hope of you to smile, sir?°

BLACK BISHOP'S PAWN Yes, at your fears, at th'ignorance of your
    power,°
The little use you make of time, youth, fortune,
Knowing you have a husband for lust's shelter;°   40
You dare not yet make bold with a friend's comfort,°
This is the plague of weakness.

WHITE QUEEN'S PAWN   So hot-burning
The syllables of sin fly from his lips,
As if the letter came new cast from hell.°

BLACK BISHOP'S PAWN Well, setting by the dish you loathe so much,   45

(Which hath been heartily tasted by your betters)°
I come to marry you to the gentleman
That last enjoyed you. I hope that pleases you?
There's no immodest relish in that office!°
WHITE QUEEN'S PAWN [*aside*] Strange of all men he should first light
    on him   50
    To tie that holy knot that sought to undo me.°
    [*To Black Bishop's Pawn*] Were you requested to perform that
    business, sir?°
BLACK BISHOP'S PAWN I name you a sure token.
WHITE QUEEN'S PAWN   As for that, sir—°
    Now you're most welcome, and my fair hope's of you,
    You'll never break the sacred knot you tie once   55
    With any lewd soliciting hereafter.°
BLACK BISHOP'S PAWN But all the craft's in getting of it knit;
    You're all on fire to make your cozening market:°
    I am the marrier and the man, do you know me?
    Do you know me, nice iniquity, strict luxury,°   60
    And holy whoredom, that would clap on marriage
    With all hot speed to solder up your game?°
    See what a scourge fate hath provided for thee:
    You were a maid; swear still, you're no worse now.°
    I left you as I found you. Have I startled you?°   65
    I am quit with you now for my discovery,
    Your outcries and your cunnings. Farewell, brokage!
WHITE QUEEN'S PAWN Nay stay, and hear me but give thanks a little,
    If your ear can endure a work so gracious;
    Then you may take your pleasure.
BLACK BISHOP'S PAWN   I have done that.°   70
WHITE QUEEN'S PAWN That power that hath preserved me from this
    devil—
BLACK BISHOP'S PAWN How?
WHITE QUEEN'S PAWN This, that may challenge the chief chair in
    hell
    And sit above his master—
BLACK BISHOP'S PAWN   Bring in merit!°
WHITE QUEEN'S PAWN That sufferedst him through blind lust to be
    led
    Last night to the action of some common bed—°   75
BLACK QUEEN'S PAWN *Within* Not over-common, neither!
BLACK BISHOP'S PAWN   Hah! what voice is that?°

WHITE QUEEN'S PAWN Of virgins be thou ever honoured.
  You may now go; you hear I have given thanks, sir.°
BLACK BISHOP'S PAWN Here's a strange game! Did not I lie with
  you?°   80
BLACK QUEEN'S PAWN (*within*) No!
BLACK BISHOP'S PAWN   What a devil art thou?
WHITE QUEEN'S PAWN   I will not answer you, sir,
  After thanksgiving.
BLACK BISHOP'S PAWN   Why, you made promise to me
  After the contract.
BLACK QUEEN'S PAWN (*within*) Yes.
BLACK BISHOP'S PAWN   Mischief confound thee!°
  I speak not to thee—and you were prepared for't°
  And set your joys more high—
BLACK QUEEN'S PAWN (*within*) Than you could reach, sir.°   85
BLACK BISHOP'S PAWN This is a bawdy pawn; I'll slit the throat
  on't.°
           Enter Black Queen's Pawn
BLACK QUEEN'S PAWN What? Offer violence to your bedfellow?
  To one that works so kindly, without rape?°
BLACK BISHOP'S PAWN My bedfellow?
BLACK QUEEN'S PAWN Do you plant your scorn against me?   90
  Why, when I was probationer at Brussels
  That engine was not known; then adoration°
  Filled up the place and wonder was in fashion.
  Is't turned to the wild seed of contempt so soon?
  Can five years stamp a bawd? (Pray look upon me,°   95
  I have youth enough to take it.) 'Tis no longer,
  Since you were chief agent for the transportation
  Of ladies' daughters, if you be remembered.
  Some of their portions I could name; who pursued'em
  too.°
  They were soon dispossessed of worldly cares   100
  That came into your fingers.
BLACK BISHOP'S PAWN   Shall I hear her?
BLACK QUEEN'S PAWN Holy derision, yes: till thy ear swell
  With thine own venom (thy profane life's vomit!)
  Whose niece was she you poisoned with child, twice,
  And gave her out possessed with a foul spirit°   105
  When 'twas indeed your bastard?
           Enter White Queen [and] the White Bishop's Pawn

BLACK BISHOP'S PAWN   I am taken°
 In mine own toils.
WHITE BISHOP'S PAWN Yes, and 'tis just you should be.°
WHITE QUEEN And thou, lewd pawn, the shame of womanhood.
BLACK BISHOP'S PAWN I'm lost of all hands.
BLACK QUEEN'S PAWN   And I cannot feel°   110
 The weight of my perdition now he's taken;
 'T'ath not the burden of a grasshopper.°
BLACK BISHOP'S PAWN Thou whore of order, cockatrice *in voto*.°
  Enter Black Knight's Pawn.
BLACK KNIGHT'S PAWN Yond's the White Bishop's Pawn; I'll play at
 his heart now.
WHITE QUEEN'S PAWN How now, black villain! Wouldst thou heap a
 murder°
 On thy first foul offence? O merciless bloodhound,°   115
 'Tis time thou wert taken.
BLACK KNIGHT'S PAWN   How! Prevented!
WHITE QUEEN'S PAWN For thy sake, and that partner in thy
 shame,°
 I'll never know man farther than by name.°
  Exeunt

5.3

  Enter the Black House [including Black King, Queen, Knight,
  Duke and Bishop]° and the White Knight and Duke
WHITE KNIGHT You have enriched my knowledge, royal sir,
 And my content together.
BLACK KING   'Stead of riot°
 We set you only welcome; surfeit is
 A thing that's seldom heard of in these parts.
WHITE KNIGHT I hear of the more virtue when I miss on't.°   5
BLACK KNIGHT We do not use to bury in our bellies°
 Two hundred thousand ducats and then boast on't,
 Or exercise th'old Roman painful-idleness°
 With care of fetching fishes far from home,°
 The golden-headed coracine out of Egypt,   10
 The salpa from Ebusus, or the pelamis
 (Which some call summer-whiting) from Chalcedon,°

Salmons from Aquitaine, elops from Rhodes,
Cockles from Chios (franked and fatted up
With far and sapa, flour and cocted wine.)   15
We cram no birds, nor (Epicurean-like)°
Enclose some creeks o'th'sea, as Sergius Orata did,°
He that invented the first stews for oysters
And other sea-fish, who, beside the pleasure
Of his own throat, got large revenues by the invention°   20
Whose fat example the nobility followed;
Nor do we imitate that arch-gormandiser,°
With two and twenty courses at one dinner
And betwixt every course he and his guests
Washed and used women, then sat down and strengthened,°   25
Lust swimming in their dishes, which no sooner
Was tasted but was ready to be vented.°
WHITE KNIGHT Most impious epicures!
BLACK KNIGHT   We commend rather
   (Of two extremes) the parsimony of Pertinax
   Who had half-lettuces set up to serve again;°   30
   Or his successor Julian that would make°
   Three meals of a lean hare, and often sup
   With a green fig and wipe his beard, as we can.°
   The old bewailers of excess in those days
   Complained there was more coin bid for a cook   35
   Than for a war-horse, but now cooks are purchased
   After the rate of triumphs, and some dishes°
   After the rate of cooks; which must needs make
   Some of your White House gormandisers (specially°
   Your wealthy, plump plebeians) like the hogs°   40
   Which Scaliger cites, that could not move for fat,°
   So insensible of either prick or goad,
   That mice made holes to needle in their buttocks°
   And they ne'er felt'em. There was once a ruler
   (Cyrene's governor) choked with his own paunch,°   45
   Which death fat Sanctius, king of Castile, fearing
   Through his infinite mass of belly, rather chose
   To be killed suddenly, by a pernicious herb
   Taken to make him lean, which old Corduba,
   King of Morocco, counselled his fear to,   50
   Than he would hazard to be stunk to death
   As that huge cormorant that was choked before him.°

WHITE KNIGHT Well, you're as sound a spokesman, sir, for parsimony,°
    Clean abstinence, and scarce one meal a day,
    As ever spake with tongue.
BLACK KING   Censure him mildly, sir,   55
    'Twas but to find discourse.
BLACK QUEEN   He'll raise of anything.°
WHITE KNIGHT I shall be half afraid to feed hereafter.
WHITE DUKE Or I (beshrew my heart) for I fear fatness,
    (The fog of fatness) as I fear a dragon;°
    The comeliness I wish for, that's as glorious.°   60
WHITE KNIGHT Your course is wondrous strict; I should transgress
      sure,°
    Were I to change my side, as you have much wrought me to't.°
BLACK KNIGHT How you misprise! This is not meant to you-ward.
    You that are wound up to the height of feeding
    By clime and custom are dispensed withal;°   65
    You may eat kid, cabrito, calf and tuns,
    Eat, and eat every day, twice if you please;
    Nay, the franked hen, fattened with milk and corn,
    (A riot which th'inhabitants of Delos
    Were first inventors of) or the crammed cockle.   70
WHITE KNIGHT Well, for the food, I'm happily resolved in;°
    But for the diet of my disposition°
    There comes a trouble; you will hardly find
    Food to please that.
BLACK KNIGHT   It must be a strange nature
    We cannot find a dish for, having policy   75
    (The master-cook of Christendom) to dress it;°
    Pray name your nature's diet.
WHITE KNIGHT   The first mess
    Is hot ambition!
BLACK KNIGHT   That's but served in puff-paste;
    Alas, the meanest of our cardinals' cooks°
    Can dress that dinner. Your ambition, sir,   80
    Can fetch no farther compass than the world?°
WHITE KNIGHT That's certain, sir.
BLACK KNIGHT   We're about that already;
    And in the large feast of our vast ambition
    We count but the White Kingdom (whence you came from)
    The garden for our cook to pick his salads;°   85
    The food's lean France, larded with Germany,

Before which comes the grave-chaste signiory°
Of Venice, served in (capon-like) in white broth;
From our chief oven, Italy, the bake-meats,°
Savoy, the salt, Geneva, the chipped manchet;   90
Below the salt the Netherlands are placed,°
A common dish at lower end o'th'table
For meaner pride to fall to; for our second course
A spit of Portugals served in for plovers,°
Indians and Moors for blackbirds; all this while   95
Holland stands ready melted to make sauce°
On all occasions; when the voider comes
And with such cheer our full hopes we suffice,°
Zealand says grace (for fashion) then we rise.

WHITE KNIGHT Here's meat enough, on conscience, for ambition!°   100
BLACK KNIGHT If there be any want, there's Switzerland,
    Polonia, and such pickled things will serve°
    To furnish out the table.
WHITE KNIGHT   You say well, sir;
    But here's the misery: when I have stopped the mouth
    Of one vice, there's another gapes for food;   105
    I am as covetous as a barren womb,
    The grave, or what's more ravenous.°
BLACK KNIGHT   We are for you, sir;
    Call you that heinous that's good husbandry?
    Why, we make money of our faiths, our prayers,
    We make the very death-bed buy her comforts,   110
    Most dearly pay for all her pious counsels,°
    Leave rich revenues for a few weak orisons
    Or else they pass unreconciled without'em.°
    Did you but view the vaults within our monasteries,
    You'd swear then Plutus (which the fiction calls°   115
    The lord of riches) were entombed within'em.
WHITE KNIGHT   Is't possible?°
BLACK DUKE You cannot walk for tuns!°
WHITE DUKE But how shall I bestow the vice I bring, sirs?
    You quite forget me, I shall be shut out
    By your strict key of life.
BLACK KNIGHT   Is yours so vile, sir?°   120
WHITE DUKE Some that are pleased to make a wanton on't°
    Call it infirmity of blood, flesh-frailty,
    But certain there's a worse name in your books for't.

BLACK KNIGHT The trifle of all vices, the mere innocent,
 The very novice of this house of clay: venery!°   125
 If I but hug thee hard I show the worst on't.°
 It's all the fruit we have here after supper;°
 Nay, at the ruins of a nunnery once
 Six thousand infants' heads found in a fishpond.°
WHITE DUKE How?°   130
BLACK KNIGHT Ay, how? How came they thither, think you?
 Huldrick, bishop of Augsburg, in's Epistle
 To Nicholas the First can tell you how;°
 Maybe he was at cleansing of the pond;°
 I can but smile to think how it would puzzle   135
 All mother-maids that ever lived in those parts°
 To know their own child's head. But is this all?
BLACK DUKE Are you ours yet?
WHITE KNIGHT   One more, and I am silenced,°
 But this that comes now will divide us, questionless;
 'Tis ten times ten times worse than the forerunners.   140
BLACK KNIGHT Is it so vile there is no name ordained for't?
 Toads have their titles, and creation gave°
 Serpents and adders those names to be known by.
WHITE KNIGHT This of all others bears the hidden'st venom,°
 The secret'st poison: I'm an arch-dissembler, sir.   145
BLACK KNIGHT How!
WHITE KNIGHT It's my nature's brand; turn from me, sir.°
 The time is yet to come that e'er I spoke
 What my heart meant.
BLACK KNIGHT   And call you that a vice?
 Avoid all profanation, I beseech you: 150
 The only prime state-virtue upon earth,°
 The policy of empires! O take heed, sir,
 For fear it take displeasure and forsake you.
 It's like a jewel of that precious value
 Whose worth's not known but to the skilful lapidary,   155
 The instrument that picks ope princes' hearts,
 And locks up ours from them with the same motion;
 You never came so near our souls as now.°
BLACK DUKE Now you're a brother to us.
BLACK KNIGHT   What we have done
 Has been a dissemblance ever.
WHITE KNIGHT   There you lie then;°   160

And the game's ours—we give thee checkmate by
Discovery, King, the noblest mate of all!°
    [*A great shout and flourish*]°
BLACK KING I'm lost, I'm taken.
WHITE KNIGHT Ambitious, covetous, luxurious falsehood!°
WHITE DUKE Dissembler includes all.   165
BLACK KNIGHT All hopes confounded!°
BLACK QUEEN Miserable condition!
    [*Flourish.*]° *Enter White King, Queen, Bishop &c*°
    [*attended*]
WHITE KING O let me bless mine arms with this dear treasure,
Truth's glorious masterpiece! See (Queen of Sweetness)°
He's in my bosom safe, and this fair structure   170
Of comely honour, his true-blessed assistant.°
WHITE QUEEN May their integrities ever possess
That powerful sanctuary.
WHITE KNIGHT   As 'twas a game, sir,°
Won with much hazard, so with much more triumph°
I gave him checkmate by discovery, sir.   175
WHITE KING Obscurity is now the fittest favour°
Falsehood can sue for; it well suits perdition.
'Tis their best course that so have lost their fame
To put their heads into the bag for shame.
    The bag opens, and the Black lost pawns appear in it°
And there behold: the bag's mouth (like hell) opens°   180
To take her due, and the lost sons appear°
Greedily gaping for increase of fellowship
In infamy (the last desire of wretches)
Advancing their perdition-branded heads
Like Envy's issue, or a bed of snakes.°   185
BLACK BISHOP'S PAWN [*in the bag*] 'Tis too apparent, the game's lost,
    King's taken.°
FAT BISHOP [*in the bag*] The White House hath given us the bag, I
    thank'em.°
BLACK JESTING PAWN [*in the bag*] They had need have given you a
    whole bag°
By yourself. This Fat Black-Bishop hath so overlaid me,
So squelched and squeezed me, I have no verjuice left in me;°   190
You shall find all my goodness (if you look for't)°
In the bottom of the bag.
FAT BISHOP   Thou malapert pawn!

The Bishop must have room, he will have room,
And room to lie at pleasure.
BLACK JESTING PAWN   All the bag, I think,°
Is room too scant for your Spalato paunch.   195
BLACK BISHOP'S PAWN Down, viper of our order! I abhor thee.
Thou show thy whorish front.
WHITE QUEEN'S PAWN [*in the bag*] Yes, monster-holiness.°
WHITE KNIGHT Contention in the pit! Is hell divided?°
WHITE KING You'd need have some of majesty and power°
To keep good rule amongst you: make room, Bishop.
          [*He puts Black King in the bag*]   200
FAT BISHOP I am not so easily moved, when I am once set;
I scorn to stir for any king on earth.
WHITE QUEEN Here comes the Queen; what say you to her?
          [*She puts Black Queen in the bag*]
FAT BISHOP Indeed a queen may make a bishop stir.°
WHITE KNIGHT Room for the mightiest Machiavel-politician   205
That e'er the devil hatched of a nun's egg.
          [*He puts Black Knight in the bag*]
FAT BISHOP He'll peck a hole i'th'bag and get out shortly.
I'm sure to be the last man that creeps out,°
And that's the misery of greatness ever.
[Foh, the politician is not sound i'th'vent;   210
I smell him hither.]°
WHITE DUKE Room for a sun-burnt, tansy-faced beloved,
An olive-coloured Ganymede, and that's all°
That's worth the bagging.
          [*He puts the Black Duke in the bag*]
FAT BISHOP   Crowd in all you can,
The bishop will be still uppermost man,   215
Maugre king, queen, or politician.
WHITE KING So let the bag close now, the fittest womb°
For treachery, pride and falsehood, whilst we (winner-like)°
Destroying, through heaven's power, what would destroy,
Welcome our White Knight with loud peals of joy.   220
          Exeunt

Epilogue

By the White Queen's Pawn

WHITE QUEEN'S PAWN My mistress, the White Queen, hath sent me
    forth
  And bade me bow (thus low) to all of worth,
  That are true friends of the White House and cause,
  Which (she hopes) most of this assembly draws.
  For any else, by envy's mark denoted,°   5
  To those night glow-worms in the bag devoted,
  Where'er they sit, stand, or in private lurk,°
  They'll be soon known by their depraving work.
  But she's assured what they'd commit to bane,
  Her White friends' loves will build up fair again.   10
    [*Exit*]

Appendix: Documents Relating to *A Game at Chess*

No play of the Elizabethan/Jacobean period generated more comment than *A Game at Chess*. Numerous letters and other documents survive, from comment on its phenomenal popularity on stage, through the record of the unusual degree of official attention it received afterwards, to a poem said to have been written by Middleton to the king to secure his release from prison (though there is no actual evidence that he was imprisoned). The most comprehensive collection of these documents appears in T. H. Howard-Hill's Revels edition of the play (Appendix 1, pp. 192–213), which makes it less necessary for me to reproduce everything.

I have confined myself here, therefore, to the two documents which tell us most about the play as it was performed in its remarkable run from 5 to 14 August 1624, excepting only Sunday, 8 August. These are a letter dated 10 August[1] by Don Carlos Coloma, the Spanish Ambassador in London, to the Conde-Duque Olivares, favourite of Philip IV of Spain, in Madrid; and a letter dated the following day by John Holles, Lord Haughton to the Earl of Somerset.[2] It is a common lament that we have very few eye-witness accounts of performances of plays from this period, and on close inspection this proves to be true even of *A Game at Chess*. Coloma himself did not see the play, though we must suppose that he took some care to get a reliable account, given that he chose to make a diplomatic incident of it. Most other accounts similarly prove to be hearsay, and are certainly less detailed and probably less accurate than what Coloma compiled. John Holles's letter thus proves to be uniquely valuable as the only true eye-witness account of the play, and quite a detailed record of the performance he saw. I have modernized the texts, removed obvious errors and repetitions, and silently expanded contractions.

---

[1] My dating of events and when letters were written is consistently in English old-style (10 days earlier than Continental new-style), though Spanish documents were actually dated new-style. The dates *within* Coloma's letter remain new-style.

[2] *Somerset:* Robert Carr, formerly favourite of James I, was disgraced with his wife, Frances Howard, after the 1615 inquiry into the murder of Sir Thomas Overbury. John Holles (*c*.1564–1637), soldier and would-be politician, was a close adherent of Somerset, even after his disgrace.

(1) Don Carlos Coloma to the Conde-Duque Olivares in Madrid, 10 August 1624

I wrote to the King a few days ago; he will now know what was worthy of report here up to the 16^{tho} of this month. Since then there has occurred an event that is not unworthy of Your Excellency's, and even of His Majesty's, knowledge, in order that the shamelessness of the English may be plainly seen, if indeed there is still any need of new examples of it. This is what 5 happened:

The actors whom they call here 'the King's Men' have recently acted, and are still acting, in London a play that so many people come to see, that there were more than 3000 persons there on the day that the audience was smallest. There was such merriment, hubbub and applause that even if I had 10 been many leagues away it would not have been possible for me not to have taken notice of it, and notorious baseness, not merely excessive tolerance, if I had paid no attention to it or neglected it. The subject of the play is a game of chess, with white houses and black houses, their kings and other pieces, acted by the players, and the king of the blacks has easily been taken for our lord the 15 King, because of his youth, dress, and other details. The first act, or rather game was played by their ministers, impersonated by the white pieces, and the Jesuits, by the black ones. Here there were remarkable acts of sacrilege and, among other abominations, a minister summoned St. Ignatius from hell, and when he found himself again in the world, the first thing he did was to rape 20 one of his female penitents; in all this, these accursed and abominable men revealed the depths of their heresy by their lewd and obscene actions. The second act was directed against the Archbishop of Spalato, at that time a white piece, but afterwards won over to the black side by the Count of Gondomar, who, brought on the stage in his little litter almost to the life, and seated on his 25 chair with a hole in it (they said), confessed all the treacherous actions with which he had deceived and soothed the king of the whites, and, when he discussed the matter of confession with the Jesuits, the actor disguised as the Count took out a book in which were rated all the prices for which hencefor- wards sins were to be forgiven. Besides this, those who saw the play relate so 30 many details and such atrocious and filthy words, that I have not thought fit to offend your excellency's ears with them. In these two acts and in the third, the matter of which I do not know in detail, they hardly showed anything but the cruelty of Spain and the treachery of Spaniards, and all this was set forth so personally that they did not even exclude royal persons. The last act ended 35 with a long, obstinate struggle between all the whites and the blacks, and in it he who played the Prince of Wales heartily beat and kicked the 'Count of Gondomar' into Hell, which consisted of a great hole and hideous figures; and the white king [drove] the black king and even his queen [into hell] almost as offensively. All this has been so much applauded and enjoyed by the mob that 40 here, where no play has been acted for more than one day [consecutively], this one has already been acted on four, and each day the crowd is greater. Had I followed the advice of the Marqués de la Hinojosa° when he advised me to go away with him, such things would not have reached my ears, nor should I have seen the sacred name of my King outraged in so many ways by such low, vile 45 people, nor his holy and glorious acts so unworthily interpreted; only this was lacking to let me describe my sufferings here as a true Hell. The greatest of these, materially, is to listen to the blasphemies uttered against God; I have been unable, too, to discover during the last two months whether I did right or wrong to stay on here; the question whether I served the King well or ill by so 50 doing keeps me in that uneasiness that your Excellency will readily understand in this true servant of his. But I leave this to Your Excellency's care, for so great a gentleman and so noble a minister of His Majesty will do me the honour of telling it to his royal ears with the due recognition of the zeal with which I have desired and striven to fulfil my duties. I report, Sir, that when I 55 had received a statement of the shamelessness of the actors, I dispatched the language-secretary to the King of England, who is at present forty miles away, where he is feasting and fawning upon the French Ambassador, with a letter in the following terms:

'Although I have not yet received orders from the King my master to 60 give His Majesty an account of my embassy,° I cannot refrain from fulfilling the obligations of my post and representing to Your Majesty what seems to be my duty. Yesterday and to-day the players called Your Majesty's men have acted in London a play that is so scandalous, so impious, so barbarous and so offensive to my royal master—if perhaps his known greatness and the inestim- 65 able worth of his royal person were capable of receiving offence from any man, least of all from such vile persons as are usually the authors and actors of such follies—that I am compelled to take up my pen and in few words and with all the humility I owe Your Majesty, to beg Your Majesty one of two things: either that Your Majesty would be pleased to order the authors and actors of the said 70 play to be publicly punished as an example, by which means Your Majesty will satisfy his own honour and the reputation of the English nation which has been so much smirched by actions that are so vile and so unworthy of honourable men; or that Your Majesty would be pleased to order that a ship be given me in which I may cross to Flanders with the necessary guarantees granted 75 to ambassadors of other sovereigns and leave to depart instantly.° I await indifferently either decision. I pray God etc.'

I do not expect a reply until the 23rd or 24th of this month as the King of England is some distance away, and the language-secretary departed in bad health. Meanwhile, although I have adopted the procedure of writing to Spain 80 every Tuesday through the Marqués de Mirabel and the ordinary Paris [courier], as I shall continue to do as long as I am detained here, I did not wish to delay until tomorrow without informing Your Excellency about this matter and reporting that if the King of England elects to give me my papers rather than punish such insolence, I shall most certainly go to Brussels and await 85 what orders His Majesty may please to send me, knowing that this decision of mine will be favourably considered as having come from the heart of a man unaccustomed to suffer insults or outrages, least of all against his King and against his country. May our Lord preserve Your Excellency many years. London, 20 August, 1624.   90

I have given the King of England this choice between punishing this roguery and sending me my papers, because every good reason and conjecture require that he should choose the first alternative, and it seemed to me that if he chose the second, he would find his actions condemned, not only by God, but also by the world. I hope that no one will consider that the cause of these   95 things' having reached such a pitch has been a slight one, when I report the injustices that were done here to the Marqués de la Hinojosa and to myself, the contempt which has been shown, and is still being shown, in writing and by word of mouth, to the greatness and power of His Majesty, and that his ambassador, who for that reason is owed so much outward respect and particu-   100 lar esteem, has for these last two months been unable to act as ambassador, shut up in his house without being able to have any dealings with the King of England or with his Ministers, either in his own person or through third parties; lastly, considering that although he can tolerate all kinds of men, the bounds of toleration are much narrower in one who, from the time of his   105 birth, took upon himself the obligations of a soldier, and that as I may be trusted in my quality as a soldier, I shall know how, with God's help, to make good those faults into which I may have fallen as an ambassador, and if, finally, I deserve blame for having put the King of England in danger of growing angry, I would rather be punished for having shown courage, despite my   110 helplessness here in so many ways, than be mildly reproved for too much toleration of insults offered not to me, but to my master the King, whom God preserve. It cannot be pleaded that those who repeat and hear these insults are merely four rogues because during these last four days more than 12,000 persons have all heard the play of *A Game at Chess*, for so they call it, includ-   115 ing all the nobility still in London. All these people came out of the play so inflamed against Spain that, as a few Catholics have told me who went secretly to see the play, my person would not be safe in the streets; others have advised me to keep to my house with a good guard, and this is being done. Let Your Excellency consider whether I could pass over this in silence; it is enough to   120 have ignored so many different things that have been said and done, even some filthy songs that Buckingham makes his musicians sing where they are now, which are such that the Marquis of Hamilton, the Earls of Montgomery and Carey, and others left a great reception in order not to hear them, as I have been told in a letter from one who saw them go. Finally, Sir, nothing else but   125 war is to be expected from these people. Let Your Excellency believe me, I beg and pray, even if for certain reasons it suits us to defer it, our best plan is to show bravery and resolution [now], rather than allow them to increase their strength . . . (Letter in Biblioteca Nacional, Madrid. Ms. 18203; translation by E. M. Wilson and O. Turner, 'The Spanish Protest against *A Game at Chess*',   130 *MLR* 44 (1949), 476–82.)

Several factors should be taken into account in weighing Coloma's version of events, apart from the fact that he had not seen the play in person. One is the diplomatic situation: with the collapse of the negotiations for a Spanish marriage for Prince Charles, and the conversion of Charles and Buckingham to an anti-Spanish foreign policy, war between Britain and Spain was now inevitable. These poor relations with Spain are in many ways what *A Game at Chess* celebrates, but also what made it seem appropriate to Coloma to turn a play into a diplomatic incident, in effect threatening to break off relations there and then if honour was not satisfied by the punishment of the King's Men. It must be probable that the persistence of King James and his ministers in following through Coloma's complaint was partly prompted by diplomatic protocol: war with Spain might be coming but had not yet been declared, and in the mean time at least a show of courtesy was called for. It is also apparent that Coloma himself was personally uncomfortable about his situation. His fellow ambassador, the Marqués de la Hinojosa, had been ignominiously sent out of England some months earlier, since when Coloma had had little contact with Madrid and was not even sure he should still be in London. This must explain some of the defensive tone of the letter, and its determination to express all the right sentiments.

Of the details of the performance he records, two warrant comment: one is that no version of the play suggests that 'when [St. Ignatius] found himself again in the world, the first thing he did was to rape one of his female penitents'. The Jesuit Black Bishop's Pawn does, however, try to rape the White Queen's Pawn. Perhaps the actor who played Ignatius Loyola also played the Black Bishop's Pawn, and to some extent carried the former role into the latter. The other point is the description of the Black House at the end of the play being driven into 'Hell, which consisted of a great hole and hideous figures'. This is sometimes advanced as evidence that the actors resurrected the hell-mouth of the morality plays for this scene. A close examination of the texts suggests something slightly different, that the Black House were put 'into the bag', in keeping with the chess motif of the play. This was obviously meant to evoke the hell-mouth, but was a variation on the theme and not quite the same thing.

(2) John Holles, Lord Haughton to the Earl of Somerset, 11 August 1624

To my Lord of Somerset at Chiswick, the 11 of August 1624. My Lord, though from Mr Whittakers, or others, this vulgar pasquin may come to your ears, yet whether he or they saw it I know not, much being the difference between eyesight and hearsay: when I returned from your Lordship hither upon Monday,° I was saluted with a report of a facetious comedy, already thrice acted with extraordinary applause: a representation of all our Spanish traffic, where Gondomar his litter, his open chair for the ease of that fistulated part, Spalato &c. appeared upon the stage.

I was invited by the reporter Sir Edward Gorge (whose balance gives all things weight to the advantage) to be also an auditor thereof, & accordingly yesterday to the Globe I rowed which house I found so thronged that by scores they came away for want of place, though as yet little past one; nevertheless loath to check the appetite, which came so seldom to me (not having been in a playhouse these 10 years) & such a dainty not every day to be found, I marched on, & heard the pasquin, for no other it was: which had been the more complete, had the poet been a better statesman; the descant° was built upon the popular opinion that the Jesuits' mark is to bring all the Christian world under Rome for the spirituality, and under Spain for the temporalty: hereupon, as a precept or legacy left those disciples from their first founder Ignatius Loyola, this their father serves for the prologue, who admiring no speedier operation of his drug, is enraged and desperate, till comforted by one of his disciples; the plot is revealed him, prosperously advanced by their design upon England: with this he vanisheth, leaving his benediction over the work.

The whole play is a chess board, England the white house, Spain the black: one of the white pawns, with an under black doublet signifying a Spanish heart, betrays his party to their advantage, advanceth Gondomar's propositions, works under hand the Prince's coming into Spain: which pawn so discovered, the white king reviles him, objects his raising him in wealth, in honour, from mean condition, next classis to a labouring man: this by the character is supposed Bristol;° yet is hard, players should judge him in jest before the State in earnest. Gondomar makes a large account of all his great feats here, describes in [earnest] scorn our vanities in diet, in apparel, in every other excess (the symptoms of a falling state); how many ladies bribed him to be groom of the stool to the Infanta, how many to be mother of the maids, with much such trash; letters from the nunnery in Drury Lane, from those in Bloomsbury &c., how many Jesuits and priests he loosed out of prison, and put again into their necessary work of seducing; how he set the king's affairs as a clock, backward and forward, made him believe and unbelieve as stood best with his business, be the cause never so clear; how he covered the roguery of the Jesuits in abusing women licentiously; how he befooled Spalato with a counterfeit letter from Cardinal Paulo his kinsman, promising to leave his

Cardinal's hat to him, himself being elected Pope; with much such like stuff, more wittily penned, than wisely staged: but at last the Prince making a full discovery of all their knaveries, Olivares, Gondomar, Spalato, Jesuit, Spanish Bishop, & a Spanish eunuch are by the Prince put into the bag, & so the play   45
ends. Your Lordship may give to this a moral; methinks this is a hardy part,° & beyond my understanding: & surely these gamesters° must have a good retreat, else dared they not to charge thus Princes' actions, & ministers, nay their intents: . . . a foul injury to Spain, no great honour to England, *rebus sic stantibus*:° every particular will bear a large paraphrase, which I submit to your better judgment &c.; Westminster 11 of August. (Reprinted from P. R.   50
Seddon, *Letters of John Holles, 1587–1637*, vol. 2, Thoroton Society Records series, xxxv (Nottingham, 1983), pp. 228–9.)

As the letter makes clear Holles was not a regular playgoer, but he fol-lowed the detail of what he saw and heard quite attentively, including the characterization of what the texts identify as the Black Jesting Pawn as a Spanish eunuch. Eunuchs in biblical and classical times could be important political figures, and in such roles were not necessarily castrated. This possibly links the clowning obscenity of scene 3.2 to the satirical politics of the rest of the play. More significantly, Holles was a minor player in, and shrewd observer of, the political scene—this report to Somerset was not just casual gossip—and he found it a major flaw of the play that it 'had been the more complete, had the poet been a better statesman'. So it is quite perplexing that he should have identified the White King's Pawn with the Earl of Bristol. Modern commentators have assumed that the pawn is a composite figure, with some characteristics pointing to a Catholic convert like Sir Toby Matthew, who might be supposed to be interested in the Cardinal's hat which the pawn is promised; and others, including those late revisions to the text which Holles paraphrases, pointing to Lionel Cran-field, who was indeed 'raised . . . From a condition next to popular labour'. Bristol was never a Catholic convert, nor was he a member of the labouring classes. Holles clearly assumed that the 'discovery' of the pawn equated to Bristol's impending examination for his part in the Spanish marriage nego-tiations (rather than, say, the impeachment of Cranfield for peculation). And this seems to speak more to his own sympathies—he felt this was unfair on the untried Bristol—than to anything in the text itself. We cannot be sure that the actor playing the Pawn did not, in some unscripted way, evoke Bristol without any warrant from what Middleton wrote. But if he did not, this is a sober warning to modern readers of the play not to be over-confident about the identification of characters in the allegory.

EXPLANATORY NOTES

A Chaste Maid in Cheapside

The Characters of the Play

Characters of the Play: based on 'The Names of the Principal Persons' in the original 1630 quarto (Q), which emphasizes the family units and the centrality of Sir Walter.

Yellowhammer: this describes his profession as a goldsmith, from the working of yellow metal. It is also a chattering bird (typical of the play's animal imagery), and slang for both a gold coin and a fool.

Maudline: her name suits both her shady past (Magdalene—sometimes pronounced 'mawdlin'—in the Bible had been a prostitute) and sentimentality ('maudlin').

Tim: commonly name of a fool.

Moll: the name is ambiguous, usually being a familiar form of Mary (and so chastity) but also a common term for a whore.

Sir Oliver Kix: Oliver means fruitful but Kix, the dry stem of a plant, implies sterility.

Allwit: his name is an inversion of wittol, a complacent cuckold, but also points to his narrow 'rationality'.

Welsh Gentlewoman: the play realistically depicts provincial women sucked into prostitution in London (the Country Wench is apparently from Derbyshire) but also perpetuates London prejudices. The Welsh are associated with dubious claims to gentility and comic lechery.

Dahumma: from Welsh, *dech yma*, come here.

Touchwood: kindling, easily inflammable.

Promoters: informers, making private profit out of policing Lent observances (mainly the prohibition against eating meat. See 2.2. and notes).

Watermen: boatmen on the Thames.

Gossips: female friends at a birth or christening.

A Chaste Maid in Cheapside: the title is a paradox or contradiction in terms, like *The Silent Woman*. Cheapside was a major commercial district, so the implication is 'chastity for sale', and a pun (*chaste = chased*) underlines the vulnerability of female chastity in this environment.

1.1 S.D. *shop being discovered*: this locates the scene in Goldsmiths' Row, in the south of Cheapside. The Swan theatre may have had a purpose-built discovery space or some such structure (a canvas booth, the front of which could be removed to reveal the actors already inside) may have been improvised.

2 *virginals*: spinets, which accomplished ladies would play. The obvious sexual quibble sets the tone of the scene.

4 *quicken*: invigorate, put life into. Maudline suggests it is high time Moll got married and had children, to get her over adolescent moping. 'Quicken' could also mean 'make pregnant' and half does so here.

7 *make salads*: become salads. In effect, to become vegetables, and not the animals they actually are (and so fit mates for the 'piece(s) of flesh' which are their husbands).

8 *cried up and down*: shouted for sale in the streets.

11 *quick*: (1) lively; (2) pregnant. The *double entendre* betrays her dubious past.

13 *spirited*: Q, 'sprited'.

14 *dancing*: another lady-like accomplishment which might hint at sexual activity.

16 *bord*: bore of a gun, condition. She means 'when I was like you' (and implicitly 'of your sexual capacity').

21 *plumber's*: plumbers used lead, so there is a lead/gold antithesis of heavy metals, since Moll is actually a goldsmith's daughter.

26 *Errors*: Yellowhammer picks up the technical legal sense of 'mistakes in law'.

27 *Westminster*: location of both court and lawcourts, so source of elaborate and expensive language.

28 *I . . . i'faith*: Yellowhammer seems to be delivering a sermon his wife has heard many times before, and she responds accordingly. He acknowledges the fact and promises to give over, but has his say none the less.

30 *half-crown piece*: valuable but rare gold coin. By analogy, 'difficult, perhaps deceptive words'.

31 *gilded twopence*: silver two-penny piece, gilded to look like gold. Counterfeiting is a recurrent theme in the play.

36 *lawns . . . bracks*: fine linens (both *lawns* and *cambrics*) have frayed places and flaws.

37 *solders up all cracks*: (1) mends all imperfections; (2) seals up all vaginas. Female genitalia are commonly described as leaking cracks or flaws, a supposed measure of women's inferiority to men.

39 *Holborn bridge*: old bridge over the Fleet, carrying the road from Wales.

47 *devotion*: zeal, enthusiasm. Maudline infuses social courtesy with misplaced zeal.

50 *before and after*: Maudline tells Moll to make a ladylike gesture, but almost certainly produces a sexually suggestive one herself. The repeated 'before and after' doubtless means that she repeats this visual *double entendre*, but also suggests coition from both front and rear. The knight will also look for this gesture both before and after sex.

51 *waving*: any provocative gesture or movement.

53 *sent*: sent word, a message.

56 *gentlemen commoners*: privileged undergraduates who paid higher fees. The Yellowhammers are social climbers.

58 *Hobson*: famous Cambridge carrier, whose policy of letting out horses in strict rotation is said to have given users 'Hobson's choice'.

60 *Amantissimis . . . matri*: 'To my father and mother, both my most loving and beloved parents'.

65 *Amantissimus charissimus*: so Q, presumably indicating that Maudline cannot even read the Latin she offers to construe, since she uses the nominative '-mus' rather than the dative '-mis' (which the Porter at least reads correctly, even if he misconstrues the meaning). There may well be some comic business here.

66 *Porter*: a traditional stage fool, whose apparent lack of intelligence masks a shrewd grasp of the main chance. The audience laughs with him, rather than at him, as he makes money out of the Yellowhammers. We cannot identify the actor in Lady Elizabeth's Men who first played the role, and so say if there is any special point in his being 'a scholar forty years ago', but cf. the Stage-Keeper in Jonson's *Bartholomew Fair* performed by the same company.

68 *no true construction*: the Latin is misconstrued. Comic misconstruction was popular, especially in school and college drama.

69 *Bell*: the Bell Inn, in Coleman Street, less than a quarter of a mile from the Yellowhammers' place in Goldsmiths' Row, connecting with Cheapside by the Old Jewry. So the Porter's pains have been much less than he makes out.

75 *hit on't*: get to the point of it. The joke, of course, is that money was always the 'point' of the exercise for him.

77–9 *Goose Fair . . . Bow*: annual goose-selling fair at Stratford-le-Bow, every Whitsun week. 'Bow' and 'boo' were closer in earlier modern pronunciation than today.

80 *Boo to a goose*: proverbial. Someone who would *not* say boo to a goose is extremely timorous or peace-loving.

83 *Maxime diligo*: I love most greatly.

86 *Inns of Court*: the law schools, nearest equivalent in London to a university. Legal/Norman French was in common use there, though there

is probably also an allusion to syphilis, 'the French disease'. A trained lawyer should certainly also be able to read elementary Latin, though a priest ought to know even more of it.

88 *papistry*: Roman Catholicism. A puritan priest might regard Latin with suspicion.

92 *Dugat a whee*: phonetic Welsh, perhaps for *Duw cadu chwi*, 'God bless you'.

93 *list*: wish. The line is an invitation to kiss him.

94 *serve . . . pass*: be sufficient to get by.

95 *'Twas*: it would be.

99 *Dahumma*: 'Dahanna' (Q). As with Moll it seems likely that Middleton had second thoughts about some names.

103 *Brecknockshire*: then a county in Wales, but 'nock' also = female genitals.

104 *mumble*: Sir Walter uses 'mumble' in the sense of 'speak indistinctly'. Davy answers in the archaic sense of 'chew softly, as with toothless gums'.

112 *brought . . . city*: as distinct from raised at court

115 *Moll*: Mary (Q). Middleton apparently started with the name Mary, then substituted Moll. It is not clear why Moll re-enters, having fled on the arrival of Sir Walter. Various stagings suggest themselves, all potentially comic. She may sneak back in and hide but be unearthed by Maudline. She may leave by one door but be caught coming through another. Or she may flee in panic, compose herself, and return to face her fate.

113–14 *quiver . . . thighs*: Maudline means to say that a handsome courtier makes the city girls nervous, but betrays herself in suggesting that they become sexually excited.

117 *your . . . servant*: the courtly phrase of a gallant suitor, purporting to be inferior to his mistress, fit only to serve her. Sir Walter tries to be charming for the sake of appearances. Middleton and Rowley ironize this trope extensively in *The Changeling*.

119 *sound*: wound (Q).

the freedom: those who are 'free' (full members) of their City companies, i.e. tradespeople.

121 *Whitehall or Greenwich*: royal palaces.

122 *serves*: Middleton commonly mixes singular and plural forms.

124 *bold . . . terms*: Sir Walter allows Yellowhammer to think of her as a 'gentlewoman' and his 'worthy niece'. She is neither of these, though he avoids an outright lie.

125 *mountains*: Jacobean joke about Wales, popularly supposed to contain little else.

127 *high as Paul's*: proverbial for great height (the old St Paul's Cathedral, destroyed in the 1666 fire, was by some margin the tallest building in London).

work: business. Davy knows that he will be called upon to back up Sir Walter's confidence trick.

130–1 *daughter ... right*: who will be our daughter-in-law, if things work out properly (i.e. if she marries Tim).

133 *ram ... London*: Touchwood Junior recognizes that Sir Walter is a rival for Moll, and that he has brought his whore to London to palm her off on an unsuspecting suitor.

hasten it: get a move on.

134 *pick*: 'picke' (Q). Often emended to 'peak a'famine'. i.e. dwindle from starvation, but 'choose a famine' makes equally good sense

blood's mine: she wants me sexually.

135 *spoil*: 'spoy' (Q). He means Moll.

136 *Sir*: Moll responds to Touchwood Junior, but it is not clear whether he signals to her, whispers from behind, or if she simply senses his presence.

136–7 *Turn ... lawfully*: do not turn around until marriage makes it lawful to turn to me as a lover.

138 *stomach*: sexual appetite, desire.

140–1 *know ... heart*: only acknowledge my ardour inwardly, do not make it public.

141–2 *send ... words*: send a very brief message of your approval.

143 *Tim, sir, Tim*: 'turn, sir, turn' (Q), probably misled by the start of Touchwood Junior's previous speech.

145 *Lent*: it is Lent by 2.1 and Tim is a BA by 3.2. If we take these clues literally, the events of the play spread over several months.

146 *Sir Yellowhammer*: 'Sir' designated BA status at Oxford and Cambridge, used only with the surname (unlike a knight). Yellowhammer's belief that the title is 'half a knight' betrays his ignorance of its real (minimal) significance but James I's wholesale creation of knights had also devalued *that* honour, so the joke is double-edged.

154 *being to him*: an odd phrase, perhaps meaning 'since she (Moll) is promised to him' (i.e. Sir Walter); or 'since she (Maudline) is favourably disposed to him'.

158 *'Twas ... in me*: it would be honourable of me (ironic, in that Yellowhammer is not to know that the ring is to marry Moll with).

164 *all ... present*: because Moll is there.

167 *stand*: 'I would have it' is understood.

168 *spark*: small stone. Wedding rings often had gems and were engraved with mottoes.

171 *finger*: fingers often have phallic implications in Middleton: cf. *The Changeling*. Touchwood Junior's following speech is a prolonged *double entendre* linking Moll's finger with his own genitalia.

173 *down*: (1) deep in the pocket; (2) detumescent.

177 *no gentlewoman*: Yellowhammer, as a tradesman, insists that his family are not gentry. The marriages he plans for his children will *make* them that.

182 *bide*: stand. Touchwood Junior agrees to pay if the ring proves does not fit.

184 *hair*: (1) nicety; (2) pubic hair. He says Moll's finger exactly 'fits' that of the lady for whom he wants the ring. Yellowhammer may have supplied him with a trial ring.

188 *How, how*: Yellowhammer is outraged by the motto but constrained by deference to his gentleman customer. Touchwood Junior apparently toys with taking offence in return, so their interchange is very prickly.

189 *Go to*: Come, come (disapprobation, but held within the bounds of respect).

191 *am . . . you*: have I guessed your secret intention? He is 'nearer' than he knows.

192 *wags*: mischievous jokers (Yellowhammer tries to contain his disapproval).

195 *wear*: 'were' (Q), but Middleton uses this spelling of 'wear' elsewhere.

200 *were . . . thee*: if I were composed of (my own) wishes, I would have gone with you.

201 *rules*: revels.

202 *lose . . . win*: in returning to Sir Walter she loses all she has 'won' in Touchwood Junior.

   s.d. *Exeunt*: here, as elsewhere, Q reads 'Exit' though there are multiple departures.

1.2 s.d. *severally*: separately (and probably by different entrances).

1 *wittol*: complacent cuckold (transposition of 'Allwit').

6 *great . . . wallow*: so large (from pregnancy) that she can only walk with a rolling gait.

7 *pickled cucumbers*: typical of the strange cravings of pregnancy, but with inevitable phallic suggestion.

12 *a table furnished to his hand*: with blasphemous echoes of the 23rd Psalm (Authorised Version, verse 5): 'Thou preparest a table before me . . . '

15 *h'as maintained . . . ten*: he has supported/paid for . . . elsewhere the figure is seven.

19 *to nothing*: at no charge.

20 *church . . . scavenger*: Sir Walter pays Allwit's church taxes for him, including parish costs of scavengers who repaired roads, cleaned pavements, etc.

27 *faggots*: bundles of brushwood, which had to be imported from ever further afield as London grew.

27–8 *o'erlooks . . . water-house*: peers over, stands higher than . . . house connected with a scheme for supplying water to London, possibly Hugh Middleton's New River at Islington, opened in September 1613 with an oration by Thomas Middleton.

29 *lies in*: is confined to bed for labour.

34 *Burse*: the Royal Exchange, built by Sir Thomas Gresham, 1566.

36 *drug shop*: shop dealing in medicinal drugs (cf. modern US 'drug store').

39 *think's*: think it's.

54–5 *strings . . . frets*: metaphors from string instruments; another instance of mixed singular and plural forms.

56 *What . . . now*: what's now got into his head to make him sing? (Scornful, alluding to the growth of cuckold's horns).

62 *Ergo*: Latin: therefore (chop logic, like that of Tim and his Tutor). The Servants show contempt for Allwit's unmanly lack of control when they bandy words as equals.

63 *Negatur argumentum*: the argument is denied.

65 *pip*: Q, 'peep'. Degree, from the marks on playing cards (cf. army rank insignia).

66 *horns*: insignia of the cuckold.

69 *nose . . . meets*: common description of pregnancy.

70 *an . . . worship*: if your worship pleases/thinks it proper.

71 *Put on*: Allwit has removed his hat, in deference to Sir Walter (the Jacobeans wore hats indoors). He waits for a second prompt, measuring the deference required.

89 *forfeited lordships*: property forfeit for non-payment of loans.

108 *legs*: prompting them to bow ('make a leg').

 kneel: the children would kneel before Sir Walter to ask a father's customary blessing on first greeting, if they knew their true relationship to him.

119 *welcome*: playing on the sense of 'well come'.

121 *heavy*: (1) sad; (2) pregnant.

124 *calf*: blockhead, with a play on 'mooncalf', phantom pregnancy.

2.1.5 *blessings*: (1) felicities; (2) children. They are simply too fruitful and cannot afford their offspring. Artificial contraception was little practised in Jacobean England.

13 *wills*: sexual desires.

16 *drinkings*: euphemism for adulteries.

17 *gear*: (1) business; (2) genitals.

19 *If . . . on't*: if you agree.

21 *honest*: chaste, honourable. Touchwood Senior praises his wife for a chastity he does not practise himself, an example of sexual double standards.

26 *sensual fool*: a thoughtless sensualist.

32 *thicker vengeance*: that is, the curse mentioned in the previous line. The line of thinking is: when he came to his senses he would have cursed for having succumbed to the temptation of sex, and then even more so when the (inevitable) child was born, because birth itself is cause enough for misery, even when the child is born to riches, yet his own face nothing but destitution.

41 *set*: game, as in tennis; i.e. 'I want to finish this now, before I change my mind'.

43–5 *This . . . approves*: [her decision to live away from him] shows not only that she is completely chaste but also that she is extremely sensible, and confirms.

45–6 *Had . . . ever*: if she had had an insatiable sexual appetite, she could not have been held to blame since it would have been totally within the law (being within marriage).

48–9 *That . . . blood*: who can moderate her desires in relation to her situation and not to her instincts.

52 *sing*: possible misprint for 'sting' (the image is of a lecherous flesh-fly who 'suck(s) out' other people's blood). But *sing* also = have sexual intercourse.

54–5 *game . . . genders*: i.e. sexual intercourse.

55–6 *ne'er . . . bastard*: never played 'the game' without 'winning' at least a bastard. (A bastard was the lesser evil since he or she might be put up for adoption or left to parish charity, but a legitimate child would have to be looked after.)

57 *pit*: Hell, but with suggestions of female pudenda, picked up in 'come', 'served' (as in 'sexually serviced'), 'finger', 'country' (with the common play on 'cunt').

58 *used . . . bargain*: (1) expected to have sex more than once before becoming pregnant; (2) were accustomed to having some say in the matter.

60 *must . . . with't*: can't help myself bringing out my 'fatal finger'/penis, so disrupting the harvest.

62 *progress*: royal tour. These usually took place in high summer, coinciding

with harvest-time. Like Touchwood Senior's sexual prodigality, which indisposes the women harvesters, progresses seriously disrupted the harvest season.

69 *pox . . . you . . . take*: may you catch venereal disease (a common curse) . . . (1) catch fire; (2) make pregnant.

72 *churchwardens*: lay officers of the parish church, not always reliable. The inference is that they have given the certificate of virginity (warrants of good conduct were needed by law for people travelling outside their own parish) in return for sexual favours which self-evidently invalidate it— hence Touchwood Senior's determination to have more proof.

74 *Nothing . . . but*: the only thing that upsets me is.

75 *cracked*: destroyed, with a pun on *crack* = female pudenda.

76 *bout*: (1) legal quarrel; (2) sexual encounter. (Touchwood Senior seizes on the latter sense.)

81–2 *gulls . . . choose one*: 'I keep some dupes [gulls] in reserve [in pickle] for whores [mutton] like her, and she can choose one for a husband.'

84 *half yard of flesh*: the baby, but with leering allusion to the phallus.

85 *wants . . . nail*: is short by a cloth measure (2½ inches). Also hints it may be syphilitic and lack finger nails. The Wench catches the latter sense.

87–8 *Do . . . deed . . . younger brother*: be kind to me . . . under the laws of primogeniture younger sons often inherited nothing. There *may* be a third, and eldest, Touchwood, but it is unlikely—this is simply a play for sympathy. Touchwood Junior is clearly a younger son, with an economic imperative in his pursuit of Moll.

89–90 *Thou . . . thankful*: the *too much* is either his genitalia or the child who is excess to requirements if Touchwood Senior is not properly grateful (*more thankful*) for it.

91 *brake . . . house*: parted from my family.

93–4 *if I . . . want it*: if I have not already eaten it, no woman shall feel the lack it. There is a *double entendre* on his penis being 'without' (just outside) his belly.

95 *word*: promise, sentiment.

96 *There's . . . on't*: There are plenty of ways to get it off your hands.

97–8 *tomorrow . . . devices*: [leave it in a rich man's doorway] before dawn tomorrow, or immediately, this evening; there are any number of ways to lose the child.

100 *ware i'the shop*: all his other bastards (possibly *all* his children?).

101 *manly*: gentlemanly (though in fact the money has been what satisfied her).

102 *This*: the baby.

104 *fifth*: i.e. her fifth child. She keeps pretending to be a virgin, then extorts money from all the possible fathers when she has a child.

105 *go . . . ride*: pass . . . (1) ride as convicted whore to prison; (2) copulate.

106 *What . . . make*: how she will manage.

107 *Lent*: the first mention of this biblically inspired period of abstinence, between Ash Wednesday and Easter, when meat-eating was forbidden by law. Touchwood Senior links illegitimate human flesh with illicit meat— a linkage explored repeatedly in the following scene, always bordering on blasphemous allusion to Christ's giving of his body in the Eucharist.

109–11 *city . . . of*: in recent years Parliament and the City Council had both passed ordinances to enforce religious observance on swearing, Lent and the Sabbath. Some of these directly affected the actors (e.g. forbidding the use of oaths on stage and restricting performances during Lent), so the enthusiasm for 'wholesome religious laws' may be ironic. Touchwood Senior is no puritan.

113 *half . . . year*: six months.

115 *Setting apart . . . promoters*: leaving aside . . . informers, who (for reward) helped enforce the laws against eating or trading in meat. They were notoriously corrupt.

119 *What's . . . do*: what is going on here? (Touchwood Senior remains unseen by them).

120 *hold . . . life*: believe on my life.

120–3 *deep passion . . . with bacon*: i.e. Lady Kix is upset that meat is unavailable and kept shut away in private rooms, but the 'meat' she bewails is the genitalia of men other than her husband. A 'calf's head' is slang for a fool, so Sir Oliver might serve as such a dish (probably sporting cuckold's horns).

124 *Hist!*: 'Be quiet'. So Q, though some editions give this to Touchwood Junior. Lady Kix would not want this intruder to hear them.

126 *licence*: necessary for a marriage for which no banns had been called in church.

129 *thirteen shillings fourpence*: the value of a 'mark', slightly more than 66p in modern sterling, and the cost of a licence.

s.d. *Exit*: it may be inferred from their dialogue that at least one Touchwood leaves, but nothing explains how Touchwood Senior learns of the Kixes' infertility, and sets up the plot with Jug the maid. I suggest he lingers long enough to hear what they say.

130 *be . . . yet*: spend even more money.

131 *blessings*: children.

135 *cut*: (1) setback; (2) female genitals.

137 *cannot do withal*: am impotent (in several senses).

137–9 *there's things . . . for nothing*: medicines (to increase potency) are being concocted, on your own doctor's advice, at the druggist's; I refrain from no expense.

142 *'bating*: reducing.

143 *bridewells and spital-houses*: prisons and hospitals, charitable works implicitly in the hope of divine assistance in begetting a child. If money was all Sir Oliver needed, he would simply stop being so charitable. While he has no children he treats 'good deeds' as his heirs.

144 *fetch . . . again*: (1) restore his fortune; (2) recover his potency.

146 S.D. *Exit*: see 2.1.129 S.D. and note. Touchwood Senior must leave early enough to arrange things with Jug and this seems a good cue.

147 *brevity*: inadequate, sexually and otherwise. Sir Oliver takes umbrage at this.

151 *kept back*: property and patronage ('lands and livings') will be lost to Sir Walter because they have no children. He stands to inherit if they die childless.

152 *play . . . woman*: behave like a woman.

153–4 *'Tis . . . knight*: it is our lack of children that aggrandises Sir Walter— only that knight gets (wealth) by your not begetting (children). Sir Walter has already borrowed ('He's made') on the strength of Sir Oliver's infertility, and will soon make a fortune from the dowry of a goldsmith's daughter, whom he would never have been able to wed without these expectations.

161 *Master . . . to . . . joy*: 'Mr', Q . . . deeply sarcastic.

162–3 *gets . . . Barthol'mew-eve*: has children . . . 23 August. As this is only Lent, the twins were conceived before the marriage.

168 *Weeping . . . railing*: crying sentimentally or abusing one another.

169 *Jug*: familiar form of Joan, commonly used for maidservants.

171 *heretics*: strictly, persons who hold false beliefs, but the maid applies this to the drugs the Kixes have been taking.

174 *haply*: (1) by chance; (2) happily.

175–6 *water . . . they*: (1) medicine; (2) semen . . . the children.

179 *run . . . much*: heavily in debt.

185 *He's . . . dear*: his charges are very expensive.

186 *True*: Q gives all the lines from here to the end of the scene to Lady Kix, also placing 'I'll about it' before 'And that's . . . sweet husband'. But Sir Oliver is the one who has talked about money and its uses, as was natural for the husband. I owe this emendation to R. B. Parker's Revels edition.

land . . . come: the land that will otherwise pass to Sir Walter.

186–7 *Put case . . . Stands . . . in*: if, for instance . . . costs me.

2.2.1 *I'll . . . presently*: I'll go and summon the godparents/guests immediately. Allwit thinks highly of himself for going to this trouble. He goes on to record self-satisfaction at having relinquished all responsibilities to Sir Walter, and all work to other people.

  7 *nurse . . . nurse*: there are at least two nurses (the Dry and Wet Nurses for the baby) and possibly as many as four, since a Midwife is present in 2.4 and a further Nurse tends Maudline in 3.2, though roles may be shared.

 14 *tailor*: a comment on her fine christening robes, but also alluding to the traditional lechery of tailors.

 15 *slut . . . correction*: 'slut' usually designates a girl of low breeding and/or with loose morals, though it could be an almost playful usage. Perhaps Allwit attempts to convey his contempt semi-jocularly, sees that Sir Walter is not pleased, and changes tack with a tacit apology (*under correction*).

 24 *Pup*: all-purpose baby-talk.

 28 *spoon-meat. Wipe your mouth*: puréed food. Don't talk foolishly. (This either shows her contempt for Allwit as a wittol, or rebukes him for suggesting weaning the baby at far too young an age.)

 30 *myself*: it was most irregular in the established churches for a parent to be godfather to his own child, but a growing practice among puritans.

 32 *'Tis . . . weapon*: it's a good idea to deal with rumour by every means possible. By standing as godfather he will deflect suspicion of being the father himself.

 35–6 *When . . . shame*: when a man become degenerate, the moral faculties themselves are extinguished; the luxury of having nothing to do blinds him to dishonour. These pieties are the first hint of the reformation that will overtake Sir Walter later.

 37–8 *studying . . . suitable to*: considering . . . appropriate for/acceptable to.

 45 *neat*: elegant.

 55 *first course*: of a meal. The promoters are behaving like dogs who know the signs of when they will eventually get rich pickings from a table.

 57 *corpse*: disguised plural.

 61 *bills in Middlesex*: dubious legal practice which extended the writ of the King's Bench by issuing warrants on false charges in Middlesex (including all of London north of the river) which could then be extended to real charges elsewhere. Allwit imagines a grotesquely extreme case, in which debtors are so pursued into their graves.

 62–3 *sweetbreads . . . lamb-stones*: pancreas and testicles of a lamb, supposed aphrodisiacs. Allwit vividly imagines the promoters, their whores, and the whores' bawds all sharing in feasts of rich meat, hypocritically seized by them.

66 *chins*: double chins were the mark of a bawd.

67 *milk of witches*: witches were supposed to give suck to the devil by a third nipple.

68 *How . . . in*: a lying-in would involve more expense on food.

69 *baffle 'em*: publicly disgrace them.

71 *carnal strictness*: the laws governing meat.

72 *tell . . . Lent*: Allwit asks for the house of someone killing animals in Lent—a seemingly gullible question directed to those supposed to suppress such activity.

73 *bird*: easy victim.

75 *veal . . . sauce*: young meat like veal, and 'green', both stress gullibility.

76 *I . . . stomach*: he pretends to have a queasy digestion.

78 *colon*: large intestine, figurative for appetite. Allwit probably rubs his stomach.

82 *answerable*: suitable.

84 *directed . . . street*: they pretend to sympathize with Allwit's needing meat for his queasy stomach, believing he can lead them to a black market trader.

86 *close*: secretly.

89–90 *kiss Newgate . . . apron*: go to prison unless he turns out the pockets of his apron (i.e. pays a bribe; butchers traditionally wore aprons).

93 *freebooters*: pirates, here preying on the baskets of ordinary shoppers.

94 *My wife lies in*: women about childbirth were exempt from the restrictions on eating meat, so Allwit may buy it unhindered. He has outsmarted them.

97–8 *I have . . . busy*: possibly an aside, but all the funnier if he is talking to himself with the promoters standing just behind him.

112 *Turnbull Street*: notorious haunt of thieves and prostitutes, near Clerkenwell Green.

113 *longs . . . crossed*: craves because pregnant . . . thwarted.

115 *booty*: prize, spoil or piece of plunder.

117 *Cry . . . mercy*: I beg your pardon (for not recognizing you).

121 *let . . . pass*: the Second Promoter has not recognized Master Oliver as someone employed by a wealthy merchant 'in fee' with them.

123 *Beggarland's*: the name suggests that he has acquired his wealth by reducing those around him to beggary.

125 *purchased . . . together*: bought an (illegal) exemption for the whole period.

126 *groats . . . Ash Wednesday*: strictly fourpenny pieces, but used of any small coin . . . first day of Lent, 21 February in 1613.

128 *shift*: (1) make a living; (2) commit a fraud; (3) palm something off on someone; (4) remove an underskirt.

130 *rump*: of the mutton.

132 *band*: collar or (more likely) cuff. The Wench is doing as poor a job of brazening out having the mutton as a murderer would if his cuff was still covered in blood.

133 *What . . . is't*: an oblique way of reminding her that it is Lent.

135 *this*: the mutton.

138 *tender*: are considerate of.

140 *true authority*: the sick, like women in childbed, could gain official exemptions.

142 *spare not*: do not spare yourself, run as fast as you can.

145 *Would . . . else*: i.e. he too solemnly swears to keep the basket.

148 *market . . . Imprimis*: purchase, deal . . . 'In the first place', Renaissance Latin word to introduce a list.

151 *Now . . . Done*: Q, 'Not'. (They bet on what they will find.) . . . the bet is agreed.

155 *I'll*: not in Q.

159 *else*: otherwise (if they had not sworn to keep it).

161 *gettings*: earnings. They are dismayed at the cost of having to bring up the baby.

163 *tallow*: for candles. The baby will need tending at night.

164–5 *We have . . . candles*: we still need to get loins of mutton for the suet to make candles (so, by implication, they cannot stop being promoters).

166–7 *Nothing . . . heads of us*: None of this upsets me, except that you felt the baby and said it was a lamb's head. She's made fools of us.

168–9 *time . . . up . . . Mid-Lent Sunday*: time to make up the money . . . 17 March in 1613.

171 *motion*: proposal.

172–3 *Checker . . . Queenhive*: inn at Queenhithe, the fish-landing quay west of Southwark Bridge.

174 *young flood . . . Brainford*: the rising tide, when the water flows up-river . . . Brentford, a suburb up the Thames where children were often put out to nurse.

2.3 S.D. *trussing*: tying the points of his hose to his doublet.

2 *kurs'ning*: christening.

3 *No . . . an*: it would not matter if. Davy plays on a secondary sense of *truss*: hang.

5 *master's . . . hair*: bawdily playing on how well Sir Walter 'fits' Allwit's wife, though the innuendo rolls off Allwit.

7 *jumped in one*: agreed, with unconscious innuendo on sharing the same woman, started by Davy in the previous speech, where *hair* = heir.

8 *comfit*: sweet made of fruit pulp and sugar, hence Allwit's 'sweet youth' joke.

11 *comes*: singular for plural, common in Middleton and generally at the time.

12 *I . . . today*: Allwit anticipates being kept busy kissing all the female guests.

13 *Underman*: stressing the lecherous nature beneath the pious exterior.

16 *become . . . faithful*: befit one of the faith (i.e. a puritan).

18 *brethren's*: Puritan sects referred to each other as brothers and sisters (see previous line), or sometimes neighbours (see below), to stress their equality as children of God.

21 *fit . . . music*: harmonize with all these tunes, or lose the benefits. He is complaining about the social role he has to perform for the sake of his easy life.

23 *sirrah*: exaggerated form of 'sir', often implying the speaker's authority.

25 *Want . . . thine*: I lack for nothing except the ability to beget children as you do.

30 *put . . . about'em*: Allwit ironically plays down his own part in the fathering of his children, which has in reality been nothing, and his *stand*(ing) (erection) non-existent.

34 *h'as . . . hour*: he has met his promised deadline.

35 *Back . . . silent*: Touchwood Junior does not want to reveal their relationship.

37 *Into one cup*: pledges both Moll and Touchwood Junior in a single drink.

43 *I . . . time*: I follow your lead (a polite deference).

2.4 S.D. *Exit . . . Child*: Throughout the scene the women squabble over precedence in the procession that follows the child to the christening.

1 *I . . . not*: Maudline refuses on oath ('In faith') to take the offered first place.

5 *You . . . creature*: an expression of exasperation, conceding the contest and going first.

10 *forbear*: indulge. She is being most condescending.

11–12 *unity . . . lowliness*: the puritans make a virtue of being last and at least not quarrelling, being one in 'spirit'.

14 *There . . . before*: proverbial put-down of those who take pride in being

lowly, but also bawdy in that *proud* = sexually excited, picked up in the closing line.

3.1.2–4 *married . . . hence*: Church of England clergymen were free to marry. He hints that he has had extra-marital relations, possibly in return for testifying to the moral character of the women concerned. So they 'will be maids', whatever their actual sexual experience. Compare this with the innuendo of the Wench at 2.1.70–3.

5 *licence*: see 2.1.126.

10 *haste*: it is essential the marriage be conducted quickly, before Moll's parents prevent it. The Parson presses on with a no-frills, rote-version of a wedding. It would not have been permitted to use the words of the Anglican wedding ceremony on stage.

12 *made . . . shift*: went to a lot of effort.

16 *heart*: the third finger of the left hand (the wedding-finger) was popularly supposed to be connected with the 'master-vein' to the heart. The Parson continues this doggerel in the final scene as if without interruption.

20 *the politic fetch . . . mystical*: your crafty stratagem . . . secretive.

21 *you*: not in Q.

25 *glasses*: presumably indicates that Yellowhammer wears spectacles throughout, suggesting literal as well as metaphorical short-sightedness.

26 *dreamed . . . still*: I always imagined what anger would be like (implying that now he is experiencing the real thing).

30 *inconscionable*: unscrupulous (sarcastic).

42 *close*: locked tightly shut.

48–52 *Your acquaintance . . . of lust*: Sir Walter stands on his feigned dignity in delivering these elegant insults. Gentlemen conventionally regretted that an acquaintance had not been made sooner, but Sir Walter implies that Touchwood Junior is no gentleman and will be avoided like the plague or (ultimate hypocrisy) 'the disease of lust'.

54 *wrong me*: Touchwood Junior warns Sir Walter not to underestimate him, even though he is in no mood to talk.

55–6 *Look . . . spare not . . . baffling*: watch him carefully and be continually on your guard . . . public disgrace. Touchwood Senior warns that Touchwood Junior is a man of integrity, and that Sir Walter is uncommonly lucky to get away with this.

58 *losers*: a play on the proverbial 'Give losers leave to speak'. Sir Walter shrugs off the threat.

3.2 S.D. *thrust out*: Middleton is using the full stage, with the bed visible from all sides, as opposed to some 'inner stage' or 'discovery space'; cf. Heywood, *The Silver Age*, beginning of 3.1, '*Enter Semele drawn out in her bed*'.

2 *I . . . pains*: thank you for your trouble.

5 *Amsterdam*: hotbed of puritanism. Such puritans abhorred 'Popish' rituals and decoration.

6–7 *At . . . forsooth . . . Look*: [I am] close by, in truth . . . make sure.

10 *As . . . mouth*: cf. 'the spitting image'.

13 *up and down*: altogether. Alludes to the constant motion of the chattering mouth, but also suggests sexual motions.

17 *mettled*: (1) courageous; (2) amorous.

20 *great speed*: good fortune.

24 *'Tis . . . spirit*: she claims Mrs Allwit as a fellow member of the faithful, reinforced by God's spirit.

S.D. *plate*: gold- or silver-ware, traditional christening presents.

26 *fatness*: richest part.

28 *Calls . . . ladies*: all the gossips are flattered by Sir Walter's grand manner to them.

30 *shows . . . to him*: seems like a boorish peasant, compared to Sir Walter.

32 *So . . . She's*: so long as . . . she has.

38 *poor*: Sir Walter's mock modesty.

42–3 *standing-cup . . . 'postle spoons*: cup with base or legs to support itself; spoons with figures of the apostles on the handle: traditional christening presents.

44 *red beard*: Judas was traditionally depicted with red hair, associated with lechery. Apostle spoons were mainly silver, but one here was *gilt*: gold-plated. The First Puritan takes *gilt* as 'guilt', and so thinks of the 'guilty' Apostle.

47 *consumes*: angers, eats up (i.e. with lust).

48 *Well said*: Well done.

50 *tasselled*: fashionably large, with showy tassels (Allwit begins a satirical commentary on the hypocritical dress and habits of the puritans and other gossips).

53 *urine*: used as a cosmetic.

62–3 *see . . . culled out . . . plums*: see if they haven't chosen . . . sugar plums.

66 *wife's . . . back*: by its own self his wife's belly (1) forced him to overwork to maintain it; (2) overtaxed his sexual powers.

70 *Bucklersbury*: street running south from Cheapside to Walbrook, 'on both sides throughout . . . possessed of grocers and apothecaries' (John Stow, *Survey of London*). Allwit smugly reflects that his own money has not been spent there.

75–6 *Courageously ... such*: she wishes Mrs Allwit many equally propitious confinements in the future.

89 *countess*: John Chamberlain wrote of the Countess of Shrewsbury, who in January 1613 'lies very richly, for the hanging of her chamber, being white satin, embroidered with gold (or silver) and pearl is valued at fourteen thousand pounds'.

91 *toward marriage*: going to be married.

92 *Lammas*: 1 August, the Christian harvest festival.

97 *lie ... bed*: she is still wetting the bed, like a child. The passage plays on the idea that women's pudenda were a 'fault', making them 'leaky vessels' and sexually incontinent.

108 *Toward*: in the making.

109 *cattle*: Q 'cattell': (1) chattel, wealth or goods; (2) literally cattle—see later discussions of 'runts'.

110 *betrayed*: Tim demonstrates the lack of 'audacity' with women which Maudline commented on earlier.

113–14 *still ... women's company*: always ... the universities were all-male institutions.

118 *freshwoman*: by analogy with freshman, first-year student, though there were no such women students.

120–1 *answered under ... thrust 'mongst*: met the requirements to become ... crowd among (with sexual suggestion).

122 *and I care not*: I will not mind the situation any longer (if you call up my tutor). He feels exposed on his own among so many women.

125 *Negatur*: it is denied (Latin).

132 *free-school*: St Paul's school, founded by John Colet, 1512. The great scholar Richard Mulcaster was headmaster from 1596 to 1608. Whipping was relatively common at such schools, but a great disgrace at university.

139–40 *in league ... Dunces*: into company ... the 'schoolmen' or scholastics, from John *Duns* Scotus (c.1300). The Tutor implies that he introduced Tim to logic but got no further. The writing of the scholastics was attacked by humanist reformers in the sixteenth century, whence *dunce* meaning a blockhead, implicitly applied here to Tim.

142 *pate*: head, brains (an archaic usage, typical of Tim's unworldliness).

144 *Naturally*: (1) spontaneously; (2) as from a 'natural' or half-wit.

144–5 *beholding ... pains*: indebted for the trouble you have taken.

145 *Non ideo sane*: Not for that reason, indeed (logicians' tag). Maudline picks up *ideo* as idiot.

151 *'Timotheus'*: Tim tries to enshroud his name with a learned, classical aura.

158 *had*: would have.

159 *comfits*: in his sexual inexperience Tim does not know that 'kissing-comfits' were eaten to take away bad breath.

161 *lower end*: i.e. greet those at the other end of the room. The Tutor is not as distressed to be in a room full of solicitous women as his student.

162 *despatch*: get through; i.e. it will be necessary, between them, to kiss all the women.

164 *waters . . . brethren*: alludes to Cambridge's strong association with puritanism, where many of its preachers were trained.

Hoist: lift yourself up. The odd choice of word suggests Tim's embarrassment.

167 *embrace our falls*: parodies Calvin's teaching that we should humbly acknowledge our fallen state.

168–9 *dropped . . . me*: suggests some comic business, in which the First Puritan perhaps puckered up for a kiss, stooped, and could not stop herself falling.

170 *parted . . . Heyday . . . looking glass*: departed . . . an exclamation, expressing high excitement (Q, 'Hyda') . . . chamber pot. Allwit is being sarcastic: the women's 'cheeks' will be reflected in the 'vessels' they now urgently need to use.

171 *in plate*: from the silver cups brought out for the christening.

173 *bravest*: most splendid.

174 *Come . . . Pissing-Conduit*: coming . . . generically named small conduit, near the Royal Exchange, invoked to round off the urinary motif. The two drums and standard-bearer suggest male genitalia.

s.d. *Exeunt . . . Puritans*: Presumably the bed is removed at this point, though it might be left to the end of the scene, with its curtains closed (and Mrs Allwit still in it).

178 *nap . . . brethren*: parodying Anabaptist teaching that men and women might lie freely together, so long as they were asleep.

181 *hare-mad*: hares are famously erratic in the breeding season, around March.

182 *bums*: (1) padded bustles; (2) posteriors. The next few exchanges are quite scatological.

184 *stools*: (1) low padded seats; (2) commode in the shape of a footstool; (3) faeces.

185 *no worse*: Allwit suspects someone has urinated.

186 *cost . . . them*: are not valued by them because they did not have to pay for them (Davy reminds us that Allwit didn't pay for them either).

189 *rushes*: strewn on the floor in houses, and also on Jacobean stages.

190 *short . . . heels*: a string of abusive terms, with bawdy and scatological associations. Low heels were associated with whores.

195 *upon*: close to.

200 *wheels*: as of a coach or machine in motion, which he desperately needs to stop.

201 *prick*: vex (him).

202 *rank toil*: (1) excessive; (2) indecent; (3) sweaty work. It is not clear whether this refers to Allwit's 'excessive' (i.e. non-existent) work—there are other hints that he is fat from being kept in luxury and not exerting himself—or to Sir Walter's copulation with Mrs Allwit. It is certainly Sir Walter whom Davy wants to keep unmarried.

3.3.1–2 *in . . . way . . . pleasure*: on the most fortunate road . . . give pleasure to.

5 *I*: not in Q.

3–7 *For though . . . me*: the gist of this passage is that Touchwood Junior is not downhearted. Though Moll is locked away from him, her vow to remain faithful means that he alone possesses her, and the weary time will be joyful ('gameful') to him.

10 *lay . . . merit*: reduce him [Sir Oliver Kix] to the bankrupt level he really deserves.

11–12 *perch . . . lap*: the image is of a harvester up in a tree, shaking ripe fruit (*golden* may allude to the golden apples of the Hesperides) into the apron of someone below.

13–14 *weep . . . goodness*: continues the orchard metaphor. If Lady Kix continues to weep and whine she will dry out, become barren, and new fruit will not grow in her.

15–16 *I find . . . provocation*: I already have more than enough inclination to do this, without prompting.

17 *might'*: as in Q. The apostrophe stands for a missing 'have'.

17–18 *eringoes . . . crab*: all supposed aphrodisiacs. *Eringoes* are sea-holly.

20–1 *an you'll . . . on me*: if you'll do what I ask and preserve my money [i.e. dowry] as well, I am a very lucky man.

22 *Finds . . . i'the common-place*: who finds such an honest friend when he needs one (literally, 'in the Westminster Court of Common Pleas').

24 *crosses*: (1) set-backs; (2) deletions (note 'additions' in the next line).

28 *will . . . straight*: shall release you from your amazement immediately.

31 *Weighing . . . own*: treating my plight as if it were her own.

39–40 *humours . . . instant*: moods they are in at this moment.

41 S.D. *'within'*: both of the Kixes are off-stage at this moment.

46 *fit*: (1) struggle; (2) part of a song; (3) seizure.

48 *Fall out . . . fall in*: quarrel . . . make up (with bawdy innuendo on *fall in*).

49 *fruit*: (lack of) children.

53 *durst but . . . justice*: dared only to . . . defence.

56 *divorced*: not a common process then, requiring an Act of Parliament. After 1613 the references to loose living at court would have brought to mind the divorce of the Earl of Essex and Lady Frances Howard, on the grounds of non-consummation though really to facilitate her marriage to the royal favourite, the Earl of Somerset.

56–7 *hanged . . . thee*: i.e. if marriage and hanging are matters of fate, it is only a matter of time before Sir Oliver is hanged.

59 *in't*: in marriage.

62 *Where . . . they*: Lady Kix is either jealously assuming this *ménage* already exists or, more likely, calling Sir Oliver's bluff about whether he could ever father children.

62–6 *When there . . . established*: the main clause of the sentence is in the last line—'Despite your mutual recriminations, I think an honourable peace could be agreed, if more friendly courses are pursued by you to beget children and be fruitful in your own house and by your own personal efforts.'

68 *like thee*: i.e. Touchwood Senior's efforts at reconciliation are as pointless as Sir Oliver's at fathering children.

69 *Singleness . . . her . . . one smock*: let divorce throw her into shame and confusion . . . i.e. with only what she stood up in.

70 *single*: implies that Sir Oliver was 'accompanied' by lice (picked up in *bit sore*), so hardly in a position to stand on his dignity.

73 *peal*: loud volley of sound or ringing of bells (he hopes they are quietening down).

74 *outcry*: auction.

79 *clap up bills*: stick up advertisements (for the auction).

80 *talk not on't*: don't talk about it.

82 *one . . . man*: one who's hardly the rear part of a man (i.e. lacking all in front).

86 *He lies that says it*: i.e. he lies who says she cannot please him.

88 *Can . . . in*: he is amused and bemused by their rapid changes of mood and direction.

89 S.D. *aside*: a relatively rare example of an aside being indicated in Q.

90 *Almond-milk . . . stood me in*: drink made from boiled sweet almonds . . . cost me.

94–5 *ought . . . had*: anything (with inevitable sexual innuendo) . . . would have.

96–7 *But . . . thee*: All I ever found in you was a contrary, ill-tempered being.

97 *grub*: (1) one of unpleasant manners; (2) dwarfish person (implying short body-parts).

103 *breed*: (1) poor education; (2) poor and unfruitful family line.

106 *yet . . . fortune*: but even so you set aside all good opportunities.

107 *in spite*: to spite you.

108 *ride . . . hours*: Touchwood Senior's device to remove Sir Oliver from the scene, but symbolically appropriate for the 'riding' he intends to do in his place.

110 *Ware*: town 20 miles north of London, notorious for assignations, famous for the 'great bed' in the Saracen's Head Inn, more than 3 metres square.

114 *standing*: (1) being upright; (2) having an erection.

115 —: Q breaks off with a dash, either due to censorship or because Middleton wanted the audience to supply the joke themselves. There are similar *lacunae* at 4.1.206, 4.1.210, 4.1.242 and 5.3.114.

118 *crossed this*: jumped over (one of the stools?) There was a fad for stool-leaping (satirised by Jonson in *Epicene*) as a way gallants showed off their physical prowess.

s.d. *capers*: capering is dancing or leaping in a frolicsome manner, and obviously absurd in these circumstances.

119 *show . . . a-horseback*: look good on horseback.

120 *joint-stool*: solidly constructed stool, about 2 feet high, made from pieces of wood designed to wedge together.

121 s.d. *Aside*: another rare instance of an 'aside' marked in Q.

126 *bad head*: he means there is nothing wrong with his memory, but ironically invokes his own imminent cuckold's horns.

129–30 *wife . . . quick . . . a-bed*: Q 'wifes' . . . pregnant . . . to her confinement.

132–3 *even . . . faster*: correct . . . Touchwood Senior mischievously urges Sir Oliver on in his capering, who is probably out of breath, though loath to admit it.

138 *anger since*: previous anger.

142 *mine . . . Clean contrary*: my (physic, medicine) . . . entirely differently (with the innuendo of 'by a different orifice').

145 *coach*: coaches had a reputation as sites for assignations.

4.1.1–17 *Negatur . . . rationale*: TIM *Your argument is denied,* tutor. TUTOR *I am proving to you, pupil, that a fool is not a rational animal.* TIM *You will certainly fail.* TUTOR *I beg you to be silent: I am proving to you*—TIM *How will you prove it, master?* TUTOR *A fool does not have reason, and therefore is not a rational animal.* TIM *Thus you argue, master: a fool has no reason,*

therefore he is not a rational animal. Your argument is denied again, tutor.
TUTOR *I will demonstrate the argument again to you, sir: whoever has no share of reason can in no way be called rational; but a fool does not have a share of reason, therefore a fool can in no way be called rational.* TIM *He does have a share.* TUTOR *So you argue: who has a share? in what way does he have a share?* TIM *As a man: I will prove it to you by a syllogism.* TUTOR *Prove it.* TIM *Thus I prove it, master: a fool is a man, just as you and I are; man is a rational animal, and just so is a fool a rational animal.*

19–20 *Sic disputas . . . rationale:* So you argue: *a fool is a man, just as you and I are; a man is a rational animal, and just so a fool is a rational animal.* The Latin disputation is ponderous and stupid, well below bachelor standard. Even non-Latin speakers will appreciate that a fool is a fool in any language, however much education he may have.

27 *I . . . now:* formal disputation phrase, inviting her into the argument.

28 *one . . . wit:* as Tim himself will be, if he does marry the 'Welsh Gentle-woman'. But it is a very broad category, into which many of the audience may feel they fall.

41 *so:* i.e. honest women.

41–2 *can . . . bastards:* he claims he can prove women honest (i.e. chaste and honourable) even if they have had three illegitimate children.

43 *tailor:* ladies' tailors had a reputation for unmanliness (though cf. note to 2.2.14), which Tim is going to offer to refute by logic.

45 *Let . . . will:* (1) Let him visit us when he chooses; (2) Let him perform sexually as he chooses. The latter sense is not intended by Tim, but understood by the audience.

48 *accidences:* books on Latin inflection, studied before the syntax covered in the grammar. Tim—surprise, surprise—was a very slow learner.

51 *haberdines:* salt dried fish. A lost allusion, possibly to a game, but perhaps (since cod = scrotum) a piece of bawdy. Relations between Maudline and the Tutor certainly warm up from this point, with much play on maturity and 'the Latin tongue'.

53 *as in praesenti:* famous *opening* phrase from William Lyly's much-used *A Short Introduction of Latin Grammar.*

56 *have . . . out:* (1) tell everything; (2) expose a man's genitalia. Tim is embarrassed by his mother's 'exposure' of him, and in meaning the first sense implies the second.

57 *Quid est grammatica?:* what is grammar? Another famous phrase from Lyly's grammar.

58 *sweet . . . token:* Maudline's memory of the 'honest gentleman' who tried to talk Latin with Tim is compounded with personal recollections of his 'tongue'.

66 *recte . . . ars*: the art of writing and speaking correctly, which is Lyly's answer to his own question. Maudline construes *ars* (art) as 'arse'.

67 *Sir-reverence*: 'Save your reverence', an apology for the indecency. Tim ought to know that it is *not* indecent.

71 *to him*: that is, to Tim, to keep him company while she and the Tutor withdraw to continue Maudline's education in Latin grammar.

73–4 *great . . . conclusion*: the Tutor responds as if commending an exercise in logic.

78 *kiff*: kith. Tim is at sea about the nature of sexual and marital relationships, unable to imagine marrying someone who is neither a family member nor an old friend.

84 *to her marriage*: as her dowry.

85 *runts*: small breed of Welsh and Highland cattle, though Tim does not know this.

88 *Rider's Dictionary*: English–Latin dictionary compiled by Bishop John Rider, 1589. The audience will appreciate that Tim should look for the word he is thinking of under 'c' rather than 'r'.

90 *Romford*: Essex town, famous for its weekly hog markets but also as a place for illicit assignations.

92 *no graduate*: Tim suggests that graduates are incapable of talking about marriage, which is either a joke about his own stupidity or about all-male universities.

96 *shall . . . her*: I will not have her saying I am so haughty that I would not even speak with her.

97 *take . . . hold*: Tim uses an archaic sense of 'take', meaning to say that she will not be able to misunderstand what he says. He actually says that she will not be able to understand his words, which proves to be most true.

98–9 *Salve . . . curo—*: Hail to you, too, most beautiful maiden; what you want I neither know nor in truth care—.

99 *Tully's . . . to a heart*: Cicero's own phrase, to the life. The phrase is not actually that of the great Roman orator, Marcus Tullius Cicero, nor anything like.

100–1 *a suitor . . . quoth a*: she mishears and does not understand the Latin . . . did he say.

103 *Ferter . . . maximis*: It is said, by Hercules, that Wales abounds in great riches. Here and below I translate what Tim is *trying* to say. The Latin is execrably bad, but I have not followed earlier editors in improving it, since it is part of the joke—*Ferter* is meaningless, for example, except as a sound for the Welsh Gentlewoman to mis-hear; *parata* (ready) should be *paratus* (Tim makes himself female); and so on.

107 *some . . . other*: I'll find one way of managing or another.

108–10 *Iterum . . . parata*: Again I say that you abound in riches, the greatest mountains and fountains and, as I may say, runts; however I am really only a very little man by nature and a bachelor (i.e. BA) by training, and not actually ready for bed.

112 *Avedera . . . foginis*: Middleton's Welsh is wholly phonetic, and worse than Tim's Latin. The first half of the line appears to represent *A fedrwch chwi Gymraeg*—'Can you speak Welsh?' But the rest is far from certain —perhaps *er Duw cog fo gennyf*, 'for God's sake, are you pretending with me?'

114 *Ego . . . cogo*: I will not come together (with you)—though he presumably thinks he is telling her he will not cheat (*cog*).

115 *Rhegosin . . . ambre*: incomprehensible, except that there is a reference to cheese and whey, supposed Welsh delicacies. She appears to be inviting him off for dinner.

117 *travelled*: with pun on 'travailed' (laboured).

119 *proceeded*: (1) to a higher degree; (2) into sexual experience (Tim again speaks more wisely than he knows).

122 *How . . . agree*: how are you getting on.

130 *recoiled*: retorted.

133 *clap*: cleave, though the sense of clap = venereal disease is probably also to be recognized by the audience.

134 *you'd . . . stranger*: you intended to marry me to a complete foreigner.

137 *Protestant tongue*: English, as distinct from the 'Catholic' Latin. As throughout this scene, 'tongue' carries the secondary sense of 'sexual equipment'.

139 *makes towards*: is approaching. That Maudline has to say this means it is not immediately apparent. She perhaps leads Tim by the ear into a kiss.

140 *country*: (1) place of origin; (2) cunt.

142 *mutton*: with the usual play on 'whore', though Welsh mutton was genuinely prized.

sing: with a secondary sense (not understood by Tim) of 'perform sexually'.

143 *British*: i.e. Welsh.

145 *good parts*: (1) accomplishments; (2) naked body—another piece of unconscious bawdy by Tim.

147 *Pray*: inviting her to start singing.

S.D. *Gentlewoman sings*: the song has no particular Welsh associations. Versions appear in Middleton's *More Dissemblers Besides Women*, and some manuscripts.

148 *Cupid*: the blind and mischievous god of love, who shoots his arrows of

desire indiscriminately, is often held responsible for the fickleness and immorality of human sexual behaviour.

152 *crests*: cuckold's horns.

156 *lips*: ambiguously the lips of the mouth and of the vagina.

161 *quick*: the tenderest part (probably to be understood as the vagina).

169 *one's . . . waste*: in the pursuit of pleasure it is a waste of time to be leisurely. The stanza contrasts the urgency of sexual passion with the desire to prolong its pleasure.

171 *We . . . find it*: Q reads 'And loose it . . . '. A line is apparently missing, probably before this one.

173 *close . . . below*: join in (a) a kiss, (b) sexual congress, (c) closing chords of music in both upper and lower registers.

175 *I . . . lodging*: Tim may be boasting that he too can sing, but is more likely responding to the sexual innuendo of the song.

177 *peals*: (1) the noise of (wedding) bells; (2) peels = matches, equals.

178 *Here's . . . conference*: there's a stranger here who wants a private word with me. Allwit *is* a stranger to Yellowhammer, though not to Maudline, who was at the christening of 'his' child. He is probably in disguise.

183 *Abingdon*: Abingdon was actually in Berkshire in Middleton's day, but only five miles south of Oxford.

185 *citizen*: a wealthy and respected inhabitant of the city (i.e. of London).

187 *zeal*: righteous commitment (to the Yellowhammers' cause).

192 *confirmed*: well established.

193–4 *Fame . . . of*: her reputation endows her with worthier qualities than you choose to mention.

201 *Resolve . . . me*: satisfy me in that one matter and you will hear what I have to say.

206 *state—*: see note to 3.3.115 above.

210 *but—*: see note to 3.3.115 above.

214 *Poulters . . . conies*: (1) poulterers by selling rabbits; (2) pimps by selling whores.

226 *Cato and Corderius*: i.e. Cato's *Disticha de Moribus* (moral precepts) and Mathurin Cordier's *Colloquia Scholastica* (1564), common versebooks, with a puritanical emphasis. Allwit indicates their age by the level of their studies.

227 *Eton College*: famous school in Windsor, founded by Henry VI in 1440.

229 *It . . . prevented*: i.e. the affair would have hurt you more deeply if Sir Walter's marriage to Moll had not been forestalled by my revelations.

232 *work*: the arrangements for the christening.

240 *call him back*: reform him.

242 *anno—*: see note to 3.3.115. Q leaves a blank here, without the dash at the other *lacunae*. It may be for the actors to supply a date suitable for the performance. Or Yellowhammer cannot or will not remember a date so distant.

244 *warden*: either a churchwarden or one of the governing body of a City Company. Either way, he has achieved a respectable standing.

247 *wholesome*: free of disease.

249 *sweat*: standard treatment for venereal disease. Yellowhammer is indifferent to the morality of the situation, resolving only to try to prevent Moll from catching disease.

4.2.5 *Trig-stairs*: landing place on the Thames, at the bottom of Trig Lane.

6–7 *common stairs . . . Puddle-wharf*: public stairs about two hundred yards upstream from Trig-stairs, all fairly unsavoury areas.

8 *silly*: foolish.

4.3.1 *had . . . sergeants*: would have . . . sheriff's officers.

2 *watermen*: boatmen, taxi-drivers of the river, still London's main thoroughfare.

3 *requitefull'st*: most eager to return favours. South Bank theatres like The Swan relied on them to ferry over many of their audience, which may explain this eulogy. The burning down of the Globe in June 1613 lost the watermen a good deal of trade until it was rebuilt.

4–5 *get their means . . . forwardest*: make their living . . . most ready.

6 *Blackfriars*: Blackfriars Theatre, the King's Men's indoor 'private house' across the river from the Swan, which used candle lighting. This apparently refers to a real event, not a show, and the swordsmen would need candles to find their way.

7 *came*: who came.

11 *bandied*: hit at.

13 *first man*: boastful trade cry of a waterman.

15–16 *Take . . . her . . . Barn Elms*: he advises his brother to take one boat himself and leave another for Moll . . . resort of lovers and duellists, opposite Hammersmith.

19 *French crown*: écu, broadly equivalent to English 5 shillings.

20–1 *take water . . . lustily*: be carried by water . . . vigorously, with a will.

26 *Paul's wharf*: between Puddle wharf and Trig-stairs.

27 *we . . . safe*: we must do everything we can to ensure our safety.

4.4.1 *call . . . keeping*: do you call this keeping (her) securely?

3 *buff sergeant*: officers supposedly as dogged as their leather jerkins were tough.

5 *Venetian uses it*: Venetian women were supposedly very amorous, and their husbands jealous, hence the use of chastity belts.

7 *looked . . . gutter*: which gave access to the watercourse.

9–10 *wise man . . . every hole*: crude mis-rendition of Ovid, *Ars Amatoria*, ii. 243–6.

11 *Verum . . . dicta . . . Dicit Virgilius*: The poet speaks truth. So says Virgil. The Tutor's smug Latin tag follows on from his just having cuckolded Yellowhammer. Tim caps the joke by ascribing all this smut to the highest minded of Latin poets.

12–13 *jills . . . jill*: wantons; played a foul trick (playing on the pronunciation of 'Vir-jil').

15 *stay . . . oars . . . smelt-boat*: wait for a proper ferry boat . . . boat for small, easily caught fish (like *gudgeons*, below), metaphoric for 'fools'.

18 *Will . . . to*: which will . . . for.

25 *Forbear . . . worse*: Sir Walter orders them to give over their assault on Moll or his temper will be even worse than it is.

26 *mermaid*: commonly slang for 'whore'. Tim's description of Moll as half-maid, half-fish emphasizes 'translation' here (literally, 'being carried over')—'death by water' begins a process of spiritual renewal.

30 *Either . . . over*: both of you stop berating Moll or I won't marry her.

31–2 *Why . . . deservèd*: Sir Walter uses exaggeratedly gallant language in asking Moll why she has so used him, and what he has done to deserve such treatment.

32 *fondly*: indulgently (with the implication 'foolishly' but Yellowhammer still has to choose his words carefully with Sir Walter).

33 *We'll . . . all*: We shall do things differently and forestall all other possibilities.

35 *trust to't*: trust to luck, allow things to go their own way.

43 *conquering metal . . . yet*: mighty weaponry, tutor, which has never yet lost a battle.

44 *Westminster*: the monuments in Westminster Abbey could be viewed for a penny. Henry V's armour had been stolen, so Tim may be thinking of Edward III's famous 7-foot sword, and typically getting it wrong.

49–50 *two . . . gold . . . maidenhead . . . forty*: the agreed dowry . . . pricing Moll's virginity as if it were on sale for prostitution.

51 *splits*: like a shipwreck.

54 *like . . . joys*: as my joys have already left me.

58 *have way*: get what I want.

59 *'twill . . . play*: your life will be at stake (in this game).

60 *at first*: (1) immediately; (2) at the formal first thrust—the moves in sword-fights had technical labels.

61–2 *There . . . pounds*: either Sir Walter acknowledges that there is no chance of negotiating and calls to mind the dowry to stiffen his resolve; or he asks Touchwood Junior if there is no chance of negotiating, offering to share the dowry with him.

62 *quit*: requited (the first wound). How badly each is wounded is not yet clear.

63 *even hand . . . play*: the sequence is shot through with gaming imagery. When each has wounded the other once (and so they are 'even'), Sir Walter withdraws.

65 *Before . . . further*: foreshadowing Sir Walter's religious doubts about duelling which surface in the next scene.

66 *ha"t out*: have it out, settle things.

5.1.3 *but*: nothing but.

5–6 *truss up . . . sheet with two knots*: pack up, settle (my) affairs . . . shroud, tied at head and feet.

15–16 *heave . . . is . . . left*: raise with effort . . . can you still remember?

34–7 *Some good . . . stays*: Sir Walter prays that someone will be kind enough to remove Mrs Allwit (now synonymous with his *sins*) from his sight.

43 *parts*: departs; Q: 'part'.

46 *thy instructor*: i.e. the devil.

51 *He . . . ever*: ironic, since this is usually said of sinners, not those repenting of sin.

57–9 *There's nothing . . . towards me*: there is only sexual passion in that sadness, you are weeping for lust; I sense it in the weakness of the spiritual comfort coming my way.

60 *shows*: looks.

62 *dalliance*: overindulgence.

64 *an't like your worship*: if it pleases your worship.

65 *last*: latest, with the implication that there could be more to come.

66 *my vengeance*: i.e. God's vengeance on me.

68 *darkens*: singular for plural. So also 'pleasures . . . hath poisoned', below.

70 *ho too*: Q, 'ho to', for which no compelling emendation has been suggested. It perhaps refers to a category of those 'Who see(s) me now', different from 'those so near me'—so a possible inference is 'God'.

73 *It*: 'my repentance'.

76 *What's he*: who.

78–80 *the round . . . soul for*: the whole earth distresses me (or: tastes bitter to me, a play on 'gall') now; its delightful delights for which I sold my soul have poisoned me.

81 *Make way . . . for me*: i.e. he hopes all his sighs will clear a path to heaven for him.

83 *hurts . . . wounds*: is making his wounds worse.

85 *death of seven*: (1) he has been the spiritual death of seven (his children by Mrs Allwit); (2) the seven have been the spiritual death of him.

93 *My . . . else*: 'will' also means 'lust', and it strikes Sir Walter how absolutely appropriate it is to write his last testament ('what else?').

99 *will*: playing on the sense 'it is what he wishes'.

100 *such . . . death*: he wants him to die a lingering death in utter misery.

103–4 *All . . . repentance*: he wishes on Mrs Allwit a lack of spiritual health ('joy', 'virtue', 'repentance') in terms echoing her sexual fruitfulness ('barrenness', 'drouth', 'dearth').

104 *for her end*: as to the means of her death (let it be).

106 *French and Dutch*: venereal diseases.

107 *Confusion*: ruin, perhaps with the specific sense of 'incest', a preoccupation of Middleton's. He wants her to see the consequences of her guilt as she dies, but to feel no remorse (*never shed a tear*), since he wants her to go to hell for it.

110–12 *Lift, lift . . . lifting*: a run of senses. Sir Walter asks to be lifted, both physically and spiritually. Allwit looks to the law to 'arrest' him instead, and declares that he has himself stopped robbing/helping/pandering for Sir Walter, who must now pay the penalty for what in law might be murder.

117 *tell yet*: she is worried that her husband is being precipitate. If Sir Walter is acquitted on grounds of self-defence he will lose nothing, so may still keep the Allwits.

120 *Hear a fool! . . . lands . . . him*: Listen to a fool talking! . . . Allwit cynically assumes Sir Walter's property will dispose the judge or the jury against him. As a murderer his lands would be forfeit to the Crown.

122 *would . . . well*: would like to see peace between you.

125 *close chamber*: small room, here privy ('place of easement'), used as an isolation chamber in times of plague. Sir Walter almost shares the fate of Dapper in Jonson's *The Alchemist* (1610), to be shut away in the house's most unsavoury room, a hell on earth, but Allwit denies him even that small comfort.

135 *undoes you . . . All ill*: denies you the inheritance of the Kixes . . . every misfortune.

140–1 *Good ... were ... officers*: it would be good if ... of the watch.

142 *I'll ... labour*: I'll shortly save you the bother (because I shall leave and/ or die).

148 *in ... extremity*: so close to death (the unintended implication being that she would never defy any man who was *not* so afflicted).

150 *Gamesters*: (1) gamblers; (2) lechers. This is how he now sees the Allwits, and he no longer wants to 'play' with them. Also a farewell to the 'gamesters' in the audience.

152–3 *head ... like ... all*: chief ... likely to lose everything.

159 *the Strand*: the most fashionable quarter of Jacobean London.

161 *bay-windows*: there was a fashion for cushions in parlour windows, but there are hints (*quaint* = 'cunt', as well as 'costly, fashionable') that Allwit has a high-class bordello in mind for these rich furnishings, supplied by Sir Walter. This is presumably what the Allwits 'were wont' to do before Sir Walter came along.

164 *close-stool*: commode, portable toilet (the unsavoury qualities of which are picked up in the suggestion of Allwit's nose being in everything).

167 *let ... stand*: let this motto be posted.

169 *box*: the implication is something like the modern maxim, 'the house always wins', in gambling, though 'box' may also evoke 'coffin' (and 'close-stool').

5.2.1 *she*: Moll, who has taken a chill from falling in the Thames.

  3 *in compass*: in the space.

  6 *curb ... humour*: rein in her wilfulness.

  7 *How now*: greeting, implicitly asking 'what are you up to?'

10–11 *means ... 'tis done*: is likely/intends ... may allude to a childish game, like 'consequences'.

13–14 *principal ... Culled ... 'de Tristibus'*: especially choice ... chosen out of Ovid's *Tristia* (a book of five mournful poems, commonly a textbook).

16 *white money*: silver, so a deterioration from gold.

19 *made*: written.

21 *get*: beget (a poem).

25 *worst ... pearl ... amber*: cheapest, least expensive ... believed to have great medicinal properties, in proportion to their rarity and expense.

27 *timely*: early, as opposed to the love that came too late.

30 *cast away*: wasted. Yellowhammer is not so grief-stricken as not to reflect on the waste of his money on the medicine.

32 *wilt ... think*: can't imagine.

33 *strive ... fit*: (1) struggle with your depressed condition; (2) do your best

with a song (music was thought to have strong therapeutic powers).

34 *You . . . goodwill*: i.e. I shall do the best I can.

45 *swan*: swans proverbially sang only before they died.

46 *By . . . leave*: with your permission. A polite way of butting into a conversation.

51 *dear*: (1) sweet; (2) costly.

65–6 *perform it . . . following*: i.e. the business of delivering the letter . . . one which shows her death will soon follow his.

69 *what . . . mean*: a polite protest, implying 'How generous'.

70 *How cheer . . . of you*: How do you feel? Your news will tell me.

72 *where . . . satisfaction*: whatever the letter leaves out.

75 *contented health*: common euphemism for death, though not so categorical that Moll cannot derive comfort from his equivocation.

81 *Look . . . up*: If you will look up only once.

88 *reward . . . thee*: gifts to the other servants were a ruse, to make it less suspicious when he makes a gift (with a letter) to Susan, who has been in Moll's confidence.

97 *private*: secret.

99 *We'll . . . catch*: the Yellowhammers take some comfort in what they think will still be a rich match for Tim, despite the loss of the alliance to Sir Walter.

5.3.2 *bestirred my stumps*: been busy, with innuendo of his own sexual potency.

4 *bells*: church bells were rung, and bonfires lit, to proclaim particularly important events, like the arrival of the Spanish Armada in 1588.

8 *monstrous*: out of proportion.

14 *land . . . after*: the land that would have gone to Sir Walter will now stay in the family (making a *poor Sir Walter* who has lived on the credit of his expected inheritance).

16 *struck it home*: struck the winning blow, with obvious bawdy innuendo.

20–3 *There's such . . . wet eyes*: the servant paints a picture of a romantic double death which has become the talk of the town, drawing throngs of sentimental mourners.

23 *helps the number*: increases the number of mourners.

28 *monopoly*: allusion to the royal practice of granting exclusive commercial rights to individuals and companies, much criticized in later Jacobean Parliaments.

30 *cast*: arranged.

5.4 S.D. *Recorders*: the most common woodwind instruments of Jacobean times, frequently mentioned in plays. The reference to the 'music-room' confirms that The Swan had this facility, a separate space for a consort of musicians.

S.D. *decked*: arrayed, probably in black.

S.D. *epitaphs*: presumably those of Tim and the Tutor. Epitaphs were pinned to notables' coffins as a mark of respect, but it was unusual for someone of Moll's status.

2 *From . . . parent*: since Adam's death.

2–3 *let the . . . hearts*: a challenge, implying that the world *cannot* bring one forth.

5 *censure*: judgement.

7 *delivered to*: (1) reported to; (2) surrendered up to the judgement of.

12–13 *monument . . . deface*: he compares her enduring reputation ('living name') to a memorial which time cannot deface.

15–17 *What nature . . . glorious*: what quality could shine, to redeem woman to the state of perfection before the Fall, but that it shone most gloriously in her?

18 *that . . . infixed*: since that jewel ('beauty') was so mounted ('in goodness') —the image harks back to the ring Yellowhammer was tricked into making for them.

20 *precedents*: exemplars. There was nothing lacking in the lives of these examples of virtue to prevent them becoming man and wife.

S.P. *ALL*: So Q marks all interjections by mourners who do not otherwise speak. They should be variously assigned.

29 *Here's . . . friends*: everyone here is a friend.

30–1 *stand from . . . this time*: give them room. If she's caught again, after this opportunity.

33 *at a push*: when things were most critical. He is referring to Susan.

33–4 *Good sir, apace . . . forever*: Q assigns this to Touchwood Senior, but most editors agree it is a more appropriate line for his brother . . . see note to 3.1.16.

38–9 *article . . . interline*: legal detail or item necessary for the contract . . . write between the lines (to supply the missing *article*).

40 *trolled*: spoken rapidly. He admires the Parson's panache.

42–3 *To you . . . wedding sheets*: a toast or blessing . . . the shrouds.

45–6 *wants utterance . . . Utter*: is beyond speech . . . (1) express; (2) ejaculate.

49 *now . . . house*: now you are to be mistress of your own house.

53–4 *ask . . . discourse . . . wrought . . . cunningly*: require an hour's talking . . . cleverly managed everything to this end.

57 *prevent*: anticipate. Yellowhammer confounds everyone's expectations by expressing his joy that they are both alive and married.

60–1 *knight's . . . arrant baggage*: Sir Walter has . . . notorious strumpet.

64 *Next to his heart*: (1) closest in love; (2) on an empty stomach, fasting.

68 *knight's ward*: there were four wards in the London Counters (debtors' prisons), depending on payment: the master's, the knight's, the two-penny, and the hole.

74 *For . . . frowns*: because of the world's disapproval.

76–7 *Say you . . . at a birth*: do you really mean what you say, sir? Put me to the test with triplets.

78–9 *Take . . . weapon*: Touchwood Senior turns the language of 'daring', associated with duels, to that of sexual weaponry.

80 *saw*: Q 'say', the old form.

84 *O . . . O mors*: Tim essays Cicero's great lament (*O tempora! O mores!*— O times! O manners! *Catiline*, I i.) but botches the Latin as usual: *O mors*—O death.

85 *jade*: (1) worn-out horse; (2) whore.

86 *to execution*: to pay off her debt to me.

85–8 *jade . . . horse-races . . . serve to carry*: riding metaphors, all suggesting that he intends to hire her out for sexual purposes.

94 *Flectere . . . mourbo*: Since I cannot move those above, I shall work on the nether regions—that, at least, is what Tim *means* to quote (Virgil, *Aeneid*, vii. 312), though he gets some of the words wrong.

104 *Uxor . . . falacis*: A wife is not a whore, therefore you lie (or words to that effect).

105–6 *Sir . . . me honest*: the Welsh Gentlewoman's point is that a wedding certificate is all the evidence of good character she needs.

109–10 *print . . . whore . . . Latin*: spelling . . . Latin for whore is 'meretrix', sounding like 'merry tricks' in English.

112 *upon—*: lacuna in Q. See note to 3.3.115. There is almost certainly an allusion to the Gentlewoman's *mons veneris*, but it is either censored, cut short by Yellowhammer, or left to the audience's imagination.

116 *Goldsmiths' Hall*: Hall of the Goldsmiths' Company, in Foster Lane, off Cheapside, and so only just round the corner from the play's fictional space. But the audience of gallants at The Swan were some way away, south of the river, and not in a position to accept Yellowhammer's invitation. So Middleton wittily offers to bring together the fictional London of the play and the actual London of its reception, but in a way that underlines the impossibility of doing so.

Women Beware Women

Preface

Preface: by the publisher, Humphrey Moseley in the 1657 Octavo edition (O).

  1 *these*: O contained *More Dissemblers Besides Women* with *Women Beware Women*.

  6 *ingenious*: intelligent. Moseley claims that works by Middleton published earlier have met with a ready welcome among discriminating readers.

  8 *recreative spirits*: minds looking for recreation.

Commendatory Verses

  2 *Drabs . . . vexed*: high-class whores, aggrieved.

  10 *in state*: with pomp and ceremony.

  12 *Nathaniel Richards*: poet and playwright, flourished 1630–54, author of *The Celestial Publican: a Sacred Poem* (1630) and *The Tragedy of Messalina, the Roman Empress* (pr. 1640). That he was a 'familiar acquaintance' of Middleton (d. 1627) and saw the play in performance links the printed text, its writing and stage history.

The Characters of the Play

Characters . . . Play: based on the list in O.

  9 *factor*: merchant's agent.

  13 *Bianca*: O reads 'Brancha' throughout, apparently a misreading of the manuscript copy. Metrically the name requires three syllables; ironically, it means 'white'. The character is based on Biannca Capello, born in Venice in 1548, who eloped with a Florentine, became mistress of Francesco de' Medici, and died in 1587.

    States: nobles.

1.1.3 *comfort . . . express*: pleasure/relief of your return . . . root sense of 'press out', 'distil'.

  5 *curse . . . sorrows*: labour of childbirth.

  8 *speak to me*: affect me.

  12 *purchase*: acquisition, with possible implication of theft.

  21 *two knots*: traditional fastening of the shroud, at head and feet, e.g. depicted in John Donne's deathbed portrait. Leantio is waxing sententious about life and its terrors.

  25 *mark*: example.

  26–7 *able . . . content*: Alexander the Great was said to have wept when there were no new worlds for him to conquer.

351

27 *in compass*: within limits. Leantio claims that Bianca's beauty keeps him from thoughts of adultery.

32 *handsomely*: properly (though with a hint of boasting).

33 *only . . . faces*: common Jacobean complaint about false motives for church-going.

35–6 *sin . . . with me*: i.e. more than original sin.

37–8 *theft . . . withal*: as noble a theft as ever a great man rose by.

40 *Though . . . death*: cf. Romans 6: 23: 'the wages of sin is death'.

46 *keep counsel*: keep it secret.

56 *too blame*: see Glossary, under 'blame'.

57 *If . . . check*: if your obedience will allow a rebuke.

60 *At . . . time*: in the fullness of time. Leantio has married Bianca without the consent of her rich parents and so lost the dowry that would have kept her in fine style.

62 *death . . . hopes*: he cannot expect to inherit much.

63–4 *means . . . single*: your income has barely supported you as a single man.

67–70 *Which . . . humours*: the Mother argues that all women seek at least to be kept in the condition to which they were born, and that most aspire to something better, swayed by desires, wishes, and whims.

69 *conditions . . . births*: circumstances, abilities, families, social standing at birth.

71 *spoil*: corrupt. He is worried that she is putting ideas in Bianca's mind.

73 *have . . . marvel*: shall be much surprised.

76 *commotion*: rebellion.

78 *once up*: once they have the upper hand.

80–1 *spirits . . . laid*: demons easily summoned but not so easily laid to rest again (but also *laid* = bedded).

83 *simple charge*: (ironic) a costly business.

84 *So ever . . . courses*: it's always (expensive) like that . . . personal actions.

90–1 *keep close . . . go . . . ability*: stay secluded at home . . . live at a rate I can afford.

93 *school-fellows*: O gives a comma, not a stop. He surely means to contrast Bianca's new intentions with the *licentious swinge* of some of her old school-fellows.

94 *sampler*: piece of embroidery used as a pattern; i.e. she will follow another example.

95 *frame the fashion*: (1) set a fashion; (2) shape the semblance.

100 *fruitful . . . wombs*: *fruitful bags* = money bags. Sterile riches/fertile poverty is a common theme. Cf. the Kixes and the Touchwood Seniors in *Chaste Maid*.

104 *perfect*: (1) contented; (2) past it.

108 *business*: with a pun on *business* = sexual intercourse.

110 *salute*: kiss.

114 *Due . . . nearness*: because I know how closely related you are.

116 *challenge*: lay claim to.

118 *few . . . mend it*: few 60-year-old mothers will improve on it.

120–1 *we are . . . welcome worth*: we are very needy and cannot give a proper welcome to people of substance.

121–2 *scurvy . . . teeth*: shabby and spoken as if a woman was toothless. The disease of scurvy leads to teeth loss.

125 *Kind*: this ends the first of several long on-stage silences in the play. What has Bianca been doing all this while? Has she heard and responded to the conversation? Readers and performers must decide. *Kind*—'natural' as well as 'considerate'—introduces a crucial theme to the play.

127–30 *Heaven . . . here*: if Heaven will allow me to live quietly with this man's love I shall be as rich as the virtuous can be poor, and that suffices—for our emotional and spiritual lives—to allow me to build sacred places of happiness here.

133 *successes*: fortunes, good or bad.

136 *has . . . sorts*: receives all sorts of people.

147 *turn . . . glass*: turn over the hour-glass (i.e. double the time).

150 *voice . . . me*: i.e. my own mother's voice.

152 *care . . . factorship*: (1) self-regard; (2) conscientiousness . . . work as a merchant's agent/clerk.

156 *leave her | Still*: so O, though both lines are metrically irregular. The extra stress on 'Still' emphasizes Leantio's reluctance to leave her sexually undisturbed so long, and also (*still* = always) his recognition that this will be repeated every week.

158 *After . . . course*: in the manner of.

163 *pride*: as often in Middleton, the word hints at sexual desire, lust in the blood.

165–6 *policy . . . places*: Jacobean commonplace about Italian husbands' treatment of their wives (cf. Corvino in Jonson's *Volpone*). *policy* = prudence, shrewd tactics.

168 *stick*: scruple.

1.2.3 *ward*: orphaned children of gentry became wards of the king. They were usually farmed out to someone, who would control (and profit

353

from) the ward's estates until he came of age at 21. A guardian might propose a suitable marriage, and levy a fine on the estate if the ward refused. But he was not liable if the prospective bride refused.

4 *time . . . me*: his guardianship, and the profits he derives from it, are almost at an end.

5 *moral*: (1) traditional, customary; (2) proper.

7–8 *I'd . . . elect . . . fair*: I'm disposed to choose . . . (1) clear; (2) pleasant.

10 *hanselled*: a 'hansel' is a New Year's gift, so ironic: 'that would be a fine present!'

12–13 *meridian . . . take*: highest point of achievement . . . catch.

17 *fools . . . foolish*: proverbial.

26 *reason . . . pleasure*: Isabella is asked to choose between her reason and Fabritio's pleasure, not her own. The limits of a father's authority over his daughter in choosing a husband was a subject of much Jacobean debate, and a recurrent theme in the drama.

34 *Counting*: considering.

37–8 *the . . . goes . . . observance*: matters (esp. sexual matters) have turned out . . . duty, obligation.

40 *sundry dishes*: i.e. men have wider experience of the world than women, but their sexual misdemeanours are overlooked where women's are not.

48 *blown*: full-blown (i.e. past it), like a flower (in contrast to 'bud').

54 *counsellor | Has*: lawyer who has.

55 *soon parted*: proverbial: 'a fool and his money are soon parted'.

56 *Light . . . brother*: it is not clear what *Light* means here, and Guardiano is not Fabritio's brother. It may be jocular encouragement of Fabritio in his battle of wits with Livia—*Light* = 'alight, settle on' and *brother* expresses male solidarity.

60 *stop*: pause, reflect.

61 *new-found land*: may refer to Newfoundland, where colonies were settled in 1610, 1617 and 1618. But other American colonies, especially Virginia, were more newsworthy enterprises. Marriages in such places were often hastily arranged.

62 *Look . . . her*: Find her uncle and you are sure to find her.

65 *walk . . . sleeps*: they walk instead of sleeping.

66–7 *those . . . in'em*: i.e. sleepwalkers.

71–2 *clean wrought . . . stranger things*: perfectly made . . . men and women not related.

76 *mean*: intend.

80 *tongues*: gossip.

85 *bushels*: ironically invokes the proverbial idea of hiding a light under a bushel (a large pile of anything). The Ward's stupidity is hidden under a great deal of money.

86 *foul . . . him*: some portion of the Ward's anatomy, probably his arse, may appear before the rest of him—an earnest of the descent into farce while he is on.

87 S.D. *trap-stick*: (also called cat-stick, below) cudgel used in the rural game of tip-cat to strike the 'cat' (a short piece of wood, tapered at both ends) and hit it again when it flew in the air.

89 *first hand*: first strike. The *him* may be the *ladies' tailor*, whom the Ward boasts of beating, though all his 'conquests' are probably fictitious.

90 *tailor*: tailors were proverbial cowards.

91–2 *beat . . . beating*: quibble on embroidering silk by beating gold and silver into it.

92–3 *tickled . . . tippings*: ironic understatement, 'thrashed' . . . the action of knocking the cat up in the air.

94 *on'em*: of them (the tippings—one of which apparently hit the child's head).

98 *get . . . furious*: make a profit (by selling) . . . impassioned.

99 *fair end*: favourable position in a game.

103 *chimney-corner*: with a play on *chimney* = cunt and *chimney-corner* = brothel.

104–5 *chimney-corner . . . coats*: an obscure piece of obscenity. *Cats* are whores, and those in love with them are said to sleep in the chimney-corner. *Burn* probably alludes to the effects of syphilis. Sordido links the Ward's love of childish games with sexual experience limited to whores.

109 *great*: fat/important.

110–11 *stoop gallantly . . . hole*: a range of obscure hunting and playing terms, all with bawdy innuendo: *stoop* = fuck; *pitch out* = ejaculate; *hole* = cunt.

111–12 *mar'l . . . have . . . bout*: marvel . . . fornicate.

112 *contract*: go through the forms of a marriage pre-contract, held to be binding in the presence of a witness (though the witness he envisages is inanimate).

113–14 *fool . . . sack-posset*: fool is made with cream and fruit. A posset is curdled milk, here mixed with sherry-sack.

116–17 *prone . . . cock-horse*: i.e. to lechery . . . hobby-horse, with obvious bawdy innuendo, pursued in the next few lines. The Ward's insistence on his virility is unconvincing.

119–20 *eggs . . . cock*: supposed aphrodisiacs . . . (1) cockerel; (2) erect penis.

130 *liberty*: district within which a Justice of the Peace's warrant was valid.

133 *the . . . alters*: the ground changes.

135–6 *set by . . . Capitol*: in early Rome geese, sacred to Juno, were kept on the Capitoline Hill. Famously their cackling once warned soldiers of a surprise attack by the Gauls, but Middleton seems to invoke them as a familiar irrelevance.

138–9 *an honest . . . staff*: i.e. a pilgrim; or an old man who uses a stick, aware of his fading strength.

140–1 *You . . . it*: Livia's first four lines seem to be spoken after the departing Fabritio, though he is not expected to hear them. She then turns to Hippolito.

143 *dwell here*: (1) live here; (2) linger over (something unstated—presumably Hippolito). Livia may well kiss Hippolito here—at all events, the intensity of the sister–brother relationship is clear.

143–4 *seat . . . parts*: estate (figurative) . . . features.

149 *thy*: O, 'that'.

156–7 *honesty . . . so*: it is not clear whom Hippolito is addressing here— certainly not Isabella, possibly God or the fates, perhaps his 'sorrows'. The most intriguing possibility is that he is openly addressing and involving the audience.

162 *idolatry*: the worship of an idol, forbidden in the Bible. Her argument is that the Ward is no true man, only a badly made image of one.

164 *neither*: as well.

168 *portions*: dowries.

171 *lies in still*: remains in prison despite the bribe. Bribery of gaolers to receive preferential treatment was common.

172 *sometimes*: in O this is the first word of the next line, and there is no full-stop.

179 *four . . . elements*: the four elements were earth, air, fire, and water, constantly in conflict in the world (macrocosm) and in the little world of man (microcosm). Cf. Marlowe: 'Nature that framed us of four elements | Warring within our breasts for regiment' (*1 Tamburlaine*, 2.7.18–19). She suggests that providence finds a way to reconcile them, even though this defies reason.

197 *arguments*: discussion points.

200 *obstinate . . . forgetfulness*: a perverse, willed blindness.

206–7 *made profession . . . but profession*: swore . . . (but) it was only words.

214 *Though . . . venture . . . come nearer*: at the risk of blushing . . . be more explicit, but resonant (as *near* repeatedly is in the play) of sexual contact and familial proximity.

216–19 *Methought . . . welcome it*: an obscure passage. Isabella distinguishes between an intuitive premonition of unwelcome news and over-strong apprehension of it when actually heard. She bids to *prevent it* (anticipate it, meet it half-way, and so avoid the full realization), however painful, to *welcome it*, knowing she will never hear it again.

224 *such*: i.e. Hippolito.

1.3.7 *poor heads*: i.e. working people.

8–9 *stick . . . does game*: make them less adept at their work, just so does love-making.

12 *expenses*: both financial and sexual.

19 *begging . . . sooner*: being reduced to beggary . . . sooner than will happen anyway.

20 *a match*: agreed.

24 *Fondness*: infatuation is only a fool (*idiot*) compared with true love (*affection*).

25 *hot-cockles*: game like blind man's buff, but sexually suggestive. Leantio tries to convince himself these are foolish pastimes for someone with a fortune still to make.

27 *cracks*: i.e. because stuffed with goods.

47 *respective . . . increase*: pays due regard to future prosperity.

48 *good . . . peace*: perhaps a glance at King James's pacific foreign policy.

52 *bore double*: obscure. Leantio seems to suggest that his fertility is such that even horses he buys bear two foals. Or 'carried two riders' may allude to his sexual stamina, but also foreshadow a second 'rider' for Bianca.

56 *care . . . forward*: proverbial failing of the prodigal.

60 *that disease*: putting pleasure before work.

69 *in . . . fountain*: reflected in a fountain / in tears.

70–1 *dressing . . . water*: tending her hair by the reflection in a bowl of water.

73 *State*: collective singular for the nobility of the realm.

75 *standing*: place to stand. The Apprentice catches the sense of a sexual erection.

82 *solemnity*: festival.

84 *fifteenth . . . April*: the Feast of St Mark actually fell on 25 April in both the English (Julian) and continental (Gregorian) calendars. The one was ten days behind the other.

86 *'Twas . . . down else*: it's lucky you asked that question, I would have gone downstairs otherwise. (They are on the balcony, 'above'.)

88–9 *I would . . . sight*: I would rather have lost the chance to be ten years younger than to have had you miss the sight.

95 *greater . . . blood*: nobler in his piety than in his birth.

98 *Against*: in time for.

103 *reverence*: dignity.

108-9 *careful . . . minds*: one with cares and duties . . . pays attention to.

2.1.7 *point*: compass-needle, direction finder, but with a pun on *point* = penis.

12 *stranger*: a sexual partner who is not a blood relation.

12-14 *bounty . . . spare*: where greatness is measured by liberality, it is bad management to be frugal.

16 *That spares . . . stock*: who refuses what is freely given [i.e. all other women], and sexually consumes his own line/kindred. She counsels him to sow his wild oats elsewhere in order to forget Isabella.

17 *sowed up*: variant of 'sewed up', meaning 'neatly encapsulated'.

19 *venture . . . change*: hazard (as always in the play a mercantile metaphor) . . . a stronger term than today, suggesting disaster or calamity.

22 *Under . . . leave*: under a reprimand, and I'll give it up.

24 *passion*: suffering.

26 *Thou keepst*: you preserve (in yourself).

28 *ministered*: Livia evokes both religion and medicine, with herself as priest/doctor.

29-30 *'tis but . . . virtue*: it's only a matter of putting at risk grace and integrity.

33 *perfect*: complete, satisfied.

34-5 *I would . . . win*: I wish that love of yours was staked on this gamble, and that you could lose it as readily as I could win hers for you.

36 *give . . . a lift*: make as cunning (depraved?) an attack on.

39 *fling*: unseat. An image from jousting, picking up 'lift'.

43-4 *handsome . . . praise me*: decent. Once you've tested what I can do, then praise me.

48 *cordials*: medicines for the heart.

54-5 *'Death . . . sealed*: by God's death . . . confirmed.

59 *'lighted*: arrived.

60 *bless . . . simple*: a much-disputed passage. O reads 'bless; you simple', which leaves 'bless' hanging ('you' understood) and has Livia addressing the servant as 'you simple' (blockhead), as my punctuation more emphatically does. Possibly Middleton wrote something like 'your stars bless you simply; lead her in'. My version signals Livia's often disguised arrogance and short temper.

65 *fondest . . . affect*: most foolish . . . love.

70–1 *liberal* . . . *ease*: (1) over-generous; (2) licentious . . . comfort, pleasure.

72 *if you question*: Livia acknowledges the involvement of the audience.

80 *make* . . . *shift*: get by well enough.

81 *he's a* . . . *in't*: he's a congenital idiot, he limps to a full stop at being a fool.

85 *Let't appear*: make it apparent (don't keep it to yourself).

91 *in* . . . *fashion*: as if from someone not a relative.

92 *It* . . . *match*: there is something within my breast which would thwart this marriage.

99–100 *sister* . . . *'twixt* . . . *eyelids*: sister-in-law . . . in my mind's eye.

108 *Not wronging*: which did not harm.

109 *fruitfulness*: O, 'fruitness'. She swears by her desire eventually to have children.

111 *once*: ever.

122–3 *that* . . . *you* . . . *cheer*: that you like . . . basic provisions (as distinct from a full meal). Livia tantalizes her with incomplete information.

125 *deal plainlier*: explain yourself more clearly.

127 *that* . . . *start*: something which would startle.

128 *How* . . . *silence*: how can I be sure of your good faith and silence?

129 *mercy*: i.e. divine mercy.

131 *how* . . . *good*: however much common usage has approved.

136 *courtesy* . . . *opinion*: i.e. people are respectful enough to assume that Isabella's mother was faithful to her husband.

140 *so* . . . *odds*: that much distance (in relationship).

143–5 *Did never* . . . *wonder*: convoluted sentence, emphasizing *wonder*. The framework is 'Did never the report . . . fill your ear . . . your time was ripe for understanding [i.e. you became an adult]'. She intends to impress Isabella with the name of *Coria*, which may allude to one of the actual holders of that title, the Dukes of Alva, like Fernando Alvarez de Toledo (1507–82) who ruled the Netherlands for Philip II of Spain.

152–3 *end* . . . *friend*: i.e. death . . . i.e. the Marquis.

155 *It had* . . . *else*: if she had not been so moved by pity it would have been a long time (i.e. until she was dying herself) until she revealed the secret.

158 *whom* . . . *father*: i.e. Fabritio.

160 *largeness*: scope, opportunity.

162 *father*: appear to be father of, and pay for.

163 *wench*: without its modern condescending inflection (e.g. serving-wench), this might be a term of endearment. But Livia uses *wench* often, especially with the Mother, and there is scope for less charitable resonances beneath apparent goodwill.

165–6 *of a . . . people . . . great canopy*: for the flawed folk we are . . . the heavens.

175 *hope . . . pity*: hope of my help and friendship again.

182 *know myself*: ironic, in that she has just lost all knowledge of her actual self.

186 *favours*: love tokens.

197 *edge . . . affection*: makes desire sharper. This reintroduces the language of food, which is usually indistinguishable in the play from that of sex.

213 *compass . . . either*: manage . . . equally readily.

214–15 *none . . . enough. So*: no fool can be wrong now if he is stupid enough. As long as.

215–16 *discretion . . . Desert . . . judgement*: all qualities of Hippolito.

217–18 *housekeeper . . . fare*: someone who runs a household . . . eat.

227 *Though . . . on't*: although you are a stranger (not actually a member of her family) yourself, and do not know it.

231 *she*: Livia.

233 *strange*: picking up Isabella's 'make our love no stranger'. Note how often the play contrasts kind/natural with strange/unnatural (the latter associated here with devilish black arts, of which one with no name was the most terrible).

2.2.1–2 *How . . . set forth, spied from*: an interjection, like the modern 'What' . . . described, seen at.

3–4 *Sunday . . . supper*: she was probably sometimes invited to these meals, a charitable act to a poor neighbour.

6–7 *prime gallant . . . follow . . . leader*: most handsome person (used of either sex) . . . are as attractive as the face.

9–10 *admiration . . . single*: wonder (cf. 'admired Miranda' in *The Tempest*) . . . only experienced by one person.

12 *draw in*: withdraw.

15–16 *tax . . . folly*: mock his enthusiasm for being foolish about something undeserving.

18 *best piece*: highest achievement.

22–3 *but . . . worth . . . work . . . peace*: highly valuable . . . help him achieve satisfaction.

25 *second*: help.

28–9 *fail . . . All means*: let you down in your plan (may) all means.

35 *absolute*: perfect.

39 *waits*: awaits.

360

42 *court passage*: a gambling game with dice, implying 'court intrigue'.

44 *alteration*: Fabritio means he has news that Isabella has changed her mind. Guardiano chooses to misconstrue it as Fabritio's own change from folly to wisdom.

48 *Another yet*: mocks the redundancy of a *new* change. It may refer to the 1609 New (Ex)change, which many thought unnecessary, given Gresham's Royal Exchange.

54 *gets before*: goes ahead of.

56 *smell*: predict.

61 *I . . . handsome*: I guarantee she will be beautiful.

67 *halter*: noose, for hanging or for leading a horse. It is an anagram of 'lather' and there is a play on lather/leather, of which a halter might be made.

69 *tricks*: trinkets.

72 *After*: at the rate of.

74 *let . . . vein*: metaphor from the old medical treatment of blood-letting, meaning that Livia is precisely right about Fabritio's 'condition'.

79 *world's end*: (being a fool is) all they are capable of; sums them up.

s.d. *battledore*: small racket.

82–3 *There's . . . battledores*: almost certainly obscene. A pair of crossed battledores might represent testes, supporting a phallus.

86 *list*: please.

87 *asked*: O, 'ask', which might just reflect the Ward's slow wits. He confuses *ask* (as in 'propose to', or 'sexually proposition') with it in 'ask the banns'. Banns were normally 'asked' (or 'called') three times in the church before a wedding. If this was not done, a special licence was necessary.

90 *nose-gays . . . pottage*: bunches of sweet-smelling herbs or flowers . . . thick soup. The Ward imagines her blowing on it with her bad breath.

94–5 *plaguy guess . . . 'way*: shrewd judgement . . . an assertive interjection, like 'anyway' or 'whatever'.

98 *in rhyme*: Sordido debases the old medieval poetic tradition of the catalogue of ideal female beauty.

103 *pearl in eye . . . ruby . . . nose*: cataracts . . . red with a pimple or carbuncle.

104 *burn . . . cut . . . shows*: suggests venereal disease . . . the one allowed 'cut' is the cunt.

107–8 *plumped . . . hopper-rumped*: O, 'plump' . . . i.e. with protuberant buttocks. The hopper of a mill is shaped like an inverted pyramid, and has a to-fro motion Sordido associates with buttocks.

111 *splay-foot*: flat feet, clumsily turned outwards in walking.

114 *bump . . . belly*: be neither hunch-backed nor pregnant.

120 *naked on record*: precedent for her to be naked. The idea of potential husbands and wives seeing their suitors naked occurs in More's *Utopia* (1516).

123 *case*: (1) situation; (2) suit of clothes; (3) outer casing, i.e. bare skin.

125 *for . . . trick*: i.e. he will not pursue the idea if it means he has to strip as well.

127 *bum-roll*: hip-cushion to hold out a full skirt.

130 *Penthouse*: sloping roof attached to the wall of the main building, blocking the light. His point is that the customer cannot see what he is buying in these situations.

133–4 *rotten stuff . . . take*: rotten cloth, suggesting venereal disease . . . succeed.

138 *come at*: visit.

146 *society*: company.

150 *tongue-discourse*: the ability to make conversation.

152 *merrily*: O, 'meerly'.

155 *nine . . . thirty*: Middleton's own age in 1619/20.

157 *knights' wives . . . account*: O, 'Knights, Wives' . . . O, 'accompt'.

161 *friend*: lover.

171 *sojourners*: staying guests.

174 *forsworn*: Livia has already sworn that the Mother will stay for dinner.

S.D. *Table and chess*: apparently a reminder of a property needed shortly, though it may have been on stage some time (e.g. the Servant might bring it on when he ushers in the Mother). Perhaps Livia goes to it here as she begins to unfold her plot.

183 *charge*: responsibility.

192 *all . . . have*: all the responsibilities you have.

201 *men*: chessmen.

203 *will*: is determined to.

206 *gentlewoman*: Bianca's precise status as a 'gentlewoman' is repeated emphatically.

217 *stranger*: foreigner.

225 *carried . . . privately*: managed with absolute secrecy.

227 *heat . . . part*: the most demanding piece of your assignment. Guardiano takes *part* as 'theatrical role' and assures her he will not *be out* (forget his lines).

231 *by this*: by now.

238 *bounty*: hospitality, generosity.

240 *'mends*: amends.

244 *the . . . you*: your appearance.

246 *An . . . condition*: bad manners.

247–8 *humanity . . . your company*: common human feeling . . . i.e. the Mother.

252 *motioned of*: suggested by.

256 *profession*: (1) occupation (Guardiano as a professional guardian stands for the 'rights' of his wards); (2) assertion.

257 *intentions*: endeavours.

261 *old quarrel*: i.e. they have regularly played each other at chess.

264 *set . . . off*: incite us (to battle), let us extricate ourselves. Both expressions have sexual connotations, foreshadowing the other 'battle' to come.

275 *monument*: possibly a carved figure in wood or stone.

283 *grace . . . honour*: Gratiano anticipates his reward from the Duke for this subterfuge.

286–7 *w'are . . . you . . . seconds*: we will join you . . . assistants.

290 *rook*: chess piece now usually known as 'castle'. Also formerly known as 'duke' (see *A Game at Chess*).

293 *cunning . . . game*: skilful at the game. Livia's replies knowingly take up the unintended sense of *game* = amorous intrigue.

297 *black . . . mine*: the Mother touches Livia's king by mistake. This clarifies who has which colour.

298 *duke*: see note above. This emphasizes the parallel with the action upstairs.

300 *Your . . . itself*: the pawn, like Bianca, cannot retreat from danger.

302 *hold*: bet.

304 *saintish king*: as opposed to the (evil) black king.

307 *simplicity . . . one*: she rather obscurely pursues the betting theme. *Simplicity* (simple honesty) perhaps receives two blows for every one it gives, so is always worsted.

310–11 *livelier . . . Venice*: more life-like . . . Bianca's birthplace.

312 *Takes . . . part*: supports you.

S.D. *above*: on the same upper stage as Guardiano and Bianca.

319 *turtle*: turtledove, proverbial for timorous innocence.

321 *brightness*: beauty.

328 *in prison*: i.e. he is imprisoned by her charms, and would remain so if she escaped. The language of enthralment is probably reinforced by his physically holding her.

332 *have . . . leisure*: only take the time.

334–6 *The lifting . . . him*: raising your voice is like a man who promotes his enemy, only to find him then plotting by all means to undermine the one who advanced him.

345 *single comfort*: a poor comfort because solitary, with a play on *single* = unmarried.

346 *friend to*: lover in addition to.

349 *Make . . . with*: do not make me unafraid of.

350–1 *fear . . . health*: frighten . . . i.e. spiritual or moral health.

348–56 *Nor, great . . . to virtue*: a difficult passage. In essence Bianca says that she recognizes and respects the moral order (described in natural metaphors of weather and health) even if the Duke does not.

357 *affect*: am especially fond of, prefer.

369–70 *tree . . . fruit*: in alluding to the Fall, the Duke inadvertently casts Bianca as Eve and himself as the Serpent.

374 *necessities . . . merely*: i.e. Leantio, whose income will never run to luxuries . . . extremely.

380 *wise*: O, 'wife'.

386 *fetch . . . over*: get the better of you.

389 *meet*: (1) encounter; (2) grapple; (3) unwitting pun on 'mate'; (4) get even.

390 *blind mate*: in effect checkmate, but the attacking player has not appreciated her victory. Livia refers ironically to the *Mother's* blindness to the 'game' above.

394 *witty*: cunning or deceitful.

398 *flesh-fly*: blow-fly (part of the common Renaissance equation of sex and death).

400 *queasy*: (1) nauseous; (2) scrupulous. As with *stomach*, the term plays on the recurrent equation of food and morality.

402 *stay*: in the rarer sense of 'whet' rather than 'subdue'.

402–7 *Well, advancement . . . endure all*: Guardiano reflects on his own motives, looking for *advancement*. The *greater title* is presumably that of the pander, a *cross* he resolves to bear until something better comes along. The image of the crest is from heraldry, a device above the shield and helmet bearing an inscription (*title*).

410 *neighbours*: i.e. Livia herself, who continues to pretend friendship.

412 *time*: age.

415 *in's kind*: in his true nature.

418 *bless . . . blasting*: save me from a withering up (i.e. scandal).

420 *mildews . . . at's*: destructive fungi on plants (i.e. disease) . . . at his.

422–3 *why . . . that fair*: O, 'who' . . . i.e. her beauty.

425 *bane . . . broods*: poison . . . breeds, hatches.

426 *smooth-browed*: hypocritically unruffled.

432 *first-fruits*: normally an offering to God from the first harvest of the year.

433–4 *His weight . . . for use*: anyone who has sex with prostitutes, even after they have been corrupted, still commits a mortal sin.

436 *more*: more guilty are.

S.D. *He . . . traitor*: a proverbial expression. It has been associated with Henry II after the death of Thomas à Beckett and Henry IV after the murder of Richard II.

442 *so*: so long as.

443 *two feasts*: presumably the Duke's reward (granted) and Bianca's (denied).

448 *since*: in the time you have been away.

448–55 *That have . . . I rose*: Bianca's deep sarcasm is lost on the Mother.

459 *may't . . . forty . . . hence*: O, 'may' . . . i.e. if she has a child by the Duke.

463–4 *bawd . . . ass*: procuress, brothel-keeper . . . alluding to the Mother's stupidity.

466 *art*: Guardiano's *art* lies in *get*(*ting*) *before*, preparing the ground.

468–9 *want . . . use . . . sea-sick*: not being used to it . . . first sexual experience is likened to a sea-voyage (further metaphors of appetite, taste, and stomach for moral choice.)

474 *wormwood water*: extremely bitter drink, flavoured with the herb wormwood—the very opposite of *nectar*.

3.1.3 *She . . . abroad*: Bianca was only one day away from home.

5 *cheer*: entertainment.

10 *agreed long*: lived in harmony for a long time.

11 *quarter*: the year was divided into four quarters for legal and financial purposes.

13–14 *takes . . . disease*: the new disease catches hold. An unrecognized fever emerged in the late sixteenth century. Ben Jonson described its effects— violent headache, distortion of memory and judgement, serious impairment of all mental functions (*Every Man In His Humour*, folio text, ed. Herford and Simpson, 2.1.46 ff).

14 *likes*: pleases.

17 *Made . . . withal*: put up with.

19–20 *cushion-cloth . . . cut-work*: Bianca is asking for expensive decoration of walls and furniture. Cushion-cloth was a cushion covering, drawn work being 'ornamental work done . . . by drawing out some of the threads . . . so as to form patterns' (*OED*); *cut-work* was openwork lace, with the pattern cut rather than woven into the material.

23–4 *To spare you . . . of duty*: not to demand from you . . . as one's due.

25–6 *offered under . . . state's*: offered less . . . estate's.

29 *orange tawny*: a vibrant colour, often associated with courtiers, hence the sarcasm.

32 *Got . . . move me to't*: begotten . . . provoke me/mention it.

37 *white boys*: darlings, with a play on the whiteness of flour.

38 *bathes . . . flour*: a vision of extravagant luxury, the bean-flour to add whiteness.

40–1 *affect . . . After . . . princes*: express itself on a princely scale.

44 *stoop*: (1) fall down; (2) kneel for a blessing.

48 *To the end*: with the intention.

53 *maid*: girl, virgin.

59 *copy*: legal term from property rights. Bianca means she has a right and ability established from birth to *wrangle* (argue with force) her due.

62 *'Twere . . . quietness*: it would be none the worse for my tranquillity.

64 *subtlest*: most difficult to understand.

74 *once*: at once (or possibly 'once and for all').

76 *by . . . will*: if she had her way.

77 *pewterer*: worker in pewter, a cheap, inferior metal for cups, pans etc.

78 *the noise*: sounds supposedly heard by those about to die.

82 S.D. *Exit the Mother*: O is unclear about what happens to the Mother here, indicating neither an exit nor a re-entry (but nor does it supply a re-entry for Bianca, so this is not conclusive). She could stay on stage, neither seeing Leantio nor being seen by him, e.g. falling asleep in a corner. But Bianca and the Mother re-enter the dialogue and address Leantio at the same time, hence my stage-directions. Leantio's entry on to an empty stage is technically the start of a new scene.

90 *banqueting-house*: common feature of Jacobean formal gardens, often places of assignation (adding unintended irony to Leantio's analogy).

93 *pride*: splendour.

98–9 *goodly temple . . . rotting*: cf. Matthew 23: 27: 'Woe unto you, scribes and Pharisees, hypocrites! for ye are like unto whited sepulchres, which indeed appear beautiful outward, but are within full of dead men's bones, and of all uncleanness.'

100 *shrink . . . again*: (1) draw back from my excitement; (2) lose my erection. Leantio claims to prefer marriage over illicit sex, but it is clear that the latter excites him.

102 *I'm as well*: either 'I'm well advised to do so' or 'I'm as well as I was before' (i.e. I'm myself again).

108 *take care*: worry.

111 *this*: i.e. 'this [indifferent welcome] is'.

118 *yet*: even now, all of a sudden.

120–1 *disliked . . . content*: displeased . . . satisfaction (alluding to the Duke).

126–7 *tumbling cast . . . Methinks . . . mind*: wrestling throw . . . (1) nothing in this house pleases me; or (2) I do not like the location of this house.

128–31 *I'd . . . gallants*: what Bianca asks is the opposite of respectable. For a woman to show herself at the window in Renaissance Italy was the mark of a whore.

132 *another . . . stranger*: another inclination, a total stranger.

135 *Too . . . unseemly*: to be foolishly infatuated is as unbecoming.

146 *'tis*: O, 'till'.

150–1 *matter . . . toy*: occasion . . . trifle.

153 *pirates . . . stirring?*: pirates, anything happening? Pirates were a concern to all Mediterranean countries, and to English traders. In October 1620 Sir Robert Mansell led an expedition against them, with moderate success (see *A Game at Chess*, 3.1.83–6). Bianca only wishes to change the subject.

154–5 *yet . . . I had lied*: at this point . . . he would have thought I lied.

157 *strange . . . wont*: distant, not encouraging (cf. the play's strange/kind antitheses) . . . your usual behaviour.

159 *pigeon-house*: dovecot. The affection of turtle-doves was proverbial.

164 *French curtsy*: the French were mocked for over-elaborate manners. The sense of *French pox* (venereal disease) is doubtless also intended; syphilis causing stooping.

170–1 *fits him . . . catched*: gets back at him appropriately . . . caught (as in 'catch a cold').

176 *Howe'er . . . on me*: however much you chose just now to look coolly upon me.

194 *return it*: report it.

196 *What . . . other*: what is her other/last name?

207 *Knows me*: Bianca fears Leantio realizes the Duke 'knows her' in the carnal sense.

209 *work*: business.

211 *kept . . . close*: remained concealed indoors (not true, of course).

213 *gadding*: wandering idly, a supposed sign of wantonness in women.

214 *court-green*: where bowls were played, a popular courtly pastime.

367

216 *masks*: Italian women wore masks or veils for modesty outdoors.

224 *hard chance*: bad luck.

226 *riddance*: way of getting rid of the problem.

232 *apprehension*: knowledge, grasp of the matter.

233 *quickened*: (1) began; (2) became pregnant. The term betrays Leantio's anxiety. Bianca picks it up in *conceived*, which ostensibly means 'included within'.

244 *artificially . . . conveyance*: ingeniously, skilfully . . . (1) a secret passage; (2) deft subterfuge, sudden disappearance.

246 *Kept . . . manslaughter*: remained indoors to escape arrest for man-slaughter: an intriguing insight into the family's past. Leantio's respectability is always suspect.

249 *choke . . . up*: (1) imprison me totally; (2) suffocate me.

254 *banquet*: such meals could be substantial affairs, or lighter ones of sweet-meats only. The latter, obviously easier to stage, seems implied here and in the next scene.

266-7 *I'm . . . mind . . . handkerchiefs*: I agree with you . . . often used to carry choice items from a feast. Cf. the 'gossips' at the christening in *Chaste Maid* (3.2).

270 *colt in marchpane*: figure of a young horse in marzipan.

277 *to . . . colour*: i.e. to ripen.

288 *spends*: punning on the sense of sexual expenditure, ejaculation.

295-6 *issue . . . perfection*: children . . . conclusion, outcome.

298 *shift . . . too*: substitute another in your place (implying underhand deal-ing). There is a tension between Leantio and the Messenger, an honest citizen and little more than a servant—but with the authority of the court behind him.

300 *theft*: he assumes the Duke wants him for stealing Bianca away from her parents.

3.2 S.D. *banquet*: see Note to 3.1.254.

1 *gentlewoman*: i.e. Isabella.

10 *express*: show.

11-12 *mark . . . deft*: distinctive feature . . . petite.

13 *lusty . . . sprig*: large, flowering spray from a plant.

20 *asked*: see note to 2.2.87.

22 *I . . . rather*: i.e. leap upon the woman. Inane bawdy, as ever, from the Ward.

25 *ev'ry . . . too*: the Bible is ambiguous on whether God gave women souls,

a favourite Renaissance debating topic; cf. Donne's 'To the Countess of Huntingdon'.

28 *light . . . arms*: embrace me.

29 *a grudging . . . you*: a man with a grudge who will rebuke you.

31 *if . . . durst*: if it dared. She implies Leantio is overawed by the Duke and his Court.

36 *so . . . fasting*: so shameless when they have had nothing to eat/inflame their passions.

37 *parts*: qualities.

39–40 *since the . . . by any*: recently vacated by the death of the holder, filled by anyone. The place and appointment are both fictitious. The episode demonstrates how casually and cynically Court posts might be distributed.

40 S.P. *GENTLEMAN*: O, 'GENTLEMEN'.

46–7 *bit . . . stomach*: morsel to appease the hunger of a cuckold (i.e. buy him off).

50 *means*: benefit, advantage.

54–5 *eats . . . plague-sore*: eats heartily even though he shows clear signs of having the plague; i.e. he feels well within himself even though he is desperately sick.

56 *barren*: dull, stupid.

58 *And . . . misery*: Leantio has taken on the traditional role of the Jacobean malcontent.

67 *goodness*: kindness, gifts.

68 *ape's*: vulgar term of endearment. Leantio and Livia speak privately, as the Ward reminds us of his different agenda. But all business revolves around the Duke.

69–70 *almost . . . ten pence*: he is thinking of her as a small doll, sold for a derisory sum.

71 *simpers it . . . marmalade*: smiles affectedly . . . a fruit preserve, not necessarily made with oranges.

73 *gilded bull*: another gold-coloured marzipan figure, like ram and goat, with lecherous associations (see note to 3.1.270).

79 *unpledged*: untoasted. The convention is that the person toasted should not drink. Bianca pretends not to recognize the compliment.

81 *plead your benefit*: plead exemption from the law, as by Benefit of Clergy or Peerage.

83 *dry*: (1) thirsty; (2) sober; (3) sexually unstimulated.

84 *Venus*: in Renaissance astrology Venus represented 'warm and moist', so

Bianca should not be 'dry'. The Duke is putting his 'prize' through her paces with inconsequential banter to impress the court.

85 *'mends*: amends, reparation.

88 *poor thief*: i.e. himself, the poor man who *stole* Bianca originally, now ignored. Leantio and the Duke are now *near kin*, having both 'stolen' her.

94–5 *equal . . . met . . . weight*: exactly just . . . balanced out my sin in full measure (on the scales of justice).

96 *All . . . breast*: he claims to feel as Bianca's friends felt when he eloped with her.

99 *sat*: should have sat.

101 *rite . . . tender*: ceremony (O, 'right') . . . betrothal. It was a custom among the Italian privileged classes for such ceremonies to be performed before the ruler.

104 *stirring*: excitement, with sexual innuendo (see *stir*, l.111).

112 *What . . . up to . . . cat-and-trap*: what are his accomplishments and expectations . . . see 1.2.87 ff.

114 *wise-acres*: a wiseacre is a foolish person who wishes to seem witty or wise. There is no actual connection with acre = measurement of land.

117 *laid . . . provision*: i.e. arranged to have a lover in addition.

118 *Fools . . . summer*: puns on fool as a creamy dessert, liable to go off in the heat.

118–19 *such . . . whores*: i.e. such wives will not keep from becoming whores.

120 *sweet breast*: a pleasant singing voice. Bianca's later comments suggest the phrase was old fashioned.

121 *wisely*: (ironic) foolishly.

122 *pricksong*: written vocal music, the notes of which were 'pricked' on the paper, not left to the singer's invention. Cf. the bawdy punning on *prick* = penis, lost on Fabritio.

124–5 *rare . . . baggage*: talented . . . playful term for a young girl.

125–6 *swell . . . puffed up*: (1) with pride; (2) with child.

128 *of man*: O, 'of a man'.

132 *of themselves*: either 'left to themselves' or 'in themselves, innately'.

136–7 *I am . . . speak*: I am now unable to speak any language but that of love, as if I had never learned to talk.

140 *paint*: put on make-up. Jacobean literature is full of denunciations of cosmetics.

S.D. *Song*: the Song and the Ward's speech are printed side by side in O, to underscore the Ward's boorishness and the fact that he does not attend to Isabella's insults to him. He prefers an unaccompanied street ballad, full of rustic news.

146 *observance*: dutiful service.

148 *make . . . work*: fit to help a laxative do its job (with mild exertion).

148–9 *blood . . . cheek*: raise a blush in an old lady's cheek (i.e. these are the limits of his sexual energy and allure).

152 *compound with . . . kitlings*: kittens, with puns on *cat* = whore and *kit* = small fiddle . . . join with.

153 *breast*: see note to 3.2.120 Bianca understands only the modern anatomical sense.

157–8 *to . . . unvalued*: bestowed on . . . priceless.

162–3 *the less . . . practised*: the fewer qualities a woman shows off, the better practised they will be.

164 *keeps*: practises (as distinct from merely 'commending' it).

167 *This . . . common*: virtue that is merely professed is common.

174 *blood*: inclination.

175 *Let whoso . . . first*: let whosoever (O, 'who's') wants to, do so, I'll not start first. The Ward means 'start to dance', but Hippolito has already *begun first* in another sense, repeatedly evoked in the next lines.

176 *took . . . order*: made better plans. He has already 'danced' with her himself (cf. Guardiano's *take*).

178 *fine-timbered*: well-built.

182 *out*: i.e. out of my resolution.

183 *I . . . myself*: i.e. I stand more closely by my own decisions (than that).

189 *office*: duty.

192 *set 'em out*: display them.

193 *mad . . . necessitous*: furious . . . poor, needy (and so having to sell the horse).

196 *mars . . . S.D. honours*: injures . . . bows.

198 *are fortunate*: have a happy outcome.

201 *prick . . . praise*: praise for the highest excellence. *Prick* runs together three senses: (1) centre of the archery target; (2) choice ('pricked') from a list of names; (3) penis.

208 *hornpipe*: lively dance, not appropriate in such aristocratic company. The Ward unwittingly alludes to cuckold's horns he has acquired even before he marries.

209 *Well*: O, 'We'll'.

211–14 *measures . . . jig*: the *measures* was a slow and stately dance; the *cinquepace* a lively galliard; the *hay* a country dance with serpentine movements; the *round* a circling dance (linked here with soldiers who kept 'the round' of the watch); the *canaries* a quick Spanish dance, allegedly from the Canary Islands (like the sweet wine—hence *drunkards*); and the *jig* a lively dance, often associated with lewdness.

214 *You . . . you*: perhaps should be 'Your . . . your' (as in 'Your soldiers') but the Ward may embrace the audience (as *drunkards*, *whore*, and *bawd*) in his bit of business.

218 *by attorney*: by proxy.

223 *glory . . . by*: the ostentation of her sin consigns to oblivion.

224 *thing . . . make shift*: i.e. the Ward will barely manage. But Bianca picks up *shift* = chemise or undergarment (hence *ill-favoured*, bad-smelling).

231 *on*: of.

233 *My . . . loves*: a general formula of goodwill as the Duke prepares to leave.

239 *save . . . woman*: preserve people's faith in the loyalty of women.

242 *punishment of after-life*: damnation.

245–6 *mistook . . . were*: inappropriate, suffered in error . . . was meant to be.

249 *watched*: kept vigil.

256–7 *only . . . life*: designed solely for that embrace, to demonstrate how well art could imitate life.

259 *madder*: even more enthusiastic/frenzied.

262 *praise*: celebrate (i.e. the *better joys*).

263 *close*: secret, furtive—but also 'nearby', as Livia indeed is.

268 *counsel*: advice, support.

273 *doubtful*: uncertain.

276 *perjurious friendship*: *perjurious* = breaks its promises. This applies as much to Livia as to Bianca.

282 *y'had . . . her*: she only brought you a small dowry.

288 *beggars*: Bianca and all the demands she would make. Perhaps also children.

288–9 *that . . . else*: who would otherwise have lived comfortably purely on your bounty.

290 *heat*: (1) toil; (2) sexual excess.

292 *pitiful*: compassionate. Livia characterizes Leantio's regard for Bianca as a selfless devotion paid to womenfolk in general, which another woman must repay.

293 *whole sex general*: the whole generality of women.

296 *bears . . . to't*: considers it a duty.

297 *blow all fortunes*: whatever fate sends; or, however the wind blows.

300 *And . . . for't*: and you shall not worry in the least about it.

313–14 *take . . . strange*: ravish . . . not yet familiar and accepted.

314 *hearse*: ornamental wooden structure temporarily placed over the coffin in church.

317 *hard measure*: harsh punishment.

326–7 *his . . . truth*: i.e. the Duke's . . . faithfulness.

331–2 *be guilty . . . abusing*: i.e. in taking the captainship he has implicitly condoned Bianca's adultery with the Duke and taken on the dishonour (*abusing*) himself.

339–41 *A place . . . with't*: a distinguished position, I concede, but not well paid; what I earn as factor more than equals it.

343–4 *not fits . . . breeding*: i.e. the position does not suit him. It befits his determination but, born into the merchant class, he has not been brought up as a soldier.

352 *spitefully . . . up*: over-ardent or thwarted passion was said to dry up the life-blood.

354 *You . . . yet*: ironically recalls for the audience the circumstances of Bianca's betrayal.

363 *true substance*: reality (not a dream).

365–6 *gallanter . . . allow*: more fashionably . . . assign.

369 *constant stuff*: consistently coloured material, unlike (e.g.) shot silk, changeable when it moves.

3.3.6 *speak*: suggest, demonstrate.

12–13 *contract . . . dispatch*: betrothal . . . settle the matter quickly.

15 *purse pays*: see note on 1.2.3.

17 *shoot . . . bolt*: (1) make my decision; (2) engage sexually. The metaphor is from the crossbow, which fired bolts. These were used in fowling, firing blunt 'bird-bolts', hence Guardiano's *birding*, a term often used of the pursuit of women.

22 *woodcock*: simpleton (since woodcock were notoriously easy to snare).

23–4 *cried . . . eggs o'the'spit*: proclaimed lost by the town crier, like a small child . . . delicate business in hand.

37 *cater's*: person in charge of buying 'cates' (provisions). The point is that the Ward will only be paying to provide for what Hippolito actually enjoys.

38–9 *curious . . . nice professor*: fastidious . . . pedantic self-proclaimed expert.

43 *what*: not in O.

46 *crabbed*: begins a long quibble on crab = crab-apple, *verjuice* being an acidic sauce made from crushed crab-apple.

51–2 *once . . . meat . . . mustard*: now . . . apparently proverbial for a feigned penance. The Ward, however, thinks he is making a real threat.

56 *enter upon*: (1) claim possession of; (2) penetrate sexually.

58 *comfit . . . shop*: comfits were spicy sweetmeats and the shops where they were made naturally sweet-smelling, unlike the streets where all manner of rubbish lay and rotted.

61 *danger . . . wits*: (1) I shall indeed run mad for you; (2) I shall be in danger of losing my mind, marrying you.

62 *For . . . forward*: a third way in which she might lose her wits—in being so *forward* with/close to the *ass*/Ward she is in danger of having her head kicked.

63 *hair . . . own*: venereal disease made the hair fall out.

65 *'Tis . . . hearing*: that's good to hear.

68 *last*: shape (cf. cobbler's last).

70–3 *strong bridge . . . once*: the running sub-text here is syphilis, to which *camp* followers were especially prone. It could eat away the nose.

75 *bate . . . tooth*: accept one tooth less than normal.

83 *two . . . lap*: the 'balls' she has caught are Hippolito's. Note how she dies (5.2.117).

84–6 *trap . . . bring . . . to*: the game of cat-and-trap . . . train me in.

92 *scurvy . . . handkerchief*: Isabella is 'mannerly' and covers her mouth.

98 *gamesters*: sexual athletes.

101 *splay-footed*: with feet pointing outwards, taken as the mark of a witch.

104–5 *cleanly shift . . . dab down*: neat trick . . . duck down flat.

109 *scaffolds*: temporary tiered seating to view processions etc. Under these Sordido would have an uncommon view of ladies' legs.

113–14 *get . . . stomach . . . fall to*: work up an appetite for love/lust . . . (1) descend to the level of; (2) feed off.

115 *clean-treading*: straight-walking (but also *tread* = copulate).

118–19 *ropes . . . rushes*: tightropes, at which the French were particularly adept . . . used as floor-coverings.

123 *simple . . . kind*: great . . . true to type (continuing the strange/kind antithesis).

124 *breed . . . teeth*: alludes to the idea that husbands of pregnant women develop 'sympathetic' toothache.

131 *break . . . action*: cannot suffer in a better cause (with a play on *nose* = penis, which will either be inflamed or rendered impotent by the drink).

4.1.1 *How . . . now*: the unreliability of personal clocks and watches, which were newish inventions, became a metaphor for unruly sexual behaviour (mainly female) in several plays, e.g. *Love's Labour's Lost* ('A woman, that is like a German clock . . .' 3.1.185–8) and Dekker's *2 The Honest Whore*, with a passage very like this one (3.1.108–27).

3 *St Anthony's*: there is a St Mark's Church in Florence, but no St Anthony's.

8 *sun*: i.e. the Duke, though his association with the sun is highly suspect.

13–15 *And too . . . work too*: much bawdy play on analogies with genitalia—*dial's point* (male), *spring* (female).

15 *wants . . . nine*: is shortly before nine.

17 *advocate*: lawyers are professional 'liars', so they are both faulty *clocks*.

21 *one . . . other*: somebody.

24 *This . . . to me*: everything that has happened is the most unlikely fate to befall me.

28 *when they . . . my hap*: when I was in their sight. Yet it is my fortune.

30 *in sadness*: seriously.

33 *flesh stirring*: (1) the renewed sale of meat; (2) sexual activity.

39 *fetch . . . about*: take a very roundabout course to fall into sin.

43–4 *simply . . . first*: absolutely . . . when they first eloped (see 1.1.49–50).

46 *silk-worm's*: mocking Leantio's new dandyish silk clothes.

48 *legs*: polite bows, but also third leg = penis, which Bianca picks up in *service* = (1) deference; (2) sexual satisfaction.

51 *wondrous brave*: splendidly dressed.

54 *proud*: magnificent.

57 *spurs*: a mark of distinction, but again with bawdy quibble (= testicles), which Bianca picks up in *ride* (= have sex).

62 *impudent*: shameless.

70 *pass that*: (1) surpass that charity; (2) pass by (Bianca's) door.

72 *erected . . . love*: (1) built charitable institutions; (2) aroused phalluses.

76 *plagued home*: punished with the very disease with which she infected others.

78 *friend*: lover.

79 *There's . . . suckling*: her devil is the Duke, characterized as a familiar spirit. Such spirits were supposedly suckled by a witch—here implicitly Bianca.

80 *breed teeth*: cut his teeth/become dangerous.

82 *great one*: the real devil, Lucifer.

84–5 *drive . . . kennels*: metaphors from greyhound coursing; *course* is a pack, *kennels* are lairs.

87 *know*: O, 'knew'.

91 *moon . . . so*: Bianca probably makes the sign of a horned moon on her forehead, reminding Leantio of his cuckoldry.

92–3 *put to't . . . all forehead . . . eyes*: troubled . . . all effrontery and no moral sense.

95 *as much*: [it is] as much.

99 *feel . . . hardness*: i.e. because they bump into them.

111 *rail*: (1) array (his clothes); (2) be abusive.

123 *Should . . . copy . . . not*: if he followed the example in the copy-book . . . i.e. not happen. Copy-books were used to teach penmanship.

126 *take . . . for't*: don't worry about it.

131–2 *He is . . . sudden*: his passion is soon aroused, and as quick as he is to feel an affront, he's bold and impetuous.

136 *goodness*: benefaction.

137 *now . . . practise*: previously thought of, but never intended to put into practice.

138–9 *base . . . drives him . . . poise*: corrupt, and that will motivate him . . . weight.

142–3 *lusty . . . sped . . . second*: (1) vigorous; (2) lecherous . . . successfully in possession of a second. But cf. 'I have buried my two husbands' (1.2.50).

148 *confessed too fast*: all too quickly made manifest.

150 *services*: with a pun on 'sexual satisfactions'.

155 *bounteous house-keepers*: those free with their hospitality.

157 *blood*: family.

161 *blood*: lust, desire.

163 *voyage*: quibbling on Leantio's mercantile profession.

171 *pities . . . surgeons*: i.e. in using anaesthetics.

176 *cure's*: picking up the medical metaphor, but playing on *cure* = care, concern.

178 *speaks*: promises.

185 *lost*: in thought.

192 *vengeance*: i.e. from heaven, for his sins.

202 *low private*: lowly, politically insignificant (O, 'love private').

203 *enclosed grounds*: fenced-off land.

206 *charged*: held accountable.

210 *popular breath*: the gossip of the common people.

216 *example*: being a (bad) example.

217–18 *scattered . . . bill*: separate items on a bill that has not been totalled.

218–19 *such . . . sums . . . all*: 'the great man' . . . i.e. completing the metaphor of the bill, the 'great reckoning'.

226–7 *Not only . . . light up*: i.e. who not only do not act virtuously themselves, but also set up a light.

232 *reprehension*: rebuke.

235 *taken*: i.e. by death.

239 *stay*: detain.

241 *wall*: of flesh (the body).

243 *it*: i.e. damnation.

246–7 *beauty . . . neither*: common Jacobean themes—female beauty is only skin-deep, and anyway achieved by cosmetics.

257–8 *there . . . grace*: there is no desolate place that portends a greater lack of sustenance than to be without God's grace.

260 *Sung . . . Heaven*: cf. Luke 15: 10 'there is joy in the presence of the angels of God over one sinner that repenteth'.

262 *First . . . glory*: see Introduction.

268 *it*: his lust for her.

270 *save my oath*: keep my word. The Duke adopts a very partial moral code.

272 *spent*: completed.

276 *stoves*: heated rooms.

4.2.4–5 *Put case . . . vicious . . . blind time*: assuming . . . a sinner . . . hours of darkness.

6 *'twere conscionable*: would show a proper regard for conscience.

7 *Art . . . closeness*: artifice, cunning . . . secrecy.

9 *apparent*: open, brazen.

15 *fear*: for fear.

20 *shines*: who shines.

22 *in state*: in great pomp.

24–5 *at . . . forth . . . an . . . draw*: (1) to begin with; (2) as you depart . . . if you'll draw your sword.

29 *no . . . valour*: he denies that it was cowardly to strike Leantio without warning, because that was what Leantio has done to him in dishonouring the family name.

30–1 *of even . . . best course*: on equal terms, mount the best attack you can.

37 *Of . . . stamp*: (1) of a base nature (because without warning); (2) like a false/counterfeit impression on a coin.

38 *mettle . . . one*: (1) temperament; (2) metal (cf. the play on coining) . . . a wound.

40 *own*: not in O.

41 *'tis . . . thee*: you have received your death wound.

44 *heart-string*: tendon thought to sustain the heart.

46 *string*: the sound of a string.

48 *Shift . . . thyself*: get away quickly. She fears he will be arrested for illegal duelling.

53 *without voice*: noiselessly.

57 *too sure*: over-careful.

60 *prodigy*: horrific portent.

65 *more . . . loves*: more lawful than the incest between Isabella and Hippolito.

67 *kept close*: been kept secret.

71 *ignorant*: wilfully not paying attention.

72 *strange notes*: cries of a new-born child. 'Strange' echoes the incestuous parentage.

74–5 *lights upon . . . His . . . home*: rebounds upon . . . Hippolito's arm has paid me in full.

81 *reprobate*: O 'rebrobate', which may reflect the Ward's clumsy pronunciation.

84 *wife . . . Sunday*: she would be wearing her best clothes to church and *look* virtuous.

89 *To*: to lift up.

89–90 *in life . . . nimbler*: i.e. in life he moved as nimbly as flames.

92 *list*: listen. He turns down Livia's invitation to talk of mournful things.

93–4 *quotha . . . sweet . . . graffing*: (sarcastic) said he . . . (ironic) your guardian's arranged marriage (*graffing* = grafting) has produced fine fruit. *Plum* supposedly resembles female genitalia; *sweet plum-tree* was slang for a loose woman.

97 *medlar-tree*: the fruit of the medlar, known as 'open arse' (cf. *open one*), looks like a small, brown-skinned apple, and is eaten when soft and pulpy (*rotten*).

99–100 *queans . . . abroach*: whores, who might be *rotten* with venereal disease by an early age . . . running, flowing (as from a pierced cask).

104 *tumble*: (1) perform acrobatics; (2) copulate.

114 *millstone*: to see through a millstone is proverbially to resolve great difficulties. Sordido is trying to convey the visual impenetrability of the farthingale.

114–15 *in the going . . . i'th'bottom*: (1) as the millwheel moves; (2) as Isabella walks . . . (1) at the bottom of the mill; (2) within Isabella's private parts.

117 *small . . . no maid*: high . . . no virgin. The Ward could not know that Isabella was pregnant when she sang, so perhaps 'the fool' steps out of the theatrical illusion to comment on the fact that Isabella's role was actually being played by a boy.

118–19 *singing . . . head*: from the cuckold's horns. Sordido picks up the allusion.

120 *cinquepace*: see note to 3.2.212–15.

123 *hogshead . . . angels*: large barrel full of gold coins bearing the image of St Michael.

124 *scrivener's sand-box*: box with a perforated top for sprinkling sand on documents to dry ink. Scriveners were professional penmen.

126 *confusion*: ruin.

129–30 *And . . . that . . . yon man*: and that's too near (i.e. too closely related) . . . Hippolito.

134 *hurt*: undermine.

140 *So . . . you*: in this way I hope to avoid meeting you again in hell (by not committing incest purposefully).

143 *least means*: smallest opportunity.

153 *Be . . . far*: be a woman to the extent of dissembling this.

154 *As*: as long as.

159 *privilege . . . triumph*: protection (afforded by confusion during) a wedding masque.

161 *all's*: all as.

162 *Not . . . natures . . . conceive*: not deliberately conceived . . . understand.

173 *resolved*: informed, satisfied.

179 *hindrance . . . I . . . mother*: incapacity (from the wound) . . . i.e. all women can dissemble.

182 *this is*: O, 'thus'.

184 *approve*: demonstrate.

191 *affectionate comfort*: loving pleasure.

200 *invention . . . his own*: it would be doubly ironic if the Duke died during a fiction of his own devising, but since it is unfamiliar to him later Guardiano must be the author.

201 *pains . . . charge bestowed*: hard work (devising and planning) . . . expenses incurred.

204 *device*: (1) stratagem; (2) allegory; (3) masque.

207 *voice*: support.

209 *make one . . . plot's full*: play a part . . . the cast is complete/the scheme is ready.

213 *Juno Pronuba*: goddess of marriage, according to Virgil. An ironic role for Livia.

218–19 *state . . . incensed*: dignity . . . (1) enraged; (2) perfumed with incense.

223–4 *project drawn . . . weigh . . . one*: the plot written out . . . am indifferent, so long as I have a role.

229 *here*: in her heart.

4.3 S.D. *pass solemnly over*: not merely a procession across the stage, but grandly entering and leaving through the playhouse yard.

12 *sure*: inevitable.

16 *great master*: God.

22 *surfeit*: over-indulgence.

26 *this . . . not*: this (reproach) is unnecessary.

33 *He*: the devil.

39 *Close . . . temple*: i.e. claiming sanctuary of the church.

47 *read . . . over*: observed you closely.

49 *severe*: (1) serious; (2) censorious.

51 *first-born . . . religion*: cf. 1 Corinthians 13.

56–7 *sinner . . . professor*: see note to 4.1.260 . . . one who professes Christianity.

65 *whether is*: is.

69 *build . . . ruins*: restore (Bianca's) honour and reputation (by marrying her).

69 *work . . . grace*: act of God's grace (punning on *Grace* = duke).

72 *controlled*: brought to book.

5.1.3 *cannot . . . feeling*: whenever I wash my face I feel (cuckold's horns, and so *abuse*).

6 *trap-door*: trap-doors were a regular feature of the Jacobean stage.

7 *triumph*: masque or pageant.

8 *devil . . . fireworks*: comic devils and exploding fireworks were a common feature of Elizabethan drama, but considered rather unsophisticated by the 1620s.

10 *squibbing*: (1) letting off fireworks; (2) tart (or foolish) talking.

13–15 *stamp . . . current . . . one hole*: puns on the stamp of a coin, and its validity/currency . . . the same trap-door.

19 *i'th'chaps on't*: in the cheeks of it.

20 *Slander . . . out-parishes*: parishes outside the city (London), where

theatres like the Red Bull and the Fortune still staged morality plays with characters like Slander.

21 *It . . . not*: the Ward cannot understand that Guardiano's plot will disrupt the play, so that the part of Slander will never be called for.

26–7 *list to . . . Stamp*: listen for . . . pound.

28–9 *present . . . headache*: immediate remedy for the pain of the cuckold's horns.

31 *As . . . nimble . . . certain*: though . . . alert . . . sure (to succeed).

32 *present*: represent.

34 *Fitting . . . part*: appropriate to Hippolito's role as a lovesick shepherd.

5.2 S.D. *Flourish . . . above*: i.e. of trumpets . . . on the upper stage, where Bianca's seduction took place.

7 *grace . . . merit*: Bianca talks the language of Protestant theology, which stresses that *divine* Grace is obtained by 'faith' and not by 'good works' (*merit*).

11 *two spirits*: those of the Cardinal and Bianca.

15 *seal*: i.e. a kiss in reconciliation, a resolution like the wax seal on a legal document.

17 *this*: this show of reconciliation.

24 *holy friend*: a mocking allusion to the Cardinal.

27 *through . . . blood*: through the medium of flesh and blood (corrupt in all men).

29 *we, poor soul*: so O, i.e. the 'poor soul' is the Cardinal. This is commonly emended to 'we poor souls'.

30 *model*: abstract or 'plot'.

32 *list . . . argument*: hear the subject-matter.

40 *How the . . . be . . . . strife*: the outcome . . . conflict.

42 *abused*: frustrated.

44 *which . . . him*: punishes him fittingly.

50 S.D. *yellow . . . powdered with stars*: Hymen, god of marriage, is usually depicted in saffron-yellow . . . sprinkled with stars, alluding to Zeus eventually making Ganymede (his page and cupbearer) into the constellation Aquarius.

59–60 *stumbling . . . Lactea*: a little-known myth explains that the Milky Way (*Via Lactea*) was created when Hebe stumbled and spilled a cup of milk, staining the heavens.

64 *parting take*: O, 'part', but a rhyme is called for.

69 *antemasque*: interlude before a masque, variously spelled 'ante-', 'antic/que-', and 'anti-', denoting respectively that it was before the masque, a

show of grotesques, or a contrast to the main masque. Bianca is responsible for this business, in her attempt to poison the Cardinal. Her *peace is perfect* because she thinks she has succeeded.

70 *entertain*: while away.

72 S.D. *in parts*: that is, each singer takes a different 'part'. They do not sing in unison.

77 *amazed*: bewildered.

83 *springs*: where the Nymphs live.

89 *one*: O, 'me', which makes little sense.

96 *design*: point out.

98 S.D. *descends*: Livia is lowered from the 'heavens' of the theatre by stage machinery, and hangs over the altar amid the poisoned fumes.

102 *keeps . . . touch*: passes the test successfully (from the touchstone used to test gold.)

103 *be long*: O, 'belong'.

106 *to*: compared to.

115 *savour*: O, 'favor'. She means the smell of the incense.

118 *brother Jove*: Juno was both sister and wife to Jove.

121 *conceit*: meaning, significance.

123 *lapful*: the flaming gold in Isabella's lap recalls Jove's violation of Danae in a shower of gold, though the circumstances are very different.

124 *swerves . . . argument*: the Duke's attempts to follow matters in the light of the 'plot' underline how little any of the characters understand the 'plots' of their own lives.

126 *fast . . . tole . . . hither*: gone to plan . . . entice him to the trap-door.

128–9 *Stark . . . How's that*: we cannot be sure exactly what happens, or in what order. Hippolito perhaps first discovers Isabella, stamps, and his 'How's that?' scornfully marks Guardiano's fall. But it is also possible that Guardiano himself stamps by accident and that Hippolito finds his body before that of Isabella.

134 *subtlety . . . sped*: my scheming is complete (but unsuccessful, unusual with 'sped').

135 *ambition*: that of aspiring to behave like a goddess, with powers of life and death.

138–9 *makes she . . . other shows*: is she doing . . . such as Jonson's masque, *Hymenaei*, where she has a prominent role.

140 *peacock's feathers*: Juno is traditionally accompanied by peacocks.

143 *spoiled*: destroyed.

146 *I worse*: because not only dying but damned.

148 *forgetfulness*: culpable disregard of moral truths.

151 *fire*: the effect of Jacobean stage poison is often described as an unbearable inner burning, foreshadowing the burning of hell from which death itself is no escape.

152 *now . . . it*: either 'now I feel the poison' or 'now I begin to have a sense of it all'.

154 *The event . . . it*: the outcome demonstrates the truth of it.

156–7 *She . . . in . . . bloods*: Livia . . . i.e. in an incestuous relationship.

160 *set match . . . plagues*: pre-arranged conspiracy . . . O, 'plague'.

162 *fawning partner . . . I reach not*: servile accomplice (i.e. Guardiano) . . . . is beyond my understanding.

166–7 *property . . . downward*: inherent tendency . . . i.e. to hell, in Guardiano's case via a trap-door.

S.D. *a Guard*: probably in the sense of a body of troops on guard duty. At least four people will be needed to make a credible job of clearing the stage of corpses.

S.D. *halberd*: O does not say what Hippolito impales himself on. An early note in a Yale Library copy suggests a halberd (cross between an axe and a spear, often carried by guards), which is very plausible.

173–4 *plays . . . prodigious*: O, 'play' . . . ill-omened.

177 *When . . . earth*: i.e. she is expecting the Cardinal to die.

180 *fell first*: i.e. Guardiano.

183–4 *let . . . down . . . at . . . him*: caused him to fall . . . when he heard him call out.

188 *way*: passage.

191 *heart . . . bigger*: the blood was thought to flow to the heart at the moment of death.

207 *blemished face*: perhaps we are to understand that the poison on the Duke's lips has scarred Bianca's face.

208 *What . . . here*: a poignant moment, as the dying Bianca remembers that she does not belong in Florence and is a 'stranger'. They are all on a private and solitary road to hell.

211 *ignorant*: reckless.

213 *heart-breaking*: i.e. at the point of death.

217 *no enemy*: the repetition may be a mistake, but it is very resonant phrasing.

222 *remove*: die.

The Changeling

The Characters of the Play

The Persons of the Play: based on Q 1653.

changeling: idiot, but see the Introduction.

Deflores: from the Latin for 'deflower'. Editors commonly print it 'De Flores', but Q consistently gives it as one word, which better reflects its derivation.

Beatrice-Joanna: Q gives the name simply as Beatrice.

Alicante: Alicante in Spain. Q, 'Allegant'.

1.1.1 *temple*: church.

4 *or*: possibly a misprint for 'of'.

6–7 *holy purpose . . . admits*: marriage . . . allows, warrants.

8 *place blest*: Paradise/the Garden of Eden. Alsemero looks to marriage to redeem man from the Fall, returning him to his 'right home back', Eden.

10 *interview*: mutual sight of each other, meeting.

12 *beginning . . . perfection*: circularity symbolizes perfection and permanence.

14–15 *passage . . . 'tis contrary*: Alsemero is expected to set sail for Malta . . . i.e. the wind is in the wrong direction.

17 *gale . . . witches*: alludes to the belief that witches could magically control the winds.

18–19 *lucky pennyworth . . . a'God's name*: bargain (of a wind) . . . free, without charge.

26 *doubt*: fear.

27–8 *inclinations . . . now*: i.e. Alsemero has always been anxious to press on with his travels. His current delay is uncharacteristic.

30 *trap . . . for the speed*: dress with trappings . . . to hasten matters.

34 *changed . . . orisons*: changed what you pray for. The play repeatedly casts love and aspiration in terms of religious devotion.

36 *stoic*: Stoics tried to suppress their passions in pursuit of an austere ethical code.

38 *snares . . . beauty*: i.e. they have tried to tempt him into marriage.

49 *critical . . . Aquarius*: crucial, propitious . . . sign of the zodiac, the water-carrier and propitious weather for sailing. Jacobeans placed much faith in astrological signs.

50–1 *smoke . . . fire*: a variation on 'where there's smoke there's fire'. Second Servant anticipates something serious from Alsemero's uncharacteristic decision.

s.d. Q adds 'Joanna' after 'Servants', suggesting that the compositor was confused by Beatrice-Joanna's double name.

58 *laws . . . Medes*: unchangeable laws. Cf. Daniel 6: 8.

60 *in . . . conscience*: on my word (a stock phrase).

62 *Valencia . . . Greece . . . Turk*: the city of Valencia (Alicante, where the action takes place, is in the wider province of Valencia, and about 75 miles from the city) . . . Greece at this time was part of the Turkish Empire.

66 *sing . . . sight*: can sight-read it immediately. 'Sight' is a critical theme in the play.

79 *Both houses*: a metaphor from Parliament. Both Houses (the 'eyes' or senses, and 'judgement' or intellect) have agreed to a bill. It now only needs the royal signature of assent—casting Beatrice-Joanna as queen.

82 *one . . . me*: she does not have the power of a queen because her father controls her.

82–3 *For . . . recalled*: would that the last five days could be undone. Presumably the time since she agreed to be betrothed to Alonzo de Piracquo.

84 *This*: Alsemero.

86–7 *carriers . . . at farthest*: by land transport, rather than by sea . . . as far as we are going to get.

88–90 *venturer . . . top-sail*: a string of nautical metaphors. Jasperino plans to emulate Alsemero as a pirate/trader in love, aiming to assault and board Diaphanta.

95–6 *stall . . . a . . . presence*: (1) forestall; (2) make stale . . . i.e. that of her father.

99 *One . . . other*: one way or another.

108–11 *Nor . . . wholesome*: I can give you no explanation except that any person might render, involving something they have to give up as deadly poisonous to themselves, though it is totally harmless to a thousand others.

115 *sound*: i.e. generally sound (healthy) but subject to one specific imperfection.

116–19 *one distastes . . . One oil*: one man dislikes the smell of roses, which to innumerable others is most pleasing and fragrant; (another one dislikes) medicinal unction.

121 *countenance*: demeanour, appearance.

126 *What*: Q, 'And what', probably by repetition from the previous line.

131–3 *I want . . . him*: I can do nothing about this, because he is a gentleman well regarded by my father, and in his service.

135–7 *mad wag . . . doctor*: merry, mischievous fellow . . . Alibius. The first link with the play's other plot.

141–3 *such a thing . . . after*: i.e. an invitation to wear each other out with sexual intercourse, totally exhausting themselves.

143–4 *profess physic . . . poppy*: declare an expertise in medicine . . . opiate.

146–7 *simple . . . cuckoo (what you call't)*: medicinal herb . . . one of the wild flowers linked in folklore with sexual impropriety and so the cuckoo. Here probably cuckoo pintle-root (with phallic associations) or ladies' smocks (with vaginal ones), the latter used as a cure for madness.

147 *discover*: reveal.

149 *Joanna*: the first time we *hear* any part of her name. Audiences are probably *meant* to be surprised by the double name, which is not voiced until 3.3.246.

151 *change . . . saint*: change who she prays to—i.e. Alsemero.

158–9 *article between . . . use . . . to*: (quasi-)legal condition to be satisfied . . . do not usually.

160 *strangers*: foreigners. The definition of such for the Spanish would have been complex, since even within Europe Spain ruled much territory beyond its own borders, including Portugal and parts of the Netherlands and of Italy.

167–9 *best love . . . truth*: Vermandero usually calls Beatrice-Joanna his 'best love', so in addressing Alsemero this way he has voiced her own thoughts.

171 *Before . . . down*: before our beards began to grow. 'Iulan' (a trisyllable) is apparently from the young son of Aeneas in Virgil's *Aeneid*, Iulus Ascanius.

173 *coined . . . silver*: turned our beards grey.

175 *went together*: were equal.

176 *Saint Jacques*: St James the Greater ('Santiago'), patron saint of Spain.

178–81 *Gibraltar . . . league*: these events date the fictional action quite closely. The battle of Gibraltar occurred on 25 April 1607, and the *league* between Spain and her Dutch subjects, providing for a twelve-year truce (*time to breathe*) was signed on 9 April 1609. British readers should note that Gibraltar did not become a colony until 1704.

205 *Did . . . wish*: if my business affairs had fallen in with my wishes in the matter.

208 *complete*: 'rounded', invoking the Renaissance ideal of the gentleman (courtier, soldier, scholar), propounded (e.g.) by Castiglione in his *Book of the Courtier*.

209–10 *gallant . . . ornaments*: man of fashion and chivalry . . . distinctions.

214 *Bound*: obliged, in your debt (for these compliments).

215 *want*: be denied, deprived of.

219 *murderers*: light cannon, ironic in view of what is to happen.

221 *serpent*: refers to Deflores, but Alsemero is the one 'tempting' her.

s.d. *glove*: Q does not indicate when she drops the glove. She may intend Alsemero to retrieve it, or the proximity of Deflores may cause an involuntary reflex.

226 *thine . . . 'em*: perhaps implying that Deflores is disfigured by some skin condition.

s.d. *Exeunt*: Q suggests everyone else leaves the stage just before Deflores's final speech, which would mean that others might see the altercation between Beatrice-Joanna and Deflores. But it can be staged otherwise.

227 *favour*: love-token (the gloves, probably meant for Alsemero).

229–30 *thrust . . . sockets*: intensely sexually suggestive, as the actor will make clear on stage.

1.2.3 *ever . . . secret*: always good at keeping (or discovering) secrets.

 15 *go about*: am concerned/engaged with.

 20 *old Lollio*: the old jokes, as they say, are the best. As a stage fool, Lollio has a degree of witlessness in character but also a superior wit that comments on the folly around him, giving him a special relationship with the audience.

 21 *this . . . sympathise*: this relationship of youth and age come together harmoniously.

 22 *old . . . plants*: a joke about old husbands growing cuckolds' horns, as Alibius sees.

 27 *my ring . . . finger*: i.e. I want to keep my wife to myself. *Ring* = vagina, *finger* = phallus, equations repeated throughout the play and picked up in Lollio's response.

 35 *look out*: (1) go out of the house on business; (2) be careful.

 38 *treadings*: (1) movements; (2) copulations. (Alibius does not intend the latter sense.)

 42 *comfortable*: comforting.

 47 *either sort*: fools, born simple-minded, and the insane.

 50 *daily visitants*: it was common for people in the seventeenth century to visit madhouses (like London's Bethlehem Hospital, 'Bedlam') as an entertainment.

 57 *serve . . . turn*: fill the role. Since Lollio is a 'fool' already, this casts Alibius as a madman, but he does not recognize the insult.

 59 *ward*: defensive guard (from fencing).

 61 *by . . . consequent*: following that logic.

387

64 *buckler*: shield (following the fencing metaphor).

71–2 *gather . . . rose*: visit the privy.

73 *lay . . . victuals*: search for food and drink.

77 *new . . . entered*: a new 'scholar' (madman) brought to the hospital.

78 *come home*: fulfilled.

S.D. *like an idiot*: this suggests that he was wearing a familiar costume.

80 *takes . . . tongue*: saves the need for me to use my tongue.

85 *patterns*: samples, earnests.

89–90 *Sir . . . hands*: Lollio is asking for a fee to ensure good service. It was a normal understanding that salaries were inadequate and that gifts/bribes would be looked for.

96 *Tony*: later in the century 'Tony' was a nickname for any fool, the *OED* thinks possibly as a result of this character's popularity. But Shakespeare uses 'Antonio' in three plays—*The Merchant of Venice*, *Twelfth Night*, and *The Tempest*—for characters who are silent, unwed, apparently unassimilated at the end of their plays, so perhaps the name had unfortunate associations even before *The Changeling*.

100–1 *laugh . . . beast*: an Aristotelian commonplace holds that laughter separates man from the beasts.

109 *discretion*: understanding and judgement.

111 *gentleman*: of good birth and social standing (who would have been heir to a 'great family' if he had not lost his wits).

113 *gentleman . . . yet*: double-edged wit from the fool: (1) fools and gentlemen are interchangeable; (2) I see through his disguise.

114 *have good . . . lodging*: be well looked after and have fresh-smelling accommodation.

117–18 *there . . . want . . . magnifico*: all expenses will be paid . . . person of high judicial authority. This starts a run of jokes on the low intelligence of officers of the law.

120 *I . . . I'll*: Q reads 'I'll warrant you make', which is clearly wrong. My amendment assumes the problem arose because the compositor conflated I/I'll.

123–4 *headborough, beadle, or watchman . . . able him*: respectively the lowest parochial, judicial, and civil officers . . . enable him to be, make him fit for.

129 *arrant*: unmitigated (with a pun on 'errant', wandering).

133 *state*: professional position (i.e. as a keeper of fools and madmen—but also a theatrical fool).

135 *none*: i.e. cares.

138 *whipped*: treatment of the insane, like that of children, could be extremely brutal.

141 *form*: school-class.

144 *true*: tailors were proverbially dishonest.

148 *deuce*: two, on cards or dice. So 'two less than a deuce' is none.

150 *goes to*: (1) make up, constitutes; (2) visit.

153–4 *lawyer . . . friends*: lawyers, then as now, were accused of exploiting the misery of others for their own gain.

166 *served yourself*: have been suitable for you (another insult unnoticed by Alibius).

168 *push-pin*: a child's game, but suggestive of Antonio's actual erotic purpose.

177 *stand there*: Lollio puts Antonio, Alibius and himself in a row, suggesting Alibius as a knave between two fools but covertly implying a fool between two knaves.

184 *we three*: the old sign of two idiots' heads with the inscription 'we three' normally involves the spectator as the third idiot—here Alibius has the honour.

187 *fly . . . swallow*: proverbial, 'Fly and you will catch the swallow'.

189 *crag*: neck. The First Madman's line relates to punishment for selling short-weight bread but this is only gibberish. Rope = string (of onions) or the hangman's noose.

190–2 *chimes of Bedlam . . . wire*: cries of the asylum inmates for food . . . whip.

193 *permasant*: Parmesan cheese, which the cat is reviled for not defending from a mouse. The joke hangs on the belief that the Welsh were inordinately fond of cheese.

196 *was*: who was.

203–4 *stultus . . . stultum*: able to decline the Latin for 'foolish'.

205 *would see*: would like to see.

211 *prove . . . myself*: suggests again that Lollio 'sees through' Antonio's disguise.

2.1 S.D. *severally*: by different doors.

1 *service*: (1) selfless duty or action (as Beatrice-Joanna intends it here); (2) sexual mating. The two senses become compromisingly confused as the play progresses.

4 *conduct*: pass.

5 *return*: give back. He asks nothing for himself.

7–8 *judgement . . . approved*: judgement parallels *service* as one of the key terms by which we interpret the action of the play . . . commendable, worthy of approval.

12 *choose . . . most discreet*: make a good choice of that close friend, with whom he shares his thoughts . . . proves to be most judicious.

14 *merit*: a slippery term here, as either a noun or a verb. 'Merit' is desert/reward or being fit for desert/reward, with theological connotations (being fit for God's grace). Beatrice-Joanna regards Alsemero as her 'merit', oblivious of the moral issues.

19–20 *intellectual eyesight . . . spends . . . for*: i.e. the eye of the mind, which can conjure up things not actually present . . . wastes his breath on.

20–3 *blessing . . . curse*: my father only blesses me as long as I follow him and enhance the family's reputation (*name*), otherwise he turns against me as an enemy and curses me.

24 *forward*: aggressive, eager. Beatrice-Joanna's complaint is that her father is so set in his attitudes, and so determined to marry her to de Piracquo as quickly as possible, that she has no opportunity to think for herself or suggest alternatives.

26 *comforts*: pleasures, delights.

35 *At no hand*: on no account.

39 *not endured . . . on*: not just tolerated but adored.

44 *wash*: medicinal lotion, here for the eyes.

46 *plucks*: Q, 'pluckt'.

46–7 *Yet . . . sweet*: but a person like that take his pleasures where he will, and then has the final satisfaction of seeming beautiful to his sweetheart. There are puns in *grace* (= blessing to a meal) and *sweet* (= last course of the meal).

48–9 *servitude . . . gentleman*: only the *gentle* (those of higher rank) could engage in courtly love. Lesser ranks found more menial service in paid employment. Deflores is a gentleman by birth but lacks means and so works in the service of Vermandero, which he calls *servitude* (and Beatrice-Joanna calls him *slave*). Being robbed of his birthright is a key element in Deflores's psychosexual obsession with Beatrice-Joanna.

57 *standing . . . pool*: foul, stagnant water, breeding place of toads (a further possible reference to skin disease).

60 *another since*: another so soon after the last.

67 *wilt*: Q, 'wil't'.

78 *qualm*: sudden access of passion.

79 *common . . . bull*: like a bull baited (*lugged*) at the Paris Garden in Southwark, a popular entertainment. 'Common' again signals his social grievance.

84–5 *his . . . Wrangling*: i.e. their . . . bitter argument or complaint.

87 *chid . . . men*: scolded themselves into bed with men.

90 *of*: for.

94 *Affliction's . . . torrent*: the return of Alonzo de Piracquo, her no longer loved fiancé.

98 *addition . . . son*: title of a son. Vermandero's eager adoption of Alonzo as his 'son' may speak volumes about his relationship with his daughter.

103 *keep . . . night*: (1) watch carefully during the night of my marriage; (2) protect myself during the night (which may mean she intends to avoid consummating the marriage).

107 *there's . . . you*: you will not learn.

108 *If . . . fault*: if lovers were to find fault with every little thing; *faults* (below) = list of errata.

128 *Unsettle*: undo, detach.

132 *pleasure*: sexual pleasure.

137 *him; and*: Q, 'him, in his | passions, and'. There is no really satisfactory explanation of *in his passions*. Words may be missing which would have made up a line.

138 *her . . . to*: the effect of restraining her may eventually become.

146 *but think*: merely entertain the notion.

148 *friends*: Alonzo is saying that he would not have taken Tomazo's slurs against Beatrice-Joanna from anyone else, and friendship with his brother remains unbroken.

150 *injury*: insult, affront to her honour.

152 *How . . . lovingly*: our duty to heaven (as brothers) requires us to depart as friends.

2.2.1 *kept . . . hour*: been punctual in your arrival.

3 *complete gentleman*: see note to 1.1 208.

4–5 *praises . . . with*: Diaphanta is flirting with Alsemero, and suspects Beatrice-Joanna would be jealous if she heard.

6–7 *ladies' cabinets . . . locked*: cases for the safe keeping of jewels etc. . . . Q, 'lock'.

9–10 *Requests . . . defects*: prayers that ascend to heaven with our requests and descend again (answered) to supply those things we lack.

17–18 *enemy . . . to't*: i.e. their kiss has an enemy (Alonzo) who would wish it poisoned.

22 *strike off*: as fetters are struck off.

23–4 *remove . . . ceases*: i.e. remove Piracquo and her father's command to marry him would cease.

25 *let . . . you*: Beatrice-Joanna has lost track of what Alsemero is suggesting.

27 *honourablest . . . valour*: the honour culture readily spilled over into

duelling and an equation of honour with physical bravery; *piece*: Q, 'peece', which could mean 'peace'.

33 *y'are*: Q, 'your'.

danger's . . . then: she rejects this (male) code of honour, since Alsemero might be killed in the duel or imprisoned for it, either thwarting her own wishes.

36–7 *one . . . condition*: one (thought) of this kind.

40–1 *becomes . . . too blame*: suits . . . see Glossary, under 'blame'.

42 *marred . . . scorn*: spoiled so good an opportunity (in Deflores) by my scorn.

46 *art*: (1) learning; (2) cunning.

49 *of*: on.

52 *opens*: becomes auspicious.

54 *Perfect*: complete, finish.

56 *firm*: the play on 'sexually aroused' underscores the level of sexual tension.

58 *t'other*: Alonzo.

59 *served . . . transgress*: satisfied (by implication 'sexually') unless she commits a sin.

59–60 *happily . . . one*: perhaps/with any luck, then, I'll bid to be one of her lovers.

61–2 *point . . . mounts*: (1) penis; (2) decimal point . . . (1) adds up, multiplies; (2) sexually engages.

64 *sutler*: seller of provisions to an army. So one who purveys sex wholesale.

66 *put case*: suppose.

69 *serve . . . turn*: use him for my own purposes.

74 *pruned yourself*: (1) preened yourself; (2) removed your deformities.

75 *amorously*: like a lover, attractive.

80 *liver*: one of the supposed seats of passion. She speaks truer than she knows.

82–3 *amber . . . water*: sweetly perfumed with ambergris . . . medicinal wash.

86 *act of pleasure*: sexual intercourse.

94 *If . . . employment*: if there were a need to employ him.

97 *mounts*: the sexual innuendo points to the ambiguity in *service* in the line before.

102 *quick*: perceptive.

105 *lend . . . word*: let it speak.

113 *occasion*: opportunity.

115 *Claim . . . me*: i.e. claim enough of the manliness in me to perform this. In doing so she unwittingly lays claim to another 'man' in Deflores, his virility.

118 *mean faithfully*: intend faithful service.

126–7 *angels' food . . . need*: bread of heaven, manna in the Old Testament, Christ's body in the New . . . need of money.

129 *As . . . forward*: in proportion as you are bold and resolute.

132 *ravishes*: enraptures.

139 *cast*: throw of the dice.

143 *bravely*: gallantly, in style.

146 *blood*: sexual passion.

150 *Slovenly*: negligently prepared.

163 *gainst . . . rising*: before your lordship has risen from dinner.

165 *beyond hopes*: in ways I could never have hoped for.

3.1 S.D. *In the . . . rapier*: Q places this stage direction after the entry direction at the head of 3.1. 'Act-time' is the time between acts 2 and 3.

2 *wanted*: lacked (the key).

3.2.2 *place . . . on*: i.e. his grave.

3 *all . . . house*: all the members of Vermandero's household.

10–11 *munition . . . bastard*: defences . . . inferior.

14 *you . . . dwell*: (1) your sight may linger; (2) your body will be kept.

16 *malice . . . on*: whose hatred have you adopted? i.e. who are you working for?

23 *approve*: give proof of.

26 *suspect*: suspicion.

3.3.6 *pipe after*: follow my lead. There is a sexual sub-text here, on Lollio's side.

9–10 *taken . . . pounded*: caught among another man's crop (like a stray animal), you might be (1) penned up; (2) pummelled (with sexual innuendo).

16 *abroad . . . to boot*: out of the house . . . into the bargain.

18 *participate*: partake (i.e. gain experience). Lollio is as much a threat to Alibius's wife as any of the daily visitors.

21 *Afford . . . bedlam*: give . . . madhouse. Bedlam was originally the Bethlehem Hospital just outside London, but was already a generic term for a madhouse.

23 *proper*: handsome.

34 *shooting . . . two*: sliding back the bolts on the doors. This alludes to the proverb 'A fool's bolt is soon shot'.

34 S.D. *Exit [Lollio]*: Q follows this immediately with '*Enter presently*', before Lollio's next sentence, so that he is directed to exit once but enter twice. There is either confusion or this reflects some now obscure stage business.

38–40 *Anacreon . . . poet*: alludes to the legend (Pliny, *Natural History*, vii. 7) of the poet Anacreon, who choked to death on a grapestone while drinking wine.

44 *forwards*: on the road (to madness).

45 *she . . . neither*: she was only a dwarf.

46–8 *Titania . . . dryades*: Franciscus is trying to tempt Isabella/Titania, suggesting that Oberon/Alibius is dallying with other women (*dryades* = wood-nymphs). Oberon and Titania were King and Queen of the Fairies, as in *A Midsummer Night's Dream*.

52 *Diomede*: either the Greek hero in The *Iliad* who captured the Thracian horses of Rhesus; or a king of the Bistonians who fed his horses with human flesh, until Hercules killed him and fed his flesh to his horses.

54 *Get . . . Bucephalus*: get up on my (horse's) back. Bucephalus was the horse of Alexander the Great, whom only he could ride.

59 *Esculapius*: Greek god of medicine. Alibius and Lollio are 'doctors' to the inmates—Lollio's 'poison' is the whip.

61 *Tiresias*: mythical Theban prophet (rather than poet), who was changed from man to woman for a seven-year period. According to Ovid (*Metamorphoses*, iii) he was blinded by Juno for revealing that sex was more pleasurable to women than to men.

63 *tame . . . geese*: nonsense, but with a contemporary allusion, now lost, since the same oxymoron appears elsewhere. Possibly a cant term for prostitutes.

68 *might*: so Q. A word like 'say' seems to have been dropped.

72 *eye*: (1) perception; (2) vagina.

75 *Luna . . . two trades*: lunacy derives from Luna, the moon . . . madness and blindness.

76–7 *big-bellied . . . Hecate*: (1) full; (2) pregnant . . . another name for Luna, especially when associated with witchcraft and magic.

79 *dog . . . bush*: nonsense, but the dog and bush traditionally go with the man in the moon.

81 *lycanthropi*: madmen who transform (or suppose they transform) into wolves at the full moon.

91 *mouse-hole*: suggestive of the vagina.

96 *aunt*: slang term for a bawd or pimp.

99 *nidget*: idiot (as with the ironic pronunciation 'ijjit').

100 *bauble*: stick, often phallic in shape, traditionally deployed by fools indecently.

103 *Cousin . . . cousins*: Isabella is too sharp-witted to be trapped in kinship with fools which the all-purpose Jacobean 'cousin' makes possible.

110 *play . . . Orlando*: imitate the violent behaviour of Orlando, hero of Ariosto's *Orlando Furioso* (though *left-handed* inadvertently suggests he would do so ineptly).

113 *Cast . . . change*: do not be astonished by my transformation. Antonio converts from fool to would-be lover, with a string of amorous poetic conceits (and falsehoods).

124 *parlous*: (1) dangerously cunning; (2) perilous.

127 *arrow*: in Antonio's conceit the arrows of Cupid (*love*) are kisses.

132 *Galaxia*: Milky Way.

134 *acquaintance*: notice.

138–9 *habit . . . becomes . . . discover you*: clothing, disguise . . . suits . . . reveal you.

143 *must again*: i.e. play the fool, given Lollio's return.

146 *Passing*: (1) surpassingly; (2) as he passes (i.e. I prefer him when he's gone).

158 *catch . . . hell*: a cry in the game of barley-break, played by three couples, hand-in-hand. Those in a centre circle, *hell*, try to catch the others as they run from one end of the court to the other.

160 *both . . . wards*: the fools' ward and the madmen's ward.

163–4 *become not . . . clothes*: do not accord with what you say, when you talk in a way not befitting your clothes.

166 *orchard . . . Hesperides*: the orchard bore golden apples, guarded by the Hesperides (daughters of Hesperus) and the hundred-headed dragon Ladon.

169 *giants*: perhaps alludes to William Rowley playing Lollio (whom Isabella seems to have spotted above). A number of the parts he is known to have played—including the Fat Bishop in *A Game at Chess*—make comic capital out of his great size.

171 *Lipsius*: the great scholar and jurist, Justus Lipsius (1547–1606), is introduced purely for the play on 'lips'.

He's . . . 'Amandi': he's beyond Ovid's *The Art of Loving*. Antonio's scholarship of love is far in advance of what Lollio expected.

174 *Do you smile*: a gentle command, not a question.

180 *bright mirrors*: i.e. her eyes.

182 *cuckoo*: Lollio recognizes that Antonio intends to cuckold Alibius.

s.d. *some . . . beasts*: imitating birds and beasts, as Isabella says. There is no evidence that they are dressed as them.

183–4 *Of . . . enough . . . schools*: dangerous enough (given our secret) . . . classes.

187 *conceit*: fancy.

191 *large one*: another apparent reference to William Rowley (see note to l. 170).

194–5 *one . . . benefices*: the practice of clergymen holding multiple livings ('pluralism') or being minister at more than one church was much condemned by puritans.

201–2 *put . . . down*: (1) get the better of you with his wit; (2) get you into bed.

204 *bankers*: those employed to tend the banks of a flooding river. Isabella reflects that Antonio offers an opportunity to break out of the restraints imposed by Alibius.

207 *needle's point*: point of a compass, always drawn to the attractive frozen north (*drawing arctics*), however far from the Pole. It has phallic connotations.

212 *degrees*: degrees of rank in fooling.

217–24 '*What should . . . . not*': there is a theatrical in-joke in Lollio's quotation of Antonio word for word: which actor is playing the fool? 'I know this shape|Becomes me not' is particularly comic, given the much-remarked size of the actor in Lollio's role.

226 *Lacedemonian*: Spartan (so someone who speaks briefly and to the point).

230 *This . . . errant*: i.e. Antonio, with his suspect protestations of chivalry.

231 *purchase*: winning.

232–3 *his . . . enjoying*: what I shall require of him to gain sexual favours from me (ironic mirroring of the 'deal' struck between Beatrice-Joanna and Deflores).

238 *bounden servant*: bitter gibe at how he keeps her imprisoned (= *bounden*).

245 *Beatrice-Joanna*: the first spoken revelation of her double name.

246 *bespoke . . . pains*: commissioned our labour.

250–1 *Only an . . . frightful pleasure*: just a brief surprise appearance, to give a pleasurably frightening entertainment. Alibius (rather incoherently) wants to make more of this than has strictly been asked for, an antic/grotesque counterpoint to the wedding harmony.

258 *bounty*: special gratuity.

266 *Madmen . . . commodity*: madmen and fools are always a source of employment.

268 *lawyers' . . . arrive*: we reach the same safe harbour (source of income) as lawyers.

3.4.3 *fellow*: twin, sister.

4 *had ... once*: an unusual personal and psychological insight. Is Vermandero referring to his dead wife, or to a lost child? Has Beatrice-Joanna been the more spoiled for being a sole surviving child? Does this suggestion of an 'alternative' Beatrice-Joanna relate in any way to her double identity as Beatrice-Joanna?

6 *vale*: i.e. vale of tears, the world. It would be sinful to want to bring her back to life, denying her heaven's bliss.

9 *I ... largely*: I hear how beautiful this house is wherever I go.

14 *that eye*: i.e. Alonzo. Cf. 'And if thine eye offend thee, pluck it out' (Matthew 18: 9).

17 *refulgent*: (1) resplendent; (2) reflecting back [on Alsemero].

18–19 *at ... deed ... feel ... weight*: overwhelmed with delight over the deed done (murder) and to come (sex with Beatrice-Joanna) ... am not oppressed by conscience.

26 *token*: (1) proof ; (2) love-token.

31–2 *A greedy ... this*: i.e. greedy people sticking their hands in the way of carving knives at court have accidentally lost a finger like this.

39 *At ... fees*: keepers traditionally received the skin, head and certain other parts of slain deer.

45 *worm*: i.e. of remorse.

47–8 *merit ... on't*: Deflores insists on the standards of aristocratic honour and service, not the fee of a paid servant. Beatrice-Joanna has real difficulty understanding him.

50 *In state*: by the way.

56 *warm*: (1) heated by exertion; (2) zealous.

65 *The ... man*: [gold] in return for a man's life.

68 *journeyman ... murder*: professional murderer.

69 *slept at ease*: Not in Q. Some such words are needed to complete the line.

67–70 *I could ... home*: the key metaphors are commercial, piecework contracted out for later return to the contractor.

84 *counsel ... ill*: give you wholly bad advice.

93 *forgetfulness*: forgetting yourself.

95 *too blame*: see Glossary, under 'blame'.

97–8 *I'm ... of you*: Deflores speaks the language of courtly love, as if he suffers from being spurned by an indifferent mistress. He means to convey sexual urgency.

101–2 *Speak ... on't*: cf. *Women Beware Women*, 1.2.216–20.

106 *put . . . spirit*: animated me, made me lustful.

108 *wrought . . . into't*: i.e. worked to obtain the task.

111–12 *Not . . . not . . . In order*: Not that I do not need it. (The second 'not' is missing in Q, probably because of the repetition.) . . . in due course.

126 *Would I*: I wish rather I.

129–30 *Think . . . mine*: consider only the difference nature established between your birth and social standing and my own.

134 *no more*: i.e. no more than what the act of murder has made you.

135 *to*: (1) in your relations with; (2) in favour of.

136 *Y'are . . . creature*: you now belong to the deed (as you once did to your parents).

137 *first condition . . . challenge*: original (1) innocence, (2) superiority of rank . . . claim.

138 *turn'd . . . out*: rejected you.

140–1 *urge . . . writ'st*: provoke . . . style yourself.

151 *shooting eye*: in the language of courtly love, the lady's eye burns her unrequited lover with amorous passion.

162 *you*: not in Q.

164–5 *Was . . . first*: was I cursed from my conception with losing my virginity to a viper?

4.1 S.D. *points to . . . choice*: the action here is the only direct indication that, with Piracquo missing (and deemed to have abandoned Beatrice-Joanna), she has undertaken to marry Alsemero instead. The ensuing dialogue takes this for granted.

S.D. *Exeunt . . . Vermandero*: not in Q, but necessary to account for the second mention of Alsemero and Jasperino.

S.D. *state*: pomp, splendour.

S.D. *accident*: event.

S.D. *pass over*: such processions often passed through the auditorium on their way to and from the stage, making as much capital as possible out of the rich clothes.

1 *undone . . . endlessly*: (1) ruined me eternally; (2) ravished me repeatedly.

3–4 *ensuing . . . cope*: the night to come, after the wedding . . . (1) meet; (2) contend.

5 *that's*: Q, 'both', probably by confusion with its occurrence later in the line.

9–10 *There is . . . distress*: the more I examine my calamity, the more I realize I can't conceal it.

11 *Stands for*: represents, i.e. a wise man brings home to a guilty person her crime.

12 *what course . . . upon*: whatever option I consider.

13 *shame . . . danger*: she is worried Alsemero will discover she is no longer a virgin, which would certainly involve dishonour, but could also lead to violent conclusions.

15 *lie by*: (1) lie in bed with; (2) speaks untruths to. Q, 'lie by by'.

16 *precious craft*: valuable skill (ironic = dangerous game).

18 *park*: large ornamental piece of land attached to a country estate, used for recreation and hunting. Not the modern public space.

21–2 *vials . . . her mark . . . physic*: phials, each one with its own label . . . medicine.

25 *'Secrets . . . Nature'*: *De Arcanis Naturae* by the French scholar Antonius Mizaldus (1520–78), though the tests described do not appear there. Similar tests do appear in his *Centuriae IX. Memorabilium.*

27–8 *if . . . though . . . folio*: but what if he should test me . . . page.

36 *know . . . hundred*: I could pick you out among a hundred phials.

38 *look to*: be on my guard for.

43–4 *That . . . proof . . . sleight*: who has not yet put it to the test . . . trick (Q 'slight').

48–9 *else . . . Where . . . been*: otherwise . . . i.e. if I had not seen this.

50–3 *'tis . . . purchase*: she's a scrupulous girl who cannot be bribed with gold.

54–5 *look . . . Would . . . too*: look for . . . i.e. she too is attracted to Alsemero, which Beatrice-Joanna does not know.

58 *roosting time*: bedtime.

60 *pit-hole*: grave. But Diaphanta's analogies have a shared sexual sub-text —men of action who roam the world or conquer it come in the end to small, confined spaces (i.e. the vagina). Hence Beatrice-Joanna's reproof about lack of modesty.

64 *set light . . . owed*: play down her delights, as if she owned.

66–7 *maid . . . You . . . behind*: virgin . . . i.e. your immodest talk makes me blush. Beatrice-Joanna tries to convince Diaphanta that she is afraid of her first sexual encounter.

68 *Do . . . sooth*: are you speaking in earnest?

71–4 *will give . . . to't*: i.e. she offers 1,000 ducats to any virgin willing to lose her virginity and tell her how she feels after it. If she enjoys it, that may be enough to attract her (Beatrice-Joanna) to the experience.

75 *Do . . . get*: i.e. Get.

84–5 *the gold . . . honour*: the gold is a side-issue to ensure that her honour remains secure (that seems to be the meaning, though 'by-bet' is unusual in this context).

86–7 *I do . . . honesty*: i.e. I cannot vouch for anyone else's faith or honesty.

90–1 *quick . . . urge*: gamesome, wanton . . . provoke.

95 *honesty*: chastity.

97–8 *She . . . jury*: perhaps alludes to the notorious divorce of Frances Howard, Countess of Essex, who was medically examined by a female jury, though such 'searches' are a common Jacobean joke/fantasy.

102 *praise itself*: prove its own effectiveness.

107 *which . . . it*: who am the one for whom the test is most significant.

109 *circumscribed . . . accident*: set on a prescribed course . . . characteristic, symptom.

114 *lays itself*: dies down.

118 *The carriage*: how to carry out.

118–19 *carry . . . burden*: she plays on 'carrying a tune' (*burden* = refrain), but really anticipates the weight of Alsemero on top of her.

121 *use . . . place*: take over the place (in bed).

123–4 *I'm for . . . fools*: I set my sights on a big fool of a justice now that I have a dowry, scorning lesser men.

4.2.1 *honour . . . question*: Alonzo's disappearance is a matter of honour, if he has been murdered. The honour of a host is impugned if a guest is murdered in his house (because he has not ensured his safety), whether or not he is actually responsible.

7 *Briamata*: in the dramatists' source this was Vermandero's country house.

9 *charge*: suspicion, accusation.

11–12 *answer . . . command . . . apprehension*: vouch for . . . order for their arrest.

16 *set on*: assaulted (i.e. he has seen Tomazo's entrance).

20 *the place*: Tomazo holds the household responsible for the disappearance of his brother, and threatens vengeance on them if he gets no satisfaction. He cites the hurried rematch of Beatrice-Joanna to Alsemero as evidence of probable murder.

24 *breach of faith*: Vermandero counters by accusing Alonzo of dishonourably deserting Beatrice-Joanna and betraying those friends who trusted him.

27 *prepared morning*: i.e. the morning set for the wedding.

33–4 *'Tis too . . . alliance*: it's too good an answer for a relation of his.

34–5 *warn . . . see you*: a formal order to leave his house and not return.

36 *more . . . on*: i.e. there are other places where I can exact revenge.

38–9 *way . . . she . . . blessed*: way did she go . . . guarded (i.e. warded off evil).

40 *fain . . . off*: be glad to get away. Deflores is uncomfortable talking with the brother of the man he murdered.

46–7 *jealousy . . . guilty person*: suspicion . . . i.e. he wants Deflores to nominate a murderer.

51 *easy . . . packed*: the sense is clear—Deflores argues Beatrice-Joanna is an average sinner, for a woman, against Tomazo's insistence she is really wicked. But the precise meaning of *round-packed* is not known—attractively plump? wide-ranging?

54 *chins and noses*: Q, 'sins and vices', which makes little sense. The 'horned-moon' profile of the old crone/witch is a common figure. He means that women are by no means (*at no hand*) wicked until old enough to consort with (or resemble?) witches.

56 *o'erlays*: oppresses.

58 *bring . . . out*: discover the secret.

59–60 *the . . . joy . . . 'Twill*: i.e. the bridegroom (*glorious* = boastful) . . . Q, 'I will'.

65–6 *none of those . . . wine*: i.e. not just here to congratulate you on your wedding.

67 *'Tis . . . lay*: i.e. the blood of the murderer is what must quench.

71–4 *I should . . . fairly*: the gist of Tomazo's charge is that, as Alsemero has taken Alonzo's place as bridegroom, impossible without foul play, he is the prime suspect.

75–6 *answer . . . word . . . it*: fight a duel over that accusation . . . the answer (i.e. a sword).

77 *Keep . . . not*: Tomazo makes great ironic play of not disturbing the sanctity of the wedding day: he can bide his time.

80 *My . . . me*: knowing that I am innocent makes this easier to bear.

83–4 *Would I . . . in't*: I wish I could keep my news to myself, if only I could honour my friendship with you in doing it.

85–6 *dispense . . . in this*: allow me to be less than usually zealous in my duty, so that I do not have to pass on the news.

86–7 *puts me . . . slowness*: provokes me and makes you reprehensible in your slowness.

88–9 *friendly fear . . . though*: over-concern of a friend . . . Q 'thou', in later printings emended to 'tho'.

91 *pretend*: profess (with no pejorative overtones).

97 *out*: mistaken (probably playing on the theatrical sense of being 'out' when an actor forgets or confuses his lines).

98 *tell . . . anon*: tell me more about this shortly. i.e. who knows about this—you or me?

   prevent: forestall. He is telling Jasperino he *must* be wrong.

103–4 *challenge . . . woman . . . Peace . . . bosom*: claim some right to a woman . . . Alsemero warns Jasperino to say no more, or he risks being run through with a sword.

108 *And touched . . . here*: yet tainted . . . in my bed.

109 *be . . . hereof*: to have my doubts on this cleared up.

113 *Chaldean*: ancient race, noted for prophecy and magic. So one skilled in the occult.

   I've made: Q, 'I've'.

117 *hang together*: make sense.

119 *Delivered . . . for*: reported her to be.

122 *That . . . bosom*: that Beatrice-Joanna might come to my embraces in the dark.

124 *grieves*: it grieves.

130 *abused, questionless*: slandered, without doubt.

141 *Treble qualitied*: with three effects.

147 *blasted*: blighted, cursed.

149 *Keeps*: Q, 'Keep'.

4.3.1 *waiting*: so Q, perhaps meaning 'lying in wait' and so 'ill-intentioned'. But 'waxing' (with the consequence that lunacy was increasing) may have been intended.

2–3 *at . . . madman . . . fool*: not in Q . . . a madman (Franciscus) like the fool (Antonio).

6 *Compare . . . out*: (1) compare the contents of the letter with its cover; (2) compare the inner man with his appearance.

7 *taste*: refers to Franciscus's attack on Lollio in 3.3.

8–11 *'To the bright . . . madness*: madness indeed, sent by an assistant of Aeolus, god of winds, though not without method. Franciscus hails Isabella as Andromeda because he casts himself as the Perseus who will rescue her from the dragon, Alibius. The Knight of the Sun is an alternative hero, from *Mirror of Knighthood*, a chivalric romance, and the chambermaid (Isabella is the only woman in the asylum) is apparently meant to be besotted with him. Scorpio is the sign of the zodiac that governs the sexual organs (so *in the middle region* is bawdy).

13 *appear to*: stand before (as someone 'appears' in court for judgement). The rest of the letter is full of perversely ingenious playing on the

language of courtly love. Her perfections have made him imperfect. Her *sun* (favour) makes him grow, her *winter* (disfavour) makes him wither, etc. The death/rebirth tropes are all sexually suggestive, clearest in *Tread* (= copulate with).

17 *made*: Q repeats 'have'.

20–1 *transshapes . . . dismantled . . . ornaments*: metamorphoses . . . stripped of my proper clothes.

26–9 *cure . . . madmen*: the claim that a beloved could cure the 'madness' of love (in effect by committing adultery) was a totally conventional literary trope, which Lollio ironically takes seriously, suggesting that Isabella should apply herself in the asylum.

32–3 *if . . . thirds*: i.e. if she sets up in trade to cure madmen and fools (as an adultress) Lollio demands his third share of any fees (she would be joining Alibius and Lollio in business). He also implies that he expects to share in her sexual favours.

35 *fall*: Isabella means 'make a mistake', but Lollio opts to construe it as 'have sex'.

38 *stand to*: (1) stand by; (2) have an erection.

39 *deal with*: (1) treat, handle (Isabella's sense); (2) have illicit relations (Lollio's).

40 *Why*: Q, 'We'.

41 *fair understanding*: she asks to be understood in the sense she honestly intends.

43 *kindly*: (1) gently; (2) naturally. So Lollio has a perfect excuse for mistreating his inmates—as the Petrarchan mistress has for scorning her suitors.

44–5 *practise . . . wardrobe*: (1) scheme; (2) perform . . . Isabella wants a suitable disguise.

46 *fit . . . 'em*: dress/prepare yourself for them, and I'll make them ready.

47–8 *outside . . . inside*: Isabella tells Lollio to observe what is going on, but only from outside. Lollio turns it into a bawdy joke about entering inside her.

53 *taken pains*: (1) taken trouble, put in effort; (2) inflicted pain on.

54–5 *miss . . . the more . . . so*: make a mistake . . . the more absurd the better, as long as.

56 *nice*: delicate.

58 *pizzles*: whips made from the dried penises of bulls, but Lollio is also thinking of the power of his own 'pizzle' to tame *the ladies*.

60 *morris*: country dance.

63 *measure*: dance.

68–9 *length . . . short*: snidely belittles Albinius's own sexual performance.

75 *elephant*: an obscure joke, which perhaps suggests that Alibius is being led by the nose, but may also imply that the length of his nose compensates for that of his penis.

81 *ride*: have intercourse.

82 *Vault in*: many Jacobean dances involved leaping and high stepping.

85 *honour*: bow, obeisance.

88 *Does . . . hams*: in asking how to bow Antonio implicitly asks whether nobles bow to their inferiors. Lollio picks this up, but also takes *bend in the hams* as 'copulate'.

89 *worship . . . yeomanry*: the social scale of honour (who bows to whom). Persons 'of honour' were nobility, those 'of worship' substantial gentry, squires lesser country gentry, and yeomen freeholders—the lowest rank whom those 'of honour' acknowledged socially.

92 *rises*: Q, 'rise'.

94 *figure*: (1) dance steps; (2) face, appearance. Antonio plays on the second sense.

96 *he*: Q, 'she'. 'Treads air' suggests high, flying steps.

96–101 *shoo . . . clue*: Isabella mixes madness with method. She identifies Antonio with Icarus, who flew from Crete with wings made by his father Daedalus, but flew too near the sun and the wax holding the wings melted. 'Shoo, shoo' may be her attempt to get Antonio to be more careful in his leaping, which fails. The wax becomes seals on legal documents (which may be *cancelled* or destroyed), perhaps her own marriage contract. One version of the myth had Icarus and Daedalus escaping from a labyrinth. A different myth placed the Minotaur in the labyrinth, and Theseus went in to slay it, only finding his way out with the thread (*clue*) given him by Ariadne. If the labyrinth is the asylum, Alibius is the Minotaur.

102 *drowned*: *drowned*, *billows*, *straits*, *pirates*, and *waves* all play off Icarus falling into the Mediterranean.

106 *tiara*: turban with a long tailpiece.

108 *straits*: Q, 'streets'. Isabella is messing with Antonio's outlandish disguise to make him look even more foolish, but there is probably also some sexual or scatological by-play in the offer to *suck out those billows in thy belly*.

112 *hadst . . . of*: were successor to.

113 *Endymion*: shepherd youth with whom Luna/the moon fell in love, subject of a play by John Lyly. Isabella casts herself as Luna, controlling the waves.

117 *antic*: grotesque clown. He does not see through her disguise.

118 *I . . . mad*: I came as one pretending to be mad, and return as one absolutely so.

131 *usher*: (1) doorkeeper; (2) under-teacher.

133 *You . . . then*: then you had better spend another period being mad.

138 *fox-skin*: cunning disguise.

139–42 *arrant a . . . ride her*: Lollio says more than anyone knows in claiming that Isabella 'loves' Antonio. He may be more attractive than Alibius. But he has failed her test of him, and neither he nor Lollio (the two 'fools') will actually get to *ride* her. Lollio's motive is to entice Antonio into the plot against Franciscus.

151 *Latona's . . . bowstring*: confused mythology. The *bowstring* suggests Cynthia/Diana, the huntress, often synonymous with Luna. But Latona was actually Diana's mother.

165 *another*: either a reference to Antonio (who will also *be hanged*), or *another trick*, presumably adultery on top of fraud.

167 *Art . . . with*: are you in the confidence of.

169 *hand*: Lollio chooses to take this as 'handwriting'. Putting Franciscus's letter in his pocket leads to puns on words being *true*, or able to *pick* (steal) and *lie*.

177 *give you over . . . cast your water*: consign you to her care . . . test your urine for signs of disease.

180 *loves you*: Lollio has even fewer grounds for saying that Isabella loves Franciscus than for saying that she loves Antonio. This is clearly just a ploy.

182 *There . . . wishes*: that accords with my own wishes.

183 *meet*: Lollio is suggesting a duel, paralleling Tomazo's calling out of Alsemero.

192 *reserve . . . past*: delay beating him until after the wedding masque.

193–4 *My master*: the stage action from this point is not easy to deduce. Lollio presumably says this because he sees Alibius (though it *could* be a mock-deference to Franciscus). Franciscus's final line seems to be gibberish for the benefit of Alibius and he has to leave the stage to rejoin the mad dancers. Lollio would seem to have to go off-stage to bring the madmen and fools back on—but Alibius never actually stops talking to him. My stage directions are thus extremely provisional.

196 *Well said*: stock phrase, meaning 'well done'.

200–1 *fool . . . begged*: to beg a fool was to become his legal guardian, and so have the use of the proceeds of his estate (cf. Guardiano in *Women Beware Women*).

202 *him*: Lollio presumably has either Franciscus or Antonio in mind.

204 *fit . . . strains*: just make ready this music.

5.1 s.d. *strikes*: Q, 'strike'.

1 *lies by't*: (1) lies with Alsemero; (2) pretends to be who she is not.

5 *havoc . . . pays*: pillages my sexual rights as a wife; but she will pay. Beatrice-Joanna is distressed by the idea that Diaphanta is actually enjoying her time with Alsemero.

6–7 *No trusting . . . promise*: I cannot allow her to live, knowing what she does, when she cannot control her sexual passion enough to keep her word.

8–10 *Beside . . . her*: apart from which I doubt her loyalty to me, since Alsemero suspected me, and that must have come from her.

11 *Pist . . . where*: it is supposed to be dark and a quiet time of night. They presumably talk in heavy stage whispers.

14 *sowed . . . her*: put his sexual appetite into her. Deflores castigates all waiting women as lustful.

17–18 *fall upon . . . first-fruits*: have voracious sex with . . . pleasures of the wedding night.

19 *You . . . royal*: you cannot beat them away from the royal game. The image is from hunting dogs (*mad whelps*) which cannot be pulled off a deer (all deer legally belonged to the crown) once they have attacked it.

20 *harsh . . . counsel*: independent and headstrong, ask no advice.

21–2 *And . . . an . . . thanked*: when . . . Q, 'a' . . . Q, 'thank'.

25 *Phosphorus*: the morning-star. Q, 'Bosphorus'.

26–7 *Advise . . . else*: tell me how to set about destruction of some kind; there is no other safe plan. Beatrice-Joanna is lapsing into (possibly suicidal) despair, and keeps seeing objections, while Deflores is brusquely practical.

27–8 *I ha't . . . no remedy*: I know what to do now; we must cause everyone in the house to get up; there is no alternative.

31 *reach*: plan.

36 *strikes . . . sure*: (which) solves everything for certain. There is a play on the implication 'by murder'.

37–46 *The chimney . . . chimney*: Deflores has thought through all the eventualities. He is going to set the chimney in Diaphanta's chamber alight and one or two small items (*light parcels*), not creating any real danger. When the alarm is raised, if Diaphanta is seen near Alsemero's room (which would normally be suspicious) people will assume she is frightened and looking for help. If not, she will head for her own chamber, where Deflores will have a fully charged gun (*piece*), ostensibly to dislodge soot and debris from the chimney (which might cause such a fire).

46 *proper*: complete, fitting. i.e. the whole plan, including the explanation for the gun.

47 *mark*: target.

48 *honour*: Beatrice-Joanna is still obsessed with the appearance of honour. Deflores insists that the stakes are more practical, *safety*, *pleasure*, *continuance*. He shows signs of exasperation with Beatrice-Joanna in the oath *'Slid*: by God's eyelid.

55–6 *conveyance . . . minute*: way of removing the body . . . cue.

59 *'Twixt . . . me*: the Ghost stands between Deflores and heaven.

65 *he*: Alsemero. Beatrice-Joanna imagines Diaphanta forcing him to bring her to climax after climax (*lives* = orgasms).

67 *Three*: she reads each hour struck as another sexual climax in Alsemero's bed.

70 *loathes*: disgusts.

72 *east*: associated with the dawn, new light and life, and the Holy Land.

75–6 *the chimney . . . piece*: the chimney is fulfilling its role; my responsibility, the gun.

78–9 *well . . . trim*: happily situated . . . fine (heavily ironic, hence Diaphanta's 'What?').

89 *well said*: well done. Vermandero typically switches from touchy bad temper (*Knave . . .*) to enthusiastic gratitude when he thinks he understands what is happening.

91 *wondrous necessary*: absolutely indispensable.

93 *Dog*: a multiple pun, emphasizing Vermandero's respect for Deflores. (1) keen like a dog in pursuit of the fire; (2) an iron (= andiron), so a useful fireplace tool; (3) an early firearm—so an ingenious way to *scour* (clean out) the chimney.

101–2 *heavy . . . She . . . mine*: slovenly, sluggish . . . she twice eluded a conflagration. These are probably fictions. Beatrice-Joanna is mainly thinking of Diaphanta's sexual near-misses (*mine* = vagina), the virginity test and undiscovered night in Alsemero's bed.

102 *Strangely*: miraculously.

103 *sluts*: slovenly young women, possibly without the slur of loose morals usual today. But it would be typical of Vermandero's abrupt judgements if it implied both.

104 *An . . . good*: however good they are.

s.d. *Enter Deflores*: conceivably 'with Diaphanta's body'. Vermandero asks 'what's that' and Deflores replies 'a thing', perhaps a body so burnt as to be unrecognizable and to disguise a gunshot wound. If so, this was the *safe conveyance for the body* Deflores earlier planned. But Q is not categorical about this, and it is equally possible that Deflores is play-acting horror and revulsion at what he has seen in the chamber.

109 *presaging*: foreseeing. She is referring to her former 'fear'.

112 *sister*: see 3.4.4 and note.

124 *call . . . me*: visit me to seek your reward.

125 *trick . . . me*: twist even I did not think of.

5.2.1-2 *I cannot . . . to do*: Tomazo, brooding on the presumed death of his brother, has developed the characteristics of a Jacobean stage melancholic, like Hamlet, having lost all appetite for life and its pleasures, and suspicious of all men and their motives.

5 *ignorant in*: do not know on.

9 *some . . . Deflores*: melancholy has put an end to Tomazo's earlier trust in Deflores.

10-11 *hard . . . lodging*: hard put to it to settle in that body. Voicing the common Jacobean assumption that an ugly body reflected a corrupt personality.

12-13 *her . . . pest-house . . . contrariety*: a plague-hospital into her palace . . . antipathy.

15 *give . . . game*: an obscure phrase—'single him out as my quarry'?

16-17 *One . . . of*: a person would scarcely touch him with a sword he loved and valued. The contorted construction requires us to supply Deflores as the object of *touch*, rendering him as a kind of non-person.

21 *In . . . manhood*: by the laws of honourable, manly behaviour. A sword so 'poisoned' by Deflores's blood would not be fit for a future duel.

24 *walks . . . up*: walks past on purpose, without doubt, to suffocate me (with his infectious breath).

29 *politician*: intriguer, schemer.

33-4 *see . . . crystal*: see in Tomazo's eyes, as in a crystal ball, Alonzo's wounds bleeding freshly (alluding to the belief that a corpse's wounds bled freshly when the murderer was near).

35-7 *injury . . . gave it*: i.e. he refuses the challenge to a duel implicit in Tomazo's blow. If Tomazo is *noble* and has a *worthy hand* no breach of honour has taken place, though this is a loss of face to himself. Deflores has perhaps lost his self-belief.

40 *instinct . . . strain*: intuition is more rarefied in nature (than reason or common sense).

42 *came near*: almost found me out (twisting the literal sense in the previous line).

43 *league . . . mankind*: association with humanity.

44-5 *not so . . . up*: I'll even renounce normal good manners (more signs of melancholy).

59 *chiefest men*: principal followers.

61 *To . . . satisfaction*: to satisfy your peace of mind even further.

63 *Name . . . in*: i.e. put to me what I should need to do to earn forgiveness.

65 *perfect*: perform, carry out.

67–8 *you overdo . . . a't'other*: you are as excessive now in your penitence as you were deficient before in courtesy.

75–6 *habits . . . agrees justly*: (1) behaviour; (2) clothing, disguise . . . fits exactly.

79–80 *both . . . leaves*: both pretended they were going to Briamata and so obtained permission to be absent (actually one was supposed to be going to Valencia: 4.2.7/8).

84 *Be . . . conduct*: be my most fortunate and blest guide (to confront the guilty men).

85–6 *Like . . . in'em*: an image of diabolical torture, based on the idea that lightning could kill by melting the marrow in the bones, without leaving a mark on the flesh.

5.3.1 *confidence . . . of proof*: belief [in my story] . . . unshakeable. Jasperino is trying to convince Alsemero to take his suspicions seriously.

2 *prospect*: view (see note to 4.1.18).

3 *black mask*: refers to Deflores's ugliness, but also to Beatrice-Joanna's deceit in pretending to despise him, a pretence that must mask something even more ugly.

6 *despite . . . bottomless*: apparently inexhaustible scorn for him.

7 *Touch . . . home*: probe it all the way to the bottom (a medical metaphor).

10–11 *meets . . . with her*: the two have watched a meeting outdoors between Beatrice-Joanna and Deflores, in which it was apparent that their relationship has changed. Alsemero is now positioned to intercept Beatrice-Joanna on her way back inside.

19 *resolve me*: settle for me.

21 *broad*: (1) wide; (2) bawdy. 'Honest' comprehended 'honourable' and 'sexually chaste', as well as its modern senses.

24 *rough brow*: frowning and angry face.

26–7 *Say . . . faith to*: if I were to force enough tears to fill the heaven, would that make you trust me more?

37–8 *let . . . Rifling*: speak (the truth) now or I will ransack your heart for it.

41–2 *ground . . . tread*: she still protests her innocence, demanding to know the *ground* (evidence) for the accusation against her. But the secondary sense of *tread* (copulate), picked up by Alsemero, betrays her insincerity.

46 *ticklish*: fickle.

48 *impudence*: shamelessness.

49–51 *How . . . Deflores*: how else can we explain this loving accord between you and the man you despised, the man you utterly loathed, Deflores?

52 *arms' supporter*: (1) someone you allow to take you by the arm; (2) a figure who supports your shield (and so family honour) in heraldic blazoning.

53 *saint*: someone to whom you pray (in kissing).

56 *counsel . . . bosom*: close confidant.

61 *Than . . . with*: than your delusive imagination is overcome by.

62–4 *To your . . . proof of*: perhaps 'To your bed's scandal' should complete the previous sentence (meaning that the 'false suspicion' is creating a scandal about Alsemero's bed). As punctuated here, the sense is: against this scandal of your bed I oppose innocence, which indeeed the guilt of another crime will establish.

67–9 *worthy in . . . employed*: deserving to my mind no better use, and he most deserving that use (she means, of course, Deflores).

72 *the place*: the temple (cf. the opening lines of the play).

75–6 *right one . . . 'twill . . . now*: i.e. right devotion, to God . . . it (the place) will have its vengeance now.

82 *true . . . bed*: just how naïve or calculating is Beatrice-Joanna being? She may have reverted to her earlier view, that sexual dishonour is worse than murder. But equally, alone with Alsemero, she may be trying to convince him that he is partly responsible for the murder and that they still have a future.

84 *it . . . pause*: I need time to consider.

86 *closet*: his private room, from which there is no other exit.

89 *put . . . in*: given me my cue.

91 *her commended*: asked to be remembered (an act of courtesy).

94 *ever . . . well*: that is how much she loved me (ironic).

98 *sword . . . school . . . 'tis out*: practice session with sword and dagger . . . (the bloodstain) has been washed out.

101–2 *What . . . murder . . . behindhand with*: what is the going rate for murder . . . slow in paying.

107 *she's . . . whore*: contradicting what she has told Alsemero, hence her *He lies*.

108 *choose . . . follow*: you couldn't have one without the other.

112 *crying crocodile*: a crocodile was thought to shed tears to lure its victims into a false sense of security; hence one who weeps without real compassion or feeling.

113 *get . . . in*: we must presume that Alsemero has drawn his sword. Deflores would hardly allow himself to be imprisoned so easily otherwise.

116 *black audience*: devils in hell.

118 *'tis . . . pilot*: i.e. she is like Charon, who ferried the dead over the Styx in Hades.

119 *Mare Mortuum*: the Dead Sea, in which bodies will not normally sink because of the heavy salt content. It was thought to be bottomless—and so like the pit of hell.

121 *a wonder for you*: something to astonish you.

131 *nearer*: nearer in blood—i.e. your kin, who will 'acquit' the servants.

134 *bandied*: tossed back and forth, like a tennis ball.

135 *in blood*: concerns my family honour and moves me passionately.

138–9 *wife with . . . adultery*: Tomazo is determined either to find his brother (1) alive, in which case he believes Beatrice-Joanna is still legally betrothed to him, or (2) dead, in which case he demands vengeance both for murder and for adultery between Alsemero and Beatrice-Joanna, since she was legally betrothed to Alonzo.

139 *Oh, oh, oh*: the 'horrid sounds' are probably firstly those of Beatrice-Joanna and Deflores willingly copulating, and latterly of her being wounded by him.

'tis . . . you: the recompense which Tomazo demanded is about to appear.

145–6 *so . . . yet . . . broken . . . mankind*: that is all the strength I have now . . . i.e. he likens Beatrice-Joanna to Eve, created from Adam's rib and *broken* by sin.

150–1 *blood . . . health*: blood let by a surgeon to purge the body of its impurities.

152 *regardlessly*: paying it no attention.

153 *from distinction*: from the state in which it can be known or identified.

154 *meteor*: Deflores. In medieval astrology the stars were fixed and unchanging, like the fates they represented. But meteors wandered in the sublunar regions, where things were unstable and 'corruptible'.

156 *it*: my fate.

162–3 *the while . . . barley-brake*: in the mean time . . . see note to 3.3.159.

164 *We . . . here*: cf. Marlowe, *Dr Faustus*: 'Hell hath no limits, nor is circum-scribed | In one self place, for where we are is hell . . . ' (Bevington and Rasmussen (eds), *Dr Faustus and Other Plays* (Oxford, 1995), A-text 2.1.121–2).

167 *honour's prize*: virginity.

171 *pledge me*: drink a toast to me.

175 *by . . . token*: by token of the wound he has just given himself. The point is perhaps that it replicates the one he gave her earlier.

180 *record*: as when Alonzo's murder was first suspected, Vermandero is probably thinking of family dishonour (*my name*) rather than divine reckoning.

182 *it*: the entry in the record.

185–7 *Justice . . . proclamation*: justice has so squarely condemned the guilty that the innocent have been acquitted by public proclamation.

190–1 *my injuries . . . no more*: those who caused me injury . . . no more vengeance.

192–3 *o'ertake . . . fugitives*: catch up with the damned souls of Beatrice-Joanna and Deflores in flight.

194–6 *wraths . . . mine . . . opacous*: i.e. those of God . . . dark, obscured, and so ominous.

201 *wantonness*: Diaphanta, whose sin was *paid before* with her death.

203 *more on's*: more of us that have undergone such marked changes.

205 *changed . . . gallows*: changed by being hung (being suspected of Alonzo's murder).

206 *innocence*: (1) lack of guilt; (2) idiocy.

208–9 *behind . . . transformation*: to come, but you deserve your change most of all.

210–11 *coxcomb . . . break . . . head*: simpleton . . . i.e. with cuckold's horns.

215–16 *Sir . . . accept it*: i.e. Alsemero as son-in-law offers himself in place of Beatrice-Joanna, whom he urges Vermandero to forget even as he weeps for her.

Epilogue 5–6 *Your only . . . dead again*: only your (the audience's) smiles can bring the dead characters to life again in a new performance, so giving Tomazo a renewed Alonzo, and Vermandero Beatrice-Joanna.

A Game at Chess

The Characters of the Play

Characters of the Play: there is no list in any early text. See the Introduction on the 'identification' of characters with known individuals. More detailed discussion of key characters is given in the notes at the points where they first enter.

Prologue

The Prologue is after the Induction in Lan., interrupting the dramatic flow, the mark of a text for readers rather than an account of the play as staged.

4 *States*: great men, (1) leading political figures; (2) chessmen more potent than pawns.

5 *Houses*: metaphor for the sides, implying families or races (and so countries) but also religious orders. They are 'well distinguished' by being respectively Black and White.

6–7 *entrapped . . . play*: in the play (unlike chess) characters are 'taken' when they are discovered to play falsely—hence *to their shame* and *Rewarded by their play*.

8 *checkmate*: the terminal play in a game of chess, when one side traps the other's king so that there is no avoiding its being taken.

9 *our . . . deck*: can grace our hopes.

10 *check*: rebuke, with an obvious play on the chess sense (threaten the king).

The Induction

Induction: placed before the Prologue in Lan., after in other witnesses.

S.D. *Ignatius . . . feet*: Ignatius Loyola (1491–1556) was founder of the Society of Jesus (Jesuits), the main Roman Catholic force in the Counter-Reformation and so particularly reviled by Protestants. Error is the main figure of untruth in Middleton's Lord Mayor's Pageant, *The Triumphs of Truth* (1613). No text precisely indicates the staging here. Tr.'s 'appearing' may suggest Loyola arose from under the stage, as from hell. But Error 'at his foot as asleep' seems to indicate a stationary discovery tableau; it also precludes use of the partly shielded upper stage—otherwise an attractive option.

1 *this*: i.e. here in the theatre, so England.

5 *As . . . institution*: both of my plots and of my established order (i.e. of the Jesuits). Loyola is surprised at finding a rare corner of the world where his plots have not flourished, nor his followers and order become established.

7–8 *Covered . . . grasshoppers*: cf. Exodus 10: 14–15 'And the locusts went up over all the land of Egypt, and rested on all the coasts of Egypt. . . . For they covered the face of the whole earth, so that the land was darkened' (1611 Authorized Version). The passage was commonly applied to Jesuits in Protestant propaganda.

10 *deflowered*: made to lose virginity, raped. Religious truth is pure and innocent, and the Jesuits seek to defile it. Hence the plot against the White Queen's Pawn.

11–12 *they . . . monarchy | Unperfect*: Loyola's followers . . . the Jesuit mission to convert all Protestants was perceived as a grand design to establish a single Catholic power, the 'universal monarchy'.

17–18 *to canonise . . . prosperous institutor*: in canonizing (admitting to the calendar of saints) . . . founder who caused them to flourish. Loyola complains that the Jesuits took too long about having him declared a saint. The Bull for his canonization was published in March 1622, only two years before the play, not five. This may be ignorance or may indicate Middleton maintaining a careful fictional distance.

19 *no . . . calendar*: Protestant propaganda ridiculed the process of modern canonization as beset by petty rivalries within the Catholic Church. Saints were assigned a feast-day but there were already more saints than days, so 'lesser' saints had to share days.

23 *saint-homily*: holy preacher. Loyola scornfully lists the pious but undistinguished saints who he feels have unjustly been given precedence (*place*) over him.

24 *Roch, Main, and Petronill*: St Roch (*c*. 1350–80) was patron of the plague-stricken, St Main (Meen, Mewan) a famed healer of skin diseases in the sixteenth century, St Petronilla an early Roman martyr.

25 *Abbess . . . Cunegund*: St Aldegundis (*c*.635–84), virgin and hermit, suffered a patient death from cancer. St Cunegund is either the founder of a convent which served the poor and the sick (1224–92) or the empress wife of Henry II (*c*.978–1033).

26 *Marcell . . . Polycarp*: St Marcella (*c*.410), Roman widow and ascetic. St Polycarp (*c*.69–110) was a martyred Bishop of Smyrna—*parson* is derogatory.

27 *Cecily . . . Ursula*: St Cecilia (second or third century), Roman martyr, patron saint of musicians. St Ursula was a legendary fourth-century British princess and virgin martyr.

28 *bisextile*: leap-year, every fourth year (not *one in three*) when an extra day, 29 February, is added to the calendar. No saint was allocated to that irregular day, but there was a rumour that Loyola was to be. St Ignatius Loyola's feast-day is actually 31 July, from which St Germanus of Auxterre was moved to give him the sole honour.

32 *lame soldier*: Loyola was a soldier in early life and lamed at the siege of Pamplona.

34 *first . . . name*: 'ign' gives us 'ignis', Latin for fire. The Gunpowder Plot (1605) had popularly associated Jesuits with explosives and arson.

35 *colleges*: religious orders (not necessarily buildings as such).

36 *Supererogation*: Catholic doctrine, much derided by Protestants, whereby good works beyond what were strictly required may constitute a store of merit which the Church can use to compensate for the failings of other sinners.

40 *saw*: in a dream, in his sleep.

42 *noblest . . . all*: chess was respected as a game requiring great intelligence, but Error hints at the greater struggle between good and evil.

46 *secular daughter*: follower of Mary Ward (1585–1645) who set up an order of religious women (suppressed in 1630). The Black Queen's Pawn is later described as a 'secular Jesuitess' (1.1.40).

48–9 *If ever . . . this*: if power can ever manifest true authority in you, let it do so in this (play). Loyola wants a grand demonstration of Jesuit success, but Error warns him it is only a *dream* or *vision*.

52 S.D. Music . . . *game*: only Ar. and Q3 indicate that there is music. It would require an exceptionally large cast (34, including Loyola and Error) to have *complete* Houses on stage and no witness suggests as much (e.g. only one knight and one duke is specified on either side, and nothing indicates a full complement of pawns). The White House presumably stood symbolically stage right and the Black stage left (the 'sinister' side), though all entrances and exits may not be so schematic.

55–9 *Dukes . . . titles*: Middleton draws loosely on J. Barbier's revision of Arthur Saul's *The Famous Game of Chess-Play* (1618) to justify the use of *duke* for the piece usually known as 'rook' or 'castle'. Buckingham had been made a duke in 1623, for the visit to Madrid which is the subject of scenes 5.1 and 5.3 in the play.

61 *Bishop's*: Tr. more explicitly 'and Black Bishop's'.

62 *argue but . . . preferments*: suggest only . . . advancements, offices.

65 *I would . . . place*: Loyola prefigures the Black House generally, who compete with each other as much as with the White House. The Bishop stands next to the Queen on the chess-board, where Loyola wants to be so as to make advances (*a love-tale*) to her. The Black House are driven by insatiable lust.

74 *reigned*: a pun on rein/reign.

75–6 *mark'em . . . Observe*: take note of them . . . regard (them) closely.

77 *longings . . . tossed*: he anticipates emotional turmoil until the 'great game' is settled.

78 S.D.: Lan. (unlike Tr.) is quite explicit that Loyola and Error leave the stage, and so do not watch or preside over the subsequent action. The actor playing Loyola may reappear as the Black Bishop's Pawn: see Appendix, p. 314.

1.1 Crane spells out in Latin all changes of scene in Lan. (except for the dumb-show 4.3). Tr. only so marks the first scenes of Acts 1 and 2, and the 'scaena ultima', 5.3.

S.D. Enter . . . *Pawn*: Tr.: '*Enter from the Black House the Black Queen's Pawn, from the White House the White Queen's Pawn.*'

1 *BLACK . . . PAWN*: attempts to identify the Black Queen's Pawn with known individuals, from Mary Ward (see note to Induction 46) to the Archduchess Isabella, are neither compelling nor necessary. This is true of many of the lesser characters.

3 *dust and ashes*: the Bible and *Book of Common Prayer* both stress that we are made from earth and return to it.

4–5 *give . . . heresy*: pronounce . . . Ar. 'ignorance'.

6 *bleeds . . . eyes*: i.e. weeps. The Black Queen's Pawn may recognize the spiritual purity of the White Queen's Pawn but this show of distress that she is damned as a Protestant (*the daughter of heresy*) is a stratagem to attract her trusting White counterpart.

WHITE . . . PAWN: many attempts have been made to 'identify' the White Queen's Pawn, ranging from Elizabeth of Bohemia (James I's daughter, whose misfortunes in the Thirty Years War stirred strong sympathies among English Protestants) to the Church of England. She embodies embattled purity and religious truth, and it is probably a mistake to read any one identification too rigidly.

6–7 *Where . . . sorrow*: she mistakes a show of emotion for true feeling.

7 *These are*: Tr. 'They're'.

9 *What . . . in't*: why should my peace (of mind) cause her so much distress?

10–14 *If I . . . her eye*: if I get lost and, even with eyes wide open, miss the path she can (through frequent practice) run down blindfolded, why should my inadvertence raise the smallest tear in her eye (even if this is the finest game (salvation v. damnation) that a Christian ever lost).

15–16 *charity . . . sooner*: an act of charity is prima-facie evidence of virtue.

17 *made . . . promise*: promised grace.

18–20 *What . . . firmer*: how little effort would raise a stronghold for virtue in that sweet creature, to be remembered forever, if the foundations (her faith) were more secure.

22 *what . . . professed*: the faith I have affirmed.

25–6 *Your . . . conflict*: your resolution in that respect (in standing by what you have always professed) makes you weaker in the true Christian battle.

26–9 *There . . . spirit*: mere moments ago (*but now*) I saw a flash of ardent, original (*primitive*) faith flying from your devout eye, with power to confute (*blow up*) all the heresies (Ar. 'errors') that have consistently given bad counsel to your soul.

29 s.d. *a Jesuit*: Tr.

30–1 *sanctimonious . . . Will*: (1) holy, sacred; (2) merely purporting to be holy. It is meant in the former sense, but the audience might well take it in the latter . . . Tr. 'Can'.

33 *Women . . . vessels*: i.e. what should women (traditionally *weaker vessels*) do, if (male) princes fall down before him?

34–5 *A comely . . . reverend*: a handsome appearance, the clerical dress compelling great respect. The 'Jesuit' is always impressively dressed, whether in clerical garb or not.

35 *the heart*: Tr. repeats 'the heart'. The inner virtue matters more than his appearance.

36–7 *pictured . . . arms*: Charity is traditionally depicted as fruitful, and the White Queen's Pawn has already admitted that Charity is a particularly attractive virtue.

40–1 *Jesuitess . . . greatness*: Ros., Lan., 'Jesuit' . . . Q1 'worth'.

42–6 *Jesuits in . . . holy pleasure*: i.e. they take oaths ('*in voto*': by vow) as novitiates, but continue to live secular lives until the Father General, head of the Jesuit order, requires them to wear its habit. Protestants thought such arrangements deeply suspicious.

54 *prove*: go on to become.

56 *serving . . . intelligence*: submitting items of secret information.

57 *As . . . bills*: parish clerks had to submit weekly lists of the dead in plague times.

58–9 *designs . . . prevented*: schemes often anticipated/forestalled.

62 *mystery . . . entrance*: the imagery is of a religious *mystery* too profound as yet for her to be initiated into, though the reality is one of political secrets.

63 *offend . . . back*: am at fault in so deflecting your enthusiasm.

66–7 *To the. . . wishes*: into the hands of the Black Bishop's Pawn [*the great worker*], to whose deep integrity I submit my obeisance, as (I submit) to you my best wishes.

68 *supple*: compliant, i.e. 'spiritually receptive' but the sexual innuendo is unmistakable.

passage: progress, though with the bawdy implication of 'opening'. This is more explicit in two cancelled lines, immediately following in Ar. The Black Queen's Pawn goes on: 'Women's poor arguments make but wimble-holes, | The auger is the man's'. Wimbles and augers are both drills for boring into the ground, but the latter (with obvious phallic connotations) is larger and extendable.

69–72 *Let me . . . goodness*: the language is of the pious man who calls on contemplation and his sense of wonder gradually to make himself fit to approach the holy place (*sanctuary*) she represents.

70 *season*: prepare.

417

74 *aspect*: appearance presented to the eye.

75 *single life*: the unwed life of the nun, more commonly Catholic than Protestant.

76–9 *Upon those . . . rose*: he sensually mixes a description of her lips, moist as with natural dew, with the idea of prayer as itself dew.

82–4 *a tender . . . frailty*: i.e. the penance should be no more intimidating than the fear a new bride has to overcome to suppress her maiden weakness (to face up to sexual intercourse). Fasts and penances, imagined here as *courteous physic* (mild medication), were religious mortifications particularly associated with Catholicism.

86–7 *merit . . . me*: the syntax here is such that the *erring ignorance* could actually be his own, and the very reason why he only sees her *merit* as *spotted righteousness*.

90 *Obedience's . . . daughter*: she agrees to become a secular Jesuitess, obedience being a particular feature of Jesuit vows.

93–4 *ever . . . judgement*: always intended to serve virtue in the proper way, but was mistaken (*transgressed* implies 'sinned') in my understanding of how to do that.

95–6 *That's . . . absolved . . . you*: that (sin) is easily forgiven . . . Tr. 'that you'.

97–101 *her ear's . . . again*: the Black Bishop's Pawn describes auricular confession, in which a sinner may confess to a priest and be absolved of her sins, which pass into the *knowledge* of the Church as if they had never been, like *vanished man*. Protestants disputed the Church's power in this.

102 *more trulier*: emphatic double comparative, 'more securely'.

102–3 *To . . . benefit*: the White Queen's Pawn worries this may be too easy on sinners.

107–14 *Now to . . . designs*: the Black Bishop's Pawn confirms a Protestant suspicion about auricular confession, that the Church uses it to pry into private desires (*inclination*) and weaknesses (*frailties*), so as to involve people in their machinations.

115 *disperse*: free yourself from.

119 *conceals*: who conceals.

120 *uncomely*: offensive, disagreeable. The analogy is of concealing the eruptions of venereal disease until it has done so much damage that cure is impossible.

124–5 *familiarly . . . nearer*: your confession must be made more intimately to me than anything you have ever told a close female friend you confide in at night.

126–7 *action . . . time*: the White Queen's Pawn picks up an implication that she might have committed a sexual indiscretion appropriate to night (*guilty of that black time*), and denies it. But she denies *action*, not thought.

128–38 *I must . . . profess now*: a difficult and protracted passage. What she mainly confesses is that she was once *about to part from . . . The single life which strongly I profess now*: i.e. that she contemplated a love relationship, which she now repents of. Before that, she likens her thoughts to a church congregation (*auditory*), some of whom come to see other people rather than hear sacred matter (*angels' food*). She admits she cannot police all her myriad thoughts, acknowledges error, foolish tenderness and guilt among them, but insists that she did not indulge such tendencies.

140–2 *no stain . . . footsteps*: i.e. she confesses to the temptation but denies any false-doing which would lead astray any modest young women modelling themselves on her.

145 *put . . . language to*: over the next sixty lines Middleton strongly implies, and finally confirms, what has happened: that the Black Knight's Pawn has castrated the man she loved, the White Bishop's Pawn. Quite how is never explained. The whole passage is central to Edgar C. Morris's 1907 theory that the allegory of the play is closely keyed to the fate of the Palatinate in the Thirty Years War (see 'The Allegory in Middleton's *A Game of Chess*', *Englische Studien* 37 (1907), 39–52.

146–9 *All actions . . . everlastingly*: nothing is too shocking for the confessor, and words used *in their proper language* are never immodest. The confessor must then keep them to himself for ever. But the Black Bishop's Pawn later reveals that he knows about the castration from the Black Knight's Pawn's confession.

149 *shut*: Tr. 'lock'.

150 *to . . . creation*: i.e. he was impotent.

151–2 *slip . . . deliver*: narrow strip (i.e. small amount) . . . report.

154 *heretic well pickled*: Protestant (Ar., 'puritan') who is (1) deeply confirmed, persistent; (2) reduced to a sorry (but appropriate) plight.

160 *I . . . heavy*: despite her hatred, she does not want him to be denied absolution for it. The Black Bishop's Pawn insists that the sinner must feel the consequences of such an unnatural (*unmanning*) crime.

163 *for defect*: because of his physical inadequacy.

165 *in ends of marriage*: in their purposes for marrying (i.e. to have sex and children).

169–70 *custom . . . possess*: normal expectation of enjoying what other women claim for themselves and do have.

173 *may redeem*: (which) may recover.

174–5 *I . . . was . . . forth*: i.e. the Black Bishop's Pawn's (sexual) interest in her has been redoubled by this evidence of her mental powers.

176 *I . . . you*: I will question you more closely.

179 *So exact*: (someone) so surpassingly accomplished (that).

187 *A . . . duty*: the duty of a woman to be schooled by her spiritual fathers in the Church.

189 *means*: methods.

190 *tract . . . obedience*: there were many such pamphlets for the instruction of novices.

194–6 *What makes . . . blessed spring*: what business does yonder stirrer of all Christian waters have so close to the holy spring (i.e. the White Queen's Pawn, a spring of religious virtues which the Black Bishop's Pawn seeks to pollute)?

202–3 *Are sacrifices . . . confined*: the subject is *suff'rings . . .* limited in sexual performance.

205 *inhuman*: unnatural.

207 *fingers*: Tr. completes the line with 'By this hand'. The Black Knight's Pawn's irritation is typical of the conflicts *within* the Black House.

208 *give . . . for*: wager my genitals against.

210–12 *I'll undertake . . . now*: I'll lay odds more bets will be laid on a money-lender's return from hell than on her (unsullied) return from the Black Bishop's Pawn.

212 *I'have*: Tr. 'have I'.

215 *savin tree*: the leaves of the savin were used to induce abortions. Protestant propaganda held it would be found in the orchards of nunneries. The Black Knight's Pawn is searching his soul and can find no wholesome *fruit* in his conscience.

217–18 *By . . . conjecture . . . I . . . resolved*: in all likelihood . . . I will have my doubts satisfied.

220 *sound*: i.e. the spoken words 'noble virgin'.

222 *out*: Tr. 'not'.

225 *leprosy*: figurative for a spiritual disease.

227–8 *set your . . . eyes*: contemplate your evil (i.e. examine it closely).

229 *shirt . . . hair*: wearing an irritant hair shirt was an extreme form of penance.

230–1 *And you . . . chasuble*: and a £3 chemise would better become you than a priest's white tunic, a sleeveless mantle suitable for either sex. He is impugning his manliness.

231–2 *felon . . . close . . . sting*: Tr. 'fellow' . . . secretly . . . i.e. of conscience.

235 *burdened*: i.e. with guilt.

238 *warned by diffidence*: made wary by suspicion.

239 *admit . . . nobleness*: agree to . . . Tr. 'a nobleness'.

240 *confusion . . . to*: ruin cling to.

    S.D. *Black Knight*: the play was widely known as 'the play of Gondomar', Spanish Ambassador to England 1613–22. There was no mistaking him as the Black Knight: 'They counter-feited his person to the life, with all his graces and faces, and had gotten (they say) a cast suit of his apparel for the purpose' (John Chamberlain).

245 *intelligencies*: Tr. 'intelligences'; secret news, information.

246 *fellow*: i.e. the Black Bishop's Pawn.

247 *incendiary, and*: see note to Induction, line 34 ('and' not in Tr.).

248 *seven year*: the possibility of a Spanish marriage for Prince Charles had been in the air since an English Ambassador Extraordinary was sent to Madrid in 1617.

249–50 *Put a . . . stands*: if you confront him with a new woman, the main enterprise stalls (though the secondary sense 'he has an erection' is also to be understood).

250–1 *minds nor . . . principality*: heeds neither royal nor ecclesiastical authorities ((being) the supreme spiritual authority). The bracketed phrase is probably a sneer at supposed Jesuit presumptions of being beyond the reach of all earthly authority.

252 *conclave*: body of cardinals. English Protestants widely regarded Gondomar as the chief architect of recent Catholic advances.

253 *Take . . . Assistant Fathers*: even taking into account the Jesuits specially charged with reporting to the Father General on matters in countries where they were stationed.

255 *facetiously*: urbanely, wittily. Gondomar was credited with great charm, said to bewitch King James and his court and make it possible for him to get away with all kinds of mischief. It is a feature of his characterization throughout.

257 *Abused . . . delight*: deceived all those who trusted me by being delightful.

258 *comfort . . . cozened*: pleasure in being hoodwinked.

265 *uphold . . . reverence*: respect his sanctity.

267–8 *Priapus . . . Venus' chit*: Priapus, child of Bacchus and Venus, was the Greek and Roman god of fertility (often depicted with an exaggerated phallus) and of gardens. *Cherry* gardens lewdly alludes to female genitalia. The bracketed line is not in Lan., possibly because of the sexual explicitness.

270 *dissimulation*: feigning, pretence. This dubious compliment may be intended to be lost on all but the audience as the Black Knight bows deeply.

272 *His . . . reverend*: his religious responsibilities must be deeply venerable.

274–80 *I do this . . . example*: i.e. the Black Knight despises the Jesuits (*guito-nens* = beggars, vagabonds (Spanish)), but astounds his enemies by the deference he shows them, maintaining the Black House reputation for piety, and also promoting obedience Jesuit-like in other easily led persons (*pusills* from the Latin *pusillus*, very small).

284 *to the . . . her*: he hopes to capture her when the game opens up (i.e. when pieces start to be taken), thus exposing the White King and Queen.

286–7 *If . . . harder*: suggesting that the Black Bishop's Pawn's motives are sexual rather than religious. *Harder* glances at the state of his phallus.

288–9 *existence . . . hope monarchal*: world empire . . . see Glossary, under 'universal monarchy'.

290–2 *You may . . . cedar*: i.e. you may also deny the movement of a clock or the force of the wind because you cannot see them.

293 *Where . . . intelligence*: why has the supply of intelligence dried up?

299 *quick flesh*: vital matter, with a play on *quick* = pregnant.

300 *butter*: probably an allusion to news-sheet reports of the Thirty Years War published by Nathaniel Butter.

298–302 *Anglica . . . Hispanica*: Anglica (England), Gallica (France), Germanica (the German states), Italica (the Italian states), Hispanica (Spain, incorporating Portugal). These were the provinces into which the Jesuits divided their missions.

301 *the Hebrew way*: i.e. backwards, like Hebrew script. The allusion is also to the Italian reputation (*pen* = penis) for anal intercourse.

302 *blind work*: invisible writing. Writing in lemon-juice is only visible when heated.

304 *purgatory*: in Roman Catholic theology, place of purging of sins after death. Its existence is denied by most Protestants.

306 *wound . . . name*: Tr. 'wounded your own fame'; *name*: reputation.

'*Curanda pecunia*': 'look out for your money'. The Black Knight's exclamation probably identifies the White King's Pawn as Lionel Cranfield, Earl of Middlesex, who as Lord Treasurer fought court corruption, but was impeached in 1624, on grounds of peculation though actually for his opposition to war with Spain. This passage is in Ar., suggesting Cranfield was a target all along, though other details complicate the picture.

308 '*in voto*': by vow, an initiate.

310 *special*: held in particular esteem.

315–19 *Believe it . . . you*: these lines are not in Ar., and refer to Cranfield's recent opposition in the Privy Council to war with Spain, represented as treason and support for Spain; *strength*: not in Tr.

S.D. *Exit*: Lan. places the 'Exit' here, but the White King's Pawn may be intended to hear the Black Knight's compliment as far as *gold*, though not the later contempt.

323 *fleet . . . home*: the yearly treasure fleet sent to Spain from the Americas was regularly raided (and so made *short*) by privateers.

324 *Jesuit-ridden*: completely inappropriate to Lionel Cranfield, this refers to the original target in the White King's Pawn, Sir Toby Matthew (1577–1655), son of an Archbishop of York, who converted to Catholicism in 1606 and became a priest in 1614. He was sent to Madrid in 1623 to help further the marriage negotiations for Prince Charles and so became a target of Protestant abuse.

326 *way*: Tr. 'path'. Whichever route he takes, he will be lost.

2.1 S.D. *Enter . . . Pawn*: Tr. 'Enter White Queen's Pawn with a book in her hand' and places the entry of the Black Bishop's Pawn after the White Queen's Pawn's speech.

1 *here*: she is reading the 'small tract of obedience' given her earlier.

3–4 *exception . . . general*: objection . . . comprehensive, all-embracing.

6 *gently reconciled*: easily justified (in relation to the stock of spiritual goodness). She has qualms about the unlimited powers of her Jesuit confessors.

8–9 *And . . . uncircumscribed*: in that light it seems good to have the power of the one who dispenses grace as unlimited (as that grace itself).

9–10 *modest . . . open . . . intents*: restrained, unobtrusive . . . broach my intentions.

11 *What . . . people*: how little effort it takes to win some people over.

12 *what . . . here*: not in Tr. or other witnesses.

14–15 *subscribes . . . unmeasurably politic*: signs . . . hugely skilled in political chicanery.

18–19 *carriage . . . These*: conduct . . . i.e. letters, instructions.

20 *by . . . devotion*: by the intense regard I feel for the seizing of devout souls. The Black King wraps his lascivious desires in pseudo-religious language.

21–2 *surprisal of . . . attempt . . . Queen's person*: unexpected attack upon . . . assault . . . see the Introduction on the identity of the White Queen.

27 *passed . . . rule*: accepted the main requirement (in reading the book).

32 *Hasten . . . redemption*: hurry to make up for the lost time.

39 *Well . . . goodness*: ('Boundless obedience', which has been) aptly described in this book as a universal goodness.

40 *holiness . . . garment*: the holy clothing of her own virtue.

55–6 *confess . . . meaning*: acknowledge myself very like an inexperienced non-lawyer pleading his own case who, assuming that words mean what they seem to.

59 *own*: Tr. 'good'.

63 *Fond . . . obey*: only undisciplined people obey when foolish men give orders.

66 *dealt . . . parcels*: sent out in small portions.

71 *look . . . colour*: be overcome with jealousy.

75 *idiot*: i.e. ignorance.

78 *put . . . one*: restricted to one. Cf. Truth in Middleton's *The Triumphs of Truth*: 'I never showed thee yet more paths than one.'

79 *wondrous faulty*: strangely misguided.

82–3 *At unawares . . . top*: unwittingly . . . ultimate conclusion. She begins to understand that her longing for more perfect virtue may have betrayed her into sin.

85–7 *three-vowed . . . forgot*: the people who take three vows [i.e. the Jesuits], for poverty, obedience and chastity, of which the last is the least observed.

91–2 *Must I . . . for*: do I have to order you to come forward for a happiness which you yourself should be pleading for?

95 *make . . . privilege*: misconstrue my considerate treatment (of your stubbornness) as giving you licence.

100 *grand monarchy*: see Glossary under 'universal monarchy'.

102 *A . . . with't*: a more powerful evil will deal with it (her scorn).

102–3 *threatens . . . strength*: he threatens me and quite disarms the power of virtue.

104–5 *doubtful of . . . jealousy*: anxious about . . . devotion, solicitude.

106 *house of meekness*: either the house of the Jesuits or the Black House.

112–13 *that . . . respect*: what . . . i.e. the respect due to me from the likes of her.

115 *thou . . . hence*: i.e. he begins to formulate a plan to preserve his reputation.

117 *depart so*: Tr.; Lan. lacks 'so'.

118 *Lay . . . reputation*: relinquish to me your good name, punning on 'lay down' for sex.

120 *love*: spiritual devotion (i.e. all my assiduous tuition; ironic).

121 *of . . . both*: her virginity in return for both his own *reputation* and his *love*.

122–3 *art to . . . thee to*: medical ways to conceal (your loss of virginity) and fools to pass you on to (when pregnancy makes marriage necessary).

123–4 *in my discovery . . . Society*: by my exposure all Jesuits suffer.

126–7 *Assurance . . . thee*: you cannot guarantee to keep matters secret, unless you lose your honour; that (sexual) act must cow you into control. *But thy*: Tr. 'But by thy'.

128 *Dost*: Tr. 'Dost thou'.

129 *this necessity*: ravishment, the only alternative to 'destroy(ing)' her.

131–2 *policy . . . life*: political future . . . Tr. 'life, sir'.

134 *vowed*: Tr. 'vowed since'.

137–8 *disperse . . . us*: make known the secrets of most rulers which we keep closely guarded; *princes*: Tr. 'nations'.

139 *confound*: thwart, bring to nothing. Lan. reads 'confound noise', Crane apparently running the line into the stage direction, which he then renders separately.

141 *upon . . . dangers*: whatever the risk.

142–5 *Let me . . . shrivelled*: let me see whoever it is, whether a pawn or his hollow, drum-like master, inflated with pompous bombast who, once pricked in the clergy-house, loses all his stale air and collapses, shrunken and wrinkled.

s.d. *Exit*: Q3.

150–1 *hopeful . . . dog-star*: promising, ambitious . . . Sirius, a star most prominent in the hottest summer months, often associated with excessive sexual ardour.

152 *wrought . . . pleasant*: made . . . Tr. 'pliant'.

155 *For . . . for*: to my own advantage, which is my only motive in everything I do.

157 *akindling*: alight. He expects everything to explode under him very soon.

159 *It's . . . mainly*: in his own interest he will defend you strongly.

s.d. *Black Bishop*: Father General of the Jesuits, the only Black Bishop to appear (until the Fat Bishop defects) though another is mentioned (2.2.77) who may be the Pope.

162–3 *fill . . . again*: give the enemy much to talk about (at our expense), and make the Protestants puffed with laughing, until they break out again.

164–5 *This . . . forward*: the Black Knight is being sarcastic.

167 *One . . . still*: some lascivious religious order now reverses in a minute. A *codpiece* is a decorative item worn over the male genitals.

168–9 *I dwell . . . partners*: I am not the only one at fault in this way; the Black House has others like me.

170–1 *'Qui cauté, casté'* . . . *word*: whoever acts prudently acts virtuously . . . motto.

172 *of . . . bottom*: despite a leaking ship (obliquely refers to Gondomar's fistula; see 2.2.46).

173–5 *I have . . . door*: I have made passionate love as often as younger men, while healthier ones have been inactive—that is, they have acted as door-keeps/look-outs.

176 *Gross*: stupid. He sardonically insists it unthinkable for a Jesuit to leave a witness.

178 *I . . . then*: then I have found the solution.

180 *Cast . . . suddenly*: put a great distance behind yourself as quickly as possible. Not Tr.

181–2 *Leave . . . this*: leave letters, dated at least ten days earlier than today, with members of our House.

182–3 *taste thee . . . on't*: understand your drift . . . of it.

185 *How for . . . check again*: how am I going to get away without anybody seeing me? There's another obstacle (chess metaphor).

188 *cabinet . . . intelligences*: case full of spies' reports.

190 *stand . . . pick'em*: wait around to sort through them.

191 *The . . . you*: you constitute the real danger.

194 *court-harbingers*: officers sent ahead when the court was on progress to prepare and assign lodgings.

195 *Anglica*: Tr. 'Hah! by this hand'.

200 *Whitefriars*: site of an old Carmelite monastery, between the Thames and the Fleet, a notorious haven for fugitives and prostitutes, often associated with Roman Catholics.

201 *Sisters of Compassion*: fictitious order of nuns.

201–3 *These . . . Drury Lane*: Tr. 'These three' . . . areas of London (like Bloomsbury) commonly associated with Catholics and Jesuits.

205–6 *state policy . . . one*: cunning political stratagem, and an extremely secure one. Grammatically it is the note which is *safe* (secure), but the *policy* proves also to be.

206 *it*: Tr. 'it, sir'.

208 *able it*: vouch for it.

212–13 *bull . . . husbands . . . shifts*: papal decree to dissolve a marriage . . . tricks, stratagems.

215–16 *Scorch'em . . . again . . . mystery*: char them thoroughly, burn them to a true red-brown, then put them back . . . secret purpose.

218–19 *Venice . . . there*: in 1606 the Jesuits were expelled from Venice after the Pope had placed the republic under an interdict, which the Jesuits supported.

220 *inquisitors . . . spectacled*: investigators all came wearing eye-glasses.

221–2 *dung . . . cherry-stones*: Paul Yachnin (unpublished 1978 Edinburgh M.Litt. thesis, 'The Literary Contexts of Thomas Middleton's *A Game at Chess*', p. 152) cites a passage from Rabelais's *Gargantua and Pantagruel* to illuminate the simile: 'those village ragamuffins who snuffle and rake through little children's shit when cherries are in season . . . in order to find the stones and sell them to the druggists, who make them into pomander oil'. Trans. J. M. Cohen (Harmondsworth, 1955), p. 278.

227 *inhuman violence*: the castration.

230 *made . . . then*: you made a joke about it at the time.

aggravation: making matters worse, adding to the list of my sins.

232 *'Cause . . . way*: the Black Bishop's Pawn has 'gone to ground', escaping via an underground vault.

233 *What's that . . . me with*: Tr. 'Come, come, in with' (omitting Black Knight's Pawn's question).

2.2 S.D. *Fat Bishop*: this character is not in Ar., and lines 1–100 of this scene are not in that version at all. He is based on Marc Antonio De Dominis, Archbishop of Spalato (1566–1624): see Introduction.

4 *the . . . alters*: that's another matter.

6 *Much . . . head*: the calcareous structure in the stomach (rather than head) of a lobster, supposed to resemble the outline of a female figure.

8 *pure . . . mount*: i.e. the soul.

11–12 *Like . . . flesh*: cf. 'The mountains travailed [laboured], and brought forth | A scornèd mouse': Horace, 'The Art of Poesy', trans. Ben Jonson, in *Ben Jonson: The Complete Poems* ed. G. A. E. Parfitt (Harmondsworth, 1975), pp. 354–71, ll. 198–9.

13–14 *invectives . . . House*: De Dominis wrote *De Republica Ecclesiastica*, an attack on Catholic doctrines, while still a Roman Catholic archbishop, but only published it when under English protection. More books followed, and he was anxious to circulate them.

15 *perfect*: finished, complete.

18 *rail*: be abusive, denounce one's enemies.

21 *marrow*: essence.

23 *cullis*: a rich broth. Cock-sparrows were noted for their lechery.

21–7 *[I have ... conception.]*: Tr.; lines missing in Lan.

25–6 *calvish ... eat*: stupid (or possibly refers to worship of a calf, one of the biblical false gods, in which case 'heretical') ... ate.

31 *cubit ... turn*: biblical measure of length, 18–22 inches (45–55 cm) ... change sides.

33–4 *preferment ... parts*: De Dominis did not believe the offices he received in England were worthy of him. He wanted to be Archbishop of York.

36 *master ... beds*: Master of the Savoy Hospital, a lucrative but undistinguished post. Beds link in his mind (via *long acre*, the street running from St Martin's Lane to Drury Lane, with a reputation for prostitution) with whorehouses and flower-beds.

38 *Flower-gentles ... love*: flouramour (i.e. flower of love), wild teasels, tomatoes—all plants suggestive of lechery.

41–3 *drabs ... clapped*: a string of terms linked with prostitution: *drabs* (whores), *trader* (pimp), *wholesale* (mass purchase of prostitutes; also, sale of orifices), *clapped* (copulated; also, slapped hands to conclude a deal).

44 *watergate*: gate giving access to the Thames adjacent to De Dominis's Savoy Hospital. The pimps and/or whores, it is suggested, gained access to his rooms by this means. The *watergate* is also a pun for the vagina.

44–51 *racked ... they*: severely stretched ... so that they (Tr. 'that they'). De Dominis was accused of being a harsh landlord.

46 *fistula*: a suppurating pipe-like anal ulcer, which afflicted Gondomar for years and for which he required special seating. Middleton makes this a key to the character.

48 *High ... halter*: High Holborn was one of the sites of public execution and a halter is a rope; so the Fat Bishop's cure for the Black Knight was hanging; see ll. 70–72.

48–51 *When he ... with me*: the Fat Bishop is proud that the Black Knight can witness that he has done well for himself since changing sides. It is a mark of his true *profession*, ostensibly a clergyman but really a kind of prostitute.

58 *'twere*: it would be.

60 *Into ... bag*: throughout the play 'bag' has the dual sense of the bag into which chess-pieces are retired when they are taken, and hell. See 5.3.180.

61 *Against*: in opposition to.

64 *prescribed*: Tr. 'provided'.

65 *provided*: Tr. 'invented'. The Black Knight is referring to the jibe about hanging.

69 *grew ... on ... observed*: became very excited about ... heeded.

73 *balloon-ball*: large inflated leather ball, struck back and forth with sticks in a game called balloon.

77 *second Bishop*: apparently the Pope, who does not appear in the play.

80 *motion*: action, intervention.

81 *'sede vacante'*: Latin, 'a seat being vacant'; i.e. the lure of a bishop's see, which he might fill.

85 *mounting*: rising to a higher position (as gunpowder will when ignited). The Black Knight marks the Fat Bishop as being dangerously and unrealistically ambitious.

86 *As . . . lecherous*: and he is as covetous and lecherous as ambitious.

87 *WHITE KING*: all versions of the allegory implicitly require the White King to be James I. But it is unlikely that the actors impersonated him in detail: see Introduction.

This: the public proof of De Dominis's conversion to the Anglican Church. It is likely that the Fat Bishop presents the White King with one of his new books.

90–3 *lump . . . fool*: in-jokes. William Rowley, who played the Fat Bishop, was a big man who often played fools (cf. Lollio in *The Changeling*); *lump* also = thing without sense.

95 *recantation . . . leaf*: formal repudiation of my earlier errors in the last page. *A Declaration of the Reasons Which Moved M.A. de Dominis to Depart from the Romish Religion*, 1616, would be a suitable book to contain such a recantation.

96 *Ciceronian*: i.e. in an ornate, rhetorical style, to which the White Bishop objects. Marcus Tullius Cicero was a noted Roman statesman and orator.

98 *Out*: Tr. 'Plague'; away with.

100 *provided*: prepared.

103 *Her . . . usurping*: taking over her appearance.

103–4 *affrightment . . . strangely*: fear have had an unaccountable effect.

105–6 *professors . . . candour*: devotees of noble and brilliant whiteness (hence purity).

107 *alone*: unaided.

111 *great incendiary*: revealing the Black Bishop's Pawn as a 'gunpowder' Jesuit.

112–13 *absolut'st . . . can*: most extreme . . . that can.

115 *making . . . door*: using my own compliant devotion to act as his pander.

117 *me*: Tr. has the White Queen gasp 'Ha!' at this point.

122 *both*: i.e. the Black Bishop's Pawn was set on both rape and murder.

126–30 *When we . . . their lives*: when we find desperate sins associated with evil men, we grieve with Christian charity, but experience and their own diseased predisposition takes away any surprise, since our expectation is matched by their actions.

132–4 *is able . . . unadmired*: is so remarkable as to focus attention solely on that deformed being, leaving the monsters that occur naturally unwondered at.

135–7 *The pride . . . fell*: the pride of Lucifer, the first fallen angel, was specifically to try to imitate the angel shape he lost when he fell.

138–9 *fixed . . . method*: sworn to holy orders, which is the spiritual way to heaven.

142 *infested*: morally corrupted, diseased.

146 *prime . . . zealot*: first and foremost religious enthusiast; *zealot* need not be pejorative.

152–3 *Nor . . . hypocrisy*: nor you be drunk with hypocrisy. He accuses the White Bishop of being a puritan hypocrite. If a literal identity is needed for the White Bishop he might be George Abbott, Archbishop of Canterbury (1562–1633), a zealous anti-Catholic and opponent of the Spanish marriage.

153 *WHITE KNIGHT*: he represents Prince Charles, as many contemporaries recognised.

154–6 *your own . . . following*: (anger is) your own festive drink, the morning drink dearest to your bishop's heart all the twelve days of Christmas, the taste of which you cannot lose throughout the following year.

157 s.d.–158 *Aside . . . burning*: the lines of the aside—*A shrewd . . . faster*—are not in Lan.; supplied here from Tr. . . . i.e. in hell-fire.

160 *Would I . . . faster*: I wish I stood further away (from the bishop: knights line up alongside bishops at the start of a game), if it were no impediment to my honour or the game; I wish they'd play faster (so that I might move).

163 *that . . . you . . . favour*: i.e. the Black Duke/Duke of Buckingham . . . permission.

164–5 *aforenamed respected . . . this cause*: previously named person to whom I offered my respects (i.e. Buckingham), I engage in this matter. While extremely courteous, the Black Knight acknowledges that the chess game is indeed a battle, and that he leads the Black House in this skirmish (after the initial formal exchanges, which irked him).

166 *Waste*: squander.

169 *leviathan*: enormous sea-monster, often identified with Satan; so, huge, inordinate.

165–75 *If with all . . . 'scape it*: a long and rhetorically charged attack. The

430

drift is that if the White Queen's Pawn does not plead mental derangement (*distraction*), which would barely mitigate her guilt, or (a better excuse, though nothing will fully excuse her) fall down and foam at the mouth with demonic possession, by that fit (*pang*) revealing the troublesome spirit of error within her, then she should prepare for damnation, since there is no move in the game by which she can avoid it.

177 *play . . . canst*: however you play.

178 *Spite . . . ostentation*: despite sin's boastful display.

181 *equivocation*: the private qualification of an uttered statement by a mental reservation, wherein the speaker *thinks* the whole truth but only speaks (a possibly misleading) part of it. This was a practice of which Jesuits were repeatedly accused, notably in respect of the 1605 Gunpowder Plot.

184 *Bring . . . conception*: i.e. tell us when this attempted rape was planned. Both *bring forth* and *conception* imply likely consequences of a rape, hence the indignant reply.

187 *Well . . . eruption . . . she*: well, when it burst forth [he responds to the charge of avoiding the real issue] . . . Tr. 'you'.

189 *strain*: style or tone of the proceedings.

191 *the . . . glory*: the glory of the Black Bishop's Pawn (perversely translated into a *wronged meek-man*) will be all the greater.

192 *hapless*: unfortunate; Tr. 'cursed' (perhaps Crane's avoidance of strong language).

194 *Ruin . . . kindred*: [I have evidence] enough to destroy your whole house.

195–6 *For honour's . . . confusion*: to protect your own honour call in more slanderers, I have so much capacity to confute slander.

197–8 *nobler . . . House*: more merciful and leave her to the judgement of her own House.

199 *cause*: judgement of the case.

202–3 *Is it . . . time . . . scandal*: i.e. is the Black Bishop's Pawn the man and yesterday evening the time? . . . scandalous charge.

204 *Shift*: change (as in 'change your clothes').

211 WHITE KING: Tr. 'WHITE KNIGHT'.

210–11 *Will't . . . unblasted . . . make . . . appear*: will this escape a thunderbolt? . . . prove this.

213 *sacred virtue*: i.e. that of the Black Bishop's Pawn, not the White Queen's Pawn.

214–15 *treasure of . . . reach*: treasure in . . . lay hold on.

215–16 *Amazement . . . forsaken . . . cause*: consternation . . . bereft of supporters in a case.

219 *staff . . . hat*: the emblems of a cardinal, the White King's Pawn's reward for his treachery. See Introduction.

220 *endeared*: made dear or precious (acknowledging the bribe).

223 *state-fig*: political insult. A *fig* was a gesture of contempt in which the thumb was thrust between closed fingers, representing the buttocks.

224 *they . . . one*: all the evidence is consistent.

226 *professed*: openly declared.

229–30 *Where . . . thence*: i.e. let those against whom the crime was committed determine its punishment.

232 *Queen*: Tr. 'friend'.

233 *th'olive . . . flower*: the precise reference is not understood, though the flower of the olive is green and may have been mistaken for leaves, which are *cast*.

234 *friendless*: Tr. 'harmless'.

238 *Thy counsel . . . cheerfully*: ambiguous. Either the White Knight calls on the White Duke to be his counsellor throughout *the fair policy I aim at* and the latter *cheerfully* agrees. Or the White Knight asks for immediate advice, and the White Duke advises him to pursue his chosen policy cheerfully (i.e. in good heart).

239 *A . . . speed*: he calls for someone to ride quickly.

240 *Make . . . her*: make me that well-feathered arrow, who owes the White Queen's Pawn.

242 *Galician brain*: Galicia is in north-west Spain, home region of Gondomar; Tr. 'sconce' (head) for brain.

243 *discovery*: exposure of crime. No actual case of a young woman being exposed in this way in Venice has been identified.

245 *Be . . . penance*: i.e. be ready to impose a penance on her.

246 *Vessel . . . freight*: bearer . . . burden. The image is of a ship which brought one item, now to be loaded with another.

247 *cabinet . . . niceness*: small chest of fastidiousness (the Black Knight's characterization of the White Queen's Pawn).

249 *swept . . . cast*: won at one throw of the dice.

250–1 *it had . . . tainted*: it would not have amounted to the smallest part of the universal good standing which you have sullied.

255 *Aretine's pictures*: famous pornographic pictures by Giulio Romano (1499–1546), accompanied by explanatory poems by Pietro Aretino (1492–1557).

256 *twice . . . luxury*: Hercules famously took on twelve heroic labours, so the

Black Knight envisages even more superhuman sexual temptations. *luxury* = lust.

258 *Lucrece' dagger*: Lucrece was a chaste Roman matron, who stabbed herself to death after being raped. The perverse point of the punishment is that she will have to kneel in a room surrounded by pornography, without the slightest mitigation of modesty. The pommel of the *dagger* she will *not* see (promising escape by virtuous suicide) obliquely suggests the phalluses she *will* see.

260 *BLACK DUKE*: represents the Spanish royal favourite, Don Gaspar de Guzman, Duque de Olivares. See 5.3.213–14 and note.

Inquisition: Roman Catholic tribunal for the punishment of heretics.

262 *Well . . . aggravated*: Tr. 'Why, well' . . . made more severe.

264 *patience . . . wrong*: virtue gives me a composure to face evil greater than the crimes being committed upon me.

3.1 S.D. *Fat Bishop*: the initial sequence of this scene, with the Fat Bishop, is not in Ar.

3 *ounce*: doctors measured the blood from medical 'bleedings' drawn in fluid ounces.

6 *while*: Tr. concludes the line with 'I ha'gaped for'. These complaints pick up from 2.2.33–45, where the Fat Bishop is unhappy with his *preferment*.

10 *biggest chair*: hinting that he could be Pope in the Catholic Church, or archbishop in the Anglican. In a literal sense, his *corpulent dignity* would fill *any* bishop's chair.

12–15 *master . . . preferments*: De Dominis was Dean of Windsor, with its Poor Knights, from 1617. This and the Mastership of the Savoy Hospital were in fact lucrative posts.

17 *merit*: sense of personal worth.

20 *that's put home*: this puzzling phrase qualifies *him* and may mean 'when he's sent home' (i.e. back to the Catholic Church) or 'given a mortal blow'.

25 *Paulus*: Pope Paul V, in office 1605–21. Protestant newsletters misled Middleton into thinking Pope Paul was a friend of De Dominis. It was his successor, Gregory XV (Pope, February 1621–June 1623), whose election lured De Dominis back to Rome. His successor in turn, Urban VIII, was responsible for turning De Dominis over to the Inquisition.

27 *side*: i.e. side of the chess-board.

29 *walk*: move. The chess knight has a distinctive 'crooked' move, one square forward or back and one square either way sideways.

32 *holy*: Tr. 'noble'.

34–5 *proves . . . cause of*: is the only current reason for.

36 *had*: would have.

37–8 *remove . . . might . . . supremacy*: removal . . . might have carried you to the Papacy.

39 *All . . . face*: i.e. he is flushed with pride and ambition.

42 *submissive*: Tr. 'submiss'.

44 *chair . . . ease*: comfortable ecclesiastical position.. This refers to the *sede vacente* (vacant seat) in the letter, though with an unintended second sense of 'commode'.

48 *watergate*: see 2.2.44 and note.

49 *recantation*: which De Dominis was required to do on his return to Rome.

55–6 *merry . . . Too . . . true*: joking . . . too jolly to be telling the truth.

57 *if . . . truly*: if you were really touched by remorse (*compunction*).

59 *primitive*: original and true. The *primitive mother* is the Catholic Church.

60–1 *points . . . sides*: cf. Christ on the cross: 'but one of the soldiers with a spear pierced his side, and forthwith came there out blood and water' (John 20: 34).

65 *adoration*: worship of divinity. The implication is that the Catholic Church sought 'adoration' for itself, not God, and that the Fat Bishop's *revolt* had undermined this.

67 *sainted sleepers*: i.e. the dead saints. Protestants condemned Catholic fondness for *statues* as idolatry, and veneration of the saints as a distraction from the true goal of knowing God.

68 *melt*: i.e. with embarrassed pride.

69 [*And . . . syrup*]: line not in Lan., copy Tr. Crane apparently overlooked it as he moved from one folio to the next. *Syrup* is any sweet, sticky liquid.

72–3 *When . . . way*: i.e. the Fat Bishop is drawn on by ambition/honour as a horse is by a small quantity (*lock*) of hay.

77 *inferior policies . . . shame'em*: lesser plots . . . disgrace them.

78–81 *But . . . restless*: but let me reassure my schemes a little by remembering some fine ones from the past, to foster all the projects to come, which must move on ceaselessly.

83–6 *Was it . . . expedition*: Gondomar got an English fleet (Tr. 'precious safeguard') sent to the Mediterranean to deal with Turkish pirates, arguing that it was in the wider interests of trade (*more necessitous expedition*) and not merely of Spain. Buckingham as Lord Admiral took credit, but the Black Knight mocks English diplomacy.

87–97 *Who made . . . relent*: cf. the Acts of the Apostles, where St Peter (12: 4–9) and St Paul (16: 23–6) are released miraculously from jail. In 1618 Gondomar got James I to release seventy-four imprisoned priests and

Jesuits as a goodwill gesture in the Spanish marriage negotiations. They were supposed to go abroad but the Black Knight represents them as locusts consuming heretic (English Protestant) corn, even in rural areas (*country-crops*) where they stick closely by their converts (*ears* puns on 'ears of corn'), who protect them, however fiercely the authorities try to shake them out. They have their hiding places in women's chambers, safely secluded refuges (where, by implication, they sleep with their female converts). Even when tracked down by government agents (*pursuivants*) they get away by bribery (*palm-oil*).

98–101 *Whose policy . . . restraint*: he takes credit for silencing puritan preachers who had denounced Spanish trickery but were now forbidden to speak on matters of state. The *pictures* seem to allude to Samuel Ward, a 'special preacher of Ipswich', imprisoned (1621) for possessing an anti-Spanish engraving called *1588 Deo Trin-uni Britanniae*.

102 *spleen*: supposed seat of mirth and laughter.

103–5 *Whilst our . . . world*: while our plans went unchallenged except in people's minds, the slightest sound (by anyone else) would be examined in the most fortunate corner (*angle*) of the globe (i.e. in England).

106–7 *The court . . . her*: i.e. he charmed courtiers, who then controlled the city so that he was able to exploit it.

107–8 *sops . . . liberties*: i.e. bribes . . . for obtaining freedom of worship.

109–10 *From some . . . air*: (bribes) from others to help them gain posts they had no earthly chance of ever achieving.

111 *mel aerium . . . manna*: airy honey . . . the divine bread which God sent for Moses to feed the children of Israel (Exodus 16). This is all but blasphemous.

116 *quick . . . on't*: if there is any sensitive flesh in a yard of (your conscience).

118 *driver*: hammer.

121–2 *Prithee . . . wound*: the Black Knight mocks the pawn's tender-hearted remorse.

124 *Three*: Tr. 'Four'. With so many plots, he does not know to which the pawn refers.

126 *yet . . . that*: yet are involved in lawsuits over (one plot of land, when the Black Knight has so many *plots* without comeback).

127 *by their names*: individually; *their*: Tr.; Lan. 'these'.

128 *the*: Tr. 'their'.

131 *some . . . oblique*: i.e. showing latitude and longitude.

132 *read . . . blindness*: Catholics did not encourage private reading of the Bible.

137 *climate . . . fastened*: region of their world where they took hold.

138 *I'm . . . that*: I agree with you about that.

140–1 *of . . . last brat*: Tr. 'use' . . . latest child.

143 *antedated letters*: see 2.1.181 and 2.2.212.

149 *I made*: so all witnesses. It makes no sense for the pawn to fit out a member of the opposing House, so presumably *made* means 'considered, reckoned'.

   S.D. *Enter . . . (severally)*: Tr. 'Enter Black Bishop and both the Houses'.

152 *The . . . down*: I'm over the surprise of it, but some will lose their places/ suffer.

153 *virtuous pawn*: i.e. the White Queen's Pawn, now exonerated.

155 *adversary*: Satan in Hebrew means 'adversary, one who plots against'.

156–8 *a title . . . comprised in*: the greatest monarch on earth might without detriment have the quality of his worth summed up in a title of that *candour* (purity). This acknowledges the White Knight as of more considerable standing than a mere knight.

159–62 *This fair . . . consecrated*: i.e. the White Knight's exoneration of the White Queen's Pawn will be commemorated like the deeds of chivalric knights in the Arthurian tales.

168 *enterpriser*: the one who undertakes it; cf. 'virtue is its own reward'.

169–71 *But you . . . gift*: but for you to demonstrate yourself to be a king of royal generosity as much as of integrity adds special distinction to what you give.

171 *desert claims*: Tr. 'deserts claim'.

174 *mak'st . . . glorious*: i.e. in the manner of a martyr.

175 *I'll take . . . here*: I'll (pretend to) know nothing about (her exoneration). What is she doing here?

178 *visiting anguish*: suffering inflicted as punishment.

179–80 *Let me alone . . . all . . . born to*: rely on me . . . the only charm it naturally has.

181 *What's this*: Tr. 'What's tis'.

182 *'mazed 'em*: confused them.

184–5 *fired . . . eighty-eight*: fire ships were *put in* by Lord Howard of Effingham to break up the order of the Spanish Armada at Calais in 1588.

187 *no sharplier righted*: no more keenly given its due.

189 *manners*: behaviour [i.e. what people actually do].

190–1 *This . . . take an answer*: Tr. 'That' . . . accept that he is wrong.

198–200 *Why may . . . confidence*: i.e. why may not the evil be artfully concealed in your version of things, just as you rashly suspected it in ours; *waked*: Tr.; Lan. 'walked'.

201 *This*: Tr. 'That'.

s.d. *Enter*: Tr.; not in Lan.

205 *I'll . . . again*: I'll bring the Black Bishop's Pawn back into the game in an unusual way. See 3.3.50.

207 *transitory . . . value*: no changeable (mortal) chess-piece can equal in value.

210 *distracted*: mentally deranged.

213 *this . . . altar*: i.e. the White Queen's Pawn.

214–15 *mark . . . end . . . taxed*: judge it by the outcome . . . censured, attacked.

217–18 *unlaid . . . How . . . flies*: unfixed, i.e. moved to act . . . whatever blame is in the air.

222–3 *If both . . . duel*: seconds commonly fought in duels, as well as the principals.

225 *joy . . . agent*: am delighted to confirm. I was an agent. Tr. ends the line with '(Sir)'.

227 *him*: Tr. 'his attempt'. See 2.1.140.

229 *mutually engaged*: equally indebted.

232 *'Las . . . done*: the Black Knight believed the White Queen's Pawn's defence long before it was completed—because he had manufactured her apparent guilt.

234 *But I*: except me [i.e. I am not beside myself].

237 *pity*: i.e. supposed pity.

239 *craft . . . machination*: cunning and intrigue.

241 *mess*: cooking pot.

242 *fain finger . . . hot*: gladly lay my hands on . . . (1) eager; (2) lustful.

245–6 *Bishop . . . diocese*: the Fat Bishop . . . area of a Bishop's jurisdiction/ 'field of play'.

247 *whip . . . pawn*: make you up a pawn (from concocting or cooking something quickly).

250 *default*: failure to attend to the game, so an accident, as against *wilful negligence*.

251 *sacred persons*: i.e. White King and Queen.

253 *third place*: in the general conventions of the game, the King's Pawn was understood to have a particular role in defending the King, Queen, and Bishop.

254 *what sure*: what a trustworthy.

256 *As . . . yours*: as readily as his elevation to a title [made him] yours.

257 *leprosy*: leprosy is characterized by shining white scales on the skin.

    S.D. *His . . . off*: Ar., not in Lan. or Tr. *His*: the White King's Pawn's.

260 *DUKE*: speech headers of this and the next line are reversed in Tr., but follow Lan. in all other copies.

260–1 *made . . . His . . . complexion*: turned . . . his true allegiance is of their colour.

261–6 *Has my . . . honour*: this passage confirms that Middleton finally identified the White King's Pawn with Lionel Cranfield. Lines 263–65, which glance at his rise from city apprentice (*popular*: common) to rich merchant trader, money-lender, and speculator (*adventures*: risks), are not in Ar., but grafted onto an account that would suit most recipients of royal favour. The 'discovery' thus equates to Cranfield's conviction for peculation.

268 *thy alone corruption*: (1) your unique corruption (i.e. no one else was corrupt); (2) your corruption alone (i.e. there were no other grounds for your fall). Either way, Cranfield is to be seen as a unique rotten apple in an otherwise blameless court, and he had qualities which warranted James's favour, but corruption was his undoing.

270 *weight*: importance.

272 *crying trespass*: a transgression that cries out for justice.

273 *Be . . . on*: even in anyone we (royal plural) favour highly.

274 *I . . . him . . . heaven's substitute*: Tr. 'I'd tear'em' . . . God's representative on earth.

276 *look better*: pay more attention.

277 *KING*: speech headers of this and the following line are reversed in Tr.

279 *FAT BISHOP*: this passage with the Fat Bishop was not in Ar. It adds to the sense of the White House under siege, with the White Queen's Pawn still not clear of the Black Queen's Pawn's scheming, the White King's Pawn 'discovered', the Black Knight plotting against the White Knight and Duke, and the Fat Bishop defecting.

280 *There . . . man*: i.e. they might have a chance of holding on to someone like the White King's Pawn who is only half-black.

291 *Douay . . . Spalato*: Jesuit books were commonly printed at Douay and Brussels, but not at Spalato, which is only mentioned for its associations with De Dominis.

292 *conveyed*: De Dominis attempted to smuggle out what he had acquired in England in an ambassador's train, but it was seized.

294 *KING*: Tr. ascribes this line to the White Knight.

297 *honour*: Tr. 'honours'; prestigious appointments.

298 *burn him*: by the time of the play De Dominis had been delivered to the

Inquisition on suspicion of heresy, and Middleton could speculate on his likely fate. In fact he died in prison, but was posthumously convicted, and his body and books burned.

302 *now*: not in Tr.

303–4 *staff . . . red hat*: see 2.2.219 and note.

305 *bag . . . first*: see 2.2.60 and note . . . the turncoat is the first black piece bagged.

314 *transcend*: exceed.

316 *mounted*: soared, like a flame.

317–18 *contaminating act . . . us*: i.e. her rape by the Black Bishop's Pawn . . . Tr. 'us all'.

321 *absolute . . . complete*: perfectly . . . see *The Changeling*, 1.1.208 and note.

322–3 *red hats . . . general hopes*: i.e. cardinals . . . wider expectations.

325–6 *in . . . affections . . . on's*: about; Tr. 'for' . . . desires . . . Tr. 'of us'.

329–30 *Egyptian . . . speculative virtue*: gypsies, traditionally associated with fortune-telling, were supposed to originate from Egypt . . . power of presenting images.

333 *never . . . enough*: am never tired/sated (with what I see).

335 *faculties*: disposition, instincts. She feels no impulse within herself to marry.

337–8 *We do . . . upward*: our faith and bodily growth may be imperceptible, but both take us upward (i.e. towards heaven).

339 *well applied*: a good analogy.

341–2 *right use . . . spectre*: proper ceremony (i.e. safe for the participants) . . . apparition.

343 *no hard . . . with me*: not a hard rule to follow, put your trust/have confidence in me.

345 *Why . . . observe*: Tr. 'Pray follow me then and . . . '. Crane amends the line so that the scene flows seamlessly into what this edition makes 3.3. In other witnesses, which all include 3.2, the Queens' Pawns move between scenes to another location for the room with its *magic glass*. In Lan. it is adjacent to where they have been talking.

s.d. *Exeunt*: Tr., not in Lan.

3.2 This scene is omitted from Lan., perhaps because of its pervasive obscenity, or because it does not read as well as it would perform. It is apparent that there is a good deal of physical action, much of it suggestive of anal intercourse. Copy-text is Tr.

s.d. *Black Jesting Pawn*: he serves the same master as the Black Knight's Pawn, but is a social inferior. John Holles records a 'Spanish eunuch' placed in the bag at the end, who is probably this pawn. He may literally be a eunuch but Holles may have meant pathic or catamite which, whatever else, he certainly is (see Appendix, p. 316).

1 *take*: (1) remove, as in chess; (2) possess sexually. The speech is a fantasy of homoerotic sexual domination, in which whiteness betokens subordination/passivity.

2 *under-drudgery*: the most menial tasks; sexual subordination.

3 *crumbed*: thickened or covered with crumbs (of cheese).

5 *jennet*: small Spanish horse. There is a play on 'jenny': 'The female name; hence sometimes applied derisively to a man' (*OED*).

6 *litter . . .* S.D. *White Pawn*: see S.D. 5.1.1 and note . . . his master is not specified.

7–8 *nightmare . . . miller's daughter*: female monster supposed to settle on people while asleep, inducing a sense of suffocation . . . the precise allusion is not clear, but it must be associated with the whiteness of flour.

10 *great snow*: there were several extremely severe winters in the early seventeenth century, when birds became tame with hunger.

11 *WHITE PAWN*: missing in Tr.

19 *fit you*: prepare you for your task (with a play on *fit* = punish).

21 *whipping*: an allusion to penitential scourging, but probably also evoking three London apprentices in 1621 whipped for abusing Gondomar and his litter.

23 *fast*: not eat meat. Scourging and fasting were not exclusively Catholic forms of penance, but were particularly associated with Catholics.

24 *lie . . . hands*: no one will take it off you.

27–8 *I'm . . . ordinary . . . frisk*: I know perfectly well a monkey's usual diet (monkeys were known to be partial to spiders) . . . move quickly.

28 S.D. *Second Black Pawn*: another pawn whose master is not specified.

29 *no . . . bargain*: you're not as well off (as you thought you were).

31 *in . . . me*: behind me. But also 'in my breech/buttocks'.

32 *birdspit*: birds skewered through the breech for roasting.

33 *russet woodcocks*: reddish brown birds, slow and easily caught, hence 'dupes'. There may also be a play on *cocks* = penises.

34 *firk*: cheat, beat, or fuck.

36 *old*: plenty of.

37 *for I . . . nobody*: (1) because, being first taken, he is first on the spit and not facing the right way to 'firk' anyone; (2) see note on S.D. at head of this scene. *for I* : so Ros, Q1; Tr. 'I'.

3.3 S.D. *Enter . . . Pawn*: Tr., not in Lan., which continues seamlessly from the end of 3.1.

2 *magical glass*: there is a scene which exploits a mirror like this in *A Shoemaker a Gentleman* (2.3) by William Rowley, who played the Fat Bishop here.

3 *motion*: impulse, changed feelings.

5 *turtle*: turtle-dove, emblem of faithfulness and trust.

8–9 *symptom . . . bride . . . vainer*: sign that a woman is to marry . . . more empty, idle.

10–11 *by my . . . least*: by my pledge of faith to friendship I relieve you of the slightest.

15 *argues*: indicates, suggests.

17 *Nay . . . else . . . halted*: not only that . . . otherwise the apparition ceased.

28 *Pray, try . . . your will*: line not in Tr. *another*: i.e. name to conjure with.

32 *With . . . same*: remaining for the same time, and in the same shape as before.

34 *My . . . clearer*: the truth of what I said is shown all the clearer.

35 *eye . . . your own*: Tr. 'eyes' . . . the man who is to be your own.

36 *well-composed*: well-formed, handsomely put together.

38–9 *met . . . issues*: matched, equal . . . children.

48 *enchanted*: put under a spell.

S.D. *Black . . . Pawn*: Tr. specifies 'the Jesuit'. He enters behind the White Queen's Pawn who, forbidden to turn round (3.1.342), sees him only in the mirror.

S.D. *presents . . . exits*: Tr., not in Lan.

51 *That's . . . hearing*: that's good to hear.

53 *shadow . . . yours*: image without substance . . . Tr. adds 'How do you?' (how are you feeling?).

55 *What . . . state*: how far can we rely on our passions or our condition of life?

56 *What . . . still*: all that we.

59–60 *passion . . . merely an*: sorrowful complaint . . . a complete.

61 *Most . . . composed*: formed exactly as one would wish.

64–5 *which is . . . emptiness*: which all appears most fine when viewed in a spirit of chaste delight (i.e. rather than 'passion'). What is lacking?

69 *She's . . . wronger*: line not in Tr.; *most wronger*: the one who has wronged her most.

4.1 S.D. *Enter . . . Pawn*: Tr. 'Enter Black Knight's Pawn meeting the Black Bishop's Pawn, richly accoutred'. Q1 specifies 'The Jesuit in his gallant habit'; i.e. he looks like a fashionable man-about-town, anything but a priest. The near-failure of the Black Knight's Pawn to recognize the Black Bishop's Pawn makes it the more credible that the White Queen's Pawn never recognizes him in this disguise.

2 *together*: on end, in a row.

3 *lettered hatband*: Jesuits were said to wear non-clerical clothes, but recognized each other by the secret sign of a gold hatband studded with letters or characters.

4–5 *to . . . Worn*: so Lan., Tr. Some witnesses read 'to be worn | By'.

6–7 *It's . . . president*: Tr. 'This'' (= This is) . . . one sworn to be a supreme example.

9 *think awry*: have an erring thought.

11 *poniard*: dagger. Like the feather (in the hat) and the spur, this was more the mark of a gallant than a priest.

14 *trim . . . glory*: dress of splendour.

16 *catholical mark*: i.e. the lettered hatband. The pawn ironically suggests it shines out as a touch of perfection amongst so much splendour. Protestant audiences would probably have associated it with the mark of the beast (Revelation 13: 16).

18 *Are . . . observance*: i.e. do you look so high?

19 *worm*: gnawing conscience.

21–2 *see . . . play*: get a clear view of his move.

25 *base fact*: mean deed. The Black Bishop's Pawn knows from confession that the Black Knight's Pawn is talking about his castration of the White Bishop's Pawn.

25 *to . . . schismatic*: done to a member of a breakaway sect (i.e. Protestant).

26 *What's . . . revenge*: how does that relate to the dignity of vengeance? An act of true revenge might claim *nobility* but this was too *base* to qualify.

29 *Penance-chamber*: the ecclesiastical office charged with dealing with penitents.

30 *tax-register*: the notorious *Taxa Sacra Poenitentiaria Apostolica*, the 'book of general pardons of all prices' (4.2.82–3). Protestants supposed it listed fines which the Catholic Church imposed for all crimes, as if forgiveness could be bought and need not be earned. The Black Bishop's Pawn refuses on principle to absolve the Black Knight's Pawn (though he seems genuinely penitent) but sends him off to the Fat Bishop's *clemency*, in effect suggesting that a bribe is his best *refuge*.

31 *Fat*: Lan., like all other copies, reads 'Black'. The scene satirizing the *Taxa Poenitentiaria* (4.2.82–130) originally involved the Black Bishop, and no one changed this cross-reference when the Fat Bishop was substituted for him.

33 *The . . . sting*: Tr. 'This' . . . i.e. of conscience.

34–5 *game . . . not seem*: amorous sport, quarry . . . pretend not.

35 *'tis he*: not in Tr.

38 *regardless*: indifferent.

39–40 *you are . . . him*: either (1) you, the chief part of him, are not heeded; or (2) you are not thought to be his chief part. Crane's brackets make the former more likely.

41 *see*: foresee.

43 *To . . . mastery*: Tr., line not in Lan.; *mastery*: power.

44 *And . . . it observe*: Tr.; Lan. 'To' . . . i.e. time obey/wait upon.

45 *proper virtue*: (1) intrinsic nature; (2) appropriate goodness.

49 *in his . . . me*: receive deflection from his natural course because of me.

52 *strait . . . stubborn*: strict . . . stiff; 'too straight' is only in Tr.—all other copies omit.

53 *traitor*: blush.

58–9 *Without the . . . fortune*: without the propitious glimmer of how much joy (he would find) if he looked on his fortunate destiny. Punning: she is the 'fortune' which fortune has decreed.

62 *'Twere pity*: it would be a pity if.

63 *What . . . do*: the implication seems to be that the White Queen's Pawn tries to prevent the Black Queen's Pawn from approaching the Black Bishop's Pawn.

65 *look . . . it*: examine the situation.

70–1 *nearer . . . you*: sooner by many days, sir, than it would reach you in the course of its own natural revelation.

71 *fix*: i.e. your eyes on the White Queen's Pawn.

74 *liked*: approved, found attractive.

76 *guess*: suppose.

78–9 *Her glory . . . on me*: my astonishment moves back and to between her splendour and the marvel of this secret.

81 *Affinity*: are we related?

82–3 *Or any . . . forward*: or is there some gracious assistance such as nature delights in advancing our relationship?

84–5 *perfection . . . one*: virtuous completion, i.e. marriage.

87 *show you*: i.e. in the mirror.

88–90 *The mystery . . . delights by*: the mystery increases, unless nature has put that delightful being before us as an ideal by whom to select a wife.

91–2 *art . . . put . . . off*: i.e. magic art . . . attach me to something and make me unable to break away from it.

93 *check . . . now*: reverse, rebuff . . . not in Tr.

94 *proportion*: figure.

101 *substance yonder*: very being over there (i.e. the White Queen's Pawn in the mirror).

106 *BLACK QUEEN'S PAWN*: Lan. gives this speech to the White Queen's Pawn (but one of the Black House is clearly speaking), and Tr. to the Black Bishop's Pawn (but he speaks immediately before and after). Q1 and Q3 support Black Queen's Pawn.

107 *beauties*: Tr. 'benefits'.

110–11 *flatter . . . more . . . assigned*: condone, gloss over . . . other than destined to be.

115 *Their . . . from 'em*: Tr., line not in Lan.

120–2 *Did not . . . should be*: if I did not know that you were destined to be mine, and that this gives you a strong prerogative, because of that immoral proposal you never would be.

127 *May*: bloom, prime.

129 *knowledge*: sexual intercourse.

130–1 *gives . . . strange imposture*: shrinks . . . elaborate pretence.

135 *contract*: a betrothal or 'pre-contract', an illicit form of marriage but often upheld by the courts, though either party could choose to deny it.

139–40 *Be . . . lavish . . . upon . . . occasion*: do not cry so much . . . for no good reason.

146 *that done . . . do reason*: the contract concluded . . . render satisfaction.

147–8 *'em . . . blood's*: Tr. 'you' . . . lust's.

4.2.1 *Fat*: Tr. 'Black'.

3 *Reach . . . cozenage*: bring me to my commode, my chair of trickery.

4 *Seven . . . woman*: he is thinking of the bribes he has received (see 3.1.106–10).

7 *foul . . . drum*: a reference to Gondomar's fistula (see 2.2.46). Q1: 'bum' for 'drum'.

8–9 *treacher . . . qualm*: cheat, deceiver . . . one with a troubled conscience.

15 *swallow*: gorge.

17 *lies . . . pipe*: sticks in the throat of penitence.

18–19 *by offices . . . gulled*: by services rendered . . . (1) achieved by trickery; (2) guzzled.

26–7 *Poisoned . . . malice*: undermined the allegiance of subjects to their king, impeded religious faith, and made women's frailer souls capable of male evil. These are all crimes Gondomar was accused of in Thomas

Scott, *The Second Part of Vox Populi*, published after May 1624, only shortly before the play was staged.

29 *stares*: starlings. Like parrots they can be taught to mimic human voices.

33 *tightly*: i.e. smartly. Some witnesses read 'lightly'.

34–5 *stirring ... Daughters ... seducement*: (1) rousing; (2) titillating ... i.e. those I have seduced.

37 *to shape ... by*: to cause remorse.

38 *I ... [nor]*: Tr. reads 'I feel no tempest, not a leaf-wind'. There is a blot in Lan. after *tempest* (= storm of conscience), and I have supplied *nor* to make sense of what seems to be Crane's own construction of the line.

41 *Sirrah*: most of this speech is put together from contemporary accusations against Gondomar, many virtually verbatim from Scott's *The Second Part of Vox Populi*.

sold ... groom o'the stool: taken bribes to secure a post with eponymous lavatorial functions in a royal Privy Chamber, prized for its ready access to royalty. John Holles assumed the post was that of 'groom of the stool to the Infanta' (see Appendix, p. 315), though Middleton may imply that Gondomar claimed influence over such appointments in England. The Black Knight has a scatological turn of mind.

43 *take ... of*: have precedence in rank over.

45 *mothership ... maids*: probably the post of Chief Gentlewoman of the Queen's Privy Chamber, who would supervise her Maids of Honour. With Queen Anne dead there was no such English post in 1624.

49 *Veronica's heads ... presses*: images of Christ on ornaments or tokens in secret cupboards (from the miraculous image on St Veronica's handkerchief when she wiped Christ's brow as he stumbled with the Cross on the way to Calvary).

52 *restraint*: period of stricter enforcement of the laws against Catholicism in England.

56 *on*: Tr. 'in'.

57 *dresser*: sideboard where food is prepared for serving. *Altar* and *dresser* are both places where bread and wine are served, so perhaps mocking the Catholic doctrine of transubstantiation, which holds that the bread and wine literally become the body and blood of Christ in the Mass.

60 *No fortification*: what follows is a list of White House military information that the Black Knight has spent his summer collecting.

62 *But ... platform*: yet I acquired (knowledge of) water level and chart.

66 *burden ... each ship ... murderers*: capacity ... Tr. 'the ships' ... small cannon.

70 *breast inhabitants*: native or long-term residents. Q1 and Q3 read 'best'.

75 *jails vomited*: see 3.1.87–97 and note.

76 *oil of toad . . . physic*: (presumably) an emetic in that purgative medicine.

78–9 *White . . . House*: a reference to the visit of Prince Charles to Madrid in 1623 to negotiate the Spanish marriage, the subject of 5.1 and 5.3. Gondomar was credited with this, although by then he was no longer in England.

81 *lie sweetly*: be favourably set.

82 *Taxa Poenitentiara*: the *Taxa Sacra Poenitentiaria Apostolica* dealt with ecclesiastical pardon for sins (see 4.1.30 and note). There was no edition in English in 1624, and Middleton probably only knew about it from Protestant propaganda.

84 *his sin*: i.e. the castration of the White Bishop's Pawn.

88–9 *thirteen . . . six pence*: English money was divided into pounds, shillings and pence, with twelve pence (pennies) to the shilling and twenty shillings to the pound. Money values might be as much as a thousand times what they are today, but the sums quoted here are all derisively cheap.

89–90 *killing &c.*: Lan. Tr. writes out 'killing' six times, other copies between three and seven times. The actor was probably meant to milk the repetition as often as it kept getting laughs.

94 *I'm in't now*: (1) I've found the place in the book; (2) I'm engaged in adultery myself.

96–7 *These . . . two . . . mend*: Tr. 'Mass, those are two' (Lan. 'too') . . . reform, redeem.

99 *Thirteen*: Tr. 'Thirty-three', and adds 'too' to the following line.

100 *threes*: probably joking about misplaced reverence for the Holy Trinity.

101 *story*: one often repeated. See Margaret of Navarre's *Heptameron*, novella 30, and Bandello's *Novelle*, Part 2, novella 35. Middleton probably expected people to equate this with scurrilous gossip about Gondomar.

107–8 *backside . . . forward*: a running joke about the alleged predilection of Italians in general, and Catholic priests in particular, for sodomy.

109 *precedents . . . encouragement*: the opposite of fines for sins, moneys paid out to encourage 'worthy' actions.

111–12 *killing . . . prince*: probably refers to the murder in 1610 of Henri IV of France. A Catholic convert, he was suspected of secretly adhering to his Protestant faith.

113 *True*: Tr. 'True, sir'.

114–17 *Promised also . . . Lisbon*: Dr Lopez, chief physician to Elizabeth I, was executed in 1594 for accepting a Spanish bribe to poison her. He came from Spanish-ruled Portugal (hence Lisbon) but Catholic associations with a nunnery are forced since he was a Jew.

118 *at*: Tr. 'of'. The 'townhouse' was a religious seminary in the Spanish

Netherlands, where Jesuit missionaries were trained for service in England.

119 *What's . . . to*: how does all this relate to.

123 *fact*: deed.

129–30 *picked . . . ever . . . riddle*: finally made sense . . . i.e. how to receive pardon for a sin not recognized by Church law.

131–2 *make away . . . And . . . absolution*: dispose of . . . line missing in Tr. His estate would be forfeit if he committed murder. But if he has disposed of it, even to his relatives, the Church can exact nothing more. And this is a sin for which he can buy absolution.

133 *removes*: (chess) moves.

137–8 *coming . . . sanctimonious*: amenable, persuadable . . . see 1.1.30–1 and note.

139 *that . . . state . . . hurry*: Tr. 'this' . . . diplomatic confusion and crazy tumult.

140 *eagle*: high-soaring.

142–3 *at . . . As . . . stand*: not in Tr. . . . given the state of the game. Cf. Q1 'As the game stands'.

143 *I'll . . . more*: I'll never trust the craft of plotting again.

4.3 s.d. *Recorders*: so Bri. and Ros. Ar. simply indicates 'Music'.

s.d. *Enter the . . . him*: Lan. Other witnesses vary slightly. Tr.: *Enter Black Queen's Pawn as conducting the White to a chamber; then fetching in the Black Bishop's Pawn, the Jesuit conveys him to another, puts out the light and she follows.* The implication in all versions is that the Black Queen's Pawn enjoys the sexual favours of the Black Bishop's Pawn unbeknownst to him, and in place of the White Queen's Pawn, who is left vainly waiting. Cf. the bed-trick in *The Changeling*.

4.4.1 *Duke*: Tr. 'Knight'.

2 *prevent . . . insinuation*: anticipate their foul allegations (about the Spanish marriage and alliance with Catholic Spain). Middleton implies that Charles and Buckingham never intended the marriage and were always working to counter Spanish intrigue and propaganda (the *glitteringest serpent*).

6 *'eighty-eight*: the year of the Spanish Armada.

11–12 *his . . . bolt*: Tr. 'their' . . . of lightning.

13 *asunning*: sunning itself (like a serpent).

19 *lost*: wasted.

27 *first*: foremost.

31 *For . . . thoughts*: line missing in Tr.

32–3 *Of a grave ... wanton*: (turned from) a grave father-politician to a frivolous son of revelry, made a 60-year-old man a sportive boy, a mere spoiled child.

34 *Savoy dame*: woman from the precincts of the Savoy Hospital, a sanctuary and haunt of disreputable people, its chapel being sometimes used for irregular weddings.

35 *lusting ... issue*: longing for a child.

38 *St ... Mechlin*: St Rumold or Rombaut was active in the eighth century around Malines, where a cathedral was dedicated to him.

41 *By ... great*: by [striding over the supposed breeches, and with the help of] a lover from the court (she) later became large (with child).

47 *surfeit*: be supplied to excess.

4.5 This scene is missing in Tr. and is not separately marked in Lan.

1–2 *he's gone ... surprised*: the White Knight's gone (to Madrid) ... suddenly attacked.

5–6 *luminaries ... interposed*: light-giving suns or stars ... i.e. eclipsed.

10–11 *watched ... advantage*: looked for a clear opportunity.

12 *hard beset*: under fierce attack.

15 *down ... deliverer*: be taken (in chess); be sexually possessed ... Ros. 'deliverance'.

18–19 *inflammation ... pleurisy ... luxury*: raging desire ... inflammation of lust.

20 *deflower*: the White Queen, as a married woman, presumably has no virginity to lose, but this adds to the sordid urgency of the Black King's lust.

22 *ring-dove*: wood-pigeon. A ring is a bishop's mark of office, doves are proverbial tokens of peace: the Fat Bishop is annoyed to be captured by a truly spiritual bishop.

27–8 *master check ... he ... you*: checkmate which, observe, the White King and his House live to give you [the Black House in general]. The king in chess cannot check an opponent, members of his House must do it for him: hence *he and his*. The White Bishop turns the Fat Bishop's near-success into a rallying cry for the White House.

30–1 *Let heaven's ... one*: let me not live longer than I am your sure sanctuary.

32 *rock*: cf. 'upon this rock I will build my church' (Matthew 16: 18). As Catholics traced the authenticity of their Church to the line of Popes from St Peter, the White King stands as security for his Queen (here = the Church of England).

34 *rank*: grossly fat or puffed up. The first four lines of this speech are not in Ar.

36 *hath*: who has.

40 *For . . . Holiness*: what follows is more appropriate to the Black Bishop, Father General of the Jesuits, the original recipient of the lines in Ar., than to the Fat Bishop.

41 *blind mole*: common image of a worker in (often metaphorical) darkness, or hell.

46 *puts . . . up*: metaphorically, removes you from the board.

48 *hope*: expectation of capturing.

51 *Give lost*: reckon to be lost.

51–4 *my strong . . . billows*: my conviction of their constant virtues is so strong that, even if you could set seas of countless lies against that fortress, it would deflate the most swollen waves.

57–8 *usurped . . . Confidence*: wrongly took possession of . . . faith.

59–60 *reverend of men . . . covetousness*: worthy of men's reverence [i.e. White Bishop] . . . i.e. the Fat Bishop.

61–2 *The bag . . . crack*: couplet not in Ar.

5.1 s.d. *Music*: Tr. Ar. describes it as 'Loud', Bri. and Ros. as 'Low'. Lan. omits.

    s.d. *litter*: Tr. indicates here that the Black Knight 'calls'.

    s.d. *as . . . stage*: Q1, Bri., Ros. only.

    s.d. *above*: discovered on the upper stage, from where he delivers his oration.

1 *Hold, hold*: stop; Tr., not in Lan.

4 *'Ecce . . . arce'*: Latin: behold me fixed on Caesar's triumphal arch.

5 *Tumbrel*: dung-cart.

7 *'Haeretici . . . sic'*: Latin: may all heretics so perish.

9 s.d. *Hautboys*: oboes. Tr., not in Lan.

    s.d. *The Black . . . oration*: Ar., not in Lan.

10–17 *Si . . . congratulamur*: 'If anything ever opened a merry and welcome day to mortal eyes, if anything ever brought joy to the most loving spirits of friends, or gave birth to happiness, most white and shining Knight, we assuredly confess that your auspicious arrival from the White House to the Black House has promised it, given birth to it, brought it. All of us are aflame with your arrival, with all the gladness, joy, congratulation and acclamation possible; and with respectful souls, most devoted feelings, and most reverent allegiance, we congratulate you on your safety.' The oration is based on extracts from *The Pope's Letter to the Prince* (with) *A Jesuit's Oration to the Prince, in Latin and English* (1623).

19–20 *affects . . . colleges . . . plots*: loves . . . holy orders and religious seminaries (unconsciously implying them to be breeding grounds of plots).

26 *endear us*: (1) show us to be important; (2) make yourself dear to us. The White Duke spells out the reciprocal quality of the welcome in his following lines.

30–1 *abstruse . . . freeness*: secret things open themselves to you freely and voluntarily. The Black Knight is trying to play down any suggestion of plots or secret agendas.

32 *seat of adoration*: residing place of worship.

33–4 *taste . . . relish*: taint of the old cup (i.e. Popery) yet. The wrong flavour (or 'the enjoyment of error'). In Tr. the White Duke does not speak here, his words completing the White Knight's line. Lan. and most other witnesses emphasize how close the White Knight and the White Duke are in their thinking.

S.D. *images . . . it*: Ar., Bri., Ros. render this as 'statues standing on each side'. Tr. adds 'with a song'.

36 *Wonder . . . delight*: may wonder perform something pleasing and astonishing.

41 *on fire*: Tr. 'afire'.

42 *May . . . approve*: may lifeless things demonstrate our joys. Statues coming to life and dancing feature in Francis Beaumont's *Masque of the Inner Temple and Gray's Inn*, performed for the marriage of Princess Elizabeth to the Elector Palatine (1613).

44–5 *Quickened . . . Or . . . strange*: given life . . . or (let) anything even stranger (happen).

46–7 *waits upon . . . right-hand*: accompanies . . . clock-wise; propitious, as distinct from the 'sinister' left-hand. Tr. alone omits these two lines.

5.2 S.D. *in . . . her*: Ar., Ros. The 'reverend habit' contrasts with the 'richly accoutred' outfit in 4.1.

1–3 *I see . . . me*: the White Queen's Pawn decides that the Black Bishop's Pawn was only testing her 'duty' (Tr. 'love') and so did not sleep with her in 4.3. Not realizing that he was the man who earlier tried to seduce her, she turns sharply on him ('the bad man') when he appears in his Jesuit's habit. Tr. marks the entry of 'the Jesuit' at l. 3.

5 *Traitor . . . holiness*: not in the versions most closely associated with Middleton. The words may have been added by Crane to complete the line of verse.

6 *marble-fronted*: with a face like marble, cold and hard, so showing no shame.

6–7 *knows . . . used*: Tr. 'he knows | How much he has wronged'.

11–12 *poor . . . only*: a poor man who suffers only for your sake.

13 *reverend*: Tr. 'reverence and'.

15 *her*: i.e. sanctity's.

18 *does with*: suits.

20 *think . . . see*: Tr.; Bri. 'count it strange to have'.

21–2 *shape . . . wanting one*: costume, theatrical dress . . . lacking [a *shape*].

29 *that habit*: i.e. the Jesuit's clerical (*reverend*) clothes, as distinct from his *richly accoutred* outfit in 4.1.

30 *fitted*: supplied with necessary (theatrical) properties.

31–2 *They must . . . it else*: they would otherwise need shrewd intelligence to tell the true from the false. Tr. 'it must be strange cunning | To find it else'.

33 *mighty auditory*: great audience.

34–5 *Nay . . . love you*: i.e. he is such a powerful actor when he 'pretends' to seduce members of an audience that they will not be able to love him as he really is.

37 *of . . . smile*: that you will smile. i.e. he responds to her earnestness by grinning.

38 *th'ignorance . . . power*: i.e. your ignorance of your own power.

40 *husband . . . shelter*: i.e. she is about to marry (himself in disguise, though she does not know that) as a convenient front to conceal her lust. He still thinks that she has had sexual intercourse with himself, though in fact the Black Queen's Pawn took her place.

41 *friend's comfort*: lover's attention.

44 *letter . . . cast*: the Black Bishop's Pawn's words are likened to printing type.

45–6 *the . . . much . . . heartily tasted*: i.e. the Black Bishop's Pawn himself . . . enthusiastically enjoyed.

49 *immodest . . . office*: smack of immodesty in that service (unlike earlier suggestions).

50–1 *Strange . . . me*: she reflects how unusual it is that, of all the men her 'richly accoutred' Black Bishop's Pawn might choose to perform the marriage, it should be 'the Jesuit' who tried to seduce her; *of all . . . first light*: Tr. 'of all others he should light'.

52 *business*: Tr. 'office'.

53 *I name . . . token*: it is not clear what *token* is meant. He may imply that his mere presence, knowing that a marriage is required, is proof enough. Or possibly he carries an unspecified item given by the White Queen's Pawn to his disguised self in 4.3.

56 *lewd soliciting*: i.e. further attempts to seduce her.

57–8 *craft's . . . on fire . . . cozening market*: skill's . . . Tr. 'afire' . . . cheating bargain.

60 *nice iniquity . . . strict luxury*: bashful wickedness . . . Tr 'hot luxury'; *luxury*: lust.

62 *clap on . . . solder up*: hurriedly undertake . . . repair, seal up.

64 *You . . . now*: you claimed to be a virgin; keep (hypocritically) insisting that you are no different now.

65 *I left . . . you*: i.e. you were already sexually experienced before I had sex with you.

70 *take . . . pleasure*: do what you will.

72–3 *may . . . master*: may claim as by right the highest seat in hell and sit above Satan.

73 *Bring . . . merit*: literally 'Fetch in someone of true worth', meaning something like 'Who are you to be calling me names?'

74–5 *That . . . bed*: who allowed himself through blind lust to be led last night to fornication in some prostitute's bed.

76 s.d. *Within*: not in Tr. (also lines 81, 83, 85 below).

78–9 *Of virgins . . . You may now*: by virgins . . . Tr. 'Now you may'.

79 *you hear . . . thanks*: i.e. he is formally to confirm he understands that she has thanked him for sparing her virginity, and so ended their relationship.

80 *Here's . . . game*: Tr. 'This a strange game'.

83 *the contract*: Tr. 'thanksgiving'. The Black Bishop's Pawn recalls a conversation with the Black Queen's Pawn after their 'contract' the night before.

83–4 *Mischief . . . prepared for't*: Tr. 'A pox' . . . ready for sexual intercourse; Tr., Bri. 'and you did prepare yourself'.

85 *And set . . . reach, sir*: her sexual expectations were higher than he was able to satisfy.

86 *This is . . . pawn*: Tr. 'Light, 'tis a bawdy voice'.

88 *works . . . kindly*: (1) acts so obligingly; (2) performs the deed of kind, i.e. has sex.

92 *engine . . . known*: device, means (i.e. rape) . . . Tr., Bri. 'seen'. It was 'not known' because she was the (willing) object of 'adoration' and 'wonder'.

95 *stamp*: mark or identify (me) as.

97–9 *chief agent . . . pursued 'em too*: i.e. in charge of transporting young ladies to nunneries, possibly against the will of their families [*pursued'em*], depriving them of their inherited goods [*portions*], and probably taking sexual advantage of them too. She speaks with the bitterness of experience.

104–6 *you poisoned . . . bastard*: you corrupted with pregnancy, twice, and pronounced her to be possessed with an evil spirit, when in fact it was your own illegitimate child.

105 *And*: Tr. 'Then'.

106–7 *taken . . . toils*: trapped in my own snares (as also in the chess-game).

109 *of . . . hands*: on all sides.

111 *burden . . . grasshopper*: cf. 'the grasshopper shall be a burden', Ecclesiastes 12: 5. The Black Queen's Pawn does not feel the weight of her own sins in her satisfaction at seeing the Black Bishop's Pawn *taken*.

112 *whore of order*: prostitute (1) of a religious order; (2) to order, on demand.

cockatrice 'in voto': the cockatrice is a legendary creature with the head of a cock and the body of a serpent, whose look was deadly, but also slang for a loose woman. On *in voto* see 1.1.42 and note. The phrase might be glossed as 'a sworn courtesan'.

113–14 *play . . . How . . . villain*: aim . . . Tr. 'Have' . . . Tr. 'Hold, Monster-impudence'.

115 *offence*: see 1.1.145 and note; Tr. 'attempt'.

O merciless bloodhound: not in Tr. This suggests a relentless seeker after blood.

116–17 *How! . . . that partner*: Tr. 'Death' . . . i.e. the Black Bishop's Pawn. Tr. 'yond' for 'that'.

118 *farther . . . name*: further than by social acquaintance, i.e. she renounces sexual 'knowledge' of men as a result of what the two black pawns have done.

5.3 S.D. *Bishop*: Tr. specifies the Black King, Queen, Knight, and Duke. The Black Bishop may not speak in the scene, but John Holles mentions him (in addition to 'Spalato') being put into the bag: see Appendix, p. 316.

1–2 *have . . . content*: Tr. 'have both' . . . pleasure, satisfaction.

2 *riot*: extravagance. There were complaints that the English had been meagrely entertained in Madrid in 1623. The Black House try to make a virtue of 'frugality'.

4–5 *that's . . . heard . . . miss on't*: Tr., Bri. 'we seldom hear' . . . am without it.

6 *We . . . use to*: it is not our custom to. Most of the detail of this speech is derived from Pliny (AD 23–79), *Historia naturalis*, especially Book 9, Chapters 18 and 54.

7–8 *Two . . . Roman painful-idleness*: Tr., Bri 'Three' . . . self-indulgent luxury of Roman patricians, underpinned by slave labour.

9 *care*: charge, concern (i.e. they had nothing more serious to think about).

12 *Chalcedon*: in Asia Minor. Venue of a major Church Council in 451 and the title of the provisional head of the Roman Catholics in England.

16 *Epicurean-like*: like Epicurus (341–270 BC), famous Athenian philosopher, who argued that pleasure (i.e. the practice of virtue) was the highest good, an argument often distorted to justify hedonistic self-indulgence.

17 *Sergius Orata*: mentioned in the *Saturnalia* of Macrobius (*fl* AD 400) as the possible originator of fish-farming (*stews*: brothels; artificial breeding-beds), specializing in oysters, and supposedly named Orata because of his passion for gilt-bream, *aurata*. All witnesses read 'Crata' for 'Orata'.

20 *large . . . invention*: i.e. he made a lot of money by selling his oysters, as well as eating them himself. When seafood was still relatively plentiful it could be seen as greed to farm it for yourself and self-indulgence to make a profit out of doing it for others.

22 *arch-gormandiser*: Roman emperor Heliogabalus (d. AD 222), famous for his imaginative orgies.

25 *strengthened*: ate more vigorously.

27 *vented*: emptied; expressed in sexual action.

29–30 *Pertinax . . . set up . . . again*: Roman emperor (d. 193), famous for his frugal habits . . . put out a second time as in a place of honour.

31 *Julian*: Didius Julianus, briefly emperor (d. 193).

33 *wipe . . . beard . . . can*: i.e. to signify the end of the meal . . . know how to. It was rare for aristocrats, in ancient Rome or early modern Europe, not to eat meat at a meal.

36–7 *purchased . . . triumphs*: hired at the same cost as lavish public spectacles.

39 *White . . . gormandisers*: the court of James I could be notoriously lavish, and Buckingham in particular was known for his extravagant banquets.

40 *plump*: Tr. Lan.'s 'fat' misses the alliteration and duplicates with the next line.

41 *Scaliger*: Julius Caesar Scaliger (1484–1558), noted humanist writer.

42–3 *prick or goad . . . needle*: essentially the same thing, sharp sticks with which to prod animals . . . bore with their teeth.

45 *choked . . . paunch*: stifled with the bulk of his own fat. Magas, king of Cyrene (a Greek colony in Africa), was reported to have died of suffocation in 258 BC.

46–52 *Which death . . . before him*: fat Sancho I, king of Leon (956–65), fearing such a death because of his great stomach, opted to die quickly by means of a swift and deadly herb he took to make himself lean, something the old king of Morocco advised him to do to allay his fears, rather than risk dying squalidly in his own excess like the huge cormorant (Magas) who suffocated before him. Cormorants are voracious sea-birds which store fish in their gullet to regurgitate later: hence, insatiable gluttons.

53 *sound*: (1) reliable; (2) healthy, robust.

56 *discourse*: conversation, something to talk about.

58–9 *I fear ... fog of fatness*: as a young man Buckingham was tall, long-limbed and athletic, but he was fond of food and inclined to put on weight. *fog*: unwholesome fat.

60 *comeliness ... as glorious*: handsomeness ... more splendid (than being fat). Buckingham was quite vain about his appearance.

61 *course ... strict ... transgress*: customs are remarkably abstemious ... go beyond the limits (of Black House frugality).

62 *Were ... to ... wrought ... to't*: Tr.; Bri. 'If I should' ... worked on me to do.

64–5 *You that ... withal*: you who have been brought up to eat lavishly because of climate and social convention are entirely excused.

71 *happily ... in*: content ... Tr. 'on'.

72 *diet ... disposition*: food of my nature, regulation of my natural inclinations.

76 *master-cook*: Ben Jonson's *Neptune's Triumph for the Return of Albion*, which celebrates the safe return of Charles and Buckingham from Madrid, features a master-cook who tries to teach 'the poet' how to please any audience.

78–9 *puff-paste ... meanest*: fine flour paste, so a light or frivolous person ... lowest.

81 *fetch ... compass*: extend no further in scope.

85 *garden ... salads*: salads were considered poor food at aristocratic tables, so 'an inconsiderable plot of land'.

86–7 *larded ... grave ... signiory*: enriched (as with fat) ... serious and chaste domain. Venetian women were notoriously anything but chaste, so he is being sardonic.

88–9 *served ... like ... our*: served up like a castrated cock ... Tr. 'her'.

91 *Below ... salt*: i.e. at the inferior end of the table, away from host and the chief guests. The salt-cellar marked the divide.

Netherlands: Spanish territory, but its Protestant provinces had been in intermittent revolt for years.

94 *spit ... plovers*: skewer-full of Portuguese served up in place of lapwings (birds commonly eaten). Spain annexed Portugal in 1580.

96 *Holland*: like Zealand, one of the provinces of the Netherlands.

98 *full*: Tr. 'crammed'.

100 *meat*: food.

102 *pickled things*: Switzerland and Poland have the status of pickled items guests might turn to if exceptionally hungry, reflecting their unimportance.

106–7 *barren . . . grave*: a woman's womb was thought naturally to yearn for a child, as the grave was said to gape for all mankind.

107 *what's more*: anything even more.

110–11 *We make . . . counsels*: we make people on their deathbeds buy their spiritual consolation, and pay through the nose for religious advice.

112–13 *Leave rich . . . without'em*: get them to bequeath large estates for a few ineffectual prayers (Tr. 'sale-orisons'), or else they will die unreconciled to God and the Church.

115 *swear*: Tr.; Bri. 'say'.

116 *Is't possible*: The Black Duke's line ('You cannot walk . . . ') precedes the White Knight's in all other witnesses.

117 *walk . . . tuns*: Tr. 'pass' . . . wine-casks; i.e. the vaults of monasteries are crammed with liquor.

119–20 *shut . . . life*: excluded by your rigorous code of conduct. Tr. 'locked' for *shut*.

120–1 *vile . . . make . . . on't*: Tr. 'foul' . . . dismiss it lightly, trifle with it.

124–5 *trifle . . . house of clay: venery*: least considerable . . . body: lust. Buckingham had a notorious sexual appetite and was quite indiscreet in his courtship.

126 *If . . . on't*: the line appears to mean 'If I embrace you closely I will show you the worst of [venery]'; i.e. I will reveal my own sexual excitement.

127 *fruit*: after-supper dessert.

128–9 *Nay, at . . . fishpond*: i.e. six thousand skulls of babies (aborted by the nuns) were found at the ruins of a nunnery, testimony to the Black House's sexual licentiousness.

130 *WHITE DUKE*: Tr. has no speech header. Bri. and Ros. give this to the White Knight.

132–3 *Huldrick . . . you how*: the Hulderius letter spelling out the scandal of the infant skulls was often cited by Protestant propagandists.

134 *at . . . of*: engaged in cleaning out.

136 *mother-maids . . . those parts*: nuns who were professed virgins but actually mothers . . . Tr.; Bri. 'that place'.

138 *One more*: i.e. admission of vice.

142 *Toads*: i.e. even things as loathsome as toads.

144 *hidden'st*: Tr. 'hiddest'.

147 *brand*: mark of infamy.

150–1 *Avoid . . . profanation . . . only . . . virtue*: don't be blasphemous (in calling dissembling a sin) . . . most important diplomatic virtue.

158 *came so . . . as*: Tr. 'yet came near our souls till'. The line means (1) you

were never so dear/closely allied to us, as you are now; (2) you never understood our private secrets so well until now—a telling ambiguity, with the 'discovery' imminent.

159–60 *BLACK DUKE . . . ever*: Tr. has no speech header for the Black Duke, and these two lines simply complete the Black Knight's previous speech.

161–2 *checkmate by | Discovery*: it is not clear whether checkmate by discovery is a special manœuvre for achieving checkmate (the trapping of the opponent's king, which concludes a game of chess), as some editors have claimed, or whether it is simply that the Black House have been manœuvred into revealing all their secrets. See N. W. Bawcutt, 'New Light on Middleton's Knowledge of Chess', *N&Q* 232 (1987), 301–2.

S.D. *A . . . flourish*: Q1 only.

164 *Ambitious . . . falsehood*: the line, not in Tr., recites the vices feigned by the White Knight and Duke but which truly belong to the Black House.

166 *BLACK KNIGHT*: Tr. gives this to the Black Queen, Bri. and Ros. to the Black King.

167 S.D. *Flourish*: in Ar. only, but royal entrances were usually marked with a fanfare.

S.D. *Bishop &c*: Tr. S.D. here mentions White Pawns but does not specify which or how many. The King and Queen must have an entourage, and it would be fitting for the White Queen's Pawn to be there to symbolize the thwarting of the plot against her. No other witness specifies the presence of the White Bishop.

168–9 *this . . . masterpiece*: i.e. Prince Charles.

170–1 *this fair . . . assistant*: i.e. Buckingham. *this*: Tr. 'yond'.

173 *powerful*: Tr. 'peaceful'.

174 *triumph*: elation of victory [all the greater because the game was so hazardous].

175–6 *I gave . . . fittest favour*: Tr. 'We gave' . . . most suitable reward.

S.D. *The bag . . . in it*: not in Tr. Other versions indicate that all the Black House other than those still on stage are in the bag, including the Fat Bishop. It is often assumed that the bag was a hell-mouth, a gaping mouth with fire and other marks of the devil, used for sinners in the old morality plays. Indeed, the Spanish Ambassador reported that 'he who played the Prince of Wales heartily beat and kicked the "Count of Gondomar" into Hell, which consisted of a great hole and hideous figures' (Appendix, p. 311). But he did not see the play himself. John Holles, who did, wrote: 'the Prince making a full discovery of all their knaveries, Olivares, Gondomar . . . are by the Prince put into the bag, & so the play ends' (Appendix, p. 316). The emphasis throughout is on putting characters 'in the bag', with all its chess resonances, and this continues even when the Black House are *physically* consigned to the 'bag'. A tent-like structure to represent the bag was presumably erected on stage, perhaps adjacent to the central trapdoor by which the Black House may make their final exit—so a witty variation on the old hell-mouth.

180 *bag's . . . hell*: Tri.; Bri. 'the bag, like hell-mouth'. See previous note: Middleton acknowledges the analogy with the old hell-mouth but distinguishes his staging from it.

181 *lost sons*: certainly the Black Bishop's Pawn, Black Queen's Pawn, Fat Bishop and Black Jesting Pawn; possibly also the White King's Pawn, anonymous White Pawn from 3.2 and the Black Knight's Pawn, though none of these says anything.

184–5 *heads . . . Envy's issue*: Tr. 'foreheads' . . . the children of Envy. Envy is presented as the champion of Error in *The Triumphs of Truth*.

186 *'Tis too apparent*: Tr. 'See, all's confounded'; Bri., Ros. 'All hope's confounded'.

187 *given . . . bag*: cheated us (colloquial).

188 *JESTING PAWN . . . had . . . have*: see 3.2.1 s.d. and note . . . should have.

189–90 *This Fat . . . squeezed me*: Tr. ''Sfoot this Fat Bishop hath so squelched and squeezed me | So overlaid me'.

191 *goodness*: life-juices.

193–4 *room . . . lie*: punning on the pronunciation of 'Rome', echoing the Fat Bishop's ambition to be Pope . . . (1) lie down; (2) tell untruths.

196–7 *I abhor . . . whorish*: Tr. 'Art thou showing | Thy impudent-whorish'. He is addressing the Black Queen's Pawn who betrayed him.

198 *pit*: Lan., Tr. This suggests the trapdoor was in use by this point. Bri. 'bag'.

199 *WHITE KING*: Tr. lacks a speech header, so the White Knight speaks these lines.

204 *Indeed . . . stir*: (1) a chess-queen may indeed make a bishop move (with her greater power and mobility); (2) a whore ('quean') can indeed arouse a bishop sexually.

208 *I'm . . . creeps out*: i.e. being so fat. Tr. 'But I'm sure I shall be the last creeps out'.

210–11 *Foh . . . hither*: Tr., not in Lan. A reference to Gondomar's fistula (*vent*: anus), presumably omitted by Crane on grounds of taste.

211 *olive-coloured Ganymede*: greenish catamite. 'Olive-coloured' identifies Don Carlos, Duke of Olivares, Philip IV's favourite, as the Black Duke. Holles recognized 'Ollivares' as one of those placed in the bag, though the Spanish Ambassador does not mention him—tactfully, since he was the recipient of his letter (see Appendix pp. 316, 311). The relationship

between Philip IV and his favourite would have meant little to English audiences, except as a final instance of Black House sodomy. Perhaps English audiences would have 'applied' their relationship to James and his own Duke/favourite.

217 *now . . . womb*: in Tr. *now* is before *let . . .* a place of darkness but (like the idea that the Black Knight will *peck a hole i'th'bag*) a reminder that the Black House will not remain in the bag forever. The White House needs to be on guard for its next *game*.

218 *falsehood*: Tr. 'malice'.

Epilogue 4–5 *most . . . draws . . . envy's mark*: has the loyalty of most of this audience . . . see 5.3.185 and note.

6–7 *devoted . . . or in private*: consigned to damnation . . . Tr. 'and in corners'.

Appendix

1.2 *16ᵗʰ*: i.e. 6th, old-style, and so for all dates within the letter.

43 *Marqués de la Hinojosa*: formerly Special Ambassador in London, along-side Coloma. The two men had not got along, but plotted together to disgrace the Duke of Buckingham, for which de la Hinojosa was required to leave the country with ignominious speed and lack of formality.

60–1 *Although . . . embassy*: Don Carlos was indeed recalled to Spain the following month, after serving in London since June 1622; that had nothing to do with the play.

74–6 *ship . . . instantly*: Don Carlos is in effect threatening a suspension, if not exactly a severance, of diplomatic relations if the play's affront to the honour of the King of Spain is not punished.

2.5 *Monday*: the 11th was Wednesday.

16 *descant*: variations on a central theme.

30 *Bristol*: John Digby, first Earl of Bristol (1580–1653), diplomat and statesman, English Ambassador to Spain during the visit of Charles and Buckingham. Charles accused him of taking the Spanish side during the marriage negotiations and of trying to persuade him to become a Catholic. He was recalled in disgrace in 1624 and at the time of the play awaited examination by Parliament. Holles's close précis of 3.1.261–6, specifically mentioning details not in the early Archdall text, confirms that the revisions to the role of the White King's Pawn were in the staged version of the play.

46 *hardy part*: bold/foolhardy affair. Holles, like several other contemporary commentators, assumed the actors were taking an awful risk.

47 *gamesters*: actors.

48–9 *'rebus sic stantibus'*: Latin: matters standing thus.

GLOSSARY

a he

a God's name free; without charge

a match agreed

able (v.) enable; make fit for

ableness ability

above on the upper stage

abroach running; flowing

abroad away from home; out of the house

absolute perfect; most noble

abused frustrated; deceived

accidence books on Latin grammar and inflection

accident characteristic; symptom; event

acquaintance notice

act of pleasure sexual intercourse

admiration wonder

admit agree to; allow; warrant

adoration worship of divinity

advance thrust forward

adventure risk

adventurer speculator; game-player

affect love; be especially fond of; prefer; have feelings for; express

affected disposed; inclined

affectionate comfort loving pleasure

affinity kinship

afford give

affrightment fear

after (prep.) at the rate of; (adv. as v.) follow

against in time for

aggravate make more severe

agree long live in harmony for a long time

agree justly fit exactly

akindling alight

alacrity cheerful readiness

a-late recently

alight land; arrive

allow assign; grant

Allwit inversion of wittol; a complacent cuckold

almond-milk sweet liquid made from boiled sweet almonds

alms charitable donations

alms-knights military pensioners

alone unaided

amain violently

amaze astound; bewilder

amazement consternation/confusion

amazing amazed

amiss wrong

amorously like a lover; attractive

an (*and*) if; even if; when

angels' food bread of heaven

angle corner

anon at once

another since yet again

answerable in agreement; suitable

answered fulfilled

answered under met the requirements to become

antemasque an interlude, usually comic, before the main masque

antic grotesque clown

any stirring anything happening

apace quickly

ape colloquial term of endearment

apparent open; brazen

appear to stand before

apple-loft enclosed; dry alcove used for storing apples

apprehend learn; understand

apprehension knowledge; grasp of the matter

approve confirm; demonstrate; give proof of

approved commendable; worthy of approval

argue indicate; suggest

argument discussion; discussion point

arrant unmitigated

art learning; artifice; cunning

article legal term

article between a (quasi-)legal condition to be satisfied

artificial ingenious; skilful

aspect the appearance presented to the eye

aspire rise up

asunning sunning itself

at a push when things were most critical

at first immediately; in swordplay, at the formal first thrust

at no hand on no account

at unawares unwittingly

aunt bawd or pimp (slang)

Bacchus Greek god of wine

baffle publicly disgrace

bags money bags

bait taunt

balloon-ball large inflated leather ball

band collar or cuff

bandy hit at; toss back and forth

bane death; ruin; destruction

bankers those employed to tend the banks of a flooding river

bankrout bankrupt

banqueting-house common feature of Jacobean formal gardens

barren dull; stupid

base corrupt

bashful modest; retiring

basilisk mythical creature whose look could kill

bastard inferior

'bating reducing

battledore small racket

bauble stick, often phallic in shape, traditionally carried by fools

bawd procuress; brothel-keeper

bawdy dirty

beadle under-officer of justice

become suit

bedlam Bethlehem Hospital outside London; generic term for a madhouse

beforehand in advance

behind to come

beholding beholden; indebted

belike perhaps; most likely

bent inclined

beshrew blame; curse; devil take

best piece highest achievement

bestead situated; positioned

bestow dispose of

betimes immediately

bid summon

bide stand

big-bellied full; pregnant

bill advertisement

bird easy victim

birding fowling

birdspit birds skewered through the breech for roasting

birth social standing at birth

bisextile leap-year

bit mouthpiece of a horse's bridle

blame commonly adjectival in the 17th cen. (i.e. blameworthy); hence 'too blame' where modern usage is 'to blame'

blasted blighted; cursed

blessings felicities; children

blest guarded

blind time hours of darkness

blind work invisible writing

blood family; kinship; lust; desire; inclination

blown full-blown

blushing business sex

bode portend

booty prize; spoil or piece of plunder

bord bore of a gun; condition

bore width of a pipe

bound (adj.) obliged; in [someone's] debt; (v. and n.) leap

bounteous free with hospitality

bounty hospitality; generosity; special gratuity

bout legal quarrel; sexual encounter

brace pair

brack flaw

brand mark of infamy

brave grand; gallant; splendid

breast inhabitants most intimate occupants

breed teeth cut one's teeth, so become dangerous

brevit inadequate, sexually and otherwise

bridewell prison

brightness beauty

British Welsh

broad wide; bawdy

brokage illicit dealer; pimp

brood (v.) breed; hatch

brook stomach; suffer

buckler shield (in fencing)

buff particularly strong leather, used for soldiers' uniforms
bum padded bustle; posterior
bum-roll hip-cushion to hold out a full skirt
burden capacity
business affair
buss kiss
but only; nothing but
but that except for the fact that
by attorney by proxy
by offices by taking fees or bribes while holding official positions
by their names individually
by this by now
by-bet side issue
cabalistic secret; conspiratorial
cabinet small case for holding letters, jewels, etc.
cabrito goat's flesh [Spanish]
calf blockhead
call back reform
caltrop = galtrop
calvish stupid; heretical
cambric kind of fine linen
can know how to
canaries quick Spanish dance
candour brilliant whiteness, and so purity; openness; lack of malice
canopy the sky
caparison clothing
capcase small container or wallet
caper dance or leap in a frolicsome manner
care self-regard; conscientiousness; charge; concern; effort
careful one with cares and duties
carnal strictness the laws governing meat consumption
caroch stately coach
carriage conduct
carry up uphold
case situation; suit of clothes
casement window
cast (p. part) arranged; (n.) throw of the dice
cast away wasted
castigation corrective punishment
casting-bottle bottle for sprinkling perfume

cat wedge of wood struck in the game of tip-cat
catched caught
cater person in charge of buying *cates*, exotic delicacies
cattle chattel; wealth or goods; cattle
cautelous crafty, circumspect
censure judgement
certificate proof of good conduct
Chaldean one skilled in the occult
chaldron cauldron; a dry measure of 32 bushels
challenge claim as a right; lay claim to
chance happen to
chandler candle-maker
change stronger term than today, suggesting disaster or calamity
changeling idiot (see Introduction)
charge expense; responsibility; suspicion; accusation
charge bestowed expenses incurred
charnel cemetery; place for bones
charwomen women hired by the day to perform odd chores
chary careful
check rebuke; threaten opponent's King in chess
check for deflection from
checkmate terminal play in a game of chess
cheer entertainment; basic provisions (as distinct from a full meal)
chide rebuke
chiefest men principal followers
Chios Greek island-port in the Aegean
chipped manchet loaf of fine white bread with the crust pared away
chopping strapping
chops cheeks
Christmas-bowl festive drink
churchwarden lay officer of the parish church
cinquepace lively galliard
circumscribe channel one way
citizen an inhabitant of the city (i.e. of London)
clap cleave; catch venereal disease
clap on hurriedly undertake
clap up stick up
classis division by rank, class

clean contrary entirely differently

clean wrought perfectly made

cleanly shift neat trick

clean-treading straight-walking (but 'tread' also = copulate)

clip embrace

close (adj.) locked tightly shut; (adv.) secretly

close chamber small room; privy

closeness secrecy

close-stool commode; portable toilet

closet cabinet for storing valuables; private quarters; chamber

cloth-stopple a plug of cloth for a jar

Coads me a mild euphemized oath

cock cockerel; erect penis

cock-horse hobby-horse

cockle shell fish

cocted boiled

cog cheat

college religious order

colon large intestine; figurative for appetite

come at visit

come home fulfilled

come nearer be more explicit

comely beautiful; handsome; proper; decent

comfit sweet made of fruit pulp and sugar

comfort pleasure; relief

comfortable comforting

commodious successful

commotion rebellion

compass (v.) achieve; manage; encompass; experience; (n.) scope

complete perfect

composition mixture; medicinal compound

compound join

comprehend contain

conceit idea; notion; fancy; meaning; significance

conceive understand

concise brief

conclave body of cardinals

conduct (v.) lead; (n.) pass

coney rabbit; whore

confirmed well established

confound thwart; bring to nothing

confusion ruin

consort servant

constant stuff consistently coloured material, unlike changeable silk

consume burn (with sexual innuendo)

content happiness; satisfaction

contract (n.) betrothal; (v.) go through the forms of a marriage pre-contract

contrariety conflict

control bring to book

contumelious insolent; offensive

conveyance a secret passage

cope meet; contend

copy legal term, from property rights

coracine black Nile fish, like perch

cordials medicines for the heart

cormorant voracious sea-bird which stores fish in its gullet to regurgitate later; hence, a glutton

counsel advice; support

counsellor lawyer

countenance (n.) demeanour; appearance; (v.) favour; patronize

counting considering

country place of origin; cunt

couple (v.) join

courses personal actions

court passage a gambling game with dice, implying 'court intrigue'

courteous physic mild medication

court-green bowling green

court-harbingers officers sent ahead when the court was on progress to prepare and assign lodgings

covetous desirous of wealth

coxcomb simpleton

coz familiar form of 'cousin'

cozen cheat

crack (v.) destroy; (n.) female pudenda

crag neck

cram stuff

crests cuckold's horns

critical crucial; propitious

crop-sick sick in the gullet

cross (n.) set-back; (vb.) oppose; impede; deny

crudity indigestion

crumbed thickened or covered with crumbs (of cheese)

cry tout for sale; shout about; declare by the town crier to be lost

crying trespass transgression that cries out for justice

cubit biblical measure of length; 18–22 inches (45–55 cm)

Cuds abbreviation of *Cud's foot* ('By God's foot'), a mild oath

cullis a rich broth

cunning (n.) sly trick; (adj.) skilful

cupid mischievous, often blindfolded son of Venus, usually depicted naked, with a bow to fire arrows of desire

cure care; concern

curious fastidious

cushion-cloth expensive cushion covering

custom repeated experience

cut setback; female genitals

cutted querulous; abrupt

cut-work openwork lace

dab down duck down flat

Dahumma from Welsh, *dech yma*, come here

dalliance over-indulgence

deal plainlier explain yourself more clearly

deal with treat; handle; have illicit relations with

dear sweet; costly

'Death by God's death

decayed fallen from prosperity

decked arrayed

default failure to attend to the game

deflower make to lose virginity; rape

deft petite

degrees degrees of rank

delight delightfulness

deliver report

deserts good qualities

design (v.) point out; (n.) plot; scheme

despatch get through; polish off

deuce two, on cards or dice

device stratagem; scheme; allegory; masque

devotion zeal; enthusiasm

die pine away with passion

dildo nonsense refrain; artificial phallus

dimple smile

diocese area of a bishop's jurisdiction

discourse conversation; something to talk about

discover reveal

discovery exposure (of crime or secrets)

discreet judicious

discretion understanding; judgement

disliked displeased

dispatch settle the matter quickly

disperse free one's self from

dissimulation feigning; pretence

distracted mentally deranged

do reason do what is required; render satisfaction

dog (adj.) keen like a dog; (n.) iron (= andiron) in the grate of a fire; early form of firearm

dog-star Sirius

done cheated

doubt (v.) fear; suspect; (n.) suspicion; uncertainty

doubtful of anxious about

down be overthrown; taken [in chess]; lose place; suffer

drab whore

draw attract

draw in withdraw

dress prepare something for eating

dresser sideboard where food is prepared for serving

driver hammer

drone idle person

drouth drought

drug shop shop dealing in medicinal drugs

dry thirsty; sober; sexually unstimulated

dry sucket crystallized fruit

dubitable doubtful

Dugat a whee phonetic rendition of Welsh, perhaps *Duw cadu chwi*, 'God bless you'

duke old name for 'rook' or 'castle' chess-piece

eagle (adj.) high-soaring

ease comfort; pleasure

easy simple; comfortable

eggs o'the'spit delicate business in hand

'eighty-eight 1588, year of the Spanish Armada

Egyptian gypsy, fortune teller

either equally readily

elixir quintessence

elops fish related to herring

else otherwise
embossings embossed ornaments
enchant put under a spell
enclosed grounds fenced-off land
endear show to be important; make dear to
engine device
enjoin to impose upon
entailed condition of inheritance or permanent state
enter upon claim possession of
entertain wile away time
entreat plead; solicit
epicure glutton
epistle letter
equal impartial; just; equitable
equivocation private qualification of an uttered statement by a mental reservation
eringo (= eryngo) sea-holly
even correct
ewe-mutton old strumpet
ewer jug for carrying water
exalt extol; raise in power or rank
exceptious prone to take exception
express press out; distil; show
extenuate weaken
extremity distress
eye perception; vagina
facetious jocular; urbane; witty
factor merchant's agent
faculties disposition; instincts
fag fag-end (from the last piece of a roll of cloth)
faggots bundle of brushwood
fain be very pleased to; gladly
fair clear; pleasant
fair end favourable position in a game
fair understanding honestly intended meaning
fall upon take up with
fame (usually good) reputation
far (n.) flour
fare eat
farthingale framework of hoops to spread out the skirts of women's dresses
fasten on take firm hold of
fatness richest part
faults list of errata

favour love-token; permission
fawning partner servile accomplice
fear frighten
feign dissemble
fellow twin; sister
fellowship company
Fie shame on you
figient fidgety
figure dance steps; face; appearance
filch steal
fine-timbered well-built
firk cheat; beat; fuck
first condition original innocence
first hand first strike
first-fruits an offering to God from the first harvest of the year; earliest produce of a master's loins
fistula suppurating pipe-like anal ulcer
fit (n.) struggle; seizure; part of a song; (v.) make ready; prepare
fit him get back at him appropriately
fitters small pieces
fittest favour best reward
flatter condone; gloss over
flesh-fly blow-fly
flight long, well-feathered arrow for accurate long shots
fling unseat
flourish fanfare of trumpets
flower-gentles flouramour (i.e. flower of love)
fog unwholesome fat
folio page
fond indulgent; infatuated; foolish
fool sweet made with cream and fruit
Foot by God's foot
for as
for defect because of physical inadequacy
for fashion for show; conventional formality
for the speed to hasten matters
for you with you; i.e. agreeing with you
forbear indulge; show mercy to; give over
forfeited lordships property forfeit for non-payment of loans
forgetfulness forgetting one's self; culpable disregard of moral truths
form school-class

formally neatly
forsooth in truth
forward (adj.) precocious; aggressive; eager; (v.) proceed
forwardest most ready
forwards on the road
founder someone who endows and maintains someone else
foutra fuck (French sexual vulgarity)
fox-skin cunning disguise
frame the fashion frame in a fashionable way; shape the semblance
frank stuff
frantic lunatic
fray frayed place in cloth
freedom membership of City companies; i.e. tradespeople
freight burden
friend lover
friendly fear over-concern of a friend
frisk move quickly
from distinction from the state in which it can be known or identified
front face
fulfil satisfy
fulsome plumply padded
furious impassioned
furnish out complete
gadding wandering idly
gallant man of fashion and chivalry
gallanter more fashionably
galtrop spiked weapon of war, mainly used against cavalry
game love-making; amorous sport; quarry
gameful joyful
gamesters gamblers; lechers; players in the game of love
gaudy-day feast-day, especially university celebration
gaudy-shop shop for finery
gear business; genitals
general comprehensive; all-embracing
general hopes wider expectations
gentleman man of good birth and social standing
gentleman-ushers gentlemen serving as ushers to men of higher social rank
gentlemen commoners privileged undergraduates

gently reconciled easily justified
get beget; conceive; make a profit (by selling)
get before go ahead of
gettings earnings
gilt gold-plated
gin trap
give pronounce; wager; shrink
glasses spectacles
glory renown
glorying proudly rejoicing
go pass
go about be concerned/engaged with
go to phrase of mild reproof
goad sharp pointed sticks with which to prod animals
God-den Good evening
go to make up; constitute; visit
golls cant for hands
good husbandry economic sense
good parts accomplishments; naked body
goodfellow roisterer
goodness benefaction; kindness; gifts; life-juices
goose prostitute (slang)
gossiping christening
gossips strictly godparents, but used for all friends invited to a christening
grace favour
gradation incrementation
great fat; important
green sickness anaemic disorder of women
green-goose young goose, suitable for baking in a pie; gullible person
groat strictly fourpenny piece, but used of any small coin
groom o'the stool post in a royal Privy Chamber with 'eponymous lavatorial functions'
gross stupid
grub person of unpleasant manners; dwarfish fellow
grudging (n.) trace; suspicion
guardiner rare form of 'guardian', possibly of rustic usage
guess suppose
guitonen beggar; vagabond (Spanish)

gull dupe
gulled guzzled
haberdines salt dried fish
habit clothing; disguise
habits behaviour
halberd cross between an axe and a spear
half-crown piece valuable but rare gold coin
halter (n.) noose, for hanging or for leading a horse; (v.) hang
handsome decent; proper
hang together make sense
hanselled given a New Year's gift
hap occur fortuitously
hapless unfortunate
haply by chance
happily perhaps; with any luck
happy fortunate
hard strenuous(ly)
hard beset seriously surrounded
hard chance bad luck
hard measure harsh punishment
harms injuries; mischiefs
hautboys/hoboys oboes
hay a country dance with serpentine movements
hazard put at risk
head chief
headborough parish constable
health toast
hearse ornamental wooden structure temporarily placed over the coffin in the church
heartily taste enthusiastically enjoy
heart-string tendon thought to sustain the heart
heat toil; sexual excess
heave raise with effort
heaven's substitute God's representative on earth
heavy sad; slovenly; sluggish; pregnant
Hebe daughter of Zeus
heinous odious
heyday exclamation, expressing high excitement
hie hurry
high weighty; serious
hindrance incapacity
hit on get the point of

hoboys = hautboys
hold bet
home to the point
honest chaste; honourable
honour (n.) bow; obeisance
hopeful in anticipation; promising; ambitious
hopper-rumped with buttocks like a hopper (i.e. protuberant)
hornpipe lively dance
horns insignia of the cuckold
hose breeches
hot eager; lustful
hot-cockles game like blind man's buff
housekeeper someone who runs a household
house side in chess and other competitions
how interjection, like the modern 'What'
How now greeting, implicitly asking 'what are you up to?'
huffs blows
humanity common human feeling
humour mood; whim; temperament
hurt undermine
i'th'chaps on't in the cheeks of it
idiot ignorance
idolatry worship of an idol
ignorant reckless; wilfully not paying attention
Imprimis 'In the first place', Renaissance Latin word to introduce a list
impudence shamelessness
in all altogether
in compass in the space; within limits
in order in due course
in practice into action
in sadness seriously
in state in great pomp; with high ceremony
incense (v.) enrage; perfume with incense
inconscionable thoughtless; inconsiderate
incontinently instantly
induce introduce
inferior policy lesser plot
infested morally corrupted; diseased
inflammation raging lust
ingenious intelligent

inhuman unnatural
injury insult; affront to honour
innocence lack of guilt; idiocy
inquisitor investigator
instance precedent
institution established order
intellectual eyesight the eye of the mind
intelligencies news; information
intention endeavour
inter bury
interview mutual sight; meeting
invention composition
issue children
jack common ruffian
jade worn-out horse; whore
jealousy suspicion
jennet small Spanish horse
jig lively dance, often associated with lewdness
jiggam-bobs knick-knacks
joint-stool solidly constructed stool
Jug familiar form of Joan
julep a cooling drink
justice defence
keep practise
keep close stay secluded at home
keep counsel keep a secret
kersten christened and so Christian
kickshaws fancy foods
kid young goat
kiff kith
kind (adj.) true to type; (n.) sex
kindly gently; naturally
kindreds peoples
kitling kitten
Kix the dry stem of a plant
knit tied
knocker good-looking person; notable copulator
knowledge sexual intercourse
lamb-stones testicles of a lamb
lamentable the cause of many tears
lapidary worker in precious stones
larded enriched by fat
largely at large; wherever I go
largeness scope; opportunity
last (adj.) latest; (n.) shape (cf. cobbler's last)
late recent

lawn fine linen
lay set watch on
lay itself die down
league association; distance of approximately 3 miles / 5 kilometres
least means smallest opportunity
leave give over
leg polite bow
leprous inclination diseased tendency
leviathan enormous sea-monster, sometimes identified with Satan
liberal over-generous; licentious
liberty district within which a Justice of the Peace's warrant was valid
lie be in bed; speak untruths
lie in come to the term of pregnancy
lie sweetly be favourably disposed
Life mild oath, contraction of 'By God's life'
Light mild oath, contraction of 'By God's light'
'light alight, arrive
lights upon rebounds upon
like (adj.) likely; (v.) please
lin cease
lips ambiguously the lips of the mouth and of the vagina
list choose; wish; listen (hence *list hither* listen here)
lively lifelike
livery distinctive clothes; uniform
loathe disgust
lock small quantity
look make sure
look better pay more attention
look for expect
look into give access to
look out go outside; take care
look to be on guard for
looking glass chamber pot
lose give up
lost wasted
lucky pennyworth bargain
lug pull by the hair or ears; bait
luminary light-giving sun or star
lump thing without sense
lurch cheat; steal
lustre radiant beauty
lusty vigorous; lecherous
luxury lust

Machiavel devious schemer
mad furious; enthusiastic; frenzied
mad wag merry, mischievous fellow
magnifico person of high judicial
  authority
maid girl; virgin
make do; write
make away get rid of
make profession swear
make shift make do
malapert impudent
manly gentlemanly
mannerly polite
manners behaviour [i.e. what people
  actually do]
mar injure
marble-fronted with a face like marble
marchpane marzipan
mark (n.) distinctive feature; example;
  target; coin worth two-thirds of a
  pound, 13s 4d; (v.) notice
market purchase; deal
mar'l marvel
marmalade a fruit preserve; not
  necessarily of oranges as usually today
marrow essence
marry name of the Virgin used as a mild
  expletive, often meaning 'certainly'
Mass 'By the mass', an oath with no
  specific Catholic overtones
master check checkmate
masterprize masterpiece (Middleton's
  own coinage)
mate (v. & n.) equal; (v) = checkmate
matter occasion
Maudline Magdalene; maudling
maugre despite
May bloom; prime
mazard head (jocular)
mean (n.) benefit; advantage; (v.) be
  likely, intend; (adj.) low, humble, little
mean faithfully intend faithful service
measure dance; (pl.) a slow and stately
  dance
meat food
meeting reconciliation
mel aerium airy honey (Latin)
men chessmen
mend reform; redeem; improve on
'mends amends

Mercury flying messenger and herald of
  the gods
mere total
merely extremely
meridian highest point of achievement
merit (n.) desert; reward; (adj.) being fit
  for desert or reward
mermaid commonly slang for whore
merry joking
mess cooking pot; portion of food
mettle temperament; metal
mettled courageous; amorous; half-
  drunk
mew confine; shut up
mighty auditory great audience
mildews destructive fungi on plants
milk-pottage milk broth
mind pay attention to
minute cue
misprise misunderstand
miss make a mistake
mistook inappropriate; suffered in error
mistrust suspect
mitigate make less severe
model play abstract or plot
Moll familiar for Mary; common term
  for a whore
monstrous out of proportion
mooncalf phantom pregnancy
moral (adj.) traditional; customary;
  proper
morris country dance
mortal deadly
mother-maid nun who professed to be a
  virgin but was actually a mother
motion proposal; action; intervention;
  impulse; changed feelings; natural
  course; inclination
motioned of suggested by
mount add up; multiply; sexually
  engage; soar like a flame
mum say not a word
mumble speak indistinctly; chew softly,
  as with toothless gums
mummy-matrons shrivelled old
  women
munition defences
murderer light cannon, common on
  ships
must need have no choice but to

GLOSSARY

mutton whores
mystery secret purpose
mystical secretive
nail cloth measure (2½ inches)
naturally spontaneously; as from a 'natural' or half-wit
nay indeed; not only that
neat elegant
necessitous poor; needy
need necessity
needle (v.) bore with teeth
needle's point point of a compass
neighbourhood living as neighbours
neither as well
new disease a previously undiagnosed fever
nice delicate; fastidious; squeamish
nice iniquity bashful wickedness
nice professor pedantic self-proclaimed expert
nidget idiot (as with the pronunciation 'ijjit')
nightmare female monster said to settle on people while asleep, inducing a sense of suffocation
night-piece bedfellow
nobler more generous or merciful
nosegay bunch of sweet-smelling herbs or flowers
not fits does not suit
not seem pretend not
not wronging which did not harm
o'erlay oppress
o'erseen mistaken
o'life by my life; exceedingly; alive
observance dutiful service; obligation
observed attended closely
occasion opportunity
of for; from; on
of duty as one's due
of force of necessity
of threescore aged sixty
offered under offered less
office duty
officers members of the watch
oil medicinal unction
oil of toad emetic
olive-coloured greenish
Oliver fruitful
on conscience in all conscience

on of
on the sudden all of a sudden
once ever; now
opacous dark; obscured and so ominous
open become auspicious
opportuneful timely; offering opportunity
orange tawny a vibrant colour, apparently often associated with courtiers
ordain prescribe
ordinary usual diet
ordnance cannon
orifex orifice
ornament distinction
ought (= aught) anything
out mistaken
out upon it emphatic exclamation, insisting that reality be faced up to
outcry auction
out-parishes parishes outside the city (of London) boundaries
over-against alongside
overtake catch up
owe own
pains effort; trouble
paint put on make-up
pairs mates
pander one who brings illicit lovers together
papistry Roman Catholicism
park large ornamental piece of land attached to a country estate
parlous dangerously cunning; perilous
parsimony carefulness; meanness
part depart
partake share in
participate partake (i.e. gain experience)
parts accomplishments; qualities; features
pass surpass; pass by.
passage progress; sexual opening
passing exceedingly
passion suffering; sorrowful complaint
pate head; brain
patrimony inheritance
pattern sample; earnest
peal loud volley of sound or ringing of bells; = peel (match, equal)

pearl in eye early modern term for cataracts

peep abroad be seen out of doors

pelamis young Mediterranean tunny

Penance-chamber ecclesiastical office charged with dealing with penitents

pennyworth bargain

penthouse sloping roof attached to the wall of a main building

penurious mean; niggardly

perdition utter destruction; damnation

perfect (adj.) contented; satisfied; past it; (v.) complete; round off (hence *perfection* conclusion; outcome)

permasant Parmesan cheese

pernicious wicked; deadly; swift

personage notable person

pewterer worker in pewter

physic medicine, often purgative

physnomy physiognomy; face

pick-haired with hard; spiky bristles

pigeon-house dovecote

pillowbeer pillowcase

pin bolt

pinching tight, like shoes

pinfold pen or fold for holding stray animals

pipe after follow [the] lead

pit-hole grave

pitiful compassionate

pizzle whip made from the dried penis of a bull

plaguily annoyingly; like a nuisance

plaguy troublesome

plaguy guess shrewd judgement

plant set up

plate gold and silverware

plead benefit plead exemption from the law

pleasure (v.) give pleasure to

plebeian commoner

pledge toast

pluck a rose pass water

ply press on with

point compass-needle; direction finder; penis; decimal point

poise weight

policy statecraft; cunning; political future

politic cunning; crafty; scheming; expedient

politician intriguer; schemer

pommel knob at the end of a sword hilt

poniard dagger

poor heads working people

poor-poached half-baked

poppy opiate

popular breath the gossip of the common people

portentously as if foretelling something important

portion dowry

posset curdled milk

postern back door

post-horse horse kept at posting inns for immediate hire

'postle spoons silver spoons with figures of the apostles on the handle

posy motto

pothecary apothecary; seller of medicinal drugs

pottage thick soup

poulterer (= poulter) one who deals in poultry; a pimp

pound (v.) pen up; pummel (with sexual innuendo)

powder sprinkle

practise scheme

praise celebrate; = 'appraise' (test, prove)

prank up smartly dress

precedent exemplar

precious craft valuable skill; dangerous game

preferments advancements; offices

presaging foreseeing

present (adj.) immediate; instant (hence, *presently* immediately) (v.) represent

press cupboard

pretend profess

prevent anticipate; forestall

prick (n.) centre of the archery target; sharp pointed stick with which to prod animals; penis; (v.) choose from a list of names; vex

pricksong written vocal music, the notes of which were 'pricked' on paper not left to the singer's invention

pride splendour

prime gallant most handsome person (used of either sex)

primitive original and true

principal especially choice

print spelling

prithee I pray thee; so 'please'

private secret; not in the public eye

privilege safety; prerogative; legal immunity

privy secret

probationer religious novice

proceed progress

procurer pander

prodigy ill-omen; horrific portent

profess openly declare

profession occupation; assertion

professor devotee

profess physic declare an expertise in medicine

progress royal tour

promont promontory

promoter informer, policing Lent observances

proneness inclination; sexual urgency

propagate breed

proper excellent; admirable; suitable, handsome; complete; thorough; personal; genuine, not counterfeit

proper virtue intrinsic nature; appropriate goodness

property inherent tendency

proportion figure

prospect view

protract delay

proud magnificent

prove turn out; become

provide prepare

prune preen; remove deformities

puff-paste fine kind of flour paste; figuratively; a light or frivolous person

pukingest most vomit-inducing

purchase acquisition; winning

purgatory in Catholic theology, place of purging of sins after death

push = pish, disdainful exclamation of contempt, impatience or disgust

push-pin a child's game

pusill child-like; easily-led person

put case assuming; suppose

put to restricted to

put to't troubled

qualm sudden access of passion; one with a troubled conscience

quarter legal and financial division of the year

quean whore

queasy nauseous; scrupulous

questionless without doubt

quick lively; gamesome; wanton; pregnant; perceptive; the tenderest part (esp. the vagina)

quick flesh vital matter

quicken invigorate; put life into; make pregnant

quit (v.) rid; (adj.) requited; even

quittance revenge

quoth a did he say

quoth's said he (sarcastic)

rack neck

racked severely stretched

rail (v.) array (clothes etc); be loudly abusive

raise promote

raise of talk about

rank excessive; indecent; sweaty; showing status

rare hardly cooked; talented

ravish carry away with rapture

reach (v.) plan; lay hold on

receipt recipe

reckon come to a reckoning

recoil retort

redeem recover; save

refulgent resplendent; reflecting back

regardless indifferent

regardlessly paying no attention

relish pleasure

remedy opportunity of changing something

remit pardon (sins)

remove (v.) die; (n.) removal

replication rejoinder

reprehension rebuke; reprimand

requitefullest most eager to return favours

resolve inform; satisfy

respect good reputation

rest depend

restorative cordial; medicine

restraint move to restrict Catholicism in England

return give back

return it report it so

revels merry-making

reverence dignity

rid remove

riddance way of eliminating (a problem)

ride be conveyed as convicted whore to prison; copulate

right use proper ceremony

right-hand clock-wise; propitious

ring-dove wood-pigeon

riot extravagance

rite ceremony

rook chess piece now usually known as 'castle'

roosting time bed time

rope tightrope

rotten stuff rotten cloth

rough brow frowning

round a circling dance

roundly energetically; thoroughly; promptly

rules revels

runlets casks of various capacities

runts small breed of Welsh and Highland cattle

russet reddish brown

sack-posset curdled milk, mixed with sherry-sack

saint someone to whom you pray for spiritual guidance

sainted sleepers the dead saints

sallet any green vegetable for a salad

salpa mollusc-like fish

salute kiss

samphire plant grown on rocky coasts, used in salads

sampler piece of embroidery used as a pattern

sanctimonious holy; sacred; merely purporting to be holy

sanctity holiness

sapa boiled wine

sauciness insolence

save my oath keep my word

savin tree tree whose leaves were used to induce abortions

Savoy dame woman from the precincts of the Savoy Hospital; whore

say saw

scaffolds temporary tiered seating to view processions etc.

scandal scandalous charge

scant inadequate

school classes

sconce small fort

scripts writings

scrutinous searching

scurvy degenerative disease from poor diet; so shabby, contemptible

sealed confirmed; ratified

season prepare

seat estate; house

second help (hence, *seconds* assistants)

sensible aware

sent sent word

sergeant sheriff's officer

service deference; selfless duty or action; work duly performed; sexual mating or satisfaction

set (v.) abate; (n.) game, as in tennis

set by regarded; set aside

set forth described

set match pre-arranged conspiracy

set on assaulted

set up put out as in a place of honour

set'em out display them

sevennight week

several distinct; different; separate (hence, *severally* via different entrances)

severe serious; censorious

shadow image without substance

shamefaced bashful

shape costume; theatrical dress

sharplier righted more strictly corrected

shelves sandbanks and ledges

shift (n.) effort; chemise or undergarment; (v.) barely manage; make a living; commit a fraud; palm something off on someone

shire county

shoot my bolt make my decision; engage sexually

shows looks

shrewd strong; dangerous

GLOSSARY

shroud disguise
silly foolish
simony sin of trading in clerical benefices
simpers it smiles affectedly
simple (adj.) great; absolute; (n.) medicinal herb
simple charge (ironic) a costly business
since in the time you have been away
sing (slang) have sexual intercourse
single only experienced by one person
single life the unwed life of the nun
sirrah exaggerated form of 'sir', implying authority on the part of the speaker
Sir-reverence 'Save your reverence', an apology
sister sister-in-law
sleight trick
Slid mild oath, 'By God's eyelid'
slip narrow strip (i.e. small amount)
slovenly negligently prepared
slut slovenly young woman
smack kiss; taste
small high
smell predict
smelt small, easily caught fish
smock chemise, woman's undergarment
smooth-browed hypocritically unruffled
smut (v.) blacken; dirty
snap gobble up; neatly catch
snap-hance flintlock on a musket
so as long as
society company
soil (v.) get dirty
soil alters that's another matter
sojourner staying guest
solder up repair; seal up
solemnity ceremony; festival
somewhat something
sops bribe
sound reliable; healthy; robust
spacious circuit wide bounds
spangling cloth decorated with spangles
spare to refrain from
spark small gemstone
speak promise; suggest; demonstrate; express
special held in particular esteem

spectacled wearing eye-glasses
spectre apparition
speculative virtue power of presenting images
spend consume; ejaculate
spent completed
spied from seen at
spiny lean
spital-house hospital
spittles hospitals for sexual diseases
splay-foot flat feet, clumsily turned outwards in walking
spleen supposed seat of mirth and laughter
spoil (v.) corrupt; ruin; destroy; (n.) ruination
spoon-meat puréed food
springe snare for game
squib (v.) to let off squibs (fireworks); (n.) tart or foolish talk
stall forestall
stamp pound
stand for represent
standing being upright; having an erection; place to stand
standing-cup cup with base or legs to support itself
stand to stand by
staple commodity principal object of employment
stare starling
start startle
starved lacking
state dignity; pomp; splendour; (= states) collective singular for the nobles of the realm
state-eyes politician's vision
state-fig diplomatic insult
stay subdue; detain; allay; (rarely) whet
stews brothels; artificial breeding-beds
stick scruple
still always; constantly
stir move; rouse; excite (sexually)
stomach sexual appetite; desire
stood me in cost me
stool-ball kind of primitive indoor cricket; with the stool as a wicket
stools low padded seats; commodes in the shape of a footstool; faeces
stop pause; reflect

stored furnished

stoves heated rooms

straight immediately

strain style or tone of proceedings

strait strict

strange distant; not encouraging; unfriendly; not yet familiar and accepted

strange imposture elaborate pretence

strange notes the cries of a new-born child

strangely greatly; very earnestly; miraculously

stranger foreigner; not a blood relation

strife conflict

stubborn stiff

studying considering

stuff material

submiss humble

subsidy bourgeois or commercial, as opposed to courtly

subtle difficult to understand

success fortune, good or bad

suckling infant

sudden impetuous; instant; immediate

suffice satisfy

suffices it is sufficient that; suffice it to say

sugar-sops bread soaked in sugar-water

suitable to appropriate for; acceptable to

supererogation Catholic doctrine whereby good works beyond what were required may constitute a store of merit which the Church can use to compensate for the failings of other sinners

supple compliant

sure inevitable

surfeit over-indulgence; excess; be supplied to excess

surprised suddenly attacked

suspect suspicion

sutler seller of provisions to an army

swapping huge

sweet breast a pleasant singing voice

sweetbreads pancreas (of a lamb)

sweetmeats confectionery; pastries etc.

swindge sway; freedom of action

'Swounds oath, 'By God's wounds'

syrup sweet, sticky liquid

take catch; capture; ravish; succeed; win; catch fire; remove, as in chess; possess sexually; make pregnant

take an answer accept that one is wrong

take care worry

take pains take trouble; put in effort; inflict pain on

take water be carried by water

tansy-faced yellow-faced

tasselled fashionably large, with showy tassels

taste detect

tax censure; attack

tax-register the *Taxa Sacra Poenitentiaria Apostolica*, the 'book of general pardons of all prices'

teeming fecund

tell count

temper disposition, inclination

tempest storm of conscience

temple church

tender (v.) be considerate of; cherish; supply for approval; (n.) betrothal

tender-hoofed like a horse with a sore hoof; thin-skinned

termagant fierce, shrewish creature

tester sixpence

tetrarch governor of a Roman province

that something which

the while in the mean time

thirst for long for vengeance upon

thraldom servitude

throughly fully, completely

thrumming idling

tiara turban with a long tailpiece

tickle thrash

ticklish fickle

tightly smartly

Tim commonly name of a fool

time age

tip-cat game in which a stick is used to knock up, then away, a cat or wedge of wood

tipping the action of knocking the cat in tip-cat up in the air

tipple tumble over

to in one's relations with; in favour of; compared to; for

to a heart to the life

to boot into the bargain

to nothing at no charge

to the end with the intention

to you-ward in your direction; applying to you

together on end; in a row

token proof; love-token

tongue-discourse the ability to make conversation

tongues gossip

too sure over-careful

touch (v.) have anything to do with

touchwood kindling

toward(s) preparing for; to come; in the making

toy trifle

tractable easily managed

traffic trade

transcend exceed

transgress go beyond limits

transshape metamorphose

trap dress with trappings; the game of cat-and-trap

trap-stick also called cat-stick, cudgel used in the rural game of tip-cat

travel (v. & n.) travail; journey; labour

treacher cheat; deceiver

treading where one treads/goes; copulation

treasury place where honour is stored and reckoned

treble qualitied with three effects

trencher plate; platter

trick trinket

tricked up dressed in finery

trim fine

triumph pageant; lavish spectacle; elation of victory

troll circulate

trolled spoken rapidly

trot into readily become

troths wedding vows

trow do you think?

truckle-beds small beds designed to stack neatly under larger ones

true substance reality (not a dream)

truss (v.) tie the points of hose to the doublet; hang

truth faithfulness

tumble copulate

tumbler acrobat; copulator

tumbling cast wrestling throw

tumbrel dung-cart

tun tunny fish; wine-cask

turn change sides

turn from look away from; abandon

turtle turtledove

uncomely offensive; disagreeable

unconscionable conscienceless; having no remorse

under-drudgery the most menial tasks; sexual subordination.

undertake venture to assert

undiscovered undisclosed

undo ruin; destroy

universal monarchy supposed scheme to establish a single all-embracing Catholic power in Europe; sometimes applied to the private ambitions of the Jesuits

unkind unnatural

unlaid moved; disturbed

unlooked-for unexpected

unpenanced unchastised

unpledged without a toast

unsettle undo; detach

unvalued priceless; invaluable

upon close to

urge provoke

use custom; practice

use it commonly do it

usher doorkeeper; under-teacher

utter express (possibly in a sexual sense, i.e. ejaculate)

vain empty; idle

vane weather-cock, usually on a church steeple

vaunt boast

vending (= venting) selling

vent express

vent'rous adventurous; bold

venture (v.) try; put at risk; (n.) trial; hazard; risk

Venus goddess of love

verjuice acidic liquor made from sour fruit

Veronica's heads images of Christ on ornaments or tokens

vessel bearer

vestal virgin Roman priestess of the temple of Vesta, dedicated to chastity

vexed irritated; troubled; aggrieved

vials phials

vicious (n.) sinner; (adj.) given to vice

virginal spinet

virtue power; quality

visiting anguish suffering inflicted as punishment

visor mask

voice support

voider servant who clears the table into a basket

vouchsafe deign

wag mischievous joker

wait await

wait upon accompany

wamble feel nauseous

want (vb.) lack; be denied; deprived of; (n.) shortage; shortcoming

want utterance be beyond speech

ward defensive guard (from fencing); orphaned child of gentry, placed in protective care

warden churchwarden; one of the governing body of a City Company

warily cautiously; secretively

warm heated by exertion; zealous

wash medicinal lotion, often for the eyes

waste miss

watch keep vigil

watchman constable of the watch

water medicine; medicinal wash; semen

water-house building relating to the water supply

watermen boatmen

way passage

we three two idiots' heads, implying the spectator as the third idiot

weigh judge

weight importance

welcome worth give a proper welcome to people of substance

well applied a good analogy made

well pickled deeply confirmed; persistent; reduced to a sorry plight

well said stock phrase, meaning 'well done'

well-favouredly soundly; severely

went together were equal

were was meant to be

white boy darling

white money silver

whitemeats food prepared from milk

wholesome free of disease

will (n.) sexual desire; (v.) be determined to

winged warrant fast-moving, reliable witness

wire whip

wise-acre foolish person who wishes to seem witty or wise

wishfully composed formed exactly as one would wish

withal with; as well

without voice noiselessly

wittol complacent cuckold

witty (dangerously) cunning or deceitful

wonder astonishment; surprise

wondrous faulty strangely misguided

wondrous necessary absolutely indispensable

wont (n.) usual behaviour; (v.) be accustomed, used (to something)

woodcock slow bird, easily caught; hence dupe; simpleton

word promise; sentiment; motto

work business

wormwood water extremely bitter drink, flavoured with wormwood

worst cheapest; least expensive

wrack ruin

wrangling bitter argument or complaint

wretch sorry person

wriggle-tail tiny

wrought made

wrought underhand worked secretly

yellowhammer a chattering bird; gold coin or fool (slang)

yet even now; at this point; all of a sudden

young flood rising tide, when the water flows up-river

zeal ardent or righteous commitment; self-sacrifice